Applied general equilibrium analysis

Applied general equilibrium analysis

Edited by

HERBERT E. SCARF
Yale University

and

JOHN B. SHOVEN
Stanford University

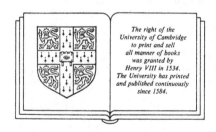

The right of the
University of Cambridge
to print and sell
all manner of books
was granted by
Henry VIII in 1534.
The University has printed
and published continuously
since 1584.

CAMBRIDGE UNIVERSITY PRESS

Cambridge
London   New York   New Rochelle
Melbourne   Sydney

CAMBRIDGE UNIVERSITY PRESS
Cambridge, New York, Melbourne, Madrid, Cape Town, Singapore, São Paulo

Cambridge University Press
The Edinburgh Building, Cambridge CB2 8RU, UK

Published in the United States of America by Cambridge University Press, New York

www.cambridge.org
Information on this title: www.cambridge.org/9780521257459

First published 1984
Reprinted 1986
This digitally printed version 2008

A catalogue record for this publication is available from the British Library

Library of Congress Cataloguing in Publication data
Main entry under title:
Applied general equilibrium analysis.
"Papers presented at the Conference on Applied
General Equilibrium Analysis, held in San Diego in
August 1981" – Pref.
1. Equilibrium (Economics) – Congresses.   I. Scarf,
H. (Herbert) II. Shoven, J. (John)   III. Conference on
Applied General Equilibrium Analysis (1981 : San Diego,
Calif.)
HB145.A66   1984   339.5   83-7614

ISBN 978-0-521-25745-9 hardback
ISBN 978-0-521-07093-5 paperback

Contents

Contributors

Antonio M. Borges
INSEAD
Boulevard de Constance
Fontainebleau 77305, France

Peter B. Dixon
Department of Economics
La Trobe University
Bundoora, Victoria 3083
Australia

Andrew Feltenstein
International Monetary Fund
700 Nineteenth Street, N.W.
Washington, DC 20431

Don Fullerton
Department of Economics
Princeton University
Princeton, NJ 08554

Victor Ginsburgh
Free University of Brussels
C.E.M.E.
Avenue F-D Roosevelt 50
B-1050 Brussels, Belgium

Lawrence H. Goulder
Department of Economics
Harvard University
Littauer Center
Cambridge, MA 02138

Glenn W. Harrison
Department of Economics
University of Western Ontario
London, Ontario N6A 5C2
Canada

Yolanda K. Henderson
Department of Economics
Amherst College
Amherst, MA 01002

Dale W. Jorgenson
Department of Economics
Harvard University
Littauer Center 122
Cambridge, MA 02138

Larry J. Kimbell
Graduate School of Business
University of California,
    Los Angeles
Los Angeles, CA 90024

Lawrence J. Lau
Department of Economics
Stanford University
Stanford, CA 94305

James MacKinnon
Department of Economics
Queen's University
Kingston, Ontario K7L 3N6
Canada

Ronald I. McKinnon
Department of Economics
Stanford University
Stanford, CA 94305

Charles E. McLure, Jr.
Hoover Institution
Stanford University
Stanford, CA 94305

Alan S. Manne
Operations Research
Stanford University
Terman Engineering Bldg.
Stanford, CA 94305

Ahsan Mansur
International Monetary Fund
700 Nineteenth Street, N.W.
Washington, DC 20431

Peter Mieszkowski
Department of Economics
Rice University
Houston, TX 77001

B. R. Parmenter
Department of Economics
La Trobe University
Bundoora, Victoria 3083
Australia

Russell J. Rimmer
Department of Economics
La Trobe University
Bundoora, Victoria 3083
Australia

Sherman Robinson
World Bank
1818 H Street, N.W.
Washington, DC 20433

Herbert E. Scarf
Department of Economics
Cowles Foundation
Yale University
New Haven, CT 06520

Jaime Serra-Puche
El Colegio de Mexico
CEE
Camino al Ajusco 20
Mexico 20, D.F. Mexico

John B. Shoven
Department of Economics
Stanford University
Stanford, CA 94305

Robert M. Stern
Department of Economics
University of Michigan
Ann Arbor, MI 48109

Michael J. Todd
Operations Research
School of Engineering
Cornell University
Ithaca, NY 14850

Laura D'Andrea Tyson
Department of Economics
University of California,
    Berkeley
Berkeley, CA 94720

Jean Waelbroeck
Free Univesity of Brussels
C.E.M.E.
Avenue F-D Roosevelt 50
B-1050 Brussels, Belgium

John Whalley
Department of Economics
University of Western Ontario
London, Ontario N6A 5C2
Canada

Preface

The general equilibrium model of an economy is the product of nearly two centuries of conceptual innovation and continued intellectual refinement. Its roots may be found in Adam Smith's description of the behavior of capitalists motivated by considerations of profitability in the selection of economic activities. The elements of demand theory appear in John Stuart Mill's treatment of international trade and in his analysis of the response of economic agents to changes in taxes and import duties. The model reaches its mature form later in the nineteenth century in the work of Leon Walras, who provided a general description of the functioning of a complex economic system based on the interaction of a number of interdependent economic units.

The fundamental themes of the general equilibrium model are extremely simple and lie at the heart of economic theory. The production side of the economy, engaged in the transformation of certain commodities into other commodities, is distinguished from the consumption side, whose goals are the acquisition and eventual consumption of goods and services. Stocks of commodities, which may be consumed directly, maintained as inventories for eventual use, or offered as factors of production, are owned by households in their physical form or by means of a variety of financial instruments. Each consumer's income, or wealth, is determined by evaluating his stock of commodities in terms of those prices at which the commodities can be sold. Income and a knowledge of relative prices permit the consumer to express his demands for goods and services and his offerings of labor and other stocks that are made available for the productive side of the economy.

That observation of daily life which recognizes the efficiency of large-scale productive enterprises has never found a congenial location in general equilibrium analysis, which requires the menu of possible choices by producers to exhibit decreasing or constant returns to scale. In the general equilibrium model, producers are assumed to be informed of the prices of all inputs and the prices at which outputs can be sold. These prices are taken to be independent of the scale and composition of productive activity; each producer then selects, from the technically available choices, the production plan that maximizes his profits.

The decisions of the production and consumption sides of the economy need not be consistent with each other if they are based on an arbitrary list of prices. If the price of a desired commodity is too low, consumers may be motivated to demand large quantities of this commodity, and producers may be averse to supplying that commodity whose sales generate insufficient revenue to cover the costs of manufacture. Equilibrium prices are those that equate demand and supply in all markets. Once they are known, in the context of a particular model of an economy, the entire range of economic decisions based on them is determined.

The formulation of the general equilibrium model offered by Walras was the most mathematically elaborate of his time, and he alone among his contemporaries seemed to recognize the need for an argument demonstrating the existence of prices that would equilibrate the large number of decentralized decisions postulated in the model. He offered two lines of argument. When translated into a formal mathematical system, the number of prices to be determined equaled the number of independent equations governing their determination. Walras was satisfied by this argument for existence, which, although it has considerable merit, is incomplete without further analysis. The second argument offered by Walras is his famous *tâtonnement* in which tentative prices are revised according to the discrepancy between demand and supply. Unfortunately, this process need not converge, and it therefore represents neither an argument for the existence of equilibrium prices nor a computational procedure for their determination.

The existence problem for the general equilibrium model was finally solved during that remarkable burst of intellectual activity in mathematical economics that took place in the late 1940s and 1950s. Based on the work of Arrow, Debreu, Gale, Kuhn, McKenzie, Nikaido, and others, the model was formalized with a high degree of precision and generality, and fixed-point arguments – originally introduced into mathematical economics by von Neumann – were used to demonstrate the existence of prices that simultaneously equated supply and demand for all commodities. A fundamental question in economic theory – the consistency of the general equilibrium model – was given a definitive answer.

But the price of this remarkable achievement in pure theory seemed extremely high. The techniques used in demonstrating the existence of equilibrium utilized mathematical arguments that were fundamentally nonconstructive. At that time, these arguments gave no indication of the way in which prices might be computed and used as a practical tool in the very types of economic analysis that had provided the original motivation for the general equilibrium model.

The present volume consists of a series of papers presented at the Conference on Applied General Equilibrium Analysis held in San Diego in August 1981. This conference and others with a similar orientation give adequate testimony to the fact that the technical problems associated with the numerical solution of large general equilibrium models have been overcome. Since the early 1970s a number of increasingly refined methods have been proposed for approximating the fixed points of continuous mappings. In their simplest form they involve decomposing the price simplex into a large number of small regions and utilizing information about the mapping to construct a pricewise linear path that can be shown to terminate at a fixed point. The chapters by Scarf and by Todd are an introduction to the mathematical techniques involved in approximating fixed points of a continuous mapping. These methods, whose development was spurred by the problem of calculating equilibrium prices, have become sufficiently rapid – in terms of computing time – so that numerical problems are no longer an effective constraint on our ability to solve general equilibrium problems of modest size, say, involving 30 to 40 disaggregated sectors. The constraints, to the extent that they exist, are to be found in the conceptual problems of formulating realistic models and in the insufficiency of data required to estimate with confidence the great number and variety of parameters of such a model.

The general equilibrium model has traditionally been used, and continues to be used, to analyze the effects of a change in economic policy such as the imposition of a tariff or quota on imported goods, the granting of export subsidies, or a modification of the tax code. It can be used to explore the consequences of an increase in the price or reduction in the supply of an imported good such as oil, the ramifications of an unexpected fall in the supply of food, or a major change in the regulation of an industry, to name several examples. In each of these cases, the parameters of the model are required to yield current prices and output levels as the solution of the general equilibrium model prior to the change. A recalculation is then done that predicts the consequences of the proposed change on a variety of economically significant variables: prices, levels of output, government receipts, and the distribution of income among the consuming units.

One of the major virtues of the general equilibrium model is its ability to trace the consequences of large changes in a particular sector throughout the entire economy. It shares this property with input–output analysis but permits a more flexible treatment of the consumer side of the economy and is less rigid in the requirements placed on the productive side. Major policy changes frequently have significant impacts on the distribution of income – indeed, they may be designed with this consequence in mind – and require, for their analysis, a conceptual framework that allows for the possibility of variations in income.

The consequences of a change in economic policy are frequently analyzed by assuming the changes to be small and using local linear approximations based on estimates of the relevant elasticities. If the number of sectors is small, diagrammatic techniques or explicit analytical results may also be available as in the two-sector models so frequently used in international trade theory. But if the model is disaggregated, and if the changes – possibly more than one – are large, there is no recourse other than the construction and explicit solution of a numerical general equilibrium model.

The imperfections of the general equilibrium model as a description of economic reality are well known to economists and in a less informed way to the general public. The model is inadequate in its treatment of money and financial institutions, it has great difficulty in allowing for unemployed resources, and it is unable to cope with large-scale industrial enterprises that are capable of exerting a significant influence on prices. Investments and roundabout methods of production are poorly treated if the model is formulated in static terms, and any attempt to rectify this by a dynamic model must find a replacement for the unrealistic assumption of perfect futures markets. But there are no competing formulations that avoid these shortcomings and provide the flexibility and conceptual wealth of the general equilibrium model. In spite of its imperfections, this method of analysis will retain its usefulness until economic theory is capable of providing compelling alternative formulations.

The chapters in the present volume deal with a variety of topics. Mansur and Whalley discuss the problems of data collection, parameter specification, and the feasibility of estimating an entire model attending to all of the cross-equation restrictions implied by the general equilibrium framework. Mansur and Whalley are pessimistic about full model estimation for all but the simplest structures and suggest the necessity of continued reliance on current methods of parameter specification. The chapter by Jorgenson is an ambitious and sophisticated attempt to estimate and report on a large general equilibrium model consisting of 36 sectors.

Fullerton, Henderson, and Shoven survey the structure of eight different applied general equilibrium models dealing with taxation. The sensitivity of such models to the level of disaggregation in production is investigated. The chapter examines several aspects of the eight models including their treatments of saving, the labor–leisure choice, foreign trade, and the household sector. The chapter by Serra-Puche develops a model of the Mexican economy that is used to analyze the effect of introducing a value-added tax of the consumption type on income distribution and resource allocation. His main result is that the welfare of rural consumer groups increases after this reform. Borges and Goulder use a model of the United States to simulate the impact of higher energy prices on economic growth and to test the relative importance of several channels through which higher-priced energy affects growth. The chapter by Kimbell and Harrison develops a regional model that predicts the incidence of fiscal policy in the California economy.

Ginsburgh and Waelbroeck discuss planning models and activity analysis. They propose that linearized economic models that can be formulated as optimization problems have advantages over computable general equilibrium models in the analysis of developing countries. The chapter by Dixon, Parmenter, and Rimmer also deals with a linearized model, but its most distinctive feature is its level of detail. The authors' model of Australia identifies 113 industries, 230 commodities, 9 types of labor, and 7 types of land. It has been used for policy evaluation by several agencies of the Australian government.

The chapter by Robinson and Tyson discusses integrating features of financial and macroeconomic models (the nonneutrality of money, asset markets, nominally denominated securities, etc.) with the structural detail of a computational general equilibrium model. Feltenstein's chapter represents a preliminary attempt to introduce monetary phenomena in a general equilibrium model of an open economy. In his formulation, the government sector issues a combination of bonds and money to finance the acquisition of public goods.

The editors would like to express their thanks to the National Science Foundation for their generous support of the conference at which these papers were presented and to Altheia Chaballa for the exceptionally fine assistance in organizing the conference and preparing this volume.

H. E. Scarf
J. B. Shoven

CHAPTER 1

The computation of equilibrium prices

Herbert E. Scarf

1   The general equilibrium model

A demonstration of the existence of equilibrium prices for a general Walrasian model of competitive behavior necessarily makes use of some variant of Brouwer's fixed-point theorem as an essential step in the argument. The strategy for calculating equilibrium prices is to render that step constructive by a numerical approximation of the fixed point implied by Brouwer's theorem or one of its alternatives. We begin this chapter with a brief review of the competitive model and the role of fixed-point theorems. (See Debreu, 1959.)

The typical consumer will be assumed to have a set of preferences for commodity bundles $x = (x_1, \ldots, x_n)$ in the nonnegative orthant of n-dimensional space. These preferences can be described either by an abstract preference relationship $\succeq$ satisfying a series of plausible axioms or by a specific utility indicator $u(x)$.

It is customary to assume that, prior to production and trade, the typical consumer will own a nonnegative vector of commodities w whose evaluation by means of market prices forms the basis for that consumer's income. More specifically, if the nonnegative vector of prices $\pi = (\pi_1, \ldots, \pi_n)$ is expected to prevail, then the consumer can obtain an income

$$I = \sum_1^n \pi_i \cdot w_i = \pi \cdot w$$

by the sale of his commodity bundle w. This income is then used by the consumer for the purchase of an alternative bundle of commodities in such a way as to provide him with the highest possible utility level.

Given a vector of prices for all of the commodities in the economy, the consumer is faced with a maximization problem: to find a vector of commodities x that maximizes his utility function (or is maximal according to his preference relationship) subject to the budget constraint

The present chapter is a revision of a chapter in the *Handbook of Mathematical Economics,* edited by K. J. Arrow and M. D. Intriligator (Scarf, 1981).

1

$$\pi \cdot x \leqslant \pi \cdot w$$

The problem faced by the consumer is clearly unchanged if the price vector π is replaced by $\lambda \pi$, with λ an arbitrary positive number. This provides us with a degree of freedom in normalizing prices in any fashion that happens to be convenient. For example, prices can be normalized so as to lie on the unit sphere $\sum_1^n \pi_i^2 = 1$ (meaningless from an economic point of view, but mathematically quite useful) or on the unit simplex $\sum_1^n \pi_i = 1$. For definiteness we shall adopt the latter normalization throughout most of this chapter.

Under quite acceptable assumptions, such as continuity and strict convexity of preferences, the solution to the consumer's maximization problem will be a single-valued demand function $x(\pi)$ that is continuous on the unit simplex and that satisfies the identity

$$\sum_1^n \pi_i \cdot x_i(\pi) \equiv \sum_1^n \pi_i \cdot w_i$$

stating that the consumer's entire income will be spent on the purchase of commodities. (This is of course not meant to rule out the possibility that the consumer may choose to save some of his current income for future purchases – an aspect of consumer behavior that can be captured by declaring that certain commodities become available in the future.)

For the purpose of computing equilibrium prices, the demand functions $x(\pi)$ are frequently more natural to work with than the underlying utility function or preference relationship. A general equilibrium model must be fully specified in order to obtain a numerical solution: On the consumer side this is typically done by providing a numerical or algebraic description of the functions $x(\pi)$. A few examples of some of the more familiar utility functions and their associated demand functions may be appropriate at this point.

$$1. \quad u(x) = x_1^{a_1} \ldots x_n^{a_n} \quad \text{with} \quad a_i \geqslant 0, \quad \sum a_i = 1$$

It is an elementary observation that a consumer with this utility function will spend the same fraction a_i of his income on the ith good, independently of relative prices. Since his income is given by $\pi \cdot w$, this implies that his demand for the ith good is given by

$$x_i(\pi) = \frac{a_i \, \pi \cdot w}{\pi_i}$$

(There is an insignificant technical problem in that these demand functions and others that are subsequently presented exhibit a discontinuity on the boundary of the unit simplex.)

2. $u(x) = \min[x_1/a_1, \ldots, x_n/a_n]$ with $a_i > 0$

A consumer with preferences exhibiting such strict complementarity wishes to purchase a commodity bundle proportional to the vector $(a_1, \ldots, a_n)$. His demands are therefore given by

$$x_i(\pi) = a_i \cdot \pi \cdot w / \pi \cdot a$$

3. $u(x_1, \ldots, x_n) = \left(\sum_1^n a_i^{1/b} x_i^{(b-1)/b} \right)^{b/(b-1)}$ with $a_i > 0$ and $b \leqslant 1$

This is the constant elasticity of substitution (CES) utility function, which includes the two previous examples for special values of the parameter b. It will be left to the reader to verify that the demand functions $x_i(\pi)$ are given by

$$x_i(\pi) = \frac{a_i \, \pi \cdot w}{\pi_i^b \sum_j \pi_j^{1-b} a_j}$$

A model of equilibrium will generally involve a number of consuming units – individuals, aggregations of individuals, or countries involved in foreign trade – each of whom has a stock of assets w, prior to production and trade, and demands that are functions of the prevailing prices π. If the jth consumer's assets are represented by w^j and his demand functions by $x^j(\pi)$, then the *market demand functions* are defined by

$$x(\pi) = \sum_j x^i(\pi)$$

The market demand functions specify the total consumer demand, for the goods and services in the economy, as a function of all prices.

Market demand functions cannot be arbitrarily specified if they are derived from individual demand functions by the process of aggregation described above. For example, if the individual demand functions are continuous, the market demand functions will be continuous as well. Moreover, the market demand functions will satisfy the identity

$$\pi \cdot x(\pi) \equiv \pi \cdot w$$

(if $w = \sum w^j$) known as the *Walras law* – resulting from the assumption that the income available for consumer purchases is accounted for fully by the sale of privately owned assets.

The market *excess* demand functions, representing the difference between market demands and the supply of commodities prior to production, are defined by

$$\xi(\pi) = x(\pi) - w$$

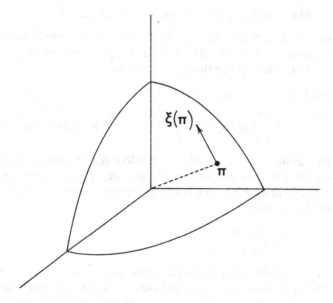

Figure 1. The excess demand vector.

Our analysis may be summarized as follows:

1.1 [Properties]. The market excess demand functions will satisfy the following conditions:

1. They are defined and continuous everywhere in the positive orthant other than the origin.
2. They are homogeneous of degree zero; that is, $\xi(\lambda\pi) = \xi(\pi)$, for any positive λ.
3. The Walras law: $\pi \cdot \xi(\pi) \equiv 0$.

In this form, the Walras law has an interesting geometrical interpretation when prices are normalized to lie on the unit sphere (Figure 1). If the excess demand $\xi(\pi)$ is drawn as a vector originating at π, the geometric interpretation of the Walras law is that this vector is tangent to the unit sphere at π. The excess demands determine, therefore, a continuous vector field on that part of the unit sphere lying in the nonnegative orthant.

A description of the consumer side of the economy, for the purposes of the general equilibrium model, is adequately provided by the market excess demand functions. To complete the model a specification of the productive techniques available to the economy must also be given. We shall return to this point, after examining the pure trade model in which production is absent and consumers simply exchange the commodities that they initially own. For such a model the total supply is given by the vector w and the market demand by the functions $x(\pi)$. An equilibrium price vector π^* is one which equilibrates supply and demand for all commodities. We have the following formal definition that allows for the possibility that some of the commodities have a zero price and are in excess supply:

1.2 [Definition]. A nonzero price vector π^* is an *equilibrium price vector* for the pure trade model if $\xi_i(\pi^*) \leqslant 0$ for all i and is equal to zero when $\pi_i^* > 0$.

If all of the coordinates of π^* are positive, then π^* is a zero of the vector field ξ on the unit sphere. The existence of a zero for an arbitrary vector field on the sphere is a subtle topological question. It is therefore a matter of some significance, in assessing the difficulty of demonstrating the existence of equilibrium prices (and in their calculation), to ask how general a vector field can be obtained by the process of aggregating individual demand functions. This question was first studied by Sonnenschein (1973) and was given a definitive answer in subsequent papers by Mantel (1974), Debreu (1974a), and McFadden et al. (1975). There are some technical difficulties on the boundary of the positive orthant, but given an arbitrary continuous vector field on the sphere and an arbitrary open subset of the positive orthant, there will be a collection of n consumers with preferences and initial holdings, whose individual demand functions sum to the preassigned vector field on the open subset. In other words, market excess demand functions are essentially arbitrary aside from the conditions described in 1.1.

Walras suggested that an equilibrium price vector could be found by a *tâtonnement* process: the continued revision of nonequilibrium prices on the basis of the discrepancy between supply and demand. If π is a price vector for which $\xi_i(\pi) \neq 0$, then a formalization of our intuitive understanding of the price mechanism would suggest that π_i be increased if $\xi_i(\pi) > 0$ and decreased if $\xi_i(\pi) < 0$. The continuous analog of this process is a system of differential equations of the following sort:

$$\frac{d\pi_i}{dt} = \xi_i(\pi)$$

with some modification if the price vector happens to lie on the boundary of the positive orthant. The solution is a curve that simply follows the vector field on the sphere. Given the arbitrariness of this vector field, however, there is no difficulty in designing a model of exchange in which the Walrasian adjustment mechanism leads to the most capricious behavior with no tendency whatsoever toward equilibrium. For example, we can prescribe an aribtrary differentiable curve on the positive part of the sphere and construct a model of exchange such that the adjustment process follows that curve. The possibilities are quite staggering in large dimensions and surely imply that the price adjustment mechanism can be used neither to provide a proof of the existence of competitive equilibria nor an effective computational procedure for the general case.

Production can be introduced in the general equilibrium model in a variety of ways. Perhaps the simplest is to describe the productive techniques available to the economy by an activity analysis model based on a matrix of the following type:

$$
A = \begin{bmatrix} -1 & 0 & \dots & 0 & \dots & a_{1j} & \dots & a_{1k} \\ 0 & -1 & \dots & 0 & \dots & a_{2j} & \dots & a_{2k} \\ \vdots & \vdots & & \vdots & & \vdots & & \vdots \\ 0 & 0 & \dots & -1 & \dots & a_{nj} & \dots & a_{nk} \end{bmatrix}
$$

Each column of A represents a known technical mode of production, which can be employed at an arbitrary nonnegative level. Inputs into production are represented by negative entries in a given column and outputs by positive entries. (The first n activities are disposal activities.) The result of using techniques 1 through k at levels $x_1, \dots, x_k$ is a net production plan Ax, where $x = (x_1, \dots, x_k)$. The negative entries in Ax represent a demand for factors of production that must be contributed by consumers from their stock of initial assets w. The positive entries represent increases in the stock of other assets, which can then be distributed among the consumers. An equilibrium price vector π^* is one that equilibrates the net consumer demand $\xi(\pi^*)$ with the net supply Ax. It also induces the correct selection of productive techniques (though not their levels) on the grounds of decentralized profit maximization. We have the following formal definition of equilibrium:

1.3 [Definition]. A nonzero price vector π^* and a nonnegative vector of activity levels, x^*, represent *equilibrium prices and activity levels* if

  1. $\xi(\pi^*) = Ax^*$
  2. $\pi^* A \leqslant 0$

The second of these conditions says that all potential activities make a nonpositive profit when evaluated by means of equilibrium prices π^*. It

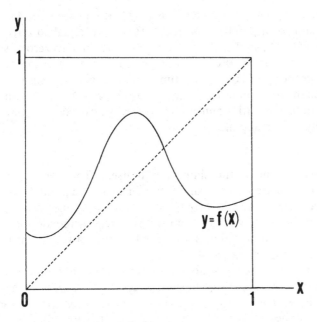

Figure 2. A mapping of the unit interval.

follows from the Walras law that $\pi^*Ax^* = 0$ and that those activities that are actually used at equilibrium make a profit of zero. The demonstration that equilibrium prices and activity levels exist – under suitable assumptions on the matrix A – is more subtle than that of the case of pure trade, and typically makes use of Kakutani's fixed-point theorem rather than Brouwer's theorem. The arguments apply equally well to a description of production given by an arbitrary closed convex cone (see, for example, Debreu, 1959) rather than the polyhedral cone implied by an activity analysis model.

2 Brouwer's fixed-point theorem

Let S be a closed, bounded convex set in n-dimensional Euclidean space, which is mapped into itself by the continuous mapping $x \rightarrow f(x)$. Brouwer's theorem asserts the existence of a fixed point, that is, a point for which $\hat{x} = f(\hat{x})$. In order to illustrate the theorem we consider a few simple examples.

1. Let S be the closed unit interval $[0, 1]$. A continuous mapping of this interval into itself is defined by an ordinary continuous function $f(x)$ whose values also lie in the unit interval (Figure 2). A fixed point of

this mapping is a point where the graph $(x, f(x))$ intersects the 45° line from the origin, or a point where $g(x) = f(x) - x$ is equal to zero. But $g(0) \geqslant 0$ and $g(1) \leqslant 0$, so that the function must be equal to zero at some point in the unit interval. Brouwer's theorem is a generalization of this well-known property of continuous functions to higher dimensions.

2. Let S be the unit simplex $\{x = (x_1, \ldots, x_n) \mid x_i \geqslant 0, \ \Sigma_j \, x_j = 1\}$, and let A be a square matrix with nonnegative entries, whose column sums are equal to unity. The mapping

$$f(x) = Ax$$

is continuous and maps the simplex into itself. The conditions for Brouwer's theorem are satisfied and there will be a fixed point $\hat{x} = A\hat{x}$. In this particular case Brouwer's theorem implies that a nonnegative square matrix with column sums of unity must have a characteristic root of 1 with an associated nonnegative characteristic vector, a result which can be obtained by simpler arguments.

3. In this example we show how Brouwer's theorem can be used to demonstrate the existence of equilibrium prices for a model of exchange. We consider prices normalized so as to lie on the unit simplex S. For each π in S, $\xi(\pi)$ will be the market excess demand associated with this price. Here ξ is assumed to be continuous on the simplex and to satisfy the identity $\pi \cdot \xi(\pi) \equiv 0$.

Define a mapping as follows:

$$f_i(\pi) = \frac{\pi_i + \max[0, \xi_i(\pi)]}{1 + \Sigma_j \max[0, \xi_j(\pi)]}$$

The fact that f is continuous follows from the continuity of the market excess demand functions. It should also be clear that $f(\pi)$ is on the unit simplex if π is. Brouwer's theorem can therefore be applied and we deduce the existence of a price vector $\hat{\pi} = f(\hat{\pi})$. We shall demonstrate that $\hat{\pi}$ is an equilibrium price for the model of exchange.

If c is defined to be

$$c = 1 + \sum_j \max[0, \xi_j(\hat{\pi})] \geqslant 1$$

then

$$c\hat{\pi}_i = \hat{\pi}_i + \max[0, \xi_i(\hat{\pi})]$$

or

$$(c-1)\hat{\pi}_i = \max[0, \xi_i(\hat{\pi})]$$

But c must be equal to 1, for if it were strictly larger, this last relationship would imply that

$$\xi_i(\hat{\pi}) > 0 \qquad \text{for each} \quad i \quad \text{with} \quad \hat{\pi}_i > 0$$

violating the Walras law $\sum \hat{\pi}_i \xi_i(\hat{\pi}) = 0$. If $c = 1$, however, it follows that $\sum_j \max[0, \xi_j(\hat{\pi})] = 0$, or $\xi_j(\hat{\pi}) \leq 0$ for all j.

We see that the existence theorem for exchange economies is an immediate consequence of Brouwer's theorem. As the following argument (Uzawa, 1962) shows, Brouwer's theorem itself follows from the existence of an equilibrium price vector for an arbitrary exchange economy.

Let $x \to f(x)$ be a continuous mapping of the unit simplex into itself. Define the functions

$$\xi_i(x) = f_i(x) - \lambda(x)x_i$$

where

$$\lambda(x) = \frac{\sum_j x_j f_j(x)}{\sum_j x_j^2}$$

Then ξ_i are defined and continuous everywhere on the unit simplex and, by construction, satisfy the Walras law $\sum x_i \xi_i(x) \equiv 0$. From the existence theorem for competitive equilibria, we conclude that there is an $\hat{x}$ with $\xi_i(\hat{x}) \leq 0$ and equal to zero if $\hat{x}_i > 0$. But then

$$f_i(\hat{x}) \leq \lambda(\hat{x})\hat{x}_i$$

with equality if $\hat{x}_i > 0$. If $\hat{x}_i = 0$, we must also have equality, since otherwise $f_i(\hat{x}) < 0$, and f would not map the unit simplex into itself. It follows that

$$f_i(\hat{x}) = \lambda(\hat{x})\hat{x}_i$$

But since $\sum f_i(\hat{x}) = \sum \hat{x}_i = 1$, we see that $\lambda(\hat{x}) = 1$ and that $\hat{x}$ is indeed a fixed point of the mapping.

Since Brouwer's theorem and the theorem asserting the existence of equilibrium prices are equivalent, any effective numerical procedure for computing equilibrium prices must at the same time be an algorithm for computing fixed points of a continuous mapping.

3   An algorithm for computing fixed points

In this section we shall present our first algorithm for approximating a fixed point of a continuous mapping of the unit simplex into itself. There is no loss in generality in restricting our attention to the unit simplex. If the mapping $f(x)$ is defined for a more general, closed, bounded, convex set C, we embed C in a larger simplex S (as in Figure 3) and define a mapping $g(x)$ of S into itself in the following way:

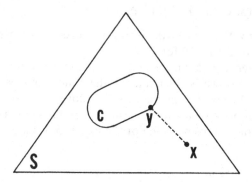

Figure 3. A mapping of a general convex set.

1.   If $x \in C$, then $g(x) = f(x)$
2.   If $x \notin C$, then $g(x) = f(y)$

where y is that unique point in C that is closest, in the sense of Euclidean distance, to x.

Since y varies continuously with x, it is clear that the new mapping satisfies the conditions of Brouwer's theorem and has a fixed point $\hat{x} = g(\hat{x})$. But since $g(\hat{x}) \in C$, it follows that $\hat{x} \in C$ and is a fixed point of the original mapping f.

A simplex is defined to be the convex hull of its n vertices $v^1, \ldots, v^n$, that is, the set of points of the form

$$x = \sum \alpha_j v^j \quad \text{with} \quad \alpha_j \geq 0 \quad \text{and} \quad \sum \alpha_j = 1$$

The vertices are assumed to be linearly independent in the sense that each vector in the simplex has one and only one representation in the above form. The simplex, which has dimension $n-1$ in our notation, has n faces of dimension $n-2$. The face opposite the vertex v^j consists of those vectors whose representation as a convex combination of the vertices has $\alpha_j = 0$.

More generally, the simplex has a number of subfaces of lower dimension. For any subset T of $(1, 2, \ldots, n)$ there is a face of the simplex consisting of those vectors with $\alpha_j = 0$ for j in T.

We now consider a finite collection of simplices $S^1, \ldots, S^k$ contained in the large simplex S. If no restriction is placed on this collection, then two of its members may have interior points in common, or their intersection may not consist of an entire face of one or the other of them (see Figure 4). For the purpose of demonstrating Brouwer's theorem we shall require the collection of simplices to form what is known as a "simplicial subdivision" by ruling out these forms of intersection.

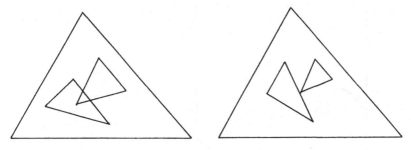

Figure 4. Inappropriate intersections.

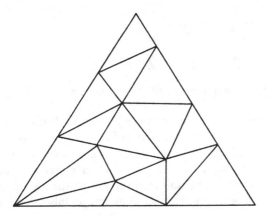

Figure 5. A simplicial subdivision.

3.1 [Definition]. A collection of simplices $S^1, \ldots, S^k$ is called a *simplicial subdivision* of S if (1) S is contained in the union of the simplices $S^1, \ldots, S^k$, and (2) the intersection of any two simplices is either empty or a full face of both of them.

Figure 5 illustrates a simplicial subdivision of the simplex.

The method we shall adopt to demonstrate Brouwer's theorem and to provide an effective computational procedure for approximating fixed points makes use of a combinatorial lemma involving simplicial subdivisions of the simplex. There are alternative computational methods, noticeably those of Kellog, Li, and Yorke (1977) and Smale (1976), that avoid simplicial subdivisions completely and use instead the methods of differential topology. These two apparently distinct approaches have much greater similarities than might appear on the surface.

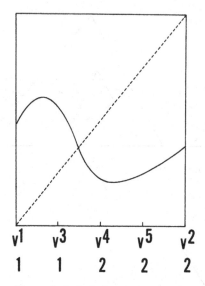

Figure 6. Labels for a mapping of the unit interval.

To appreciate the combinatorial approach to Brouwer's theorem let us examine the simplest case, a continuous mapping of the unit interval into itself. A simplicial subdivision of the unit interval is given by a monotonic sequence of points, say $v^3 < v^4 < \cdots < v^k$ (I have used the notation v^1 for the lower endpoint of the unit interval and v^2 for the upper). In Figure 6, I have placed below each vertex v^j an integer label that is either 1 or 2. The rule for associating the integral label is to label v^j with 1 if $f(v^j) \geqslant v^j$ and 2 if $f(v^j) < v^j$. The combinatorial lemma, which is trivial for this one-dimensional problem, is simply that there must exist at least one small interval, in this case (v^3, v^4), whose two endpoints are differently labeled. If the grid were very fine, this combinatorial lemma would permit us to select two points, very close together, for which $f(x) - x$ has opposite signs. Any point in the interval will then serve as an approximate fixed point of the mapping, with the degree of approximation [the closeness of x to $f(x)$] controlled by the fineness of the grid, and the modulus of continuity of f. Of course, a proof of the existence of a true rather than approximate fixed point involves continued refinement of the grid and the selection of a convergent subsequence of approximants.

Our first generalization of this elementary combinatorial observation will involve the special class of simplicial subdivisions specified in the following definition.

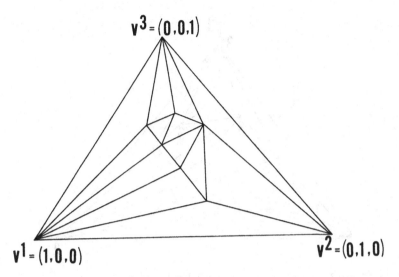

Figure 7. A restricted subdivision.

3.2 [Definition]. A simplicial subdivision of the simplex

$$S = \{x \mid x = (x_1, \ldots, x_n) \mid x_i \geqslant 0, \ \sum x_i = 1\}$$

will be said to be *restricted* if no vertices of the subdivision, other than the n unit vectors, lie on the boundary of S.

An example of a restricted simplicial subdivision is given in Figure 7.

Let us consider a restricted subdivision of S, with $v^1, \ldots, v^n$ representing the first n unit vectors, and with remaining vertices $v^{n+1}, \ldots, v^k$. We shall assume that each vertex of the subdivision has associated with it an integer label $l(v^j)$ selected from the set $(1, 2, \ldots, n)$. When, in a moment, we apply our argument to Brouwer's theorem, the label associated with a given vertex will depend on the continuous mapping $f(x)$. For the present, however, the labels will be completely arbitrary aside from the condition that $l(v^j) = j$ for $j = 1, 2, \ldots, n$. In other words, the only vertices whose labels are prescribed in advance are those on the boundary of S.

The remarkable combinatorial lemma that lies behind Brouwer's theorem is the following:

3.3 [Lemma]. Let the simplicial subdivision be restricted, and let the integer labels $l(v^j)$ be arbitrary members of the set $(1, 2, \ldots, n)$ aside

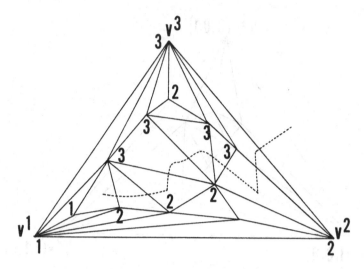

Figure 8. The path to a completely labeled simplex.

from the condition that $l(v^j) = j$ for $j = 1, 2, \ldots, n$. Then there exists at least one simplex in the simplicial subdivision all of whose labels are distinct.

Avoiding for the moment the question of why one would want to find a simplex with distinct labels, we shall demonstrate the existence of such a simplex by an explicit computational procedure based on an argument that first appears in Lemke and Howson (1964) and Lemke (1965).

We begin by considering that unique simplex in the subdivision whose vertices are the $n-1$ unit vectors $v^2, v^3, \ldots, v^n$ and a single other vertex, say v^j. The vertices $v^2, v^3, \ldots, v^n$ will have the labels $2, 3, \ldots, n$. If the vertex v^j is labeled 1, the algorithm terminates immediately with a simplex whose labels are distinct, that is, a *completely labeled simplex*. Otherwise $l(v^j)$ will be one of the integers $2, 3, \ldots, n$. We proceed by eliminating the vertex whose label agrees with $l(v^j)$, arriving at a new simplex in the subdivision. Again we determine the label associated with the new vertex that has just been introduced. If this label is 1, we terminate; otherwise the process continues by eliminating that old vertex in the simplex whose label agrees with that of the vertex just introduced.

At each stage of the algorithm we will be faced with a simplex in the subdivision whose n vertices bear the $n-1$ labels $2, 3, \ldots, n$. A pair of the vertices, one of which has just been introduced, will have a common label. We continue by removing that member of this pair that has not just been introduced.

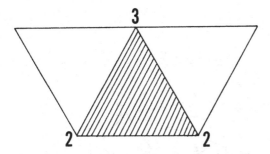

Figure 9. A revisited simplex.

Figure 8 illustrates a typical example of a path of simplices followed by the algorithm.

There are a finite number of simplices in the subdivision. We shall demonstrate that the algorithm never returns to a simplex that it previously encounters. Assuming this to be correct, the algorithm must terminate after a finite number of iterations. But termination can only occur if we have reached a simplex all of whose labels are different, or if we arrive at a simplex $n-1$ of whose vertices lie on the boundary of S, with the remaining vertex about to be removed. Such a boundary simplex would, however, have to contain the vertices $v^2, \ldots, v^n$, since if the vertex v^1 appears in a simplex encountered in the algorithm, the label 1 would have been obtained and the algorithm would have terminated.

We see, therefore, that a proof that the algorithm terminates in a finite number of iterations, with a simplex whose labels are distinct, consists in showing that the algorithm never returns to the same simplex. Consider the *first* simplex that is revisited (as in Figure 9). If it is not the initial simplex, it can be arrived at in one of two possible ways – through one or another of the adjacent simplices with $n-1$ distinct labels. But both of these adjacent simplices would have been encountered during the first visit and our simplex is therefore not the first simplex to be revisited. A similar argument demonstrates that the initial simplex (with vertices $v^2, v^3, \ldots, v^n$ and one other vertex) is not the first simplex to be revisited. This concludes the proof of Lemma 3.3.

The customary proofs of Brouwer's theorem make use of a combinatorial lemma known as Sperner's lemma (see, for example, Berge, 1959), which is a generalization of 3.3 to arbitrary simplicial subdivisions of the simplex. Consider now a simplicial subdivision many of whose vertices lie on the boundary of S. The vertices v^j will again be labeled with integer labels $l(v^j)$ selected from the set $(1, 2, \ldots, n)$. The vertices that are interior to S will have arbitrary labels (as in Figure 10). In order

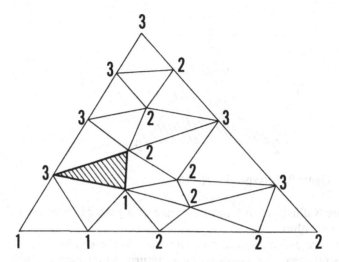

Figure 10. Sperner's lemma.

to guarantee the existence of a simplex all of whose labels are distinct, the vertices on the boundary faces of S will have labels that are restricted according to the following theorem:

3.4 [Sperner's lemma]. Let v be an arbitrary vertex in the subdivision and assume that $l(v)$ is one of the indices i for which $v_i > 0$. Then there exists a simplex in the subdivision with distinct labels.

The assumption of Sperner's lemma is that a vertex on a face of S generated by a subset of the unit vectors must have a label corresponding to one of these unit vectors. The assumption is illustrated in Figure 10, in which the shaded simplex is completely labeled.

Sperner's lemma may be demonstrated from Lemma 3.3 by the following simple argument. We embed the unit simplex in a larger simplex S' with vertices $s^1, \ldots, s^n$. We then extend the simplicial subdivision of S to a *restricted* simplicial subdivision of S' by introducing a number of simplices obtained in the following way: Take an arbitrary subset T of $(1, 2, \ldots, n)$ with $t < n$ members. Consider a collection of $n - t$ vertices that are on the face of S defined by $x_i = 0$ for $i \in T$ and that lie in a single simplex of the subdivision of S. These $n - t$ vertices in S are augmented as in Figure 11 by the t vertices s^i for $i \in T$ in order to define a simplex in the larger subdivision.

Lemma 3.3 will be applied to the subdivision of S'. We must associate

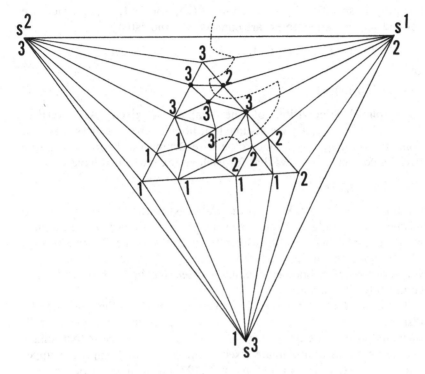

Figure 11. An embedding in a larger simplex.

a distinct label with each of the new vertices $s^1, \ldots, s^n$, and we wish to do this in such a fashion that the completely labeled simplex obtained by applying 3.3 will contain none of the new vertices.

Let us define $l(s^i)$ to be equal to $i+1$ modulo n. In other words, $l(s^1) = 2, l(s^2) = 3, \ldots, l(s^n) = 1$. A completely labeled simplex may then contain the vertices s^i for i in T, and $n-t$ other vertices on the face $x_i = 0$ for $i \in T$. Since these remaining vertices will, by the assumption of Sperner's lemma, have labels different from the members of T, it follows that the collection of vertices s^i in the completely labeled simplex must bear all of the labels in T. This is in contradiction to $l(s^i) = i+1$ modulo n, unless T is the empty set and the completely labeled simplex is a member of the original simplicial subdivision of S. This completes the proof.

Having demonstrated Sperner's lemma by means of an explicit computational procedure, we turn now to Brouwer's theorem. Let us consider a continuous mapping $x \to f(x)$ of the unit simplex into itself. The mapping is specified by n functions $f_i(x)$, for $i = 1, \ldots, n$, which are defined on the unit simplex, are continuous, and satisfy

$$f_i(x) \geqslant 0 \qquad \text{for} \quad i = 1, \ldots, n$$

and

$$\sum f_i(x) \equiv 1$$

A simplicial subdivision of the simplex is given, with vertices $v^1, \ldots, v^n, v^{n+1}, \ldots, v^k$. We assume that none of these vertices is a fixed point of the mapping f, since otherwise Brouwer's theorem would be trivially correct. It follows that for each vertex v we must have

$$v_i > f_i(v)$$

for at least one index i. We define the label associated with the vertex v to be one of these indices. If the vertex lies on the boundary of the simplex, with say $v_j = 0$, then the label associated with v must be different from j. The assumptions of Sperner's lemma are satisfied and the algorithm on which our proof of Sperner's lemma is based may be used to determine a completely labeled simplex.

If the simplicial subdivision has a very fine mesh, in the sense that the distance between any pair of points in the same simplex is quite small, then any point in the completely labeled simplex will be close to its image and serve as an approximate fixed point of the mapping. [An upper bound for $\|f(x) - x\|$ is given in Scarf (1973) as a function of the mesh size and the modulus of continuity of the mapping.] In order to demonstrate Brouwer's theorem completely we must consider a sequence of subdivisions whose mesh tends to zero. Each such subdivision will yield a completely labeled simplex, and as a consequence of the compactness of the unit simplex there is a convergent subsequence of completely labeled simplices all of whose vertices tend to a single point x^*. (This is, of course, the nonconstructive step in demonstrating Brouwer's theorem, rather than providing an approximate fixed point.) The point x^* is the limit of points bearing all of the labels $1, 2, \ldots, n$. Since f is continuous, it follows that

$$x_i^* \geqslant f_i(x^*) \qquad \text{for all} \quad i$$

But $\sum x_i^* = \sum f_i(x^*)$, and therefore $x_i^* = f_i(x^*)$, for $i = 1, \ldots, n$. This concludes the proof of Brouwer's theorem.

Let us now show that the existence of equilibrium prices for a model of exchange follows directly from Sperner's lemma without using Brouwer's theorem as an intermediary tool. We consider the continuous excess demand functions $\xi_1(\pi), \ldots, \xi_n(\pi)$ defined on the unit price simplex

$$S = \{ \pi = (\pi_1, \ldots, \pi_n) \mid \pi_i \geqslant 0, \ \sum \pi_i = 1 \}$$

and satisfying the Walras law

$$\sum \pi_i \xi_i(\pi) \equiv 0$$

Now S is subjected to a simplicial subdivision of fine mesh, with vertices $\pi^1, \ldots, \pi^n, \pi^{n+1}, \ldots, \pi^k$. We shall label a vertex π of this subdivision with an integer i for which $\xi_i \leqslant 0$.

In order to satisfy the hypothesis of Sperner's lemma we must show that for any price vector π, there is at least one coordinate with $\pi_i > 0$ and $\xi_i(\pi) \leqslant 0$; this will provide us with a labeling consistent with 3.4. But this is certainly correct, since otherwise every coordinate i with $\pi_i > 0$ would have $\xi_i(\pi) > 0$, violating the Walras law.

We may therefore conclude that there is a simplex with distinct labels. If the subdivisions are refined, we may select a subsequence of these completely labeled simplices whose vertices tend, in the limit, to a price vector π^*. Since the excess demand functions are continuous, $\xi_i(\pi^*) \leqslant 0$ for all i, and π^* is indeed an equilibrium price vector.

4   The nonretraction theorem

Brouwer's theorem is frequently demonstrated by an appeal to a well-known topological theorem that asserts that there is no continuous mapping of the unit simplex that carries all points in the simplex into the boundary and that maps each boundary point into itself (Hirsch, 1963). It will be instructive for us to see the relationship between these two theorems and to interpret our combinatorial Lemma 3.3 as an example of the nonretraction theorem.

To see that Brouwer's theorem follows from the nonretraction theorem let $x \rightarrow f(x)$ be a continuous mapping of the unit simplex into itself. If the mapping has no fixed points, we can define a continuous retraction to the boundary of S in the following way (see Figure 12).

For each x draw the straight line originating at the image $f(x)$ and passing through x. The straight line will intersect the boundary of the simplex at a point which we call $g(x)$. Clearly $g(x)$ is a continuous function of x, and for any x on the boundary of the simplex $g(x) \equiv x$; g is therefore a continuous retraction of x onto the boundary. Since this cannot be, the original mapping must have a fixed point.

Conversely Brouwer's theorem may be used to demonstrate the non-existence of a continuous retraction g. We simply compose g with a continuous mapping of the boundary of the simplex into itself, which has no fixed points. [For example, the mapping $(x_1, x_2, \ldots, x_n) \rightarrow (x_n, x_1, \ldots, x_{n-1})$.] The composite mapping will have no fixed points and therefore will contradict Brouwer's theorem.

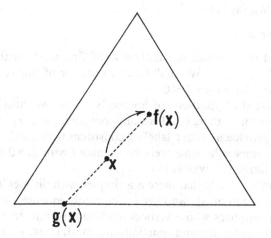

Figure 12. Brouwer's theorem and the nonretraction theorem.

Now let us return to the situation described in Lemma 3.3. The unit simplex is given a *restricted* simplicial subdivision with vertices $v^1, \ldots, v^n, v^{n+1}, \ldots, v^k$. All of these vertices, aside from the first n, are assumed to be strictly interior to the simplex. In addition, each vertex is given an integer label $l(v)$, which is selected without restriction from the set $(1, 2, \ldots, n)$, aside from the requirement that $l(v^j) = j$ for $j = 1, \ldots, n$.

These integer labels may be used to define a continuous piecewise-linear mapping $g(x)$ of the unit simplex into itself. For each vertex v in the subdivision we define $g(v) = v^{l(v)}$, in other words, to be that one of the first n vertices whose label agrees with that of v. We then extend the mapping linearly throughout each simplex in the subdivision, in the following way: If a simplex in the subdivision has vertices $v^{j_1}, v^{j_2}, \ldots, v^{j_n}$, then a point in the simplex has the form

$$x = \alpha_1 v^{j_1} + \alpha_2 v^{j_2} + \cdots + \alpha_n v^{j_n}$$

with $\alpha_i \geqslant 0$, $\sum \alpha_i = 1$ (see Figure 13). We then define

$$g(x) = \alpha_1 g(v^{j_1}) + \alpha_2 g(v^{j_2}) + \cdots + \alpha_n g(v^{j_n})$$

The mapping g is clearly continuous, and as a consequence of the assumption that the subdivision is restricted, $g(x) \equiv x$ for every boundary point of the simplex. This follows from the observation that a boundary point of S is a convex combination of a subset of the first n vectors, each of which is mapped into itself by g.

If Lemma 3.3 were false, no simplex in the subdivision would have a full set of labels. But the n vertices of a simplex for which, say, the label 1

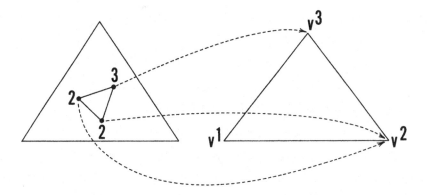

Figure 13. A piecewise linear mapping.

is missing would all be mapped, under g, into that face of the boundary of S given by $x_1 = 0$. Every point on such a simplex would also be mapped, by our construction, into the same face. We see, therefore, that the absence of a simplex with a complete set of labels permits us to construct a continuous piecewise-linear retraction of the simplex into itself.

The constructive argument given for Lemma 3.3 may also be interpreted in terms of $g(x)$, as first suggested by Hirsch (1963). Let c be a vector on the boundary of S, whose first coordinate is zero and whose remaining coordinates are strictly positive. We shall demonstrate that there exists a continuous path $x(t)$ that is linear in each simplex of the subdivision of the simplex through which it passes and which satisfies $g(x(t)) \equiv c$. Moreover, the path will have one endpoint at c, the other endpoint in a completely labeled simplex, and trace out precisely that sequence of simplices that appear in the proof of 3.3.

The simplices arising in 3.3 have the property that their n vertices bear the $n-1$ labels $2, 3, \ldots, n$. One of these labels will appear on two distinct vertices. Two faces of the simplex can be constructed by dropping either one of these two vertices; the $n-1$ vertices on each of these faces will have a full set of labels $2, 3, \ldots, n$. It follows that there is an interior point on each of these two faces for which $g(x) = c$. Since the mapping is linear, the straight-line segment connecting these two points will also satisfy $g(x) = c$ (see Figure 14).

This continuous piecewise-linear path starts at the boundary point c and passes through a sequence of simplices bearing the $n-1$ labels $2, 3, \ldots, n$. It terminates upon reaching a completely labeled simplex since such a simplex would have no other face on which $g(x) = c$ has a solution. This does in fact provide an alternative proof for Lemma 3.3

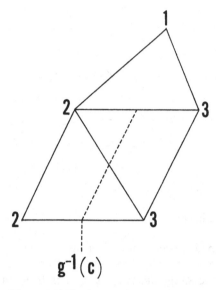

Figure 14. The inverse image of a point.

since if there were no completely labeled simplex, the path could never terminate.

The relationship between fixed-point theorems and the solution of systems of equations will be explored later in this chapter.

5   A specific subdivision

The algorithm described in Section 3 approximates a fixed point of a continuous mapping by moving systematically through a sequence of simplices in the simplicial subdivision. At each iteration we are given a particular simplex with vertices, say, $v^{j_1}, \ldots, v^{j_n}$. Depending on the particular assignment of integer labels, a specific vertex in the simplex is removed; we move to that unique simplex in the subdivision that has $n-1$ vertices in common with the remaining vertices of the original simplex. If the method is to be implemented effectively on a computer, the simplicial subdivision must be such that this replacement operation is easy to carry out. Moreover, the vertices of the simplicial subdivision must be scattered with some regularity throughout the unit simplex so that the degree of approximation is independent of the region of the simplex in which the approximate fixed point happens to lie. The particular subdivision, which was brought to the attention of researchers in this

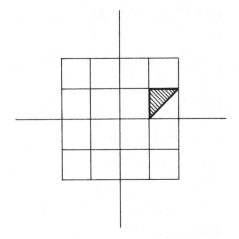

Figure 15. A simplicial subdivision of R^2.

field by Hansen (1968) and Kuhn (1968), solves these two problems admirably. (It should be remarked that many other subdivisions, which are superior in practice to the Hansen–Kuhn subdivision, have been proposed since the early 1970s.)

We begin our discussion by describing this particular simplicial subdivision for n-dimensional Euclidean space. The n unit vectors will be denoted by $e^1, e^2, \ldots, e^n$. With this notation a simplex will have $n+1$ vertices $v^0, v^1, \ldots, v^n$, which will consist of the points in R^n with integral coordinates.

5.1 [Definition]. A typical *simplex* in the subdivision will be defined by an integral point b (called the *base point*) and a permutation $(\phi_1, \ldots, \phi_n)$ of the integers $1, 2, \ldots, n$. The vertices are then given by

$$
\begin{aligned}
v^0 &= b \\
v^1 &= v^0 + e^{\phi_1} \\
v^2 &= v^1 + e^{\phi_2} \\
&\ \ \vdots \\
v^n &= v^{n-1} + e^{\phi_n}
\end{aligned}
$$

Figure 15 illustrates this simplicial subdivision for the plane. The shaded simplex has the base point $b = (1, 0)$ and the permutation $(\phi_1, \phi_2) = (2, 1)$. Its vertices consist therefore of

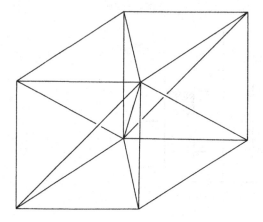

Figure 16. A simplicial subdivision of R^3.

$$v^0 = b \qquad = (1, 0)$$
$$v^1 = v^0 + e^2 = (1, 1)$$
$$v^2 = v^1 + e^1 = (2, 1)$$

These are two distinct types of simplices in the plane: one for each of the two permutations of $(1, 2)$. In general, there will be $n!$ distinct simplices with every simplex in the subdivision equivalent under translation to one of them. Figure 16 illustrates the six distinct simplices for $n = 3$.

One of the major virtues of this particular simplicial subdivision is that the replacement operation has a remarkably simple form, which can be programmed for the computer with great ease. (See Scarf, 1973, for a proof of the following theorem and a demonstration that this construction is indeed a simplicial subdivision.)

5.2 [Theorem]. Let the vertices of a simplex in the simplicial subdivision be given be $v^0, v^1, \ldots, v^n$, according to 5.1. The replacement for an arbitrary vertex v^j is given by

$$v^{j-1} + v^{j+1} - v^j$$

with the superscripts interpreted modulo n.

In practice we store the vertices of the current simplex as columns in a matrix. When a given column is removed it is replaced by the sum of its two adjacent columns minus itself, with the interpretation that columns 0 and n are adjacent. The following examples illustrate this remark:

$$\begin{bmatrix} 0 & 1 & 1 & 1 \\ 0 & 0 & 1 & 1 \\ 0 & 0 & 0 & 1 \end{bmatrix}$$

$\downarrow$

$$\begin{bmatrix} 0 & 1 & 1 & 1 \\ 0 & 0 & 0 & 1 \\ 0 & 0 & 1 & 1 \end{bmatrix}$$

$\downarrow$

$$\begin{bmatrix} 2 & 1 & 1 & 1 \\ 1 & 0 & 0 & 1 \\ 1 & 0 & 1 & 1 \end{bmatrix}$$

$\downarrow$

$$\begin{bmatrix} 2 & 2 & 1 & 1 \\ 1 & 1 & 0 & 1 \\ 1 & 2 & 1 & 1 \end{bmatrix}$$

In order to implement our constructive approach to fixed-point theorems, we require a simplicial subdivision of the unit simplex,

$$S = \left\{ x = (x_0, \ldots, x_n) \mid x_i \geq 0, \ \sum_0^n x_i = 1 \right\}$$

and with two vectors in the same simplex close to each other. We shall construct such a simplicial subdivision with vertices $(k_0/D, k_1/D, \ldots, k_n/D)$, where D is a large positive integer and $k_0, \ldots, k_n$ nonnegative integers summing to D. To do this we simply modify the definition given in 5.1 by letting the base point b be an integral vector in R^{n+1} whose coordinates sum to D and by redefining $e^1, \ldots, e^n$ to be the n vectors in R^{n+1} given by

$$e^1 = (1, -1, 0, \ldots, 0)$$
$$e^2 = (0, 1, -1, \ldots, 0)$$
$$\vdots$$
$$e^n = (0, 0, 0, \ldots, 1, -1)$$

The simplices defined by

$$k^0 = b$$
$$k^1 = k^0 + e^{\phi_1}$$
$$\vdots$$
$$k^n = k^{n-1} + e^{\phi_n}$$

will have all of their vertices on the plane $\sum_0^n k_j = D$ and will form a simplicial subdivision of this plane since they are obtained from our previous subdivision of R^n by a linear transformation.

It should be noticed that the replacement operation described in 5.2 holds, in precisely the same form, for this simplicial subdivision. A sequence of replacements is illustrated in Figure 17.

In Figure 17, $D = 5$; the numerators of the vertices in the sequence of simplices are as follows:

$$\begin{bmatrix} 5 & 4 & 4 \\ 0 & 0 & 1 \\ 0 & 1 & 0 \end{bmatrix}$$
$$\downarrow$$
$$\begin{bmatrix} 3 & 4 & 4 \\ 1 & 0 & 1 \\ 1 & 1 & 0 \end{bmatrix}$$
$$\downarrow$$
$$\begin{bmatrix} 3 & 3 & 4 \\ 1 & 2 & 1 \\ 1 & 0 & 0 \end{bmatrix}$$
$$\downarrow$$
$$\begin{bmatrix} 3 & 3 & 2 \\ 1 & 2 & 2 \\ 1 & 0 & 1 \end{bmatrix}$$
$$\downarrow$$
$$\begin{bmatrix} 3 & 2 & 2 \\ 1 & 1 & 2 \\ 1 & 2 & 1 \end{bmatrix}$$
$$\downarrow$$
$$\begin{bmatrix} 1 & 2 & 2 \\ 2 & 1 & 2 \\ 2 & 2 & 1 \end{bmatrix}$$

6   A numerical example

In this section we shall give an example of a general equilibrium model that we shall solve by the use of Lemma 3.4 and the particular simplicial subdivision of the last section. Our previous discussion of Sperner's lemma involved embedding the unit simplex in a larger simplex and extending the simplicial subdivision to a restricted subdivision of the larger simplex (see Figure 11). Since the new subdivision will not be of the type described in the previous section, the very elementary replacement operation cannot be employed without some modification. Before presenting the numerical example I shall describe Kuhn's method (1968) for initiating the algorithm, which avoids this difficulty and in addition permits us to start our calculation at any boundary point of the simplex.

Let the unit simplex

$$S = \left\{ x = (x_1, \ldots, x_n) \mid x_i \geq 0, \ \sum_{i=1}^{n} x_i = 1 \right\}$$

be given a simplicial subdivision of the type described in the previous section. We select a large positive integer D and consider as vertices in the

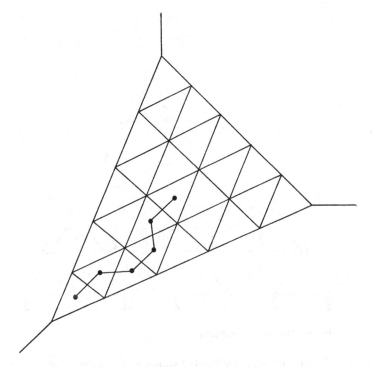

Figure 17. A sequence of replacements.

subdivision the points $(k_1/D,\ldots,k_n/D)$ with $k_1,\ldots,k_n$ nonnegative integers summing to D. The numerators of the vertices of any particular simplex in the subdivision can be written as the columns in an $n \times n$ matrix

$$K = \begin{bmatrix} k_1^1 & \cdots & k_1^n \\ \vdots & & \vdots \\ k_n^1 & & k_n^n \end{bmatrix}$$

The arguments of the previous section imply that the columns of K can be ordered in such a way that $k^j = k^{j-1} + e^{\phi_j}$, where e^i is a vector whose $(i-1)$st coordinate is $+1$, whose ith coordinate is -1, and whose remaining coordinates are 0. Moreover, $\phi_2,\ldots,\phi_n$ is a permutation of the set $(2,\ldots,n)$. In other words, each column is identical with its predecessor (interpreted modulo n) except for the entries in two successive rows the first of which is a single unit higher and the second a single unit lower than the entries in the preceding column.

The vertices k^j/D are given an integer label $l(k^j)$ taken from the set $(1,2,\ldots,n)$ and subject to the requirement that a vector receive a label corresponding to one of its positive coordinates. Let us attempt to initiate

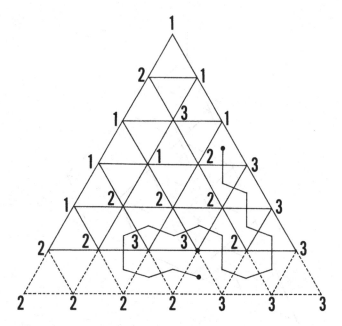

Figure 18. Kuhn's method.

our search for a completely labeled simplex at a point $(0, k_2^*, \ldots, k_n^*)$ on that face of the simplex whose first coordinate is 0.

We begin by extending the simplex to include those vertices whose first coordinate is given by $k_1 = -1$ (see Figure 18). These additional vertices will be given an integer label, from the set $(2, \ldots, n)$, in such a way that there is a *unique* simplex in the extended subdivision, which consists of a single vertex with $k_1 = 0$, $n-1$ vertices with $k_1 = -1$, and with the latter set of vertices bearing all of the labels $2, \ldots, n$.

6.1 [Labeling rule]. A vertex given by $(-1, k_2, \ldots, k_n)$, with $k_i \geq 0$, for $i = 2, \ldots, n$ and $\sum_2^n k_j = D + 1$, will be labeled with the first integer for which $k_i > k_i^*$.

The columns of the matrix

$$
\begin{bmatrix}
-1 & \cdots & -1 & -1 & 0 \\
k_2^* & & k_2^* & k_2^* + 1 & k_2^* \\
k_3^* & & k_3^* + 1 & k_3^* & k_3^* \\
\vdots & & \vdots & \vdots & \vdots \\
k_n^* + 1 & & k_n^* & k_n^* & k_n^*
\end{bmatrix}
$$

Table 1

Consumer	Initial stock of commodities									
1	.6	.2	.2	20.0	.1	2.0	9.0	5.0	5.0	15.0
2	.2	11.0	12.0	13.0	14.0	15.0	16.0	5.0	5.0	9.0
3	.4	9.0	8.0	7.0	6.0	5.0	4.0	5.0	7.0	12.0
4	1.0	5.0	5.0	5.0	5.0	5.0	5.0	8.0	3.0	17.0
5	8.0	1.0	22.0	10.0	.3	.9	5.1	.1	6.2	11.0

represent a simplex in this extended subdivision. The first $n-1$ vectors bear the labels $n, n-1, \ldots, 2$; the final vector bears a label different from 1. The algorithm will be initiated at this simplex and can only run into difficulty if it encounters another simplex

$$\begin{bmatrix} -1 & \cdots & -1 & 0 \\ k_2^1 & & k_2^{n-1} & k_2^n \\ \vdots & & \vdots & \vdots \\ k_n^1 & & k_n^{n-1} & k_n^n \end{bmatrix}$$

whose first $n-1$ columns bear all of the labels $n, \ldots, 2$, say in that particular order. For this to be true, however, we must have

$$k_{n-j+1}^j > k_{n-j+1}^* \qquad \text{for} \quad j=1, \ldots, n-1$$

Since no two entries in the same row of this matrix differ by more than unity,

$$k_i^j \geqslant k_i^* \qquad \text{for} \quad j=1, \ldots, n-1 \quad \text{and} \quad i=2, \ldots, n$$

But

$$\sum_{i=2}^n k_i^j = \sum_{i=2}^n k_i^* + 1$$

and it follows that the second matrix is identical to the one initiating the algorithm, a form of cycling ruled out by our general arguments.

Let us now consider an example of an exchange economy involving 5 types of consumers and 10 commodities. The ith consumer will own, prior to trade, a specific vector w^i, as given by Table 1.

The ith consumer's demand functions will be derived from a utility function

$$u_i(x) = \sum_{j=1}^{10} a_{ij}^{1/b_i} x_j^{1-(1/b_i)}$$

Table 2

Consumer	Utility parameters									
1	1.0	1.0	3.0	.1	.1	1.2	2.0	1.0	1.0	.07
2	1.0	1.0	1.0	1.0	1.0	1.0	1.0	1.0	1.0	1.0
3	9.9	.1	5.0	.2	6.0	.2	8.0	1.0	1.0	.2
4	1.0	2.0	3.0	4.0	5.0	6.0	7.0	8.0	9.0	10.0
5	1.0	13.0	11.0	9.0	4.0	.9	8.0	1.0	2.0	10.0

Table 3

Consumer	b
1	2.0
2	1.3
3	3.0
4	.2
5	.6

Table 2 describes the parameters a_{ij} for each consumer. The parameters b are given by Table 3.

The problem was solved by selecting $D = 200$ and initiating the algorithm as the center of the face $x_1 = 0$. After 6063 iterations the following matrix, whose columns are the numerators of the vertices of a completely labeled simplex, was found:

$$\begin{bmatrix}
39 & 39 & 39 & 39 & 40 & 39 & 39 & 39 & 39 & 39 \\
22 & 22 & 22 & 22 & 22 & 23 & 22 & 22 & 22 & 22 \\
19 & 19 & 19 & 19 & 19 & 19 & 20 & 19 & 19 & 19 \\
8 & 8 & 8 & 8 & 8 & 8 & 8 & 9 & 8 & 8 \\
23 & 23 & 23 & 23 & 23 & 23 & 23 & 23 & 24 & 23 \\
15 & 15 & 15 & 15 & 15 & 15 & 15 & 15 & 15 & 16 \\
24 & 23 & 23 & 23 & 23 & 23 & 23 & 23 & 23 & 23 \\
21 & 22 & 21 & 21 & 21 & 21 & 21 & 21 & 21 & 21 \\
20 & 20 & 21 & 20 & 20 & 20 & 20 & 20 & 20 & 20 \\
9 & 9 & 9 & 10 & 9 & 9 & 9 & 9 & 9 & 9
\end{bmatrix}$$

Each of these columns, after division by 200, may be used as an approximate equilibrium price vector, yielding a vector of excess demands that is fairly close to zero. A better approximation is obtained by averaging these prices, using a variation of Newton's method, to yield

$$\pi = (.187, .109, .099, .043, .117, .077, .117, .102, .099, .049)$$

At this price vector the excess demands are equal to zero for two decimal places.

As can be seen, the algorithm requires a fairly substantial amount of computation in order to yield a modest accuracy. In the next several sections we shall describe a number of variations of the basic algorithm that provide a dramatic improvement in computational speed in addition to extending the class of problems to which these methods can be applied.

7 Vector labels

The algorithm with which we have been concerned associates with each vertex of a simplicial subdivision an integer label selected from the set $(1, 2, \ldots, n)$. When applied, for example, to determining equilibrium prices for a model of exchange the excess demands $\xi_1(\pi), \ldots, \xi_n(\pi)$ are evaluated, and the associated label corresponds, say, to a commodity with negative excess demand.

It is clearly inefficient from a computational point of view to replace the vector of excess demands, whose evaluation may in itself be quite time-consuming, by a single integer. The vector-labeling procedures to be discussed in this section permit us to utilize all of the information in the excess demand vector with the expectation of greater accuracy in less computing time. In addition, they are applicable to a large class of problems, including, for example, the approximation of a fixed point implied by Kakutani's theorem, to which the earlier methods cannot readily be applied.

Let us consider, as in Figure 19, a *restricted* simplicial subdivision of the unit simplex, with vertices $v^1, \ldots, v^n, v^{n+1}, \ldots, v^k$.

Each vertex v^j will have associated with it a label $l(v^j)$, which is a vector in n-dimensional space. In the applications of the vector-labeling algorithms these labels will depend on the particular problem being solved. For the moment, however, the labels are arbitrary, aside from the stipulation that the unit vectors defining the simplex receive the labels $l(v^j) = v^j$ for $j = 1, 2, \ldots, n$. We shall also be given, in advance, a specific positive vector b in R^n.

Our previous algorithms attempted to determine a simplex in the subdivision with vertices $v^{j_1}, v^{j_2}, \ldots, v^{j_n}$ and whose labels $l(v^{j_1}), l(v^{j_2}), \ldots, l(v^{j_n})$ were distinct. By a solution to the vector-labeling problem we mean the

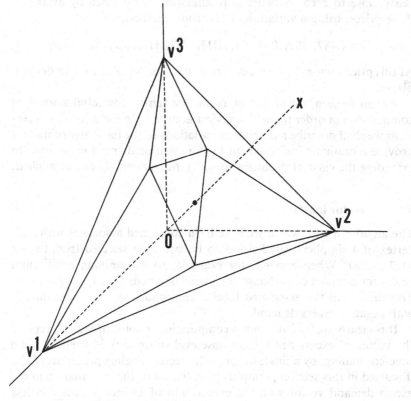

Figure 19. Vector labels.

determination of a simplex with vertices $v^{j_1}, \ldots, v^{j_n}$, for which the system of linear equations

$$y_{j_1} l(v^{j_1}) + \cdots + y_{j_n} l(v^{j_n}) = b$$

have a nonnegative solution $y_{j_1}, \ldots, y_{j_n}$. The following theorem provides sufficient conditions on the labels $l(v^j)$ for the problem to have a solution:

7.1 [Theorem]. Consider a restricted subdivision of the unit simplex with vertices $v^1, \ldots, v^n, v^{n+1}, \ldots, v^k$. Each vertex v^j has associated with it a label $l(v^j) \in R^n$; the first n vectors have as labels $l(v^j) = v^j$. Assume that

$$\sum_{j=1}^{k} y_j l(v^j) \leqslant 0$$

and $y_j \geq 0$ for $j = 1, \ldots, k$ imply $y_j = 0$ for all j. Then for any positive vector $b \in R^n$, there is a simplex in the subdivision with vertices $v^{j_1}, \ldots, v^{j_n}$ such that

$$\sum_i y_{j_i} l(v^{j_i}) = b$$

has a nonnegative solution.

There are several methods for demonstrating Theorem 7.1 and its generalizations to an arbitrary simplicial subdivision. We shall make use of the path-following techniques that produce a completely labeled Sperner simplex based on the nonretraction theorem. In that argument the integer labels associated with the vertices of a restricted subdivision were used to construct a piecewise-linear mapping of the simplex $g(x)$ with $g(x) \equiv x$ on the boundary. The algorithm for finding a Sperner simplex was then shown to be equivalent to following the piecewise-linear path $g^{-1}(c)$, with c a specified point on the boundary of the simplex.

There are many applications of the basic idea of following the inverse image of a mapping from a given set to an image set of one-lower dimension. Eaves and Scarf (1976) discuss a number of these applications in detail when the mappings are piecewise-linear. Similar algorithms for differentiable mappings were introduced in the mid-1970s and have provided an extremely fertile field of research. (See Allgower and Georg, 1980, in addition to the previously mentioned references.)

Let us begin by defining a mapping $g(x_1, \ldots, x_n)$ from the nonnegative orthant of R^n into R^n in the following way:

7.2 [Definition]. The mapping $g(x)$ is defined to be the unique mapping satisfying

1. $g(v^j) = l(v^j)$ for each vertex in the subdivision.
2. $g(x)$ is linear in each simplex in the subdivision.
3. $g(x)$ is homogeneous of degree 1, that is, $g(\lambda x) = \lambda g(x)$ for $\lambda \geq 0$.

To determine $g(x)$ for any nonnegative x (different from 0) we find that λ for which λx is on the unit simplex, and therefore contained in a particular simplex with vertices $v^{j_1}, \ldots, v^{j_n}$. We then write

$$\lambda x = y_{j_1} v^{j_1} + \cdots + y_{j_n} v^{j_n}$$

with $y \geq 0$ and summing to 1, and define

$$g(\lambda x) = y_{j_1} l(v^{j_1}) + \cdots + y_{j_n} l(v^{j_n})$$

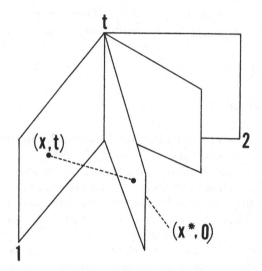

Figure 20. Pieces of linearity.

With this interpretation we see that Theorem 7.1 is equivalent to assert-ing the existence of a vector x^* with $g(x^*)=b$. The validity of this asser-tion is a consequence of the following two properties, which are imme-diate from the definition of $g(x)$:

7.3 [Properties]

    1. $g(x)=x$ for x on the boundary of the positive orthant.
    2. $g(x)\leqslant 0$ implies $x=0$.

The mapping $g(x)$ is piecewise-linear. The nonnegative orthant of R^n is partitioned into a finite set of polyhedral cones – each one of which has n extreme rays through the origin – and such that g is linear in each cone.

Let $P=R_+^n\times[0,1]$, the product of the nonnegative orthant and the closed unit interval. The set P is naturally subdivided into a finite num-ber of "wedges" (products of cones and the unit interval) as Figure 20 indicates for $n=2$.

We shall extend g to a mapping G of the set P into n space in such a way that G is linear in each wedge.

7.4 [Definition]. Let c be a vector in R^n, strictly larger than b in each coordinate. For $(x_1,\ldots,x_n,t)\in P$ we define

$$G(x,t)=g(x)+tc$$

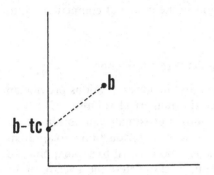

Figure 21. The boundary solution.

With this definition a solution to the vector-labeling problem is a vector x^* for which $G(x^*, 0) = b$. The mapping G will permit us to trace out the one-dimensional family of solutions to $G(x, t) = b$ and to show that there is at least one member of the family with $t = 0$.

The boundary of the set P consists of a number of hyperplanes: the two hyperplanes given by $t = 0$ and $t = 1$ and the n hyperplanes defined by $x_i = 0$. Let us ask whether there are any solutions to $G(x, t) = b$ on the boundary of P – other than $t = 0$.

A solution on the upper boundary would require $g(x) + c = b$, and since $c > b$ this implies $g(x) < 0$, contrary to the second property in 7.3. To examine the solutions on that part of the boundary defined by $x_i = 0$, we make use of the first property in 7.3, that is, that $g(x) = x$ on the boundary of the nonnegative orthant. For such points $G(x, t) = b$ is equivalent to $x + tc = b$. These equations have a unique solution obtained by selecting that index, say i^*, for which b_i/c_i is minimal, setting $t = b_{i^*}/c_{i^*}$ and $x = b - ct$ (Figure 21).

We see that there is a unique solution to the equations $G(x, t) = b$ on the boundary of P, other than that part of the boundary on which $t = 0$. The algorithm for finding x^* consists simply of following the piecewise-linear path defined by $G(x, t) = b$ from this particular boundary point until it intersects a point on the boundary with $t = 0$. Quite elementary arguments may be used to show that generically the path $G^{-1}(b)$ is well defined and terminates on the lower boundary; the actual mechanics used in following the path are elementary modifications of linear programming pivot steps. These general methods are also extremely useful in discussing "index theory" and its implications for counting the number of solutions. [See, for example, the paper by Eaves and Scarf (1976) for a discussion of index theory in the piecewise-linear case and

Kehoe (1979, 1980) for an application to the model of competitive equilibrium.]

8   The general equilibrium model with production

The method of the preceding section and its generalizations provide an exceptionally flexible technique for the numerical solution of a wide variety of problems. They can be used to approximate equilibrium prices in a general Walrasian model – with or without production – to approximate fixed points of an upper semicontinuous point to set mapping, to solve nonlinear programming problems, and to determine a vector in the core of an n-person game. Limitations of space make it impossible to describe anything other than the application of vector-labeling methods to the determination of equilibrium prices, and even in this example we shall be forced to restrict our attention to one of the many approaches that have been suggested. The reader who is curious about other applications can consult Scarf (1973) or other items in the Bibliography at the end of the chapter.

Consider a general equilibrium model specified by a strictly positive vector w of assets prior to production, a set of market demand functions $x(\pi)$ [continuous, homogeneous of degree 1, and satisfying the Walras law $\pi \cdot x(\pi) \equiv \pi \cdot w$], and an activity analysis matrix

$$A = \begin{bmatrix} -1 \dots & 0 \dots & a_{1j} \dots \\ 0 \dots & 0 \dots & a_{2j} \dots \\ \vdots & \vdots & \vdots \\ 0 \dots & -1 \dots & a_{nj} \dots \end{bmatrix}$$

We make the conventional assumption that $Ay \geqslant 0$, $y \geqslant 0$ implies $y = 0$. A price vector π^* and a nonnegative vector of activity levels y^* will be a solution to the general equilibrium problem if

1. $x(\pi^*) = w + Ay^*$ and
2. $\pi^* A \leqslant 0$

The following assignment of vector labels to the vertices of a simplicial subdivision of the price simplex will provide an approximate solution. (The boundary labels require a slight generalization of 7.1.)

8.1 [Labeling rule]. Let π be a vertex of the simplicial subdivision. If π is on the boundary of the simplex, then $l(\pi)$ is the ith unit vector, where i is the first coordinate of π equal to zero. If π is interior to the simplex, we find that column a^j in the activity analysis matrix for which $\pi \cdot a^j$ is maximal. If $\pi \cdot a^j > 0$, then $l(\pi) = -a^j$. If $\pi \cdot a^j \leqslant 0$, then $l(\pi) = x(\pi)$. Moreover, the vector b is defined to be w.

In order to apply 7.1 we must verify that the vector labels $l(\pi^j)$ satisfy the condition that $\sum y_j l(\pi^j) \leqslant 0$, $y_j \geqslant 0$ implies $y_j = 0$ for all j. This can easily be shown to be a consequence of the assumption made about the activity analysis matrix plus the fact that for each price vector π, $x(\pi) \geqslant 0$ and is positive for at least one coordinate.

When the algorithm is applied, we determine a simplex with vertices $\pi^{j_1}, \ldots, \pi^{j_n}$. Several of these vertices will have associated vector labels that are the market demand functions evaluated at the corresponding price; the remaining vertices have labels that are the negatives of certain columns in the activity analysis matrix. With an obvious change in notation the equations $Ly = b$ can be written as

$$\sum y_j x(\pi^j) - \sum y_l a_l \leqslant w$$

Labeling Rule 8.1 permits us to make the following statement: In the above inequality $y_j > 0$ if at prices π^j *all* activities make a profit $\leqslant 0$, and $y_l > 0$ if for some vertex of the final simplex a^l is the activity that makes the largest profit and it is positive. Moreover, the ith row will be an equality unless some vertex of the final simplex has its ith coordinate equal to zero.

It may be shown that the activity levels y_l and a suitable average of the prices in the final simplex are an approximate equilibrium in the sense that the two defining properties are approximately satisfied (Scarf, 1973).

In order to illustrate this algorithm we consider an example, discussed in detail in Scarf (1967a), of a general equilibrium model with production. There are six commodities that can be described as follows:

1. Capital available at the end of the period
2. Capital available at the beginning of the period
3. Skilled labor
4. Unskilled labor
5. Nondurable consumer goods
6. Durable consumer goods

The activity analysis model of production is given by Table 4, in which the six columns representing disposal activities have been omitted.

In addition to the specification of production possibilities, we assume that there are five consumers who at the beginning of the period own positive quantities of goods 2, 3, 4, 6 according to Table 5. Each

Table 4

Commodity	Activity							
	7	8	9	10	11	12	13	14
1	4	5	1.6	1.6	1.6	.9	7	8
2	−5.3	−5	−2	−2	−2	−1	−4	−5
3	−2	−1	−2	−4	−1	0	−3	−2
4	−1	−6	−3	−1	−8	0	−1	−8
5	0	0	6	8	7	0	0	0
6	4	3.5	0	0	0	0	0	0

Table 5

Consumer	Commodity			
	2	3	4	6
1	3	5	.1	1
2	.1	.1	7	2
3	2	6	.1	1.5
4	1	.1	8	1
5	6	.1	.5	2

consumer will be assumed to have a CES utility function of the type used in Section 6 and Table 6. The parameters b are given by Table 7.

To solve this problem, a denominator $D = 200$ was selected and labeling rule 8.1 was used. After approximately 2200 iterations the simplex whose numerators are given by the columns of the following matrix was obtained:

$$\begin{bmatrix} 44 & 44 & 44 & 44 & 44 & 45 \\ 47 & 48 & 48 & 48 & 48 & 47 \\ 35 & 34 & 35 & 35 & 35 & 35 \\ 12 & 12 & 11 & 12 & 12 & 12 \\ 22 & 22 & 22 & 21 & 22 & 22 \\ 40 & 40 & 40 & 40 & 39 & 39 \end{bmatrix}$$

Five of these six columns have associated vector labels that are the negatives of activities 7, 9, 10, 11, and 13. The corresponding weights y_j' can be used as approximations to the equilibrium activity levels. In order

Table 6

Consumer	Utility parameters					
1	4	0	.2	0	2	3.6
2	.4	0	0	.6	4	1
3	2	0	.5	0	2	1.5
4	5	0	0	.2	5	4.5
5	3	0	0	.2	4	2

Table 7

Consumer	b
1	1.2
2	1.6
3	.8
4	.5
5	.6

Table 8

Activity	Level	Profit
7	.468253	.006000
8	0	− .143333
9	3.127146	.005833
10	.188899	− .005833
11	.165613	− .006667
12	0	− .039583
13	.365860	.010833
14	0	− .246667

to obtain an approximate equilibrium price vector the columns were averaged,

Equilibrium prices:

.22083   .238333   .174167   .059167   .109167   .198333

These prices were used to calculate the profitabilities in Table 8 and to evaluate the consumer market demand functions in Table 9.

Table 9

Commodity	Demand	Supply
1	11.188389	10.004686
2	0	1.191501
3	1.099712	2.090414
4	2.731755	3.970645
5	23.079518	21.433357
6	9.705318	9.373014

As can be seen, the approximation is not exceptionally accurate; in particular, the discrepancy between supply and demand is fairly large for certain commodities. An improvement in accuracy can be obtained by selecting a much finer grid, but this is a very expensive procedure since it requires us to initiate the algorithm at a vertex of the simplex and to discard the information we have already obtained as to the approximate location of the equilibrium price vector. Alternatively, there are numerical methods – essentially adaptations of Newton's method to systems of nonlinear inequalities – that can be used to improve the current approximation. But neither of these approaches is remotely as good as the algorithms of Merrill, of Eaves, and of van der Laan and Talman that are described in the next section.

9 The algorithms of Merrill, Eaves, and van der Laan and Talman

The computational methods we have discussed in the previous sections have two major drawbacks. First of all they require the algorithm to be initiated at a vertex of the unit simplex – or as in Kuhn's version of integer labeling at a boundary point of the simplex. If an answer is obtained with a fixed grid whose accuracy is inadequate for the problem at hand, the algorithm must be restarted with a finer grid and the results of the previous calculations discarded completely. The algorithms introduced by Merrill (1972), van der Laan and Talman (1979a, 1979b), and Eaves (1972) permit the computation to be initiated at an arbitrary point on the simplex and allow a continual refinement of the grid. They yield a vast improvement in computational speed over the earlier algorithms that require a fixed simplicial decomposition, and are used in virtually all practical applications of fixed-point methods.

Merrill's method, which is essentially identical to the "sandwich" method subsequently introduced by Kuhn (1975), is particularly simple

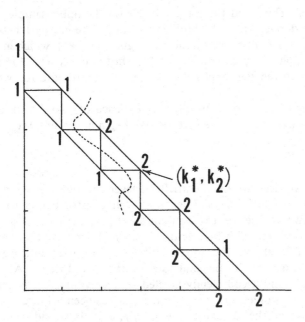

Figure 22. Merrill's algorithm.

to describe. In order to introduce the basic idea of Merrill's method, let us consider the case in which the unit simplex is one-dimensional and where the basic problem is to be solved by integer-labeling techniques. The interval $\{(x_1, x_2) \mid x_i \geqslant 0, \; x_1 + x_2 = 1\}$ is subdivided with some pre-assigned grid size D. The vertices in the subdivision will be of the form $(k_1/D, k_2/D)$, with k_1 and k_2 nonnegative integers summing to D. The numerators of the vertices of a typical simplex in the subdivision will be given by

$$\begin{bmatrix} k_1 & k_1 + 1 \\ k_2 & k_2 - 1 \end{bmatrix}$$

The vertex defined by $(0, D)$ will be given the label 1 and $(D, 0)$ the label 2. The customary integer-labeling methods starts at one of these extreme vertices and moves into the simplex until we first encounter a vertex with the other label.

Let us imagine that we have an initial guess as to where the true answer lies, given by the vector $(k_1^*/D, k_2^*/D)$, with k_1^*, k_2^* nonnegative integers adding to D. Merrill's algorithm incorporates this additional information by drawing the simplex $k_1 + k_2 = D - 1$ and subdividing the resulting two-dimensional figure (see Figure 22).

In Figure 22, $D=6$ and the integer labels on the upper simplex are assumed to be derived from the problem at hand. The integer labels on the lower simplex will be based on the initial guess (k_1^*, k_2^*), which in this particular example we assume to be $(3, 3)$. On the lower level the pair (k_1, k_2) will be given the label i if i is the first coordinate for which $k_i < k_i^*$.

Merrill's algorithm moves through a sequence of two-dimensional simplices, each defined by three vertices. We begin at the simplex

$$\begin{bmatrix} k_1^* & k_1^* - 1 & k_1^* \\ k_2^* & k_2^* & k_2^* - 1 \end{bmatrix}$$

two of whose vertices are on the artificial level and one vertex on the original simplex. The initial simplex has been constructed in such a way that the two vertices on the artificial level bear the labels 1 and 2, one of which is shared with the vector (k_1^*, k_2^*). We remove that vertex on the artificial level with the doubled label and continue until we are forced to exit through the original face of the "sandwich." At that point we have found a completely labeled simplex whose labels derive from the original problem. If the accuracy that has been achieved is not adequate, we repeat the calculation, with, say, a doubled grid size, and with the new guess given by a choice of one of the vertices in the completely labeled simplex. Since the grid size grows exponentially, we can expect a high degree of precision in a relatively small number of iterations.

The layer that is subdivided is part of a two-dimensional simplex, obtained by introducing an additional coordinate $k_0 = D - k_1 - k_2$. With this notation the initial simplex may be represented by

$$\begin{bmatrix} 0 & 1 & 1 \\ k_1^* & k_1^* - 1 & k_1^* \\ k_2^* & k_2^* & k_2^* - 1 \end{bmatrix}$$

This permits us to make use of the regular simplicial subdivision based on the vertices (k_0, k_1, k_2) with $\sum_0^2 k_i = D$, and in particular to exploit the simplicity of the replacement step. Of course, vectors on the artificial level will have $k_0 = 1$ and those on the original level $k_0 = 0$.

Let us generalize these observations by considering a problem of size n and by making use of vector labeling. We are concerned with the set of nonnegative integers $(k_1, \ldots, k_n)$ summing to D. Each such vector has associated with it a vector label $l(k)$ in R^n, derived from the problem at hand and satisfying the condition that $l(k)$ is the ith unit vector in R^n if k_i is the first coordinate equal to zero. We wish to determine a simplex in the subdivision such that a nonnegative linear combination of the associated vector labels equals a preassigned positive vector b. In addition, we are given an initial guess $(k_1^*, \ldots, k_n^*)$ as to the solution.

The set of vertices is enlarged by considering an additional coordinate k_0 and the regular simplicial decomposition based on the set of vertices $(k_0, k_1, \ldots, k_n)$ with $k_i \geq 0$, $\sum_0^n k_i = D$. Only those vertices with $k_0 = 0, 1$ are relevant for the computation, and these are associated with vector labels in R^n (not R^{n+1}) according to the following rule:

9.1 [Labeling rule for Merrill's algorithm]. A vector $k = (k_0, k_1, \ldots, k_n)$ will, if $k_0 = 0$, receive the label $l(k_1, \ldots, k_n)$. If $k_0 = 1$, the vector label is the ith unit vector in R^n if i is the first coordinate for which $k_i < k_i^*$.

The initial simplex is given by the columns of the following $(n+1) \times (n+1)$ matrix:

$$
\begin{bmatrix}
0 & 1 & \ldots & 1 \\
k_1^* & k_1^* - 1 & & k_1^* \\
\vdots & \vdots & & \vdots \\
k_n^* & k_n^* & & k_n^* - 1
\end{bmatrix}
$$

If the rows and columns of this matrix are indexed $0, \ldots, n$, we see that columns $1, \ldots, n$ have as vector labels the n unit vectors in R^n. These vector labels form a feasible basis for the system $Ly = b$. The vector label associated with the zeroth column derives from the original problem.

The first step of the algorithm is to introduce this latter vector into the feasible basis by a pivot step. One of the other vectors is eliminated and its replacement found by determining an adjacent simplex. The vector label associated with the new vertex is brought into the feasible basis and we continue.

The algorithm terminates when the simplex contains n vectors whose zeroth coordinate is 0 (i.e., vectors whose labels come from the original problem) and a single vector whose zeroth coordinate is 1 and whose associated column has just been removed from the feasible basis by a pivot step. The labels associated with these n vectors therefore form a feasible basis for $Ly = b$, and we have obtained a solution to the original problem. If the accuracy is not adequate, the algorithm is repeated with a higher value of D.

It can be shown that we never depart from the "sandwich" other than through the top face. Demonstrating that the algorithm cannot cycle is also a simple application of the types of analysis used in previous sections.

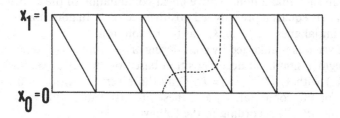

Figure 23. The path followed by Merrill's algorithm.

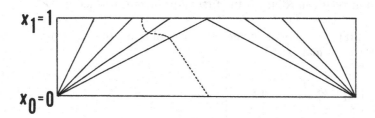

Figure 24. The algorithm of van der Laan and Talman.

In Merrill's method we take the product of the unit simplex and the closed unit interval $[0, 1]$ and subject it to a simplicial subdivision all of whose vertices lie on one of the two bounding planes. We then construct a piecewise-linear mapping of this product into the unit simplex that approximates the true mapping on the face $x_0 = 1$. On the face $x_0 = 0$ the mapping is chosen so as to have a unique fixed point. Merrill's method essentially traces the fixed point from one face to another, as in Figure 23.

The variable-dimension method of van der Laan and Talman may be viewed as working with an alternative subdivision of the product of the unit simplex and the interval $[0, 1]$ (see Figure 24). The vertices of an arbitrary subdivision on the level $x_0 = 1$ are joined, in a systematic way, to the vertices of the large simplex on the level $x_0 = 0$. The simplicial subdivision of the product is constructed in such a way that the algorithm begins in the vicinity of a region in which the fixed point is expected to lie. If the accuracy furnished by the completely labeled simplex on the level $x_0 = 1$ is not adequate, we simply restart the algorithm with a finer subdivision.

Eaves's method, on the other hand, involves a simplicial decomposition of the product of the unit simplex and the half-line $[0, \infty)$ with the grid becoming finer as the coordinate x_0 increases (Figure 25). Eaves's method has the distinct advantage that the vector labels obtained at the previous level are retained. This means that the Jacobian of the mapping

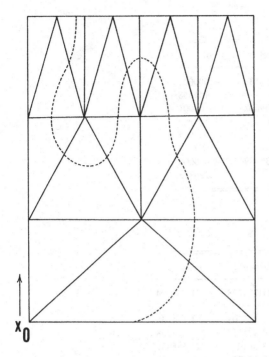

Figure 25. Eaves's algorithm.

is utilized rather than a single estimate of the fixed point. Eaves's method does, however, require the construction of a simplicial decomposition of the product space with exponentially decreasing grid size, and this is slightly more complicated to work with.

In applying Merrill's algorithm to the general equilibrium model of the preceding section we began with a small value of D and an initial estimate of $k^* = (9, 9, 8, 8, 8)$. The grid size was then tripled a total of nine successive times. In roughly 2000 iterations – essentially the same as that required by a fixed grid size of 200 – the following simplex was obtained:

$$
\begin{bmatrix}
216827 & 216827 & 216827 & 216827 & 216827 & 216828 \\
247077 & 247077 & 247077 & 247078 & 247078 & 247077 \\
158471 & 158472 & 158472 & 158471 & 158471 & 158471 \\
54073 & 54072 & 54072 & 54072 & 54073 & 54073 \\
104398 & 104398 & 104399 & 104399 & 104398 & 104398 \\
203304 & 203304 & 203303 & 203303 & 203303 & 203303
\end{bmatrix}
$$

Any of these columns can be taken as an estimate of the equilibrium price vector after division by the sum of the entries in the column:

Table 10

Activity	Level	Profit
7	.463533	− .000003
8	0	− .141668
9	3.939607	− .000001
10	.006050	− .000002
11	0	− .007615
12	0	− .052769
13	.438389	− .000006
14	0	− .254323

Table 11

Commodity	Demand	Supply
1	11.234238	11.235904
2	0	− .001595
3	1.155703	1.154355
4	2.974338	2.973208
5	23.682987	23.686038
6	9.354235	9.354134

Equilibrium prices:

.220319 .251057 .161024 .054943 .106080 .206578

These prices may then be used to calculate the profits in Table 10 in which the activity levels are derived from the weights in the final feasible basis.

Table 11 illustrates the relationship between supply and demand based on these prices and activity levels. As can be seen, the degree of approximation has been substantially improved – with no increase in computational cost – over the answer based on a fixed grid size.

REFERENCES

Allgower, E. L. (1977). "Application of a Fixed Point Search Algorithm to Nonlinear Problems Having Several Solutions." In *Fixed Points: Algorithms and Applications,* ed. S. Karamardian and C. B. Garcia. New York: Academic Press.

Allgower, E. L., and Kurt Georg (1980). "Simplicial and Continuation Methods for Approximating Fixed Points and Solutions to Systems of Equations." *SIAM Rev., 22,* 27–85.

Allgower, E. L., and M. M. Jeppson (1973). "The Approximation of Solutions of Nonlinear Elliptic Boundary Value Problems with Several Solutions." *Springer Lecture Notes, 333,* 1-20.

Berge, C. (1959). *Espace Topologiques, Functions Multivoques.* Paris: Dunod.

Cohen, D. I. A. (1967). "On the Sperner Lemma." *J. Comb. Theory, 2,* 585-7.

Cottle, R. W., and G. B. Dantzig (1970). "A Generalization of the Linear Complementarity Problem." *J. Comb. Theory, 8*(1), 79-90.

Dantzig, G. B., and A. S. Manne (1974). "A Complementarity Algorithm for an Optimal Capital Path with Invariant Proportions." *J. Econ. Theory, 9,* 3, 312-23.

Debreu, G., (1959). *Theory of Value.* New York: Wiley.

   (1974a). "Excess Demand Functions." *J. Math. Econ., 1,* 15-21.

   (1974b). "Four Aspects of the Mathematical Theory of Economic Equilibrium." In *Proceedings of the International Congress of Mathematicians, Vancouver,* pp. 65-77.

Dohmen, J., and J. Schoeber (1975). *Approximated Fixed Points.* EIT 55. Tilburg, Holland: Department of Econometrics, Tilburg University.

Eaves, B. C. (1970). "An Odd Theorem." *Proc. AMS, 26*(3), 509-13.

   (1971a). "Computing Kakutani Fixed Points." *SIAM J. Appl. Math., 21*(2), 236-44.

   (1971b). "On the Basic Theory of Complementarity." *Math. Progr., 1*(1), 68-75.

   (1972). "Homotopies for Computation of Fixed Points." *Math. Progr., 3*(1), 1-22.

Eaves, B. C., and R. Saigal (1972). "Homotopies for Computation of Fixed Points on Unbounded Regions." *Math. Progr., 3*(2), 225-37.

Eaves, B. C., and H. Scarf (1976). "The Solution of Systems of Piecewise Linear Equations." *Math. Op. Res., 1*(1), 1-27.

Fisher, M. L., and J. F. Gould (1974). "A Simplicial Algorithm for the Nonlinear Complementarity Problem." *Math. Progr., 6*(3), 281-300.

Fisher, M. L., F. J. Gould, and J. W. Tolle (1974). "A New Simplicial Approximation Algorithm with Restarts: Relations between Convergence and Labelling. In *Fixed Points: Algorithms and Applications,* ed. S. Karamardian and C. B. Garcia. New York: Academic Press, pp. 149-64.

Freidenfelds, J. (1974). "A Set Intersection Theorem and Applications." *Math. Progr., 7*(2), 199-211.

Garcia, C. B. (1975). *Continuation Methods for Simplicial Mappings.* Chicago: Graduate School of Business, University of Chicago.

   (1976). "A Hybrid Algorithm for the Computation of Fixed Points." *Manage. Sci., 22*(5), 606-13.

Garcia, C. B., and W. I. Zangwill (1979). "Determining All Solutions to Certain Systems of Nonlinear Equations." *Math. Op. Res., 4,* 1-14.

Ginsburgh, V. and J. Waelbroeck (1975). "A General Equilibrium Model of World Trade, Part I: Full Format Computation of Economic Equilibria." Cowles Discussion Paper No. 412, Yale University.

   (1974). "Computational Experience with a Large General Equilibrium Model." CORE Discussion Paper No. 7420, Heverlee, Belgium.

Hansen, T. (1968). "On the Approximation of a Competitive Equilibrium." Ph.D. Thesis, Yale University.

   (1974). "On the Approximation of Nash Equilibrium Points in an N-Person Noncooperative Game." *SIAM J. Appl. Math., 26*(3), 622-37.

48   Herbert E. Scarf

Hansen, T., and T. C. Koopmans (1972). "On the Definition and Computation of a Capital Stock Invariant under Optimization." *J. Econ. Theory, 5,* 487-523.
Hansen, T., and H. Scarf (1969). "On the Application of a Recent Combinatorial Algorithm." Cowles Foundation Discussion Paper No. 272, Yale University.
Hirsch, M. W. (1963). "A Proof of the Nonretractibility of a Cell onto Its Boundary." *Proc. AMS, 14,* 364-5.
Jeppson, M. M. (1972). "A Search for the Fixed Points of a Continuous Mapping." In *Mathematical Topics in Economic Theory and Computation,* ed. R. H. Day and S. M. Robinson. New York: Academic Press, pp. 122-9.
Kannai, Y. (1970). "On Closed Coverings of Simplexes." *SIAM J. Appl. Math., 19*(2), 459-61.
Karamardian, S. (1969). "The Nonlinear Complementarity Problem with Applications, Parts I and II." *J. Opt. Theory Appl., 4*(2, 3), 87-98, 167-81.
Karamardian, S., and C. B. Garcia (eds.) (1977). *Fixed Points: Algorithms and Applications.* New York: Academic Press.
Kehoe, T. (1979). "Regularity and Index Theorem for Economic Equilibrium Models." Ph.D. diss., Yale University.
    (1980). "An Index Theorem for General Equilibrium Models with Production." *Econometrica, 48,* 1121-32.
Kellogg, R. B., T. Y. Li, and J. Yorke (1977). "A Method of Continuation for Calculating a Brouwer Fixed Point." In *Fixed Points: Algorithms and Applications,* ed. S. Karamadian and C. B. Garcia. New York: Academic Press.
Kojima, A. (1975). "A Unification of the Existence Theorems of the Nonlinear Complementarity Problem." *Math. Progr., 9*(3), 257-77.
Kuhn, H. W. (1960). "Some Combinatorial Lemmas in Topology." *IBM J. Res. Dev., 4*(5), 518-24.
    (1968). "Simplicial Approximation of Fixed Points," *Proc. Nat. Acad. Sci., U.S.A., 61,* 1238-42.
Kuhn, H. W., and J. G. MacKinnon (1975). "The Sandwich Method for Finding Fixed Points." *J. Opt. Theory Appl., 17,* 189-204.
van der Laan, G., and A. J. J. Talman (1979a). "A Restart Algorithm for Computing Fixed Points without an Extra Dimension." *Math. Progr., 17,* 74-84.
    (1979b). *Interpretation of the Variable Dimensions Fixed Point Algorithm with an Artificial Level.* Amsterdam: Interfacultiet der Actuariële Wetenschappen an Econometrie, Onderzoekverslag 47, Vrije Universitiet.
Lemke, C. E. (1965). "Bimatrix Equilibrium Points and Mathematical Programming." *Manage. Sci., 11*(7), 681-9.
Lemke, C. E., and J. T. Howson, Jr. (1964). "Equilibrium Points of Bimatrix Games." *SIAM J. Appl. Math., 12*(2), 413-23.
McFadden, D., A. Mas-Colell, R. Mantel, and M. K. Richter (1975). "A Characterization of Community Excess Demand Functions." *J. Econ. Theory, 9,* 361-74.
MacKinnon, J. G. (1975). "Solving Economic General Equilibrium Models by the Sandwich Method." In *Proceedings of the Conference on Computing Fixed Points with Applications.* Clemson, S. C.: Department of Mathematical Sciences, Clemson University.

Mantel, R. R. (1968). "Toward a Constructive Proof of the Existence of Equilibrium in a Competitive Economy." *Yale Econ. Essays, 8,* 155–200.

(1974). "On the Characterization of Aggregate Excess Demand." *J. Econ. Theory, 9,* 348–53.

Merrill, O. H. (1972). "Applications and Extensions of an Algorithm that Computes Fixed Points of Certain Upper Semi-Continuous Point to Set Mappings." Ph.D. diss., Department of Industrial Engineering, University of Michigan.

Saigal, R. (1976). "On Paths Generated by Fixed Point Algorithms." *Math. Op. Res., 1*(4), 359–80.

Saigal, R., and C. B. Simon (1973). "Generic Properties of the Complementarity Problem." *Math. Progr., 4*(3), 324–35.

Scarf, H. (1967a). "On the Computation of Equilibrium Prices." In *Ten Economic Studies in the Tradition of Irving Fisher.* New York: Wiley.

(1967b). "The Approximation of Fixed Points on a Continuous Mapping." *SIAM J. Appl. Math., 15*(5), 1328–43.

(1967c). "The Core of an N Person Game." *Econometrica, 35*(1), 50–69.

Scarf, H. (with the collaboration of T. Hansen) (1973). *Computation of Economic Equilibria.* New Haven: Yale University Press.

Scarf, H. (1981). "The Computation of Equilibrium Prices: An Exposition." In *The Handbook of Mathematical Economics,* Vol. 2, ed. K. J. Arrow and M. D. Intrilligator. New York: North-Holland, pp. 1007–61.

Shapley, L. S. (1974). "A Note on the Lemke-Howson Algorithm." *Math. Progr. Study, 1,* 175–89.

Shoven, J. B., and J. Whalley (1972). "A General Equilibrium Calculation of the Effects of Differential Taxation of Income from Capital in the U.S.." *J. Publ. Econ., 1,* 281∴321.

Smale, S. (1976). "A Convergent Process of Price Adjustment and Global Newton Methods." *J. Math. Econ., 3,* 107–20.

Sonnenschein, H. (1973). "Do Walras' Identity and Continuity Characterize the Class of Community Excess Demand Functions?" *J. Econ. Theory, 6,* 345–54.

Todd, M. J. (1976a). *The Computation of Fixed Points and Applications.* Lecture Notes in Economics and Mathematical Systems No. 124 (Mathematical Economics). New York: Springer-Verlag.

(1976b). "Orientation in Complementary Pivot Algorithms." *Math. Op. Res., 1*(1), 54–66.

(1976c). "On Triangulations for Computing Fixed Points." *Math. Progr., 10,* 322–46.

Uzawa, H. (1962). "Walras' Existence Theorem and Brouwer's Fixed Point Theorem." *Econ. Studies Q., 13,* 1.

Wilmuth, R. J. (1973). "The Computations of Fixed Points." Ph.D. thesis, Department of Operations Research, Stanford University.

Wilson, R. (1971). "Computing Equilibria of N-Person Games." *SIAM J. Appl. Math., 21*(1), 80–87.

CHAPTER 2

Efficient methods of computing economic equilibria

Michael J. Todd

1   Introduction

Because Scarf (Chapter 1, this book) has given an excellent introduction to the computation of economic prices, we will concentrate on some of the techniques that have been devised since the early 1970s to make the algorithms based on piecewise-linear approximations more efficient. In discussing these improvements we will restrict ourselves to models of pure trade economies and of economies with activity analysis models of production, as discussed in Section 1 of Scarf (Chapter 1, this book). Little or no change is required to adapt these techniques to more complicated models with taxes, public goods, tariffs, and so forth. The cumulative effect of these improvements is that equilibrium problems in models with production with a few dozen commodities are computationally tractable.

We will not discuss methods based on differentiable path-following, heuristic adjustments of prices or of utility weights, or local approximations such as Newton's method, although such algorithms can be very effective for well-behaved problems. Nor can we give many details of the algorithms we do consider, which we like to call piecewise-linear homotopy methods – for survey articles, see Todd (1976), Eaves (1976), and Allgower and Georg (1980).

Suppose that there are $n+1$ goods, indexed $0, 1, \ldots, n$. Then the price simplex is $S^n = \{x = (x_0, x_1, \ldots, x_n)^T \in R^{n+1} : x_i \geqslant 0$ for all i, $\sum_i x_i = 1\}$. Let the excess demand be described by the function $z: S^n \to R^{n+1}$, so that z is continuous and satisfies Walras's law: $x^T z(x) = 0$ for all $x \in S^n$. (We ignore the purely technical problem of demand being undefined when some price is zero.) Then x^* is an equilibrium price vector for the pure trade economy that gives rise to z if $z(x^*)$ is nonpositive. If there is production, we assume that it is modeled by a finite set of activities, so that

Research for this chapter was supported in part by National Science Foundation grant ECS–7921279.

the production set is $\{Ay: y \geq 0\}$ for some $(n+1) \times m$ matrix A. We suppose that the first $n+1$ columns of A form the negative identity (free disposal) and that for some $\hat{x} \in S^n$, $\hat{x}^T A < 0$ (equivalent to irreversibility). Then x^* is an equilibrium price vector for the economy described by z and A if $z(x^*) = Ay$, $y \geq 0$, and $A^T x^* \leq 0$.

The problem of computing equilibria in such models can be reduced to the search for fixed points of continuous functions (or upper semicontinuous correspondences) defined on S^n. The function or correspondence used will clearly depend on the excess demand function z. We will take the view that evaluation of z requires at least of order n^2 arithmetical operations – this implies that "vector-labeling" methods will almost certainly be more efficient than "integer-labeling" methods. Computation of z is at least this burdensome if each consumer has a constant elasticity of substitution (CES) utility function and the number of consumers is of the same order of magnitude as n, or if a pure trade model is derived from a larger model with production. The latter situation arises when, apart from a small number of factors of production, the rest of the production side of the economy can be described by a Leontief input–output model, as in several other chapters in this volume. Thus we consider only "vector-labeling" methods.

However, it is frequently preferable to view these methods from a different viewpoint. Rather than assign vector labels to vertices of some simplicial subdivision, we shall consider fixed points or zeros of continuous functions of upper hemicontinuous correspondences. This approach does not disguise the structure of the problem and helps us in devising suitable functions and correspondences. We describe this homotopy viewpoint in Section 2 and discuss the algorithms of Merrill (1972), Eaves (1972), and van der Laan and Talman (1979) in this context.

The remaining sections describe how improvements can be made to these algorithms when applied to equilibrium problems. In Section 3 we discuss how the search for an equilibrium price vector can be formulated as a fixed-point or zero-finding problem – the particular formulation can have a profound effect on computational efficiency. Section 4 is concerned with different subdivisions that have been suggested.

In Section 5 we discuss acceleration procedures that have been developed to give fast local convergence for smooth problems. Finally, Section 6 considers the equilibrium problem with production that gives rise to a zero-finding problem for a correspondence and describes how the structure of this correspondence can be exploited to yield efficient algorithms.

To establish the gains that result from the improvements we will give numerous results of computational experience using the author's code

PLALGO (Todd, (1980c)). This program contains all of the improvements to be discussed; however, it is far from simple. I believe the time has come for those who wish to compute equilibria in economic models to use such codes as black boxes rather than write their own – they can then concentrate on the formulation of their model as a zero-finding problem in the most natural and smoothest fashion. The gains to be realized are significant – the improved codes are at least an order of magnitude faster than earlier versions. Thus models with a few dozen commodities and a general (rather than input–output) activity analysis model of production are certainly reasonable. The modeler can therefore be free to develop the most accurate model without concerning himself too much with computational limitations. As an example, the production model of Scarf with Hansen (1973) with 14 commodities was solved in under 5 seconds using an IBM 370/168 (the program was compiled by the FORTRAN H extended computer using OPT = 3). This run did not use the dimension-reducing trick of Scarf with Hansen (1973), section 5.5 – it was applied in the full commodity space. The final price vector x^* had $\|z(x^*) - Ay\| \leqslant 10^{-12}$ and $(A^T x^*)_j \leqslant 10^{-16}$ for all j.

In demonstrating the significance of each improvement, we shall proceed backwards: The result of a run with PLALGO will be compared with a run when the specific improvement is deleted. For comparison with early algorithms, see the computational results cited in Scarf (Chapter 1, this book). The examples used are the test problems in Scarf with Hansen (1973): a pure trade economy with 10 commodities and 2 production economies, one with 6 and one with 14 commodities. The first two are also described in Scarf (Chapter 1, this book). The last is included to demonstrate the feasibility of computation in models of reasonable size.

2   The homotopy viewpoint

Suppose for simplicity we are trying to find a fixed point of a continuous function $f: S^n \to S^n$. We choose a linear function $q: S^n \to S^n$ with a unique, known, fixed point x^0. For example, we may choose $q(x) = x^0$ for all $x \in S^n$. The algorithms we consider, those of Merrill (1972), Eaves (1972), and van der Laan and Talman (1979), can all be viewed as approximating the fixed points of a function that is deformed from q to f. It is often convenient instead to consider zeros of functions. Thus let $g(x) = f(x) - x$, $r(x) = q(x) - x$. The homotopy function h, taking $S^n \times [0, 1]$ into R^{n+1} (in fact, into a subset of the tangent space $U^n = \{x \in R^{n+1}: \Sigma_j x_j = 0\}$ to S^n), is defined by

$$h(x, t) = tg(x) + (1 - t)r(x)$$

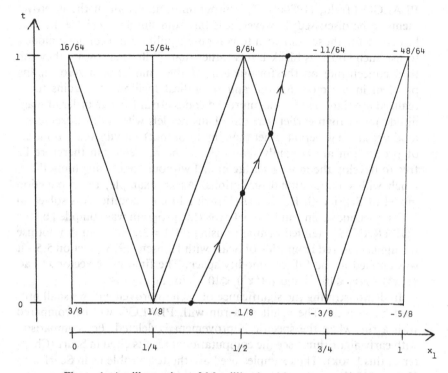

Figure 1. An illustration of Merrill's algorithm.

We wish to approximate paths of zeros of h. Note that $(x^0, 0)$ is one such zero, and that if $(x^*, 1)$ is a zero of h, then $g(x^*) = 0$ and $f(x^*) = x^*$. In order to approximate paths of zeros of h, we make a piecewise-linear approximation h_T to h using a triangulation T of $S^n \times [0, 1]$. That is, for vertices v of T we set $h_T(v) = h(v)$, and we extend h_T linearly on each simplex of T, so that if w is a convex combination $\sum \lambda_i v^i$ of the vertices $v^0, v^1, \ldots, v^{n+1}$ of a simplex of T, $h_T(w)$ is the same convex combination $\sum \lambda_i h_T(v^i)$ of the function values.

This framework embraces the algorithms of Merrill (1972) and of van der Laan and Talman (1979), which differ only in their choice of the triangulation T. In this case, barring degeneracy, a path of zeros of h_T starting at $(x^0, 0)$ will lead to a point $(x^1, 1)$, where x^1 is an approximate zero of g. We then usually restart the algorithm with a triangulation T_1 giving better approximations and a new linear function $r_1(\cdot)$ with a unique zero at x^1, to obtain x^2, and so on. Each application of the algorithm to get a new iterate x^k is called a major cycle.

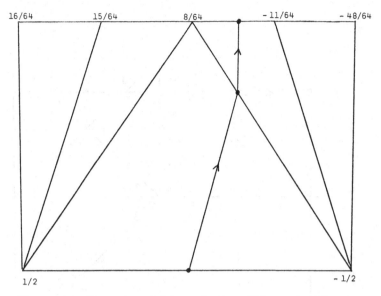

16/64   15/64   8/64   - 11/64   - 48/64

1/2   - 1/2

Figure 2. An illustration of the van der Laan-Talman algorithm.

We illustrate one major cycle of Merrill's algorithm for the case $n = 1$, with $f(x_0, x_1)^T = (x_0 + x_1^3 - \frac{1}{4}, x_1 - x_1^3 + \frac{1}{4})^T$, starting with $q(x) \equiv x^0 = (\frac{5}{8}, \frac{3}{8})^T$. When $n = 1$, we can associate S^n naturally with the interval $[0, 1]$ using the correspondence $((1 - x_1), x_1)^T \leftrightarrow x_1 \in [0, 1]$. We therefore seek a fixed point of $\hat{f}: [0, 1] \to [0, 1]$, $\hat{f}(x_1) = x_1 - x_1^3 + \frac{1}{4}$, starting from the fixed point of $\hat{q}: [0, 1] \to [0, 1]$, $\hat{q}(x_1) \equiv \frac{3}{8}$. Figure 1 illustrates a particular triangulation T of $[0, 1] \times [0, 1]$, the value of $h(x_1, t)$ at each vertex of T and the path of zeros of h_T, starting at $x_1^0 = \frac{3}{8}$ and ending at $x_1^1 = \frac{23}{38}$. The path traverses three triangles of T and is linear within each such triangle. Note that the path is in fact linear in the union of the first two triangles it traverses. This fact is not coincidental; it will be discussed further in Section 4.

Figure 2 illustrates the type of triangulation used in van der Laan and Talman's algorithm (1979) and the corresponding path for the same problem. [Here we have used $x^0 = (\frac{1}{2}, \frac{1}{2})^T$.]

The continuous deformation algorithm of Eaves (1972) uses a very special type of triangulation of $S^n \times [0, 1)$ to avoid restarting. As the simplices approach $S^n \times \{1\}$, they get smaller and smaller, thus providing more and more accurate approximations to f and g. For the example considered above, Eaves's algorithm is illustrated in Figure 3. Here we have arranged the homotopy h to go from r to g as t goes from 0 to $\frac{1}{2}$,

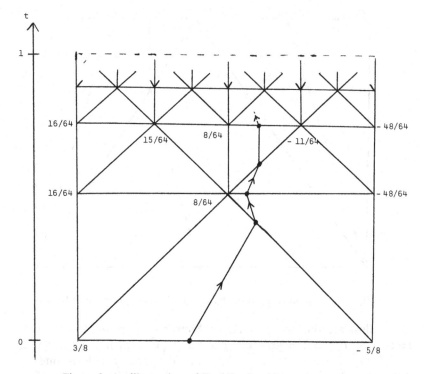

Figure 3. An illustration of Eaves's algorithm.

and then to stay at g from $t = \frac{1}{2}$ to $t = 1$. It is important to note that, for $n > 1$, the progression of the algorithm toward $t = 1$ may not be monotonic.

For the problem of approximating a fixed point of an upper hemicontinuous correspondence $F : S^n \to S^{n^*}$, we proceed analogously. (We use C^* to denote the collection of nonempty convex compact subsets of C.) We define G by $G(x) = F(x) - \{x\} = \{f - x : f \in F(x)\}$ and the homotopy $H : S^n \times [0, 1] \to U^{n^*}$ by

$$H(x, t) = \{tg + (1 - t)r(x) : g \in G(x)\}$$

We define a piecewise-linear approximation to H with respect to a triangulation T to be *some* function H_T that is linear on each simplex of T and that satisfies $H_T(v) \in H(v)$ for each vertex of T - the selection is arbitrary. As before, we trace a path of zeros of H_T.

To conclude this section, let us discuss what the homotopy viewpoint tells us about designing algorithms and about the types of function f or correspondence F that we would most like to encounter. Note that the algorithms require one evaluation of h (or H) – equivalently, one evaluation of g (or G) or of the linear function r – and one linear algebra step (analogous to a linear programming pivot step) to traverse each simplex. Thus we wish to minimize the number of simplices traversed to obtain a certain accuracy of solution. For this purpose it is natural to ask that f (or g) be as smooth a function as possible, and that r be in some sense similar to g, to avoid introducing an extreme deformation from r to g. We would also suspect that problems involving a correspondence F would be much harder to solve than those with a continuous function f. These considerations guide us in our choice of formulation for the economic equilibrium problem.

3   Reformulations of the economic equilibrium problem

Let us consider first the case of a pure trade economy. We are then given an excess demand function $z: S^n \to R^{n+1}$, and we seek $x^* \in S^n$ with $z(x^*) \leq 0$. Scarf (Chapter 1, this book) has given one formulation of this problem as a fixed-point problem: Define $\hat{f}: S^n \to S^n$ by

$$\hat{f}_i(x) = \frac{x_i + z_i(x)^+}{1 + \sum_{j=0}^{n} z_j(x)^+}$$

where λ^+ denotes $\max\{0, \lambda\}$ for any scalar λ. Certainly, $\hat{f}$ is continuous and its fixed points correspond to equilibria. On the other hand, let x^* be an equilibrium price vector. Then it is likely that for some i, $z_i(x^*) = 0$, but its gradient, $\nabla z_i(x^*)$, is not zero. This means that $\hat{f}$ as defined above is not differentiable at equilibria, even if z is smooth. An alternative formulation (see, e.g., Arrow and Hahn, 1971) is to define

$$f_i(x) = \frac{(x_i + \lambda z_i(x))^+}{\sum_{j=0}^{n} (x_j + \lambda z_j(x))^+}$$

for any positive scalar λ. Note that if x^* is an equilibrium price vector with all components positive, then as long as λ is sufficiently small,

$$f(x) = \frac{x + \lambda z(x)}{1 + \lambda \sum_{j=0}^{n} z_j(x)}$$

for x close to x^*; thus f will be smooth if z is. It may be thought that small values of λ lead to round-off errors and cancellation; however, the formula

$$g_i(x) = \frac{\max\{\lambda z_i, -x_i\} - x_i \sum_j \max\{\lambda z_j, -x_j\}}{\sum_j (x_j + \lambda z_j)^+}$$

Table 1.

Run: Problem P1	Statistics	Residual
Using f with acceleration	70/84	10^{-14}
Using $\hat{f}$ with acceleration	282/287	10^{-2}
Using f without acceleration	195/201	10^{-2}
Using $\hat{f}$ without acceleration	321/320	10^{-5}

[where $z = z(x)$] shows that g can be calculated without excessive cancellation.

We now demonstrate the computational improvement achieved by using f rather than $\hat{f}$. The test problem is the pure trade economy in Scarf with Hansen (1973) with 10 commodities, henceforth called problem P1. We give results for a version of PLALGO that attempts to accelerate using approximations to the derivatives of f and $\hat{f}$ (see Section 5) and for a version that eschews such acceleration. (Note that acceleration is not strictly valid when using $\hat{f}$, which is not differentiable.) Here and in the following computational results, an entry p/q in the Statistics column indicates that p linear programming pivot steps and q evaluations of the nonlinear function f or $\hat{f}$ were required. The termination criterion was the generation of a zero of a piecewise-linear approximate to g based on a simplex of diameter $(.37)^{10} \times .3 \approx 4 \times 10^{-5}$, or of some x^* with $g_i(x^*) \leqslant 10^{-12}\lambda$ for all i. The results appear in Table 1. The Residual column gives the approximate maximum value of excess demand at the computed equilibrium price vector x^*.

Before we add production to the model, let us briefly address a technique for converting our problem to one on R^n. Many algorithms are more conveniently expressed for problems on R^n; moreover, it is simpler to write a single code for such problems and apply it to problems on other domains by suitable transformations. Let e be a vector of ones of appropriate dimension. Then $S^n = \{x \in R^{n+1}: x \geqslant 0, e^T x = 1\}$, its tangent space is $U^n = \{x \in R^{n+1}: e^T x = 0\}$, and its affine hull is $T^n = \{x \in R^{n+1}: e^T x = 1\}$. We wish to find a zero of $g: S^n \to U^n$. It is usually easy to extend g to a function $\bar{g}: T^n \to U^n$ whose zeros are exactly those of g. For example, we can take $\bar{g}(x) = f(p(x)) - x$, where $p(x)$ is any convenient projection from T^n onto S^n, for example, $p(x) = x^+/e^T x^+$ with $x^+ = (x_i^+)$. Now let the nonsingular linear transformation $L: R^n \to U^n$ be given. Then we can translate the zero-finding problem for $\bar{g}: T^n \to U^n$ into one for $\bar{g}: R^n \to R^n$ by setting

$$\tilde{g}(y) = L^{-1}(\bar{g}(x^0 + L(y)))$$

In order that the conditioning of $\tilde{g}$ be no worse than that of $\bar{g}$, it is advisable to choose for L an orthogonal transformation. One convenient choice, which requires only $0(n)$ operations to evaluate L or L^{-1}, is given by $L(y) = My$, $L^{-1}(x) = M^T x$, where M is the $(n+1) \times n$ matrix given by the last n columns of the orthogonal matrix $I - aa^T/\alpha$, where $\alpha = n+1 + (n+1)^{1/2}$ and $a = [1 + (n+1)^{1/2}, 1, 1, \ldots, 1]^T \in R^{n+1}$.

We now add an activity analysis model of production to our economy. Thus we have an $(n+1) \times m$ matrix A, whose first $(n+1)$ columns are the negatives of the unit vectors. We seek $x^* \in S^n$ with $z(x^*) = Ay$, $y \geqslant 0$, and $x^{*T}A \leqslant 0$. Let $a^1, \ldots, a^m$ be the columns of A, and assume there is some $\hat{x}$ with $\hat{x}^T A < 0$. We will convert this problem directly into a zero-finding problem for a correspondence $G: T^n \to U^{n^*}$; as above, we can then equivalently find a zero of a correspondence $\tilde{G}: R^n \to R^{n^*}$. Although it is possible to proceed via a correspondence $F: S^n \to S^{n^*}$ whose fixed point is sought, the approach we follow is simpler, although it is not immediately apparent that G has a zero in S^n.

The basic idea in constructing G is simple; we define appropriate adjustments to prices that are not in equilibrium. Thus define the polyhedra $X_0, \ldots, X_m$ subdividing T^n as follows: $X_0 = \{x \in T^n : x^T A \leqslant 0\}$ and $X_j = \{x \in T^n : x^T a^j = \max\{x^T a^k : 1 \leqslant k \leqslant m\} \geqslant 0\}$ for $j = 1, 2, \ldots, m$. An equilibrium price vector must lie in the set $X_0 \subseteq S^n$ of prices where no activity makes a positive profit; X_j is the set of "prices" (possibly not nonnegative) at which activity j makes maximum profit, which is nonnegative. In X_j we modify x to decrease the profit of activity a^j; in X_0 we modify x to increase (decrease) the prices of goods in excess demand (supply). Thus we would like to put $-a^j$ in $G(x)$ for x in X_j and $z(x)$ in $G(x)$ for x in X_0. To stay within T^n we must change these modifications to stay within U^n. Thus define

$$\hat{z}(x) = \left(I - \frac{ee^T}{n+1}\right)z(x), \qquad \hat{A} = \left(I - \frac{ee^T}{n+1}\right)A$$

Now $\hat{z}(x)$ and $\hat{a}^j$ are the orthogonal projections of $z(x)$ and a^j into U^n. We now define $g^0(x) = \hat{z}(x)$ and $g^j(x) \equiv -\hat{a}^j$ and set

$$G(x) = \text{conv}\{g^j(x) : 0 \leqslant j \leqslant m \text{ and } x \in X_j\}$$

We leave it to the reader to check that if $0 \in G(x^*)$, then $x^* \in X_0 \subseteq S^n$ and that the weight on $g^0(x^*)$ is positive. Thus $\hat{z}(x^*) - \hat{A}y = 0$ for some $y \geqslant 0$. It is then easy to verify that $z(x^*) = Ay$ and $A^T x^* \leqslant 0$.

The equilibrium problem can also be formulated as a fixed-point problem for a continuous function, as described by Todd (1979), using an idea of Eaves (1971). Let $p: T^n \to X_0$ be the projection map: $p(x)$ is the closest point in X_0 to $x \in T^n$, using the Euclidean metric. Then we can define $f: X_0 \to X_0$ by $f(x) = p(x + \hat{z}(x))$ and verify that fixed points of f are equilibrium price vectors. However, it may be more convenient to deal with a function $\bar{f}$ defined on all of T^n: Let $\bar{f}(x) = p(x) + z(p(x))$. Then if x^* is a fixed point of $\bar{f}, p(x^*)$ is an equilibrium price vector. We can therefore calculate equilibria by computing fixed points of continuous (and piecewise-smooth) functions; however, note that each evaluation of f or of $\bar{f}$ requires not only an evaluation of z but also the solution of a least-distance programming problem to compute $p(y)$ for some y. Very little computational experience has been obtained with this formulation; but it appears to be more efficient to work directly with G, as long as its structure is exploited as discussed in Section 6.

4   Different subdivisions

We pointed out in Section 2 that, from the homotopy viewpoint, the only distinction between the algorithm of Merrill (1972) and that of van der Laan and Talman (1979) was the use of different subdivisions. During a single major cycle of Merrill's algorithm, one might expect about half the evaluations of h to be at vertices in $S^n \times \{1\}$ and half at vertices in $S^n \times \{0\}$. The latter evaluations are trivial, since r is usually a simple linear function; however, associated with each evaluation of h is a linear algebra step to traverse the new simplex. Thus computational testing of Merrill's algorithm typically showed that one-and-a-half times as many linear programming pivot steps were taken as function evaluations of g. The idea of van der Laan and Talman (1979) was to minimize the number of evaluations of h on $S^n \times \{0\}$ (and hence the extra linear programming pivot steps) by using a triangulation with few vertices on the artificial level $S^n \times \{0\}$. Indeed, they used a subdivision in which the "base" simplex $S^n \times \{0\}$ was not subdivided at all, and thus there were only $n + 1$ vertices on the artificial level. In the example of Section 2, it can be seen that both Merrill's and van der Laan and Talman's algorithms require two evaluations of g, but that the latter requires only two linear programming pivot steps (corresponding to the two triangles traversed) whereas the former seems to need three. However, as we pointed out in that example, while the path of zeros of h_T traverses three triangles, it is composed of just two linear pieces. The reason for this is that h_T is exactly the same linear function on both of the first two triangles, and this follows from the linearity of the function r. Although this seems a very minor improvement for $n = 1$, in fact full exploitation of this idea leads to a drastic reduction in the amount of work associated with the extra dimension and the corresponding artificial layer $S^n \times \{0\}$. A complete description of how this technique can be implemented is beyond the scope of this paper – for details, see Todd (1980a). How the different simplices join up to form large pieces of linearity of h_T (which may not be simplices) clearly depends to a great degree on the initial triangulation T (for example, try putting all the diagonals from southwest to northeast in Figure 1 and examine the effect) and suggests that for maximum advantage to be taken of the linearity of r, the so-called Union Jack triangulations (see Todd, 1977) are preferable to those popularized by Kuhn (1960). The code PLALGO is based on these ideas.

The practical result of this observation is that Merrill's algorithm, when the linearity of r is exploited, exacts very little penalty for the extra dimension, and computational results are very similar to those obtained with van der Laan and Talman's algorithm.

However, there is a subtle distinction between the two approaches that might lead one to prefer Merrill's algorithm. We have stated that the only difference between Merrill's and van der Laan and Talman's methods is in the subdivisions used, and this is formally true. However, because of the shape of some of the simplices in the subdivision used by van der Laan and Talman, it may be helpful to view the distinction in another way. In Figure 4 we have drawn a subdivision of the simplex $S^2 \times \{1\}$ and marked on it three cones C_0, C_1, and C_2. Each cone C_j is associated with the vertex $(e^j, 0)$ of $S^n \times \{0\}$, where e^j, $j = 0, 1, \ldots, n$, denotes the jth unit vector in R^{n+1}. In the subdivision of van der Laan and Talman, the vertex $(e^j, 0)$ is connected to every vertex and every simplex in C_j. Thus we may think of $(e^j, 0)$ as "representing" all points $(x, 0)$, $x \in C_j$, and with this interpretation the homotopy considered is really

$$h(x, t) = t g(x) + (1-t) \hat{r}(x)$$

where $\hat{r}$ is the piecewise-constant (and discontinuous) function $\hat{r}(x) = r(e^j)$ if $x \in C_j$ (undefined on the intersection of two or more C_i terms). [Note that Scarf (Chapter 1, this book) gives a labeling rule for Merrill's algorithm (9.1) that is very similar. Such piecewise-constant functions are also analogous to "integer labeling."] We would prefer to use a homotopy from a linear function r, which can better model the nonlinear function g locally or globally.

It would be hard to modify PLALGO to implement the algorithm of van der Laan and Talman (1979). However, they have developed a related algorithm (van der Laan and Talman, 1981; see also Todd, 1980b) that is an option of the code PLALGO. The idea is very similar to that of their earlier algorithm, but instead of the subdivision having one large

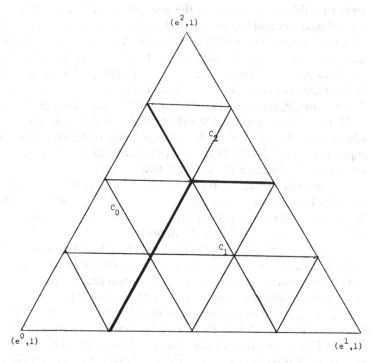

Figure 4. A subdivision for van der Laan and Talman's algorithm.

simplex on the artificial layer $S^n \times \{0\}$, it has one large hypercube. The 2^n vertices of this hypercube are joined to vertices according to a partition of $S^n \times \{1\}$ into 2^n, rather than $n+1$, cones. Results are given in Table 2. Here P2 and P3 are the two economic models with production in Scarf and Hansen (1973). They have respectively 6 and 14 commodities. Here, in the Statistics columns, an entry $p/q/r$ indicates that p linear programming pivot steps, q evaluations of G, and r evaluations of z were required; we distinguish the latter because the remaining $q-r$ evaluations of G are much simpler. The Residual columns contain the norm $\|z(x^*) - Ay\|$ with $y \geqslant 0$ for the computed equilibrium price vector x^*; in all cases, $A^T x^* \leqslant 0$ up to round-off error. The termination criterion was $\|z(x^*) - Ay\| \leqslant 10^{-10}$.

We must now explain the difference between the last two rows of Table 2. PLALGO has as options the algorithm of van der Laan and Talman (1981) with the triangulations J_1, K', and K_1 (see, e.g., Todd, 1978). A comparison of algorithms with both using J_1 might seem fairer, but in fact van der Laan and Talman designed their algorithm to employ the triangulation K'; it should be more efficient implemented this way than with either J_1 or K_1. However, using K_1 allows the "optimal" linear

Table 2

Algorithm	P1		P2		P3	
	Statistics	Residual	Statistics	Residual	Statistics	Residual
Merrill's algorithm using triangulation J_1	70/84	10^{-14}	124/132/53	10^{-14}	842/802/96	10^{-14}
van der Laan and Talman's algorithm using triangulation K'	62/77	10^{-13}	124/133/57	10^{-14}	839/817/91	10^{-12}
van der Laan and Talman's algorithm using triangulation K_1^*	49/61	10^{-13}	170/173/60	10^{-14}	438/424/47	10^{-13}

transformation of K_1, here denoted K_1^* (see van der Laan and Talman, 1980), to be used. Although this entails some distortion of the "artificial hypercube" and the associated cones, it seems to lead to better performance, particularly on the large problem arising from an economy with production. Implementing K_1^* requires only a simple modification of the method in Section 3 to convert a zero-finding problem involving $\bar{g}: T^n \to U^n$ to one involving $\tilde{g}: R^n \to R^n$.

Other computational results comparing different triangulations for economic equilibrium problems can be found in Todd (1978).

5   Acceleration for smooth problems

For this section, suppose we wish to compute a zero of a smooth function $g: R^n \to R^n$; this setting is more natural for describing the acceleration procedures. Suppose that Merrill's algorithm has given us an approximate zero x^k of g; in fact, x^k is an exact zero of a piecewise-linear approximation to g based on a simplex σ containing x^*; let $v^0, v^1, \ldots, v^n$ be the vertices of σ. With almost all currently used triangulations, the v^i terms can be ordered so that the edge vectors $v^i - v^{i-1}$, $i = 1, 2, \ldots, n$, are scaled versions of the n unit vectors in R^n. Since we have evaluated g at each vertex, we automatically obtain, in addition to x^k, an approximation D_k to the derivative matrix $Dg(x^k)$ of g at x^k, based on finite differences. This matrix can be used in several ways.

First, we may take an approximate Newton step from x^k to $\bar{x}^k = x^k - (D_k)^{-1}g(x^k)$. If desired, we may continue with approximate Newton or quasi-Newton steps (updating D_k using only values of g), possibly converging to a zero x^* of g. However, Saigal (1977) showed how D_k could be used to accelerate homotopy algorithms and demonstrated that quadratic convergence could be achieved (i.e., $\|x^{k+1} - x^*\| \leqslant \rho\|x^k - x^*\|^2$ for some ρ) and that, asymptotically, only $n+1$ evaluations of g were required to obtain x^{k+1} from x^k. The basic idea, as refined by Saigal and Todd (1978), is to use a homotopy from $r_k(\cdot) = D_k(\cdot - \bar{x}^k)$ to g at the kth restart and to use a triangulation T_k whose simplices, when projected from $R^n \times [0, 1]$ into R^n, have diameter of the order of $\|\bar{x}^k - x^k\|$.

Note how the homotopy viewpoint makes such a choice of r_k natural; r_k not only has a zero close (one hopes) to one of g, but also its derivative matrix is close to that of g. Thus the homotopy proceeds smoothly from r_k to g, and this leads to paths of zeros that traverse only $n+1$ simplices asymptotically. It is possible also to accelerate van der Laan and Talman's algorithms (see Todd, 1980b). Whereas Eaves's algorithm (1972) has the advantage of not using an artificial linear function for $t \geqslant \frac{1}{2}$ and thus naturally has a smooth homotopy, the triangulations that have been proposed generally shrink their diameters at only a linear rate. Thus it is complicated to perform acceleration with this type of algorithm; see, however, Saigal and Todd (1978).

Table 1 has already shown the gains to be achieved using acceleration. PLALGO attempts a sequence of quasi-Newton steps at the end of each major cycle, but monitors their performance closely. As soon as these iterations begin to degrade, the code reverts to the homotopy algorithm.

6   Exploiting the structure of a correspondence

We have already alluded to two techniques for converting the equilibrium problem for an economy with production into a zero-finding problem for a continuous function. The first can be used when, apart from a small number of factors, production is described by an input–output model; in this case, it is possible to define an equivalent pure trade economy, with the number of goods equal to the number of factors. The second technique is more general and was described at the end of Section 3.

Besides these, Scarf and Hansen (1973) have described two ways to exploit structure; in their section 5.5, they perform a search in just the space of prices of goods that enter into some consumer's uitility function, whereas in section 6.4 they apply an integer-labeling algorithm to the space of convex weights on vertices of the polyhedron $X_0 = \{x \in T^n : A^T x \leqslant 0\}$. Both are remarkably effective for problem P3. Here, however, I want to outline another technique that can be used in general and possesses quadratic convergence; for details and more computational results, see Awoniyi and Todd (1983).

Recall the formulation in Section 3 of the equilibrium problem as a

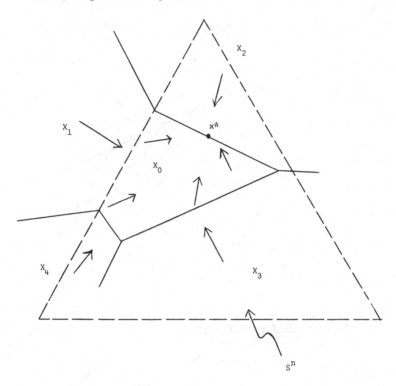

Figure 5. The form of $G(x)$.

zero-finding problem for a correspondence G. This formulation can be illustrated for the case $n=2$ (see Figure 5). Here the arrows in each X_j denote elements of $G(x)$; note that G agrees with a smooth function g^j in X_j and that g^j is constant for $j>0$.

It is likely that a few major cycles of Merrill's algorithm will generate a small simplex close to x^* and that this small triangle will have vertices in X_0 and X_2. We then guess that x^* lies in $X_{02} \equiv X_0 \cap X_2$ and orient our triangulation so that it has line segments along X_{02}. We can then define $H_T(x,1)$, for $x \in X_{02}$, to be a member of $G(x)$, that is, a convex combination of g^0 and g^2, that lies in the tangent space to X_{02} (see Figure 6). The resulting $H_T(x,1)$ is a continuous *function* on a subset of X_{02}, and the algorithm can be implemented so as to compute an approximate zero of this function efficiently. We may use all the acceleration techniques of Section 5 to improve convergence. However, it is important to note that, although the algorithm is designed to operate efficiently within X_{02}, it is applied to the whole set T^n, and thus recovers automatically from the

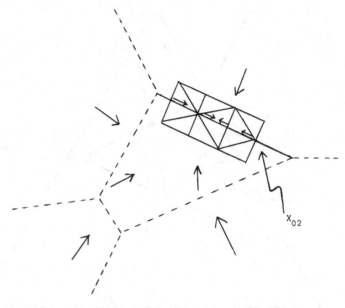

Figure 6. The form of $H_T(x,1)$.

Table 3.

	P1		P2		P3	
Version	Statistics	Residual	Statistics	Residual	Statistics	Residual
Accelerated version	93/101/101	10^{-13}	124/132/55	10^{-14}	842/802/97	10^{-14}
Unaccelerated version	—	—	344/319/70	10^{-2}	1895/1818/156	10^{-1}

choice of an incorrect set of X_j terms. Asymptotically, it locates a correct index set and from then on operates implicitly in a space of far lower dimension – in fact, $n-t$, where t is the number of production activities used in the equilibrium.

We applied PLALGO, both with and without this acceleration feature, to the two economic equilibrium problems P2 and P3. We also applied the accelerated version to problem P1, the exchange economy problem, with an artificial activity amounting to disposing of all commodities added to the free disposal activities. The results are given in Table 3. For the accelerated version, the termination criterion was

$\|z(x^*) - Ay\| \leqslant 10^{-10}$, whereas the unaccelerated version was stopped when it generated a simplex of diameter $(.5)^{10} \times \sqrt{n}/(n+1)$.

7 Conclusions

Piecewise-linear homotopy algorithms can provide accurate approximations to equilibria in a reasonable amount of computer time, even for models with general (linear) production technologies and a few dozen commodities. However, these sophisticated algorithms are quite complicated, and therefore are best used as "black-box" programs by economic modelers, who can then concentrate on formulating their problem as accurately and smoothly as possible.

REFERENCES

Allgower, E. L., and Georg, Kurt. 1980. Simplicial and continuation methods for approximating fixed points and solutions to systems of equations. *SIAM Review* 22:28–85.

Arrow, K. J., and Hahn, F. H. 1971. *General competitive analysis*. San Francisco: Holden-Day.

Awoniyi, S. A., and Todd, M. J. 1983. An efficient simplicial algorithm for computing a zero of a convex union of smooth functions. *Mathematical Programming* 25:83–108.

Eaves, B. C. 1971. On the basic theorem of complementarity. *Mathematical Programming* 1:68–75.

1972. Homotopies for computation of fixed points. *Mathematical Programming* 3:1–22.

1976. A short course in solving equations with PL homotopies. In R. W. Cottle and C. E. Lemke, eds., *Nonlinear programming,* Proceedings of the Ninth SIAM-AMS Symposium in Applied Mathematics. Philadelphia: SIAM, pp. 73–143.

Kuhn, H. W. 1960. Some combinatorial lemmas in topology. *IBM Journal of Research and Development* 4:518–24.

van der Laan, G., and Talman, A. J. J. 1979. A restart algorithm for computing fixed points without an extra dimension. *Mathematical Programming* 17:74–84.

1980. An improvement of fixed point algorithms by using a good triangulation. *Mathematical Programming* 18:274–85.

1981. A class of simplicial restart fixed point algorithms without an extra dimension. *Mathematical Programming* 20:33–48.

Merrill, O. H. 1972. Applications and extensions of an algorithm that computes fixed points of certain upper semi-continuous point to set mappings. Ph.D. diss., University of Michigan, Ann Arbor.

Saigal, R. 1977. On the convergence of algorithms for solving equations that are based on methods of complementary pivoting. *Mathematics of Operations Research* 2:108–24.

Saigal, R., and Todd, M. J. 1978. Efficient acceleration techniques for fixed-point algorithms. *SIAM Journal on Numerical Analysis* 15:997–1007.

Scarf, H. E. (with the collaboration of T. Hansen) 1973. *Computation of economic equilibria.* New Haven: Yale University Press.

Todd, M. J. 1976. *The computation of fixed points and applications.* Berlin: Springer-Verlag.

——— 1977. Union jack triangulations. In S. Karamardian, ed., *Fixed points: Algorithms and applications.* New York: Academic Press, pp. 315-36.

——— 1978. Improving the convergence of fixed-point algorithms. *Mathematical Programming Study* 7:151-69.

——— 1979. A note on computing equilibria in economies with activity analysis models of production. *Journal of Mathematical Economics* 6:135-44.

——— 1980a. Traversing large pieces of linearity in algorithms that solve equations by following piecewise-linear paths. *Mathematics of Operations Research* 5:242-57.

——— 1980b. Global and local convergence and monotonicity results for a recent variable-dimension simplicial algorithm. In W. Forster, ed., *Numerical solution of highly nonlinear problems.* Amsterdam: North-Holland, pp. 43-70.

——— 1980c. PLALGO: a FORTRAN implementation of a piecewise-linear homotopy algorithm for solving systems of nonlinear equations. Technical Report No. 454, School of Operations Research and Industrial Engineering, Cornell University.

CHAPTER 3

Numerical specification of applied general equilibrium models: estimation, calibration, and data

---

Ahsan Mansur and John Whalley

1   Introduction

Most recent work on applied general equilibrium models has focused on solution of models and interpretation of findings in terms of policy implications. Only limited attention has been given to the issue of deciding upon an appropriate numerical specification before computation proceeds.

In this chapter we discuss alternative approaches to parameter specification in applied general equilibrium models. Although the models currently in use span a number of applied fields,[1] a standard procedure has evolved among modelers of "calibration" of the whole model to a benchmark observation coupled with use of literature estimates for certain key parameters (particularly elasticities). A sequence of data adjustments is frequently used to "force" equilibrium conditions on observed data before calibration begins. Most of these models involve dimensionalities that are quite outside those which econometricians are used to, and estimation of all model parameters using a stochastic specification and time series data is usually ruled out as infeasible.

We explore some of the issues raised by these procedures. We consider whether for small-scale general equilibrium models stochastic estimation procedures can be used. We discuss both system estimation and estimation of subsystems of models, and in the process review some of the econometric literature that seems to us relevant. For models of the scale currently being used, stochastic estimation of complete models appears to us to be infeasible. For smaller-scale variants time series econometric

We are grateful to France St-Hilaire for help with Tables 1 and 3 and the Bibliography. The Academic Development Fund of the University of Western Ontario has provided financial support. Although this is a joint chapter, we note that the first author has principally prepared Sections 2 and 4 and the second author Section 3.

69

estimation appears possible, and we report some estimates for a two-sector model of the United States. Because the calibration procedures in use in existing "large" models are somewhat sparsely documented, we also describe these methods, summarizing some of the characteristics of the data sets used.

In Section 2 of this chapter we discuss econometric approaches to model estimation in small-scale, simple general equilibrium systems. We discuss estimation of a classical pure exchange economy and extend the analysis to incorporate production. We discuss both system and subsystem estimation, reviewing some of the literature on demand and production functions. We also comment on estimation of linear demand–supply systems.

In Section 3 we outline the broad characteristics of some of the applied general equilibrium models currently in use and describe the calibration procedures used. We present a numerical example of a "benchmark equilibrium" and outline how data of this type are used to generate parameter values. In practice, construction of a benchmark data set for a particular model involves a substantial reorganization of conventional national income and other accounts, and we discuss this, suggesting the label *general equilibrium accounting* to differentiate benchmark accounts from traditional accounts. We comment on the absence of any statistical test of the specifications chosen through such a procedure.

In Section 4 we report on comparisons of some preliminary results due to Mansur (1981) of both stochastic estimation and deterministic calibration for a small-dimensional general equilibrium tax model of the U.S. economy. In the final section, we synthesize the discussion and evaluate alternative approaches to parameter selection. We also emphasize the limits that data availability and reliability place on the modeling exercise.

2   Stochastic estimation

The natural reaction of anyone faced with the problem of specifying parameter values for a general equilibrium model to be used for counter-factual policy or other analyses is to think in terms of stochastic estimation of the model (through either system or single-equation methods). This, however, is not the procedure generally adopted for existing applied models where "calibration" of the model to an equilibrium data set is followed, combined with a literature search or "best-guess" procedure for key parameters (usually elasticities). No test of model to data is employed, and sensitivity analysis is widely used for parameters whose values are uncertain and/or pivotal to results.

In this section we outline some approaches to stochastic estimation of general equilibrium models, highlighting some of the problems that have motivated the widespread use of calibration. Before discussing possible estimation procedures, we first outline stochastic formulations of two widely used simple general equilibrium models to put the material that follows in better focus.

2.1 Simple general equilibrium models in stochastic form

(a) *Classical pure exchange economy:* The simplest general equilibrium structure is the traditional two-person pure exchange economy represented in an Edgeworth box diagram. Each of two consumers has an endowment of each of two goods. The endowment point usually does not coincide with the contract curve, and trade between the individuals moves the consumption point from the initial endowment point to a point on the contract curve (which is also Pareto-optimal). Diagrammatically this can be represented by the intersection of the offer curves of the two individuals, the intersection point characterizing a competitive equilibrium.

This model can be formulated algebraically in terms of the excess demand functions $f_i^j(\pi)$ for the two individuals $j = A, B$ for each of the two goods $i = X, Y$. Each individual's set of excess demand functions will separately satisfy budget balance; $\sum_{i=X,Y} \pi_i f_i^j(\pi) = 0$, $j = A, B$ for any pair of nonnegative prices π_i. Because relative prices are all that are relevant in such models, a common normalization used is that the sum of prices equal unity, that is, $\pi_X + \pi_Y = 1$.

A convenient functional form that can be used to represent individual excess demand functions is the constant elasticity offer curve (see Johnson, 1953, and Gorman, 1957). In the two-good case, the restriction of budget balance implies that the elasticities of the two excess demand functions are not independent but are related to the elasticity of the offer surface. Thus, in constant elasticity form, the deterministic two-good model can be written as

$$f_X^A = X^A \pi^{\sigma_X^A} \qquad f_X^B = X^B \pi^{\sigma_X^B}$$
$$f_Y^A = Y^A \pi^{\sigma_Y^A} \qquad f_Y^B = Y^B \pi^{\sigma_Y^B}$$
$$\sigma_Y^A + \sigma_X^A = -1 \qquad \sigma_X^B + \sigma_Y^B = -1$$

where π is the relative price of good X in terms of Y, the σ terms are the elasticities of excess demand functions for each good by each agent, and X^A, Y^A, X^B, Y^B are unit parameters. In stochastic form, assuming multiplicative disturbances, this model becomes

$$f_X^A = X^A \pi^{\sigma_X^A} V_X^A \qquad f_X^B = X^B \pi^{\sigma_X^B} V_X^B$$

$$f_Y^A = Y^A \pi^{\sigma_Y^A} V_Y^A \qquad f_Y^B = Y^B \pi^{\sigma_Y^B} V_Y^B$$

$$\sigma_X^A + \sigma_Y^A = -1 \qquad \sigma_X^B + \sigma_Y^B = -1$$

$$E[V_X^A] = E[V_Y^A] = 1 \qquad E[V_X^B] = E[V_Y^B] = 1$$

This model as specified is not identified, though if it is estimated in the presence of changing policies it can become identified. A natural area of application for such a model is to the simultaneous estimation of import demand and export supply elasticities in a two-region model, and the incorporation of changing tariffs in both regions can serve to identify the model. Another approach to use of the model is to specify a functional form for agent demand functions for each commodity rather than excess demand functions (such as Cobb–Douglas or CES). In this case exogenous shifts in the endowment point for both consumers serve to identify the model.

Although one would perhaps have thought that the two-person pure exchange economy would be widely used in econometric work since it is the most basic model in general equilibrium analysis (and, some would say, in all of economics), we find it remarkable that (to our knowledge) no stochastic analog of this model has ever been estimated.

(b) *One-person, two-good, general equilibrium with production:* A second widely used general equilibrium (GE) model is the two-good, two-factor general equilibrium model incorporating one consumer (or multiple consumers with identical homothetic preferences). Equilibrium in this economy involves demand–supply equality conditions for both goods and factors, along with zero-profit conditions.

This model in deterministic form can be specified as follows:[2]

Demand side	Demands X^D, Y^D determined from max $U(X, Y)$ (subject to $P_X X + P_Y Y = P_L \bar{L} + P_K \bar{K}$)
Production side	$Y^S = F_Y(K_Y, L_Y), \quad X^S = F_X(K_X, L_X)$
Zero-profit conditions	$P_Y Y^S = P_K K_Y + P_L L_Y,$ $P_X X^S = P_K K_X + P_L L_X$
Demand–supply equalities	$Y^D = Y^S, \quad X^D = X^S, \quad \bar{K} = K_X + K_Y,$ $\bar{L} = L_X + L_Y$

This system is represented diagrammatically by the familiar production possibilities frontier diagram. In order to work with such a system, "convenient" functional forms (such as Cobb–Douglas or CES) are frequently used for demands and production. In stochastic form, additive disturbances usually appear in demand functions whereas multiplicative disturbances enter production functions.

In contrast to conventional estimation of sets of demand functions that satisfy budget balance, estimation of the above model involves simultaneously estimating demand functions (subject to budget balance) and a production system subject to fixed factor endowments. By using data on fixed factor endowments in each period and assuming the functional form for production functions to be unchanged through time, the model is identified and estimation can proceed. As with the pure exchange economy, to our knowledge there have been no attempts to estimate the standard two-good production model.

2.2   System estimation of simple GE models

We now suppose that an attempt is to be made to estimate an entire general equilibrium model through system full-information maximum likelihood methods. We consider a simple two-factor, two-good model with fixed endowments of labor ($\bar{L}_t$) and capital ($\bar{K}_t$) in period t. The model will also incorporate utility maximization by consumers and cost minimization by producers, along with the relevant policy structure (if any). Let us suppose, for now, that we can specify a complete stochastic model in general form as

$$F_t[Y_t, X_t, B] = e_t \qquad (2.1)$$

where Y_t is a $(1 \times M)$-dimensional row vector of endogenous variables and X_t is a $(1 \times K)$ vector of exogenous variables. Now $F_t[\cdot]$ is a $(1 \times M)$ vector function $[f_{1t}, f_{2t}, \ldots, f_{mt}]$ that, in the neighborhood of the true parameter values B, is assumed to be uniformly bounded and twice differentiable with uniformly bounded derivatives. The $(1 \times M)$ vector of errors, e_t, is assumed to be multivariate-normal with expected value zero and variance–covariance matrix Σ. The identifiability of the parameters of this system has to be ensured but for now is assumed to be satisfied.[3]

Equation (2.1) can be rewritten

$$f_{it}[y_{1t}, \ldots, y_{Mt}, x_{1t}, \ldots, x_{Kt}, B_i] = e_{it}$$

where $i = 1, \ldots, M$ and $t = 1, \ldots, T$; $\{x_{kt}\}$, $k = 1, \ldots, K$ are predetermined variables; $\{y_{mt}\}$, $m = 1, \ldots, M$ are endogenous variables; and $\{B_i\}$ is a vector of parameter values.

Under the assumption that the Jacobian of the transformation from the disturbances to the observed random variables y_t is nonvanishing and the errors follow a multivariate-normal distribution, a likelihood function can be derived. The concentrated likelihood function can be expressed as

$$L^*(B) = \text{constant} + \sum_t \log|\det \cdot J_t| - \tfrac{1}{2}\log|\det \cdot \hat{\Sigma}|$$

Here it is assumed that $E(e_{it}) = 0$ for all $i = 1,\dots,M$, $t = 1,\dots,T$; $E(e_t e_{t'}) = \Sigma$ is of full rank; $E(e_t e_{t'}) = 0$ if $t = t'$; and $\hat{\Sigma}_{mi} = \hat{\Sigma}_{im} = (1/T)\sum_t f_{it} f_{mt}$ is derived from the first-order conditions of the likelihood function

$$J_{i,m,t} = \left(\frac{\delta f_i}{\delta y_m}\right)_t$$

Now J_t is the matrix of such derivatives.

A number of algorithms are available to maximize such a likelihood function such as Eisenpress and Greenstadt (1966) or Chow (1973), who use a Newton method, or Berndt et al. (1974), who use a gradient maximization method. The later algorithm by Berndt et al. has the advantage that convergence to a local maximum of the likelihood function is guaranteed and, unlike the Newton method employed by Eisenpress and Greenstadt (1966) and Chow (1973), does not involve the evaluation of third derivatives. This method requires the evaluation of the model up to second derivatives while third derivatives are eliminated by taking advantage of the fundamental statistical relation that the asymptotic variance–covariance matrix of a maximum likelihood estimator is equal to the variance–covariance matrix of the gradient of the likelihood function.

Although most satisfactory from a statistical point of view, such a system approach is of limited applicability for most general equilibrium models. A number of reasons are involved:

(i) For a wide class of GE models the likelihood function is not well defined. For example, a complete general equilibrium model normally has market-clearing conditions requiring that labor and capital employed in all sectors together add up to the exogenously given factor endowments. Errors in the input demand functions are thus not independent of each other and we cannot define a likelihood function for the model since we do not have independently distributed error terms.

(ii) For most applied GE models the number of parameters to be estimated increases very rapidly with each increase in the number of sectors or consumers. With a moderate sample size, for most applied GE models the number of independent parameters to be estimated will exceed the number of available data points. Some of the larger models to be discussed in the next section have numbers of parameters in the thousands. The degrees-of-freedom problem is especially acute if the translog framework is used in modeling both the production and consumer behavior.

For example, in the 36-sector model of Jorgenson and Fraumeni (1980) there are 38 relative share parameters for each sector (these are relative shares of inputs in the value of the output of each sector) and also relative shares of commodity groups in the value of total consumer expenditure. Besides these share parameters, there are "second-order" parameters that correspond to the measures of substitutability in production and consumption. Jorgenson and Fraumeni estimate these parameters subject to separability restrictions, leading to a hierarchy of submodels. In their empirical implementation about 50 such parameters are estimated for each sector. An additional 50 or so parameters are needed to specify the consumer behavior, the total number of second-order (or elasticity) parameters being approximately 2000 for the 36-sector model considered by Jorgenson and Fraumeni. Thus for models of this scale, any full information method for complete model estimation has limited implementation possibilities.

An obvious procedure in light of these problems is to apply full information methods to subsystems of the complete general equilibrium model, dividing the model in such a way that structural equations whose coefficients or error variances are related to each other are part of the same subsystem. This hopefully enables cross-equation constraints for each of the subsystems to be imposed. The most natural choice of subsystems consists of demand systems and production structures that are embedded into the complete GE formulation. We now turn to methods for separate estimation of subsystems and return later to review literature on demand and production subsystem estimates.

2.3 *Estimation of GE subsystems (method I)*

The specification of subsystems in any general equilibrium model will vary from case to case. Subsystems may be linear or nonlinear in variables, nonlinear in parameters, or nonlinear in both variables and parameters.

Let us consider a subsystem of the general model (2.1) that consists of $L (<M)$ equations that in normalized form can be expressed as

$$y_{it} = f(G_{it}, B) + e_{it} \tag{2.2}$$

where y_{it} is the tth observation on the dependent variable in the ith equation and e_{it} follows a normal distribution as described earlier. Now G_{it} is a g_i-component vector of observations at time t on endogenous functions appearing in the ith equation. Each of these functions contains endogenous variables (i.e., random variables correlated with e_{it}) and exogenous variables or combinations of the two. There $G_{it} = [g^i_{1,t}, \ldots, g^i_{g_i,t}]$, where in general $g_{jt}^i = g_j^i[y_t, x_t]$ and $y_t = (y_{1,t}, \ldots, y_{M,t})$ is the set of endogenous variables of the system (2.1). Now x_t is the set of all predetermined variables.

Implicit in the construction of the subsystems is the assumption that some of the y values are determined outside the subsystem but remain endogenous to the complete model. In a demand or expenditure system, for instance, income is not endogenously determined, but is endogenously in the larger complete GE model. In general terms, if we treat $y_1, \ldots, y_L$ as endogenous variables, then the subsystem predetermined variables $y_{L+1,t}, \ldots, y_{M,t}$ need careful treatment. One might hope that it is possible to treat the variables $y_{L+1,t}, \ldots, y_{M,t}$ as exogenous or predetermined for this subsystem and proceed with nonlinear FIML estimation.[4] However, strictly speaking, this would give us consistent estimators only if the variables $y_{L+1,t}, \ldots, y_{M,t}$ are uncorrelated with e_{it} values (of the relevant subsystem), a condition that would not generally be satisfied for GE models. In general, these variables are correlated in these models.

In this case we can use a nonlinear three-stage least squares estimator – a form of instrumental variable estimator often referred to as a minimum distance estimator. Here we first transform the structural form of any given subsystem and then minimize the sum of squares of errors through an iterative procedure. We begin with the structural form of the subsystem (2.1) represented as

$$y - f(G, B) = e \qquad (2.2')$$

Premultiplying each equation by a matrix $Z'(K \times T)$ such that

$$E(Z' \cdot e) = 0 \qquad (2.3)$$

the transformed system is

$$(I_L \otimes Z')[y - f(G, B)] = [I_L \otimes Z']e$$

Let

$$E[ee'] = \Omega \otimes I_T$$

where

$$\Omega = \begin{bmatrix} \omega_{11} & \cdots & \omega_{1L} \\ \vdots & \ddots & \\ \omega_{L1} & & \omega_{LL} \end{bmatrix}$$

and

$$E(e_{it} \cdot e_{jt'}) = 0 \qquad \text{for} \quad i \neq j \quad \text{and/or} \quad t = t'$$

$$= \omega_{ij} \qquad \text{for} \quad i = j \quad \text{and} \quad t = t'$$

For the transformed system the variance–covariance matrix can be represented as

$$E[I_L \otimes Z'] \cdot ee' \cdot [I_L \otimes Z] = [I_L \otimes Z'][\Omega \otimes I_T][I_L \otimes Z]$$

$$= \Omega \otimes (Z'Z)$$

The minimum distance estimator can be obtained by minimizing

$$J(B) = [y - f(G, B)]'[I_L \otimes Z][\Omega \otimes Z'Z]^{-1}[I_L \otimes Z'][y - f(G, B)]$$

$$= (y - f)'S(y - f) \tag{2.4}$$

where

$$f = f(G, B) \quad \text{and} \quad S = [I_L \otimes Z][\Omega \otimes Z'Z]^{-1}[I_L \otimes Z']$$

Under certain regularity conditions [following Amemiya (1977, 1974) and Jorgenson and Laffont (1974)] it can be shown that the estimated value $\hat{B}$ converges in probability to the corresponding true value B^* and that $\sqrt{T} \ (\hat{B} - B^*)$ converges in distribution to[5]

$$N[0, \{H'(\Omega \otimes M)^{-1}H\}^{-1}]$$

where $M = \lim_{T \to \infty} (1/T)Z'Z$, which is assumed to exist and be nonsingular, and

$$H_i = \operatorname*{plim}_{T \to \infty} \frac{1}{T} Z' \frac{\delta f_i}{\delta B'}$$

uniformly in B. This implies

$$\operatorname*{plim}_{T \to \infty} \frac{1}{T} Z' \frac{\delta f}{\delta B'} = \begin{bmatrix} H_1 \\ \vdots \\ H_L \end{bmatrix} = H$$

is of rank R uniformly in B, where

$$\left[\frac{\delta f_i}{\delta B'}\right] = \frac{\delta f_i'}{\delta B} = \begin{bmatrix} \dfrac{\delta f_i}{\delta B'}(Z_{i1}, B), \ldots, \dfrac{\delta f_i}{\delta B'}(Z_{iT}, B) \\ \vdots \\ \dfrac{\delta f_i}{\delta B^R}(Z_{i1}, B), \ldots, \dfrac{\delta f_i}{\delta B^R}(Z_{iT}, B) \end{bmatrix}$$

Minimization of Equation (2.4) is usually performed by an iterative procedure as the equation system is highly nonlinear in both parameters and variables. A Gauss–Newton method, or a variant, is normally used. The iterations take the form

$$\hat{B}_{(n)} = \hat{B}_{(n-1)} + \left[\frac{\delta f'}{\delta B} \cdot S \cdot \frac{\delta f}{\delta B'} \right] \cdot \frac{\delta f'}{\delta B} \cdot S \cdot (y - f) \qquad (2.5)$$

where $f(\cdot)$ and $\delta f/\delta B$ are evaluated at the estimated parameter values of the $(n-1)$th iteration, that is, at $\hat{B}_{(n-1)}$. Further discussion of the properties of this estimator occurs in Amemiya (1974, 1977), Berndt et al. (1974), and Jorgenson and Laffont (1974).

2.4 Selection of instruments in subsystem estimation (method II)

In the discussion in the previous section we ignored the issue of selecting the components of the matrix Z, the matrix of instruments. Any set of variables that are uncorrelated with the errors [so as to satisfy condition (2.3)], but at the same time are highly correlated with the endogenous functions G_{jt}, should qualify as instruments. We suggest two methods of selecting the instruments. The first method, somewhat analogous to that suggested by Goldfeld and Quandt (1968), Kelejian (1971), and Amemiya (1974), is to regress each G_{jt} on the elements of a polynomial of degree r in X_t. The underlying regression model can be expressed as

$$G_{jt} = Z_{jt} + \eta_{jt}$$

where

$$Z_{jt} = \theta_{0,j} + \theta_{1,1} X_{1,t} + \cdots + \theta_{1,K_1} X_{K_1,t} + \cdots + \theta_{r,1} X_{1,t}^r + \cdots + \theta_{r,K_1} X_{K_1,t}^r$$

$$j = 1, \ldots, g_1, \qquad t = 1, \ldots, T$$

Here the X terms are the elements of X_t, and the η_{jt} terms are residuals that are not correlated with the elements Z_{jt}. Defining

$$Q_t = [1, X_{1,t}, \ldots, X_{K_1,t}, \ldots, X_{K_1,t}^r]$$

and θ_j, the associated vector of parameters, the instruments we are considering are

$$\hat{Z}_{jt} = Q_t \hat{\theta}_j$$

where $\hat{\theta}_j = (Q'Q)^{-1} Q'G_j$, Q being the matrix formed with the vectors Q_t, and G_j is the vector with corresponding elements G_{jt} for $t = 1, \ldots, T$. The matrix Z would then consist of low-order polynomials of all the exogenous variables of the complete system.

In the method above, the instruments are obtained by regressing the endogenous functions (g_{jt}) on the lower-order polynomials of the exogenous variables of the complete system. The procedure accommodates the simultaneity, and thus the estimators are consistent. This method does not, however, directly incorporate the restrictions of the general equilibrium model, such as full employment of factors.

An alternative method is to impose general equilibrium restrictions directly on the instruments. Using the method described earlier, a set of consistent estimators can be obtained for the subsystems of the model. Adopting the parameters from one set of subsystem estimates, we can impose the conditions specified in the others that would ensure the restrictions of the general equilibrium model. General equilibrium solution algorithms can be employed at this stage to produce appropriate sets of instruments. Using these equilibrium magnitudes (prices, income, etc.) as instruments, we can reestimate earlier subsystems repeating the methods outlined above. In applications, solution algorithms apply to each year's data separately as the endowments of factors change from year to year. The process is repeated for each year's data with changed values of exogenous variables, yielding a time series for the instruments to be used in subsystem reestimation in the next round.

In terms of our generalized notation for the complete model, $F_t(Y_t, X_t, B) = U_t$, we first estimate $\hat{B}$ by some suitable method (e.g., the method outlined above) to produce consistent estimators. We then produce forecasts

$$\hat{Y}_t = g(X_t, B)$$

The estimates of the endogenous variables from this solved reduced form can be used as instruments (or in constructing appropriate instruments) for each of the submodels in reestimation.

This alternative method is in essence an extension and partial modification of the methods described earlier. Reduced form estimates of endogenous functions (g_{jt}) are used in the formation of the matrix Z and once again minimum-distance estimation is used on this newly constructed matrix. Properties of the estimators remained essentially the same as described for the earlier method.

2.5   Literature on demand and production systems

Whereas the previous section highlighted some of the conceptual issues in estimation of general equilibrium systems or subsystems, perhaps the simplest way to obtain parameter values for use in a simple equilibrium model with production is to separately estimate the commodity demand system and the production functions (the production system). The literature on applied consumption and production analysis is clearly relevant in this context, and in this section we briefly refer to some of this literature.

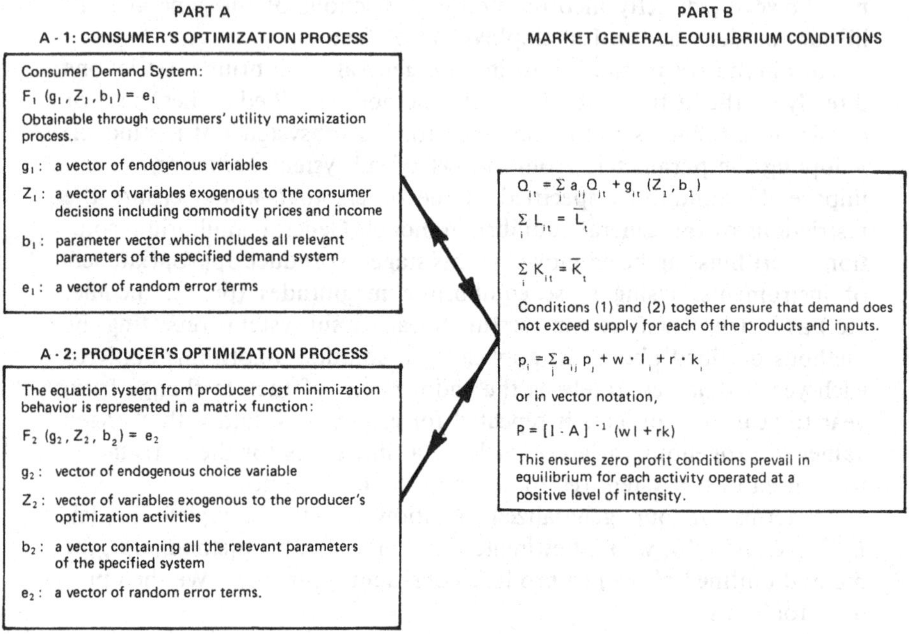

PART A
A - 1: CONSUMER'S OPTIMIZATION PROCESS

Consumer Demand System:

$F_1 (g_1, Z_1, b_1) = e_1$

Obtainable through consumers' utility maximization process.

g_1 : a vector of endogenous variables

Z_1 : a vector of variables exogenous to the consumer decisions including commodity prices and income

b_1 : parameter vector which includes all relevant parameters of the specified demand system

e_1 : a vector of random error terms

A - 2: PRODUCER'S OPTIMIZATION PROCESS

The equation system from producer cost minimization behavior is represented in a matrix function:

$F_2 (g_2, Z_2, b_2) = e_2$

g_2 : vector of endogenous choice variable

Z_2 : vector of variables exogenous to the producer's optimization activities

b_2 : a vector containing all the relevant parameters of the specified system

e_2 : a vector of random error terms.

PART B
MARKET GENERAL EQUILIBRIUM CONDITIONS

$Q_{it} = \sum_j a_{ji} Q_{jt} + g_{it} (Z_1, b_1)$

$\sum_i L_{it} = \bar{L}_t$

$\sum_i K_{it} = \bar{K}_t$

Conditions (1) and (2) together ensure that demand does not exceed supply for each of the products and inputs.

$p_i = \sum_j a_{ij} p_j + w \cdot l_i + r \cdot k_i$

or in vector notation,

$P = [1 - A]^{-1} (wl + rk)$

This ensures zero profit conditions prevail in equilibrium for each activity operated at a positive level of intensity.

Figure 1. General equilibrium subsystem decomposition from Mansur (1981): consumer's and producer's optimization separated from market equilibrium conditions. (The decomposition represents a class of general equilibrium models with two primary factors of production and fixed-coefficient intermediate inputs.)

A complete general equilibrium system can be disaggregated into two broad subsystems interrelated through the equilibrium conditions. We consider a commodity demand system derived from the underlying (direct or indirect) utility function as characterizing consumer behavior. The production system characterizing producer behavior, given the technology underlying the production function, forms the second subsystem. The market equilibrium conditions then coordinate the separate subsystems.

The model decomposition used by Mansur (1981) is outlined in Figure 1. Within Part A, A-1 describes the consumer's optimization process and A-2 the optimizing behavior of producers. The two subsystems of Part A can be expressed in general notation as

$$F_1(g_1, Z_1, b_1) = e_1 \tag{A.1}$$

$$F_2(g_2, Z_2, b_2) = e_2 \tag{A.2}$$

Here g_s ($s = 1, 2$) are vectors of endogenous variables; prices and income are subsumed under the vector Z along with other predetermined variables. By construction, different subsystems in Part A do not have common parameters, and errors in one can be assumed to be independent of those of others. These two subsystems are linked to each other indirectly through the market equilibrium conditions in Part B.

Independent estimation of commodity demand and production systems would provide estimates of all the parameters that are needed to solve a complete general equilibrium model. If equilibrium conditions are ignored, we could restrict ourselves to the separate estimation of demand and production systems. The issue facing users of subsystem estimates is thus to determine exactly what the degree of unreliability is if the simultaneity between subsystems is ignored.

Demand systems: In empirical analyses of demand systems, income (Y) and prices ($\mathbf{P}$, in vector form) are taken to be exogenously given. The budget balance condition along with other restrictions taken from the theory of consumer demand act as constraints on the system, which in compact notation can be represented as

$$\mathbf{X} = \mathbf{f}(Y, \mathbf{P}) + \mathbf{u}$$

$$Y = \mathbf{P}'\mathbf{x}$$

where $\mathbf{x}$ is a vector of quantities of n goods and services demanded.

There are a large number of possible functional forms for the demand system, and different approaches can be adopted in specifying the system. Two classes of functional form for utility functions are direct and indirect utility functions with demand functions generated from utility maximization.[6] A third approach starts with directly specified demand equations and imposes theoretical restrictions from utility maximization in the process of estimation (see Nasse, 1973; Barten, 1964; etc.).

The theoretical restrictions from utility maximization (which depend on the form of the utility function), along with the budget constraint, imply cross-equation restrictions. Joint estimation is thus necessary and full information methods such as FIML or variants of generalized least squares (GLS) methods (e.g., Zellner, 1962) can be employed. One equation is conventionally dropped from the system to avoid the problem of singularity of the variance–covariance matrix (due to the budget constraint). These issues are widely discussed in applied consumption analysis, an overall survey of which also reveals that variations in income and prices generally can explain only some of the variation in observed demand (see Barten, 1977; Desai, 1976; and Bridge, 1971). The role of prices in determining demand behavior would seem, on the basis of econometric studies on demand, to be less than theory might suggest, although prices become somewhat more important if a finely divided classification of commodities is used. For broad aggregates, however, price indices over time tend to move in the same direction following similar patterns, making substitution possibilities hard to detect from the data.

It is now widely believed (Barten, 1977) that since consumer demand models (in the forms in which these are currently estimated) concentrate only on one side of the market, simultaneous consideration of demand and supply might be a desirable step. Although little work along these lines has been undertaken by econometricians, thinking in this area can be said to be moving toward general equilibrium considerations. Currently, most applied consumption literature reports independent demand-side estimation exercises, with little attention being given to this as a part or subsystem of an overall GE model. Nevertheless, the degree of understanding developed over the last three decades on estimation of sets of demand equations does provide a valuable starting point to applied general equlibrium model builders in specifying the consumption side of models.

Production systems: On the production side, there are a number of well-known papers on the estimation of production functions. Most of these emphasize the Marschak–Andrews (1944) approach that utilizes the optimizing behavior of the producer in estimation.[7] The estimation of the parameters of any production system should be based on the derived input demand system since firms cost-minimize. The input demand functions employed in this empirical literature are obtained either directly from the production function using cost minimization or indirectly from cost functions using Shephard's lemma. If we simultaneously estimate production functions for several sectors and impose the condition that factors are fully employed, the endowment constraint (if relevant) would be binding and impose further cross-equation restrictions across the errors of input demand equations. In existing econometric literature the focus is only on the input demand functions for particular sectors.

For both production and cost function approaches a variety of functional forms have been used. Using the CES specification of Arrow et al. (1961) (under constant returns to scale) and cost minimization, the production system in intensive form (i.e., per unit of labor) can be expressed as

$$q_i = \frac{Q_i}{L_i} = A_i [\alpha_i k_i^{-\rho_i} + (1-\alpha_i)]^{-1/\rho_i}$$

$$k_i = \frac{K_i}{L_i} = \left(\frac{1-\alpha_i}{\alpha_i}\right)^{1/(1+\rho_i)} \cdot \left(\frac{P_L}{P_K}\right)^{1/(1+\rho_i)}$$

where

Q_i = value added in the ith sector
K_i = amount of capital used in ith sector
L_i = amount of labor used in ith sector
α_i = share parameters
ρ_i = elasticity parameters
A_i = scale parameters
P_K, P_L = prices of capital and labor inputs

The CES production system can be estimated either in the direct form or in its intensive form (with or without logarithmic transformations).

Berndt and Wood (1975) and Christensen et al. (1971, 1973) use translog cost functions, whereas other forms such as generalized Cobb-Douglas cost functions are discussed by Diewert (1971, 1973). In its general form the cost function can be expressed as

$$C = C(Q, P_1, \ldots, P_m)$$

where C is total cost, the P_i terms ($i = 1, \ldots, m$) are the input prices, and Q is the flow of gross output of the jth product. Using a translog cost function with symmetry and constant returns to scale imposed, the cost function can be expressed as

$$\ln C = \ln \alpha_0 + \ln Q + \sum_i \alpha_i \ln P_i + \tfrac{1}{2} \sum_i \sum_j \gamma_{ij} \ln P_i \ln P_j$$

Linear homogeneity in prices imposes the restrictions

$$\sum \alpha_i = 1$$

and

$$\sum_j \gamma_{ij} = 0 \quad \text{for all} \quad i$$

Using Shephard's lemma, input demand equations are obtained that can be expressed in cost share form as

$$S_i = \alpha_i + \sum_j \gamma_{ij} \ln P_j, \quad i, j = 1, \ldots, m$$

and

$$\sum_i S_i = 1$$

where the S_i are the shares of inputs in the total cost of producing Q.

In a recent piece Jorgenson and Fraumeni (1980) employ translog price functions, impose homogeneity (of degree 1) and derive sectoral value shares of factors. Since share elasticities with respect to prices are symmetric, further cross-equation restrictions are imposed. As the cost or value shares of the factors of production for each sector always sum to unity, in both Berndt and Wood (1975) and Jorgenson and Fraumeni (1980) the sum of the disturbances across the input cost shares or value share equations is zero at each observation. To avoid singularity of the covariance matrix they drop one equation arbitrarily (for each sector) and assume the disturbances in the remaining equations to be independently and identically normally distributed with zero mean and variance–covariance matrix Ω.

This literature on input demand systems emphasizes producer behavior and cost minimization but ignores economywide restrictions that the general equilibrium approach suggests. This is perfectly consistent with the behavior of a single competitive price-taking firm, but limits the potential use of these methods for general equilibrium models that incorporate analysis of broad aggregate sectors with economywide restrictions. At an aggregate industry level input prices are unlikely to be exogenous, and exogenously given factor endowments introduce additional cross-equation restrictions (among different sectors), particularly across the errors.[8] Thus in estimating production systems for use in multisector general equilibrium analyses it may be inappropriate to assume that prices are exogenous and that regressors in the input demand system are uncorrelated with the disturbances. If we are interested in obtaining consistent estimates of the parameters of the production subsystem of a general equilibrium model, this simultaneity should be taken into account.[9]

2.6   System estimation of linear demand–supply systems: Allingham's approach

Most econometric work on commodity and production (or input demand) systems proceeds separately and is not developed in the context of general equilibrium modeling where classifications of the two systems must match and restrictions from the general equilibrium model need to be incorporated. Using an alternative approach, Allingham (1973) attempts to capture the general equilibrium market-clearing process while giving somewhat less attention to the detailed specification of production and demand systems.

Allingham estimates a form of general equilibrium model where he uses a variant of a "Keynesian-type" consumption function not based on utility maximization. Income or expected income determines aggregate consumption; its division among different categories then depends on relative prices (represented by the price for the category relative to the general consumer price level). Moreover, to avoid nonlinearities in both parameters and variables he uses a linear production function (linear in inputs). This has the two features that the marginal product of any factor is constant and the elasticity of substitution (between the factors) is undefined. Because of these simplifications and the limited treatment of commodity and input demand systems (along with underlying cross-equation restrictions), this model reduces to a system of linear simultaneous equations. This system does not, however, satisfy the usual properties of production and consumer demand systems, such as homogeneity, Walras's law, and other restrictions that are key elements in much of the recent general equilibrium literature.

All these simplifications enable Allingham to use conventional limited-information (single-equation) methods, two-stage least squares (2SLS) or limited-information maximum likelihood (LIML). The lack of incorporation of prior restrictions coming from economic theory necessarily reduces the attractiveness of his model; however, this is (to our knowledge) the first attempt to incorporate both demand-side and production-side features of general equilibrium modeling into a complete systems approach and estimate the model parameters using time series data.

Allingham evaluates the performance of his systems approach by comparing predictive performance against traditional macro models. He estimates his model with the U.K. data over the period 1956 through 1966, distinguishing 10 producing agents (or industries) based on the Standard Industrial Classification (SIC) for 1958. After estimating the unknown parameters by using standard (linear) limited-information methods, the estimated model is solved and quantitative static and dynamic properties of the system are analyzed.

His conclusion is that the complexities associated with general equilibrium modeling are justified in predicting equilibrium values of broad aggregates and individual components and for investigating the process whereby equilibrium is attained. Allingham's approach, however, is quite different from the applied models currently in use for policy appraisal. As demand functions do not come from utility maximization, no welfare analysis of policy alternatives is possible; the absence of Walras's law as a restriction on demand functions raises issues as to the internal feasibility of model solutions, and the absence of clearly defined production functions suggests that economywide production possibility sets may not be well defined. Nonetheless, Allingham's work represents a bold first step toward a desirable systems approach.

3   Deterministic "calibration" procedures

From the discussion in the preceding section, system or subsystem estimation might seem the natural way to proceed in specifying a numerical general equilibrium model to be used for policy or other analyses.[10] The "facts of life" of applied general equilibrium modeling, however, are that less sophisticated procedures are usually employed. The common procedure is to "calibrate" the model to a base year observation, "calibration" meaning the ability of the model to reproduce base year data as a model solution. Calibration is augmented by literature search (and on occasion econometric estimation) for key model parameters, whose value is required before calibration can proceed. In practice, due to the widespread use of CES functions in applied models, "key" parameters are more or less synonymous with elasticities, and in some cases literature search provides limited, contradictory, or (at times) no information. Resort is usually made to "sensitivity" analysis, in which alternative values of key variables are tried and model findings crudely evaluated for their robustness. In this section we outline these procedures and in the process briefly describe the structure of some of the applied models currently in use.

3.1   Summary of existing applied general equilibrium models in which calibration is used

To provide background for the later discussion in this section, we begin by outlining the main characteristics of some of the recent applied general equilibrium models. In Table 1 we briefly summarize the main characteristics of a number of models constructed for use in counterfactual policy analysis. The main areas of use are international trade, public finance, and development, but increasingly other areas of economic activity including energy and financial market activity are being examined. Examples of issues to which these models have been applied are analyses of the incidence of taxes in domestic economies and the effects of changes in tariffs on the international economy.

In these applications modifications to existing policies are expected to change relative prices in the (domestic and international) economy. The use of the model allows comparison between a historical equilibrium generated by existing policies that is assumed to be observable and a hypothetical or counterfactual equilibrium that the model produces under a changed policy regime. Comparison of equilibria leads directly to applied welfare analysis producing estimates of welfare gains and losses for the groups identified in the model. In an alternative use the model may simply be interpreted as providing indications as to how the structure of the economy could be affected by the policy change.

The central characteristic of these models is the price-endogenous equilibrium framework that typically involves separate specification of equation systems representing the demand and production sides of the economy. In equilibrium all behavior is consistent with the equilibrium prices in that consumers maximize utility, producers maximize profits, and market demands equal market supplies. Policy evaluation proceeds by comparing a "benchmark" equilibrium under existing policies to a new equilibrium under new policies. As the new policy alternatives considered are usually hypothetical, such an equilibrium is termed "counterfactual." The benchmark equilibrium is assumed to be reflected in observable behavior, and a micro consistent equilibrium data set is constructed using national accounts and other data sources for purpose of both making the comparison possible and providing a data base for model calibration.

The most common specification in this type of modeling involves demand and production functions drawn from the family of so-called convenient functional forms. Cobb–Douglas are the simplest of these, but this group also includes CES, linear expenditure (LES), and constant ratios of elasticities of substitution (homothetic) (CRESH) systems, and may incorporate nesting involving hierarchical functions. A major difference in these models from more conventional input–output analysis is that they explicitly incorporate extensive substitutability on both the demand and production sides of the model.

An important ingredient in these models is the amount of detail that is incorporated. Whereas some seek to provide a general-purpose capability so that many different policy alternatives can be analyzed, others are oriented more to specific issues. With multipurpose models, incorporation of a large number of commodity and household groupings is usually viewed as important because of the complex commodity differentiation contained in the policy instruments to be analyzed. The Dixon et al. (1980) model of Australia, for instance, separately identifies 109 industries in an attempt to accomodate the detail of Australian tariff and other policies. In their model of the U.K. tax system, Piggott and Whalley (1980) identify 100 household types stratified by income, occupation, and family size in order to perform detailed distributional analysis of the effects of tax changes. In the multipurpose models the level of detail identified on the demand and production sides frequently reflects the maximum available detail in basic data.

For the selection of parameter values these models all employ procedures that we loosely describe as "calibration." For the particular functions assumed for demand and production, parameter values are chosen so that the model will exactly reproduce an assembled equilibrium data set as a solution to the model, assuming there are no changes in policies from those in operation in the base year. This "observed"

Table 1. *Summary of model characteristics and uses*

Model	Demand side		Production side		Policy interventions incorporated
	Demand functions	Disaggregation	Functions for production structure	Number of industrial commodities	
Adelman & Robinson (1978)	CES with elasticities "adjusted" to satisfy budget and other constraints	15 socioeconomic categories of income recipients	Two-level CES using a Cobb–Douglas aggregation function for labor; fixed coefficients for intermediate production involving "composite" goods	29 producing sectors, 4 firm sizes, 7 labor skill categories	Tax and transfer experiments; agricultural experiments; trade and industrialization experiments; technology and manpower experiments; land reform; urban policy; development strategies
Dervis & Robinson (1978)	Cobb–Douglas demands for "composite" goods, CES aggregation functions over "comparable" domestic and imported products	1 household	Two-level CES functions; fixed-coefficient intermediate production involving "composite" goods	19 sectors, 3 labor groups	Higher exchange rate; manufactured exports; and investment-oriented policy package

Study	Treatment of demand	Consumers	Production structure	Sectors	Application
Carrin, Gunning, & Waelbroek (1980)	CES aggregation over comparable domestic and imported products, 2 sets of ELES coefficients for household demands for composites	2 groups of consumers (rural/urban)	Cobb-Douglas value-added functions plus fixed-coefficient intermediate production involving "composites"	5 sectors (2 rural, 3 urban)	Simulation experiments, considering the impact of an increase in oil prices under price rigidity and flexibility
Deardorff & Stern (1979)	Cobb-Douglas demands for "composite" goods, CES aggregation functions over "comparable" domestic and imported products	18 OECD countries and rest of the world	CES value-added functions; fixed-coefficient intermediate use for CES composites of home imports	22 tradeable, 7 nontradeable industries and commodities	Tokyo Round tariff changes, under fixed-exchange-rate nontariff barriers, agricultural concessions, procurement liberalization
Whalley (1980)	Nested CES	41 households (in largest variant)	CES value-added functions; fixed-coefficient intermediate use for CES composites of home imports	33 commodities and industries in each of 4 regions	Changes in tariffs and nontariff barriers and taxes in EEC, U.S., and Japan
Fullerton, Shoven, & Whalley (1980)	Nested CES/Cobb-Douglas	12 households	CES value-added functions	16 commodities, 17 industries	Variations in U.S. tax policies (represented by 1973 data)
Piggott & Whalley (1980)	Nested CES	100 households (income, occupation, and family characteristics)	CES value-added functions; fixed-coefficient intermediate production	33 commodities and industries	Alterations in U.K. tax and subsidy policies (represented by 1973 data)

Table 1 *(cont.)*

| | Demand side | | Production side | | |
Model	Demand functions	Disaggregation	Functions for production structure	Number of industrial commodities	Policy interventions incorporated
Manne (1980)	Derived demands from energy CES production functions	3 regions	Nested CES production functions, energy and nonenergy		3 assumptions on energy supply; 1 assumption on energy demand; 3 variations in trade elasticities
Dixon et al. (1980)	Nested CES	1 household	Three-level functions: (1) Leontief assumption (between inputs of composite products); (2) CES (a) between imported and domestic products; (b) between primary factors; (3) CES between labor inputs	109 industries and commodities, 9 labor groups	Change exchange rate, tariff increase
Serra-Puche (1979)	Cobb–Douglas	8 consumer groups, 4 income class rural/urban	CES value-added functions with fixed-coefficient specification for intermediate production	8 industries and commodities plus imports plus investment	Substitute value-added tax for sales tax; substitute sales tax for income tax; lump-sum rebate for poor; lump-sum transfer to poor; change in income tax progressivity

equilibrium is frequently termed a benchmark equilibrium data set, and we next turn to an elaboration of this concept.

3.2   *The concept of a benchmark equilibrium data set*

In counterfactual equilibrium analysis, the numerical analog of traditional comparative statics, the assumption of an "observable" equilibrium leads directly to the construction of a data set that fulfills the equilibrium conditions for some form of general equilibrium model. A natural accounting framework consistent with general equilibrium models is to record transactions occurring in the separate markets that comprise the economy. A benchmark equilibrium data set is a collection of data in which equilibrium conditions of an assumed underlying equilibrium model are satisfied.

General equilibrium analysis is perhaps the most widely used theoretical framework for economywide microeconomic analysis, but is only explicitly recognized in the construction of current national income accounts in the aggregate income–expenditure identity, not in any of the subaggregate detail in the accounts. The orientation of conventional national accounts can reasonably be described as the determination of macroeconomic aggregates. The detailed information presented in most national accounts, although clearly of enormous value to economists, nonetheless is largely a by-product of the process of assembly of macro aggregates and typically does not aim at consistency in the various areas of detail that general equilibrium analysis requires.

If equilibrium is reflected in an assembled set of accounts, demands equal market supplies for all commodities, and supplies and demands can be separately disaggregated by agent. Each agent, in turn, has incomes and expenditures consistent with its budget constraint.

Four sets of equilibrium conditions satisfied by most of the constructed benchmark equilibrium data sets are:

 i.   Demands equal supplies for all commodities.
 ii. Nonpositive profits are made in all industries.[11]
 iii. All domestic agents (including the government) have demands that satisfy their budget constraints.
 iv. The economy is in zero external sector balance.

These conditions are not all satisfied in intermediate transactions accounts (input–output data) and other data published by agencies that produce national accounts data. In input–output data, sector budget conditions are not explicit, nor is an external sector balance condition satisfied. Demand–supply equalities by commodity do not appear in national accounts data. Household expenditure data are usually inconsistent with production-side data; classifications differ and totals do not agree.

In constructing benchmark data sets various adjustments are therefore necessary to the blocks of data involved that are available separately but are not arranged on any synchronized basis. The nature of these adjustments varies from case to case as alternate sets of benchmark accounts are constructed to fit differing models.

Differences in measurement concepts from national accounts practice frequently arise for particular items. One example is the measurement of input use by industry since unadjusted national accounts measures of the use of capital by industry are inappropriate for use in general equilibrium models. Another example arises with the imputation of retained earnings through to households as savings, which is necessary to examine production and exchange in terms of underlying real counterparts.

Further difficulties arise with differences in classification between various inconsistent data sets. An example is the incompatibility between categories of consumers' expenditures in family expenditure data and the classification of products of industries in gross domestic product (GDP) accounts on which final consumer expenditures by product are recorded in input–output data. A further difficulty is that producer output classifications refer to measures of the value of output on the basis of net of retail and wholesale margin and net of transportation costs, whereas consumer expenditure classifications are on a gross basis. Classification difficulties also arise with taxation data, which in a number of instances are collected on an administrative rather than statistical basis.

Another form of adjustment arises with the need to guarantee mutual consistency between inconsistent data sets. Most benchmark data sets rely heavily on the RAS adjustment method[12] for these modifications. Examples of areas where this technique is applied are where household demands for individual products do not equal the supplies of firms, where costs of industries are not equal to sales (after modifications to published intermediate transactions accounts), and where household incomes do not equal expenditures.

In Table 2 we provide an example of interlocking benchmark accounts for an artificial economy with four industries, four goods, and three consumer groups taken from Piggott and Whalley (1980). In the consistent set of production-side accounts in this economy the value of GNP at market prices is 29, GNP at factor cost is 22, and the total value of production is 49. Zero-profit conditions are satisfied for each industry as is a zero external sector balance condition. On the left side of the table we highlight the equilibrium consistency conditions satisfied by the data.

The data sets used in the applied models typically contain much more detail and complexity than in the example discussed above. The data usually refer to a single year, although some averaging across years is done in constructing portions of those data sets where substantial volatility occurs.

In Table 3 we list the types of data used in the models outlined in Table 1. The documentation of data sources and adjustments used in these models is in varying states of completeness since complex, detailed modifications are often involved. The paper by St-Hilaire and Whalley (1980), however, is worth mentioning at this point since it is solely concerned with describing data modifications and procedures used in the construction of a benchmark data set for tax policy analysis for Canada. The benchmark approach is also outlined in this paper.

Although benchmark data sets are usually constructed with one particular model in mind, many different model specifications are consistent with the same benchmark data set. In the following sections we discuss choice of model and specifications of parameter values consistent with benchmark data.

3.3 Choice of functional form and selection of parameter values

The choice of functional forms for demand and production functions in applied general equilibrium models is guided in practice by the restrictions that ease of solution impose. The major considerations in choice of functional form are that they be consistent with the basic model assumptions and the maximizing responses of agents must be able to be repeatedly solved for in the sequences of calculations involved in equilibrium computations. Tractable functional forms must clearly be used to describe behavior patterns of both producers and consumers. Household utility maximization problems must be readily soluble, as must industry cost minimization problems.[13]

Inevitably, the well-known family of convenient functional forms provides the candidate specifications for general equilibrium policy models of the form discussed here. Demand and cost functions derived from Cobb–Douglas, Stone–Geary, and CES (either single-stage or nested) utility and production functions tend to be used. More complex variants (such as generalized Leontief functions) may also be considered, although such functions substantially increase execution times required for equilibrium calculations. The widespread choice of CES functions reflects a tradeoff that model builders face between complexity and tractability. The use of CES functions (nested or unnested) allows corresponding

Table 2. A simple example of a benchmark equilibrium data set

Demand side

1. Purchases of products by consumer groups at consumer prices

	Consumer groups A	B	C	Value of purchases at consumer prices
Products 1	4	2	1	7
2	2	3	1	6
3	4	1	3	8
4	1	3	4	8
Disposable incomes	11	9	9	29

Production side

1. Interindustry transactions

	Industries 1	2	3	4	Output for intermediate use	Final consumer demands
Products 1	2	2	2	3	8	6
2	4	3	1	0	10	4
3	3	1	1	0	5	7
4	2	1	1	0	4	5
					27	22
Intermediate costs	10	6	5	6		
Factor value added	4	8	7	3		

Public sector

Receipts

Consumer purchase taxes	Income taxes	Business taxes
7	7	5

19

Expenditures

Transfers to groups

A	B	C
6	7	6

19

Consistency conditions satisfied by data

1. Demands equal supplies for all products.
2. Each industry's total costs equal total sales.
3. Each consumer group's purchases equal disposable income for the group.
4. The endowments of consumers match factor usage.
5. The government's budget is balanced.
6. The value of final demands equals the sum of value added.

2. Consumer disposable incomes

	Consumer groups			Total
	A	B	C	
Income from capital	5	1	1	7
Labor income	3	3	4	10
Transfers received less income tax paid	6	7	6	19
	3	2	2	7
Disposable incomes	11	9	9	29

2. Composition of value added by industry

	1	2	3	4	Total
Capital service usage	1	2	3	1	7
Labor service usage	2	4	3	1	10
Indirect business taxes	1	2	1	1	5
Total	4	8	7	3	22

3. Consumer taxes paid

	Value of purchases at consumer prices	Con- sumer taxes	Value of purchases at producer prices
Products 1	7	1	6
2	6	2	4
3	8	1	7
4	8	3	5
Total	29	7	22

Note: A number of features not included in this example must be incorporated into the data set used in the model, such as: (1) real government expenditures; (2) foreign trade; (3) consumer savings; (4) investments by business, consumers, and government; (5) depreciation; (6) inventory accumulation; (7) financial transactions between the personal business, public, and external sectors; (8) more complex taxation and subsidy arrangements (e.g., a value-added tax).
Source: Piggott and Whalley (1980).

Table 3. *Data used in applied models listed in Table 1*

Model	Countries	Year	Base year data	Extraneous use of elasticities	Production data	Demand data	Policy data
Adelman & Robinson (1978)	Korea	1968	Data reconciled to 1968 input–output data and selected national accounts estimates	Expenditure elasticities, price elasticities of demand, labor supply elasticities	Input–output, national accounts, capital stock, employment survey, financial survey, wage survey	Urban household survey; farm household survey; input–output accounts	Policy scenarios, no data required
Dervis & Robinson (1978)	Turkey	1973	Approximate calibration to base year (1973)	Production-side and trade elasticities	Input–output, capital stock, wage and employment, governmental expenditure and income	Input–output, final demand	Policy scenarios, no data required
Carrin, Gunning, & Waelbroek (1980)	9 groups of developing countries and the rest of the world	1978	Data used for projections in World Bank Development Report for 1978	Income and price elasticities, trade elasticities	World Bank base year data	World Bank data	Simulation experiments, no data required

					U.S. input-output, national account (GDP),[a] trade data, tariffs, employment	Trade data for each industry; level of aggregate expenditure by country	Post-Kennedy Round tariffs; MTN offer rate tariffs (ad valorem);[b] non-tariff barriers data
Deardorff & Stern (1979)	18 OECD countries and rest of the world	1976	Comparative static analysis rather than calibration to base year data set	Import demands, production function elasticities			
Whalley (1980)	EEC, U.S., Japan, rest of the world	1973	Constructed benchmark data set for international and domestic economies for 1973	Production function elasticities, demand elasticities, trade elasticities	Input-output plus value-added data	Household expenditure data disaggregated using foreign trade data	Tariffs, ad valorem equivalent of non-tariff barriers, and domestic taxes
Fullerton, Shoven, & Whalley (1980)	U.S.	1973	Constructed benchmark data set for 1973	Production and demand elasticities	Input-output plus value-added data	Household expenditure data	Production, expenditure, and income taxes
Piggott & Whalley (1980)	U.K.	1973	Constructed benchmark data set for 1973	Production and demand elasticities	Input-output plus value-added data	Household expenditure data	U.K. taxes and subsidies

Table 3 *(cont.)*

Model	Countries	Year	Base year data	Extraneous use of elasticities	Production data	Demand data	Policy data
Manne (1980)	3 regions: industrialized; LDC oil-exp.;[c] LDC oil-imp.	1976 projection to 1990	Approximate calibration to 1976 data in World Development Report	Trade elasticities	GNP, energy production and consumption, exports and imports, trade deficit (World Development Report)	Energy consumption; imports	Various quantity scenarios
Dixon et al. (1977)	Australia	1968–69	1968–69 input–output data base	Extensive elasticities file (estimation and literature search)	Input–output accounts	Input–output accounts	1% devaluation; 1% increase in all ad valorem tariff rates
Serra-Puche (1979)	Mexico	1968	Approximate consistency of model to 1968 data from Mexico	Production side only	Input–output and value-added data	Household survey adjusted to national account	Ad valorem taxes

[a] GDP = gross domestic product.
[b] MTN = multilateral trade negotiations.
[c] LDC = less developed countries.

98

Cobb–Douglas functions to be separately considered as special cases. The CES function is a directly additive function that implies certain restrictions on the corresponding demand functions.[14] Nested CES utility functions are widely used (additive functions of additive functions) to derive demand functions, which modify the nature of these restrictions somewhat, but they still apply within nests. The derived CES demand functions have unitary income elasticities that for some policy issues may be inappropriate. Although this feature can be relaxed through the use of a Stone–Geary variant of CES, these functions are not widely used. These models can therefore be thought of as drawing heavily on CES functions for demand and production, and the main issue in practice faced in model specification is the choice of parameter values in these functions.

The procedure of calibration of the model to a benchmark data set follows from the structural characteristic that utility and production functions yield household demand and industry cost functions that depend directly or indirectly upon all prices. Even if we are able to conceive of a reduced form for one of these models being represented by tractable interdependent excess demand functions, estimation of the model using conventional methods rapidly becomes difficult if not impossible for the reasons mentioned in Section 2. For the parameters of any particular structural equation to be identified, a large number of excluded exogenous variables or other identifying restrictions are required, and even if identification is possible, time series are required of a length infeasible for estimation of even modest models. Although partitioning of the model prior to estimation partially overcomes some of these problems, a major objection to partitioning is that in estimating production and demand functions the exogeneity of variables not central to the equation(s) being considered is assumed; and the estimates so determined are then used in a model that explicitly recognizes their joint endogeneity.

Estimation also produces difficulties with the compatibility of units used in the general equilibrium model and separate estimation exercises. Units for capital and labor services are defined in some of these models as those amounts capable of generating a return of one dollar in any possible use, net of taxes and gross of subsidies. These units are defined for a particular year for which the data are assumed to represent an equilibrium for the economy. Although physical units are implied by such an assumption, they cannot be specified in a form that makes a conversion to other well-defined physical units (such as tons) possible. Single-equation estimation that produces unit-dependent estimates are of limited value in the model unless the units involved are capable of being converted from one to another.

For all these reasons, the equilibrium solution concept of the model is used as the dominant restriction in the process of parameter selection by "calibrating" the model to the benchmark equilibrium data set. The fundamental assumption made is that the economy is in equilibrium in a particular year. By modifying the national accounts and other blocks of data for that year, a benchmark data set is generated in which all equilibrium conditions inherent in the model are satisfied. The requirement that the set of parameter values used in the model be capable of replicating this "observed equilibrium" as an equilibrium solution to the model is then imposed as a restriction on parameter values selected. Parameter values are determined in a nonstochastic manner by solving the equations that represent the equilibrium conditions of the model using the data on prices and quantities that characterize the benchmark equilibrium.

One potential difficulty with this procedure is that the models used may exhibit multiplicity of equilibria, so that even if the test of replication is not satisfied, there is no way to rule out the admissibility of a given specification. This is one of the several difficulties that the possibility of multiplicity of equilibria causes in the use of these models. A number of ad hoc procedures designed to investigate the possibility of nonuniqueness in these models have been used (starting computational procedures at different places, approaching solutions at different speeds and along different paths, displacing solutions once found and testing the successful relocation). In no case known to the authors has nonuniqueness been established in these models, although this does not "prove" that it is absent.[15]

3.4   Determination of parameter values through calibration to a benchmark equilibrium data set

Whether the observed equilibrium alone is sufficient to uniquely determine the parameter values depends upon the functional forms used. The benchmark equilibrium data set, which contains "equilibrium" share observations, can only be generated by one set of Cobb–Douglas functions. For CES production and demand functions, however, extraneous estimates of elasticities of substitution (which are unit-free) need to be incorporated into the procedure to serve with the equilibrium replication requirement as identifying restrictions on the model. The choice of elasticity values critically affects results obtained with these models, and the values chosen are discussed later. Additional functional complexity thus implies calibration using an expanding set of previously specified extraneous parameter estimates.

The requirement placed on the set of estimated parameter values for production and demand functions in the process of calibration is that they be capable of reproducing the complete benchmark data set as an equilibrium solution to the model. The calibration procedure thus uses the equilibrium conditions of the model and the benchmark equilibrium data set to solve for parameter estimates.

After selection of functional forms for the model, the first step in calibration involves the separation of the benchmark transactions data into separate price and quantity observations. The benchmark equilibrium data set obtained by adjusting diverse data sets into a mutually consistent form provides observations on equilibrium transactions in value terms. To obtain information separately on equilibrium prices and quantities, a unit's convention must be adopted to separate observations on price quantity combinations into component parts.

Factors of production are treated in most of the applied models as perfectly mobile between alternative uses, and the allocation of factors by industry in equilibrium will equalize the returns received net of taxes and gross of subsidies in all industries. A convenient and widely used definition of physical units for all factors is that amount of a factor that can in equilibrium earn a reward of 1 currency unit ($1) net of taxes and before receipt of subsidies in any of its alternative uses. Units for commodities are similarly defined as those amounts that in equilibrium sell for $1 net of all consumer taxes and subsidies.

The assumption that marginal revenue products of factors are equalized in all uses in equilibrium permits factor payments data by industry to be used as observations on physical quantities of factors for use in the determination of parameters for the model.[16] In this way observed equilibrium transactions (products of prices and quantities) are separated out into price and quantity observations. An observed equilibrium is characterized by an equilibrium price vector of unity, and ownership of a unit of labor or capital services yields a net income of $1.

Using these data it is then possible to calculate production function parameters from the benchmark equilibrium observations of capital and labor services in each industry. We consider the case of CES value-added functions for each of j industries. These functions are given by

$$Y_j = \gamma_j [\delta_j K_j^{-\rho_j} + (1 - \delta_j) L_j^{-\rho_j}]^{-1/\rho_j} \tag{3.1}$$

where γ_j is a constant defining units of measurement, δ_j is a weighting parameter, $\sigma_j = 1/(1 + \rho_j)$ is the elasticity of substitution, K_j and L_j are capital and labor service inputs, and Y_j is the industry scale of operation.

From the benchmark equilibrium data set, values for K_j and L_j can be obtained and (in the case of a tax model) factor tax rates t_j^K and t_j^L calculated. As units are chosen for productive factors such that $P_K = P_L = 1$

(where P_K and P_L refer to the net-of-tax factor prices) at the benchmark equilibrium, prices associated with the equilibrium quantities are known.

Once a value of the elasticity parameter σ_j is selected for each industry,[17] the values of the share parameters δ_j are given by

$$\delta_j = \left[\frac{K_j^{1/\sigma_j}(1+t_j^K)}{L_j^{1/\sigma_j}(1+t_j^L)} \right] \div \left\{ 1 + \left[\frac{K_j^{1/\sigma_j}(1+t_j^K)}{L_j^{1/\sigma_j}(1+t_j^L)} \right] \right\}$$

Values for γ_j are then derived from the zero-profit conditions for each industry given the units definition for outputs.

Parameters for household demand functions are estimated in a similar manner from the benchmark equilibrium data on purchases of commodities by households. The procedure is analogous to that for production functions, except that individual consumer demand functions rather than first-order conditions for cost minimization problems are used to estimate parameter values.

Taking a two-nested variant of CES consumer demand functions, the ratio of expenditures by household q on any two commodities i, j, within the same nest l, gives an equation involving the bottom-level weighting parameters in each household utility function,

$$\frac{(p_i^q)^{\sigma_l} X_i^q}{(p_j^q)^{\sigma_l} X_j^q} = \frac{(b_i^q)^{1/\sigma_l}}{(b_j^q)^{1/\sigma_l}}$$

where the x terms represent benchmark demands, the b terms are weighting parameters of the lower-level CES utility function, and σ_l is the value of the elasticity of substitution within the nest l.

Using the elasticity value within the nest σ_l, the ratios of the coefficients b_i^q, b_j^q can be calculated. A normalization of the coefficients within the nest is frequently used.

For top-level utility function weighting parameters, the benchmark data on the sum of expenditures on components of the nest can be used. If $\bar{P}_l \bar{X}_l^q$ is the expenditure by household q on the nest l, the ratio of expenditures on any two nests l, l' gives a similar equation involving top-level weighting parameters

$$\frac{\bar{P}_l \bar{X}_l^q}{\bar{P}_{l'} \bar{X}_{l'}^q} = \frac{(b_l^q)^{1/\sigma}}{(b_{l'}^q)^{1/\sigma}} \cdot \frac{(p_{l'}^q)^\sigma}{(p_l^q)^\sigma}$$

A value for σ, the elasticity of substitution across nests, is selected and the coefficients b_l^q calculated as for lower-level nests. This same procedure can be extended to three- or higher-level nested CES functions.

By using the complete benchmark equilibrium data set in this way to generate parameter values for production and demand functions,[18] the equilibrium computed by the model before any policy changes will replicate the benchmark equilibrium data set exactly. This is assured as the equilibrium conditions have been used directly in the nonstochastic determination of parameter values. A practical advantage of this procedure is that the equilibrium solution of the estimated model is known ex ante and its recalculation serves as a check on the correctness of programming and on error propagation difficulties.

A typical procedure of parameter selection thus involves the construction of a benchmark equilibrium data set consistent with the model along with a set of extraneously chosen elasticities of substitution in demand and production functions. These two pieces of information are then combined to give a procedure for selecting nonelasticity parameter values such that the entire set of parameters chosen for the model equations produce an equilibrium solution identical in all respects to the benchmark equilibrium data.

3.5 Specifying extraneous elasticity values

Because of the widespread use of CES functions in applied models, calibration procedures need elasticity values to be prespecified and heavy reliance is placed on literature searches (or extraneous estimation of elasticities of substitution) in production and demand functions. The set of elasticity values used are critical parameters in determining the general equilibrium impacts of policy changes generated by these models. Discussion of their values usually precedes presentation of model results, and sensitivity analysis on key parameters is frequently employed. Here we review some of the values used in the hope this may provide useful information to other researchers.

i. *Production function elasticities:* Most models incorporate CES value-added functions for each industry. For each industry in the model it is therefore necessary to specify a separate value for the elasticity of substitution between capital and labor.

Since the introduction of the CES function in the early 1960s, there has been a continuing debate as to whether the elasticity of substitution for manufacturing industry is approximately unity. If unity is a correct value, the more complex CES form can be replaced by the simpler Cobb–Douglas form that has unitary elasticity of substitution. This debate has concentrated primarily on substitution elasticities for aggregate manufacturing rather than component industries as specified in these models. This debate is nonetheless important in assessing the choice of values.

Early estimation of the elasticity of substitution in manufacturing industry by Arrow et al. (1961) involved a pooled cross-country data set of observations on output per man and wage rates for a number of countries. The same production function was assumed to apply in all countries, and the first-order condition from the industry cost minimization problem equating the marginal product of labor to the wage rate was used to estimate the elasticity of substitution. Their results indicated that the elasticity of substitution was below 1, but that the difference between the estimated coefficient and unity was not significant at a 90% level. This was used as support for the position that Cobb–Douglas production functions are a reasonable specification of aggregate production functions.

Following Arrow et al. (1961), a number of econometric studies have estimated substitution elasticities for manufacturing industry (primarily in the United States) by a variety of methods and produced results with substantial disagreement.[19] Cross-section studies, many of which use statewide data, produce estimates that are close to unity, but time series studies produce lower estimates, typically differing from cross-section studies by a factor of around 2. Also, estimates of substitution elasticities appear to vary systematically with the choice of estimating equation. Using the marginal product of capital relationship produces lower estimates than using the marginal product of labor.

A number of explanations of this difference have been offered, such as lagged adjustment, technical change and problems in measurement of inputs, serial correlation in time series data, and cyclical variations in utilization rates. At present no single explanation is widely accepted. A recent attempt by Berndt (1976) to reconcile alternative elasticity estimates used six different functional forms, five alternate measures of capital prices, and two estimation methods. His main finding was that estimates of substitution elasticities "are extremely sensitive to differences in measurement and data construction," and he concurred with an earlier remark of Nerlove (1967) that "even slight variations in the period or concepts tend to produce drastically different estimates of the elasticity." Given this degree of uncertainty over estimates for manufacturing in aggregate, obtaining estimates for individual industries is indeed hazardous.

A common procedure is to construct "central tendency" tables for elasticity estimates by industry drawn from the literature. A catalog of industry estimates of substitution elasticities has been recently compiled by Caddy (1976) in connection with the IMPACT project and is currently one of the most widely used sources in the applied models. Table 4 was constructed by Piggott and Whalley (1980) for use in their model of the U.K. economy and tax system. This table is compiled for all estimates in a given industry and separately for cross-section and time series esti-

Table 4. *"Central tendency" estimates of elasticities of substitution by industry*

Industry	Central tendency value (plus number of estimates used and their variance)		
	Overall	Cross section	Time series
Agriculture and fishing	.607 (29, .13)	.809 (17, .10)	.322 (12, .03)
Food	.789 (58, .17)	.937 (14, .13)	.433 (17, .08)
Drink	.657 (30, .15)	.879 (17, .11)	.368 (13, .06)
Tobacco	.848 (12, .24)	1.309 (3, .24)	.694 (9, .13)
Mineral oils	.827 (24, .17)	1.002 (13, .15)	.621 (11, .13)
Chemicals	.827 (42, .16)	1.009 (26, .11)	.531 (16, .12)
Metals	.806 (79, .16)	.967 (51, .09)	.511 (28, .14)
Mech. engineering	.587 (35, .11)	.663 (21, .11)	.451 (14, .09)
Instr. engineering	.893 (16, .14)	1.053 (10, .12)	.627 (6, .06)
Elec. engineering	.750 (32, .13)	.811 (24, .11)	.568 (8, .17)
Shipbuilding	.808 (21, .35)	1.043 (14, .33)	.341 (7, .04)
Vehicles	.810 (25, .31)	1.040 (15, .33)	.471 (9, .08)
Textiles	.914 (67, .18)	1.093 (46, .11)	.520 (21, .11)
Clothing	1.106 (25, .17)	1.221 (20, .14)	.649 (5, .05)
Leather, fur, etc.	.940 (50, .13)	1.058 (35, .09)	.664 (15, .08)
Timber, furniture, etc.	.843 (76, .13)	.974 (56, .07)	.475 (20, .10)
Paper, printing, and publishing	.908 (65, .14)	1.057 (48, .08)	.489 (17, .08)
Other manufacturing	.944 (76, .17)	1.067 (54, .11)	.641 (22, .196)

Source: Piggott and Whalley (1980) based on estimates from Caddy (1976).

mates. In building the table a small number of estimates are rejected as being implausible (due to a wrong sign, for instance), and the remainder are classified according to the industries used in the model. An important point to note is that for some of the industries used in the applied models no estimates exist in the literature because of the problems of measurement of outputs (such as financial services, government, and other service industries).

A further point worth noting is that these elasticity values represent technological relationships, and when alternate general equilibria are calculated for policy variations the adjustments between equilibria are assumed to be complete. An assumption of smooth substitutability between capital and labor services in any industry in the short run is clearly not appropriate. Much capital is industry-specific and cannot be easily adapted for alternative use, and complete substitution only takes place in the longer run as capital depreciates and is not replaced. Some adjustments between equilibria may be relatively small and thus are capable of being made quickly; others may require much longer periods of time.[20] The time scale for the adjustments in applied models is usually left ill defined, although it is assumed that sufficient time elapses for all adjustments between equilibria to be complete.

ii. *Demand function elasticities:* On the demand side, household demand functions derived from staged CES utility functions are commonly used in the applied models. These functions specify constant substitution elasticities between subgroups from the list of commodities. Where a multi-level "nesting" structure is used for each household, the "bottom"-level nest may contain comparable domestically produced and imported goods between which a degree of substitutability is assumed consistent with import demand price elasticity estimates. In the "intermediate" nest would be blocks of commodities between which various elasticities of substitution are assumed. A constant elasticity of substitution then prevails at the top level between commodity blocks. As many as four levels of hierarchical nesting are currently in use in some models.

Few econometric estimates of substitution elasticities for CES demand functions of the staged variety exist, and few (if any) demand function systems are separately estimated by household type. Therefore, a set of indirect procedures has been used in the applied models to obtain elasticity values that have some claim to plausibility. These procedures involve collection of central tendency estimates from a literature survey of (both compensated and uncompensated) own-price elasticities of demand, by product, for aggregate household sector demand functions. Substitution elasticities are then chosen for the various levels of nests to approximately calibrate to these as point estimates of the demand functions of the model at the benchmark equilibrium.

The procedure of calibrating point estimates of own-price elasticities at the benchmark equilibrium to estimates of substitution elasticities can be illustrated most simply in the case of a single-stage CES demand function. The N-commodity demand functions derived from maximization of a single-stage CES utility function subject to a household budget constraint are

$$X_i = \frac{a_i I}{p_i^\sigma \cdot \Sigma_j a_j p_j^{1-\sigma}} \qquad (I = 1, \ldots, N)$$

where I is household income, a_i are weighting parameters, σ is the elasticity of substitution, and P_i is the commodity price of good i.

Taking derivatives through the demand function

$$\frac{\partial X_i}{\partial p_i} = -\sigma a_i I p_i^{-\sigma-1} \cdot \left(\sum_j a_j p_j^{1-\sigma} \right)^{-1} - a_i I p_i^{-\sigma} \left(\sum_j a_j p_j^{1-\sigma} \right)^{-2} \cdot (1-\sigma) a_i p_i^{-\sigma}$$

gives the expression for the uncompensated own-price elasticity

$$\frac{\partial X_i}{\partial p_i} \cdot \frac{p_i}{X_i} = -\sigma - \frac{a_i \cdot (1-\sigma)}{p_i^{(\sigma-1)} \cdot \sum_j a_j p_j^{(1-\sigma)}}$$

The (uncompensated) cross-price elasticities can be shown to be

$$\frac{\partial X_i}{\partial p_k} \cdot \frac{p_k}{X_i} = -\frac{a_k(1-\sigma)}{p_k^{(\sigma-1)} \cdot \sum_j a_j p_j^{(1-\sigma)}}$$

At the benchmark equilibrium, producer prices are equal to unity because of the units definition adopted for outputs. Consumer prices may not exactly equal unity because of the consumer taxes; however, if they are assumed to be approximately equal to unity, and the a_i are chosen such that $\sum_j a_j = 1$, then

$$\frac{\partial X_i}{\partial p_i} \cdot \frac{p_i}{X_i} \approx -\sigma - a_i(1-\sigma)$$

$$\frac{\partial X_i}{\partial p_k} \cdot \frac{p_k}{X_i} \approx -a_k(1-\sigma)$$

In those cases where weighting parameters are small (and σ is not too different from unity),

$$\frac{\partial X_i}{\partial p_i} \cdot \frac{p_i}{X_i} \approx -\sigma, \qquad \frac{\partial X_i}{\partial p_k} \cdot \frac{p_k}{X_i} \approx 0$$

In the case of two-level staged CES functions, an expression for the uncompensated own-price elasticity at the benchmark equilibrium is obtained,

$$\frac{\partial X_i}{\partial p_i} \cdot \frac{p_i}{X_i} \approx -\sigma_k - a_{jk} \cdot (1-\sigma_k) - a_{jk} \cdot (1-\sigma)[-\sigma - b_k(1-\sigma)]$$

where commodity i is the jth commodity in the kth nest; a_{jk} and b_k are the bottom- and top-level weighting parameters, respectively; and σ_k and σ are bottom- and top-level elasticity values, respectively. If each a_{jk} is reasonably small and σ_k and σ are not too far from 1, this gives

$$\frac{\partial X_i}{\partial p_i} \cdot \frac{p_i}{X_i} \approx -\sigma_k$$

Under these approximations the own-price elasticity of a commodity or composite of commodities is determined primarily by the elasticity of substitution in the lowest level of the nesting in which it appears. Similar but more complex expressions can be obtained from three-level staged CES functions.

The procedure used for specifying substitution elastiticities is to utilize these expressions to generate values for elasticities of substitution from own-price elasticity estimates by product. Because all commodities within any nest have the same compensated own-price elasticity, this procedure is somewhat limited in scope unless extensive nesting is used to provide sufficient elasticity parameters to prespecify. Frequently the nesting is arranged so that elasticities for "key" commodities or commodity blocks can be set (e.g., labor supply, savings, energy demand).

Central tendency estimates are obtained from literature estimates in a manner similar to that adopted for production function elasticities. The values used on the demand side by Piggott and Whalley (1980) in their U.K. model are shown in Table 5. The majority of elasticity estimates reported in the literature are for demand function systems for which price elasticity estimates are only available as the point estimates at sample means. For this reason, the central tendency figures are differentiated by estimating equation. Moreover, these estimates relate to aggregate demand functions rather than household demand functions. Most estimates are based on time series data, and the stratification between time series and cross-section estimates important for production function estimates does not appear in this table.

iii. *Other elasticities:* Depending upon the orientation of the particular applied model, other elasticities besides those discussed are also important elements of the parameter set and are treated in a similar way with literature search followed by some form of calibration as needed.

In the trade models import and export demand price elasticities are critical parameters, and parameters of CES functions are calibrated to literature estimates. The recent compendium of estimates due to Stern, Francis, and Schumacher (1976) is widely used. In some of the trade modeling income elasticities of import demand functions are important, and LES variants of CES forms are used with calibration of intercept LES parameters to literature income elasticities.

In the tax models two important elasticities parameters are labor supply and savings elasticities. In analysis of labor supply taxation issues, the common procedure is to define utility functions over leisure and goods and choose a value for the leisure–goods substitution elasticity consistent with literature estimates of labor supply elasticities with respect to the net of tax wage. Literature estimates on this elasticity vary sharply by the group involved, with prime-age males having low if not negative elasticities, and secondary and older workers having higher elasticities (around .5). Fullerton, Shoven, and Whalley (1980) use an elasticity of .15 for the whole workforce.

With intertemporal taxation issues the elasticity of savings with respect to the real net-of-tax rate of return becomes important. The approach in

Table 5. *Central tendency values for own-price elasticities of house-hold demand functions*

Industry	LES estimates	Log-linear demand estimates	Other	Total
Agriculture and fishing	.334 (17, .03)	.420 (25, .05)	.562 (44, .08)	.468 (86, .07)
Coal mining	—	.321 (1, 0)	1.265 (2, .01)	.950 (3, .76)
Other mining and quarrying	.425 (1, 0)	.905 (3, .06)	.257 (2, .01)	.609 (6, .13)
Food	.353 (15, .03)	.580 (30, .19)	.476 (27, .08)	.494 (72, .13)
Drink	.617 (5, .07)	.780 (12, .25)	.464 (15, .06)	.607 (32, .16)
Tobacco	—	.611 (8, .15)	.431 (11, .04)	.507 (19, .10)
Mineral oils	.425 (1, 0)	.905 (3, .07)	.257 (2, .01)	.609 (6, .13)
Other coal and petroleum products	1.283 (2, .01)	1.404 (3, .80)	1.978 (3, 1.41)	1.589 (8, .90)
Chemicals	.685 (1, 0)	.890 (1, 0)	.680 (3, .07)	.724 (5, .05)
Metals	—	1.522 (19, .42)	.989 (18, .40)	1.083 (51, .48)
Mech. engineering	—	1.296 (16, .61)	1.068 (15, .43)	1.005 (45, .48)
Instr. engineering	.606 (14, .15)	1.099 (17, .57)	1.240 (11, .54)	.972 (42, .49)
Elec. engineering	—	1.388 (19, .377)	1.049 (17, .410)	1.060 (50, .44)
Vehicles	.606 (14, .15)	1.137 (19, .55)	1.099 (18, .40)	.985 (51, .44)
Clothing	.277 (16, .03)	.491 (26, .16)	.564 (19, .15)	.458 (61, .18)
Timber, furniture etc.	.570 (14, .09)	1.258 (19, .23)	.974 (20, .39)	.969 (53, .33)
Paper, printing, and publishing	.191 (1, 0)	.343 (5, .02)	.416 (5, .02)	.362 (11, .02)
Other manufacturing	.578 (14, .02)	.527 (7, .11)	.626 (17, .12)	.592 (38, .09)
Gas, electricity, and water	1.203 (1, 0)	.921 (9, .02)	.369 (10, .01)	.659 (20, .10)
Transport	.761 (4, .23)	1.027 (14, .26)	.994 (10, .16)	.977 (28, .23)
Banking and insurance	—	.559 (3, .02)	.894 (1, 0)	.642 (4, .04)
Housing services (private)	.461 (15, .11)	.550 (29, .45)	.434 (9, .09)	.505 (53, .29)
Professional services, other services	.488 (7, .08)	1.09 (16, .39)	.946 (16, .39)	.961 (50, .48)

Note: All uncompensated own-price elasticity estimates; figures in parentheses refer to the number of studies included and the variance of estimate.
Source: Piggot and Whalley (1980).

Fullerton, Shoven, and Whalley (1980) is to consider a sequence of equilibria through time with savings decisions depending on expected rates of return. Savings today augments the capital stock in all future periods. Fullerton, Shoven, and Whalley place substantial reliance on Boskin's (1978) recently estimated elasticity of .4, although the use of this elasticity in an alternative model by Summers (1980) has sharply different implications.

In other areas critical elasticities also arise. In energy modeling a major issue is the substitutability (or complementarity) between energy, capital, and labor. In development models regional features are sometimes incorporated and the elasticity of outward migration from rural areas becomes important.

In all these cases the procedure seems to be similar to the discussion above. Share parameters come from calibration, and elasticity values come from a literature search or extraneous estimation.

4   Comparison between stochastic estimation and calibration for a one-consumer, two-sector GE tax model using U.S. data

In this section we present some results obtained by Mansur (1981) from time series estimation of a two-sector general equilibrium tax model of the United States. We are then able to compare his parameter estimates to estimates obtained by calibration to a benchmark data set for alternative years. Although such a comparison is by no means conclusive, it does provide some initial indications as to how large the differences may be between the two procedures.

Mansur focuses on the well-known one-consumer, two-sector general equilibrium model with differential taxation of income from capital due to Harberger (1962). Although the literature on this model is primarily concerned with measuring the costs of distortions in capital use arising from nonneutralities of tax system, its use in the present context serves three purposes: (a) as an illustration of how estimation procedures suggested in Section 2 can be applied; (b) to allow comparison between parameter estimates obtained from "calibration" to a benchmark equilibrium and those produced by estimation; (c) to allow comparison of measures of the cost of capital tax distortions for the alternative parameter estimates and further compare them with cost estimates due to Harberger (1966), Shoven and Whalley (1972), and Shoven (1976).

Mansur uses time series data for the U.S. economy (1948–65), most of the information coming from U.S. Department of Commerce publications (e.g., various issues of the *Survey of Current Business*). A similar

Table 6. *Calculated parameters of the Cobb–Douglas production and demand system from benchmark calibration to individual years' data*

Year	a_1	a_2	b_1	b_2
1948	.516	.330	.160	.840
1950	.564	.333	.143	.857
1955	.600	.276	.126	.874
1960	.633	.298	.109	.891
1962	.636	.271	.115	.885
1965	.687	.280	.115	.885

Notes:

$Q_i = A_i K_i^{a_i} L_i^{1-a_i} =$ sector production functions

$U = X_1^{b_1} X_2^{b_2} =$ household utility function

Sector 1 is lightly and sector 2 heavily taxed.

commodity classification as used by Harberger (1962, 1966) and Shoven and Whalley (1972) is adopted. The two sectors are the predominantly corporate (heavily taxed) sector and the lightly taxed sector (agriculture, housing or real estate, crude oil and gas). The corporate sector includes mining, manufacturing, transport, communication, contract construction, electric, gas and sanitary services, wholesale and retail trade, finance and insurance (except real estate), and services.[21]

Mansur considers two simple specifications:[22]

i.   Demand and production systems derived from Cobb–Douglas utility and production functions.

ii. The demand system derived from a Cobb–Douglas utility function while the sector production functions are CES. The associated input demand system is derived accordingly.

Table 6 reports calibrated benchmark equilibrium parameter estimates for the Cobb–Douglas case for alternative benchmark years. For each year reported data have to be adjusted to ensure the conditions of general equilibrium accounting (as described above). The RAS method has been applied to yearly data obtained from national income accounts to ensure the equilibrium conditions and "calibration" used to determine parameter values.

Table 7 presents parameter estimates obtained by employing a nonlinear

Table 7. *Parameter values for different estimation methods
(Cobb–Douglas production and demand systems)*

Parameter	FIML[a] (ignoring simultaneity)	NLIV[a] (method I)	NLIV[a] (method II)	Benchmark equilibrium parameters[b]
a_1	.606	.627	.647	.516–.678 (.609)
a_2	.369	.307	.325	.332–.272 (.292)
b_1	.122	.124	.124	.160–.109 (.124)
b_2	.878	.876	.876	.890–.840 (.876)

Note: FIML = full-information maximum likelihood; NLIV = nonlinear instrumental variable.
[a] All coefficients are statistically significant at 1% level of significance.
[b] The numbers shown side by side represent the range of estimated values over different years as obtained under the benchmark equilibrium method. The numbers within the parentheses represent the arithmetic mean of the whole range of estimated values.

instrumental variable (NLIV) method as described above (in Section 2). Unlike the use of calibration methods, there is no prior adjustment to data as involved in benchmarking. Estimates are also shown as obtained by applying FIML method to the subsystems of the complete model, ignoring the simultaneity.

Comparison of estimates in Tables 6 and 7 indicate that these different methods have somewhat similar parameter estimates. Benchmark equilibrium parameters show some degree of variation from year to year, but if we take the average of these yearly values, the mean is not very different from the values obtained by estimation. For the Cobb–Douglas case, the initial impression would seem to be that calibration to a benchmark is not too bad; although if one is to apply the benchmark method, it may be best to apply consistency adjustments to time-averaged data. The treatment of technical change, however, may dictate further modifications to such a procedure.

In the CES case, benchmark calibration cannot be a complete substitute for econometric estimation because of the need to prespecify substitution elasticities. Benchmark calibration when applied to average data may give reasonably good estimates of the share and scale parameters but cannot estimate the elasticity parameters. The values selected for elasticity parameters influence calibration-determined values of share and scale parameters. In the Cobb–Douglas case this issue does not arise because the elasticity of substitution in both demand and production is unity.

Table 8. *Sensitivity of share and scale parameters due to variations in elasticity values under benchmark calibration*

Elasticity value	a_1	a_2	A_1	A_2
.333	.547	.048	4.0988	3.6383
.500	.531	.136	4.1008	3.9338
1.000	.516	.329	4.1028	4.4412
2.000	.508	.464	4.1038	4.7885

Note: These figures are based on the benchmark equilibrium data set constructed for the year 1948. The elasticity values are arbitrarily chosen to assess the impact of variations on other parameters.

Table 8 shows how share and scale parameters calculated through calibration are influenced by the variations in adopted elasticity values for the U.S. data used by Mansur. We note that estimated share parameter in sector 2 is surprisingly sensitive to changes in the adopted values of substitution elasticities. This point is important to keep in mind because of the limited consensus from literature searches on relevant elasticity values. Benchmark calibration, by using only elasticity values from literature searches, can give the appearance of "removing" the need for estimation. However, the fact remains that errors committed at the stage of elasticity selection then tend to be propagated onto other estimated parameters.

Table 9 reports estimated parameters for a model with CES production functions under different methods of estimation. For NLFIML method applied to model subsystems ignoring subsystem simultaneity, the estimators would generally be biased and estimates obtained appear to be biased downward. For the corporate sector (sector 2), both the elasticity of substitution and share parameters are statistically insignificant in this case. For the NLIV methods both sets of estimated parameters are not very different from one another, although method I (NLIV) is computationally much simpler and involves significantly less work compared to NLIV method II. This table once again lends support to the observation that when averaged over time, the share parameters from calibration (with same elasticity value) tend to be not much different from those of NLIV methods, but the dependence on preselected elasticities is worth reemphasis.

Table 10 reports welfare costs due to differential rates of taxation in

Table 9. *Stochastic estimates of the elasticity and share parameters under various methods of estimation*

Stochastic method	Elasticity (production)		Share parameter (production)		Share parameter (demand)	
	σ_1	σ_2	α_1	α_2	b_1	b_2
NLFIML[a]	.2419	.2465[b]	.8648	.0015[b]	.122	.878
NLIV (method I)	1.45	.485	.623	.18	.124	.876
NLIV (method II)	1.489	.535	.620	.16	.124	.876
Calibration[c] (with elasticities obtained by NLIV method I)	1.45	.485	.574	.15	.124	.876
Calibration[c] (with elasticities obtained by NLIV method II)	1.489	.535	.574	.12	.124	.976

[a] NLFIML applied to the subsystems ignoring the underlying simultaneity.
[b] The parameter is not statistically significant.
[c] The share parameters are the average figures and the elasticity estimates are taken from NLIV (method II).

the U.S. economy using a Cobb–Douglas production and utility function and using estimated parameter values obtained under different methods. Harberger's approximation formulas and the Shoven–Whalley algorithmic approach are both used to calculate welfare costs.

This table shows that the measures of loss in the Shoven–Whalley algorithmic approach tend to be lower with benchmark equilibrium parameters than those with NLIV estimators. The extent of underestimation increases rapidly in both absolute and relative terms over time. Whereas for 1949 the benchmark parameters underestimate the loss by 25%, by 1965 this figure (for underestimation) increases to 162%. For Harberger's formula for measuring the costs of the tax distortion, we use parameter values close to those used by Harberger, which are then compared to loss estimates from use of the NLIV estimators. There are represented in column 3 and column 1, respectively, of Table 10. The difference between the two outcomes is not very significant, and although the Harberger parameters tend to underestimate the measured costs, the difference tends to be reduced over time (as indicated in column 4). The surprising degree of closeness in the measured costs is due to the fact that Harberger's method of assigning the parameter values for this Cobb–Douglas case yields parameters very close to the NLIV estimators.

For CES production functions the welfare costs are reported in Table 11

Table 10. *Comparison of the estimates of welfare loss due to nonneutrality of taxes on income from capital in the U.S. economy with Cobb–Douglas production and demand systems*

	Harberger formulation				Shoven–Whalley formulation		
	NLIV estimators (method II):		Harberger parameter: loss ($ million)[a] (3)	% Variation between cols. 3 and 1: $\frac{(3)-(1)}{(1)}\times100$ (4)	NLIV parameter: % loss (FI)[b] (5)	Benchmark equilibrium parameter: % loss (FI)[c] (6)	% Variation between cols. 5 and 6: $\frac{(5)-(6)}{(5)}\times100$ (7)
Year	loss ($ million) (1)	% loss (2)					
1949	5451	2.29	5175	−5.06	.558	.446	20.07
1952	6159	2.19	5874	−4.63	.558	.387	30.65
1955	6501	2.15	6246	−3.92	.569	.340	40.25
1958	6563	2.05	6328	−3.58	.558	.368	34.05
1962	7841	2.09	7577	−3.37	.598	.340	43.14
1965	9573	2.14	9292	−2.94	.900	.343	61.88

[a] Share of capital (fK_2) in sector 2 is .2; $fK_1 = .54$; $T = .53$, the surcharge, share of labor in sector 2; $fL_1 = .54$; $fL_2 = .8$; elasticity of substitution is unity for both sectors; and price elasticity of demand for commodity 2 is unity.

[b] The estimates are based on the parameters reported in Table 6.

[c] FI = Fisher's index (the geometric mean of Laspeyre's and Paasche's indices) with no-tax situation as the base.

Table 11. *Comparison of the estimates of welfare loss due to nonneutrality of taxes on income from capital in the U.S. economy, using CES production functions*

| | Harberger formulation | | | | | Harberger parameter[a] | | | | |
| | NLIV estimates (method I) | | NLIV estimates (method II) | | | | | | | |
Year	Loss ($ million) (1)	% Loss (2)	Loss ($ million) (3)	% Loss (4)	% Variation: $\frac{(3)-(1)}{(1)} \times 100$ (5)	Loss ($ million) $E2 = -\frac{1}{7}$ (6)	% Loss $E2 = -\frac{1}{7}$ (7)	Loss ($ million) $E2 = -1.0$ (8)	% Loss $E2 = -1.0$ (9)	% Variation: $\frac{(8)-(3)}{(3)} \times 100$ (10)
1948	3611.44	1.48	3838.27	1.55	5.9	1962.09	.79	5216.27	2.11	35.9
1949	3531.64	1.48	3711.11	1.56	4.8	1890.75	.80	5175.26	2.17	39.0
1950	3967.91	1.52	4169.16	1.60	4.8	2094.46	.80	5804.53	2.22	39.2
1951	3922.97	1.45	4124.11	1.52	4.9	2096.95	.77	5777.59	2.13	40.1
1952	3937.96	1.40	4144.38	1.47	5.0	2102.93	.75	5873.89	2.09	41.7
1953	3942.48	1.35	4155.58	1.43	5.1	2103.11	.72	5988.36	2.06	44.1
1954	3834.56	1.35	4043.25	1.42	5.2	2062.12	.72	5850.98	2.05	44.7
1955	4071.10	1.35	4294.92	1.42	5.2	2157.76	.72	6245.83	2.07	45.4
1956	4353.95	1.35	4594.33	1.42	5.2	2283.38	.72	6693.53	2.07	45.7
1957	4301.81	1.32	4542.51	1.39	5.3	2284.21	.71	6672.29	2.04	46.9
1958	4075.13	1.28	4302.97	1.35	5.3	2230.31	.70	6327.46	1.98	47.0
1959	4855.15	1.41	5124.64	1.49	5.3	2530.25	.73	7486.32	2.17	46.1
1960	4455.74	1.27	4708.80	1.34	5.4	2398.35	.68	6980.91	1.99	48.3
1961	4536.70	1.27	4794.30	1.34	5.4	2464.10	.69	7109.92	1.99	48.3
1962	4839.37	1.29	5113.96	1.36	5.4	2603.04	.69	7577.06	2.01	48.2
1963	5025.98	1.29	5311.17	1.36	5.4	2692.84	.69	7867.23	2.01	48.1
1964	5508.85	1.31	5829.70	1.39	5.5	3025.36	.72	8779.90	2.09	50.6
1965	5846.41	1.30	6185.27	1.38	5.5	3229.28	.72	9291.49	2.07	50.2

116

Shoven–Whalley formulation

Year	NLIV estimate (method I)		NLIV estimate (method II)		Benchmark parameter		% Variation: $\frac{(13)-(15)}{(13)} \times 100$
	Loss (FI) (11)	% Loss (FI) (12)	Loss (FI) (13)	% Loss (FI) (14)	Loss (FI) (15)	% Loss (FI) (16)	(17)
1948	1522.60	.515	1397.8	.491	1392.8	.50	.4
1949	1649.6	.567	1359.3	.49	1280.2	.47	5.8
1950	2354.0	.74	2247.5	.74	1331.5	.456	40.8
1951	1870.8	.53	2046.3	.61	1893.6	.49	7.5
1952	2101.8	.56	2162.0	.62	1907.4	.55	11.8
1953	2299.3	.57	1998.2	.54	1605.1	.45	19.7
1954	1844.7	.42	2254.5	.62	1592.8	.46	29.4
1955	2437.7	.58	2094.8	.55	1780.0	.49	15.0
1956	2680.8	.61	2244.1	.54	1676.1	.43	25.3
1957	2958.4	.72	4280.3	1.0	1733.7	.43	59.5
1958	2461.7	.56	2254.6	.54	1765.0	.45	21.7
1959	2498.1	.54	2409.4	.56	1700.4	.42	29.4
1960	2617.5	.56	2409.4	.52	1920.4	.44	20.3
1961	3405.5	.63	2525.4	.54	2017.1	.46	20.1
1962	3447.5	.58	2838.9	.56	2348.5	.47	17.3
1963	3517.2	.57	2844.3	.551	2138.4	.41	24.8
1964	3773.3	.60	5026.6	.939	2445.1	.48	51.4
1965	3393.8	.58	8289.1	1.36	2595.1	.45	68.9

Notes: The parameters used in this table are based on the estimates reported in Table 9. The same figures as shown in the footnote of Table 10 have been used as Harberger parameters; the price elasticities of demand for both commodities are assumed to be unity. E2 = price elasticity for corporate sector products. FI = Fisher's Index (the geometric mean of Laspeyres and Paasche's indices), with no-tax situation as the base.

[a] We consider two situations, the original Harberger assumption the demand elasticity for this corporate sector is only $-(\frac{1}{7})$ and the other more reasonable assumption that demand elasticity is -1.0 for both sectors.

117

in a manner similar to those of Table 10. The figures in Table 11 are based on the parameters reported in Table 9. In the first 10 columns we report Harberger's measures of costs under three different sets of parameter values. It appears that loss estimates are very sensitive to the price elasticity of demand for corporate sector products (see columns 6 and 8 of Table 11). NLIV method I parameters slightly but systematically underestimate the welfare loss compared to those from NLIV method II parameters. Whereas the Harberger parameters with the price elasticity of corporate sector products (E2) set at $\frac{1}{7}$ underestimate the welfare loss compared to NLIV methods, the figures with E2 = 1.0 are significantly higher than those of NLIV counterparts.

With the Shoven–Whalley algorithmic approach the loss estimates are somewhat similar to each other. Under all three sets of parameters the values of welfare loss tend to increase over time, following the pattern observed with the Harberger formulation. The absolute measures of loss are not significantly different from the others, though the benchmark method yields figures that are slightly downward-biased compared to other methods. The small differences may once again be due to the fact that for the benchmark case we use elasticities from NLIV (method II) estimation procedure. As has been indicated above in the discussion of the Cobb–Douglas case, as long as the elasticities are the same, benchmark calibration tends to produce share parameters close to those from stochastic methods.

5   Implications for existing applied models and specification procedures

Any assessment of implications of our chapter for current general equilibrium modeling efforts must inevitably be both inconclusive and highly subjective.

Our perspective on the issues raised can be summarized as follows:

1. Literature on numerical application of general equilibrium analysis (primarily to policy issues) appears to us to have progressed from a concern with computational methods in the late 1960s and early 1970s to a recent spate of model building where the ability to solve and manipulate large models has taken primacy. While we see this as both a valuable and natural progression, the contribution this work can make to policy issues ultimately lies in the numerical perspectives offered on policy choices. The "value" of these attempts at quantification depends crucially on the reasonableness or otherwise of the numerical specifications used, and it seems natural to us that more attention be given in this area to the question of how one numerically specifies a general

equilibrium model in a "reasonable" manner, in addition to how one solves it.[23]

2. Modelers seem to be increasingly conscious of the key role played by elasticities in these models. The widespread use of CES and other tractable forms seems to us to be a natural development in these models,[24] but the paucity of econometric literature on many required parameters poses serious problems and dilemmas. "Assumed" elasticities for "illustrative" calculations do not provide convincing policy conclusions. On the other hand, it does not seem reasonable to suggest modelers suspend their work in order to devote themselves to prior estimation of elasticities. The accommodation might be to clearly display the absence of estimates where this occurs and to limit modeling efforts where elasticities are the bottleneck (e.g., perhaps not work with detailed commodity or industrial groupings if no estimates exist for that detail, but use a more aggregated model).

3. Calibration, as a method for selecting parameter values, appears to have the two weaknesses of requiring preselection of elasticities and not providing any basis for a test of the specification since it fits perfectly the single data point used. Exclusive reliance on stochastic estimation also appears to have problems associated with it. For even "mildly" elaborate models (commodity and industry groups each less than 10), prohibitively long time series are needed for system estimation, yet subsystem (or single-equation) estimation will typically neglect some of the cross-equation restrictions that are the essence of general equilibrium. Statistically well-grounded estimation procedures may indeed only be implementable for models so simplified that they remove much (or even most) of the detail that interests the policy makers. This we see as a dilemma and offer no clear guidance.

4. Our instinct is that numerical general equilibrium modeling for some time to come will remain the subjective elasticity-dependent "art" into which it seems to be evolving. Despite that, it has a major contribution to make to policy evaluation, much of which even today seems to proceed on hunches, prior belief, and data exercises with unclear (or missing) theoretical underpinnings. It is ridiculous to claim that numerical general equilibrium analysis can definitely "solve" policy problems, especially as the assumptions (let alone the numerical applications) can be and are frequently questioned. However, taken with the appropriate grain of salt at the right time, we believe there is enormous potential for both extending and raising the level of debate on many social issues. If this potential is to be realized, existing procedures for choosing between alternative numerical specifications for their models would seem to need further refinement.

NOTES

1. In tax policy, the models of the United States by Fullerton, Shoven, and Whalley (1978, 1980) and of the United Kingdom by Piggott and Whalley (1976, 1980) have been used in a range of tax change evaluations. In trade policy, models by Miller and Spencer (1977), Boadway and Treddenick (1978), Carrin, Gunning, and Waelbroeck (1980), Deardorff and Stern (1979), and Brown and Whalley (1980) have been applied to evaluation of changes in protectionist policies. In development, alternative policy strategies for South Korea, Turkey, Colombia, and other countries have been studied by Adelman and Robinson (1978), Dervis and Robinson (1978), de Melo (1978), and others. A closely related modeling project in Australia (Dixon, Parmenter, Ryland, and Sutton, 1977) has developed a multipurpose modeling capability for analysis of a wide range of policy options.
2. The notation used is self-evident and left undefined to conserve space.
3. General equilibrium systems usually contain a large number of endogenous variables along with relatively few exogenous ones, which can cause identification problems. Restrictions on parameters enter through constant returns to scale, budget balance, homogeneity, and symmetry. We assume, for now, that these independent restrictions along with exclusion restrictions provide enough information to identify the complete model.
4. It is worth noting that this would give us the conventional estimates of demand and production systems (as described later).
5. For the existence of such an estimator with this property further regularity assumptions are needed (see Amemiya, 1974, 1977; Jorgenson and Laffont 1974). These are that the e_t terms are identically independently distributed random vectors and $(1/T)(\delta^2 F/\delta B_i \delta B_i') \cdot Z$ converges in probability to a constant matrix uniformly in B for $i = 1, 2, \ldots, R$, where B_i is the ith element of B.
6. Stone (1954), Pollak and Wales (1969), and Deaton (1972) deal with demand systems originated from direct utility functions. Johansen (1969) formulates a general additive utility function that implies that the direct translog of Christensen et al. (1975), Stone–Geary, and Cobb–Douglas types of utility functions are special cases. Houthakker (1960) introduced the indirect utility function and empirically estimated the derived demand system. Various forms of Leontief reciprocal indirect utility functions are suggested and estimated by Diewert (1969, 1974), Gussman (1972), and Darrough (1975); for translog utility functions, see Christensen et al. (1975), Jorgenson and Lau (1975), and Christensen and Manser (1977).
7. Marschak and Andrews (1944) showed that under perfect competition and profit-maximizing conditions ordinary least squares (OLS) does not yield consistent estimates of the parameters of Cobb–Douglas production functions. For a competitive firm maximizing profit (or minimizing cost) the choice of inputs reflects cost minimization, along with the technological relation characterizing the production function. Thus independent estimation of the technological relation alone does not provide consistent estimates. Hoch (1958), Kmenta (1964), and Mundlak (1963) provided consistent estimators for Cobb–Douglas production function parameters assuming that the "technical" disturbance (associated with the production function) and the "economic" disturbance (in the profit-maximizing equations) are uncorrelated.

In another classic paper, Zellner and Drèze (1966) show that under the assumption of expected profit maximization and perfect competition, OLS does provide consistent and unbiased estimates of the parameters. Most of this literature, although cast in terms of Cobb–Douglas production functions, can be applied to other specifications such as CES.

8. In terms of the production system specified earlier, $\sum_i L_{it} = \bar{L}_t$ and $\sum_i K_{it} = \bar{K}_t$ imply that all the errors to be associated with L_{it} or K_{it} terms (for all $i = 1, \ldots, n$) are not independent of each other. In the intensive form, $\sum_i \theta_i k_{it} = \bar{k}_t$, where $\sum_i \theta_i = 1$, which implies that $\sum_i \theta_{it} u_{it} = 0$ for all t.

9. Berndt and Wood (1975) use instrumental variable methods to deal with the simultaneity. The values of instruments are formed by regressing each of the regressors on a set of variables considered to be exogenous to the aggregate sector.

10. Discussions similar to that in this section, of "calibration" in applied models appear in St-Hillaire and Whalley (1980) and chapters 4 and 6 of Piggott and Whalley (1980). We also use three tables drawn from Piggott and Whalley (1980) by way of illustration in this section.

11. This typically involves treating the residual profit return to equity as a contractual cost, as is implicit in most input–output transactions tables.

12. The term *RAS* derives from the row and column sum method discussed in detail in Bacharach (1970). This is a method of using an initial guess of a matrix where given row and column constraints must be met and moving to a consistent matrix. This procedure is typically followed in updating input–output tables from previous years' tables to take account of new national accounts data.

13. In fact, to determine equilibria computationally it is simpler to work directly with the consumer demand functions for commodities and the per unit output factor demand functions of producers.

14. An important property of the demand functions derived from a single-stage CES utility function is what Deaton (1974) refers to as "Pigou's law." This is an approximate constant proportionality between income and own-price elasticities for any demand functions derived from directly additive preferences (of which a single-stage CES function is an example). Other restrictions are also imposed by additivity, most notably the absence of inferiority and the unambiguous sign of compensated cross-price elasticities. If preference functions are nested rather than single-stage CES functions, these restrictions apply only to demands for the implied composite goods rather than for the individual goods. With this structure the restrictions implied by direct additivity will no longer hold exactly, although they still apply within nests.

15. Kehoe (1980) has shown that for general equilibrium models with production an index can be associated with any equilibrium that is either $+1$ or -1 with the property that the sum of the indices will be $+1$. There is a suggestion that -1 equilibria are unstable. In a simple numerical example involving four commodities and four households with Cobb–Douglas demands and activities, Kehoe has also shown a case of nonuniqueness that does not seem to be in any way an extreme or implausible specification. In this example, the equilibrium prices are widely separated between the equilibria, suggesting that nonuniqueness may possibly not be as likely an occurrence as the numerical ad hoc tests seem to indicate.

16. Although underlying physical units of measurement are implied by such a procedure, their physical dimensions remain undefined, as there are no weight or volume measures one can appeal to. With labor services, for instance, different people will be of different productivities and provide different quantities of labor services; counting the number of workers in an industry is an inappropriate measure of labor used by industry.
17. The selection of these values is discussed later.
18. Ignoring the problem of nonuniqueness mentioned earlier.
19. The discussion here draws heavily on the summary presented by Berndt (1976) in his attempt to reconcile alternative estimates of elasticities of substitution in aggregate production functions.
20. Given depreciation rates on the housing stock of a little over 1% per year, removal of tax preferences to owner-occupied housing, for instance, could result in adjustments which may take 30 years or more to complete.
21. Personal and business services and wholesale and retail trade are not overwhelmingly corporate in structure but treated as heavily taxed. Rosenberg (1969) has an approximate 30% tax rate on income from capital in these activities.
22. On the demand side other variations were tried such as linear expenditure system (LES) and CES demand system, but the estimation procedure either did not converge or produced estimates that were not of proper sign.
23. And, we might add, a question almost totally ignored in the Hayek–Robbins–Lange debate in the 1930s on the feasibility of centralized calculation of solutions to "Paretian equations."
24. Although we note the reservations expressed by some authors as to the restrictions these functions imply.

REFERENCES

Adelman, I., and S. Robinson. 1978. *Income Distribution Policy in Developing Countries.* Stanford: Stanford University Press.

Allingham, M. 1973. *Equilibrium and Disequilibrium; A Quantitative Analysis of Economic Interaction.* Cambridge, Mass.: Ballinger.

Amemiya, T. 1974. "The Nonlinear Two Stage Least Squares Estimator." *Journal of Econometrics* 2(2), 105–10.

    1977. "The Maximum Likelihood and the Nonlinear Three Stage Least Squares Estimation in the General Nonlinear Simultaneous Equation Model." *Econometrica* 45(4), 955–68.

Armington, P. 1969. "A Theory of Demand for Products Distinguished by Place of Production." *IMF Staff Papers* 16(1), 159–78.

Arrow, K. J., H. B. Chenery, B. Minhas, and R. M. Solow. 1961. "Capital-Labor Substitution and Economic Efficiency." *Review of Economics and Statistics* 43, 225–50.

Bacharach, M. 1970. *Biproportional Matrices and Input–Output Change.* Cambridge: Cambridge University Press.

Barku, A. P., 1964. "Consumer Demand Functions under Conditions of Almost Additive Preferences." *Econometrica* 32, 1–38.

Barten, A. P. 1964. "Consumer Demand Functions under Conditions of Almost Additive Preferences." *Econometrica,* 32(1–2).

1967. "Evidence on the Slutsky Conditions for Demand Equations." *Review of Economics and Statistics* 49, 77–84.

1969. "Maximum Likelihood Estimation of a Complete System of Demand Equations." *European Economic Review* 1(1), 7–73.

1977. "The Systems of Consumer Demand Functions Approach: A Review." In M. D. Intriligator (ed.), *Frontiers of Quantitative Economics*. Amsterdam: North-Holland, pp. 24–58.

Berndt, E. R. 1976. "Reconciling Alternative Estimates of the Elasticity of Substitution." *Review of Economics and Statistics* 58, 59–68.

Berndt, E. R., B. Hall, and J. A. Hausman. 1974. "Estimation and Inference in Non-Linear Structural Models." *Annals of Economic and Social Measurement* 3(4), 653–65.

Berndt, E. R., and D. O. Wood. 1975. "Technology, Prices, and the Derived Demand for Energy." *Review of Economics and Statistics* 57(3), 259–68.

Boadway, R., and J. Treddenick. 1978. "A General Equilibrium Computation of the Effects of the Canadian Tariff Structure." *Canadian Journal of Economics* 11(3), 424–46.

Boskin, M. J. 1978. "Taxation, Savings, and the Rate of Interest." *Journal of Political Economy* 86 (April), s3–s28.

Bridge, J. L. 1971. *Applied Econometrics*. Amsterdam: North-Holland.

Brown, A., and A. Deaton. 1972. "Surveys in Applied Economics: Models of Consumer Behavior." *Economic Journal* 82(328), 1145–236.

Brown, F., and J. Whalley. 1980. "General Equilibrium Evaluations of Tariff Cutting Proposals in the Tokyo Round and Comparisons with More Extensive Liberalization of World Trade." *Economic Journal* 90 (December), 838–66.

Caddy, V. 1976. "Empirical Estimation of the Elasticity of Substitution: A Review." Mimeo. Industries Assistance Commission, Melbourne, Australia.

Carrin, G., J. W. Gunning, and J. Waelbroek. 1980. "A General Equilibrium Model for the World Economy: Some Preliminary Results." Paper prepared for the 8th IIASA Global Modelling Conference, Laxenburg, Austria.

Chow, G. 1973. "On the Computation of Full-Information Maximum Likelihood Estimates for Nonlinear Equation Systems." *Review of Economics and Statistics* 55(1), 104–9.

Christensen, L. R., D. W. Jorgenson, and L. J. Lau. 1971. "Conjugate Duality and Transcendental Logarithmic Production Function." *Econometrica* 39(4–6), 255–6.

1973. "Transcendental Logarithmic Production Frontiers." *Review of Economics and Statistics* 55(1), 28–45.

1975. "Transcendental Logarithmic Utility Functions." *American Economic Review* 65(3), 367–83.

Christensen, L. R., and M. E. Manser. 1977. "Estimating the U.S. Consumer Preference for Meat with Flexible Utility Function." *Journal of Econometrics* 5(1), 37–53.

Darrough, M. N. 1975. "Intertemporal Allocation of Consumption, Savings, and Leisure: The Japanese Case." Ph.D. diss., University of British Columbia.

Deardorff, A. V. and R. M. Stern. 1979. "An Economic Analysis of the Effects of the Tokyo Round of Multilateral Trade Negotiations on the United States and the Other Major Industrialized Countries." Report prepared for the Committee on Finance, United States Senate.

Deaton, A. S. 1972. "The Estimation and Testing of Systems of Demand Equations: A Note." *European Economic Review* 3(4), 399–411.

Deaton, A. 1974. "A Reconsideration of the Empirical Implications of Additive Preferences." *Economic Journal* 84 (June), 338–49.

De Melo, J. 1978. "Estimating the Cost of Protection: A General Equilibrium Approach." *Quarterly Journal of Economics* 92(2), 209–27.

De Melo, J., and K. Dervis. 1977. "Modelling the Effects of Protection in a Dynamic Framework." *Journal of Development Economics* 4, 149–72.

Dervis, K. 1975. "Substitution, Employment, and Intertemporal Equilibrium in a Nonlinear Multi-Sectoral Planning Model for Turkey." *European Economic Review* 6(1), 77–96.

Dervis, K., and S. Robinson. 1978. "The Foreign Exchange Gap, Growth, and Industrial Strategy in Turkey: 1973–83." World Bank Staff Working Paper No. 306. Washington, D.C.

Desai, M. 1976. *Applied Econometrics.* Oxford: Philip Allan Publisher Limited.

Dhrymes, P. 1962. "On Devising Unbiased Estimators for the Parameters of the Cobb–Douglas Production Function." *Econometrica* 76, 264–78.

Diewert, W. E. 1969. "Functional Form in the Theory of Production and Consumer Demand." Ph.D. diss., University of California, Berkeley.

    1971. "An Application of the Shephard Duality Theorem: The Generalized Leontief Production Function." *Journal of Political Economy* 79(3), 481–507.

    1973. "Separability and a Generalization of the Cobb–Douglas Cost, Production, and Indirect Utility Functions." Technical Report No. 86. Institute of Mathematical Studies in Social Sciences, Stanford University. Mimeo.

    1974. "Applications of Duality Theory." In M. D. Intriligator and D. A. Kendrick (eds.), *Frontiers of Quantitative Economics,* Vol. 2. Amsterdam: North-Holland, pp. 106–99.

Dixon, P. B., B. R. Parmenter, G. J. Ryland, and J. Sutton. 1977. *ORANI: A General Equilibrium Model of the Australian Economy: Current Specification and Illustrations of Use for Policy Analysis.* Canberra: Australian Government Publishing Service.

Dixon, P. B., B. R. Parmenter, D. P. Vincent, and J. Sutton. 1980. *ORANI: A Multisectoral Model of the Australian Economy.* Amsterdam: North-Holland.

Eisenpress, H., and J. Greenstadt. 1966. "The Estimation of Nonlinear Econometric Systems." *Econometrica* 34(4), 851–61.

Fisher, F. M. 1966. *The Identification Problem in Econometrics.* New York: McGraw-Hill.

Fullerton, D., J. B. Shoven, and J. Whalley. 1978. "General Equilibrium Analysis of U.S. Taxation Policy." In *1978 Compendium on Tax Research.* Washington, D.C.: Office of Tax Analysis, U.S. Treasury.

    1980. "Dynamic General Equilibrium Impacts of Replacing the U.S. Income Tax with a Progressive Consumption Tax." National Bureau of Economic Research Conference Paper No. 55, October.

Goldfeld, S., and R. Quandt. 1968. "Nonlinear Simultaneous Equations: Estimation and Prediction." *International Economic Review* 9, 113–36.

Gorman, W. M. 1957. "Tariffs, Retaliation, and Elasticity of Demand for Imports." *Review of Economic Studies* 25, 137–62.

Gussman, T. K. 1972. "The Demand for Durables, Nondurables, Services, and the Supply of Labor in Canada: 1946–1969." Department of Economics, University of British Columbia. Mimeo.

Harberger, A. C. 1962. "The Incidence of Corporate Income Tax." *Journal of Political Economy* 70, 215–40.

　　1966. "Efficiency Effects of Taxes on Income from Capital." In M. Krzyzaniak (ed.), *Effects of Corporation Income Tax.* Detroit: Wayne State University Press.

Hausman, J. A. 1975. "An Instrumental Variable Approach to Full-Information Estimators for Linear and Certain Nonlinear Econometric Models." *Econometrica* 43(4), 727–38.

Hoch, I. 1958. "Simultaneous Equation Bias in the Context of the Cobb–Douglas Production Function." *Econometrica* 26, 566–78.

Houthakker, H. S. 1960. "Additive Preferences." *Econometrica* 28, 244–57.

Johansen, L. 1960. *A Multi-Sectoral Study of Economic Growth.* Amsterdam: North-Holland.

　　1969. "On the Relationship between Some Systems of Demand Functions." *Liiketaloudellinen Aikakauskirga* 18(1), 30–41.

Johnson, H. G. 1953. "Optimum Tariffs and Retaliation." *Review of Economic Studies* 21, 142–53.

　　1956. "General Equilibrium Analysis of Excise Taxes: Comment." *American Economic Review* 46, 151–6.

Jorgenson, D. W., and B. Fraumeni. 1980. "Relative Prices and Technical Change." Discussion Paper Series, Harvard Institute of Economic Research, Harvard University.

Jorgenson, D. W., and Jean J. Laffont. 1974. "Efficient Estimation of Nonlinear Simultaneous Equations with Additive Disturbances." *Annals of Economic and Social Measurement* 3(4), 615–40.

Jorgenson, D. W., and L. J. Lau. 1975. "The Structure of Consumer Preferences." *Annals of Economic and Social Measurement* 4(1), 49–101.

Kehoe, T. J. 1980. "An Index Theorem for General Equilibrium Models with Production." *Econometrica* 48(5), 1211–33.

Kelejian, H. 1971. "Two Stage Least Squares and Econometric Systems Linear in Parameters but Nonlinear in Endogenous Variables." *Journal of the American Statistical Association* 66(334), 373–4.

Kendrick, J. W. 1973. "Postwar Productivity Trends in the United States, 1948–1969." National Bureau of Economic Research, General Series 98, New York.

Kmenta, J. 1964. "Some Properties of Alternative Estimators of the Cobb–Douglas Production Function." *Econometrica* 32, 183–8.

Lau, L. J. 1976. "Complete Systems of Consumer Demand Functions through Duality." In M. D. Intriligator (ed.), *Frontiers of Quantitative Economics,* Vol. IIIA. Amsterdam: North-Holland, pp. 59–86.

Lewis, H. G. 1975. "Economics of Time and Labour Supply." *American Economic Review* 65(2), 29–34.

Manne, A. S. 1980. "A Three-Region Model of Energy, International Trade, and Economic Growth." Department of Operations Research, Stanford University.

Manne, A. S. (with S. Kim). 1980. "Energy, International Trade, and Economic

Growth." In P. Auer (ed.), *Energy and the Developing Nations.* New York: Pergamon Press.

Mansur, A. 1981. "On the Estimation of General Equilibrium Models." Department of Economics, University of Western Ontario, London. Mimeo.

Marschak, J., and W. Andrews. 1944. "Random Simultaneous Equations and the Theory of Production." *Econometrica* 12, 143–205.

Miller, M. H., and J. E. Spencer. 1977. "The Static Economic Effects of the UK Joining the EEC: A General Equilibrium Approach." *Review of Economic Studies* 44(1), 71–93.

Mundlak, Y. 1963. "Estimation of Production and Behavioral Functions from a Combination of Cross-Section and Time Series Data." In *Measurement in Economics.* Stanford, Calif.: Stanford University Press, pp. 138–65.

Nasse, Ph. 1973. "Un Système Complet de Functions de Demande: Les Equations de Fourgeand et Nataf." *Econometrica* 41(6), 1137–58.

Nerlove, M. 1967. "A Survey of Recent Evidence on C.E.S. and Related Production Functions." In *Studies in Income and Wealth,* Vol. 31, *The Theory and Empirical Analysis of Production.* New York: N.B.E.R.

Parks, R. W. 1969. "Systems of Demand Equations: An Empirical Comparison of Alternative Functional Forms." *Econometrica* 37(4), 629–50.

Piggott, J. R., and J. Whalley. 1976. "General Equilibrium Investigations of U.K. Tax-Subsidy Policy: A Progress Report." In M. J. Artis and A. R. Nobay (eds.), *Studies in Modern Economic Analysis.* Oxford: Blackwell, pp. 259–300.

——— 1977. "The Numerical Specification of Large Scale Walrasian Policy Models." University of Western Ontario, London. Mimeo.

——— 1980. "Economic Effects of U.K. Tax-Subsidy Policies: A General Equilibrium Appraisal." Mimeo.

Pollak, R. A., and T. Wales. 1969. "Estimation of the Linear Expenditure System." *Econometrica* 37(4), 611–28.

Rosenberg, L. G. 1969. "Taxation of Income from Capital by Industry Group." In Arnold C. Harberger and M. J. Bailey (eds.), *The Taxation of Income from Capital.* Washington, D.C.: Brookings Institution, pp. 123–79.

St-Hilaire, F., and J. Whalley. 1980. "A Microconsistent Equilibrium Data Set for Canada for Use in Tax Policy Analysis." University of Western Ontario, London. Mimeo.

Scarf, H. 1973. *The Computation of Economic Equilibria.* Cowles Foundation Research Monograph No. 24. New Haven: Yale University Press.

Serra-Puche, J. J. 1979. "A Computational General Equilibrium Model for the Mexican Economy: An Analysis of Fiscal Policies." Ph.D. diss., Yale University.

Shoven, J. B. 1976. "The Incidence and Effects of Taxes on Income from Capital." *Journal of Political Economy* 84(6), 1261–83.

Shoven, J. B., and J. Whalley. 1972. "A General Equilibrium Calculation of the Effects of Differential Taxation of Income from Capital in the U.S." *Journal of Public Economics* 1, 281–321.

Stern, R. M., J. Francis, and B. Schumacker. 1976. *Price Elasticities in International Trade: An Annotated Bibliography.* London: Macmillan, for the Trade Policy Centre.

Stone, R. D. 1954. "Linear Expenditure Systems and Demand Analysis: An Application to the Pattern of British Demand." *Economic Journal* 64, 511–27.

Summers, Lawrence H. 1980. "Tax Policy in a Life-Cycle Mode." Paper presented at the NBER Conference on Taxation of Capital, November 16–17, 1979, Cambridge, Mass.

Whalley, J. 1980. "Discriminatory Features of Domestic Factor Tax Systems in a Goods Mobile-Factors Immobile Trade Model: An Empirical General Equilibrium Approach." *Journal of Political Economy* 88(6), 1177–202.

Zellner, A. 1962. "An Efficient Method of Estimating Seemingly Unrelated Regressions and Tests for Aggregation Bias." *Journal of the American Statistical Association* 57(298), 348–68.

Zellner, A., J. Kementa, and J. Drèze. 1966. "Specification and Estimation of Cobb-Douglas Production Function Models." *Econometrica* 34, 784–95.

Comments

Lawrence J. Lau

Unlike most of the authors in this book, I am not a producer of applied general equilibrium models; I am only a consumer, but an extremely enthusiastic one. I am therefore very happy to see the large (and increasing) number of applied general equilibrium models that have come into being barely a decade since Professor Herbert Scarf first made the computation of such models feasible.

The parameters of most of the "first-generation" applied general equilibrium models, however, have not been econometrically estimated. Rather, they are derived through a technique described as "calibration" by Mansur and Whalley. In their chapter, Mansur and Whalley provide good expositions of both the econometric and the "calibration" approaches to the numerical specification of applied general equilibrium models. In particular, they have identified most of the pitfalls of the econometric approach. However, in my opinion, they have not distinguished sufficiently between what is done generally (which may be wrong) and the state of econometric art. They have not described the "best econometric practice." The fact that econometric estimation is frequently implemented incorrectly does not imply that it cannot be done right, and certainly does not imply that it should not be done at all. In what follows I shall attempt to compare the econometric and "calibration" approaches under the assumption that both approaches are correctly implemented as intended.[1]

1 The problem of numerical specification

The problem of numerical specification of a model arises in every application. It is not unique to applied general equilibrium models. The standard form of the problem may be stated as follows:

Given a system of n equations

$$F(y, X; \beta, \epsilon) = 0 \qquad (1)$$

where y is a vector of the n endogenous variables, X is a vector of exogenous variables, β is a vector of unknown parameters, and ϵ is a vector of n stochastic disturbances of either known, partially known, or unknown distribution, how should the vector β be specified numerically? In general equilibrium models in the sense used in this book the vector y typically consists of the quantities and prices of all the distinguished commodities (and thus is of even dimensionality).

The choice of a value for β is frequently up to the modeler. It can be simply "drawn out of a hat,"[2] or it can be adopted from the results of other empirical studies, or it can be based on the subjective prior beliefs of the modeler. However, we shall confine our attention to *data-based* numerical specification, that is, the selection of a value for β on the basis of one or more observations on y and X. Numerical specification then reduces to the following problem: Given the assumed form of the vector-valued function $F(y, X; \beta, \epsilon)$ (which is unique up to a transformation that takes the origin into the origin), and *one* or *more* observations on y and X, and appropriate assumptions on the distribution of ϵ, select a value for β which is "best" in some sense.

One may raise the question of why the vector ϵ belongs in Equation (1). There are at least two reasons. First, no model can possibly capture *all* the factors that affect or may affect the values of the endogenous variables. For example, the weather may affect the output of wheat, and unanticipated increases in the foreign demand for wheat may increase the price of wheat. Few if any modelers seriously insist that their model specifications encompass all possible factors that may affect the values of the endogenous variables. Thus ϵ represents the effects of all the omitted factors. Second, the endogenous variables and sometimes even the so-called exogenous variables may be measured with errors. This is especially the case if, as Mansur and Whalley point out in their chapter, the standard published national income and product account data have to be further transformed and adjusted, sometimes by ad hoc procedures.[3]

In the econometric approach, typically a distribution is specified, often only partially, for the unknown ϵ, in Equation (1), and β is estimated from the resulting system of equations using *all available observations* on y and X. In the "calibration" approach, ϵ is simply set equal to zero in Equation (1). Here β is solved from the resulting system of equations using a single observation of y and X. This amounts to saying that absolutely no factors other than those already included in the model affected the values of the endogenous variables in the benchmark period and none are expected to affect them in any future period. This is a very strong assumption indeed.[4] To mitigate partially the effects of this strong assumption, some modelers using the "calibration" approach would derive different sets of values for β from observations of different periods and then average them to obtain a single estimate of β. This averaging procedure, although similar in spirit to the econometric approach, does not seem to be rigorously justifiable on a statistical basis. In any event, if an average value is used for β, one of the major advantages claimed by the proponents of the "calibration" approach – the identical satisfaction of the so-called general equilibrium constraints in the benchmark period – is lost.

What does it mean for an applied general equilibrium model with an estimated vector of parameters $\hat{\beta}$ to satisfy the general equilibrium constraints in the benchmark period? It implies that for this value of $\hat{\beta}$, the value of y in the benchmark period should solve the model exactly given the value of X in the benchmark period. It is evident that if the "calibration" approach is used to derive $\hat{\beta}$, then

$$F(y, X; \hat{\beta}, 0) = 0 \tag{2}$$

identically for y and X in the benchmark period since that is the way in which $\hat{\beta}$ is constructed. By contrast, if the econometric approach is used, then, in general,

$$F(y, X; \hat{\beta}, 0) \neq 0$$

for the benchmark period, and certainly not for all observations.[5] Thus, the general equilibrium constraints are not identically satisfied for the benchmark period. This has often been identified as one of the major advantages of the "calibration" approach over the econometric approach.

However, a moment's reflection suggests that this is not a real issue. It is often possible to choose a parametric specification so that some or all of the general equilibrium constraints are identically satisfied for $\epsilon = 0$ in Equation (1). In any case, if it is desirable to have the model solved exactly in some benchmark period, the time-honored procedure known as "constant adjustments" can be used.[6] In other words, for given y and X in the benchmark period and an econometrically or otherwise estimated $\hat{\beta}$, one can simply set ϵ equal to a constant vector k so that

$$F(y, X; \hat{\beta}, k) = 0$$

In this way, the general equilibrium constraints are identically satisfied. The real issue is whether and how well β can be estimated by using either approach and not the identical satisfaction of the model equations for some benchmark observation.

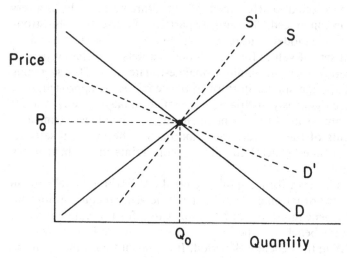

Figure 1. Underidentification of supply and demand functions: the case of a single observation.

2   "Calibration" versus econometric estimation

Even if one were willing to make the strong assumption that $\epsilon = 0$ in the benchmark period as well as in all future periods, there are additional problems with the "calibration" approach. The first is underidentification – that is, the inability to determine all the parameters of a model given the data. In general, whether there is identification depends on the specification of the model, the nature of the data, and the number and type of observations. It should be noted that underidentification can be a problem for the econometric approach as well. We shall illustrate the problem of underidentification by presenting two examples.

First we consider a simple two-equation model of supply and demand. Let there be a supply curve and a demand curve, labeled S and D, respectively, in Figure 1.

With only one observation, (P_0, Q_0), it is impossible to determine S and D uniquely. In fact S' and D' are just as consistent with the data as S and D. The "calibration" approach cannot yield unique estimates of the slopes and intercepts of the supply and demand curves. They will have to be assigned values based on extraneous information.

With additional observations, the econometric approach can be used. However, underidentification can still be a problem, depending on the presence or absence of exogenous variables. If there were no exogenous variables, then the underidentification problem persists, as illustrated in

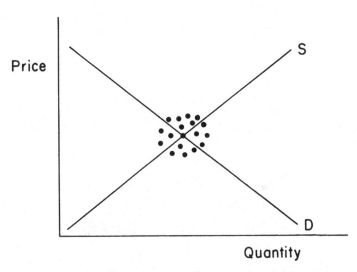

Figure 2. Underidentification of supply and demand functions: the case of multiple observations.

Figure 2, in which each point represents an observation. The cluster of data points yields no information on the slopes and intercepts of the supply and demand curves.

It is only in the presence of exogenous variables that shift one curve without shifting the other that the supply and demand curves can be identified from data. In the econometric approach, considerable attention is paid to the identification problem. The "calibration" approach, however, cannot accommodate exogenous variables whose effects are not known a priori. In fact, the greater the number of exogenous variables, the more serious is the underidentification problem for the "calibration" approach. This is because the "calibration" approach depends on the solution of Equation (2) for $\hat{\beta}$. In order that $\hat{\beta}$ can be determined uniquely from Equation (2), the number of independent unknown components of $\hat{\beta}$ cannot exceed n, the number of equations. Adding exogenous variables whose effects are not known a priori increases the number of independent unknown components of $\hat{\beta}$ that must be estimated and thus worsens the underidentification problem.

This limitation on the total number of independent unknown parameters that can be estimated by using the "calibration" approach leads to a second problem, that is, the lack of "flexibility" of the assumed functional forms. In order to use the "calibration" approach, the average number of independent unknown parameters per equation cannot be greater than unity. This implies that each of the n functions

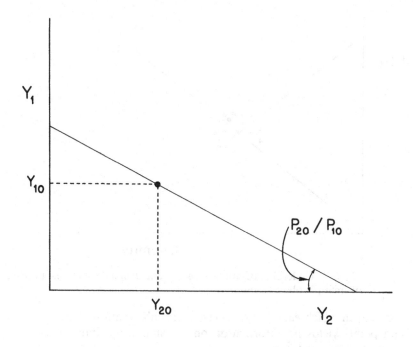

Figure 3. Data for a two-commodity general equilibrium model.

$$F_i(y, X; \beta, 0), \qquad i = 1, \ldots, n$$

can only depend, on average, on a single parameter. All the properties of the function $F_i(\cdot)$, including in particular all its first-, second-, and higher-order derivatives, depend only on this single parameter. This restricts the ability of $F_i(\cdot)$ to mimic its counterpart in the real world. In practice, this limitation on the number of parameters dictates the use of simple functional forms such as the Cobb–Douglas and the Leontief utility and production functions. Although I do not object to simplicity per se, the use of these simple inflexible forms can often affect or bias the conclusions of the model. If the econometric approach is used, the assumed functional forms can be much more "flexible" – a far greater number of independent unknown parameters can be estimated from the data, limited only by the number of observations.

Second, we consider a two-commodity, Y_1 and Y_2, general equilibrium model with *given* aggregate endowments of capital $\bar{K}$, labor $\bar{L}$, and population $\bar{N}$. The data available for the benchmark period consist of Y_{10}, Y_{20}, and p_{20}/p_{10} and can be represented in Figure 3. The problem of "calibration" essentially consists of finding an indifference curve U_1 that is

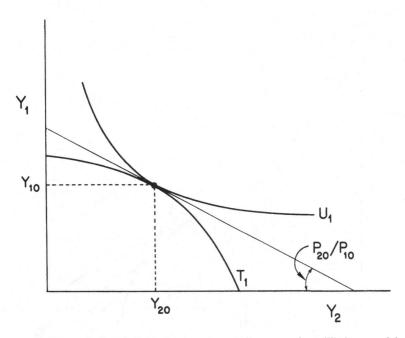

Figure 4. Calibration of a two-commodity general equilibrium model.

tangent to the price line at Y_{10} and Y_{20} and a production possibility frontier T_1 that is also tangent to the price line at Y_{10} and Y_{20}. Figure 4 depicts this situation.

It is easy to see that given only one observation, an uncountably infinite number of pairs (U_1, T_1) can serve as calibration candidates for the indifference curve and the production possibility frontier. Thus, in general, it is not possible to identify either the indifference curve U_1 or the production possibility frontier T_1 without additional a priori non–data-based restrictions on the form of U_1 and T_1.

Even if one were willing to make strong a priori assumptions on the form of U_1 and T_1, it remains the case that the indifference curve and the production possibility frontier can each depend on only a single independent unknown parameter if one were to have identification. There are, in effect, two independent equations of the model:

$$\frac{(\partial U/\partial Y_1)(Y, \beta_U)}{(\partial U/\partial Y_2)(Y, \beta_U)} = \frac{p_{10}}{p_{20}}$$

and

$$\frac{(\partial F/\partial Y_1)(Y, \beta_F)}{(\partial F/\partial Y_2)(Y, \beta_F)} = \frac{p_{10}}{p_{20}}$$

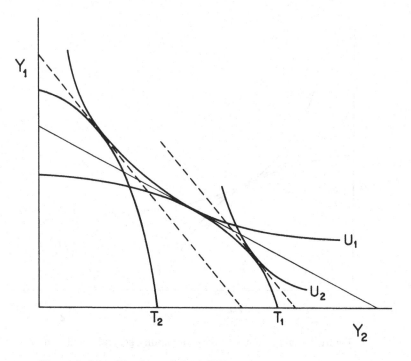

Figure 5. Identification of the indifference curve and the production possibility frontier through shifts in the exogenous variables.

from which the parameters β_U and β_F are to be determined. In order for them to be uniquely determinable, the numbers of independent unknown parameters in β_U and β_F must be one each. We may further note that under the "calibration" approach it is impossible to determine the effects of alternative levels of $\bar{K}$ and $\bar{L}$ on T or of alternative levels of $\bar{N}$ on U from the data.

With the econometric approach, identification of U and T can be achieved from the shifts of U due to changes in $\bar{N}$ and the shifts of T due to changes in $\bar{K}$ and $\bar{L}$. In fact, shifts in U help to identify T and vice versa.[7] This situation is depicted in Figure 5.

A third problem with the "calibration" approach has to do with the lack of a measure of the degree of reliability of the model and its parameters. If the parameters are determined completely by the solution of Equation (2) for the benchmark period, they may be quite sensitive to the choice of the benchmark period. If the parameters are partially based on other estimates in the literature, there may be a serious issue of comparability due to differences in the definitions of variables and in the scope of the models. For example, the other estimates may be based on partial rather than general equilibrium models.

In any case, the potential consumer of the applied general equilibrium model must be reasonably convinced of the reliability, stationarity, and stability of the model and its parameters before he can have any degree of confidence in its results. With the "calibration" approach, no measures of the reliability of the model and its parameters are available. With the econometric approach, such measures are readily available in the forms of the estimated variance–covariance matrix of the estimator of the parameters and other within-sample goodness-of-fit statistics. Measures of stationarity and stability are not so readily available. With the "calibration" approach, such measures may be based on the predictive performance of the "calibrated" model outside the benchmark period. Some additional assumptions on the nature of the stochastic disturbance terms appear necessary for the construction and evaluation of these measures. With the econometric approach the question of stationarity and stability may be tackled by subdividing the sample as well as by postsample predictive tests.

Does the "calibration" approach have any virtues? The first and foremost virtue is the parsimony of the data requirement – only one observation is needed. The second is the ease with which the values of the independent unknown parameters can be determined. There is a relatively small number of parameters to start with – approximately one per equation – and the determination requires only a numerical solution of Equation (2) for $\hat{\beta}$. Third, if one were to do a sensitivity analysis of the model with respect to the values of the independent unknown parameters, the results would be much easier to interpret and to understand because of both the smaller number of parameters and the simpler functional forms used.

However, many of the estimation problems identified by Mansur and Whalley with the econometric approach have to do not so much with the level of effort required but with the use of "shortcut" methods that are known to be inappropriate. For example, "simultaneous-equations bias" is a problem only if the ordinary least squares estimator is used in situations where a simultaneous-equations estimator is called for. The singularity of the variance–covariance matrix of the stochastic disturbance terms (across equations) can also be easily accommodated if recognized. Nor does "complexity" of a model present any real conceptual problem in estimation unless the degrees of freedom are exhausted or drastically reduced.[8] And whereas it is true that, in general, econometrically estimated applied general equilibrium models tend to be too "complex" to be "calibrated," there is no reason why a "calibrated" model should not be econometrically estimated. After all, any model that can be "calibrated" can be econometrically estimated but not vice versa. Finally, it is pointed out by Mansur and Whalley, quite correctly, that certain full-information estimators, in particular the "full-information maximum likelihood" estimator, may not be implementable for certain models because of size and degrees of freedom limitations. However, it should also be recognized that this does not mean the model cannot be estimated by other consistent simultaneous-equations methods, which may or may not have the same efficiency properties as these "full-information" estimators.

3   Concluding remarks

Although an example is presented by Mansur and Whalley in which the econometric approach and the "calibration" approach yield similar results, it is definitely not sufficient to establish the robustness of the "calibration" approach in general. It does demonstrate that the econometric approach can be successfully implemented. In addition, the econometric approach provides error statistics that can be used as a basis for judging the reliability of the parameters.

What would I recommend? I would recommend that first, whenever it is possible, use the econometric approach. Then use constant adjustments to ensure that the model is exactly satisfied for the benchmark observation. Second, identify the parameters that are critical to the question in hand. Focus on improving the precision of the estimators of these parameters. Third, do lots and lots of sensitivity analyses, especially with respect to the critical parameters. Finally, whenever possible, perform postsample predictive tests based on known exogenous variables. If all these things are done, the modeler will have a fairly good idea of the values of the parameters and their reliability as well as the properties of his model.

However, the econometric approach does require a great deal of work – from data assembly, model specification, and estimation to postsample prediction.[9] The major advantages of the "calibration" approach consist of minimal data requirements – one observation will do – and minimal computation requirements relative to the econometric approach. Thus, it is ideally suited to situations in which data are scarce and a quick answer is required. It is a useful shortcut for a modeler in a hurry.

NOTES

1. It is, however, generally true that "calibration" takes far less time and effort than econometric estimation, a factor that may explain the relative popularity of the "calibration" approach.

2. This is precisely what is done in sensitivity analysis.
3. Note that in the general form of Equation (1), the vector X may be interpreted to include the initial values of the lagged endogenous variables. Thus, it is not necessary to assume that the actual observed data pertain to a long-run equilibrium. The modeler, however, may wish to impose this additional assumption.
4. Setting ϵ equal to zero is just as arbitrary as setting ϵ equal to any other constant k.
5. For example, not all observations will lie on a regression surface.
6. This procedure has been and continues to be widely used by almost all macroeconometric modelers.
7. There are indeed plausible circumstances under which identification is not possible even with an infinite number of observations. In these cases, the econometric approach does not help either. A Bayesian approach with an informative prior may be the only possibility.
8. For example, D. W. Jorgenson and his collaborators have actually estimated a rather "complex" general equilibrium model econometrically.
9. To the extent that there is reason to believe that a sharp break has occurred between the past and the present so that the historical data are no longer helpful, the usefulness of the econometric approach will be limited.

CHAPTER 4

Econometric methods for applied general equilibrium analysis

Dale W. Jorgenson

1 Introduction

The development of computational methods for solving nonlinear general equilibrium models along the lines pioneered by Scarf (1973; Chapter 1, this book) has been the focus of much recent research. By comparison the development of econometric methods for estimating the unknown parameters describing technology and preferences in such models has been neglected. The purpose of this chapter is to summarize the results of recent research on econometric methods for estimating the parameters of nonlinear general equilibrium models. For this purpose we present econometric models of producer and consumer behavior suitable for incorporation into a general equilibrium model of the U.S. economy. The most important feature of these models is that they encompass all of the restrictions implied by economic theories of producer and consumer behavior.

At the outset of our discussion it is essential to recognize that the predominant tradition in applied general equilibrium modeling does not employ econometric methods. This tradition originated with the seminal work of Leontief (1941, 1953), beginning with the implementations of the static input–output model half a century ago. Leontief gave a further impetus to the development of general equilibrium modeling by introducing a dynamic input–output model. Empirical work associated with input–output analysis is based on estimating the unknown parameters of a general equilibrium model from a single interindustry transactions table.

The usefulness of the "fixed-coefficients" assumption that underlies input–output analysis is hardly subject to dispute. By linearizing technology and preferences it is possible to solve at one stroke the two fundamental problems that arise in the practical implementation of general equilibrium models. First, the resulting general equilibrium model can be solved as a system of linear equations with constant coefficients. Second,

139

the unknown parameters describing technology and preferences can be estimated from a single data point.

The first successful implementation of an applied general equilibrium model without the fixed-coefficients assumption of input–output analysis is due to Johansen (1960). Johansen retained the fixed-coefficients assumption in modeling demands for intermediate goods, but employed linear-logarithmic or Cobb–Douglas production functions in modeling the substitution between capital and labor services and technical change. He replaced the fixed-coefficients assumption for household behavior by a system of demand functions originated by Frisch (1959).

Linear-logarithmic production functions imply that relative shares of inputs in the value of output are fixed, so that the unknown parameters characterizing substitution between capital and labor inputs can be estimated from a single data point. In describing producer behavior Johansen employed econometric methods only in estimating constant rates of technical change. Similarly, the unknown parameters of the demand system proposed by Frisch can be determined from a single data point, except for one parameter that must be estimated econometrically.

The essential features of Johansen's approach have been preserved in the applied general equilibrium models surveyed by Fullerton, Henderson, and Shoven (Chapter 9, this book) and by Mansur and Whalley (Chapter 3, this book). The unknown parameters describing technology and preferences in these models are determined by "calibration" to a single data point. Data from a single interindustry transactions table are supplemented by a small number of parameters estimated econometrically. The obvious disadvantage of this approach is that highly restrictive assumptions on technology and preferences are required in order to make calibration feasible.

As an example of the restrictive assumptions on technology employed in the calibration approach, we first observe that almost all applied general equilibrium models retain the fixed-coefficients assumption of Leontief and Johansen for modeling demand for intermediate goods. This assumption is directly contradicted by recent evidence of changes in energy utilization in response to the higher energy prices that have prevailed since 1973. As an example of restrictive assumption on preferences employed in the calibration approach, we observe that preferences are commonly assumed to be homothetic, which is contradicted by empirical evidence on consumer behavior going back more than a century.

To implement models of producer and consumer behavior that are less restrictive than those of Johansen, it is essential to employ econometric methods. A possible econometric extension of Johansen's approach would be to estimate elasticities of substitution between capital and labor inputs along the lines suggested by Arrow, Chenery, Minhas, and Solow (1961). Unfortunately, constant elasticity of substitution (CES) production functions cannot easily be extended to encompass substitution among capital, labor, and intermediate inputs or among intermediate inputs. As Uzawa (1962) and McFadden (1963) have shown, constant elasticities of substitution among more than two inputs imply, essentially, that elasticities of substitution among all inputs must be the same.

An alternative approach to the implementation of econometric models of producer behavior is to generate complete systems of demand functions for inputs in each industrial sector. Each system gives quantities of inputs demanded as functions of prices and output. This approach to modeling producer behavior was first implemented by Berndt and Jorgenson (1973). As in the descriptions of technology by Leontief and Johansen, production is characterized by constant returns to scale in each sector. As a consequence, commodity prices can be expressed as function-of-factor prices, using the nonsubstitution theorem of Samuelson (1951). This greatly facilitates the solution of the econometric general equilibrium model constructed by Hudson and Jorgenson (1974) by permitting a substantial reduction in dimensionality of the space of prices to be determined by the model.

The implementation of econometric models of producer behavior is very demanding in terms of data requirements. These models require the construction of a consistent time series of interindustry transactions tables. By comparison, the noneconometric approaches of Leontief and Johansen require only a single interindustry transactions table. Second, the implementation of systems of input demand functions requires methods for the estimation of parameters in systems of nonlinear simultaneous equations. Finally, the restrictions implied by the economic theory of producer behavior require estimation under both equality and inequality constraints.

Similarly, econometric models of consumer behavior can be employed in applied general equilibrium models. Econometric models stemming from the pathbreaking contributions of Schultz (1938), Stone (1954b), and Wold (1953) consist of complete systems of demand functions giving quantities demanded as functions of prices and total expenditure. A possible approach to incorporating the restrictions implied by the theory of consumer behavior is to treat aggregate demand functions as if they could be generated by a single representative consumer. Per capita quantities demanded can be expressed as functions of prices and per capita expenditure.

The obvious difficulty with the representative consumer approach is that aggregate demand functions can be expressed as the sum of individual demand functions. Aggregate demand functions depend on prices and total expenditures, as in the theory of individual consumer behavior. However, aggregate demand functions depend on individual total expenditures rather than aggregate expenditure. If individual expenditures are allowed to vary independently, models of aggregate consumer behavior based on a single representative consumer imply restrictions that severely limit the dependence of individual demand functions on individual expenditure.

An alternative approach to the construction of econometric models of aggregate consumer behavior is provided by Lau's (1977b, 1982) theory of exact aggregation. In this approach, systems of aggregate demand functions depend on statistics of the joint distribution of individual total expenditures and attributes of individuals associated with differences in preferences. One of the most remarkable features of models based on exact aggregation is that systems of demand functions for individuals can be recovered uniquely from the system of aggregate demand functions. This feature makes it possible to exploit all the implications of the economic theory of the individual consumer in constructing an econometric model of aggregate consumer behavior.

The implementation of an econometric model of aggregate consumer behavior based on the theory of exact aggregation has been carried out by Jorgenson, Lau, and Stoker (1980, 1981, 1982). Their approach requires time series data on prices and aggregate quantities consumed. This approach also requires cross-section data on individual quantities consumed, individual total expenditures, and attributes of individual households, such as demographic characteristics. By comparison, the non-econometric approaches of Leontief and Johansen require only a single data point for prices and aggregate quantities consumed. The implementation of a system of aggregate demand functions requires methods for combining time series and cross-section data for the estimation of parameters in systems of nonlinear simultaneous equations.

In Section 2 we present an econometric model of producer behavior, originally implemented for 35 industrial sectors of the U.S. economy by Jorgenson and Fraumeni (1981). This model is based on a production function for each sector, giving output as a function of inputs of intermediate goods produced by other sectors and inputs of the primary factors of production, capital, and labor services. Output also depends on time as an index of the level of technology. Producer equilibrium under constant returns to scale implies the existence of a sectoral price function, giving the price of output as a function of the input prices and time. To incorporate the restrictions implied by the economic theory of producer behavior we generate our econometric model from a price function for each sector.

Sectoral price functions must be homogeneous of degree one, non-decreasing, and concave in input prices. In addition, we assume that these price functions are homothetically separable in the prices of capital, labor, energy, and materials inputs. Under homothetic separability our model of producer behavior is based on a two-stage allocation process. In the first stage the value of sectoral output is allocated among capital, labor, energy, and materials inputs. In the second stage the value of each of the inputs is allocated among individual types of that input. Two-stage allocation makes it possible to determine the rate of technical change and the shares of 35 intermediate goods and two primary factors of production in the value of output as functions of input prices.

Our model of producer behavior consists of a system of equations giving the shares of all inputs in the value of output and the rate of technical change as functions of relative prices and time. To formulate an econometric model we add a stochastic component to these equations. Since the rate of technical change is not directly observable, we consider a form of the model with autocorrelated disturbances. We can transform the data to eliminate the autocorrelation. We treat the prices as endogenous variables and estimate the unknown parameters by means of econometric methods appropriate for systems of nonlinear simultaneous equations. Finally, we impose restrictions on the parameters that assure that the underlying sectoral price functions are homogeneous, nondecreasing, and concave in input prices.

In Section 3 we present an econometric model of aggregate consumer behavior that has been implemented for the U.S. economy by Jorgenson, Lau, and Stoker (1980, 1981, 1982). This model is based on a utility function for each consumer, giving utility as a function of quantities of individual commodities. Consumer equilibrium implies the existence of an indirect utility function for each consumer. The indirect utility function gives the level of utility as a function of prices of individual commodities, total expenditure, and attributes of the consumer associated with differences in preferences among consumers. To incorporate the restrictions implied by the economic theory of consumer behavior we generate our econometric model from an indirect utility function for each consumer.

Indirect utility functions must be homogeneous of degree zero in prices and expenditure, nonincreasing in prices and increasing in expenditure, and quasi-convex in prices and expenditure. In addition, we assume that these indirect utility functions are homothetically separable in the prices of five commodity groups – energy, food and clothing, consumer services, capital services, and other nondurable expenditures. Under homothetic separability our model of consumer behavior is based on a two-stage allocation process. In this first stage total expenditure is allocated among commodity groups. In the second stage the expenditure on each commodity group is allocated among individual commodities within the group. Two-stage allocation makes it possible to determine the shares of 35 commodities in total expenditure as functions of prices, total expenditure, and consumer attributes.

Our model of individual consumer behavior consists of a system of equations giving the shares of all commodities in total expenditure as functions of relative prices, total expenditure, and consumer attributes. To obtain a model of aggregate consumer behavior we multiply individual expenditures shares by expenditure for each consuming unit, add over all consuming units, and divide by aggregate expenditure. Our model of aggregate consumer behavior consists of equations giving the shares of all commodities in aggregate expenditure as functions of relative prices. The aggregate expenditure shares also depend on the joint distribution of total expenditure and attributes of individual consumers, such as demographic characteristics. The impact of changes in this distribution is summarized by means of certain statistics of the joint distribution.

To formulate an econometric model of individual consumer behavior we add a stochastic component to the equations for the individual expenditure shares. Aggregation over individuals results in disturbances that are heteroscedastic. We can transform the data on aggregate expenditure shares to eliminate the heteroscedasticity. We estimate the unknown parameters by means of econometric methods for combining cross-section data on patterns of individual expenditures with time series data on patterns of aggregate expenditures. As before, we treat the prices as endogenous variables and employ methods appropriate for systems of nonlinear simultaneous equations. Finally, we impose restrictions on the parameters that assure that the underlying indirect utility functions are homogeneous, nonincreasing in prices and increasing in expenditures, and quasi-convex in prices and expenditure.

In Section 4 we present the empirical results of implementing our econometric models of producer and consumer behavior for the U.S. economy. We give empirical results of implementing the model of producer behavior described in Section 2 for 35 industrial sectors. We limit our presentation to the first stage of the two-stage process for the allocation of the value of sectoral output. Similarly, we give empirical results of implementing the model of consumer behavior described in Section 3, limiting our presentation to the first stage of the two-stage process for the allocation of total expenditure. We employ family size, age of head, region of residence, race, and urban versus rural residence as attributes of individual households associated with differences in preferences.

2   Producer behavior

In this section our objective is to analyze technical change and the distribution of the value of output for 35 industrial sectors of the U.S. economy. Our most important conceptual innovation is to determine the rate of technical change and the distributive shares of productive inputs simultaneously as functions of relative prices. We show that the effects of technical change on the distributive shares are precisely the same as the effects of relative prices on the rate of technical change.

Our methodology is based on a model of production treating substitution among inputs and changes in technology symmetrically. The model is based on a production function for each industrial sector, giving output as a function of time and of capital, labor, energy, and materials inputs. Necessary conditions for producer equilibrium in each sector are given by equalities between the distributive shares of the four productive inputs and the corresponding elasticities of output with respect to each of these inputs.

Producer equilibrium under constant returns to scale implies that the value of output is equal to the sum of the values of capital, labor, energy, and materials inputs into each sector. Given this identity and equalities between the distributive shares and the elasticities of output with respect to each of the inputs, we can express the price of output as a function of the prices of capital, labor, energy, and materials inputs and of time. We refer to this function as the sectoral price function.

Given sectoral price functions for all 35 industrial sectors, we can generate econometric models that determine the rate of technical change and the distributive shares of the four productive inputs endogenously for each sector. The distributive shares and the rate of technical change, like the price of sectoral output, are functions of relative prices and time. We assume that the prices of sectoral outputs are transcendental-logarithmic or, more simply, translog functions of the prices of the four inputs and time.

Although technical change is endogenous in our models of production and technical change, these models must be carefully distinguished from models of induced technical change, such as those analyzed by Hicks (1932), Kennedy (1964), Samuelson (1965), von Weizsäcker (1962), and many others.[1] In those models the biases of technical change are endogenous and depend on relative prices. In our models the biases of technical change are fixed, whereas the rate of technical change is endogenous and depends on relative prices.

As Samuelson (1965) has pointed out, models of induced technical change require intertemporal optimization, since technical change at any point of time affects future production possibilities. In our models myopic decision rules are appropriate, even though the rate of technical change is endogenous, provided that the price of capital input is treated as a rental price for capital services.[2] The rate of technical change at any point of time is a function of relative prices, but does not affect future production possibilities. This vastly simplifies the modeling of producer behavior and greatly facilitates the implementation of our econometric models.

2.1   *Translog model of producer behavior*

Given myopic decision rules for producers in each industrial sector, we can describe all of the implications of the theory of production in terms of the sectoral price functions.[3] The sectoral price functions must be homogeneous of degree one, nondecreasing, and concave in the prices of the four inputs. A novel feature of our econometric methodology is to fit econometric models of sectoral production and technical change that incorporate all of these implications of the theory of production.

To represent our models of producer behavior we first require some notation. There are I industrial sectors, indexed by $i = 1, 2, \ldots, I$. We denote the quantities of sectoral outputs by $\{Z_i\}$ and the quantities of sectoral capital, labor, energy, and materials inputs by $\{K_i, L_i, E_i, M_i\}$. Similarly, we denote the prices of sectoral outputs by $\{q_i\}$ and the prices of the four sectoral inputs by $\{p_K^i, p_L^i, p_E^i, p_M^i\}$. We can define the shares of inputs in the value of output for each of the sectors by

$$v_K^i = \frac{p_K^i K_i}{q_i Z_i}, \qquad v_L^i = \frac{p_L^i L_i}{q_i Z_i}, \qquad v_E^i = \frac{p_E^i E_i}{q_i Z_i},$$

$$v_M^i = \frac{p_M^i M_i}{q_i Z_i} \qquad (i = 1, 2, \ldots, I)$$

Outputs are valued in producers' prices, while inputs are valued in purchasers' prices. In addition, we require the following notation:

$v_i = (v_K^i, v_L^i, v_E^i, v_M^i)$ – vector of value shares of the ith industry ($i = 1, 2, \ldots, I$)

$\ln p_i = (\ln p_K^i, \ln p_L^i, \ln p_E^i, \ln p_M^i)$ – vector of logarithms of prices of sectoral inputs of the ith industry ($i = 1, 2, \ldots, I$)

$t = $ time as an index of technology

We assume that the ith industry allocates the value of its output among the four inputs in accord with the price function:

$$\ln q_i = \alpha_0^i + \ln p_i' \alpha_p^i + \alpha_t^i \cdot t + \tfrac{1}{2} \ln p_i' \beta_{pp}^i \ln p_i + \ln p_i' \beta_{pt}^i \cdot t$$
$$+ \tfrac{1}{2} \beta_{tt}^i \cdot t^2 \qquad (i = 1, 2, \ldots, I) \qquad (2.1)$$

For these price functions, the prices of outputs are transcendental or, more specifically, exponential functions of the logarithms of the prices of inputs. We refer to these forms as *transcendental-logarithmic* price functions or, more simply, translog price functions,[4] indicating the role of the variables that enter the price functions. In this representation the scalars $\{\alpha_0^i, \alpha_t^i, \beta_{tt}^i\}$, the vectors $\{\alpha_p^i, \beta_{pt}^i\}$, and the matrices $\{\beta_{pp}^i\}$ are constant parameters that differ among industries, reflecting differences among sectoral technologies. Differences in technology among time periods within an industry are represented by time as an index of technology.

The value shares of the ith industry can be expressed in terms of the logarithmic derivatives of the sectoral price function with respect to the logarithms of the prices of the corresponding inputs:

$$v_i = \frac{\partial \ln q_i}{\partial \ln p_i} \qquad (i = 1, 2, \ldots, I) \qquad (2.2)$$

Applying this relationship to the translog price function, we obtain the system of sectoral value shares:

$$v_i = \alpha_p^i + \beta_{pp}^i \ln p_i + \beta_{pt}^i \cdot t \qquad (i = 1, 2, \ldots, I) \qquad (2.3)$$

We can define the *rate of technical change* for each of the sectors, say $\{v_t^i\}$, as the negative of the rate of growth of the price of sectoral output with respect to time, holding the prices of sectoral capital, labor, energy, and materials inputs constant:

$$v_t^i = -\frac{\partial \ln q_i}{\partial t} \qquad (i = 1, 2, \ldots, I) \qquad (2.4)$$

For the translog price function this relationship takes the form

$$-v_t^i = \alpha_t^i + \beta_{pt}^{i\prime} \ln p_i + \beta_{tt}^i \cdot t \qquad (i = 1, 2, \ldots, I) \qquad (2.5)$$

Given the sectoral price functions, we can define the *share elasticities with respect to price*[5] as the derivatives of the value shares with respect to the logarithms of the prices of capital, labor, energy, and materials inputs. For the translog price functions the matrices of share elasticities with respect to price $\{\beta_{pp}^i\}$ are constant. We can also characterize these functions as *constant share elasticity* or CSE price functions, indicating the role of fixed parameters that enter the sectoral price functions.[6] Similarly, we can define the *biases of technical change with respect to price* as derivatives of the value shares with respect to time.[7] Alternatively, we can define the biases of technical change with respect to price as derivatives of the rate of technical change with respect to the logarithms of the prices of capital, labor, energy, and materials inputs.[8] These two definitions of biases of technical change are equivalent. For the translog price functions the vectors of biases of technical change with respect to price $\{\beta_{pt}^i\}$ are constant. Finally, we can define the *rate of change of the negative of the rate of technical change* as the derivative of the rate of technical change with respect to time.[9] For the translog price functions these rates of change $\{\beta_{tt}^i\}$ are constant.

The negative of the average rates of technical change in any two points of time, say t and $t-1$, can be expressed as the difference between successive logarithms of the price of output, less a weighted average of the differences between successive logarithms of the prices given by the average value shares:

$$-\bar{v}_t^i = \ln q_i(t) - \ln q_i(t-1) - \bar{v}_K^i[\ln p_K^i(t) - \ln p_K^i(t-1)]$$

$$- \bar{v}_L^i[\ln p_L^i(t) - \ln p_L^i(t-1)] - \bar{v}_E^i[\ln p_E^i(t) - \ln p_E^i(t-1)]$$

$$- \bar{v}_M^i[\ln p_M^i(t) - \ln p_M^i(t-1)] \qquad (i=1,2,\dots,I) \qquad (2.6)$$

where

$$\bar{v}_t^i = \tfrac{1}{2}[v_t^i(t) + v_t^i(t-1)] \qquad (i=1,2,\dots,I)$$

and the average value shares in the two periods are given by

$$\bar{v}_K^i = \tfrac{1}{2}[v_K^i(t) + v_K^i(t-1)]$$

$$\bar{v}_L^i = \tfrac{1}{2}[v_L^i(t) + v_L^i(t-1)]$$

$$\bar{v}_E^i = \tfrac{1}{2}[v_E^i(t) + v_E^i(t-1)]$$

$$\bar{v}_M^i = \tfrac{1}{2}[v_M^i(t) + v_M^i(t-1)] \qquad (i=1,2,\dots,I)$$

We refer to the expressions for the average rates of technical change $\{\bar{v}_t^i\}$ as the *translog price indexes of the sectoral rates of technical change.*

Our model of producer behavior is based on two-stage allocation. In the first stage the value of sectoral output is allocated among sectoral capital, labor, energy, and materials inputs. In the second stage the value of each of the four inputs is allocated among individual types of that input. We have characterized the behavior of the ith industry $(i=1,2,\dots,I)$ in terms of the price function that underlies the two-stage allocation process. In addition to homogeneity, monotonicity, and concavity, this price function has the property of homothetic separability in prices of individual types of capital, labor, energy, and materials inputs.

We can regard each of the input prices $\{p_K^i, p_L^i, p_E^i, p_M^i\}$ as a function of its components. These functions must be homogeneous of degree one, nondecreasing, and concave in the prices of the individual inputs. We can consider specific forms for price indexes of each of the four inputs as functions of the individual types of that input. If each of these prices is a translog function of its components, we can express the differences between successive logarithms of the prices as a weighted average of differences between successive logarithms of prices of individual types of that input with weights given by the average value shares. We can refer to the resulting expressions as *translog indexes of the prices of capital, labor, energy, and materials inputs.*[10]

2.2   Integrability

Our next step in representing our models of producer behavior is to employ the implications of the theory of production in specifying econometric models of technical change and the distribution of the value of output. If a system of equations, consisting of sectoral value shares and the rate of technical change, can be generated from a sectoral price function, we say that the system is *integrable.* A complete set of conditions for integrability expressed in terms of the system of equations is the following:

1. *Homogeneity.* The sectoral value shares and the rate of technical change are homogeneous of degree zero in the input prices.

We can write the sectoral value shares and the rate of technical change in the form

$$v_i = \alpha_p^i + \beta_{pp}^i \ln p_i + \beta_{pt}^i \cdot t$$
$$-v_t^i = \alpha_t^i + \beta_{pt}^{i\prime} \ln p_i + \beta_{tt}^i \cdot t \qquad (i=1,2,\ldots,I) \qquad (2.7)$$

where the parameters $\{\alpha_p^i, \alpha_t^i, \beta_{pp}^i, \beta_{pt}^i, \beta_{tt}^i\}$ are constant. Homogeneity implies that these parameters must satisfy

$$\beta_{pp}^i \iota = 0$$
$$\beta_{pt}^{i\prime} \iota = 0 \qquad (i=1,2,\ldots,I) \qquad (2.8)$$

For four sectoral inputs there are five restrictions implied by homogeneity.

2. *Product exhaustion.* The sum of the sectoral value shares is equal to unity:

$$v_i' \iota = 1 \qquad (i=1,2,\ldots,I)$$

Product exhaustion implies that the value of the four sectoral inputs exhausts the value of the product. Product exhaustion implies that the parameters must satisfy the restrictions:

$$\alpha_p^{i\prime}\iota=1$$

$$\beta_{pp}^{i\prime}\iota=0$$

$$\beta_{pt}^{i\prime}\iota=0 \qquad (i=1,2,\ldots,I) \tag{2.9}$$

For four sectoral inputs there are six restrictions implied by product exhaustion.

3. *Symmetry*. The matrix of share elasticities and biases and rate of change of technical change must be symmetric.

Imposing homogeneity and product exhaustion restrictions we can write the system of sectoral value shares and the rate of technical change without imposing symmetry in the form

$$v_i=\alpha_p^i+\beta_{pp}^i\ln p_i+\beta_{pt}^i\cdot t$$

$$-v_t^i=\alpha_t^i+\beta_{tp}^{i\prime}\ln p_i+\beta_{tt}^{i\prime}\cdot t \qquad (i=1,2,\ldots,I) \tag{2.10}$$

A necessary and sufficient condition for symmetry is that the matrix of parameters must satisfy the restrictions

$$\begin{bmatrix} \beta_{pp}^i & \beta_{pt}^i \\ \beta_{tp}^{i\prime} & \beta_{tt}^i \end{bmatrix} = \begin{bmatrix} \beta_{pp}^i & \beta_{pt}^i \\ \beta_{pt}^{i\prime} & \beta_{tt}^i \end{bmatrix}' \tag{2.11}$$

For four sectoral inputs the total number of symmetry restrictions is 10.

4. *Nonnegativity*. The sectoral value shares must be nonnegative:

$$v_i\geqq 0 \qquad (i=1,2,\ldots,I)$$

By product exhaustion the sectoral value shares sum to unity, so that we can write

$$v_i\geqslant 0 \qquad (i=1,2,\ldots,I)$$

where $v_i\geqslant 0$ implies $v_i\geqq 0$ and $v_i\neq 0$.

Nonnegativity of the sectoral value shares is implied by monotonicity of the sectoral price functions:

$$\frac{\partial \ln q_i}{\partial \ln p_i}\geqq 0 \qquad (i=1,2,\ldots,I)$$

For the translog price function the conditions for monotonicity take the form

$$\frac{\partial \ln q_i}{\partial \ln p_i}=\alpha_p^i+\beta_{pp}^i\ln p_i+\beta_{pt}^i\cdot t\geqq 0 \qquad (i=1,2,\ldots,I) \tag{2.12}$$

Since the translog price functions are quadratic in the logarithms of sectoral input prices $\ln p_i$ $(i=1,2,\ldots,I)$, we can always choose prices so that the monotonicity of the sectoral price functions is violated. Accordingly, we cannot impose restrictions on the parameters of the translog price functions that would imply nonnegativity of the sectoral value shares for all prices and time. Instead we consider restrictions on the parameters that imply concavity of the sectoral price functions or monotonicity of the sectoral value shares for all nonnegative value shares.

5. *Monotonicity.* The matrix of share elasticities must be nonpositive-definite.

Concavity of the sectoral price functions implies that the matrices of second-order partial derivatives, say $\{H_i\}$, are nonpositive-definite,[11] so that the matrices $\{\beta_{pp}^i + v_i v_i' - V_i\}$ are nonpositive-definite:[12]

$$\frac{1}{q_i} \cdot N_i \cdot H_i \cdot N_i = \beta_{pp}^i + v_i v_i' - V_i \qquad (i = 1, 2, \ldots, I) \qquad (2.13)$$

where the sectoral price functions are positive and

$$N_i = \begin{bmatrix} p_K^i & 0 & 0 & 0 \\ 0 & p_L^i & 0 & 0 \\ 0 & 0 & p_E^i & 0 \\ 0 & 0 & 0 & p_M^i \end{bmatrix}, \quad V_i = \begin{bmatrix} v_K^i & 0 & 0 & 0 \\ 0 & v_L^i & 0 & 0 \\ 0 & 0 & v_E^i & 0 \\ 0 & 0 & 0 & v_M^i \end{bmatrix} \qquad (i = 1, 2, \ldots, I)$$

and $\{\beta_{pp}^i\}$ are matrices of constant share elasticities as defined above.

Without violating the product exhaustion and nonnegativity restrictions on the sectoral value shares we can set the matrices $\{v_i v_i' - V_i\}$ equal to zero, for example, by choosing one of the value shares to be equal to unity and the other value shares equal to zero. Necessary conditions for the matrices $\{\beta_{pp}^i + v_i v_i' - V_i\}$ to be nonpositive-definite are that the matrices of constant share elasticities $\{\beta_{pp}^i\}$ must be nonpositive-definite. These conditions are also sufficient, since the matrices $\{v_i v_i' - V_i\}$ are nonpositive-definite for all nonnegative value shares summing to unity and the sum of two nonpositive-definite matrices is nonpositive-definite.

To impose concavity in the translog price functions the matrices of constant shares elasticities $\{\beta_{pp}^i\}$ can be represented in terms of their Cholesky factorizations:

$$\beta_{pp}^i = T_i D_i T_i' \qquad (i = 1, 2, \ldots, I)$$

where $\{T_i\}$ are unit lower triangular matrices and $\{D_i\}$ are diagonal matrices. For four inputs we can write the matrices $\{\beta_{pp}^i\}$ in terms of their Cholesky factorizations as follows:

$\beta_{pp}^i =$

$$
\begin{bmatrix}
\delta_1^i & \lambda_{21}^i \delta_1^i & \lambda_{31}^i \delta_1^i & \lambda_{41}^i \delta_1^i \\
\lambda_{21}^i \delta_1^i & \lambda_{21}^i \lambda_{21}^i \delta_1^i + \delta_2^i & \lambda_{21}^i \lambda_{31}^i \delta_1^i + \lambda_{32}^i \delta_2^i & \lambda_{41}^i \lambda_{21}^i \delta_1^i + \lambda_{42}^i \delta_2^i \\
\lambda_{31}^i \delta_1^i & \lambda_{31}^i \lambda_{21}^i \delta_1^i + \lambda_{32}^i \delta_2^i & \lambda_{31}^i \lambda_{31}^i \delta_1^i + \lambda_{32}^i \lambda_{32}^i \delta_2^i + \delta_3^i & \lambda_{41}^i \lambda_{31}^i \delta_1^i + \lambda_{42}^i \lambda_{32}^i \delta_2^i + \lambda_{43}^i \delta_3^i \\
\lambda_{41}^i \delta_1^i & \lambda_{41}^i \lambda_{21}^i \delta_1^i + \lambda_{42}^i \delta_2^i & \lambda_{41}^i \lambda_{31}^i \delta_1^i + \lambda_{42}^i \lambda_{32}^i \delta_2^i + \lambda_{43}^i \delta_3^i & \lambda_{41}^i \lambda_{41}^i \delta_1^i + \lambda_{42}^i \lambda_{42}^i \delta_2^i + \lambda_{43}^i \lambda_{43}^i \delta_3^i + \delta_4^i
\end{bmatrix}
$$

$$(i=1,2,\ldots,I)$$

where

$$
T_i = \begin{bmatrix}
1 & 0 & 0 & 0 \\
\lambda_{21}^i & 1 & 0 & 0 \\
\lambda_{31}^i & \lambda_{32}^i & 1 & 0 \\
\lambda_{41}^i & \lambda_{42}^i & \lambda_{43}^i & 1
\end{bmatrix}, \quad
D_i = \begin{bmatrix}
\delta_1^i & 0 & 0 & 0 \\
0 & \delta_2^i & 0 & 0 \\
0 & 0 & \delta_3^i & 0 \\
0 & 0 & 0 & \delta_4^i
\end{bmatrix} \quad (i=1,2,\ldots,I)
$$

The matrices of constant share elasticities $\{\beta_{pp}^i\}$ must satisfy symmetry restrictions and restrictions implied by product exhaustion. These restrictions imply that the parameters of the Cholesky factorizations must satisfy the following conditions:

$$1 + \lambda_{21}^i + \lambda_{31}^i + \lambda_{41}^i = 0$$

$$1 + \lambda_{32}^i + \lambda_{42}^i = 0$$

$$1 + \lambda_{43}^i = 0$$

$$\delta_4^i = 0 \quad (i=1,2,\ldots,I)$$

Under these conditions there is a one-to-one transformation between the matrices of constant share elasticities $\{\beta_{pp}^i\}$ and the parameters of the Cholesky factorizations $\{T_i, D_i\}$. The matrices of share elasticities are nonpositive-definite if and only if the diagonal elements of the matrices $\{D_i\}$, the so-called Cholesky values, are nonpositive.

Similarly, we can provide a complete set of conditions for integrability of the systems of sectoral value shares for individual inputs for the second stage of the two-stage allocation process. For example, the sectoral value shares for individual capital inputs are homogeneous of degree zero in the prices of these inputs, the sum of the sectoral value shares is equal to unity, and the matrix of share elasticities with respect to prices of individual capital inputs must be symmetric. These conditions can be used to generate restrictions on the parameters of the translog price indexes for capital input. The restrictions are analogous to those for the first stage of the two-stage allocation process, except that restrictions on the equation for the rate of technical change are omitted.

The sectoral value shares for individual capital inputs must be non-negative; as before, we cannot impose conditions on the parameters of the translog price indexes for capital input that would imply nonnegativity of the sectoral value shares for all prices and time. Instead we can consider restrictions on the parameters that imply concavity of the sectoral price functions for capital input for all nonnegative value shares. These restrictions are precisely analogous to those for concavity of the sectoral price functions. These restrictions can be imposed by representing the matrices of constant share elasticities in terms of their Cholesky factorizations and requiring that the corresponding Cholesky values are nonpositive. Similar restrictions can be imposed on the parameters of translog price functions for labor, energy, and materials inputs.

2.3   Stochastic specifications

Our models of producer behavior are generated from translog price functions for each industrial sector. To formulate an econometric model of production and technical change we add a stochastic component to the equations for the value shares and the rate of technical change. We associate this component with unobservable random disturbances at the level of the individual industry. The industry maximizes profits for given prices of inputs, but the value shares of inputs are chosen with a random disturbance. This disturbance may result from errors in implementation of production plans, random elements in sectoral technologies not reflected in the models of producer behavior, or errors of measurement in the value shares. We assume that each of the equations for the value shares and the rate of technical change have two additive components.[13] The first is a nonrandom function of the prices of capital, labor, energy, and materials inputs and time; the second is an unobservable random disturbance that is functionally independent of these variables.

To represent an econometric model of production and technical change we require some additional notation. We consider observations on expenditure patterns by I industries, indexed by $i = 1, 2, \ldots, I$, for T time periods, indexed by $t = 1, 2, \ldots, T$. The vector of value shares of the ith industry in the tth time period is denoted v_{it} $(i = 1, 2, \ldots, I;$ $t = 1, 2, \ldots, T)$. Similarly, the rate of technical change of the ith industry in the tth time period is denoted v_{it}^t $(i = 1, 2, \ldots, I; t = 1, 2, \ldots, T)$. The vector of price indexes for capital, labor, energy, and materials inputs for the ith industry in the tth time period is denoted p_{it} $(i = 1, 2, \ldots, I;$ $t = 1, 2, \ldots, T)$. Similarly, the vector of logarithms of input price indexes is denoted $\ln p_{it}$ $(i = 1, 2, \ldots, I; t =, 2, \ldots, T)$. As before, time as an index of technology is denoted by t.

We obtain econometric models of production and technical change corresponding to translog price functions by adding random disturbances to the equations for the value shares and the rate of technical change in each industry:

$$v_{it} = \alpha_p^i + \beta_{pp}^i \ln p_{it} + \beta_{pt}^i \cdot t + \epsilon_{it}$$

$$-v_{it}^t = \alpha_t^i + \beta_{pt}^{it} \ln p_{it} + \beta_{tt}^i \cdot t + \epsilon_{it}^t \qquad (i=1,2,\ldots,I; \ t=1,2,\ldots,T) \quad (2.14)$$

where $\{\epsilon_{it}\}$ is the vector of unobservable random disturbances for the value shares of the ith industry and the tth time period and $\{\epsilon_{it}^t\}$ is the corresponding disturbance for the rate of technical change. Since the value shares for all inputs sum to unity for each industry in each time period, the random disturbances corresponding to the four value shares sum to zero in each time period:

$$\iota' \epsilon_{it} = 0 \qquad (i=1,2,\ldots,I; \ t=1,2,\ldots,T) \quad (2.15)$$

so that these disturbances are not distributed independently.

We assume that the unobservable random disturbances for all five equations have expected value equal to zero for all observations:

$$E\begin{pmatrix} \epsilon_{it} \\ \epsilon_{it}^t \end{pmatrix} = 0 \qquad (i=1,2,\ldots,I; \ t=1,2,\ldots,T) \quad (2.16)$$

We also assume that these disturbances have a covariance matrix that is the same for all observations; since the random disturbances corresponding to the four value shares sum to zero, this matrix is nonnegative-definite with rank at most equal to 4. We assume that the covariance matrix of the random disturbances, say $\{\Sigma^i\}$, for instance, has rank 4, where

$$V\begin{pmatrix} \epsilon_{it} \\ \epsilon_{it}^t \end{pmatrix} = \Sigma^i \qquad (i=1,2,\ldots,I; \ t=1,2,\ldots,T)$$

Finally, we assume that the random disturbances corresponding to distinct observations in the same or distinct equations are uncorrelated. Under this assumption the covariance matrix of random disturbances for all observations has the Kronecker product form

$$V\begin{bmatrix} \epsilon_{K1}^i \\ \epsilon_{K2}^i \\ \vdots \\ \epsilon_{KT}^i \\ \epsilon_{L1}^i \\ \vdots \\ \epsilon_{iT}^t \end{bmatrix} = \Sigma^i \otimes I \qquad (i=1,2,\ldots,I; \ t=1,2,\ldots,T) \quad (2.17)$$

The sectoral rates of technical change $\{v_{it}^l\}$ are not directly observable; however, the equation for the translog price indexes of the sectoral rates of technical change can be written

$$-\bar{v}_{it}^l = \alpha_t^i + \beta_{pt}^{i\prime}\,\overline{\ln p_{it}} + \beta_{tt}^i \cdot \bar{t} + \bar{\epsilon}_{tt}^l$$

$$(i=1,2,\ldots,I;\ t=2,3,\ldots,T) \qquad (2.18)$$

where $\bar{\epsilon}_{it}^l$ is the average disturbance in the two periods:

$$\bar{\epsilon}_{it}^l = \tfrac{1}{2}[\epsilon_{it}^l + \epsilon_{i,t-1}^l] \qquad (i=1,2,\ldots,I;\ t=2,3,\ldots,T)$$

Similarly, $\overline{\ln p_{it}}$ is a vector of averages of the logarithms of the prices of the four inputs and $\bar{t}$ is the average of time as an index of technology in the two periods.

Using our new notation, the equations for the value shares of capital, labor, energy, and materials inputs can be written

$$\bar{v}_{it} = \alpha_p^i + \beta_{pp}^i\,\overline{\ln p_{it}} + \beta_{pt}^i \cdot \bar{t} + \bar{\epsilon}_{it} \qquad (i=1,2,\ldots,I;\ t=2,3,\ldots,T) \quad (2.19)$$

where $\bar{\epsilon}_{it}$ is a vector of averages of the disturbances in the two periods. As before, the average value shares sum to unity, so that the average disturbances for the equations corresponding to value shares sum to zero:

$$\iota'\bar{\epsilon}_{it}=0 \qquad (i=1,2,\ldots,I;\ t=2,3,\ldots,T) \qquad (2.20)$$

The covariance matrix of the average disturbances corresponding to the equation for the rate of technical change for all observations, say Ω, is proportional to a Laurent matrix:

$$V\begin{pmatrix} \bar{\epsilon}_{t2}^i \\ \bar{\epsilon}_{t3}^i \\ \vdots \\ \bar{\epsilon}_{tT}^i \end{pmatrix} \sim \Omega \qquad (i=1,2,\ldots,I) \qquad (2.21)$$

where

$$\Omega = \begin{bmatrix} \tfrac{1}{2} & \tfrac{1}{4} & 0 & \cdots & 0 \\ \tfrac{1}{4} & \tfrac{1}{2} & \tfrac{1}{4} & \cdots & 0 \\ 0 & \tfrac{1}{4} & \tfrac{1}{2} & \cdots & 0 \\ \vdots & \vdots & \vdots & & \vdots \\ 0 & 0 & 0 & \cdots & \tfrac{1}{2} \end{bmatrix}$$

The covariance matrix of the average disturbance corresponding to each equation for the four value shares is the same, so that the covariance matrix of the average disturbances for all observations has the Kronecker product form

$$
V \begin{pmatrix} \bar{\epsilon}^i_{K2} \\ \bar{\epsilon}^i_{K3} \\ \vdots \\ \bar{\epsilon}^i_{KT} \\ \bar{\epsilon}^i_{L2} \\ \vdots \\ \bar{\epsilon}^i_{tT} \end{pmatrix} = \Sigma^i \otimes \Omega \qquad (i=1,2,\ldots,I) \qquad (2.22)
$$

Although disturbances in equations for the average rate of technical change and the average value shares are autocorrelated, the data can be transformed to eliminate the autocorrelation. The matrix Ω is positive-definite, so that there is a matrix P such that

$$P\Omega P' = I$$

$$P'P = \Omega^{-1}$$

To construct the matrix P we can first invert the matrix Ω to obtain the inverse matrix Ω^{-1}, a positive-definite matrix. We then calculate the Cholesky factorization of the inverse matrix Ω^{-1},

$$\Omega^{-1} = TDT'$$

where T is a unit lower triangular matrix and D is a diagonal matrix with positive elements along the main diagonal. Finally, we can write the matrix P in the form

$$P = D^{1/2}T'$$

where $D^{1/2}$ is a diagonal matrix with elements along the main diagonal equal to the square roots of the corresponding elements of D.

We can transform equations for the average rates of technical change by the matrix $P = D^{1/2}T'$ to obtain equations with uncorrelated random disturbances[14]

$$
D^{1/2}T' \begin{pmatrix} \bar{v}^i_{t2} \\ \bar{v}^i_{t3} \\ \vdots \\ \bar{v}^i_{tT} \end{pmatrix} = D^{1/2}T' \begin{pmatrix} 1 & \overline{\ln p^i_{K2}} & \cdots & 2-\frac{1}{2} \\ 1 & \ln p^i_{K3} & \cdots & 3-\frac{1}{2} \\ \vdots & \vdots & & \vdots \\ 1 & \ln p^i_{KT} & \cdots & T-\frac{1}{2} \end{pmatrix} \begin{pmatrix} \alpha^i_t \\ \beta^i_{Kt} \\ \vdots \\ \beta^i_{tt} \end{pmatrix} + D^{1/2}T' \begin{pmatrix} \bar{\epsilon}^i_{t2} \\ \bar{\epsilon}^i_{t3} \\ \vdots \\ \bar{\epsilon}^i_{tT} \end{pmatrix}
$$

$$(i=1,2,\ldots,I) \qquad (2.23)$$

since

$$P\Omega P' = (D^{1/2}T')\Omega(D^{1/2}T')' = I$$

The transformation $P = D^{1/2} T'$ is applied to data on the average rates of technical change $\{ \bar{v}_i^j \}$ and data on the average values of the variables that appear on the right-hand side of the corresponding equation.

We can apply the transformation $P = D^{1/2} T'$ to the equations for average value shares to obtain equations with uncorrelated disturbances. As before, the transformation is applied to data on the average value shares and the average values of variables that appear in the corresponding equations. The covariance matrix of the transformed disturbances from the equations for the average value shares and the equation for the average rate of technical change has the Kronecker product form

$$(I \otimes D^{1/2} T')(\Sigma^i \otimes \Omega)(I \otimes D^{1/2} T')' = \Sigma^i \otimes I \qquad (i = 1, 2, \ldots, I) \qquad (2.24)$$

To estimate the unknown parameters of the translog price function we combine the first three equations for the average value shares with the equation for the average rate of technical change to obtain a complete econometric model of production and technical change. We estimate the parameters of the equations for the remaining average value share, using the restrictions on these parameters given above. The complete model involves 14 unknown parameters. A total of 16 additional parameters can be estimated as functions of these parameters, given the restrictions. Our estimate of the unknown parameters of the econometric model of production and technical change is based on the nonlinear three-stage least squares estimator introduced by Jorgenson and Laffont (1974).

2.4 Summary and conclusion

In this section we have presented a model of producer behavior based on transcendental-logarithmic or translog price functions for all industrial sectors. These price functions incorporate restrictions on producer behavior that result from maximization of profit subject to a production function. Our model of producer behavior is based on a two-stage allocation process. For each stage of the allocation process the behavior of the industry is generated by sectoral price functions that are homogeneous of degree one, nondecreasing, and concave in prices.

For all industrial sectors we have employed conditions for producer equilibrium under perfect competition. We have assumed constant returns to scale at the industry level. Finally, we have employed a description of technology that leads to myopic decision rules. To incorporate differences in technology among industrial sectors into our model of producer behavior, we allow the parameters of the translog price functions to differ among sectors. Similarly, to permit differences in technology among time periods for a given sector, we introduce time as an index of technology into the sectoral price functions.

Given translog price functions for each industrial sector, we derive value shares of inputs and the rate of technical change for that sector by logarithmic differentiation. For the first stage of the two-stage allocation process this results in value shares for inputs and a rate of technical change that are linear in the logarithms of input prices and in time. Since the translog price functions for the second stage of the two-stage allocation process depend only on prices of individual inputs, the value shares for inputs are linear in the logarithms of input prices.

The value shares of inputs and the rate of technical change at the first stage of the two-stage allocation process are homogeneous of degree zero in input prices. For four sectoral inputs homogeneity implies five restrictions on the parameters of the translog price functions. Second, the sum of the sectoral value shares is equal to unity, so that the value of the four sectoral inputs exhausts the value of the product. Product exhaustion implies six restrictions on the parameters for four inputs. Third, the matrix of share elasticities and biases and the rate of change of technical change must be symmetric, implying 10 restrictions on the parameters.

Monotonicity of the sectoral price function implies that sectoral value shares must be nonnegative. Similarly, concavity of the price function implies that the matrix of share elasticities must be nonpositive-definite. Since it is always possible to choose prices so that monotonicity of the price function or nonnegativity of the value shares is violated, we consider restrictions that imply monotonicity of the value shares wherever they are nonnegative.

3   Consumer behavior

We now turn to models of aggregate consumer behavior. Before proceeding with the presentation, we first set down some notation. There are J consumers, indexed by $j = 1, 2, \ldots, J$. There are N commodity groups in the economy, indexed by $n = 1, 2, \ldots, N$; p_n is the price of the nth commodity group, assumed to be the same for all consumers. We denote by $p = (p_1, p_2, \ldots, p_N)$ the vector of prices of all commodity groups. The quantity of the nth commodity group demanded by the jth consumer is x_{nj} and total expenditure of the jth consumer is $Y_j = \sum_{n=1}^{N} p_n x_{nj}$. Finally, A_j is a vector of individual attributes of the jth consumer.[15]

We assume that the demand for the nth commodity group by the jth consumer x_{nj} can be expressed as a function f_{nj} of the price vector p, total expenditure Y_j, and the vector of attributes A_j:

$$x_{nj} = f_{nj}(p, Y_j, A_j) \tag{3.1}$$

Aggregate demand for the nth commodity group is given by

$$\sum_{j=1}^{J} x_{nj} = \sum_{j=1}^{J} f_{nj}(p, Y_j, A_j)$$

In models of consumer behavior based on aggregate quantities consumed, the aggregate demand function depends on the price vector p, aggregate expenditure $\sum_{j=1}^{J} Y_j$, and possibly some index of aggregate attributes, say $\sum_{j=1}^{J} A_j$. Thus, we may write

$$\sum_{j=1}^{J} f_j(p, Y_j, A_j) = F\left(p, \sum_{j=1}^{J} Y_j, \sum_{j=1}^{J} A_j\right) \qquad (3.2)$$

where f_j is a vector-valued individual demand function:

$$f_j = \begin{bmatrix} f_{1j} \\ f_{2j} \\ \vdots \\ f_{Nj} \end{bmatrix} \qquad (j=1,2,\ldots,J)$$

giving the vector of demands for all N commodities by the jth consumer, and F is a vector-valued aggregate demand function, giving the vector of demands for all N commodities by all J consumers.

The conditions under which Equation (3.2) holds for all expenditures $\{Y_j\}$, all prices, and all possible attributes have been derived by Gorman (1953) under the assumption of utility maximization by individual consumers. Gorman's conditions imply

1. $f_j(p, Y_j, A_j) = h_1(p)Y_j + h_2(p)A_j + C_j(p) \qquad (j=1,2,\ldots,J)$

2. $F\left(p, \sum_{j=1}^{J} Y_j, \sum_{j=1}^{J} A_j\right) = h_1(p) \sum_{j=1}^{J} Y_j + h_2(p) \sum_{j=1}^{J} A_j + \sum_{j=1}^{J} C_j(p)$

where the vector-valued function $h_1(p)$ is homogeneous of degree -1 and the vector-valued functions $\{h_2(p), C_j(p)\}$ are homogeneous of degree 0. In other words, the individual demand functions are linear in expenditure and attributes. They are identical up to the addition of a function that is independent of expenditure and attributes. Furthermore, if aggregate demands are equal to zero when aggregate expenditure is equal to zero, individuals must have identical homothetic preferences.[16]

Homothetic preferences are inconsistent with well-established empirical regularities in the behavior of individual consumers, such as Engel's law, which states that the proportion of expenditure devoted to food is a decreasing function of total expenditure.[17] Identical preferences for individual households are inconsistent with empirical findings that expenditure patterns depend on demographic characteristics of individual households.[18] Even the weaker form of Gorman's results, that quantities consumed are linear functions of expenditure with identical slopes for all individuals, is inconsistent with empirical evidence from budget studies.[19]

Despite the conflict between Gorman's characterization of individual consumer behavior and the empirical evidence from cross-section data, this characterization has provided an important stimulus to empirical research based on aggregate time series data. The linear expenditure system, proposed by Klein and Rubin (1947) and implemented by Stone (1954a), has the property that individual demand functions are linear in total expenditure. The resulting system of aggregate demand functions has been used widely as the basis for econometric models of aggregate consumer behavior. Generalizations of the linear expenditure system that retain the critical property of linearity of individual demand functions in total expenditure have also been employed in empirical research.[20]

Muellbauer (1975, 1976a, 1976b) has substantially generalized Gorman's characterization of the representative consumer model. Aggregate expenditure shares, interpreted as the expenditure shares of a representative consumer, may depend on prices and on a function of individual expenditure not restricted to aggregate or per capita expenditure. In Muellbauer's model of the representative consumer, individual preferences are identical but not necessarily homothetic. Furthermore, quantities consumed may be nonlinear functions of expenditure rather than linear functions, as in Gorman's characterization. An important consequence of this nonlinearity is that aggregate demand functions depend on the distribution of expenditure among individuals. Berndt, Darrough, and Diewert (1977) and Deaton and Muellbauer (1980a, 1980b) have implemented aggregate models of consumer behavior that conform to Muellbauer's characterization of the representative consumer model, retaining the assumption that preferences are identical among individuals.

Lau (1977b, 1982) has developed a theory of exact aggregation that makes it possible to incorporate differences in individual preferences. We first generalize the concept of an aggregate demand function to that of a function that depends on general symmetric functions of individual expenditures and attributes:

$$\sum_{j=1}^{J} f_j(p, Y_j, A_j)$$

$$= F(p, g_1(Y_1, Y_2, \ldots, Y_J, A_1, A_2, \ldots, A_J),$$

$$g_2(Y_1, Y_2, \ldots, Y_J, A_1, A_2, \ldots, A_J), \ldots, g_I(Y_1, Y_2, \ldots, Y_J, A_1, A_2, \ldots, A_J))$$

$$(3.3)$$

where each function g_i $(i = 1, 2, \ldots, I)$ is symmetric in individual expenditures and attributes, so that the value of this function is independent of the ordering of the individuals. We refer to the functions $\{g_i\}$ as index functions. These functions can be interpreted as statistics describing the population. To avoid triviality we assume also that the functions $\{g_i\}$ are functionally independent.

The fundamental theorem of exact aggregation establishes conditions for Equation (3.3) to hold for all prices, individual expenditures, and individual attributes. These conditions are the following:

1. All the individual demand functions for the same commodity are identical up to the addition of a function independent of individual attributes and expenditure.
2. All the individual demand functions must be sums of products of separate functions of the prices and of the individual attributes and expenditure.
3. The aggregate demand functions depend on certain index functions of individual attributes and expenditures. The only admissible index functions are additive in functions of individual attributes and expenditures.
4. The aggregate demand functions can be written as linear functions of the index functions.[21]

Specializations of the fundamental theorem of exact aggregation have appeared earlier in the literature. For example, if there is only one index function and we take $g_1 = \sum_{j=1}^{J} Y_j$, aggregate expenditure for the economy, then this theorem implies that for given prices, all consumers must have parallel linear Engel curves. Restricting demands to be nonnegative for all prices and expenditures implies that for given prices, all consumers have identical linear Engel curves. These are the results of Gorman (1953). Muellbauer's condition for the existence of a representative consumer,

$$\sum_{j=1}^{J} f_{nj}(p, Y_j) = F_n(g_2(Y_1, Y_2, \ldots, Y_J), p)\left(\sum_{j=1}^{J} Y_j\right) \quad (n = 1, 2, \ldots, N)$$

can be viewed as a special case of Equation (3.3) with the number of indexes I equal to 2 and the first index function $g_1(Y_1, Y_2, \ldots, Y_j) = \sum_{j=1}^{J} Y_j$ equal to aggregate expenditure. The representative consumer interpretation fails for the case of more than two index functions.

3.1 *Translog model of consumer behavior*

We next present individual and aggregate models of consumer behavior based on the theory of exact aggregation. The theory of exact aggregation requires that the individual demand functions must be linear in a number of functions of individual attributes and expenditure. Representing aggregate demand functions as the sum of individual demand functions, we find that the aggregate demand functions depend on the distribution of expenditure among individuals as well as the level of per capita expenditure and prices. The aggregate demand functions also depend on the joint distribution of expenditures and demographic characteristics among individuals.

In our model of consumer behavior the individual consuming units are households. We assume that household expenditures on commodity groups are allocated so as to maximize a household welfare function. As a consequence, the household behaves in the same way as an individual maximizing a utility function.[22] We require that the individual demand functions are integrable, so that these demand functions can be generated by Roy's (1943) identity from an indirect utility function for each consuming unit.[23] We assume that these indirect utility functions are homogeneous of degree zero in prices and expenditure, nonincreasing in prices and nondecreasing in expenditure, and quasi-convex in prices and expenditure.

To allow for differences in preferences among consuming units, we allow the indirect utility functions for the jth unit to depend on a vector of attributes A_j; each attribute is represented by a dummy variable equal to unity when the consuming unit has the corresponding characteristic and zero otherwise. In our model of consumer behavior there are several groups of attributes. Each consuming unit is assigned one of the attributes in each of the groups.

To represent our model of consumer behavior we require the following additional notation:

$w_{nj} = p_n x_{nj}/Y_j$: Expenditure shares of the nth commodity group in the budget of the jth consuming unit $(j=1,2,\ldots,J)$

$w_j = (w_{1j}, w_{2j}, \ldots, w_{Nj})$: Vector of expenditure shares for the jth consuming unit $(j=1,2,\ldots,J)$

$\ln(p/Y_j) = (\ln(p_1/Y_j), \ln(p_2/Y_j), \ldots, \ln(p_N/Y_j))$: Vector of logarithms of ratios of prices to expenditure by the jth consuming unit $(j=1,2,\ldots,J)$

$\ln p = (\ln p_1, \ln p_2, \ldots, \ln p_N)$: Vector of logarithms of prices

We assume that the jth consuming unit allocates its expenditures in accord with the transcendental logarithmic or translog indirect utility function,[24] say U_j, where

$$\ln U_j = G(A_j) + \ln\left(\frac{p}{Y_j}\right)' \alpha_p + \frac{1}{2} \ln\left(\frac{p}{Y_j}\right)' \beta_{pp} \ln \frac{p}{Y_j}$$

$$+ \ln\left(\frac{p}{Y_j}\right)' \beta_{pA} A_j \quad (j=1,2,\ldots,J) \tag{3.4}$$

In this representation the function G depends on the attribute vector A_j but is independent of the prices p and expenditure Y_j. The vector α_p and the matrices β_{pp} and β_{pA} are constant parameters that are the same for all consuming units.

The expenditure shares of the jth consuming unit can be derived by the logarithmic form of Roy's identity:

$$w_{nj} = \frac{\partial \ln U_j}{\partial \ln(p_n/Y_j)}$$

$$\div \sum \frac{\partial \ln U_j}{\partial \ln(p_n/Y_j)} \qquad (n=1,2,\dots,N;\ j=1,2,\dots,J) \qquad (3.5)$$

Applying this identity to the translog indirect utility function, we obtain the system of individual expenditure shares:

$$w_j = \frac{1}{B_j}\left(\alpha_p + \beta_{pp}\ln\frac{p}{Y_j} + \beta_{pA}A_j\right) \qquad (j=1,2,\dots,J) \qquad (3.6)$$

where the denominators $\{B_j\}$ take the form

$$B_j = \iota'\alpha_p + \iota'\beta_{pp}\ln\frac{p}{Y_j} + \iota'\beta_{pA}A_j \qquad (j=1,2,\dots,J) \qquad (3.7)$$

and ι is a vector of ones.

We first observe that the function G that appears in the translog indirect utility function does not enter into the determination of the individual expenditure shares. This function is not identifiable from observed patterns of individual expenditure allocation. Second, since the individual expenditure shares can be expressed as ratios of functions that are homogeneous and linear in the unknown parameters – $(\alpha_p, \beta_{pp}, \beta_{pA})$, these shares are homogeneous of degree zero in the parameters. By multiplying a given set of the unknown parameters by a constant we obtain another set of parameters that generates the same system of individual budget shares. Accordingly, we can choose a normalization for the parameters without affecting observed patterns of individual expenditure allocation. We find it convenient to employ the normalization

$$\iota'\alpha_p = -1$$

Under this restriction any change in the set of unknown parameters will be reflected in changes in individual expenditure patterns.

The conditions for exact aggregation are that the individual expenditure shares are linear in functions of the attributes $\{A_j\}$ and total expenditures $\{Y_j\}$ for all consuming units.[25] These conditions will be satisfied if and only if the terms involving the attributes and expenditures do not appear in the denominators of the expressions given above for the individual expenditure shares, so that

$$\iota'\beta_{pp}\iota = 0$$

$$\iota'\beta_{pA} = 0$$

These restrictions imply that the denominators $\{B_j\}$ reduce to

$$B = -1 + \iota'\beta_{pp}\ln p$$

where the subscript j is no longer required, since the denominator is the same for all consuming units. Under these restrictions the individual expenditure shares can be written

$$w_j = \frac{1}{B}(\alpha_p + \beta_{pp}\ln p - \beta_{pp}\iota \cdot \ln Y_j + \beta_{pA}A_j) \qquad (j = 1, 2, \ldots, J) \qquad (3.8)$$

The individual expenditure shares are linear in the logarithms of expenditures $\{\ln Y_j\}$ and the attributes $\{A_j\}$, as required by exact aggregation.

Aggregate expenditure shares, say w, are obtained by multiplying individual expenditure shares by expenditure for each consuming unit, adding over all consuming units, and dividing by aggregate expenditure:

$$w = \frac{\sum Y_j w_j}{\sum Y_j} \tag{3.9}$$

The aggregate expenditure shares can be written

$$w = \frac{1}{B}\left(\alpha_p + \beta_{pp}\ln p - \beta_{pp}\iota\frac{\sum Y_j \ln Y_j}{\sum Y_j} + \beta_{pA}\frac{\sum Y_j A_j}{\sum Y_j}\right) \tag{3.10}$$

Aggregate expenditure shares depend on prices p. They also depend on the distribution of expenditures over all consuming units through the function $(\sum Y_j \ln Y_j)/\sum Y_j$, which may be regarded as a statistic of the distribution. This single statistic summarizes the impact of changes in the distribution of expenditures among individual consuming units on aggregate expenditure allocation. Finally, aggregate expenditure shares depend on the distribution of expenditures among demographic groups through the functions $\{\sum Y_j A_j / \sum Y_j\}$, which may be regarded as statistics of the joint distribution of expenditures and attributes. Since the attributes are represented as dummy variables, equal to one for a consuming unit with that characteristic and zero otherwise, these functions are equal to the shares of the corresponding demographic groups in aggregate expenditure. We conclude that aggregate expenditure patterns depend on the distribution of expenditure over all consuming units through the statistic $(\sum Y_j \ln Y_j)/\sum Y_j$ and the distribution among demographic groups through the statistics $\{\sum Y_j A_j / \sum Y_j\}$.

Our model of individual consumer behavior is based on two-stage allocation. In the first stage total expenditure is allocated among N commodity groups. In the second stage total expenditure on each commodity group is allocated among the individual commodities within each group.[26] We have characterized the behavior of the individual consumer in terms of properties of the indirect utility function. In addition to the properties of homogeneity, monotonicity, and quasi-convexity, the indirect utility function that underlies the two-stage allocation process is homothetically separable in prices of the individual commodities.

We can regard each of the prices of commodity groups $\{p_n\}$ as a function of the prices of individual commodities within the group. These functions must be homogeneous of degree one, nondecreasing, and concave in the prices of the individual commodities. We can consider specific forms for price indexes for each commodity group. If each of these prices is a translog function of its components, we can express the difference between successive logarithms of the price of each commodity group as a weighted average of the differences between successive logarithms of prices of individual commodities within the group with weights given by the average value shares. We refer to these expressions for the prices of the N commodity groups $\{p_n\}$ as *translog price indexes* for these groups.[27]

3.2   *Integrability*

Systems of individual expenditure shares for consuming units with identical demographic characteristics can be recovered in one and only one way from the system of aggregate expenditure shares under exact aggregation. This makes it possible to employ all the implications of the theory of individual consumer behavior in specifying an econometric model of aggregate expenditure allocation. If a system of individual expenditure shares can be generated from an indirect utility function by means of the logarithmic form of Roy's identity, we say that the system is *integrable*. A complete set of conditions for integrability, expressed in terms of the system of individual expenditure shares, is the following:

1. *Homogeneity*. The individual expenditure shares are homogeneous of degree zero in prices and expenditure.

We can write the individual expenditure shares in the form

$$w_j = \frac{1}{B}\left(\alpha_p + \beta_{pp}\ln p - \beta_{pY}\ln Y_j + \beta_{pA}A_j\right) \qquad (j=1,2,\ldots,J)$$

where the parameters $\{\beta_{pY}\}$ are constant and the same for all consuming units. Homogeneity implies that this vector must satisfy the restrictions

$$\beta_{pY} = \beta_{pp}\iota \tag{3.11}$$

Given the exact aggregation restriction, there are $N-1$ restrictions implied by homogeneity.

2. *Summability*. The sum of the individual expenditure shares over all commodity groups is equal to unity:

$$\sum w_{nj} = 1 \quad (j = 1, 2, \ldots, J)$$

We can write the denominator B in the form

$$B = -1 + \beta_{Yp} \ln p$$

where the parameters $\{\beta_{Yp}\}$ are constant and the same for all commodity groups and all consuming units. Summability implies that these parameters must satisfy the restrictions

$$\beta_{Yp} = \iota'\beta_{pp} \tag{3.12}$$

Given the exact aggregation restrictions, there are $N-1$ restrictions implied by summability.

3. *Symmetry*. The matrix of compensated own- and cross-price effects must be symmetric.

Imposing homogeneity and summability restrictions, we can write the individual expenditure shares in the form

$$w_j = \frac{1}{B}\left(\alpha_p + \beta_{pp} \ln \frac{p}{Y_j} + \beta_{pA} A_j\right) \quad (j = 1, 2, \ldots, J)$$

where the denominator B can be written

$$B = -1 + \iota'\beta_{pp} \ln p$$

The typical element of the matrix of uncompensated own- and cross-price effects takes the form

$$\frac{\partial x_{nj}}{\partial(p_m/Y_j)} = \frac{1}{(p_n/Y_j)(p_m/Y_j)}\left[\frac{1}{B}(\beta_{nm} - w_{nj}\beta_{Ym}) - \delta_{nm}w_{nj}\right]$$

$$(n, m = 1, 2, \ldots, N; \; j = 1, 2, \ldots, J)$$

where

$$\beta_{Ym} = \sum \beta_{nm} \quad (m = 1, 2, \ldots, N)$$

$$\delta_{nm} = 0 \quad \text{if} \quad n \neq m$$

$$= 1 \quad \text{if} \quad n = m \quad (n, m = 1, 2, \ldots, N)$$

The corresponding element of the matrix of compensated own- and cross-price effects takes the form

$$
\frac{\partial x_{nj}}{\partial (p_m/Y_j)} - x_{mj} \sum \frac{\partial x_{nj}}{\partial (p_l/Y_j)} \cdot \frac{p_l}{Y_j}
$$

$$
= \frac{1}{(p_n/Y_j)(p_m/Y_j)} \left[\frac{1}{B} (\beta_{nm} - w_{nj}\beta_{Ym}) - \delta_{nm} w_{nj} \right]
$$

$$
- x_{mj} \sum \frac{1}{(p_n/Y_j)(p_l/Y_j)} \left[\frac{1}{B} (\beta_{nl} - w_{nj}\beta_{Yl}) - \delta_{nl} w_{nj} \right] \frac{p_l}{Y_j}
$$

$$
(n, m = 1, 2, \ldots, N; \; j = 1, 2, \ldots, J)
$$

The full matrix of compensated own- and cross-price effects, say S_j, becomes

$$
S_j = P_j^{-1} \left[\frac{1}{B} (\beta_{pp} - w_j \iota' \beta_{pp} - \beta_{pp} \iota w_j' + w_j \iota' \beta_{pp} \iota w_j') + w_j w_j' - W_j \right] P_j^{-1}
$$

$$
(j = 1, 2, \ldots, J) \qquad (3.13)
$$

where

$$
P_j^{-1} = \begin{bmatrix} \dfrac{1}{p_1/Y_j} & 0 & \cdots & 0 \\ 0 & \dfrac{1}{p_2/Y_j} & \cdots & 0 \\ \vdots & \vdots & & \vdots \\ 0 & 0 & \cdots & \dfrac{1}{p_N/Y_j} \end{bmatrix}, \qquad W_j = \begin{bmatrix} w_{1j} & 0 & \cdots & 0 \\ 0 & w_{2j} & \cdots & 0 \\ \vdots & \vdots & & \vdots \\ 0 & 0 & \cdots & w_{Nj} \end{bmatrix}
$$

$$
(j = 1, 2, \ldots, J)
$$

The matrices $\{S_j\}$ must be symmetric for all consuming units.

If the system of individual expenditure shares is to be generated from a translog indirect utility function, a necessary and sufficient condition for symmetry is that the matrix β_{pp} must be symmetric. Without imposing the condition that this matrix is symmetric we can write the individual expenditure shares in the form

$$
w_j = \frac{1}{B} \left(\alpha_p + \beta_{pp} \ln \frac{p}{Y_j} + \beta_{pA} A_j \right) \qquad (j = 1, 2, \ldots, J)
$$

Symmetry implies that the matrix of parameters β_{pp} must satisfy the restrictions

$$\beta_{pp} = \beta'_{pp} \tag{3.14}$$

The total number of symmetry restrictions is $\frac{1}{2}N(N-1)$.

4. *Nonnegativity.* The individual expenditure shares must be nonnegative:

$$w_{nj} \geqq 0 \qquad (N=1,2,\ldots,N; \; j=1,2,\ldots,J)$$

By summability the individual expenditure shares sum to unity, so that we can write:

$$w_j \geqslant 0 \qquad (j=1,2,\ldots,J)$$

where $w_j \geqslant 0$ implies $w_{nj} \geqq 0$ $(n=1,2,\ldots,N)$ and $w_j \neq 0$.

Nonnegativity of the individual expenditure shares is implied by monotonicity of the indirect utility function:

$$\frac{\partial \ln U_j}{\partial \ln(p/Y_j)} \leqq 0 \qquad (j=1,2,\ldots,J)$$

For the translog indirect utility function the conditions for monotonicity take the form

$$\frac{\partial \ln U_j}{\partial \ln(p/Y_j)} = \alpha_p + \beta_{pp} \ln \frac{p}{Y_j} + \beta_{pA} A_j \leqq 0 \qquad (j=1,2,\ldots,J) \tag{3.15}$$

Summability implies that not all the expenditure shares are zero, so that

$$B = -1 + \iota'\beta_{pp} \ln p < 0 \tag{3.16}$$

Since the translog indirect utility function is quadratic in the logarithms of prices $\ln p$, we can always choose the prices so that the individual expenditure shares violate the nonnegativity conditions. Alternatively, we can say that it is possible to choose the prices so the monotonicity of the indirect utility function is violated. Accordingly, we cannot impose restrictions on the parameters of the translog indirect utility function that would imply nonnegativity of the individual expenditure shares or monotonicity of the indirect utility function for all prices and expenditure. Instead we consider restrictions on the parameters that imply quasi-convexity of the indirect utility function or monotonicity of the system of individual demand functions for all nonnegative expenditure shares.

5. *Monotonicity.* The matrix of compensated own- and cross-price effects must be nonpositive-definite.

We first impose homogeneity, summability, and symmetry restrictions on the expenditure shares. We restrict consideration to values of the prices p, expenditures $\{Y_j\}$, and attributes $\{A_j\}$ for which the individual expenditure shares satisfy the nonnegativity restrictions, so that $w_j \geq 0$ $(j = 1, 2, \ldots, J)$. The summability restrictions imply that $\iota'w_j = 1$ $(j = 1, 2, \ldots, J)$. We can write the matrix of price effects in the form

$$S_j = P_j^{-1} \left[\frac{1}{B} (I - \iota w_j')' \beta_{pp} (I - \iota w_j') + w_j w_j' - W_j \right] P_j^{-1} \qquad (j = 1, 2, \ldots, J)$$

A necessary and sufficient condition for monotonicity of the systems of individual expenditure shares is that the matrices

$$\left\{ \frac{1}{B} (I - \iota w_j') \beta_{pp} (I - \iota w_j') + w_j w_j' - W_j \right\}$$

are nonpositive-definite for all expenditure shares satisfying the nonnegativity and summability conditions.

We next consider restrictions on the parameters of the translog indirect utility function implied by monotonicity of the individual expenditure shares. If $\iota'\beta_{pp} = 0$, the denominator B is independent of prices and the translog indirect utility function is homothetic; otherwise, for a given value of the individual expenditure shares we can make the denominator B as large or as small as we wish by a suitable choice of prices p. A necessary and sufficient condition for monotonicity of the systems of individual expenditure shares is that the matrices

$$\left\{ \frac{1}{B} (I - \iota w')' \beta_{pp} (I - \iota w_j') \right\} \quad \text{and} \quad \{ w_j w_j' - W_j \}$$

are both nonpositive-definite.

The matrices $\{ w_j w_j' - W_j \}$ are nonpositive-definite for all expenditure shares satisfying the nonnegativity and summability restrictions. A sufficient condition for nonpositive definiteness of the matrices

$$\left\{ \frac{1}{B} (I - \iota w_j')' \beta_{pp} (I - \iota w_j') \right\}$$

is that the matrix β_{pp} is nonnegative-definite. However, if the quadratic form $z'\beta_{pp} z$ achieves the value zero, which must be a minimum, for any vector z not equal to zero, then z is a characteristic vector of β_{pp} corresponding to a zero characteristic value if β_{pp} is nonnegative-definite. Hence, $\beta_{pp}\iota = 0$ and the translog indirect utility function is homothetic.

Next, we introduce the definition due to Martos (1969) of a *merely positive-subdefinite matrix*. A merely positive-subdefinite matrix, say P, is a real symmetric matrix such that

$$x'Px < 0$$

implies $Px \geqslant 0$ or $Px \leqslant 0$ and P is not nonnegative-definite. Similarly, a *strictly merely positive-subdefinite* matrix is a real symmetric matrix such that

$$x'Px < 0$$

implies $Px > 0$ or $Px < 0$. A complete characterization of merely positive-subdefinite matrices has been provided by Cottle and Ferland (1972), who have shown that such matrices must satisfy the conditions:

1. P consists of only nonpositive elements; and
2. P has exactly one negative characteristic value.

A complete characterization of strictly merely positive-subdefinite matrices has been provided by Martos (1969), who has shown that a strictly merely positive-subdefinite matrix must satisfy the additional condition:

3. P does not contain a row (or column) of zeros.

We observe that this condition does not imply in itself that a strictly merely positive-subdefinite matrix is nonsingular.

A necessary and sufficient condition for monotonicity is either that the translog indirect utility function is homothetic or that β_{pp}^{-1} exists and is strictly merely positive-subdefinite. To impose restrictions on the matrix β_{pp} implied by monotonicity of the systems of individual expenditure shares, we first provide a Cholesky factorization of this matrix:

$$\beta_{pp} = TDT'$$

where T is a unit lower triangular matrix and D is a diagonal matrix.

Since the matrix β_{pp}^{-1} is strictly merely positive-subdefinite, all the elements of this matrix are nonpositive. We can express the nonpositivity constraints on these elements in terms of the elements of the Cholesky factorization of the matrix β_{pp}, where

$$\beta_{pp} = TDT'$$

Finally, we include restrictions on the Cholesky values; the matrix β_{pp} has exactly one negative Cholesky value, the last in order, and $N-1$ positive Cholesky values. Combining these restrictions with nonpositivity restrictions on the elements of β_{pp}^{-1}, we obtain a complete set of restrictions implied by the monotonicity of the systems of individual expenditure shares.

Similarly, we can provide a complete set of conditions for integrability of the system of individual expenditure shares for the second stage of the two-stage allocation process. For example, the individual expenditure shares for commodities within each group are homogeneous of degree zero in commodity prices, the sum of these shares is equal to unity, and the matrix of compensated own- and cross-price effects must be symmetric for each group. These conditions can be used to generate restrictions on the parameters of the translog price indexes for each group. The restrictions are analogous to those for price indexes we have employed in models of producer behavior.

The individual expenditure shares must be nonnegative for each commodity group; as before, we can always choose prices so that the monotonicity of the indirect utility function for each commodity group is violated. We can consider restrictions on the parameters that imply quasi-convexity of the homothetic translog indirect utility function or monotonicity of the system of individual demand functions for all nonnegative expenditure shares for each commodity group. Again, the conditions for monotonicity for expenditure shares that satisfy the nonnegativity restrictions are precisely analogous to those we have employed for models of producer behavior.

3.3   Stochastic specification

The model of consumer behavior presented in Section 3.2 is generated from a translog indirect utility function for each consuming unit. To formulate an econometric model of consumer behavior we add a stochastic component to the equations for the individual expenditure shares. We associate this component with unobservable random disturbances at the level of the individual consuming unit. The consuming unit maximizes utility, but the expenditure shares are chosen with a random disturbance. This disturbance may result from errors in implementation of consumption plans, random elements in the determination of consumer preferences not reflected in our list of attributes of consuming units, or errors of measurement of the individual expenditure shares. We assume that each of the equations for the individual shares has two additive components. The first is a nonrandom function of prices, expenditure, and demographic characteristics. The second is an unobservable random disturbance that is functionally independent of these variables.

To represent our econometric model of consumer behavior we introduce some additional notation. We consider observations on expenditure patterns by J consuming units, indexed by $j = 1, 2, \ldots, J$, for T time periods, indexed by $t = 1, 2, \ldots, T$. The vector of expenditure shares for the jth consuming unit in the tth time period is denoted w_{jt} ($j = 1, 2, \ldots, J$; $t = 1, 2, \ldots, T$). Similarly, expenditure for the jth unit on all commodity groups in the tth time period is denoted Y_{jt} ($j = 1, 2, \ldots, J$; $t = 1, 2, \ldots, T$). The vector of prices faced by all consuming units in the tth time period is denoted p_t ($t = 1, 2, \ldots, T$). Similarly, the vector of logarithms of prices in the tth time period is denoted in $\ln p_t$ $(t=1,2,\ldots,T)$. The vector of logarithms of ratios of prices to expenditure for the jth consuming unit in the tth time period is denoted $\ln(p_t/Y_{jt})$ $(j=1,2,\ldots,J; t=1,2,\ldots,T)$.

Using our notation, the individual expenditure shares can be written:

$$w_{jt} = \frac{1}{B_t}\left(\alpha_p + \beta_{pp}\ln\frac{p_t}{Y_{jt}} + \beta_{pA}A_j\right) + \epsilon_{jt}$$

$$(j=1,2,\ldots,J; t=1,2,\ldots,T) \qquad (3.17)$$

where

$$B_t = -1 + \iota'\beta_{pp}\ln p_t \qquad (t=1,2,\ldots,T)$$

and $\{\epsilon_{jt}\}$ are the vectors of unobservable random disturbances for all J consuming units and all T time periods. Since the individual expenditure shares for all commodities sum to unity for each consuming unit in each time period, the unobservable random disturbances for all commodities sum to zero for each unit in each time period:

$$\iota'\epsilon_{jt} = 0 \qquad (j=1,2,\ldots,J; t=1,2,\ldots,T) \qquad (3.18)$$

These disturbances are not distributed independently.

We assume that the unobservable random disturbances for all commodities have expected value equal to zero for all observations:

$$E(\epsilon_{jt}) = 0 \qquad (j=1,2,\ldots,J; t=1,2,\ldots,T) \qquad (3.19)$$

We also assume that these disturbances have the same covariance matrix for all observations:

$$V(\epsilon_{jt}) = \Omega_\epsilon \qquad (j=1,2,\ldots,J; t=1,2,\ldots,T)$$

Since the disturbances sum to zero for each observation, this matrix is nonnegative-definite with rank at most equal to $N-1$, where N is the number of commodities. We assume that the covariance matrix has rank equal to $N-1$.

Finally, we assume that disturbances corresponding to distinct observations are uncorrelated. Under this assumption the covariance matrix of the disturbances for all consuming units at a given point of time has the Kronecker product form

$$V\begin{bmatrix} \epsilon_{1t} \\ \epsilon_{2t} \\ \vdots \\ \epsilon_{jt} \end{bmatrix} = \Omega_\epsilon \otimes I \qquad (3.20)$$

The covariance matrix of the disturbances for all time periods for a given individual has an analogous form. The unknown parameters of the system of equations determining the individual expenditure shares can be estimated from time series data on individual expenditure shares, prices, total expenditure, and demographic characteristics.

At any point of time the aggregate expenditure shares are equal to the individual expenditure shares multiplied by the ratio of individual expenditure to aggregate expenditure. Although the data for individual consuming units and for the aggregate of all consuming units are based on the same definitions, the aggregate data are not obtained by summing over the data for individuals. Observations on individual consuming units are based on a random sample from the population of all consuming units. Observations for the aggregate of all consuming units are constructed from data on production of commodities and on consumption of these commodities by households and by other consuming units such as businesses, governments, and the rest of the world. Accordingly, we must introduce an additional source of random error in the equations for the aggregate expenditure shares, corresponding to unobservable errors of measurement in the observations that underly the aggregate expenditure shares.

We assume that each of the equations for the aggregate expenditure shares has three additive components. The first is a weighted average of the nonrandom functions of prices, expenditure, and demographic characteristics that determine the individual expenditure shares. The second is a weighted average of the unobservable random disturbances in equations for the individual expenditure shares. The third is a weighted average of the unobservable random errors of measurement in the observations on the aggregate expenditure shares.

Denoting the vector of aggregate expenditure shares at time t by w_t $(t = 1, 2, \ldots, T)$, we can express these shares in the form

$$w_t = \frac{1}{B_t}\left(\alpha_p + \beta_{pp}\ln p_t\right) - \frac{1}{B_t}\beta_{pp}\iota\frac{\sum_{j=1}^{J} Y_{jt}\ln Y_{jt}}{\sum_{j=1}^{J} Y_{jt}}$$

$$+ \frac{1}{B_t}\beta_{pA}\frac{\sum_{j=1}^{J} Y_{jt} A_j}{\sum_{j=1}^{J} Y_{jt}} + \epsilon_t \qquad (t = 1, 2, \ldots, T) \qquad (3.21)$$

where

$$B_t = -1 + \iota'\beta_{pp}\ln p_t \qquad (t = 1, 2, \ldots, T)$$

as before, and $\{\epsilon_t\}$ are the vectors of unobservable random disturbances for the tth time period.

The aggregate disturbances ϵ_t can be expressed in the form

$$\epsilon_t = \frac{\sum_{j=1}^{J} Y_{jt}\epsilon_{jt}}{\sum_{j=1}^{J} Y_{jt}} + \frac{\sum_{j=1}^{J} Y_{jt}\nu_{jt}}{\sum_{j=1}^{J} Y_{jt}} \qquad (t = 1, 2, \ldots, T) \qquad (3.22)$$

where $\{\nu_{jt}\}$ are the vectors of errors of measurement that underlie the data on the aggregate expenditure shares. Since the random disturbances for all commodities sum to zero in each time period,

$$\iota'\epsilon_t = 0 \qquad (j=1,2,\ldots,J;\ t=1,2,\ldots,T) \tag{3.23}$$

these disturbances are not distributed independently.

We assume that the errors of measurement that underlie the data on the aggregate expenditure shares have expected value equal to zero for all observations:

$$E(\nu_{jt}) = 0 \qquad (j=1,2,\ldots,J;\ t=1,2,\ldots,T)$$

We also assume that these errors have the same covariance matrix for all observations:

$$V(\nu_{jt}) = \Omega_\nu \qquad (j=1,2,\ldots,J;\ t=1,2,\ldots,T)$$

and that the rank of this matrix is equal to $N-1$.

If the errors of measurement are distributed independently of expenditure and of the disturbances in the equations for the individual expenditure shares, the aggregate disturbances have expected value equal to zero for all time periods:

$$E(\epsilon_t) = 0 \qquad (t=1,2,\ldots,T) \tag{3.24}$$

and have a covariance matrix given by

$$V(\epsilon_t) = \frac{\sum_{j=1}^{J} Y_{jt}^2}{(\sum_{j=1}^{J} Y_{jt})^2}\,\Omega_\epsilon + \frac{\sum_{j=1}^{J} Y_{jt}^2}{(\sum_{j=1}^{J} Y_{jt})^2}\,\Omega_\nu \qquad (t=1,2,\ldots,T)$$

so that the aggregate disturbances for different time periods are heteroscedastic.

We can correct for heteroscedasticity of the aggregate disturbances by transforming the observations on the aggregate expenditure shares as follows:

$$\rho_t w_t = \frac{\rho_t}{B_t}(\alpha_p + \beta_{pp}\ln p_t) - \frac{\rho_t}{B_t}\beta_{pp}\iota \frac{\sum_{j=1}^{J} Y_{jt}\ln Y_{jt}}{\sum_{j=1}^{J} Y_{jt}}$$

$$+ \frac{\rho_t}{B_t}\beta_{pA}\frac{\sum_{j=1}^{J} Y_{jt} A_j}{\sum_{j=1}^{J} Y_{jt}} + \rho_t \epsilon_t \qquad (t=1,2,\ldots,T)$$

where

$$\rho_t^2 = \frac{(\sum_{j=1}^{J} Y_{jt})^2}{\sum_{j=1}^{J} Y_{jt}^2} \qquad (t=1,2,\ldots,T)$$

The covariance matrix of the transformed disturbances, say Ω, becomes

$$V(\rho_t \epsilon_t) = \Omega_\epsilon + \Omega_\nu = \Omega$$

This matrix is nonnegative-definite with rank equal to $N-1$. Finally, we assume that the errors of measurement corresponding to distinct observations are uncorrelated. Under this assumption the covariance matrix of the transformed disturbances at all points of time has the Kronecker product form

$$V \begin{bmatrix} \rho_1 \epsilon_1 \\ \rho_2 \epsilon_2 \\ \vdots \\ \rho_T \epsilon_T \end{bmatrix} = \Omega \otimes I \tag{3.25}$$

We next discuss the estimation of the translog model of aggregate consumer behavior, combining a single cross section of observations on individual expenditure patterns with several time series observations on aggregate expenditure patterns. Suppose first that we have a random sample of observations on individual expenditure patterns at a given point of time. Prices for all consumers are the same. The translog model (3.17) takes the form

$$w_j = \gamma_1 + \gamma_2 \ln Y_j + \Gamma_3 A_j + \epsilon_j \qquad (j=1,2,\ldots,J) \tag{3.26}$$

where we drop the time subscript. In this model γ_1 and γ_2 are vectors of unknown parameters and Γ_3 is a matrix of unknown parameters. Random sampling implies that disturbances for different individuals are uncorrelated. We assume that the data matrix with $(1, \ln Y_j, A_j)$ as its jth row is of full rank.

The parameters of γ_1, γ_2, and Γ_3 are identified in the cross section. Moreover, the model 3.26 is a multivariate regression model, except that the vector of disturbances ϵ_j has a singular distribution. A model where one equation has been dropped is a multivariate regression model so that the unique, minimum-variance, unbiased estimator of the unknown parameters γ_1, γ_2, and Γ_3 is obtained by applying ordinary least squares to each equation separately.

To link the parameters γ_1, γ_2, and Γ_3 to the parameters of the translog model of aggregate consumer behavior we first observe that the parameters of the translog model can be identified only up to a normalization, since multiplying all of the parameters by the same nonzero constant leaves the expenditure shares unchanged. The usual normalization is $\iota'\alpha_p = -1$, giving the unknown parameters the same sign as those in the translog indirect utility function. Second, without loss of generality we can take the prices of all goods to be equal to unity for a particular period of time. In the application to a single cross section we take all prices at the date of the survey to be equal to unity. The prices for all other time periods are expressed relative to prices of this base period.

Given the normalization of the parameters and the choice of base period for measurement of the prices, we obtain the following correspondence between the unknown parameters of the cross-section model and the parameters of the translog model of aggregate consumer behavior:

$$\gamma_1 = -\alpha_p$$

$$\gamma_2 = \beta_{pp}\iota$$

$$\Gamma_3 = -\beta_{pA} \tag{3.27}$$

The constants α_p and the parameters associated with demographic characteristics of individual households β_{pA} can be estimated from a single cross section. The parameters associated with total expenditure $\beta_{pp}\iota$ can also be estimated from a single cross section. The remaining parameters, those associated with prices, can be estimated from time series data on aggregate expenditure patterns. Since the model is linear in parameters for a cross section, we can use ordinary least squares regression to estimate the impact of the demographic structure on aggregate expenditure patterns.

After correction for heteroscedasticity the translog model of aggregate consumer behavior is given by

$$\rho_t w_t = \frac{\rho_t}{B_t}(\alpha_p + \beta_{pp}\ln p_t) - \frac{\rho_t}{B_t}\beta_{pp}\iota \frac{\sum_{j=1}^{J} Y_{jt}\ln Y_{jt}}{\sum_{j=1}^{J} Y_{jt}}$$

$$+ \frac{\rho_t}{B_t}\beta_{pA}\frac{\sum_{j=1}^{J} Y_{jt}A_j}{\sum_{j=1}^{J} Y_{jt}} + \rho_t \epsilon_t \qquad (t=1,2,\ldots,T) \tag{3.28}$$

where

$$B_t = -1 + \iota'\beta_{pp}\ln p_t \qquad (t=1,2,\ldots,T)$$

and ϵ_t is a vector of unobservable random disturbances. We have time series observations on prices p_t, the expenditure statistic $\sum Y_{jt}\ln Y_{jt}/\sum Y_{jt}$, the vector of attribute-expenditure statistics $\{\sum Y_{jt}A_j/\sum Y_{jt}\}$, and the heteroscedasticity correction ρ_t $(t=1,2,\ldots,T)$.

The translog model in (3.28) might appear to be a nonlinear regression model with additive errors, so that nonlinear regression techniques could be employed.[28] However, the existence of supply functions for all commodities makes it more appropriate to treat some of the right-side variables as endogenous. For example, shifts in prices due to demand–supply interactions may cause significant shifts in the distribution of expenditure. To obtain a consistent estimator for this model we could specify supply functions for all commodities and estimate the complete model by full-information maximum likelihood.

Alternatively, to estimate the model in (3.28) we can consider limited information techniques utilizing instrumental variables. In particular, we can introduce a sufficient number of instrumental variables to identify all parameters. We estimate the model by nonlinear three-stage least squares (NL3SLS).[29] Application of NL3SLS to our model would be straightforward except for the fact that the covariance matrix of the disturbances is singular. We obtain NL3SLS estimators of the complete system by dropping one equation and estimating the resulting system of $N-1$ equations by NL3SLS; we derive an estimator for parameters of the remaining equation from the conditions for summability. The parameter estimates are invariant to the choice of the equation omitted in the model for aggregate time series data and the model for individual cross-section data.

In the analysis of the model to be applied to cross-section data on individual expenditure patterns, we have assumed that individual disturbances and individual total expenditure are uncorrelated. If aggregate demand–supply interactions induce shifts in the distribution of expenditure, the zero correlation assumption cannot be strictly valid for all consumers at the individual level. However, the cross section is a random sample that includes a minute percentage of the total population, so that it is reasonable to assume that the correlations between total expenditure and disturbances at the individual level are negligible.

The NL3SLS estimator can be employed to estimate all parameters of the model of aggregate expenditures, provided that these parameters are identified. Since we wish to obtain a detailed characterization of the impact of changes in the demographic structure of the population, the model (3.28) contains a large number of parameters and requires a large number of time series observations for identification. The technical conditions for identification are quite complicated. A sufficient condition for underidentification is that the number of instruments is less than the number of parameters. For the translog model of aggregate consumer behavior, this occurs if

$$(N-1)(1+S) = \frac{(N+1)N}{2} - 1 > (N-1)\min(V, T) \qquad (3.29)$$

where N is the number of commodities, S is the number of components of A_{jt}, and V is the number of instruments. The left-hand side of (3.29) is the number of free parameters of the translog model under symmetry of the matrix β_{pp} and the right-hand side is the number of instruments, assuming that no collinearity exists among the instruments.

Condition (3.29) is met in our application, so that not all parameters are identified in the model for aggregate time series data. We next consider methods utilizing individual cross-section data together with aggregate time series data to obtain identification. As we have seen, cross-section data can be used to identify the constant α_p, the coefficients of total expenditure $-\beta_{pp}\,\iota$, and the demographic coefficients β_{pA}. Only the price coefficients β_{pp} must be identified from aggregate time series data. A necessary condition for identification of these parameters is

$$\frac{(N-1)N}{2} < (N-1)\min(V,T) \tag{3.30}$$

or

$$\frac{N}{2} < \min(V,T) \tag{3.31}$$

This condition is met in our application. Sufficient conditions amount to the nonlinear analog of the absence of multicollinearity. These conditions are quite weak and hold in our application.

In order to pool cross-section and time series data, we combine the model for individual expenditures and the model for aggregate expenditure and apply the method of NL3SLS to the whole system. The instruments for the cross-section model are the micro data themselves; for the aggregate model the instruments are variables that can be taken to be distributed independently of the aggregate disturbances. The data sets are pooled statistically, where estimates of the covariance matrix of the aggregate disturbances from time series data and the covariance matrix of the individual disturbances from cross-section data are used to weight aggregate and cross-section data, respectively. The resulting estimator is consistent and asymptotically efficient in the class of instrumental variable estimators utilizing the instruments we have chosen.

3.4   Summary and conclusion

In this section we have presented a model of aggregate consumer behavior based on transcendental logarithmic or translog indirect utility functions for all consuming units. These indirect utility functions incorporate restrictions on individual behavior that result from maximization of a utility function subject to a budget constraint. Our model of individual consumer behavior is based on a two-stage allocation process. For each stage of the allocation process the individual consuming unit has indirect utility functions that are homogeneous of degree zero in prices and expenditure, nonincreasing in prices and nondecreasing in expenditure, and quasi-convex in prices and expenditure.

To incorporate differences in individual preferences into our model of aggregate consumer behavior we allow the indirect utility functions for all consuming units to depend on attributes, such as demographic characteristics, that vary among individuals. Each attribute is represented by a dummy variable equal to unity when the consuming unit has the corresponding characteristic and zero otherwise.

Given translog indirect utility functions for each consuming unit, we derive the expenditure shares for that unit by means of Roy's identity. For the first stage of the two-stage allocation process this results in expenditure shares for commodity groups that can be expressed as ratios of two functions that are linear in the logarithms of ratios of price indexes to total expenditure and in attributes. The denominators for these ratios are functions that are the same for all commodity groups.

Under exact aggregation the individual expenditure shares are linear in functions of attributes and total expenditure. The denominators are independent of total expenditure and attributes and are the same for all individuals. The translog indirect utility functions for the second stage of the two-stage allocation process correspond to homothetic preferences. This results in expenditure shares for individual commodities that are linear in the logarithms of prices; these shares satisfy the conditions required for exact aggregation.

To derive aggregate expenditure shares for commodity groups, we multiply the individual expenditure shares by total expenditure for each consuming unit, sum over all consuming units, and divide by aggregate expenditure. The aggregate expenditure shares, like the individual shares, can be expressed as ratios of two functions. The denominators are the same as for individual expenditure shares. The numerators are linear in the logarithms of price indexes of all commodity groups, in a statistic of the distribution of expenditure over all consuming units $\{ \sum Y_j \ln Y_j / \sum Y_j \}$, and in the shares of all demographic groups in aggregate expenditure $\{ \sum Y_j A_j / \sum Y_j \}$.

The individual expenditure shares are homogeneous of degree zero in prices and expenditure. Given the restrictions implied by exact aggregation, this implies an additional $N - 2$ restrictions on the parameters of the translog indirect utility functions, where N is the number of commodities. Second, the sum of individual expenditure shares over all commodity groups is equal to unity. Again, given the exact aggregation restrictions, there are $N - 2$ additional restrictions implied by summability. Third, the matrix of compensated own- and cross-price effects must be symmetric. This implies $\frac{1}{2} N(N-1) - 1$ additional restrictions on the parameters of the translog indirect utility functions.

Monotonicity of the indirect utility functions implies that the individual expenditure shares must be nonnegative. Similarly quasi-convexity of the indirect utility functions implies that the individual expenditure shares must be monotonic or, equivalently, that the matrix of compensated own- and cross-price substitution effects must be nonpositive-definite. It is always possible to choose prices so that monotonicity of the indirect utility functions or nonnegativity of the individual expenditure shares is violated. Accordingly, we consider restrictions that imply monotonicity of the expenditure shares whenever they are nonnegative.

4   Empirical results

In Sections 2 and 3 we have presented econometric models of producer and consumer behavior suitable for incorporation into general equilibrium models of the U.S. economy. The most important innovation in these econometric models is that they encompass all restrictions on the parameters implied by the economic theories of producer and consumer behavior. These restrictions take the form of equalities required for homogeneity, product exhaustion or summability, and symmetry. They take the form of inequalities required for monotonicity subject to nonnegativity restrictions.

Our model of producer behavior is based on industries as producing units. Each industry behaves like an individual producer, maximizing profit subject to a production function characterized by constant returns to scale. The allocation of the value of output among inputs can be generated from a translog price function for each industry. In addition, our model of producer behavior determines the rate of technical change endogenously for each industry. Time is included in the price function for each sector as an index of technology.

Our model of consumer behavior is based on households as consuming units. Expenditures within the household are allocated so as to maximize a household welfare function. Each household behaves in the same way as an individual maximizing a utility function subject to a budget constraint. All consuming units are classified by demographic characteristics associated with differences in preferences among households. For each of these characteristics households are divided among mutually exclusive and exhaustive groups. Each demographic characteristic is represented by a qualitative or dummy variable, equal to unity when the household is in the group and zero otherwise.

4.1   *Producer behavior*

Our first objective is to present the empirical results of implementing the model of producer behavior described in Section 2 for 35 industrial sectors of the United States. This model is based on a two-stage process for the allocation of the value of output in each sector among capital, labor, energy, and materials inputs. The value of inputs from these four commodity groups exhausts the value of the output for each of the 35 sectors. We limit our presentation of empirical results to the first stage of the two-stage process.

To implement our econometric models of production and technical change we have assembled a time series data base for 35 industrial sectors of the United States. For capital and labor inputs we have first compiled data by sector on the basis of the classification of economic activities employed in the U.S. Census Bureau's National Income and Product Accounts. We have then transformed these data into a format appropriate for the classification of activities employed in the U.S. Census Bureau's Interindustry Transactions Accounts. For energy and materials inputs we have compiled data by sector on interindustry transactions on the basis of the classification of activities employed in the U.S. Interindustry Transactions Accounts.[30]

The endogenous variables in our models of producer behavior are value shares of sectoral inputs for four commodity groups and the sectoral rate of technical change. We can estimate four equations for each industry, corresponding to three of the value shares and the rate of technical change. As unknown parameters we have 3 elements of the vector $\{\alpha_p^i\}$, the scalar $\{\alpha_t^i\}$, 6 share elasticities in the matrix $\{\beta_{pp}^i\}$, which is constrained to be symmetric, 3 biases of technical change in the vector $\{\beta_{pt}^i\}$, and the scalar $\{\beta_{tt}^i\}$, so that we have a total of 14 unknown parameters for each industry. We estimate these parameters from time series data for the period 1958–74 for each industry, subject to the inequality restrictions implied by monotonicity of the sectoral input value shares. The results are given in Table 4.1.

Our interpretation of the empirical results reported in Table 4.1 begins with an analysis of the estimates of the parameters $\{\alpha_p^i, \alpha_t^i\}$. If all other parameters were set equal to zero, the sectoral price functions would be linear-logarithmic in prices and linear in time. The parameters $\{\alpha_p^i\}$ would correspond to constant-value shares of inputs and the negative of the parameters $\{\alpha_t^i\}$ to constant rates of technical change. The parameters $\{\alpha_p^i\}$ are nonnegative for all 35 sectors included in our study and are estimated very precisely. The parameters $\{\alpha_t^i\}$ are estimated less precisely and are negative in 15 sectors and are positive in 20 sectors.

The estimated share elasticities with respect to price, $\{\beta_{pp}^i\}$, describe the implications of patterns of substitution for the distribution of the value of output among capital, labor, energy, and materials inputs. Positive share elasticities imply that the corresponding value shares increase with an increase in price; negative share elasticities imply that the value shares decrease with price; zero share elasticities correspond to value

Table 4.1. *Parameter estimates: sectoral models of production and technical change*

Parameter[a]	Agriculture, forestry, and fisheries	Metal mining	Coal mining	Crude petroleum and natural gas	Nonmetallic mining	Construction
AK	.170 (.00445)	.216 (.0108)	.237 (.00643)	.449 (.00559)	.270 (.00346)	.0686 (.000640)
AL	.254 (.00475)	.313 (.0226)	.469 (.0121)	.103 (.00272)	.310 (.00963)	.439 (.00310)
AE	.0243 (.000580)	.0393 (.00251)	.121 (.00279)	.0565 (.000676)	.0746 (.000921)	.0254 (.000393)
AM	.551 (.00430)	.432 (.0242)	.173 (.0102)	.391 (.00736)	.345 (.00882)	.467 (.00350)
AT	−.0329 (.0546)	.0151 (.0602)	.00643 (.0757)	.0246 (.0759)	.0767 (.0271)	.0471 (.00565)
BKK						
BKL						
BKE						
BKM						
BKT	−.00247 (.000603)	.000775 (.00147)	.00868 (.000873)	−.000795 (.000759)	.00187 (.000470)	.000295 (.0000868)
BLL	−.220 (.0356)	−.405 (.265)				−.433 (.0420)
BLE	.00158 (.00427)	.0255 (.0224)				−.0526 (.00585)
BLM	.222 (.0342)	.379 (.244)				.485 (.0459)
BLT	.00530 (.00147)	.0154 (.00671)	.00472 (.00165)	−.000914 (.000369)	−.00189 (.00131)	−.00923 (.00158)
BEE	−.0000114 (.0000620)	−.00161 (.00181)				−.00639 (.00113)
BEM	.00159 (.00433)	−.0239 (.0206)				.0590 (.00689)
BET	.000210 (.000175)	−.000104 (.0000607)	−.00731 (.000378)	.000814 (.0000916)	.00172 (.000125)	−.00159 (.000222)
BMM	−.223 (.0333)	−.356 (.224)				−.544 (.0507)
BMT	−.00798 (.00139)	−.0160 (.00639)	−.00609 (.00138)	.000895 (.000998)	−.00170 (.00120)	.0105 (.00174)
BTT	−.000966 (.00741)	.000849 (.00815)	.00180 (.0103)	.00291 (.0103)	.00781 (.00364)	.00343 (.000771)

182

Parameter[a]	Food and kindred products	Tobacco manufacturers	Textile mill products	Apparel and other fabrics; textile production	Lumber and wood products	Furniture and fixtures
AK	.0548 (.000404)	.162 (.00238)	.0698 (.00158)	.0405 (.000285)	.151 (.00192)	.0635 (.000857)
AL	.146 (.00267)	.136 (.00345)	.200 (.00476)	.306 (.00225)	.267 (.00583)	.360 (.00516)
AE	.0114 (.000457)	.00347 (.000345)	.0150 (.000216)	.00628 (.0000910)	.0178 (.000828)	.00912 (.000217)
AM	.788 (.00290)	.699 (.00495)	.715 (.00634)	.647 (.00229)	.564 (.00530)	.568 (.00547)
AT	.0188 (.0115)	.0850 (.119)	−.0183 (.0126)	−.0126 (.0299)	−.00477 (.0357)	−.00306 (.0203)
BKK						
BKL						
BKE						
BKM						
BKT	−.00130 (.0000548)	.000955 (.000322)	−.000395 (.000214)	.000240 (.0000386)	.00456 (.000260)	−.000677 (.000116)
BLL	−.132 (.0205)	−.0269 (.0158)				−1.022 (.0830)
BLE	.00631 (.00352)	.00126 (.00154)				−.0687 (.00393)
BLM	.126 (.0214)	.0256 (.0157)				1.090 (.0814)
BLT	.00104 (.000569)	.00456 (.000955)	−.000195 (.000646)	−.00232 (.000306)	−.00120 (.000791)	.0189 (.00170)
BEE	−.000301 (.000348)	−.0000588 (.000143)		−.00185 (.000651)		−.00462 (.000768)
BEM	−.00601 (.00318)	−.00120 (.00140)		.00185 (.000651)		.0733 (.00463)
BET	−.0000788 (.0000977)	.0000296 (.0000914)	.000291 (.0000293)	.000267 (.0000155)	.000625 (.000112)	.00144 (.0000744)
BMM	−.120 (.0226)	−.0244 (.0157)		−.00185 (.000651)		−1.164 (.0794)
BMT	.000332 (.000603)	−.00555 (.00107)	.000299 (.000860)	.00181 (.000310)	−.00399 (.000719)	−.0197 (.00169)
BTT	.00230 (.00156)	.0157 (.0161)	−.000871 (.00168)	−.00203 (.00405)	.000383 (.00483)	.00110 (.00276)

Table 4.1 *(cont.)*

Parameter[a]	Paper and allied products	Printing, publishing, and allied industries	Chemicals and allied products	Petroleum refining	Rubber and miscellaneous plastic products	Leather and leather products
AK	.111 (.000562)	.103 (.000741)	.128 (.00135)	.105 (.00582)	.0982 (.00151)	.0467 (.00143)
AL	.242 (.00292)	.362 (.00450)	.201 (.00311)	.0670 (.0199)	.271 (.00334)	.342 (.00469)
AE	.0322 (.000333)	.00822 (.000218)	.0885 (.00165)	.599 (.00373)	.0261 (.000279)	.00795 (.000188)
AM	.615 (.00280)	.526 (.00494)	.582 (.00412)	.229 (.00268)	.605 (.00431)	.604 (.00469)
AT	.0372 (.0301)	−.0129 (.0233)	.0130 (.0206)	.00582 (.0375)	.0318 (.0291)	−.00105 (.0239)
BKK						
BKL						
BKE						
BKM						
BKT	−.00208 (.0000762)	.000400 (.000101)	−.00545 (.000183)	.000133 (.000789)	−.00356 (.000204)	−.000401 (.000193)
BLL	−.316 (.0393)	−.327 (.0704)	−.0237 (.0449)	−.280 (.0208)		
BLE	−.0196 (.00578)	−.00875 (.00384)	−.000362 (.0164)	.0346 (.00870)		
BLM	.336 (.0382)	.335 (.0726)	.0240 (.0520)	.246 (.0272)		
BLT	.00708 (.00107)	.00948 (.00234)	−.00241 (.00160)	−.00130 (.000291)	−.0238 (.000453)	−.00141 (.000636)
BEE	−.00122 (.000772)	−.00339 (.00100)	−.00000555 (.000499)	−.00428 (.00237)		
BEM	.0208 (.00654)	.0121 (.00436)	.000368 (.0169)	−.0304 (.00635)		
BET	.00109 (.000156)	.000493 (.000129)	.00177 (.000610)	.000948 (.000508)	.000591 (.0000378)	.000225 (.0000255)
BMM	−.357 (.0378)	−.347 (.0751)	−.0244 (.0631)	−.215 (.0325)		
BMT	−.00610 (.00104)	−.0104 (.00242)	.00608 (.00186)	.000217 (.000407)	.00535 (.000584)	.00159 (.000637)
BTT	.00916 (.00409)	−.00181 (.00316)	.00440 (.00281)	.00135 (.00509)	.00651 (.00395)	−.000777 (.00326)

Parameter[a]	Stone, clay, and glass products	Primary metal industries	Fabricated metal	Machinery (except electrical)	Electrical machinery	Motor vehicles and motor vehicle equipment
AK	.119 (.00139)	.0893 (.00110)	.0874 (.000893)	.0966 (.00211)	.0923 (.00187)	.108 (.00185)
AL	.371 (.00189)	.277 (.00302)	.337 (.00253)	.311 (.00193)	.343 (.00342)	.188 (.00290)
AE	.0432 (.00100)	.0407 (.000492)	.0115 (.000194)	.0115 (.000158)	.0104 (.000215)	.00737 (.0000757)
AM	.467 (.00281)	.593 (.00361)	.564 (.00293)	.581 (.00343)	.554 (.00278)	.697 (.00429)
AT	.0132 (.0180)	−.00898 (.0257)	.0312 (.0199)	.0187 (.0133)	−.00690 (.0178)	.0208 (.0327)
BKK						
BKL						
BKE						
BKM						
BKT	−.00405 (.000189)	−.00226 (.000149)	.000220 (.000121)	−.00156 (.000286)	−.000289 (.000254)	−.000485 (.000251)
BLL	−.738 (.0696)		−.174 (.0229)	−.455 (.0488)		−.174 (.0510)
BLE	−.114 (.0119)		−.0302 (.00276)	−.0280 (.00596)		−.000469 (.00181)
BLM	.852 (.0778)		.204 (.0221)	.483 (.0524)		.174 (.0509)
BLT	.0209 (.00169)	.00176 (.000409)	.00505 (.000554)	.00746 (.00104)	−.00252 (.000464)	.00959 (.00186)
BEE	−.0176 (.00288)		−.00526 (.00137)	−.00173 (.000646)		−.00000126 (.00000977)
BEM	.132 (.0145)		.0355 (.00402)	.0298 (.00659)		.000470 (.00182)
BET	.00262 (.000317)	−.000389 (.0000667)	.000634 (.0000489)	.000854 (.000125)	.000195 (.0000292)	.000150 (.0000652)
BMM	−.983 (.0883)		−.239 (.0208)	−.513 (.0567)		−.175 (.0509)
BMT	−.0194 (.00191)	.000893 (.000490)	−.00590 (.000582)	−.00675 (.00118)	.00262 (.000378)	−.00926 (.00190)
BTT	.00273 (.00243)	−.00121 (.00348)	.00537 (.00271)	.00119 (.00181)	.00226 (.00241)	.00428 (.00444)

185

Table 4.1 *(cont.)*

Parameter[a]	Transportation equipment and ordinance	Instruments	Miscellaneous manufacturing industries	Transportation	Communications	Electric utilities
AK	.0371 (.00160)	.123 (.00276)	.0905 (.00242)	.169 (.00126)	.364 (.00275)	.324 (.00249)
AL	.371 (.00497)	.325 (.00391)	.329 (.00295)	.425 (.00174)	.388 (.00252)	.229 (.00187)
AE	.00933 (.000148)	.00676 (.000162)	.0112 (.000198)	.0550 (.000879)	.0125 (.000821)	.247 (.00513)
AM	.583 (.00482)	.545 (.00627)	.569 (.00253)	.351 (.00226)	.236 (.00329)	.201 (.00480)
AT	−.0259 (.0235)	.0348 (.0382)	.0273 (.0182)	−.0367 (.0112)	−.00449 (.0299)	.0303 (.0203)
BKK						
BKL						
BKE						
BKM						
BKT	−.00173 (.000217)	−.00145 (.000375)	.000132 (.000328)	−.000768 (.000170)	−.00280 (.000373)	−.00604 (.000338)
BLL	−.327 (.0771)	−.645 (.0298)				
BLE	.00982 (.00247)	−.00159 (.00194)				
BLM	.317 (.0778)	.646 (.0298)				
BLT	.00389 (.00164)	.00974 (.000661)	−.000581 (.000400)	−.00131 (.000236)	.0000186 (.000342)	−.00681 (.000254)
BEE	−.000295 (.000181)	−.00000392 (.00000956)			−.00481 (.00258)	−.0905 (.0183)
BEM	−.00953 (.00230)	.00159 (.00195)			−.00481 (.00258)	.0905 (.0183)
BET	−.0000433 (.0000533)	.0000853 (.0000338)	.000316 (.0000269)	.000712 (.000119)	−.000272 (.000115)	.00796 (.000679)
BMM	−.308 (.0785)	−.648 (.0299)			−.00481 (.00258)	−.0905 (.0183)
BMT	−.00212 (.00165)	−.00837 (.000937)	.000134 (.000344)	.00136 (.000307)	.00306 (.000448)	.00488 (.000631)
BTT	−.00263 (.00319)	.00569 (.00518)	.00264 (.00247)	−.00257 (.00151)	.00188 (.00406)	.00754 (.00275)

Parameter[a]	Gas utilities	Trade	Finance, insurance, and real estate	Services	Government enterprises
AK	.219 (.00410)	.148 (.00144)	.244 (.00784)	.0984 (.000536)	.0954 (.00669)
AL	.180 (.00188)	.560 (.00460)	.238 (.00196)	.509 (.00356)	.567 (.0112)
AE	.548 (.00485)	.0230 (.00128)	.0175 (.000357)	.0204 (.000435)	.0336 (.00166)
AM	.0527 (.00137)	.270 (.00466)	.501 (.00852)	.372 (.00346)	.304 (.00723)
AT	.0153 (.0201)	.00327 (.0148)	−.0429 (.0567)	−.0136 (.00797)	−.0166 (.0519)
BKK	−.00609 (.000556)				
BKL					
BKE					
BKM					
BKT	.00779 (.000255)	.000106 (.000195)	−.00429 (.00106)	.000676 (.0000727)	.00437 (.000908)
BLL	−.0767 (.00705)	−1.023 (.0905)	−.0414 (.0491)	−.335 (.102)	−.194 (.184)
BLE	.0767 (.00705)	.0303 (.0106)	−.00109 (.00797)	.0444 (.0108)	.0306 (.0308)
BLM	.00155 (.000659)	.992 (.0929)	.0425 (.0492)	.330 (.0978)	.164 (.156)
BLT	−.0767 (.00705)	.0320 (.00261)	.00140 (.00102)	.0121 (.00256)	.0215 (.00972)
BEE	−.00325 (.000190)	−.000900 (.000646)	−.0000289 (.000425)	−.0000590 (.000279)	−.00481 (.00572)
BEM	.00213 (.00272)	−.0294 (.00993)	.00112 (.00839)	−.00439 (.0105)	−.0258 (.0254)
BET		−.00150 (.000353)	.0000309 (.000160)	−.0000105 (.000270)	−.00222 (.00163)
BMM		.963 (.0961)	−.0436 (.0506)	−.326 (.0949)	−.138 (.133)
BMT		−.0306 (.00266)	.00286 (.00151)	−.0128 (.00245)	−.0237 (.00818)
BTT		.240 (.00200)	.000351 (.00764)	−.00142 (.00108)	−.00157 (.00706)

[a] See notation footnote on p. 188.

shares that are independent of price. The concavity constraints on the sectoral price functions contribute substantially to the precision of our estimates, but require that the share of each input be nonincreasing in the price of the input itself.

By imposing monotonicity on the sectoral input value shares or concavity of the sectoral price functions, we have reduced the number of share elasticities to be fitted from 350, or 10 for each of our 35 industrial sectors, to 132, or an average of less than 5 per sector. All share elasticities are constrained to be zero for 11 of the 35 industries, so that our representation of technology reduces to a price function that is linear-logarithmic in the input prices at any given time for these industries. For 15 of the 35 industries the share elasticities with respect to the price of labor input are set to equal to zero. Finally, for all 35 industries the share elasticities with respect to the price of capital input are set to equal to zero.

We continue the interpretation of the parameters estimates given in Table 4.1 with estimated biases of technical change with respect to price $\{\beta_{pt}^i\}$. These parameters can be interpreted as the change in the share of each input with respect to time, holding prices constant. Alternatively, they can be interpreted as the change in the negative of the rate of technical change with respect to the price of the corresponding input. For example, if the bias of technical change with respect to the price of capital input is positive, we say that technical change is capital-using; if the bias is negative, we say that technical change is capital-saving.

A classification of industries by patterns of the biases of technical change is given in Table 4.2. The patterns that occur with greatest frequency are capital-saving, labor-saving, energy-using, and materials-using technical change and capital-saving, labor-using, energy-using, and materials-saving technical change. Each of these patterns occurs for 8 of the 35 industries for which we have fitted biases. We find that technical

---

Notation:

Text	Table 4.1		Text	Table 4.1			
α_p^i =	$\begin{bmatrix} AK \\ AL \\ AE \\ AM \end{bmatrix}$		β_{pp}^i =	$\begin{bmatrix} BKK & BKL & BKE & BKM \\ \cdot & BLL & BLE & BLM \\ \cdot & \cdot & BEE & BEM \\ \cdot & \cdot & \cdot & BMM \end{bmatrix}$			
α_t^i =	AT						
			β_{pt}^i =	$\begin{bmatrix} BKT \\ BLT \\ BET \\ BMT \end{bmatrix}$			
			β_{tt}^i =	BTT			

Table 4.2. *Classification of industries by biases of technical change*

Pattern of biases	Industries
Capital-using Labor-using Energy-using Materials-saving	Tobacco; printing and publishing; fabricated metal; services
Capital-using Labor-using Energy-saving Materials-saving	Metal mining; coal mining; trade; government enterprises
Capital-using Labor-saving Energy-using Materials-using	Apparel; petroleum refining; miscellaneous manufacturing
Capital-using Labor-saving Energy-using Materials-saving	Nonmetallic mining; lumber and wood
Capital-using Labor-saving Energy-saving Materials-using	Construction
Capital-saving Labor-using Energy-using Materials-using	Finance, insurance, and real estate
Capital-saving Labor-using Energy-using Materials-saving	Agriculture; furniture; paper; stone, clay, and glass; nonelectrical machinery; motor vehicles; instruments; gas utilities
Capital-saving Labor-using Energy-saving Materials-using	Food; primary metal; communications
Capital-saving Labor-saving Energy-using Materials-using	Crude petroleum and natural gas; textiles; chemicals; rubber and plastic; leather; electric machinery; transportation; electric utilities
Capital-saving Labor-using Energy-saving Materials-saving	Transportation equipment

change is capital-saving for 21 of the 35 industries, labor-using for 21 industries, energy-using for 26 industries, and materials-saving for 24 industries.

The final parameter in our models of producer behavior is the rate of change of the negative of the rate of technical change $\{\beta_{tt}^i\}$. We find that the rate of technical change is decreasing with time for 24 of the 35 industries and increasing for the remaining 10. Whereas the biases of technical change with respect to the prices of capital, labor, energy, and materials inputs are estimated very precisely, we find that the rates of change are estimated with much less precision. Overall, our empirical results suggest a considerable degree of similarity across the industries, especially in the qualitative character of the distribution of the value of output among inputs and of changes in technology.

4.2   *Consumer behavior*

We next present the empirical results of implementing the model of consumer behavior described in Section 3. This model is based on a two-stage process for the allocation of consumer expenditures among commodities. As for producer behavior, we limit our presentation of empirical results to the first stage of the two-stage allocation process. At the first stage we divide consumer expenditures among five commodity groups:

1. *Energy:* Expenditures on electricity, gas, heating oil, and gasoline
2. *Food and clothing:* Expenditures on food, beverages, and tobacco; clothing expenditures; and other related expenditures
3. *Other nondurable expenditure:* The remainder of the budget, which includes some transportation and trade margins from other expenditures
4. *Capital services:* The service flow from consumer durables as well as a service flow from housing
5. *Consumer services:* Expenditures on services, such as entertainment, maintenance and repairs of automobiles and housing, tailoring, cleaning, and insurance

We employ the following demographic characteristics as attributes of individual households:

1. *Family size:* 1, 2, 3, 4, 5, 6, and 7 or more persons
2. *Age of head:* 15–24, 25–34, 35–44, 45–54, 55–65, 65 and over
3. *Region of residence:* Northeast, North-Central, South, and West
4. *Race:* White, nonwhite
5. *Type of residence:* Urban, rural

Our cross-section observations on individual expenditures for each commodity group and demographic characteristics are for the year 1972 from the 1972-73 Survey of Consumer Expenditures.[31] Our time series observations on prices and aggregate expenditures for each commodity group are based on data on personal consumption expenditures from the U.S. Interindustry Transactions Accounts for the period 1958-74.[32] We employ time series data on the distribution of expenditures over all households and among demographic groups based on *Current Population Reports*. To complete our time series data set we compile data for our heteroscedasticity adjustment from the *Current Population Reports*.[33]

In our application we have expenditure shares for five commodity groups as endogenous variables at the first stage, so that we estimate four equations. As unknown parameters we have 4 elements of the vector α_p, 4 expenditure coefficients of the vector $\beta_{pp}\iota$, 16 attribute coefficients for each of the four equations in the matrix β_{pA}, and 10 price coefficients in the matrix β_{pp}, which is constrained to be symmetric. The expenditure coefficients are sums of price coefficients in the corresponding equation, so that we have a total of 82 unknown parameters. We estimate the complete model, subject to inequality restrictions implied by monotonicity of the individual expenditure shares, by pooling time series and cross-section data. The results are given in Table 4.3.

The impacts of changes in total expenditures and in demographic characteristics of the individual household are estimated very precisely. This reflects the fact that estimates of the expenditure and demographic effects incorporate a relatively large number of cross-section observations. The impacts of prices enter through the denominator of the equations for expenditure shares; these price coefficients are estimated very precisely since they also incorporate cross-section data. Finally, the price impacts also enter through the numerators of equations for the expenditure shares. These parameters are estimated less precisely, since they are based on a much smaller number of time series observations on prices.

Individual expenditure shares for capital services increase with total expenditure, whereas all other shares decrease with total expenditure. As family size increases, the shares of energy, food and clothing, and other nondurable expenditures increase, whereas the shares of capital services and consumer services decrease. The energy share increases with age of head of household, whereas the consumer services decrease. The shares of food and clothing and other nondurables increase with age of head, whereas the share of capital services decreases.

The effects of region of residence on patterns of individual expenditures is small for energy and other nondurables. Households living in the North-Central and South regions use relatively more capital services and slightly more energy; these households use less consumer services. The only difference between whites and nonwhites is a smaller share of

Table 4.3. *Pooled estimation results*

Variable	Numerator coefficient	Standard error
For equation W_{EN}		
Constant	−.17874	.005363
ln p_{EN}	.01805	.003505
ln p_{FC}	−.08745	.014618
ln p_O	.02325	.011342
ln p_{CAP}	−.02996	.009905
ln p_{SERV}	.05898	.015862
ln M	.01712	.000614
$F2$	−.01784	.000971
$F3$	−.02281	.001140
$F4$	−.02675	.001243
$F5$	−.02677	.001424
$F6$	−.02861	.001723
$F7$	−.02669	.001808
$A30$	−.00269	.001348
$A40$	−.00981	.001440
$A50$	−.00844	.001378
$A60$	−.01103	.001374
$A70$	−.00971	.001336
RNC	−.00727	.000909
RS	−.00481	.000906
RW	.00621	.000974
BLK	.00602	.001157
RUR	−.01463	.000890
For equation W_{FC}		
Constant	−.56700	.011760
ln p_{EN}	−.08745	.014618
ln p_{FC}	.58972	.094926
ln p_O	−.11121	.064126
ln p_{CAP}	.00158	.057450
ln p_{SERV}	−.44384	.101201
ln M	.05120	.001357
$F2$	−.03502	.002030
$F3$	−.05350	.002390
$F4$	−.07016	.002605
$F5$	−.08486	.002987
$F6$	−.08947	.003613
$F7$	−.11520	.003799
$A30$	−.02189	.002813
$A40$	−.04961	.003015
$A50$	−.05067	.002878
$A60$	−.05142	.002870
$A70$	−.03929	.002791
RNC	.01993	.001897
RS	.01511	.001893
RW	.01854	.002038
BLK	−.01026	.002419
RUR	.01547	.001878

Table 4.3 *(cont.)*

Variable	Numerator coefficient	Standard error
For equation W_O		
Constant	$-.32664$	.010446
$\ln p_{EN}$	.02325	.011342
$\ln p_{FC}$	$-.11121$	.064126
$\ln p_O$	.19236	.083095
$\ln p_{CAP}$	$-.16232$	.023397
$\ln p_{SERV}$	.03887	.028097
$\ln M$	.01903	.001203
$F2$	$-.01616$	.001821
$F3$	$-.02748$	.002143
$F4$	$-.03584$	.002336
$F5$	$-.03882$	.002678
$F6$	$-.04298$	.003239
$F7$	$-.05581$	.003406
$A30$	$-.01293$	.002524
$A40$	$-.02584$	.002703
$A50$	$-.02220$	.002582
$A60$	$-.02199$	.002574
$A70$	$-.00826$	.002503
RNC	.01160	.001702
RS	.00278	.001698
RW	.01375	.001827
BLK	$-.00320$	.002169
RUR	.00783	.001680
For equation W_{CAP}		
Constant	.85630	.026022
$\ln p_{EN}$	$-.02996$	.009905
$\ln p_{FC}$	.00158	.057450
$\ln p_O$	$-.16232$	.023397
$\ln p_{CAP}$	.51464	.053931
$\ln p_{SERV}$	$-.20176$	.079587
$\ln M$	$-.12217$	.002995
$F2$	.00161	.004557
$F3$	.01074	.005361
$F4$	.01928	.005843
$F5$	.02094	.006700
$F6$	.02976	.008106
$F7$	.05885	.008522
$A30$	.03385	.006320
$A40$	.05225	.006761
$A50$	.04761	.006463
$A60$	.03685	.006444
$A70$	.00492	.006267
RNC	$-.04438$	.004261
RS	$-.03193$	.004250
RW	$-.02574$	.004574
BLK	.02338	.005431
RUR	$-.05752$	.004198

Table 4.3 *(cont.)*

Variable	Numerator coefficient	Standard error
For equation W_{SERV}		
Constant	−.78391	.024099
ln p_{EN}	.05898	.015862
ln p_{FC}	−.44384	.101201
ln p_O	.03887	.028097
ln p_{CAP}	−.20176	.079587
ln p_{SERV}	.51293	.143707
ln M	.03481	.002772
F2	.06742	.004242
F3	.09306	.004989
F4	.11348	.005437
F5	.12952	.006234
F6	.13130	.007543
F7	.13886	.007928
A30	.00367	.005885
A40	.03301	.006292
A50	.03371	.006018
A60	.04758	.006001
A70	.05233	.005836
RNC	.02011	.003968
RS	.01884	.003957
RW	−.01277	.004258
BLK	−.01592	.005055
RUR	.04885	.003907

Notation:

W = budget share   ln p = log price

In order to designate the proper good to which W or ln p refers, we append the following subscripts where appropriate:

EN = energy   CAP = capital services
FC = food and clothing   SERV = consumer services
O = other nondurable goods

Further notation is given as

ln M = log total expenditure   A40 = dummy for age class 35–44
F2 = dummy for family size 2   A50 = dummy for age class 45–54
F3 = dummy for family size 3   A60 = dummy for age class 55–64
F4 = dummy for family size 4   A70 = dummy for age class 65 and older
F5 = dummy for family size 5   RNC = dummy for region North-Central
F6 = dummy for family size 6   RS = dummy for region South
F7 = dummy for family size 7   RW = dummy for region West
     or more   BLK = dummy for nonwhite head
A30 = dummy for age class 25–34   RUR = dummy for rural residence

$$D(p) = -1 - .01712 \ln p_{EN} - .05120 \ln p_{FC} - .01903 \ln p_O$$
$$ (.000614) \quad\quad (.001357) \quad\quad (.001203)$$

$$+ .12217 \ln p_{CAP} - .03481 \ln p_{SERV}$$
$$(.002995) \quad\quad (.002772)$$

capital services and a larger share of consumer services for nonwhites. Finally, shares of food and clothing, consumer services, and other nondurables are smaller for rural families, whereas the shares of capital services and energy are much larger. Our overall conclusion is that differences in preferences among consuming units are very significant empirically and must be incorporated into models of aggregate consumer behavior.

4.3 Conclusion

Our empirical results for sectoral patterns of production and technical change are very striking and suggest a considerable degree of similarity across industries. However, it is important to emphasize that these results have been obtained under strong simplifying assumptions. First, for all industries we have employed conditions for producer equilibrium under perfect competition; we have assumed constant returns to scale at the industry level; finally, we have employed a description of technology that leads to myopic decision rules. These assumptions must be justified primarily by their usefulness in implementing production models that are uniform for all 35 industrial sectors of the U.S. economy.

Although it might be worthwhile to weaken each of the assumptions we have enumerated above, a more promising direction for further research appears to lie within the framework provided by these assumptions. First, we can provide a more detailed model for allocation among productive inputs. We have disaggregated energy and materials into 35 groups – 5 types of energy and 30 types of materials – by constructing a hierarchy of models for allocation within the energy and materials aggregates. The second research objective suggested by our results is to incorporate the production models for all 35 industrial sectors into a general equilibrium model of production in the U.S. economy. An econometric general equilibrium model of the U.S. economy has been constructed for 9 industrial sectors by Hudson and Jorgenson (1974). This model is currently being disaggregated to the level of the 35 industrial sectors included in our study.

In this chapter we have presented an econometric model of aggregate consumer behavior and implemented this model for households in the United States. The model incorporates aggregate time series data on quantities consumed, prices, the level and distribution of total expenditures, and demographic characteristics of the population. It also incorporates individual cross-section data on the allocation of consumer expenditures among commodities for households with different demographic characteristics. We have obtained evidence of very significant differences in preferences among households that differ in demographic characteristics in the United States.

Our next research objective is to provide a more detailed model for allocation of consumer expenditures among commodity groups. For this purpose we have disaggregated the 5 commodity groups into 36 individual commodities by constructing a hierarchy of models for allocation within each of the 5 groups – energy, food and clothing, other nondurable goods, capital services, and consumer services. Our final research objective is to incorporate our model of aggregate consumer behavior into the 35-sector general equilibrium model of the U.S. economy now under development. The resulting model can be employed in assessing the impacts of alternative economic policies on the welfare of individuals with different levels of income and different demographic characteristics, including family size, age of head, region, type of residence and race.[34]

NOTES

1. A review of the literature on induced technical change is given by Binswanger (1978a). Binswanger distinguishes between models, like ours and those of Ben-Zion and Ruttan (1978), Lucas (1967), and Schmookler (1966), with an endogenous rate of technical change, and models, like those of Hicks (1932), Kennedy (1964), Samuelson (1965), von Weizsäcker (1962), and others, with an endogenous bias of technical change. Additional references are given by Binswanger (1978a).
2. For further discussion of myopic decision rules, see Jorgenson (1973).
3. The price function was introduced by Samuelson (1953).
4. The translog price function was introduced by Christensen, Jorgenson, and Lau (1971, 1973). The translog price function was first applied at the sectoral level by Berndt and Jorgenson (1973) and Berndt and Wood (1975). References to sectoral production studies incorporating energy and materials inputs are given by Berndt and Wood (1979).
5. The share elasticity with respect to price was introduced by Christensen, Jorgenson, and Lau (1971, 1973) as a fixed parameter of the translog price function. An analogous concept was employed by Samuelson (1973). The terminology is due to Jorgenson and Lau (1983).
6. The terminology *constant share elasticity price function* is due to Jorgenson and Lau (1983), who have shown that constancy of share elasticities with respect to price, biases of technical change with respect to price, and the rate of change of the negative of the rate of technical change are necessary and sufficient for representation of the price function in translog form.
7. The bias of technical change was introduced by Hicks (1932). An alternative definition of the bias of technical change is analyzed by Burmeister and Dobell (1969). Binswanger (1974) has introduced a translog cost function with fixed biases of technical change. Alternative definitions of biases of technical change are compared by Binswanger (1978b).
8. This definition of the bias of technical change with respect to price is due to Jorgenson and Lau (1983).
9. The rate of change of the negative of the rate of technical change was introduced by Jorgenson and Lau (1983).

10. The price indexes were introduced by Fisher (1922) and have been discussed by Tornquist (1936), Theil (1965), and Kloek (1966). These indexes were first derived from the translog price function by Diewert (1976). The corresponding index of technical change was introduced by Christensen and Jorgenson (1970). The translog index of technical change was first derived from the translog price function by Diewert (1980) and by Jorgenson and Lau (1983). Earlier, Diewert (1976) had interpreted the ratio of translog indexes of the prices of input and output as an index of productivity under the assumption of Hicks neutrality.

11. The following discussion of share elasticities with respect to price and concavity follows that of Jorgenson and Lau (1983). Representation of conditions for concavity in terms of the Cholesky factorization is due to Lau (1978).

12. The following discussion of concavity for the translog price function is based on that of Jorgenson and Lau (1983).

13. The following formulation of an econometric model of production and technical change is based on that of Jorgenson and Lau (1983).

14. The Cholesky factorization is used to obtain an equation with uncorrelated random disturbances by Jorgenson and Lau (1983).

15. Note that when we consider only a single commodity or a single consumer, we can suppress the corresponding commodity or individual subscript. This is done to keep the notation as simple as possible; any omission of subscripts will be clear from the context.

16. If aggregate demands are zero when aggregate expenditure is equal to zero, $C_j(p) = 0$.

17. See, for example, Houthakker (1957) and the references given there.

18. Alternative approaches to the representation of the effects of household characteristics on expenditure allocation are presented by Barten (1964), Gorman (1976), and Prais and Houthakker (1955). Empirical evidence on the impact of variations in demographic characteristics on expenditure allocation is given by Lau, Lin, and Yotopoulos (1978), Muellbauer (1977), Parks and Barten (1973), and Pollak and Wales (1980). A review of the literature is presented by Deaton and Muellbauer (1980b, pp. 191–213).

19. Alternative approaches to the representation of the effects of total expenditure on expenditure allocation are reviewed by Deaton and Muellbauer (1980b, pp. 148–60). Gorman (1981) shows that Engel curves for an individual consumer that are linear in certain functions of total expenditure, as required in the theory of exact aggregation considered below, involve at most three linearly independent functions of total expenditure. Evidence from budget studies on the nonlinearity of Engel curves is presented by Leser (1963), Muellbauer (1976b), Pollak and Wales (1978), and Prais and Houthakker (1955).

20. See, for example, Blackorby, Boyce, and Russell (1978) and the references given there.

21. We omit the proof of this theorem, referring the interested reader to Lau (1977b, 1982).

22. See Samuelson (1956) for details.

23. The specification of a system of individual demand functions by means of Roy's identity was first implemented empirically in a path-breaking study by Houthakker (1960). A detailed review of econometric models of consumer behavior based on Roy's identity is given by Lau (1977a).

24. Alternative approaches to the representation of the effects of prices on expenditure allocation are reviewed by Barten (1977), Deaton and Muellbauer (1980b, pp. 60–85), and Lau (1977a). The indirect translog utility function was introduced by Christensen, Jorgenson, and Lau (1975) and was extended to encompass changes in preferences over time by Jorgenson and Lau (1975).

25. These conditions are implied by the fundamental theorem of exact aggregation presented in Section 1, above.

26. Two-stage allocation is discussed by Blackorby, Primont, and Russell (1978, especially pp. 103–216); they give detailed references to the literature.

27. See Diewert (1976) for a detailed justification of this approach to price index numbers.

28. See Malinvaud (1980, chapter 9) for a discussion of these techniques.

29. Nonlinear two-stage least squares estimators were introduced by Amemiya (1974). Subsequently, nonlinear three-stage least squares estimators were introduced by Jorgenson and Laffont (1974). For detailed discussion of nonlinear three-stage least squares estimators, see Amemiya (1977), Gallant (1977), Gallant and Jorgenson (1979), and Malinvaud (1980, chapter 20).

30. Data on energy and materials are based on annual interindustry transactions tables for the United States, 1958–74, compiled by Jack Faucett and Associates (1977) for the Federal Preparedness Agency. Data on labor and capital are based on estimates by Fraumeni and Jorgenson (1980).

31. The cross-section data are described by Carlson (1974).

32. The preparation of these data is described in detail in Jack Faucett and Associates (1977).

33. This series is published annually by the U.S. Bureau of the Census. For our study, numbers 33, 35, 37, 39, 41, 43, 47, 51, 53, 59, 60, 62, 66, 72, 75, 79, 80, 84, 85, 90, 96, 97, and 101 were employed together with technical report numbers 8 and 17.

34. See, for example, Jorgenson, Lau, and Stoker (1980, 1981).

REFERENCES

Amemiya, T. 1974. "The Nonlinear Two-Stage Least Squares Estimator." *Journal of Econometrics,* Vol. 2, No. 2, July, pp. 105–10.

(1977). "The Maximum Likelihood Estimator and the Nonlinear Three-Stage Least Squares Estimator in the General Nonlinear Simultaneous Equation Model." *Econometrica,* Vol. 45, No. 4, May, pp. 955–68.

Arrow, K. J., H. B. Chenery, B. S. Minhas, and R. M. Solow (1961). "Capital-Labor Substitution and Economic Efficiency." *Review of Economics and Statistics,* Vol. 43, No. 3, August, pp. 225–50.

Barten, A. P. (1964). "Family Composition, Prices, and Expenditure Patterns." In P. Hart, G. Mills, and J. K. Whitaker, eds., *Econometric Analysis for National Economic Planning: 16th Symposium of the Colston Society.* London, Butterworth, pp. 277–92.

(1977). "The Systems of Consumer Demand Functions Approach: A Review." In M. D. Intriligator, ed., *Frontiers of Quantitative Economics,* Vol. IIIA. Amsterdam, North-Holland, 1977, pp. 23–58.

Ben-Zion, Uri, and Vernon W. Ruttan (1978). "Aggregate Demand and the Rate of Technical Change." In Hans P. Binswanger and Vernon W. Rutton, eds., *Induced Innovation*. Baltimore, Johns Hopkins University Press, pp. 261-75.

Berndt, Ernst R., and Dale W. Jorgenson (1973). "Production Structure." In Dale W. Jorgenson and Hendrik S. Houthakker, eds., *U.S. Energy Resources and Economic Growth,* Washington, D.C., Energy Policy Project, chapter 3.

Berndt, Ernst R., and David O. Wood (1975). "Technology, Prices, and the Derived Demand for Energy." *Review of Economics and Statistics,* Vol. 56, No. 3, August, pp. 259-68.

(1979). "Engineering and Econometric Interpretations of Energy–Capital Complementarity." *American Economic Review,* Vol. 69, No. 3, September, pp. 342-54.

Berndt, E. R., M. N. Darrough, and W. E. Diewert (1977). "Flexible Functional Forms and Expenditure Distributions: An Application to Canadian Consumer Demand Functions." *International Economic Review,* Vol. 18, No. 3, October, pp. 651-76.

Binswanger, Hans P. (1974). "The Measurement of Technical Change Biases with Many Factors of Production." *American Economic Review,* Vol. 64, No. 5, December, pp. 964-76.

(1978a). "Induced Technical Change: Evolution of Thought." In Hans P. Binswanger and Vernon W. Ruttan, eds., *Induced Innovation*. Baltimore, Johns Hopkins University Press, pp. 13-43.

(1978b). "Issues in Modeling Induced Technical Change." In Hans P. Binswanger and Vernon W. Ruttan, eds., *Induced Innovation*. Baltimore, Johns Hopkins University Press, pp. 128-63.

Blackorby, C., R. Boyce, and R. R. Russell (1978). "Estimation of Demand Systems Generated by the Gorman Polar Form: A Generalization of the S-Branch Utility Tree." *Econometrica,* Vol. 46, No. 2, March, pp. 345-64.

Blackorby, C., D. Primont, and R. R. Russell (1978). *Duality, Separability, and Functional Structure.* Amsterdam, North-Holland.

Bureau of the Census (various annual issues). *Current Population Reports, Consumer Income, Series P-60,* Washington, D.C., U.S. Department of Commerce.

Burmeister, Edwin, and A. Rodney Dobell (1969). "Disembodied Technological Change with Several Factors." *Journal of Economic Theory,* Vol. 1, No. 1, June 1969, pp. 1-8.

Carlson, M. D. (1974), "The 1972-1973 Consumer Expenditure Survey." *Monthly Labor Review,* Vol. 97, No. 12, December, pp. 16-23.

Christensen, Laurits R., and Dale W. Jorgenson (1970). "U.S. Real Product and Real Factor Input, 1929-1967." *Review of Income and Wealth,* Series 16, No. 1, March, pp. 19-50.

Christensen, Laurits R., Dale W. Jorgenson, and Lawrence J. Lau (1971). "Conjugate Duality and the Transcendental Logarithmic Production Function." *Econometrica,* Vol. 39, No. 4, July, pp. 255-6.

(1973). "Transcendental Logarithmic Production Frontiers." *Review of Economics and Statistics,* Vol. 55, No. 1, February, pp. 28-45.

(1975). "Transcendental Logarithmic Utility Functions." *American Economic Review,* Vol. 65, No. 3, June, pp. 367-83.

Cottle, R. W., and J. A. Ferland (1972). "Matrix-Theoretic Criteria for the Quasi-Convexity and Pseudo-Convexity of Quadratic Functions." *Linear Algebra and Its Applications,* Vol. 5, pp. 123-36.

Deaton, A., and J. S. Muellbauer (1980a). "An Almost Ideal Demand System."
    American Economic Review, Vol. 70, No. 3, June, pp. 312–26.
    (1980b). *Economics and Consumer Behavior.* Cambridge, Cambridge University Press.
Diewert, W. Erwin (1976). "Exact and Superlative Index Numbers." *Journal of
    Econometrics,* Vol. 4, No. 2, May, pp. 115–46.
    (1980). "Aggregation Problems in the Measurement of Capital." In Dan
    Usher, ed., *The Measurement of Capital.* Chicago, University of Chicago
    Press, pp. 433–528.
Faucett, Jack, and Associates (1977). *Development of 35 Order Input–Output
    Tables, 1958–1974, Final Report.* Washington, Federal Emergency Management Agency, October.
Fisher, I. (1922). *The Making of Index Numbers.* Boston, Houghton Mifflin.
Fraumeni, Barbara M., and Dale W. Jorgenson (1980). "The Role of Capital in
    U.S. Economic Growth, 1948–1976." In George M. von Furstenberg, ed.,
    Capital, Efficiency, and Growth. Cambridge, Ballinger, pp. 9–250.
Frisch, R. (1959). "A Complete Scheme for Computing All Direct and Cross
    Demand Elasticities in a Model with Many Sectors." *Econometrica,* Vol.
    27, No. 2, April, pp. 177–96.
Gallant, A. R. (1977). "Three-Stage Least Squares Estimation for a System of
    Simultaneous, Nonlinear, Implicit Equations." *Journal of Econometrics,*
    Vol. 5, No. 1, January, pp. 71–88.
Gallant, A. R., and D. W. Jorgenson (1979). "Statistical Inference for a System
    of Simultaneous, Nonlinear, Implicit Equations in the Context of Instrumental Variable Estimation." *Journal of Econometrics,* Vol. 11, No. 2/3,
    October/December, pp. 275–302.
Gorman, W. M. (1953). "Community Preference Fields." *Econometrica,* Vol.
    21, No. 1, January, pp. 63–80.
    (1976). "Tricks with Utility Functions." In M. J. Artis and A. R. Nobay, eds.,
    *Essays in Economic Analysis: Proceedings of the 1975 AUTE Conference,
    Sheffield.* Cambridge, Cambridge University Press, pp. 211–43.
    (1981). "Some Engel Curves." In A. S. Deaton, ed., *Essays in the Theory and
    Measurement of Consumer Behavior.* New York, Cambridge University
    Press, pp. 7–29.
Hicks, John R. (1932). *The Theory of Wages.* London, Macmillan. (2nd edition,
    1963.)
Houthakker, H. S. (1957). "An International Comparison of Household Expenditure Patterns Commemorating the Centenary of Engel's Law." *Econometrica,* Vol. 25, No. 4, October, pp. 532–51.
    (1960). "Additive Preferences." *Econometrica,* Vol. 28, No. 2, April,
    pp. 244–57.
Hudson, E. A., and D. W. Jorgenson (1974). "U.S. Energy Policy and Economic
    Growth." *Bell Journal of Economics and Management Science,* Vol. 5,
    No. 2, Autumn, pp. 461–514.
Johansen, L. (1960). *A Multi-Sectoral Study of Economic Growth.* Amsterdam,
    North-Holland.
Jorgenson, Dale W. (1973). "Technology and Decision Rules in the Theory of
    Investment Behavior." *Quarterly Journal of Economics,* Vol. 87, No. 4,
    November, pp. 523–43.
Jorgenson, Dale W., and B. M. Fraumeni (1981). "Relative Prices and Tech-

nical Change." In E. Berndt and B. Field, eds., *Modeling and Measuring Natural Resource Substitution.* Cambridge, MIT Press, pp. 17-47.

Jorgenson, D. W., and J. J. Laffont (1974). "Efficient Estimation of Nonlinear Simultaneous Equations with Additive Disturbances." *Annals of Social and Economic Measurement,* Vol. 3, No. 4, October, pp. 615-40.

Jorgenson, D. W., and L. J. Lau (1975). "The Structure of Consumer Preferences." *Annals of Economic and Social Measurement,* Vol. 4, No. 1, January, pp. 49-101.

(1983). *Transcendental Logarithmic Production Functions,* Amsterdam, North-Holland.

Jorgenson, D. W., L. J. Lau, and T. M. Stoker (1980). "Welfare Comparison under Exact Aggregation." *American Economic Review,* Vol. 70, No. 2, May, pp. 268-72.

(1981). "Aggregate Consumer Behavior and Individual Welfare." In D. Currie, R. Nobay, and D. Peel, eds., *Macroeconomic Analysis.* London, Croom-Helm, pp. 35-61.

(1982). "The Transcendental Logarithmic Model of Aggregate Consumer Behavior." In R. L. Basmann and G. Rhodes, eds., *Advances in Econometrics,* Vol. 1. Greenwich, JAI Press, pp. 97-238.

Kennedy, Charles (1964). "Induced Bias in Innovation and the Theory of Distribution." *Economic Journal,* Vol. 74, No. 295, September, pp. 541-7.

Klein, L. R., and H. Rubin (1947-8). "A Constant-Utility Index of the Cost of Living." *Review of Economic Studies,* Vol. 15(2), No. 38, pp. 84-7.

Kloek, T. (1966). *Indexcijfers: Enige methodologisch aspecten.* The Hague, Pasmans.

Lau, L. J. (1977a). "Complete Systems of Consumer Demand Functions through Duality." In M. D. Intriligator, ed., *Frontiers of Quantitative Economics,* Vol. III A. Amsterdam, North-Holland, pp. 59-86.

(1977b). "Existence Conditions for Aggregate Demand Functions." Technical Report No. 248, Institute for Mathematical Studies in the Social Sciences, Stanford University, Stanford, Calif., October. (Revised 1980 and 1982.)

(1978). "Testing and Imposing Monotonicity, Convexity, and Quasi-Convexity Constraints." In Melvin Fuss and Daniel McFadden, eds., *Production Economics: A Dual Approach to Theory and Applications,* Vol. 1. Amsterdam, North-Holland, pp. 409-53.

(1982). "A Note on the Fundamental Theorem of Exact Aggregation." *Economics Letters,* Vol. 9, No. 2, pp. 119-26.

Lau, L. J., W. L. Lin, and P. A. Yotopoulos (1978). "The Linear Logarithmic Expenditure System: An Application to Consumption-Leisure Choice." *Econometrica,* Vol. 46, No. 4, July, pp. 843-68.

Leontief, W. W. (1941). *The Structure of the American Economy, 1919-1939.* New York, Oxford University Press. (2nd edition, 1951.)

Leontief, W. W., ed. (1953). *Studies in the Structure of the American Economy.* New York, Oxford University Press.

Leser, C. E. V. (1963). "Forms of Engel Functions." *Econometrica,* Vol. 31, No. 4, October, pp. 694-703.

Lucas, Robert E., Jr. (1967). "Tests of a Capital-Theoretic Model of Technological Change." *Review of Economic Studies,* Vol. 34, No. 98, April, pp. 175-80.

Malinvaud, E. (1980). *Statistical Methods of Econometrics,* 3rd ed. Amsterdam, North-Holland.

Martos, B. (1969). "Subdefinite Matrices and Quadratic Forms." *SIAM Journal of Applied Mathematics,* Vol. 17, pp. 1215–23.

McFadden, D. (1963). "Constant Elasticity of Substitution Production Functions." *Review of Economic Studies,* Vol. 30, No. 83, June, pp. 73–83.

Muellbauer, J. S. (1975). "Aggregation, Income Distribution, and Consumer Demand." *Review of Economic Studies,* Vol. 42, No. 132, October, pp. 525–43.

  (1976a). "Community Preferences and the Representative Consumer." *Econometrica,* Vol. 44, No. 5, September, pp. 979–99.

  (1976b). "Economics and the Representative Consumer." In L. Solari and J. N. DuPasquier, eds., *Private and Enlarged Consumption.* Amsterdam, North-Holland, pp. 29–54.

  (1977). "Testing the Barten Model of Household Composition Effects and the Cost of Children." *Economic Journal,* Vol. 87, No. 347, September, pp. 460–87.

Parks, R. W., and A. P. Barten (1973). "A Cross Country Comparison of the Effects of Prices, Income, and Population Composition on Consumption Patterns." *Economic Journal,* Vol. 83, No. 331, September, pp. 834–52.

Pollak, R. A., and T. J. Wales (1978). "Estimation of Complete Demand Systems from Household Budget Data: The Linear and Quadratic Expenditure Systems." *American Economic Review,* Vol. 68, No. 3, June, pp. 348–59.

  (1980). "Comparison of the Quadratic Expenditure System and Translog Demand Systems with Alternative Specifications of Demographic Effects." *Econometrica,* Vol. 48, No. 3, April, pp. 595–612.

Prais, S. J., and H. S. Houthakker (1955). *The Analysis of Family Budgets.* Cambridge, Cambridge University Press. (2nd ed., 1971.)

Roy, R. (1943). *De l'Utilite: Contribution a la theorie des choix.* Paris, Herman.

Samuelson, Paul A. (1951). "Abstract of a Theorem Concerning Substitutability in Open Leontief Models." In T. C. Koopmans, ed., *Activity Analysis of Production and Allocation.* New York, Wiley.

  (1953). "Prices of Factors and Goods in General Equilibrium." *Review of Economic Studies,* Vol. 21, No. 1, October, pp. 1–20.

  (1956). "Social Indifference Curves." *Quarterly Journal of Economics,* Vol. 70, No. 1, February, pp. 1–22.

  (1965). "A Theory of Induced Innovation along Kennedy–Weizsacker Lines." *Review of Economics and Statistics,* Vol. 47, No. 4, November, pp. 343–56.

  (1973). "Relative Shares and Elasticities Simplified: Comment." *American Economic Review,* Vol. 63, No. 4, September, pp. 770–1.

Scarf, H. (1973). *The Computation of Economic Equilibrium.* New Haven, Yale University Press.

Schmookler, Jacob (1966). *Invention and Economic Growth.* Cambridge, Harvard University Press.

Schultz, H. (1938). *The Theory and Measurement of Demand.* Chicago, University of Chicago Press.

Stone, Richard (1954a). "Linear Expenditure Systems and Demand Analysis: An Application to the Pattern of British Demand." *Economic Journal,* Vol. 64, No. 255, September, pp. 511–27.

  (1954b). *Measurement of Consumers' Expenditures and Behaviour in the United Kingdom,* Vol. 1. Cambridge, Cambridge University Press.

Theil, H. (1965). "The Information Approach to Demand Analysis." *Econometrica,* Vol. 33, No. 1, January, pp. 67–87.

Tornquist, Leo (1936). "The Bank of Finland's Consumption Price Index." *Bank of Finland Monthly Bulletin,* No. 10, pp. 1–8.

Uzawa, H. (1962). "Production Functions with Constant Elasticities of Substitution." *Review of Economic Studies,* Vol. 29, No. 81, October, pp. 291–9.

von Weizsäcker, C. C. (1962). "A New Technical Progress Function." Manuscript, Massachusetts Institute of Technology.

Wold, H. O. A. (with L. Jureen) (1953). *Demand Analysis: A Study in Econometrics.* New York, John Wiley.

Comments

James MacKinnon

The ongoing program of research that Professor Jorgenson describes in his chapter surely represents the most ambitious and sophisticated attempt ever made to estimate a general equilibrium model of a national economy. Most researchers who have constructed applied general equilibrium models have been content to choose the parameters of their models rather than to estimate them. This makes specifying the model very much easier, but often leads to very restrictive specifications of substitution possibilities. Moreover, the observer may reasonably wonder whether a model that has been constructed in this way actually describes the real world at all. Professor Jorgenson, by contrast, describes a project to estimate a reasonably large model of the United States economy, using econometric estimates exclusively.

The amount of effort that must have gone into this project is clearly very great. The models and estimating techniques that are employed are representative of the very best contemporary work on the estimation of demand and production systems. The chapter provides an excellent discussion of the models employed, and could well serve as a reference for researchers interested in doing further work in this area. It is certainly a fine example of the current state of the art in the estimation of systems of demand functions and production relationships.

In the introduction to his chapter, Professor Jorgenson discusses the reasons for using econometrically estimated general equilibrium models. The alternative is to use a model of which all or most of the parameters are chosen rather than estimated, usually in such a way that the model replicates a base year observation. He stresses the fact that models which are constructed in the latter fashion tend to be excessively restrictive in the substitution possibilities that they allow. If our models are to incorporate interesting patterns of substitution between inputs on the production side and between final goods on the demand side, they must involve a great many parameters that cannot be observed from a single year's data, but can, in principle, be estimated econometrically. This is, it would appear, the major reason why Professor Jorgenson prefers the econometric approach.

In my view, the econometric approach has another major advantage over conventional approaches to the construction of general equilibrium models. It can allow us to test, in a formal statistical manner, whether our model is in fact consistent with the real world. Unfortunately, Professor Jorgenson reports almost no efforts to test the adequacy of his model. This is, I think, the major direction in which the work described in this chapter should be extended.

The fundamental question we must ask ourselves about any economic model – econometrically estimated, guesstimated, or purely theoretical – is simply this: Can we believe the results? If not, the model may be very interesting, but it will also be perfectly useless from a practical point of view. We use demand and supply analysis every day because numerous observations of the real world have convinced most of us that demand curves really do slope downward and supply curves really do slope upward. If we employ macroeconometric models, it is presumably because we believe that they adequately describe the operation of the macroeconomy; and if we observe that they fail to do so, we reject them in favor of new models with different theoretical underpinnings. Can we then believe that the model Professor Jorgenson presents adequately describes those features of the American economy that it sets out to represent? It does not seem to me that this chapter provides enough information to allow us to do so. This is not to say that there is necessarily anything wrong with the model. On the contrary, the model is theoretically sound and extremely sophisticated. The problem is simply that no evidence has been presented to show that the model and the data used to estimate it are indeed compatible. Without such evidence, the observer is in no position to judge the model's adequacy.

We all know, in the context of single-equation linear regression models, that several different models may fit well, yield plausible parameter estimates with good t-statistics, and yet have strikingly different implications. If we accept one of the models without testing it thoroughly, we risk putting our faith in a model that is false and thoroughly misleading. Unfortunately, this well-known phenomenon is just as true for nonlinear multiequation models, like the ones estimated by Professor Jorgenson, as it is for the familiar case of linear regressions. The problem, in both cases, is to distinguish models that really do provide an adequate description of the data from models that merely look plausible.

This is of course a difficult task, especially when the model in question is as complicated as the one described by Professor Jorgenson. But it is a task that must be undertaken if we are to employ the model with any degree of confidence to answer questions that matter.

How then could the models discussed by Professor Jorgenson be tested to see whether they are in fact satisfactory representations of the data? There are many ways to do so, some of which I will now briefly discuss.

The models Professor Jorgenson estimates incorporate a number of restrictions: homogeneity, product exhaustion, symmetry, nonnegativity, and monotonicity in the case of the production model, for example. These restrictions, and similar ones for the demand model, must hold if the model is to make economic sense. Testing them will of course be time-consuming, but should not be difficult in most cases (provided we are willing to use asymptotic tests that may be too prone to reject the restrictions when they are true). Of course, it would be unrealistic to expect every restriction to hold for every one of the 36 industries studied by Professor Jorgenson; simply by chance we would expect to get a certain number of rejections. But if, by and large, the restrictions are accepted or only marginally rejected for all but a few industries, we may feel fairly confident about the model. Moreover, if we then look more closely at the few industries where the model did not perform well, we may find that there are special circumstances that explain this, and that can be taken account of to produce more realistic estimates for these industries. On the other hand, if the restrictions are decisively rejected for many industries, we simply have to conclude that the model, theoretically attractive though it may be, is just not compatible with the real world.

One of the most interesting innovations in Professor Jorgenson's paper is that the demand system he estimates uses both aggregate and household data. This is a very attractive way to overcome the inherent limitations of both types of data: lack of price variability in household data taken at a single point in time and aggregation over income classes in aggregate time series data. However, Professor Jorgenson does not report any test of the hypothesis that those parameters that are separately identifiable from both sets of data are in fact the same. If they are not the same, then pooling the two data sets is not legitimate (or else the model is inappropriate).

There are many other ways in which the adequacy of Professor Jorgenson's models could be tested. In particular, it would surely be desirable to examine the residuals to see if they look more or less like white noise, as they should if the models are specified correctly. Pronounced serial correlation would be cause for serious concern, since it very often indicates dynamic misspecification. Professor Jorgenson has of course already transformed his production sector equations for the moving average errors induced by his specification, but that merely implies that the resulting transformed residuals *should* be serially independent, not that they *will* be. Since there are only 17 annual observations for the production sector equations and the aggregate part of the demand system, it would probably not be very useful to test for serial correlation in each equation separately. Unless the residuals were very strongly correlated over time, it would tend to be very difficult to reject the hypothesis of serial independence from such a short sample. However, it should be easy enough to formulate overall tests for serial correlation, pooling all 5 times 17 observations for each industry, or all 17 times 36 observations for each equation, and using nonparametric methods to test for serial independence.

One final way to test the model would be to use it to simulate the postsample period. The data used extend only to 1974, so that virtually the entire sample period consists of years in which the real price of energy was falling. There is casual evidence to suggest that the structure of the U.S. economy has changed in recent years as a result of the dramatic increase in energy prices since 1974. Once more recent data become available, it would clearly be of great interest to simulate the model over the postsample period, to see if it continues to fit adequately. If it does, then it probably captures at least the main important features of the economy. On the other hand, if the model cannot be made to fit the recent data without substantial changes in estimated parameter values, then its validity and usefulness would be very much in doubt.

One reason why one might wonder about the model's ability to fit postsample data is that, except for technical progress on the production side, the model is entirely static. There are of course good reasons for this. Most applied general equilibrium models are static, because dynamic models would be formidably difficult to deal with and because these models are generally designed to answer long-run questions. Moreover, the difficulties of estimating a dynamic model with the available data are formidable. Nevertheless, there is certainly reason to suspect that in the real world firms and households do not respond immediately to relative price changes, so that a model that assumes that they do may well yield misleading results. One reason to test the model in the various ways that I have suggested is to see how seriously a static model does in fact misrepresent the data.

In summary, then, the model discussed in this chapter is very ambitious, very interesting as an exercise in applied econometrics, and potentially very valuable. However, this observer is not prepared to regard it as anything more than an interesting exercise until a good deal of evidence is presented to show that the model and the data are reasonably consistent with each other. I look forward to seeing this evidence.

CHAPTER 5

Money and bonds in a disaggregated open economy

Andrew Feltenstein

1   Introduction

A number of economic models have been advanced in order to represent
the open economy. Although it is not the intention of this chapter to review the extensive literature that concerns itself with these models, let us
note that it may be divided into two different categories, the first of
which concerns itself primarily with the real side of the economy and is in
the Walrasian tradition. There is generally no monetary asset in these
types of model, or if there is, it is neutral so that it will have no impact on
any real variables, and in addition there is no price level, as the models
typically deal only with relative prices of commodities. The main strength
of recent versions of this type of model is that they are able to deal with
large numbers of commodities and to consider complex tax and tariff
systems, while also allowing disaggregated consumer types, and hence a
detailed analysis of the welfare implications of changes in the exogenous
parameters of the model.[1] The attempt to introduce a monetary asset into
the Walrasian system leads to a number of difficulties, which have been
treated with considerable success within the context of a pure exchange
economy, but which are still essentially unsolved in the context of an
economy with production.[2]

The second type of model emphasizes the interaction between the financial and real sectors of the economy and does not necessarily consider
financial assets as being neutral. Essentially all Keynesian and monetarist
models may be included in this general category in which there are normally three items (e.g., commodities, money, and bonds) between which
the consumer chooses. Unlike the Walrasian system, models of this type
admit the existence and, consequently, determination of a price level, of
capital flows, of government monetary policy, and, in particular, allow

I would like to thank Mario Blejer, Michael Dooley, Morris Goldstein, Glenn
Harrison, Mohsin Khan, and Vito Tanzi for a number of important contributions to this paper. The usual disclaimers of course apply.

the consideration of intertemporal choice between current and future consumption. Since they generally assume a single (composite) good, they cannot be used for the study of relative price change or the effects of differential tariff or tax changes.[3]

Recent papers by Clements (1980) and Dornbusch and Mussa (1975) have moved in the direction of combining the Walrasian and monetary-Keynesian approaches. Clements, in particular, allows the theoretical possibility of disaggregated commodity prices, although for empirical work considers only a single good. He has, however, no factor mobility and does not introduce taxes, either levied directly upon consumers or upon individual goods, and thus is unable to analyze fiscal policies. In addition, there is not an explicit government agency, so that domestic credit expansion is purely exogenous and is not dependent upon government behavior.[4] More particularly, government behavior cannot affect the overall savings rate. Finally, and perhaps most important, the Clements model takes the country in question to be a price-taker for all traded goods, an assumption that is of doubtful validity when applied to the United States, the focus of his empirical analysis. From the point of view of a government policy maker who wishes to be able to estimate the impact of both fiscal and monetary policies, where the fiscal policies may include, for example, differential taxes, the shortcomings of the Clements and Dornbusch–Mussa models are apparent. The purpose of this chapter is therefore to set forth a model of a disaggregated open economy that is connected to the Arrow–Debreu model in its general structure, but contains a number of significant differences of a basically monetary nature. The model, which extends Feltenstein (1980), goes considerably beyond Clements in allowing mobile factors of production, many commodities, and an explicit tax structure. The interaction between the behavior of the government and the expansion of domestic credit is also considered, so that simulations reflecting different government policies may be carried out.

Private firms are assumed to have linear technologies in intermediate and final goods (an assumption that could easily be changed to one of smooth technologies), but have the possibility for substitution among the scarce factors that enter their value added, and maximize profits at given market prices subject to taxes on profits, viewed as returns to capital. These taxes are collected by the government, which also levies income and sales taxes and which uses them to finance its production of public goods. We shall not specify the composition of these public goods, but simply treat them as a single commodity produced by a smooth production function.[5] The government decides in advance on a particular level of the output, in real terms, of public goods. It receives no revenue from the sale of these public goods, but must finance their production from tax revenues and the issuance of financial instruments. At an arbitrary set of prices the government tax revenues may differ from the cost of producing the specified level of public goods, and if the revenues are more than the cost, then the government surplus is distributed to consumers as subsidies, whereas if there is a deficit, then the government will issue a combination of money and bonds. These bonds will pay a fixed return, that is, a coupon in terms of money, one period hence and will have a current price that will be determined by the market. We assume that the government finances a fixed fraction of the deficit by selling bonds or by borrowing abroad, that is, selling bonds to foreigners, while the remainder of the deficit will be covered by the issuance of money, the numeraire in the model.[6] Thus domestic credit expansion will be endogenous to the model, as will be the rate of growth of the national debt.[7] There will be no private creation of debt, that is, private enterprises issuing equity, since the problem of modeling private debt creation in an economy with production has not yet been dealt with in the general equilibrium literature, and from the point of view of the focus of this chapter is not essential. Thus, by issuing a fixed quantity of bonds the government will know what the nominal value of its debt creation will be, but because it does not know what the eventual structure of relative prices or the price level will be, it does not know what the real value of this indebtedness will be. Similarly, it cannot anticipate what the inflationary impact of its money creation will be.

There are two types of consumers in the model, domestic and foreign, and there may be a large number of different domestic consumer categories distinguished by demand characteristics. Consumers are assumed to have constant elasticity of substitution utility functions and domestic consumers require their money holdings to be a constant fraction of the value of their consumption in order to cover transaction costs. We have not, however, explicitly modeled transaction costs, but have only assumed that their existence is reflected by consumers' demand for money, a good that yields them no direct utility.[8] Consumers demand bonds, which may be viewed as being essentially a proxy for future consumption and, in the consumer's utility, will be discounted by whatever his rate of time preference may be. The consumer knows what the coupon payment will be on the bond he purchases, but he, of course, does not know what its real purchasing power will be. There are two types of bonds, domestic and foreign, each with its own coupon payment, and both domestic and foreign consumers choose between these types of bonds in order to store a portion of their wealth for future consumption. If both types of bonds were truly perfect substitutes in the eyes of the consumers, then they would purchase only the bond yielding the higher rate of return; in actual practice, however, they are not perfect substitutes for a variety of reasons. We will therefore specify a choice mechanism for consumers by which they always select a positive amount of each bond, according to their relative prices, while the relative weights given to each bond will reflect the consumer's underlying uncertainties concerning risk factors of the two bonds.

Finally, there is only a single type of money, a world currency, so that our model is formally equivalent to one with fixed exchange rates. The home country is viewed as influencing world prices for its exports and hence as facing downward-sloping demand curves for these exports, while it is a price-taker for its imports. We use a modified version of the Armington (1969) assumption, in which goods are distinguished both by type and by place of origin, so that imports are imperfect substitutes for corresponding domestic goods as inputs to production.[9] Trade will not change the total money supply, because of its universal nature, and the only changes in this money supply will be caused by the deficit of the home country's government. We will demonstrate that there exists an equilibrium in this economy at which there may be deficits in both the balance of payments and the budget of the government. The next section will give a technical description of the model; Section 3 will derive excess demand functions, and Section 4 will outline the proof of an existence of an equilibrium. Section 5 will demonstrate how a solution to a numerical example may be derived, and Section 6 will conclude with a brief discussion of possible policy questions that may be examined within the context of the model.

2   The model

It is the normal procedure in work on general equilibrium models to deal separately with the supply and demand sides of the economy in question and to then construct excess demand functions. Our goal is also to construct excess demand functions, but because of the interaction that takes place between production and consumption, it is not possible to treat these two sectors as being independent of each other. We will therefore describe the structure of the production technology and the characteristics of public and private consumption in the next two subsections, respectively, and the third subsection will construct an excess demand function by simultaneously deriving supply and demand functions.[10]

2.1 *Production*

It would be possible to use virtually any standard representation of the
production technology of our economy; smooth production functions,
activity analysis, or input–output are possible choices. Since we wish to
be able to empirically apply the model, we shall construct a particular
version of the supply technology that is closely related to the availability
of data. We will therefore assume that there are three types of physical
commodities in our model: scarce factors, which include all nonproduced
goods and, in addition, capacity constraints; intermediate and final
goods, which are the outputs of, and inputs to, production activities; and
imported goods, which may include both inputs to production and consumption goods. Intermediate and final production is represented by an
input–output matrix so that there are fixed coefficients and no joint production for each activity that produces an intermediate or final good.[11]
We shall suppose that there are $M > 0$ such goods, so that the input–
output matrix is of dimension $M \times M$.

Each input–output activity requires inputs of scarce factors, of which
we will consider only three types: capital, labor, and capacity constraints. There may be several categories of each of the first two, so that,
for example, we may have sector-specific, partially immobile capital and
different skill categories of labor. These scarce factors are combined into
a single output, value-added, via neoclassical production functions, the
parameters of which will differ from sector to sector. Although it would
once again be possible to use any number of such functions, for the sake
of being specific we shall assume that they are Cobb–Douglas, hence of
the form

$$VA_j = \prod_{i=1}^{k} K_i^{\alpha_i^j} \prod_{i=1}^{q} L_i^{\alpha_{k+i}^j} \qquad \text{for all } j \tag{2.1}$$

such that

$$\alpha_i^j \geqq 0 \qquad \text{for all } j$$

and

$$\sum_{i=1}^{k+q} \alpha_i^j = 1.0 \qquad \text{for all } j$$

where VA_j is the total output of value-added of the jth sector; K_i and L_i
are the different categories of capital and labor; α_i^j are the relative shares
in production of capital and labor in the jth sector, and hence are sector
specific; and there are $k > 0$ types of capital and $q > 0$ types of labor.

Each sector requires a certain fixed number of units of value added in order to operate at unit level, but will vary the mix of capital and labor required to produce this value added according to changes in relative prices.[12]

In addition to physical inputs of value added, certain sectors, let us say the first $c \geq 1$, may have capacity constraints, that is, maximum levels at which they are capable of operating because of some unspecified limitation. When the sector operates at unit level it is then viewed as using one unit of capacity constraint, a scarce resource. The production technology may thus be thought of as a set of smooth production functions plus capacity constraint inputs "sitting on top of" an input–output technology, and may be represented in the form of a $(M+c+1) \times M$ matrix:[13]

$$\begin{bmatrix} VA_L & \cdots & VA_c & VA_{c+1} & \cdots & VA_M \\ -1 & \cdots & 0 & 0 & \cdots & 0 \\ \vdots & & \vdots & \vdots & & \vdots \\ 0 & \cdots & -1 & 0 & \cdots & 0 \\ a_{11} & & \cdots & & & a_{1M} \\ \vdots & & & & & \vdots \\ a_{M1} & & \cdots & & & a_{MM} \end{bmatrix}$$

where a_{ij} is an element of the I-A matrix.

There is one modification that remains to be made in our discussion of the domestic production technology. Let us consider a particular good that is an input to production and that may be both imported and domestically produced. We will use a modified version of the Armington (1969) model, which assumes that traded goods are distinguished both by their physical characteristics and place of origin, and we will treat domestic and foreign versions of an input to production as being imperfect substitutes, so that the domestic manufacturers will purchase a combination of the domestically produced good and its imported counterpart. The reason for doing so could be a degree of product[14] differentiation.

Because it has generally been the case, at least in the United States, that relative shares of imports and domestically produced goods have not been constant in production, we shall asssume that inputs of them are combined in production via constant elasticity of substitution (CES) functions in the following way. Suppose that the ith commodity in the input–output matrix has a foreign counterpart, denoted by i_f, which may be imported. If a_{ij} is negative for some j, then the ith good is an input to production in the jth sector.[15] Suppose then that y_{ij} represents inputs of the ith domestically produced good and y_{i_fj} inputs of its foreign counterpart. Total inputs of good i to the jth sector, a_{ij}, are given by

$$a_{ij} = [b_i^{1/s_i} y_{ij}^{(s_i-1)/s_i} + b_{i_f}^{1/s_i} y_{i_f j}^{(s_i-1)/s_i}]^{s_i/(s_i-1)} \tag{2.2}$$

We will shortly derive the demand for domestic inputs as a function of p_i and pf_i, the domestic and world price of the ith good and its foreign counterpart, and of a_{ij}, the total input requirements, but suppose for now that this is given by $y_{ij}(p)$.[16] The lower matrix of domestic production is then modified so that the jth column has coefficients $(a_{1j}, \ldots, a_{i-1,j}, y_{ij}(p), a_{i+1,j}, \ldots, a_{Mj})$. The firms' demand for the foreign input to production is treated separately from the input–output technology in a manner to be described in the section developing the excess demand function, but let us note here that the firm requires a constant amount a_{ij} of the composite commodity.

There is one other production agent that we have not yet mentioned, namely, the government, which produces a single public good, again via a smooth production function that we shall, for simplicity, take to be Cobb–Douglas. This function requires inputs of capital and labor, and so is of the same form as specified in Equation (2.1), whereas its output does not enter into production.[17]

Finally, there are several types of goods in our model that do not enter the productive process, these being three financial assets: money, domestic bonds, and foreign bonds. Both money and domestic bonds are produced costlessly by the government in a manner that we will describe later, but suffice it to say for now that the supply function that produces money and bonds will depend upon the size of the government deficit. Our model thus goes beyond Clements (1980), where the rate of growth of the domestic money supply is exogenous. There are also foreign traded goods that are not used as inputs to domestic production, and since the country is assumed to be a price-taker for all imported goods, the supply function for all imports, including those used for domestic production, is chosen so that the supply of these goods is always equal to the domestic demand for them.[18]

2.2   Consumption

There are $I \geq 1$ domestic consumers and one foreign consumer. Domestic consumers are assumed to have positive initial holdings of all scarce resources and financial assets and no initial holdings of any intermediate or final good, whereas the foreign consumer has holdings of financial assets only. All domestic consumers are assumed to have CES utility functions of the form

$$U^i(x^i) = \left[\sum_j d_{ij}^{1/s_i} x_{ij}^{(s_i-1)/s_i} \right]^{s_i/(s_i-1)} \qquad \text{for all } i \qquad (2.3)$$

where U^i is the ith consumer's level of utility, x_{ij} his consumption of the jth good, s_i his elasticity of substitution, and d_{ij} are constants. In addition, j ranges over those goods that are consumed, primary, intermediate-final and imported, but does not include financial assets, which the consumer does, however, demand. Although we do not explicitly introduce transaction costs into the model, we will claim that for certain unspecified reasons, the consumer must hold an amount of money equal to a fixed fraction of the value of his consumption in order to cover the costs of transactions.[19] Thus, if $\bar{p}$ is the vector of market prices for all goods, primary, intermediate/final, and foreign, and $\bar{x}^i$ the vector of the ith consumer's consumption of the corresponding goods, then if there were no taxes, the consumer would demand $k(\bar{p}\cdot\bar{x}^i)$, $0 \leqslant k \leqslant 1$ units of domestic money, where k represents the fraction of the value of consumption needed to be held in the form of money and is assumed to be constant across consumers.

The consumer is assumed to demand bonds in order to finance part of his consumption next period, and his demand for bonds would presumably be dependent upon his anticipation of future salaries, rate of inflation, and so forth. Suppose then that a coupon price of c_d and a corresponding principal value p_d are announced for a domestic bond. This principal value will typically be different from the market price pm_d of the bond, and the value of the income that the consumer receives from this bond next period is then $p_d + c_d$. If the consumer's rate of time preference is δ, assumed to be constant across domestic consumers, then, ignoring for the moment foreign bonds and dropping the superscript i, he will choose a quantity x_d of domestic bonds such that

$$(p_d + c_d) \cdot x_d + r_L w^E = \frac{1}{1+\delta} \bar{p} \cdot \bar{x}(1 + \pi^E) \qquad (2.4)$$

where w^E is the consumer's expected wage for the next period, r_L is the amount of labor he can offer, and π^E is the anticipated rate of inflation.[20] If, in addition, foreign bonds with nominal price p_f, coupon payment c_f, and quantity demanded x_f are also included, then Equation (2.4) becomes

$$(p_f + c_f) \cdot x_f + (p_d + c_d) \cdot x_d + r_L w^E = \frac{1}{1+\delta} \bar{p} \cdot \bar{x}(1 + \pi^E) \qquad (2.5)$$

The consumer also faces sales taxes on the goods he purchases, so let t^c denote the vector of sales tax rates levied upon all goods. The tax will be paid by the consumer upon his consumption of all intermediate-final and imported goods, while he does not directly pay income taxes, since these will be withheld at the source.[21] If t^c denotes the vector of sales tax rates, then the total cost to the consumer in purchasing the bundle $\bar{x}$ is then given by[22]

$$\bar{p} \cdot \bar{x} + (t^c \bar{p}) \cdot (\bar{x}) = \bar{p}(1 + t^c) \cdot \bar{x} \tag{2.6}$$

The consumer's demand for money will thus be given by

$$k[\bar{p}(1 + t^c) \cdot \bar{x}] \tag{2.7}$$

Thus the consumer requires money to cover transaction costs, but does not require money to pay his income taxes.[23] If pm_d and pm_f represent the prices of domestic and foreign bonds, respectively, if TR represents whatever transfer payments the government may make to consumers and s represents this consumer's share in those payments, if r represents the vector of the consumer's initial holdings as defined above, and p the corresponding price vector, then his overall budget constraint becomes[24]

$$\bar{p}(1 + t^c) \cdot \bar{x} + k[\bar{p}(1 + t^c) \cdot \bar{x}] + pm_d \cdot x_d + pm_f \cdot x_f \leqq p \cdot r + s \cdot TR \tag{2.8}$$

The consumer's maximization problem is

$$\max U(x) \tag{2.9}$$

subject to

1. $\bar{p}(1 + t^c) \cdot \bar{x} + k[\bar{p}(1 + t^c) \cdot \bar{x}] + pm_d \cdot x_d + pm_f \cdot x_f \leqq p \cdot r + s \cdot TR$
2. $(p_d + c_d) \cdot x_d + (p_f + c_f) \cdot x_f + r_L w^E = [1/(1 + \delta)] \bar{p} \cdot \bar{x}(1 + \pi^E)(1 + t^c)$
   (see note 25)
3. $w^E = w(1 + \pi^E), \qquad \pi^E = \Delta VAI$

where ΔVAI, the change in the consumer price index, will be derived in Section 3.

Since domestic and foreign bonds do not enter the consumer's utility function directly, how are we to determine his relative demand for them? We will suppose, quite simply, that

$$pm_d x_d = a \cdot pm_f x_f \qquad a \geqq 0 \tag{2.10}$$

so that the consumer chooses to maintain constant fractions of the value of his total holdings of bonds in domestic and foreign bonds. One could, of course, claim that the consumer would buy only the bond with the lower relative price, but we will assert that, because of various uncertainties, he always wishes to hold at least some of each type of bond.[26] If $a > 1$, then the consumer prefers domestic bonds to foreign bonds, all other things being equal, while if $a < 1$, then the opposite is true.[27]

Let us now consider the foreign consumer, who has an initial holding only of money and of domestic and foreign bonds. It would be possible to have the foreign consumer be a replica of his domestic counterpart, but to do so would imply the construction of a world model, something that is beyond the scope of this exercise. We will therefore develop a highly simplified representation of the foreign consumer, who has a utility maximization problem that consists in the choice of goods exported by the home country plus his own demands for financial assets. The home country is taken to be a price-setter (actually an influencer of prices), for all goods that it exports, so that the foreign consumer will play a role in determining the level of output of exports. In order to represent the foreign demand for exports from the home country we will use a simple elasticities approach, rather than specifying a complete demand function, so that the foreign demand for exports of good i, E_i, is then given by

$$E_i = \{n_i(p_i/p_{i0}-1)+1\}E_{i0} \tag{2.11}$$

where n_i is the world elasticity of demand for exports of good i from the home country, p_i is the current domestic price of good i, p_{i0} is the price of good i in some previous base period, and E_{i0} is the demand for exports of good i in that base period. The value of consumption will thus represent a changing fraction of the foreign consumer's holdings of financial assets and we will eliminate the theoretical possibility that he may demand a value of exports greater than the value of his initial holdings of financial assets in the following way:

$$E_i = \{n_i(p_i/p_{i0}-1)+1\}\cdot E_{i0} \qquad \text{if} \quad \sum_i p_i E_i \leqq p\cdot r_f + M$$

$$= \frac{\{n_i(p_i/p_{i0}-1)+1\}E_{i0}(p\cdot r_f+M)}{\sum_i \{n_i(p_i/p_{i0}-1)+1\}E_{i0}p_i}$$

$$\text{if} \quad \sum_i \{n_i(p_i/p_{i0}-1)+1\}E_{i0} > p\cdot r_f + M \tag{2.12}$$

where r_f is the vector of the foreign consumer's initial holding of financial assets and M is the income he receives from exports he sells to the home country.[28] Thus foreign demand for each export will be scaled uniformly in the case that the value of the total demand is greater than the initial holdings of money. For any empirical application, where the foreign consumer would represent the rest of the world, this would not, of course, take place.[29]

Since we are not attempting to describe foreign consumption of foreign goods, we cannot treat the foreign consumer's demand for money in the same way as we did that of the domestic consumer, namely, as a requirement for transactions. Rather, we specify a two-part choice mechanism in which the foreign consumer first chooses a consumption bundle of domestically produced exports in a manner defined in Equation (2.12), and then divides the remainder of his income among money and domestic and foreign bonds. Suppose that g_i, $i = 1, 2, 3$ are the demand parameters, as a percentage of income, of the foreign consumer, for these three assets, respectively. The foreign consumer's demand for these assets, F_i, $i = 1, 2, 3$, is then given by

$$F_i = g_i \left(p \cdot r_f + M - \sum_j p_j E_j \right) \bigg/ p_i, \qquad i = 1, 2, 3,$$

$$0 \leq g_i \leq 1, \qquad \sum_{i=1}^{3} g_i = 1 \tag{2.13}$$

Thus the foreign consumer spends a constant fraction of the remainder of his income on each of the three financial assets.[30] Obviously there would be many other ways to represent the foreign consumer's demand for financial assets, but we will use this simple formulation for the sake of being specified. As in the case of the domestic consumer's choice of bonds, g_i could be almost any positive continuous functions summing to 1.

2.3   Taxes and the government

The government in our model has several functions. It collects taxes from businesses and consumers and uses these taxes to finance its production of public goods. Since it cannot determine in advance what the precise level of its tax revenues will be, it cannot be sure that they will be sufficient to cover the cost of its expenditures on public goods. The government therefore also functions as a central bank and a treasury in that it finances whatever deficit it may incur via the sale of bonds and the emission of money. If the government runs a surplus, then this surplus will be distributed to consumers in the form of transfer payments. Let us first consider the structure of taxes.

There will be three types of taxes in the model, the first of which is a profits tax that is levied upon returns to capital and upon inputs of labor.[31] If this tax rate is denoted by t_j^k for the jth sector when applied to capital (so that different sectors may face different profit tax rates) and by t_i^L when applied to the ith type of labor,[32] then suppose that $(y_i^j, \ldots, y_{k+q}^j, y_{k+q+j}^j)$ represents the inputs of capital and labor, as in Equation (2.1), to the value added of the jth sector, whereas y_{k+q+j}^j represents usage of the jth sectors' capacity constraint. The total cost to the firm of producing this level of value added is then given by

$$(1 + t_j^k) \sum_{i=1}^{k} p_i y_i^j + \sum_{i=k+1}^{k+q} (1 + t_i^L) p_i y_i^j + p_{k+q+j} y_{k+q+j}^j \tag{2.14}$$

and the corresponding tax paid is given by T^j, where

$$T^j \equiv t_j^k \sum_{i=1}^{k} p_i y_i^j + \sum_{i=k+1}^{k+q} t_i^L p_i y_i^j \tag{2.15}$$

The second general type of tax in our model is a consumption tax that is paid by the individual consumer and that we mentioned briefly in the previous section. In this case a tax rate t_i^c is levied upon consumption of the ith good, so that if the jth consumer's consumption of that good is x_i^j, then the tax he pays on his consumption of the ith good, c_i^j, is given by

$$c_i^j \equiv t_i^c p_i x_i^j \tag{2.16}$$

The ith commodity referred to here may be either an intermediate/final or imported good.

The third type of tax is one that is levied upon imports, that is, a tariff. A tariff is treated as a consumption tax, hence paid by the consumer, and is levied upon the sales price of the imported good, which is fixed in terms of domestic currency. Thus tariffs may be formally represented as in Equation (2.16). We will assume that there are no taxes levied upon exports,[33] so that total taxes collected by the government, T, are now given by

$$T \equiv \sum_{j=1}^{M} T^j + \sum_{j=1}^{I} \sum_{i} c_i^j \tag{2.17}$$

where i in the second summation ranges over all intermediate/final and imported goods.

Let us now turn to the government's role as a provider of public goods and suppose that it produces an output of public goods via a Cobb–Douglas production function using capital and labor as inputs. Clearly other types of production functions could be used, but we will choose this for simplicity. Thus

$$Q = \prod_{i=1}^{k} K_i^{\alpha_i} \prod_{i=1}^{q} L_i^{\alpha_{k+i}}$$

where Q is the physical output of public goods and $0 \leq \alpha_i \leq 1$, $\sum_{i=1}^{k+q} \alpha_i = 1$. Suppose then that the planners decide upon a fixed level $\bar{Q}$ (fixed in physical terms) of the output of the public good.[34] If p_i, $i = 1, \ldots, k+q$ are the prices of capital and labor, then by the usual marginality conditions,

$$L_j = \frac{1 - \alpha_{k+j} \, p_i}{\alpha_i \, p_{k+j}} K_i \tag{2.18}$$

Substituting, we obtain

$$K_i = \left(\frac{p_i}{\alpha_i}\right)^{\alpha_i - 1} \prod_{j=1}^{i-1} \left(\frac{p_j}{\alpha_j}\right)^{\alpha_j} \prod_{j=i+1}^{k+q} \left(\frac{p_j}{\alpha_j}\right)^{\alpha_j} \bar{Q}$$

$$L_j = \left(\frac{p_j}{\alpha_j}\right)^{\alpha_j - 1} \prod_{i=1}^{j-1} \left(\frac{p_i}{\alpha_i}\right)^{\alpha_i} \prod_{i=j+1}^{k+q} \left(\frac{p_i}{\alpha_i}\right)^{\alpha_i} \bar{Q}$$

(2.19)

so that the cost of producing $\bar{Q}$ is given by G, where

$$G \equiv \sum_{i=1}^{k} p_i K_i + \sum_{i=k+1}^{k+q} p_i L_i \qquad (2.20)$$

The government deficit is then given by D, where

$$D = G - T \qquad (2.21)$$

so that if D is negative, then the government runs a surplus. The government will then finance whatever deficit it incurs through a combination of bond sales and money creation. We will not make a distinction between a central bank and a treasury, but rather will assume that they are both contained in the same governmental body. In actual practice – in the United States, for example – the treasury would sell a certain number of bonds at the market price. If the revenues from this sale were not sufficient to cover the deficit, then the treasury would have another round of bond sales, driving the price of bonds lower and the interest rate higher. If, at the same time, the central bank felt that the interest rate was becoming too high, higher than its target for the rate of inflation, then it would purchase bonds by issuing money until the interest rate fell to the desired level. Since we are dealing, however, with a static model, it is not possible to capture this dynamic mechanism. Instead we will assume that the planners decide to finance some fixed fraction of the deficit, if there is one, by selling bonds, while the remainder of the deficit will be covered by issuing money.[35] Suppose that the fraction of the deficit to be covered by the creation of bonds is given by f and the market price of domestic bonds is pm_d. Then the quantity of domestic bonds that the government will put up for sale, y_d, is given by

$$y_d = f \frac{D}{pm_d} \qquad (2.22)$$

whereas the quantity of money that it issues, y_M, is given by

$$y_M = (1 - f) D \qquad (2.23)$$

if we recall that money is the numeraire.

Formally, the government in our model operates as both a consumer and a producer. It purchases capital and labor from the market and is treated as a producer in doing so, and its income, as a consumer, is made up of the taxes it collects. If we view the creation of bonds and money as being the outputs of costless production, then the profits, that is, the total value of the money and bonds created, will go to the government. Thus the cost of government expenditures will be covered and, as we will show in the next section, Walras's law will hold. If, at a particular set of prices, there is a surplus, then the money- and bond-creating activities do not operate and the surplus is distributed among consumers.[36]

3   Excess demand functions

In this section we will develop excess demand functions for the model we have described. We will demonstrate that these functions are continuous, homogeneous of degree zero, and satisfy Walras's law and may thus be shown to have a fixed point that will correspond to the competitive equilibrium. This section is of more than technical interest, since a considerable portion of the model will be developed here.

As we recall from the previous section, our model consists of three types of goods: "primary," which includes financial assets; intermediate/final; and foreign.

We will number the set of primary goods in the following way:

$$\text{Goods } 1,\ldots,k = \text{types of capital}$$

$$\text{Goods } k+1,\ldots,k+q = \text{types of labor}$$

$$\text{Goods } k+q+1,\ldots,k+q+3 = \text{money, domestic bonds, and foreign bonds, respectively}$$

$$\text{Goods } k+q+4,\ldots,k+q+3+c = \text{capacity constraints on the first } c \geq 1 \text{ activities} \tag{3.1}$$

In addition, we will shortly define two more commodities that will be proxies for transfer payments and the value of imports used as inputs to production. Let H, the total number of primary goods, be defined by

$$H \equiv k+q+3+c \tag{3.2}$$

and let $p \equiv p_i,\ldots,p_H$ be an arbitrary vector of market prices for these primary goods.

Suppose now that the jth sector (i.e., column) in the input–output matrix requires $\overline{VA}_j$ physical units of value added to operate at unit level, and, as we recall from the previous section, the jth sector faces a tax rate t_j^k on its capital inputs, corresponding to taxes on profits, and tax rates t_i^L on the ith class of labor, corresponding to income taxes. The cost-minimizing inputs of capital and labor to the jth sector are then given by

$$K_i^j = \left[\frac{p_i}{\alpha_i^j}\right]^{\alpha_i^j-1} \prod_{t=1}^{i-1} \left[\frac{p_t}{\alpha_t^j}\right]^{\alpha_t^j} \prod_{t=i+1}^{k+q} \left[\frac{p_t}{\alpha_t^j}\right]^{\alpha_t^j} [1+t_j^k]^{\sum_{t=1}^{k}\alpha_t^j-1}$$

$$\times \prod_{t=k+1}^{k+q} [1+t_t^L]^{\alpha_t^j} \overline{VA}^j$$

$$L_s^j = \left[\frac{p_j}{\alpha_s^j}\right]^{\alpha_s^j-1} \prod_{t=1}^{s-1} \left[\frac{p_t}{\alpha_t^j}\right]^{\alpha_t^j} \prod_{t=s+1}^{k+q} \left[\frac{p_t}{\alpha_t^j}\right]^{\alpha_t^j} [1+t_j^k]^{\sum_{t=1}^{k}\alpha_t^j}$$

$$\times \prod_{t=k+1}^{s-1} [1+t_t^L]^{\alpha_t^j} \prod_{t=s+1}^{k+q} [1+t_t^L]^{\alpha_t^j} [1+t_s^L]^{\alpha_s^j-1} \overline{VA}^j \tag{3.3}$$

Hence the total cost, that is, nominal value added $va^j(p)$, to the jth sector is[37]

$$va^j(p) = \sum_{i=1}^{k} p_i K_i + \sum_{i=k+1}^{k+q} p_i L_i + p_{k+q+3+j} \tag{3.4}$$

We now have the nominal value added for each column in the input-output matrix A, and if this matrix were composed entirely of constant coefficients, it would now be possible to calculate corresponding Leontief prices. Recall, however, that we are allowing for substitution between certain domestically produced and imported inputs to production, so we must first form the coefficients corresponding to these goods. We will suppose that domestic producers "follow" the world price of imported inputs to production in the following sense. Let ΔX denote the percentage change in the variable X, and let w_j, with $\sum w_j = 1$, $w_j \geq 0$ be the exogenously given weight of the jth good, and hence jth sector, in the domestic price index. We may then form a proxy for the domestic price index by weighting $\{va^j(p)\}$ by these $\{w_j\}$ to obtain $VAI(p)$, defined by[38]

$$VAI(p) \equiv \sum_{j=1}^{M} w_j va^j(p) \tag{3.5}$$

Suppose that the consumer price index at time 0 is given by VAI_0, so that the proxy for the rate of inflation at prices p, $\Delta VAI(p)$, is defined by

$$\Delta VAI(p) = \frac{VAI(p) - VAI_0}{VAI_0} \tag{3.6}$$

Suppose also that ϵ_i is the price elasticity of demand for imports of the ith good as an input to production, assumed to be uniform across sectors.[39] It is assumed that changes in demands for imported inputs to production are functions of changes in the real price of good, so let pf_j be the exogenously given world price of the jth commodity, and let Δpf_j denote the corresponding rate of increase from period 0 in this price.

Recall that we assumed that the aggregate requirements a_{ij} for the combined domestic and foreign inputs of the ith commodity to the jth sector are given by Equation (2.2), and we will assume that $b_{ij} = b'_{ij}$, $s_{ij} = s'_{ij}$, that is, that coefficients and elasticities are uniform across sectors.[40] If $y^0_{ij}, y^0_{i_f j}$ represent respectively the domestic and imported inputs to production of the ith good in sector j in period 0, then

$$\Delta y_{i_f j} = \epsilon_i (\Delta pf_i - \Delta VAI(p)) \tag{3.7}$$

so that the percentage change in use of imports of the ith good as an input to production is given by the real change in that good's world price. Since a_{ij} is a constant, it may easily be shown that

$$\Delta y_{ij} = -(b_{i_f}/b_i)^{1/s_i} (y^0_{i_f j}/y^0_{ij})^{(s_i-1)s_i} \Delta y_{i_f j} \tag{3.8}$$

Thus an increase in the real-world price of the imported counterpart of good i will lead to a decrease in that good's use as an input to production and an increase in the use of the corresponding domestically produced good. The new coefficient in the input–output matrix, $a_{ij}(p)$, is then given by

$$a_{ij}(p) = (1 + \Delta y_{ij}) y^0_{ij} \tag{3.9}$$

Let $A(p)$ represent the input–output matrix formed by these variable coefficients. Since the enterprise must purchase the imported input to production, the total cost of the jth sector's value added plus nondomestically produced inputs to production, $\overline{va}^j(p)$, will be given by

$$\overline{va}^j(p) \equiv va^j(p) + \sum pf_i \cdot (1 + \Delta y_{i_f j}) \cdot y^0_{i_f j} \tag{3.10}$$

where the summation is taken over all goods for which there is a corresponding import used as an input to production, and $va^j(p)$ was defined in Equation (3.4).

Define $\overline{va}(p)$ as

$$\overline{va}(p) = (\overline{va}^1(p), \dots, \overline{va}^M(p)) \tag{3.10a}$$

We may now calculate the Leontief prices $pL(p)$ corresponding to this set of value-addeds and foreign prices by

$$pL(p) = \overline{va}(p) \cdot (I - A(p))^{-1} \tag{3.11}$$

These prices will then be such that each sector in $A(p)$ earns exactly zero after-tax profit. Now let $\bar{p}$ denote the set of factor prices p augmented by Leontief pL and imported goods prices pF, so that[41]

$$\bar{p} \equiv (p, pL, pF) \tag{3.12}$$

We now have a complete set of prices for all goods, including financial assets, and imports, and may now derive each domestic consumer's demand for real and financial assets. The consumer's utility maximization problem as given in Equation (2.9) may be reduced to

$$\max U^i(x) \quad \text{subject to}$$

$$\left[(1+t)(1+t^c) + \frac{(a+1)p_{k+q+3}(1+\pi^E)}{(1+\delta)\lambda}\right]\bar{p}\cdot\bar{x}(1+t^c)$$

$$\leqq p\cdot r + s\cdot TR + \frac{(a+1)p_{k+q+3}r_L w^E}{\lambda} \tag{3.13}$$

where

$$\lambda = (p_d + c_d)a\frac{p_{k+q+3}}{p_{k+q+2}} + p_f + c_f$$

Let $I^i(p)$ denote the right-hand side of the constraint in (3.13). It is then straightforward to show that the consumer's demand for good j, $x_{i,j}$, is given by[42]

$$x_{i,j} = \frac{I^i(p)}{\sum_j a_{i,j}\cdot(\bar{p}_j)^{(1-s_i)}} \cdot \frac{d_{i,j}}{\gamma_j\,\bar{p}_j^{s_i}} \tag{3.14}$$

where

$$\gamma = \frac{(1+t)(1+t^c) + (a+1)p_{k+q+3}(1+\pi^E)(1+t^c)}{(1+\delta)\lambda}$$

and where the summation is taken over all goods.

In particular, the consumer's demand for imported goods is now well defined and hence the total value of imports, $M(\bar{p})$, demanded by domestic consumers is given by

$$M(\bar{p}) = \sum_{i=1}^{I} \sum_{j\in G} pf_j\cdot x_{ij}, \quad G = \text{set of all imported goods} \tag{3.15}$$

The foreign consumer will receive income from the home country from two sources. He will receive $M(\bar{p})$, the value of those imported goods used for final consumption, and, in addition, let S stand for the value of those goods imported for use as inputs to production, which we will take to be the $(H+2)$nd price in the set of factor prices.[43] The total wealth, that is, income of the foreign consumer at prices $\bar{p}$, $I^{l+1}(\bar{p})$, is then given by

$$I^{l+1}(\bar{p}) = \sum_{j=1}^{3} r_{k+q+j}^{l+1} + M(\bar{p}) + S \tag{3.16}$$

where r_{k+q+j}^{l+1} is his initial holding of the jth financial asset. The demand of the foreign consumer for the ith immediate or final good is then defined by Equation (2.12), whereas Equation (2.14) defines the foreign consumer's demand for domestic and foreign financial assets. We may now derive the aggregate demand for intermediate and final goods, xL, by

$$xL_j = \sum_{i=1}^{I+1} xL_{i,j} \tag{3.17}$$

Given these levels of demand, we may derive activity levels z needed to satisfy them by

$$z = (I - A(p))^{-1} \cdot xL \tag{3.18}$$

so that z is a $(1 \times M)$ vector of activity levels corresponding to the matrix $A(p)$. Recall that in Equation (3.3) we derived the capital and labor requirements for a particular activity to produce at unit level, corresponding to the prices p. Let y_{ij}, $i = 1, \ldots, k + q$ be these requirements for the jth column. We may then derive the aggregate supplies of capital and labor as

$$y_i = \sum_{j=1}^{M} z_j \cdot y_{ij} + r_i, \qquad i = 1, \ldots, k + q \tag{3.19}$$

where z_j is the activity level as defined in Equation (3.18) and r_i is the aggregate initial holding of good i. The supplies of each of the capacity constraints are given by

$$y_i = -z_i + r_i, \qquad i = k + q + 4, \ldots, H \tag{3.20}$$

since these activities are defined to use one unit of scarce capacity when operating at unit level. Total tax revenues paid out may now be calculated, defined by T in Equation (2.18), and hence the value of the deficit (or transfer payments) D, defined in Equation (2.22), may also be derived.[44] The "production" of money and domestic bonds, goods $k + q + 1$, $k + q + 2$, has been described in Equations (2.23) and (2.24), and in the terminology of this section is given by

$$\left. \begin{array}{l} y_{k+q+1} = (1-f)D, \\[2ex] y_{k+q+2} = f \dfrac{D}{p_{k+q+2}} \end{array} \right\} \quad 0 \leq f \leq 1 \quad \text{if} \quad D > 0$$

$$y_{k+q+1} = y_{k+q+2} = 0 \quad \text{if} \quad D \leq 0 \tag{3.21}$$

where D is the government deficit. The aggregate supply function y may now be augmented by the negative of the value of the government deficit (transfer payments), D, and the negative of the value of total imports used as inputs to production, F.[45] This augmented supply vector $\bar{y}(\bar{p})$ is thus given by

$$\bar{y}(\bar{p}) \equiv (y, -D, -F) \qquad \text{if} \quad D \leqq 0$$
$$\equiv (y, 0, -F) \qquad \text{if} \quad D > 0 \qquad (3.22)$$

The augmented demand function $\bar{x}(\bar{p})$ is similarly defined as

$$\bar{x}(\bar{p}) = (x, -TR, -S) \qquad (3.23)$$

where TR and S are respectively the price proxies for transfer payments and the value of imported inputs to production and x is the vector of aggregate demands for primary goods and financial assets. The aggregate excess demand function $u(\bar{p})$ is then defined as

$$u(\bar{p}) = \bar{x}(\bar{p}) - \bar{y}(\bar{p}) \qquad (3.24)$$

so we must show that there is some value of $\bar{p}, \bar{p}^*$, for which $u(\bar{p}) \leqq 0$, that is, for which supply is equal to or greater than demand and amount paid out in transfer payments and revenues going to foreign consumers is equal to or greater than the amounts actually collected.

4   The existence of an equilibrium in the model

In this section we will sketch a proof of the existence of an equilibrium in our model. The methodology we use is inspired by Shoven (1974), but contains a number of critical differences from his approach. Our aim is to demonstrate that the excess demand function $u(\bar{p})$, defined in (3.24), is continuous, homogeneous of degree zero, and satisfies Walras's law. An equilibrium price vector may then be shown to exist.[46] We will state a number of lemmas without proof.

Lemma 1: Total government expenditures G is a continuous function of p.

Lemma 2: $I^i(p)$, the income of the ith consumer as defined in Equation (3.13), is a continuous function of p.

Lemma 3: The nominal value added to the jth sector, $va^j(p)$, as defined in Equation (3.4), is a continuous function of p.

We now wish to show that the input–output matrix $A(p)$ is a continuous function of p. To this end we notice that $VAI(p)$ in Equation (3.5) is continuous by Lemma 3, and hence so are $\Delta VAI(p)$ in Equation (3.6) and $\Delta y_{i_f j}$ in Equation (3.7). It then follows that Δy_{ij} in Equation (3.8) and hence $a_{ij}(p)$ in Equation (3.9) are continuous. We thus have

Lemma 4: $A(p)$, the input–output matrix that allows for substitution between domestic and foreign inputs to production, is a continuous function of p.

Lemma 5: $\overline{va}^j(p)$, defined in Equation (3.10), is continuous also.

It is now immediate that the Leontief prices corresponding to $A(p)$ are continuous also.

Lemma 6: $pL(p)$ as defined in Equation (3.11) is continuous.

Proof: $\overline{va}(p)$ is continuous by Lemma 5. $A(p)$ is also continuous, and since the original matrix A is assumed to be nonsingular, it may easily be shown that $A(p)$ remains nonsingular so that $(I-A(p))^{-1}$ is also continuous.

We now have that $(p, pL(p))$, the prices for all domestic goods that the consumer purchases, is a continuous function of p, the prices of scarce factors. The prices of foreign goods, p_F, are exogenous, so $I(p)$, the right-hand side of Equation (3.13), is easily seen to be a continuous function of p, and hence so is the ith consumer's demand function $\{x_{ij}\}$ as defined in Equation (3.14), so that we have:

Lemma 7: $x_j(\bar{p}) = \sum_{i=1}^{I} x_{ij}(\bar{p})$, the aggregate demand by domestic consumers for the jth good, is a continuous function of p.

Let $x_j(\bar{p})$, the aggregate demand by domestic consumers for the jth imported good, be a continuous function of $\bar{p}$. We thus have:

Lemma 8: $I^{l+1}(\bar{p})$, the income of the foreign consumer, as defined in Equation (3.16), is continuous.

Proof:

$$M(\bar{p}) = \sum_{i=1}^{I} \sum_{j} pF_j \cdot x_{ij}(\bar{p})$$

where the inner summation is taken over the set of all imported goods, is continuous by Lemma 7. Since S in Equation (3.16) is the $(H+2)$nd element in $\bar{p}$, $I^{l+1}(\bar{p})$ is continuous.

We thus have that $x_{l+1,j}(\bar{p})$, the foreign consumer's demand for exports of goods from the home country, defined in Equation (2.12), is continuous, so that the aggregate consumer demand for good j, $x_j(p) = \sum_{i=1}^{I+1} x_{ij}(p)$, is also continuous. In addition, the foreign consumer's demands for financial assets, goods $k+q+1, \ldots, k+q+3$ as defined in Equation (2.13), are also continuous, as are those of the domestic consumer.

If we denote by xL the vector of aggregate levels of demand for intermediate and final goods, then by Lemma 4 the activity levels z defined in Equation (3.18) are continuous functions of p. It is easily seen in Equation (3.3) that the scarce resource requirements $\{y_{ij}\}$ are continuous functions also, so that we have:

Lemma 9: $y_i(p) = \sum_{j=1}^{M} z_j \cdot y_{ij}(p) + r_i$ is a continuous function of p.

Here y_i, as originally defined, is the aggregate supply of the ith scarce resource. There is, however, one further source of changes in aggregate supply, namely the inputs required by the government in its production of public goods. These inputs, as defined in Equation (2.19), are clearly seen to also be continuous functions of p, so that we may redefine y_i in Lemma 9 so that we have:

Lemma 10: $y_i(p) = \sum_{j=1}^{M} z_j \cdot y_{ij} + y_{i,M+1}(p) + r_i$ is continuous, where $y_{i,M+1}(p)$ represents the input of the ith good to government production.

In addition to using scarce goods as inputs to its production, the government produces money and bonds in the case where it incurs a deficit, given by $D = G - T > 0$. By Lemma 1, G, government expenditure, is continuous, and T, tax revenues, is also continuous because of the continuity of the aggregate supply and demand functions. Thus the supplies of money and domestic bonds are continuous. Thus we have that y, the vector of aggregate supply, is a continuous function of p. Since $\Delta y_{i_f j}$ in Equation (3.7) and z, the activity levels of the variable input–output matrix $A(p)$, have already been shown to be continuous, F, the value of imported inputs to production, given by

$$F = \sum_{j=1}^{M} z_j \sum p_i (1 + \Delta y_{i_f j}) \cdot y_{i_f j}^0 \tag{4.1}$$

where the inner summation is taken over all domestically produced goods for which there is an imported counterpart, is also continuous.

We thus have:

Theorem 1: The augmented supply function $\bar{y}(p)$, as defined in Equation (3.22), is a continuous function of p.

Since $\bar{x}(\bar{p})$, the vector of aggregate demands, has already been shown to be continuous, we also have:

Theorem 2: The augmented demand function $\bar{x}(\bar{p})$, as defined in Equation (3.23), is continuous.

Theorem 3: The augmented excess demand function $u(\bar{p})$, as defined in Equation (3.24), is continuous.

The components of $u(\bar{p})$ are easily shown to be homogeneous of degree 0 in $\bar{p}$, so it remains for us to show that Walras's law holds for $u(\bar{p})$.[47] To this end notice that the value of total supply $\bar{p} \cdot y(p)$ is given by[48]

$$[pL(p) \cdot (I - A(p)) - p \cdot va(p)] - G + M(p) + p \cdot r$$
$$= [T + F] - G + M(p) + p \cdot r$$
$$= [T - G] + F + M(p) + p \cdot r \quad \text{if} \quad T - G = -D \geqq 0$$
$$= [T - G] + F + M(p) + p \cdot r + y_{k+q+1} + p_{k+q+2} \cdot y_{k+q+2} \quad \text{if} \quad T - G < 0$$
$$= F + M(p) + p \cdot r \tag{4.2}$$

Here y_{k+q+1}, y_{k+q+2} are respectively the money and domestic bonds created by the government in the case of a deficit. Thus

$$p \cdot y(p) + D - F = M(p) + p \cdot r \quad \text{if} \quad T - G = -D \geqq 0$$
$$p \cdot y(p) - F = M(p) + p \cdot r \quad \text{if} \quad T - G < 0 \tag{4.3}$$

On the demand side, the value of total demand, $\bar{p} \cdot x(p)$, given by the value of total income, is

$$M(p) + S + TR + p \cdot r \tag{4.4}$$

and

$$p \cdot x(p) - TR - S = M(p) + p \cdot r \tag{4.5}$$

so that we have equality for the values of the augmented supply and demand functions, which are now defined to include all goods. We must show that Walras's law holds also on the smaller space of primary goods and financial assets, as defined in Equations (3.22)–(3.24). To this end notice that $yL_j \equiv xL_j$, $yF_j \equiv xF_j$ by construction,[49] so that, in particular,

$$\bar{p} \cdot y(p) - p \cdot yL - p \cdot yF = p \cdot x - p \cdot xL - p \cdot xF$$

Thus

$$p \cdot \bar{y}(p) = p \cdot \bar{x}(p)$$

so we have the required result.

Table 1

	Sector		
	1	2	3
Labor	.3	.2	.5
Capital	.7	.8	.5

Table 2

	Sector		
Good	1	2	3
1	4.0	− .2	− .1
2	− 2.0	1.5	.0
3	− 1.0	− 3.0	.5

The analysis of Shoven (1974) may now be followed to demonstrate the existence of an equilibrium on the space of scarce resources and financial assets.

5 A numerical example

In this section we will present a very simple numerical example, which should serve to clarify the mechanics of our model. The production side of the economy has only three sectors, each of which has a Cobb–Douglas function for value-added, as in Equation (2.1), with coefficients $[\alpha_{ij}]$ given by Table 1. In addition, the first sector has a capacity constraint with a total of 7 units of capacity. The input–output structure, $I - A$, of the economy is given by Table 2. There is one imported good that may be used for both consumption and as an input to production, where it competes with input–output good 1. We will assume that this good has a fixed world price of 1, in terms of units of money; and as in Equation (2.2), the coefficients and elasticity of substitution are $b_1 = .5$, $b_{1_f} = .5$, $s_1 = 1.8$.

There are only two consumers in the model, one domestic and one foreign. The domestic consumer's demand coefficients (α_{ij}) are given in Table 3, while his elasticity of substitution is $s = 1, 2$. We need also to specify the parameter k, representing the domestic consumer's demand for money, as in Equation (2.7), and which we will take to be equal to

Table 3

Good									
Primary[a]						Input–output			Imported
1	2	3	4	5	6	1	2	3	1
.1	.1	0	0	0	0	.15	.25	.2	.2

[a] Goods 3–6 are money, domestic bonds, foreign bonds, and the capacity constraint, respectively, which, as we have noted, do not enter the consumer's utility function.

Table 4

Input–output good		
1	2	3
− .02	− .04	− .01

Table 5.

Financial assets		
3	4	5
.8	.1	.1

.05, and also the parameter a, as in Equation (2.10), which we will take to be equal to .3.

The foreign consumer's elasticities of demand for the input–output goods, as in Equation (2.11), are given by Table 4, so that an increase in the domestic price of a good will lead to a decline in the foreign demand for it. The percentages of the foreign consumer's income remaining after his consumption expenditure going to the three financial assets, primary goods 3, 4, 5 [F_i, as in Equation (2.13)], are given in Table 5. Finally, each consumer has initial holdings given by Table 6, so that the foreign consumer holds only financial assets at the beginning of the period.

The government levies taxes upon consumption of input–output and imported goods, with a uniform tax rate of .2, whereas it charges a tax on each sector's use of labor, at a uniform rate of .1, equivalent to withholding income taxes at the source. The government produces public goods via a Cobb–Douglas production function, as specified in Equation (2.1), whose parameters for labor and capital are, respectively, $\alpha_1 = \alpha_2 = .5$. In the case where the government incurs a deficit, the parameter f, as in Equation (2.22), which determines what fraction of the deficit will be financed by the sale of bonds, is given by $f = .4$, so that 40% of the deficit will be financed by the emission of money, while 60% will be covered by the sale of domestic bonds.

Table 6

	Initial allocations	
Good	Domestic consumer	Foreign consumer
1	2.0	.0
2	3.0	.0
3	.034	.97
4	2.0	1.0
5	.5	.1
6	7.0	.0

Table 7

Good	Price	Supply	Excess demand[a]
Primary goods[b]			
1. Labor	.0796	1.028	0
2. Capital	1.056	.737	0
3. Money	1.0	1.004	0
4. Domestic bonds	.045	3.0	0
5. Foreign bonds	.382	.6	0
6. Capacity constraint	.0	6.785	− 6.785
7. Transfer payments	.518	—	—
8. Imported inputs to production	.954	—	—
Input–output goods			
1	3.705	.243	—
2	9.429	.181	—
3	74.138	.021	—
Imported good			
1	1.0	1.116	—

[a]Using Merrill's (1971) method of a shrinking grid subdivision, the grid size had reached 314,928, and excess demands were less than .001% of supplies.
[b]Prices are normalized so that good 3, money, is the numeraire.

We will solve this model under two different assumptions concerning the level $\bar{Q}$ of government production of public goods. In the first simulation, $\bar{Q} = .1$, leading to the results given in Table 7.

On the demand side the corresponding results are given in Table 8, whereas the remainder of the supply of labor and capital goes to the government's production of public goods. Total government revenues are

Table 8

Good	Demand	
	Domestic consumer	Foreign consumer
Primary goods		
1	.912	0
2	.650	0
3	.258	.746
4	.913	2.087
5	.356	.244
6	.0	.0
Input-output goods		
1	.174	.069
2	.094	.087
3	.006	.015
Imported good		
1	1.116	0

$T = .702$, whereas expenditures are $G = .184$, so that the government runs a surplus of .518, equal to the price of good 7, transfer payments. There is .954 unit of imported inputs to production, the value of which is thus equal to the price of good 8.

The current account is defined as the value of the demand of the foreign consumer for domestic goods (exports), minus the demand of the domestic consumer for foreign goods (imports), and in this case is equal to $2.190 - 2.069 = .121$. The capital account is given by the change in the foreign consumer's holding of domestic bonds (if positive representing a capital inflow), minus the change in the domestic consumer's holdings of foreign bonds (if positive representing a capital outflow), and in this case is equal to $.049 - (-.055) = 0.104$, so that the overall balance of payments is .225 in terms of units of domestic currency and thus is in surplus.

We may also form a measure of the domestic price index by calculating consumption weights and combining them with the corresponding prices. The resulting price index P in this case is $P = 10.244$.

As a second case, let us suppose that the government decides to quadruple the level of its output of public goods, so that $\bar{Q} = .4$, but all other exogenous parameters remain unchanged. The new outcomes are given in Table 9.

The total revenues of the government are $T = .764$, whereas its expend-

Table 9.

Good	Price	Supply	Excess demand
Primary goods			
1. Labor	.966	1.199	0
2. Capital	1.175	.962	0
3. Money	1.0	1.056	0
4. Domestic bonds	.011	10.168	0
5. Foreign bonds	.225	.600	0
6. Capacity constraint	.0	6.812	−6.812
7. Transfer payments	.0	—	—
8. Imported inputs to production	.861	—	—
Input–output goods			
1	4.086	.230	—
2	10.268	.172	—
3	80.673	.017	—
Imported good			
1	1.0	1.168	—

	Demand	
Good	Domestic consumer	Foreign consumer
Primary goods		
1	.758	0
2	.599	0
3	.266	.790
4	1.007	9.161
5	.161	.439
6	0	.011
Input–output goods		
1	.162	.068
2	.089	.083
3	.006	—
Imported good		
1	1.168	0

itures are $G=.852$, leading to a deficit of .088. This deficit has been covered by the emission of money and domestic bonds, the supply of which has increased, as compared with the previous case, in which the government was in surplus. The fact that there is a deficit is also reflected in the 0 price of transfer payments. Finally, there is .861 unit of imported inputs to production, again equal to the price of good 8.

In this case the current account has become $2.044 - 2.029 = .015$, whereas the capital account has become $.088 - (-.076) = .164$, leading to an overall balance of payments surplus of $.179$, a decline of 20% from the surplus of the previous example. The fact that the current account is almost in deficit, as compared to the large surplus of the previous example, reflects the fact that the competitive position of domestic industry has been weakened by the inflation induced by the government deficit. In addition, consumer demand for the imported good has risen from 1.116 to 1.168, reflecting the shift in relative prices in favor of imports. The improvement in the capital account follows from the large capital inflows brought about by the lower price (and hence higher interest rates) of domestic bonds caused by the deficit-induced increase in the supply of domestic bonds. The decline in the overall balance of payments is consistent with a simple version of the monetary approach to the balance of payments, in which consumers will not hold all of the money that has been created by the government. Finally, the overall consumer price index has risen to 11.544, representing an inflation of 12.7%.

6   Summary and conclusion

This chapter has discussed the general features of the Walrasian and the macroeconomic approaches to modeling an open economy and has briefly considered their relative strengths and weaknesses in coping with the type of questions that might be of interest to a government policy maker. A model has been constructed of a dissaggregated open economy that is a price-taker for some goods and a price-setter for others, an advance over the most recent macroeconomic general equilibrium models that assume the country to be a price-taker for all goods. There is an active government that produces public goods and pays for its purchases of factor inputs from the tariffs and taxes (income, profit, and sales) that it collects. Since these taxes will not necessarily be sufficient to finance the cost of the public goods, the government issues a combination of money and bonds to finance whatever deficit it incurs, so that the rates of change of both the nominal money supply and the level of public indebtedness are endogenous. This endogeneity is an advance over the current Walrasian general equilibrium literature, which, with rare exceptions, has not considered economies with production and financial assets. Current macroeconomic models, on the other hand, that have provisions for disaggregated commodities also require the money supply to be exogenous, thus precluding any investigation of the impact of government behavior on the financial sector. The model also contains foreign consumers and foreign bonds and can therefore generate endogenous capital flows.

The model is able to address a number of policy questions. What will be the impact on the savings and consumption behavior of the economy if the government changes its output of public goods? How will a differential change in tax rates affect the output and welfare levels of the economy through its direct impact on relative prices? How will a change in the government's method of financing its deficit, that is, changing the proportions financed by money and bonds, change the overall balance of payments? Since the model allows for substitution between domestic and imported inputs to production, depending upon relative prices, it is also able to investigate the impact upon the economy of an exogenous change in the world price of an imported good. There are a number of other questions that might be of interest to a government that could be examined within the context of the model.

The existence of a market-clearing equilibrium for the model, corresponding to any (reasonable) set of government policies, has been demonstrated. We have developed an algorithm, based upon the method of proof of the previous section, that calculates a numerical solution to the equilibrium of the model, so that explicit policy simulations may be carried out.[50] A small numerical example has been presented and has been solved using this indication. The example should clarify the workings of the model and should also indicate how an empirical application might be implemented. The example clearly indicates the nonneutrality of money in the model and how it might be used to analyze the real impacts of different government spending programs.

NOTES

1. The theoretical foundations of the modern versions of this model are given in Debreu (1959), while recent computational examples, some with empirical content, are given in Dervis and Robinson (1978), Feltenstein (1979, 1980), Fonseca (1978), Miller and Spencer (1977), Richter (1978), Shoven (1976), and Whalley (1977).
2. A survey of the attempts to introduce money into the Walrasian system is given in Grandmont (1977).
3. This is, of course, a great oversimplification of the characteristics of and differences between these types of models.
4. Aghevli and Khan (1978) and Tanzi (1978) have constructed monetary models that incorporate endogenous public sector deficits. They do not, however, consider differentiated commodity types.
5. Richter (1978) has constructed a computational general equilibrium model that emphasizes the production of public goods.
6. This particular financing rule is not necessarily required, and the government might instead, for example, choose to set the quantity of bonds it will issue, while letting the market price fluctuate. In addition, the rule for determining the quantity of bonds to be issued could be *any* continuous function of the

government deficit. This point should be emphasized, lest it be thought that the rule of constant fractions is essential to the model.

7. The connection between the government deficit and monetary expansion has been made in a very ad hoc manner in most of the recent literature, where there is no behavioral explanation of this expansion, but rather an econometric estimate is made of the parameter connecting the government deficit and the change in the money supply. For an example, see Aghevli and Khan (1978).

8. Hahn (1971, 1973) and Kurz (1974) are the basic papers introducing transaction costs into the general equilibrium framework. Grandmont (1977) offers a survey of the current state of the subject. Our treatment of transaction costs is admittedly ad hoc as it is not derived from axiomatic reasoning. As in the case of deficit financing, the consumer's demand for money could be a much more complicated function than the simple fraction we specify. One might, for example, specify a functional form that incorporates an anticipated rate of inflation. Such added complexity makes no qualitative change in our analysis, however.

9. Ideally we would like to be able to consider imported goods for which the country is a price-setter, but doing so would require us to specify a world supply function for that good, a task we wish to avoid.

10. This is also the procedure developed in Feltenstein (1980).

11. Our production coefficients are not, actually, completely fixed since, as we shall discuss shortly, a certain degree of substitution is allowed between domestically produced inputs to production and their imported counterparts.

12. A similar methodology is described in Whalley (1977) and Whalley and Yeung (1980). It is not the case that scarce factors will have a constant share in the value of final output, since relative prices will change.

13. The input–output matrix we refer to is $I-A$, so that negative entries represent inputs to a particular sector, whereas positive entries represent net outputs.

14. At the degree of aggregation that would be used in any empirical study, the price indices for domestic goods and their foreign counterparts are very different, indicating that they are not perfectly comparable.

15. Here a_{ij} represents the total input requirements of the ith type of good to the jth sector, a requirement that may be made up from foreign and domestic sources.

16. These are considered functions of p, domestic prices, only, since world prices of imports are taken to be exogenous. In Equation (2.2) we have assumed that for a particular commodity the coefficients and elasticity of substitution are constant across sectors, since in any empirical work it would generally be possible to estimate these parameters only on an economywide basis.

17. We are thus ignoring the government's role in, for example, training human capital or building highways. Such roles, although obviously of great importance to the modern economy, are not germane to our model.

18. This approach is described in greater detail in Whalley and Yeung (1980).

19. This admittedly ad hoc introduction of money has appeared in somewhat different form in various macroeconomic models of trade. See, for example, Weiss (1980). In Weiss's model, however, the nominal stock of money is exogenously given, so that there is no possibility of analyzing changes in the money supply. Glenn Harrison has pointed out to me that there has been

recent work on systemwide demand models that simultaneously deal with the consumer's allocation of money holdings and consumption. See, for example, Clements (1976).

20. Both w^E and π^E might, in practice, be generated in a variety of ways. For our purpose, as we shall explain in greater detail in the next section, the consumer will be perfectly myopic, so that $w^E = (1 + \pi^E)w$, where w is his current wage and π^E is equal to the current rate of inflation.

21. Here income taxes will be paid by the firm when it purchases labor and capital from the consumer.

22. Thus $t^c = (0, \ldots, 0, t_1^c, \ldots, t_M^c, \ldots, t_{M+F}^c)$, if these are F imported goods, whereas the zeros correspond to primary goods and financial assets.

23. An empirical study of the impact on money demand of withholding at the source has been made by Tanzi (1974).

24. It may be felt that we are adding stocks and flows in (2.8). For a justification of this approach see Harrison (1980).

25. We have assumed that the consumer includes sales taxes, at their current rates, in evaluating the cost of his future bundle of consumption.

26. As we mentioned earlier, the parameter a could be essentially any continuous function, since, as we shall see, the only requirement is that the excess demand functions be continuous.

27. If there were a possibility of a change in the exchange rate, then the parameter a would presumably reflect the consumer's perception of exchange rate risk, perhaps in a nonlinear fashion.

28. Here p refers only to the prices of the financial assets.

29. Because the foreign consumer receives income from his sale of exports to the home country, his own levels of demand are subject to a wealth effect. This specification of foreign demand for exports is given in Boadway and Treddenick (1978).

30. When the asset in question is money, $p_i = 1$, since money is the numeraire. This is not an explanation of why the foreign consumer holds financial assets. Such an explanation poses no theoretical problems within the context of this model, but would require an equally complete characterization of him as of the domestic consumer, which would be virtually impossible in any empirical application.

31. When the tax is levied upon inputs of labor, it represents the income tax withheld at the source that we mentioned earlier, whereas when it is levied upon capital it may be interpreted as a profits tax.

32. There is thus the same tax rate applied to different types of capital, whereas different tax rates may be applied to different types of labor, although the rates will be uniform across sectors. We will avoid introducing progressive income taxes for reasons of simplicity.

33. The introduction of export taxes (or subsidies) would pose no technical problem, but they are not currently in use in most industrial countries.

34. Our notion of public goods is, for example, defense.

35. As we mentioned in the introduction, the rule for issuing bonds could be essentially any continuous function of the deficit.

36. Thus the introduction of a government allows the existence of a central bank that creates money. Unlike Grandmont and Laroque (1975), we do not allow consumers to borrow directly from this central bank, thereby creating their own indebtedness.

37. Recall that goods $k+q+3+1, \ldots, k+q+3+c$ are capacity constraints on the first c sectors. Thus $p_{k+q+3+j} \equiv 0$ if $j > c$.

38. Because of the possibility of substitution between domestic and imported goods in production, $VAI(p)$ is not a totally satisfactory substitute for the domestic price index, as would be the case if there were completely fixed co-efficients in intermediate and final production. Our justification for the use of this proxy is that producers look at, for example, changes in domestic labor costs in making initial decisions concerning the purchases of inputs.

39. Such elasticities are typically estimated in econometric studies. See, for example, Goldstein and Khan (1978).

40. This assumption is not a technical necessity, but rather is motivated by empirical considerations.

41. Recall that prices of imported goods are exogenously given in terms of money, the numeraire.

42. Recall that TR, total transfer payments, is being treated as the $(H+1)$st price, and that the parameters defining λ are those given in Equation (3.13).

43. These are not really factor prices, since domestic financial assets may be produced. Rather they are the set of prices on which we will be calculating an equilibrium.

44. It should be recalled that in the case where $D < 0$, the transfer payments going to consumers, $-D$, is not, in general, equal to TR, the $(H+1)$st price that enters the consumer's budget constraint, as in Equation (3.13). We will demonstrate that at the equilibrium to be shown to exist they are, in fact, equal.

45. As in Equation (3.10), this amount may be calculated as

$$F = \sum_i \sum_j pf_i (1 + \Delta y_{i_f j}) y_{i_f j}^0$$

where the inner summation is taken over the set of all domestically produced goods for which there is an imported substitute.

46. We will ignore certain problems that are typically dealt with in the demonstration of the existence of an equilibrium in such models – infinite demands when a particular price goes to zero, for example. Such problems may be solved here in the same way as they have been solved elsewhere in the general equilibrium literature. In addition, this section will present only an outline of the method of proof, since the necessary details may easily be supplied by the reader.

47. The only possible problem with the homogeneity of the excess demand function comes because of the exogeneity of the foreign prices, pF. If we recall, however, that money is the numeraire, then we may define the foreign prices in terms of money as $pF_i = p_{k+q+1} pF_i'$, where pF_i' gives the price of the imported good in terms of units of money. Homogeneity is then immediate.

48. Here $y(p) \equiv (\bar{y}(p)yL, yF)$, where yL denotes the supply of intermediate/final and yF the supply of imported goods. Similarly, $x(p) \equiv (\bar{x}(p), xL, xF)$.

49. It is precisely in order to obtain these identities that we have used the input–output structure of domestic intermediate and final production and have allowed consumers to have initial allocations of primary and financial assets only.

50. The algorithm used here is based upon Merrill (1971) and Scarf (1973). Manne et al. (1980), Eaves (1976), and Mansur and Whalley (1981), among others, have constructed somewhat different algorithms to solve similar

problems. A different approach, based on Newton's method, has been employed by a number of other economists.

REFERENCES

Aghevli, Bijan B., and Mohsin S. Khan. 1978. "Government Deficits and the Inflationary Process in Developing Countries." *International Monetary Fund Staff Papers,* Vol. 25, pp. 383–416.

Armington, Paul S. 1969. "A Theory of Demand for Products Distinguished by Place of Production." *International Monetary Fund Staff Papers,* Vol. 16, pp. 159–76.

Atsumi, Hiroshi. 1981. "Taxes and Subsidies in the Input–Output Model." *Quarterly Journal of Economics,* Vol. 46, No. 1, pp. 27–46.

Boadway, R., and J. M. Treddenick. 1978. "A General Equilibrium Computation of the Effects of the Canadian Tariff Structure." *Canadian Journal of Economics,* Vol. 11, No. 3, pp. 424–46.

Clements, Kenneth W. 1976. "A Linear Allocation of Spending-Power System: A Consumer Demand and Portfolio Model." *Economic Record,* Vol. 52, pp. 182–98.

1980. "A General Equilibrium Econometric Model of the Open Economy." *International Economic Review,* Vol. 21, pp. 469–88.

Clements, Kenneth W., and Phuong Nguyen. 1980. "Money Demand, Consumer Demand, and Relative Prices in Australia." *Economic Record,* Vol. 56, pp. 338–46.

Debreu, Gerard. 1959. *Theory of Value: An Axiomatic Analysis of Economic Equilibrium.* New York, Wiley.

Dervis, Kemal, and Sherman Robinson. 1978. "The Foreign Exchange Gap, Growth, and Industrial Strategy in Turkey, 1973-1983." World Bank Staff Working Paper No. 306. Washington, D.C.

Dornbusch, R., and M. Mussa. 1975. "Consumption, Real Balances, and the Hoarding Function." *International Economic Review,* pp. 415–21.

Eaves, Curtis. 1976. "A Finite Algorithm for the Linear Exchange Model." *Journal of Mathematical Economics,* Vol. 3, pp. 197–203.

Feltenstein, Andrew. 1979. "Market Equilibrium in a Model of a Planned Economy of the Soviet Type: A Proof of Existence and Results of Numerical Simulations." *Review of Economic Studies,* Vol. 46, pp. 631–52.

1980. "A General Equilibrium Approach to the Analysis of Trade Restrictions, with an Application to Argentina." *International Monetary Fund Staff Papers,* Vol. 27, No. 4, pp. 749–84.

Fonseca, Marcos G. 1978. "The General Equilibrium Effects of International Trade Policies." Ph.D. diss., Yale University.

Goldstein, Morris, and Mohsin S. Khan. 1978. "The Supply and Demand for Exports: A Simultaneous Approach." *Review of Economics and Statistics,* May, pp. 275–86.

Grandmont, J. M. 1977. "Temporary General Equilibrium Theory." *Econometrica,* Vol. 45, pp. 535–72.

Grandmont, J., and G. Laroque. 1975. "On Money and Banking." *Review of Economic Studies,* Vol. 42, No. 130, pp. 207–36.

Hahn, Frank H. 1971. "Equilibrium with Transaction Costs." *Econometrica,* Vol. 39, pp. 417–39.

1973. "On Transaction Costs, Inessential Sequence Economies, and Money." *Review of Economic Studies,* Vol. 40, pp. 449-61.

Harrison, Glenn W. 1980. "The Stock-Flow Distinction: A Suggested Interpretation." *Journal of Macroeconomics,* Vol. 2, No. 2, pp. 111-28.

Kurz, Mordecai. 1974. "Equilibrium in a Finite Sequence of Markets with Transaction Cost." *Econometrica,* Vol. 41, pp. 1-20.

Manne, Alan S., Hung-Po Chao, and Robert Wilson. 1980. "Computation of Competitive Equilibria by a Sequence of Linear Programs." *Econometrica,* November, No. 7, pp. 1595-615.

Mansur, Ashan, and John Whalley. 1981. "A Decomposition Algorithm for General Equilibrium Computation with Application to International Trade Models." University of Western Ontario. Mimeo.

Merrill, O. H. 1971. "Application and Extensions of an Algorithm That Computes Fixed Points of Certain Non-Empty Convex Upper Semi-Continuous Point to Set Mappings." Ph.D. diss., University of Michigan.

Miller, Marcus H., and John E. Spencer. 1977. "The Static Economic Effects of the U.K. Joining the EEC: A General Equilibrium Approach." *Review of Economic Studies,* Vol. 44, pp. 71-93.

Neary, J. Peter. 1980. "Nontraded Goods and the Balance of Trade in a Neo-Keynesian Temporary Equilibrium." *Quarterly Journal of Economics,* Vol. 45, No. 3, pp. 403-30.

Richter, Donald K. 1978. "Existence and Computation of a Tiebout General Equilibrium." *Econometrica,* Vol. 49, pp. 779-805.

Scarf, H. (with T. Hansen). 1973. *The Computation of Economic Equilibria.* New Haven, Yale University Press.

Shoven, John B. 1974. "A Proof of the Existence of a General Equilibrium with ad Valorem Commodity Taxes." *Journal of Economic Theory,* Vol. 8, pp. 1-25.

1976. "The Incidence and Efficiency Effects of Taxes on Income from Capital." *Journal of Political Economy,* Vol. 84, pp. 1261-83.

Tanzi, Vito. 1974. "Demand for Money, Interest Rates, and Income Taxation." *Banca Nazionale del Lavoro Quarterly Review,* No. 111, pp. 319-28.

1978. "Inflation, Real Tax Revenue, and the Case for Inflationary Finance: Theory with an Application to Argentina." *International Monetary Fund Staff Papers,* Vol. 25, pp. 417-51.

Weiss, Lawrence. 1980. "A Model of International Trade and Finance." *Quarterly Journal of Economics,* Vol. 45, No. 2, pp. 277-92.

Whalley, John. 1977. "The United Kingdom Tax System, 1968-70: Some Fixed Point Indications of Its Economic Impact." *Econometrica,* Vol. 45, pp. 1837-58.

Whalley, John, and Bernard Yeung. 1980. "External Sector 'Closing' Rules in Applied General Equilibrium Models." University of Western Ontario.

CHAPTER 6

Modeling structural adjustment: micro and macro elements in a general equilibrium framework

Sherman Robinson and Laura D'Andrea Tyson

1   Introduction

The division of economic theory into macroeconomics and microeconomics, although now commonplace, is of relatively recent origin. Certainly, the classical economists through Marshall would not have tolerated a separate theory of macroeconomics not arising naturally from microeconomic descriptions of the behavior of the various actors in an economic system. However, such a separation has occurred in practice, and a large body of theory has been developed about relationships among economic aggregates that is only loosely, if at all, supported by well-articulated theories of relationships among microeconomic behavioral units.

Economics is not the only science to tolerate such a dichotomy in its basic theory. There are many examples in physics and chemistry, but perhaps a good analog for economics – especially considering the current state of macro theory – is provided by the science of meteorology. Although the underlying principles of physics and thermodynamics are well understood, the macro theory of weather prediction is certainly less than exact.[1] There is, of course, a tension in any science that demands a reconciliation between theories dealing with aggregates and theories about the behavior of their component units. This tension is clearly evident in economics, and there is a growing literature that reflects dissatisfaction with the current situation (for example, see Phelps, 1979; Clower, 1965; and Weintraub, 1977). Although this literature is instructive, it cannot be said to have produced an acceptable (or even widely accepted) reconciliation, and we remain a long way from an integrated theory of the way entire economies function.

We would like to thank Jaime de Melo and Adrian Wood for very helpful comments on an earlier draft. Neither they nor the World Bank can be held responsible for any views expressed in the paper.

Given the lack of an adequate integrated theory, what is one to do when faced with policy problems that clearly involve both structural issues that are essentially microeconomic in nature and aggregate flow-of-funds issues that are essentially macroeconomic? Consider, for example, the impact on an economy of a rise in the price of a crucial import such as oil. Given the large nominal magnitudes involved, there will have to be various macroeconomic adjustments. The real exchange rate must fall, aggregate income must fall, total absorption must fall, and there will be significant changes in various nominal flow-of-funds magnitudes that affect macroeconomic equilibrium. For example, the balance of payments and the government accounts will be affected, and perhaps the money supply and various capital accounts as well. Variables that are typically included in macro models, such as the exchange rate, the aggregate price level, interest rates, average wages, aggregate employment, and output, are expected to adjust.

In addition to these macroeconomic effects, a change in the price of oil will also have important effects that work through individual markets and are essentially microeconomic in nature. The increase in the relative price of oil will lead to substitution away from oil and toward other goods by both final demanders and industries that use oil as an intermediate input. The extent of this effect will depend on elasticities of substitution between oil and other goods both in consumption and in intermediate use. The change in the exchange rate will change the relative prices of tradables with respect to nontradables in the economy and hence affect the sectoral allocation of resources. The ultimate structural impact will depend on relative factor intensities and substitution elasticities in production among sectors, as well as on conditions on the demand side. These microeconomic, structural effects work through a network of interrelated markets and can only be captured by a multisectoral general equilibrium model.

The interdependence of structural or sectoral policy issues and stabilization issues suggested by this oil example is clear in policy discussions in both developing and developed countries in contemporary economic circumstances. A similar interdependence is reflected in the new emphasis on "supply-side" considerations in macro policy discussion in the advanced industrial countries. Planning strategies at the microeconomic or multisectoral level are often formulated with aggregate objectives in mind, such as a reduction in the inflation rate or in monetary outflows caused by a trade imbalance. In addition, medium- to long-term planning strategies are sometimes jettisoned in response to unexpected macro developments and the introduction of stabilization policies that make the realization of sectoral planning targets impossible. As this discussion suggests, the conventional separation between stabilization issues and development issues in the theoretical and empirical literature is no longer appropriate to many major policy problems.[2]

From the point of view of modeling and policy analysis, the implication of the interdependence between short-term stabilization objectives and medium-term structural objectives is clear: It is necessary to formulate models that allow one to analyze this interdependence and its implications for policy tradeoffs and policy effectiveness. The lack of an integrated economic theory to analyze micro and macro issues makes this modeling strategy difficult to realize in practice. Actual empirical models designed for policy analysis can be split into those that focus on short-term macro stabilization issues and those that focus on medium-term, multisectoral planning issues. Input–output models, linear programming models, and, most recently, computable general equilibrium models fall into the latter category. These models provide tools for examining the effects of policy at a micro or sectoral level. Their focus is on disaggregated behavior and relative prices rather than on economic aggregates and the nominal price level. Although their results can be added up to yield aggregate magnitudes – such as aggregate employment, unemployment, real income, and expenditure – their theory of the determinants of these aggregates focuses on underlying behavior in individual markets. In addition, because their focus is on real rather than nominal magnitudes, such models abstract from the determinants of the absolute price level or its variability over time.

In contrast, macro models focus on aggregate performance and nominal magnitudes rather than on individual markets and relative prices. In current modeling practice, most empirical attempts to extend a macro model to include a multisectoral economic structure rely on the use of an input–output framework to derive the sectoral implications of alternative macro scenarios. This has been the approach in some large-scale macroeconometric models, such as the Wharton model of the United States or the SOVMOD model of the Soviet Union (Green and Higgins, 1978). The weakness of this approach is that the disaggregation from macro to micro levels is an accounting disaggregation that does not capture the possible impacts of changing macro conditions on sectoral relative prices and the resulting modifications of production and expenditure decisions at the microeconomic level.

In addition to differences in their focus, applied micro and macro models also differ in terms of their time horizon. Most microeconomic multisector planning models are avowedly medium-run to long-run, whereas most applied macro models are short-run. Many of the variables that are usually assumed given in short-run macro models – such as tastes, technology, the capital stock, and the aggregate labor supply, to name only a few – are allowed to vary over the horizon of medium- to long-run multisector models. In addition, in micro models in which market-clearing adjustment is assumed, the medium- to long-run focus implies a periodization for the model solution that is long enough for relative prices to adjust to clear markets. In micro models that allow for the existence of barriers to price clearance in one or more markets, this translates into a periodization for the model solution that is long enough for both price and quantity adjustments to make individual decisions mutually consistent.[3] In either case, the medium- to long-run focus of most economywide micro models reflects their emphasis on the outcomes of the adjustment process rather than on its dynamics. In this sense, such models focus on the equilibrium tendencies of an economy over time rather than on its disequilibrium dynamics.[4] Model solutions are most often in the form of a series of temporary equilibria that move over time in response to changes in underlying economic conditions.

In contrast, many applied macro models focus on the short run and on the dynamics of the adjustment process. Their emphasis is on the behavior of an economy in which individual decisions have not had time to adjust to become mutually consistent – that is, on the behavior of an economy that is out of equilibrium in the sense Malinvaud (1977) discusses. In such models, the patterns and relative speeds of adjustment of different variables that move the economy toward a position of full adjustment or equilibrium are frequently the focus of the model equations and structure. This is, of course, especially true of forecasting models in which the short-term dynamics of the adjustment process provide the primary policy focus. Moreover, even in macro models with an equilibrium focus, the periodization for a model solution frequently implies a shorter period of time than the period implied for a solution of a longer-term micro planning model. Most empirical macro models assume an adjustment period between one quarter and one year, whereas most economywide micro models assume an adjustment period of at least one year.

As the preceding discussion suggests, there are several important differences in both the policy focus and conceptualization underlying empirical micro and macro models. In addition, such models usually draw on different branches of economic thought, micro models most often starting from a Walrasian general equilibrium orientation and macro models from the more recent Keynesian or monetarist theories of aggregate economic performance. An empirical model that combines both micro and macro policy concerns must be sensitive to all of these differences if inconsistencies in its underpinnings and specification are to be avoided.

In this chapter, we offer some suggestions for a modeling strategy designed to avoid such inconsistencies while, at the same time, providing a framework for empirical analysis of the interdependence between macro-stabilization issues and microstructural issues in developing economies. We begin with a computable general equilibrium (CGE) model that has been developed to study processes of real structural change in such economies. In our opinion, a multisectoral model of the CGE variety rather than a simple one- or two-sector model is required to address the questions of sectoral choice that are the essence of much development policy. These questions can only be analyzed in a model that has enough disaggregation to distinguish the critical sectors that compete for economic resources during the development process. Indeed, the development process is defined by structural transformations in production that cannot be adequately captured in one- or two-sector models. Depending on the problem under study, a multisector model might include (with some overlapping), at the very least, agriculture, consumer goods, intermediate inputs, capital goods, export industries, import-substituting industries, nontradables, and services.[5]

In the second section of the chapter, we summarize the macro features of the CGE model and identify its implicit and explicit macro assumptions. In the third section, we present a formal schematic framework for integrating economywide micro models with alternative macro models, and we present some simple illustrations of the framework using the particular CGE model of Section 2. Finally, in Section 3 we present a preliminary specification of complementary macro and CGE models that we are developing to analyze the interaction between micro and macro policy concerns in various semiindustrial countries. The specification chosen for policy analysis in a particular country will depend on the actual characteristics of that country. Nonetheless, the general specification suggests a menu of theoretical and policy choices that face the model builder, regardless of the particular country application in question.

2   A CGE model and its macro assumptions

2.1   *A brief outline of a representative CGE model*

Our starting point is a class of CGE models developed by Dervis, de Melo, and Robinson that focus on issues of foreign trade in semiindustrial countries. The models have been applied to various countries to analyze the impact of different trade adjustment policies on growth, economic structure, and the distribution of income.[6] In this section, we will present a simple version of the core CGE model and then go on to discuss in some detail its explicit and implicit macroeconomic features and their shortcomings.

A summary of the model is presented in Table 1. Given its emphasis

Table 1. Core CGE model

I. Prices	II. Production and employment	III. Foreign trade
(1) $PM_i = \overline{PW}_i(1+tm_i)ER$	(6) $X_i^S = \bar{A}_i F_i(\bar{K}_i, L_i)$	(11) $E_i = \bar{E}_i(\Pi_i/PWE_i)^{\eta_i}$
(2) $PWE_i = PD_i/[(1+te_i)ER]$	(7) $L_i = \lambda_i(L_{1i}, \ldots, L_{mi})$	(12) $M_i/D_i = g_i(PD_i/PM_i)$
(3) $P_i = p_i(PM_i, PD_i)$	(8) $PN_i(\partial X_i^S/\partial L_{ki}) = W_k$	(13) $\Sigma_i \overline{PW}_i M_i - \Sigma PWE_i E_i - \bar{F} = 0$
(4) $PN_i = PD_i - \Sigma_j P_j a_{ji} - td_i PD_i$	(9) $L_k^D = \Sigma_i L_{ki}$	
(5) $\Sigma \Omega_i P_i = \bar{P}$	(10) $L_k^D - \bar{L}_k^S = 0$	

	II.		III.	
	X_i^S	sectoral output	E_i	exports
	$\bar{A}_i$	productivity parameter in production	M_i	imports
	$\bar{K}_i$	exogenous sectoral capital stock	D_i	domestic demand for domestic production
	L_{ki}	labor of category k in sector i	$\bar{E}_i, \eta_i$	parameters of export demand function
	L_i	aggregate labor in sector i	Π_i	exogenous world price of other-country goods
	W_k	average wage of labor category k	$\bar{F}$	exogenous net inflow of foreign exchange
	L_k^D	total demand for labor category k		
	$\bar{L}_k^S$	exogenous labor supply for category k		

	I.	
ER	exchange rate
tm_i	tariff rate
$\overline{PW}_i$	world price of imports
PM_i	domestic price of imports
te_i	export subsidy rate
PD_i	domestic price
PWE_i	world price of exports
P_i	composite good price
td_i	indirect tax rate
a_{ji}	input-output coefficients
PN_i	net price or value added
Ω_i	price index weights
$\bar{P}$	exogenous level of aggregate price index

IV. Income and investment

(14) $R_L = \Sigma_i \Sigma_k W_k L_{ki}(1 - t_k)$

(15) $R_K = \Sigma_i (PN_i X_i^S - \Sigma_k W_k L_{ki})(1 - tk_i)$

(16) $R_G = \Sigma_i \Sigma_k t_k W_k L_{ki} + \Sigma_i tk_i(PN_i X_i^S - \Sigma_k W_k L_{ki}) + \Sigma_i tm_i \overline{PW}_i ER\, M_i$
$\quad - \Sigma_i te_i PWE_i ER\, E_i + \Sigma_i td_i X_i^S PD_i$

(17) $TINV = \bar{S}_L R_L + \bar{S}_K R_K + \bar{S}_G R_G + \bar{F} ER$

(18) $Y_i = \theta_i TINV$

(19) $Z_i = \Sigma_j b_{ij} Y_j / \Sigma_j b_{ij} P_j$

t_k	tax rate on labor income, category k
R_L	after-tax labor income
tk_i	tax rate on nonwage income in sector i
R_K	after-tax capital income
R_G	government revenue net of export subsidies
$\bar{S}_L, \bar{S}_K, \bar{S}_G$	exogenous savings rates
$TINV$	total investment
Y_i	investment by sector of destination
θ_i	sectoral investment allocation shares
b_{ij}	capital composition coefficients
Z_i	investment by sector of origin

V. Product markets

(20) $C_i = C_{iL} + C_{iK} + C_{iG}$

(21) $C_{ij} = \bar{q}_{ij}(1 - \bar{S}_j)R_j / P_i$ $\quad j = L, K, G$

(22) $V_i = \Sigma_j a_{ij} X_j$

(23) $D_i = S_i^d(Z_i + C_i + V_i)$

(24) $S_i^d = 1/f_i(M_i/D_i, 1)$

(25) $X_i^D = D_i + E_i$

(26) $X_i^D - X_i^S = 0$

C_{ij}	consumption, sector i, demander j
C_i	consumption demand, sector i
$\bar{q}_{ij}$	expenditure share parameters
V_i	intermediate demand
S_i^d	domestic demand ratio
X_i^D	total demand for domestic production

Notes: Endogenous variables are denoted by capital letters. Greek letters, and letters with a bar are exogenous variables or parameters. In Equation (24), $f(\ )$ denotes the CES trade aggregation function $f(M, D)$ evaluated at $(M/D, 1)$. In Equation (12), $g(\ )$ is derived from the associated first-order conditions and $p(\ )$ in Equation (3) is the associated dual cost function. $F(\ )$ and $\lambda(\ )$ in Equations (6) and (7) are CES functions.

on issues of foreign trade, an important feature of the model is that foreign and domestically produced goods are assumed to be imperfect substitutes in use. Such a specification implies that the domestic price system has a degree of autonomy from world markets that is not found in models in which all (or most) goods are assumed to be tradable (i.e., perfect substitutes). The model allows for a continuum of "tradability" and provides a much more realistic framework for analyzing issues of trade adjustment than models that only allow imports to be either perfect substitutes or perfect complements to domestically produced goods.

To distinguish between domestic goods and foreign goods the model defines a composite commodity that is a CES aggregation of imports and domestic goods (see Armington, 1969, for a full discussion of this specification). Consumers and producers demand this composite commodity so that the demand for imports and domestic tradable goods become derived demands. Assuming that demanders seek to minimize the cost of acquiring a given amount of the composite good, the desired ratio of imports to the domestic good is derived from first-order conditions and is a function of the relative prices of the domestic good and the imported substitute. Following the small-country assumption, the world price of the imported substitute is fixed, and the supply of imports is infinitely elastic at that price. These assumptions about import behavior are contained in Equations (1), (3), (12), and (24) in Table 1. On the export side, the distinction between domestic tradables and imperfect foreign substitutes is reflected in the assumption of a downward-sloping foreign demand curve for exports, where exports of tradables depend on the world price of domestically produced tradables relative to the world price of imperfect foreign substitutes. This specification is contained in Equations (2) and (11) of Table 1.

Except for the special treatment of the degree of substitutability between domestic and foreign goods, the microeconomic specification of supply and demand conditions on commodity and labor markets contained in the core CGE model is quite similar to the microeconomic structure embedded in the two-sector variants of Patinkin's macro model developed by Dornbusch (1973) and Bruno (1976). The main difference between the models arises, as we shall see, at the macroeconomic level.

For each market identified in the CGE model, an explicit formulation of supply and demand conditions must be made. For the product markets, the specification of production functions [Equation (6)] and enterprise behavioral rules (profit maximization) gives rise to domestic product supply relationships and, assuming a solution period sufficiently short so that physical capital is treated as fixed, these relationships give rise to labor demand equations [Equation (8)]. In the specification chosen for illustrative purposes in Table 1, these labor demand equations, along with labor supplies by skill type that are set exogenously for each model solution, give rise to a set of excess demand equations for each labor type [Equation (10)]. The solution of these equations in turn yields market-clearing wage rates. In alternative specifications of the model, the assumption of labor market clearance can be relaxed to allow for Keynesian-type nominal wage rigidities or possible real wage rigidities in some or all labor markets. Such specifications are more appropriate than market clearance for many developing countries.

For each product market, the model distinguishes between and specifies all categories of final demand, including consumption, investment, government expenditures, and exports [Equations (11), (17)–(24)]. The supply and demand equations for product markets together yield a set of simultaneous market clearance conditions (26), the solutions of which provide market-clearing relative prices. Finally, the price-sensitive import and export flows, along with an exogenous specification of foreign exchange inflows, yields the market clearance condition for foreign exchange [Equation (13)]. In the flexible exchange rate specification of Table 1, this condition provides the additional equation needed to solve for the exchange rate.

A model solution represents a temporary equilibrium position for the economy, a position that depends on the exogenous variables whose values are assumed to remain fixed during a given model period. Most important among such variables are sectoral capital stocks, aggregate labor supplies by skill, and foreign capital inflows. In actual empirical use, the static CGE model in Table 1 is combined with a dynamic inter-temporal adjustment model that updates the values of the exogenous variables from model solution to model solution, using the endogenous solution of the static model as input to the updating process. In terms of time horizon, a temporary equilibrium of the static model is assumed to be realized during the course of a year. Dynamic runs of the model yielding a sequence of temporary equilibrium positions trace out the medium- to long-term evolution of the economy in accordance with the rules specified in the dynamic adjustment model. In terms of the terminology suggested in the Introduction, the CGE model in Table 1 thus has a medium- to long-term policy focus, which is important to keep in mind when considering the appropriate specification of a complementary macro model.

2.2   The macro assumptions of the CGE model

As written, the product demand functions embody several assumptions that either rest on macroeconomic theory or are formulated with macro-economic concerns in mind. First, the demand model assumes that each of the three types of income recipients identified – worker households, capitalist households, and the government – save a constant fraction of their disposable income [Equations (14)–(17)]. This is a standard Keynesian assumption as far as private households are concerned, and it has been widely adopted in empirical macroeconometric work. It has also been found to be consistent with macroeconomic evidence drawn from a large number of institutionally diverse economies. Nonetheless, it is an assumption without a foundation in microeconomic theory. As Clower (1965) and others have noted, confronting income recipients with disposable income that they must then decide to spend or save diverges from the microeconomist's procedure of confronting households with wages, prices, and rates of return on alternative assets on the basis of which they allocate consumption over time. Moreover, even as a macroeconomic assumption, the specification of disposable income as the sole determinant of savings is questionable. Since the saving decision is a decision to add to the stock of wealth, theory suggests that it should depend in part on the expected returns on alternative forms of wealth. At the very least, it would seem that the simple savings behavior in the CGE specification should be modified to allow for the possible effects of changes in these returns on savings behavior. This, of course, would require the extension of the CGE model in Table 1 to include specifications of alternative asset markets. As the model now stands, only product markets are explicitly specified, and the only asset choice is whether to add to physical capital stocks. An extended model would encompass financial asset choices as well. Which asset markets should be included and how returns on financial assets affect the savings decision are questions open to empirical analysis at the macroeconomic level.

A second macro assumption embedded in the CGE model in Table 1 is the specification of macroeconomic "closure," that is, the mechanism equating the aggregate volume of savings and the aggregate volume of investment. Such a mechanism is necessary to maintain macroeconomic balance in the nominal flow of funds generated by the model solution. The closure rule adopted in Table 1 is classical in spirit – given the fixed saving rates, the endogenously determined volume of aggregate savings determines the volume of aggregate investment [Equation (17)]. Alternative closure rules can easily be adopted in the simple model formulation of Table 1, for example, the exogenous specification of aggregate investment either with savings rates determined endogenously or, in Kaldorian fashion, with fixed saving rates for groups and the endogenous determination of the distribution of income to validate the exogenously specified investment. The main point is that the choice of closure rule is essentially a macroeconomic issue since it concerns the mechanisms whereby aggregate savings and aggregate investment are balanced. Thus the closure rule adopted should reflect the macroeconomic theory most appropriate for the economy whose performance is to be analyzed and for the problems to be addressed.

Once aggregate investment is established, its sectoral allocation must be specified. In the CGE model in Table 1, which abstracts from the workings of financial markets in the investment allocation process, fixed coefficients are used to divide up the total volume of investment among sectors [Equation (18)]. Although these coefficients are fixed for a given year, they can be changed in the dynamic adjustment model to reflect assumptions about the intersectoral mobility of investment resources in response to changing sectoral capital rental or profit rates over time. This approach is classical in spirit, reflecting the view that over time the shares of investment gradually adjust to equalize profitability across sectors. Other CGE models have taken a more extreme approach and have assumed that investment (or, indeed, capital) is perfectly mobile across sectors and is instantaneously allocated so as to equate sectoral rental rates (see, for example, Fullerton et al., 1981, and Hudson and Jorgenson, 1978). This specification implicitly assumes that capital markets work perfectly, which is a rather extreme assumption even by neoclassical standards.

In either case, however, the process of investment allocation is not explicitly modeled and the role of financial markets in the allocation of loanable funds is ignored. An extension of the CGE model to include such markets would allow for a theoretically more appealing approach that explicitly models both desired investment demand in each sector and the allocation process by which aggregate investment and desired sectoral investment are reconciled. As this discussion and the discussion of the savings decision indicate, the addition of a financial structure to the CGE model is necessary to enhance the model's ability to deal with important macroeconomic issues, including the determination of aggregate savings, the equating of aggregate savings and investment, and the sectoral allocation of investment.

The CGE model in Table 1 can be demonstrated to be consistent with a very simple macro financial structure in which there is a single non-interest-earning asset, namely money. To see this, it is necessary to analyze the normalization rule adopted in the model. Together, the product demand and supply conditions yield excess demand equations for the domestically produced goods, and these equations can be solved for domestic prices. The balance-of-payments equilibrium condition gives an excess demand equation for foreign exchange, the solution of which yields the nominal exchange rate (given the exogenously specified foreign capital inflow). With the balance-of-payments condition, there are as many excess demand equations as there are prices, wages, and the exchange rate. By Walras's law, however, the excess demand equations are not independent, and some price normalization rule is required to complete the system. The CGE specification in Table 1 chooses an aggregate index of composite prices as the normalization rule [Equation (5)].

In principle, in a Walrasian CGE model with all prices flexible and with all excess-demand equations homogeneous of degree zero, the choice of an aggregate price index is arbitrary. Any nominal magnitude, such as the nominal wage or the nominal exchange rate or the nominal price of one of the domestically produced goods, could have been used as the numeraire with no effect on relative prices or real production and employment. The choice of an aggregate price index as the normalization rule in Table 1, however, provides a link between the CGE model – with its emphasis on microeconomic activity – and macro models in which the determination of the aggregate price index is an important element. The aggregate price index, which is exogenous in the CGE model in Table 1, would normally be endogenous in a macro model. The CGE specification, however, is consistent with a simple monetary model of price level determination. This can be demonstrated by comparing the CGE model with the two-sector macro models of Dornbusch and Bruno mentioned earlier. These models differ from the CGE model in their explicit modeling of an asset market for money. In the absence of an alternative interest-earning asset, the portfolio balance condition for the money market is given by assuming a simple proportional demand function for money, leading to an equation of the form

$$\bar{M}^S = M^D = kPY$$

where $\bar{M}^s$ is exogenously given, P is the aggregate price index relevant to a transactions demand for money, Y is real income generated in the domestic production process, and k is a parameter. This equilibrium condition, along with a definition of the aggregate price index as

$$P = \Omega P_T + (1 - \Omega) P_N$$

(where P_T is the price of the traded good and P_N refers to the nontraded good) allows the model to solve for the equilibrium aggregate price index endogenously, given an exogenously specified money supply.

Comparing this formulation to the CGE model, it is apparent that the normalization rule of the traditional two-sector model is the exogenous specification of a nominal money supply that determines the nominal value of the aggregate price index endogenously. In the CGE model, in contrast, the portfolio balance condition is suppressed, and the value of the aggregate price level is set exogenously by the specified normalization rule. By Walras's law, however, at the CGE solution, simultaneous equilibria in the product markets, the labor market, and the foreign exchange market imply that the portfolio balance condition in the money market is also satisfied and this, along with the exogenous aggregate price index and the endogenous CGE solution for Y, determines M^S endogenously.

As this discussion indicates, the CGE model of Table 1 is consistent with a classical equilibrium macro model in which changes in the aggregate price index are determined by changes in the money supply. The defining characteristic of such a macro formulation is its neutrality assumption, in which the solution values of the real variables are independent of changes in nominal magnitudes. As long as this neutrality assumption is maintained, the extension of the CGE model to include the endogenous determination of the aggregate price level explicitly is superfluous. In most developing countries, however, there are rigidities in important nominal magnitudes, and nonneutrality is likely to be more the rule than the exception, even in the medium term. The task facing the model builder, then, is to adjust the CGE specification to take into account the interactions between real and nominal variables that are critical to understanding policy choices. Both macroeconomic theory and macroeconometric results are necessary for the judicious completion of this modeling task.

3   A micro–macro modeling system

As the preceding discussion indicates, if the CGE model is to be useful as a tool to analyze macrostabilization issues in developing countries, its simple macro specification must be broadened to incorporate features such as nonneutrality, asset markets, interest rates, and rigidities in various nominal variables. It is important to note, however, that the justification for such features is most often to be found in macroeconomic theory and rarely in the corpus of neoclassical general equilibrium theory on which the CGE model is originally based. As a consequence, although macro extensions of the CGE model appear worthwhile from a policy point of view, on a theoretical level it is important to distinguish extensions whose justification comes from macro theory from those whose justification comes from micro theory. In this section, we propose an analytic framework and associated modeling strategy that explicitly recognizes this distinction while at the same time combining the microeconomic and macroeconomic issues that are critical to a policy understanding of structural adjustment. The aim of our discussion is to present a general modeling methodology that makes the micro and macro theoretical foundations of economywide models transparent.

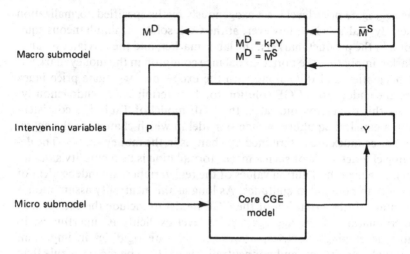

Figure 1. Micro and macro submodels: a CGE model with money.

We begin with the task of specifying an economywide model that focuses on equilibrium tendencies in the medium run. We thus assume away possible inconsistencies in the appropriate periodization for the realization of macro and micro equilibrium. For empirical purposes, this assumption is not too unrealistic, since the CGE model has a solution period of one year during which sectoral capital stocks are assumed constant. A similar solution period for a complementary macro model is in keeping with current empirical practice in macroeconomic model building. It should be understood, however, that the macro model we shall discuss is appropriate to an analysis of medium-term equilibrium tendencies rather than to an analysis of short-term disequilibrium dynamics.

Our strategy is based on the observation that an economywide model incorporating both microeconomic and macroeconomic policy concerns over the same assumed time horizon can be analytically divided into two distinct submodels.[7] First, there is a micro submodel that specifies the behavioral and institutional rules governing supply and demand conditions on the individual markets included in the model. Second, there is a macro submodel that specifies relationships among various nominal and/or real economic aggregates. These two submodels can be illustrated with the core CGE model contained in Table 1, combined with a classical macro model of money market equilibrium to replace the exogenous specification of the aggregate price index in Equation (5).

In Figure 1, the macro submodel contains two endogenous variables, M^D and P, and two exogenous variables, $\bar{M}^S$ and Y. The micro CGE model delivers Y to the macro submodel, which in turn delivers P back.

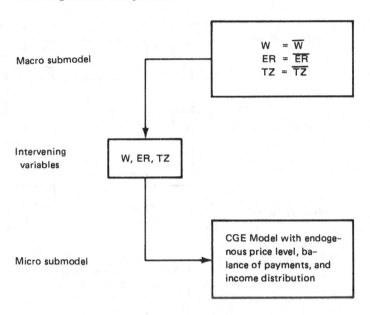

Figure 2. Micro and macro submodels: a Taylor–Kaldor model.

Given that the CGE model is neutral (and hence Y does not depend on P), real variables are determined in the CGE model and the macro submodel determines prices and hence nominal magnitudes. The two submodels are functionally separable, with no real interaction required between them to yield a consistent solution.

Figure 2 gives another example of an economywide model broken down into its component micro and macro submodels. The micro submodel is similar to the core CGE model in Table 1, combined with a macro model that embodies the standard assumptions appearing in Taylor's recent works – namely, a fixed nominal wage, a fixed nominal exchange rate, a fixed volume of real aggregate investment, and a macro closure rule to make savings equal that volume of investment. These macro assumptions have been built into the CGE model of Brazil developed by Lysy and Taylor (1980) and the CGE model of Malaysia by Ahluwalia and Lysy (1981). See also Taylor (1979).

Although based on an appeal to Keynesian and Kaldorian macro theory, the macro submodel has no explicit behavioral equations. The action is all in the CGE model in which the price level is determined so that, given the fixed nominal wage, the resulting real wage leads to a distribution of income that generates the savings required to finance the fixed level of investment. The fact that the nominal exchange rate is also

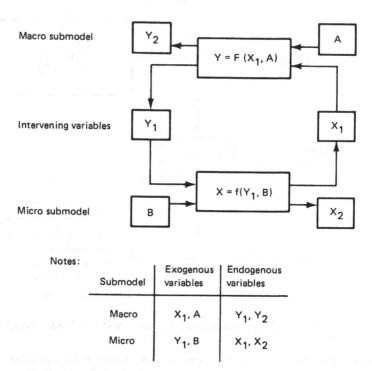

Submodel	Exogenous variables	Endogenous variables
Macro	X_1, A	Y_1, Y_2
Micro	Y_1, B	X_1, X_2

Figure 3. Micro and macro submodels: a general framework.

fixed implies that the balance of payments is determined endogenously in the CGE model, thus allowing foreign savings to adjust also. Note that because the aggregate price level is determined endogenously, the real exchange rate varies even though the nominal rate is fixed. Note also that the excess-demand equations are not homogenous of degree zero in the included prices – given the macro assumptions, the CGE model solution no longer satisfies the neutrality condition.

The schematic framework suggested by these two examples is generalized in Figure 3. Formally, the two submodels of an economywide model are segmented by dividing the variables so that the micro submodel generates endogenously the values for variables X_1 that are exogenous in the macro submodel whereas the macro submodel generates values for Y_1 that are exogenous in the micro submodel. Each submodel also has other exogenous and endogenous variables that are not passed between them.

The two submodels are defined to be functionally separable if the endogenous variables X_1 in the micro submodel do not depend on the variables Y_1 that are generated in the macro submodel. Functional separability of the submodels arises because the function summarizing the micro submodel is separable and can be written as $X_1 = f_1(B)$ and $X_2 = f_2(Y_1, B)$. The simple monetary model in Figure 1 yields separable submodels because the CGE model is neutral – that is, the excess-demand equations are homogeneous of degree zero.[8] On the other hand, the submodels in Figure 2 are not separable. As mentioned above and discussed in more detail below, neutrality – or more generally functional separability – is not a desirable property for models used to analyze the effects of changes in nominal magnitudes on real economic variables. In our opinion, at least for the group of developing economies that form the focus of our applied interests, such effects are important determinants of economic performance in the medium run. Therefore, for empirical relevance, it is necessary to drop the neutrality assumption of the standard Walrasian general equilibrium model even though doing so raises some problems in theory and empirical implementation.[9]

The two submodels are defined to be theoretically disjoint if they have no endogenous variables in common – if there are no common variables in X_2 and Y_2. It is desirable that the submodels be theoretically disjoint since otherwise the complete model is overdetermined – the two submodels are redundant – and there is no mechanism for ensuring consistency of the shared endogenous variables. On a theoretical level, such redundancy reflects the existence of two competing theoretical approaches to the determination of the same endogenous variables. Specifying a particular pair of submodels implies a particular resolution to the underlying theoretical conflict. No general resolution is available; consequently, the applied modeler must choose a specification that is reasonable for the analysis of a particular class of problems.

There are tradeoffs in empirical implementation that may lead a modeler to specify submodels that are not theoretically disjoint. Consider the nature of the different submodels. Macro models usually consist of relationships among aggregates that are estimated from time series data whereas micro CGE models typically rely on cross-section or point estimates for most of their parameters. Given the present state of theory and empirical practice, it is by no means obvious that in some cases one should have more confidence in a macro flow-of-funds variable generated by aggregation in a micro CGE model than in the same variable generated directly from an empirical relationship in an econometric macro model. In such cases, one might tolerate some redundancy.

An interesting example is provided by Cooper and McLaren (1980) in a model of Australia. In their linking of macro and CGE models they have made a virtue out of the apparent necessity of specifying theoretically redundant submodels. They use the common endogenous variables – aggregate employment, the aggregate price level, real GDP, and the dollar values of imports and exports – to calibrate the time interval implicit in comparative statics experiments with the CGE model. Given similar exogenous shocks, comparable changes in the common endogenous variables correspond to 12- to 18-month projections in the macro model. Thus they conclude that for such shocks the CGE model requires 12–18 months to reach a new equilibrium.

In formulating an integrated set of submodels, a modeler thus faces a variety of difficult choices. Existing theory simply cannot provide definitive criteria for assigning variables and behavioral relations to the two submodels. There are, however, a number of practical criteria that one might use. First, for some variables, one might assert that the current state of microeconomic theory is simply inadequate, and one must thus rely on relatively ad hoc empirical relationships with, at best, anecdotal support. Some people, for example, simply reject the neoclassical theories of wage determination and/or savings and would prefer to rely on macroeconomic theory and econometric estimates of empirical regularities to determine variables such as nominal wages and/or aggregate savings.

Second, given current computational and data limitations, there are relationships for which microeconomic theory is highly developed, but which cannot be incorporated in an empirical model. For example, questions of uncertainty and expectations (rational or otherwise) have generated much theoretical literature, but it is currently beyond the state of the art to incorporate such effects into computable microeconomic models. One must then rely on a macroeconomic specification whose results are imposed on the micro submodel and accept some inconsistency in theoretical underpinnings. A good example is sectoral investment allocation where intertemporal equilibrium and expectations play a large part in the theoretical literature, but with few exceptions, empirical models – either macro or micro – do not adequately incorporate the existing theories.[10]

Even where it would be feasible to include a theoretically more sophisticated specification in the micro submodel, it may be worthwhile to rely on a simpler macroeconomic specification. For example, CGE models have typically embodied very simple models of the supply of labor. In most models, the aggregate supply of labor of a given skill category is assumed either to be fixed exogenously or to be infinitely elastic at an exogenously fixed wage. There is, of course, a large and growing theoretical and empirical literature on labor supply decisions by households based on utility maximization and labor–leisure choices. It is certainly feasible to incorporate such models into the micro submodel. Such an extension, however, would only complicate most existing CGE models, adding little of interest, given their particular aims. There is a modeler's version of Occam's razor: Always use the simplest model adequate for the task at hand. If a simple, macro specification will suffice, then use it.

Finally, in some cases there are strong theoretical reasons for specifying behavioral relations at the macro level. For example, certain economic actors, such as the government and the central bank, actually base their behavior on aggregate information. Typically, the behavior of policy makers in models is specified exogenously, but there is a growing concern, for example, about the need to "endogenize" government. In terms of our schema, such behavior is conceptually a part of the macro submodel and is better included there than in the micro submodel.

4   General issues in the specification of a macro submodel

On an empirical level, nothing very general can be said about the exact specification of a macro submodel to be combined with a micro CGE model to analyze macroeconomic issues. Much depends on the particular policy concerns that motivate the modeler and on the particular characteristics of the country in question. For example, a macro submodel designed to analyze the dynamics of inflation or the determination of aggregate savings and investment and the mechanism equilibrating them is likely to look quite different from a macro submodel designed to analyze Keynesian involuntary unemployment. Similarly, a macro submodel designed to analyze the workings of the financial–monetary system in a highly developed market economy with a variety of asset markets is likely to look quite different from a macro submodel designed to analyze the financial–monetary system in a developing economy where asset choices are limited and the central bank plays a preponderant role in the credit allocation process.

Because the specification of a macro submodel will vary from country to country and from policy concern to policy concern, in this section we will continue the discussion by reference to a particular example, beginning with the CGE model introduced in the first section. As noted there, this model implicitly or explicitly incorporates macroeconomic relationships that determine the aggregate price level and the aggregate volume of savings and investment. Therefore, in this section we shall discuss the specification of a macro submodel that focuses on these relationships. For practical policy-making purposes, such a submodel will have to go beyond the simple money market formulation implicit in Table 1 (and made explicit in Figure 1) to incorporate equations that explain the workings of alternative financial asset markets and the effects of expected rates of return on savings and investment decisions.[11] Even in rudimentary capital markets, like those that characterize most developing countries, important asset choices exist, such as choices between holding money, interest-earning savings accounts, or loans, and choices between holding domestic money or foreign exchange or inventories in nonproductive assets. The introduction of financial asset alternatives requires a portfolio balance model of the decision-making rules according to which actors in the economy determine the composition of their asset portfolios. For the purpose of this discussion, the addition of a portfolio balance model of financial markets is treated as part of the macro submodel. This classification reflects the fact that the distinction between household flow savings decisions and portfolio decisions is a hallmark of Keynesian macroeconomic theory.

Because the CGE model in Table 1 incorporates what are essentially macro theories of savings and investment determination, a complementary macro submodel must include not only portfolio balance equations of asset market equilibrium but also specifications of flow savings and investment decisions. As far as the savings decision is concerned, the CGE formulation of savings behavior as a function of disposable income is grounded in Keynesian macroeconomic theory, supported by statistical research from a variety of countries. This theory and its statistical verification are more widely accepted than contending explanations of savings rooted in microeconomic theories of thrift. Hence, it seems reasonable to assign the behavior of savings to the macro rather than to the micro submodel. From an empirical point of view, this means that the macro submodel should contain relationships explaining the savings behavior of the agents identified in the CGE submodel and summarized in Equation (17) in Table 1. With the inclusion of the portfolio balance model in the macro submodel, these relationships can be adjusted to allow for the sensitivity of savings decisions to expected real rates of return on alternative assets.

On the investment side, the introduction of financial assets in the macro submodel requires a complete formulation of investment flow decisions as the outcome of comparisons between the expected real rates of return on alternative financial and physical assets. In particular, it is necessary to specify how changes in expected real rates of return on financial assets, which reflect the opportunity cost of investment funds, affect desired demand for additions to physical capital stocks. Investment decisions, conceived of in this way as part of a broader portfolio balance problem, are properly in the realm of macroeconomic theory and hence they are assigned to the macro submodel rather than to the micro submodel. Several alternative theories of investment behavior consistent with this conception are developed in the macro literature, and the choice between them rests on an evaluation of their relative validity for a particular empirical application. To illustrate, if it is reasonable to assume that there is no perfect capital maket for the existing stock of capital in which firms can purchase or sell (or rent) capital at a moment of time, then a traditional Keynesian approach suggests itself. This approach relates the flow demand for investment positively to the expected marginal productivity of capital and negatively to the expected cost of capital or the expected real interest rate. Such an approach can be applied in the macro submodel either at the aggregate level or at the disaggregated market level, provided, in the latter case, that the modeler has a means of measuring the expected marginal product of capital at the necessary level of disaggregation. When applied at the aggregate level, however, the theory of investment must be accompanied by a supporting theory and set of behavioral rules in the macro submodel that divide total investment into its sectoral allocation. In other words, the sectoral allocation of investment by sector of destination is properly assigned to the macro submodel as the outcome of the working of the markets for physical capital and alternative financial assets.

In addition to the relationships analyzing the savings and investment behavior of private economic actors, the macro submodel should include relationships analyzing the behavior of the government. The basic rationale for the assignment of government behavior to the macro submodel is the fact that what little theory we have of this behavior is rooted in macroeconomics. Furthermore, since government reactions are usually fashioned or triggered in response to various indicators of macroeconomic performance (such as inflation, unemployment, or the balance of payments deficit), these reactions are most appropriately analyzed in the macro submodel where performance of economic aggregates is analyzed and tracked. Finally, since government expenditure and borrowing decisions have important effects on money and other financial markets, it is reasonable to model these decisions in the macro submodel where financial market activity is analyzed. In the simplest formulation, a model of government activity in the macro submodel should contain relationships explaining government taxation, expenditure, and borrowing decisions as well as an accounting relationship of the government budget constraint.

A final component of the macro submodel must focus on the external sector of the economy. Aggregate balance-of-payments relationships are appropriately assigned to the macro submodel since they reflect the aggregate performance of the economy with the rest of the world. Similarly, the aggregate supply and demand conditions for foreign exchange that reflect both the flow and asset decisions of individual actors are appropriately analyzed in a macro model of the foreign exchange market. The foreign exchange rate that emerges in this market in response to supply and demand forces as modified by government behavior is an important determinant of relative prices and behavior on individual markets in the CGE submodel. Of course, commodity transactions involving exports

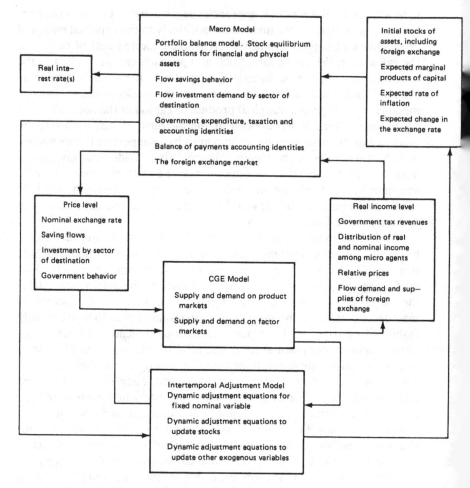

Figure 4. Macro and micro submodels for a developing country.

and imports are an important part of the micro submodel, as is also the complete specification of the institutional flow of funds involving foreign exchange.

The general form of the macro submodel suggested in this discussion is illustrated in Figure 4. The macro model delivers to the micro CGE model the aggregate price level, the exchange rate, and aggregate and sectoral levels of savings and investment in nominal terms. The model also solves for the real interest rate(s) that leaves financial markets in equilibrium and that plays a role in the balancing of aggregate savings and aggregate investment. The exogenous variables underlying the solution of the macro submodel include (1) the initial stocks of alternative financial assets, including the money supply and foreign exchange, and the initial stocks of physical assets; (2) the expected rate of inflation; (3) the expected rate of depreciation or appreciation of the exchange rate; (4) the expected marginal product of capital for the different types of physical capital identified; (5) the level and distribution of real income; and (6) the flow demands and supplies of foreign exchange arising from product market transactions with the rest of the world. The last two sets of endogenous variables are delivered from the solutions of the micro submodel, whereas the others are specified exogenously and are updated over time as part of a separate dynamic intertemporal adjustment model.

In the micro submodel, the price level, the nominal exchange rate, aggregate and sectoral savings and investment, and government expenditures and tax rates are taken as exogenous inputs from the macro model solution. Given these inputs, the micro submodel finds a microeconomic market solution of relative prices and real output that is consistent with the variables delivered to it by the macro model and delivers this solution back to the macro model. Because, as specified, both the macro and micro submodels contain nominal and real variables, they are not functionally separable in the sense defined earlier.[12] Hence, some simultaneous or iterative solution technique is required to provide a mutually consistent solution for both of them. It is important to note that the lack of separability in this case is not a result of dropping the neutrality assumption with respect to nominal magnitudes. Rather, it is the result of the particular assignment rules whereby the determination of real interest rate(s) and the exchange rate to clear financial markets and the market for foreign exchange is assigned to the macro submodel and the determination of relative prices and wages to clear product and labor markets is assigned to the micro submodel. So far, the discussion of the two submodels is consistent with a strict neutrality assumption in which changes in the aggregate price level produce offsetting changes in all other nominal magnitudes, leaving all real magnitudes unchanged.

We have argued above that the assumption of neutrality in the macroeconomic structure of most contemporary developing economies is unrealistic and unwarranted. Consequently, in empirical applications, complementary micro and macro submodels should allow for nonneutrality and important interactions between nominal and real variables. Pure theory has little to offer about the specification of models with nonneutrality since the dichotomy between nominal and real magnitudes tends to break down for institutional reasons. Several examples of circumstances of nonneutrality have been identified in the macro literature, including (1) the presence of real wealth effects in the savings and consumption functions; (2) nominal wage rigidity; and (3) irrational or lagged expectations. In addition to these, observed experience in a variety of developing countries suggests other reasons for nonneutrality in practice, including (1) controls on nominal interest rates; (2) controls on the prices of individual products; and (3) fixed nominal exchange rates. Which channels of nonneutrality apply in a particular applied model-building exercise depend on the characteristics of the economy in question. As a general statement, however, it is probably true that the sources of nonneutrality arise most often in markets that are politically sensitive. Such markets most often concern "fair" access to the factors of production – labor, land, capital, and foreign exchange.[13] Not surprisingly, these are precisely the markets where classical economic theory is weakest and where the traditional Walrasian market-clearing assumption is least likely to apply.

In most cases, nonneutrality will be the result of rigidity in some important nominal variables, such as prices, wages, the exchange rate, or the interest rate. Such rigidity builds in potential imbalances between supply and demand in the affected markets, and such imbalances – whether they occur at the macro or the micro level – may be viewed as inconsistent with the general equilibrium orientation of the models discussed in this chapter. This view, however, seems to us to stem from a misinterpretation of the concept of equilibrium. Although economists have been brought up to think that the very notion of equilibrium implies balance between supply and demand, this is not the only or even the proper interpretation, as Malinvaud (1977) has elegantly argued. As discussed above, an alternative, broader interpretation applies the notion of equilibrium to a situation in which, given price rigidities and supply-demand imbalances, individual decisions have had time to adjust to one another so as to be mutually consistent. This concept of equilibrium is static and temporary, implying a period of analysis that is sufficiently long to permit such adjustments to occur. It is most suitable for period analysis and also implies that the model builder is more interested in the outcomes of an adjustment that yields a new temporary static equilibrium position than in the dynamics of the adjustment process itself. All of these conditions are satisfied by the general equilibrium models discussed in this chapter whose primary focus is on medium-term structural change. In such models, the period of analysis is a year, long enough to allow for significant adjustments to built-in rigidities. Moreover, the focus is on medium-term tendencies – on the outcomes of the adjustment process rather than on its dynamics. The purpose of the modeling exercise is to do policy analysis, not to forecast.

Emphasis on the equilibrium configuration of the economy with built-in rigidities does not imply, however, that the modeler can overlook the issue of adjustment. Adjustment rules must be specified even when the dynamics of such rules are not explicitly modeled. Indeed, for every rigidity and supply–demand imbalance built into the model, the modeler must specify the behavioral, policy, and other rules whereby adjustment occurs. For example, in the presence of nominal wage rigidity leading to excess supply in labor markets, the model must specify how the unemployed adjust. Alternatively, in the presence of nominal interest rate controls and/or exchange rate controls resulting in excess demand for investment resources or foreign exchange, the model must specify the behavioral and policy adjustments that yield consistency in market outcomes.

Finally, in addition to specifying the within-period rules for adjustment in the presence of rigidities, a general equilibrium model incorporating such rigidities will have to contain a dynamic specification of how they change over time. Each period solution of the model yields a temporary equilibrium in the micro and macro submodels given values of the fixed nominal variables. How the solution changes from period to period – in other words, the sequence of temporary within-period solutions – depends on the dynamic adjustment processes that explain how these nominal values change over time. For example, if a nominal exchange rate or a nominal volume of government expenditure is set in the macro model, a dynamic adjustment process showing how these nominal values are expected to change over time is required. Similarly, if a price is fixed for a particular product market in the micro submodel, this too will require the specification of a dynamic rule for changes in this price level over time. Finally, both the micro and the macro submodels have to be complemented by dynamic equations that are really accounting identities – such as equations that update the initial stocks of financial and physical assets and factors over time – and by dynamic behavioral equations that update other exogenous variables taken as given in model solutions – such as equations explaining how inflationary expectations and exchange rate expectations change over time.

In the illustrative model laid out in Figure 4, the various dynamic adjustment processes are shown as providing inputs into both the macro and micro submodels on which their temporary equilibrium solutions are based. As formulated, the model solutions vary over time in accordance with these processes and form a series of temporary, period equilibria. The notion of equilibrium is a static rather than a dynamic one, however – that is, there is nothing in the formulation to guarantee equilibrium in the dynamic sense that expectations are fulfilled at every temporary equilibrium solution or that the economy is on some kind of steady-state path. Such a period analysis is especially appropriate for a model that attempts to incorporate macroeconomic stock flow adjustments in order to address issues of structural change.[14]

5   Conclusion

Despite the religious fervor with which micro and macro theorists carry on their debates, the day of judgment has not yet arrived. Barring the second coming of a Marshall or a Keynes, those interested in the analysis of events that have significant microeconomic and macroeconomic policy implications must draw from both bodies of theory and make some hard choices. There have, however, been major advances since the early 1970s that have substantially widened the choices available to the empirical modeler. The development of techniques for the empirical solution of Walrasian general equilibrium models has opened up the field of applied modeling and has permitted the application of multimarket, general equilibrium models in the analysis of a variety of problems. Similar, but perhaps not as profound, advances have been made in the solution of simultaneous-equation, nonlinear macro models.

In a period where macroeconomic theory is in something of a crisis and microeconomic theory is becoming steadily more abstract, the ability to implement empirically sophisticated macro and micro specifications poses a serious challenge to theorists. The need to find areas of reconciliation between micro and macro theory and the theoretical tension that demands such a reconciliation have never been greater. The kind of framework proposed in this chapter helps to delineate the problem and to point to fruitful areas for future research, but can provide only a framework for analysis, not a solution.

NOTES

1. One should probably not overemphasize the quality of microeconomic theory. Another analogy might be the science of medicine.
2. Chenery makes this point convincingly in comments presented to the recent Brookings conference on stabilization and development in Latin America. See Cline and Weintraub (1981).
3. Perhaps contrary to expectations, not all economywide micro models of developing countries assume market-clearing rules. Indeed, given their roots in the analysis of structural change, most of these models assume persistent barriers to price clearance in several important markets.
4. Throughout this chapter, we adopt Malinvaud's concept of equilibrium as a situation in which, given price rigidities, individual decisions have had time to adjust so as to be mutually consistent. This notion of equilibrium is broader than, but includes, the usual notion of equilibrium as a position of balance

between demand and supply realized by price variations alone. See Malin-vaud (1977) for a more detailed treatment of different interpretations of equilibrium.

5. We do not agree with the view recently suggested in the development liter-ature that most of the economic content of multisectoral CGE models can be captured by simple one- or two-sector analogs that can then be used for policy analysis (Taylor, 1980). While this may be true for the objective of understanding the fundamental theoretical structure of such models, espe-cially at the macro level, it is not true for the objective of using them for empirical analysis of development choices.

6. See Dervis, de Melo, and Robinson (1981, 1982). For particular country ap-plications, see Dervis and Robinson (1978) (Turkey), de Melo and Robinson (1980) (Colombia), de Melo and Robinson (1982) (archetype semiindustrial economies), and Robinson and Tyson (1981) (Yugoslavia).

7. The same analytic distinction is used by Powell (1981) in order to compare the scope and applicability of various macroeconomic and CGE models, with special emphasis on particular models of Australia. Adelman and Robinson (1978) use the same basic idea in their model of Korea, specifying three dis-tinct submodels.

8. In this case, functional separability is equivalent to Sargent's notion of di-chotomous monetary and real models. See Sargent (1979). Formally, separa-bility could also arise from functional separability in the macro submodel (Y_1 not depending on X_1), but it is hard to think of any interesting examples.

9. For example, existence proofs suffer. See Arrow and Hahn (1971). There also may be problems in computing simultaneous solutions to the paired sub-models, although experience to date indicates that nonneutrality causes fewer problems for solution algorithms than for theorists.

10. For exceptions, see Dervis (1975), who incorporated intertemporally consis-tent investment allocation rules into a CGE model, and Fair (1974), who ex-plicitly models investment decisions as being based on intertemporal expecta-tions in a macro model.

11. To our knowledge, with the exception of a recent CGE model for Argentina that includes money and savings accounts, there are no examples of empirical CGE models that directly incorporate alternative financial markets. See Felt-enstein (1980) for a discussion of the Argentina model. Adelman and Robin-son (1978), however, have an explicit model of the loanable funds market as part of their macro submodel.

12. The submodels are, however, theoretically disjoint, which reflects the for-mal nature of the specification and might well be abandoned in an empirical application.

13. The notions of "fair access" and "political sensitivity" really refer to issues of income distribution, and there is some work that directly addresses such issues. See, for example, de Melo and Robinson (1980) who use a nonneutral CGE model to analyze the distributional impact of different foreign ex-change rationing schemes, and Adelman and Robinson (1978).

14. Dixit (1981, p. 282) has recently put the point succinctly: "Any actual econ-omy has several stock magnitudes fixed by its history, and they are typically not in a steady-state configuration. Models which confine themselves to steady states are therefore simply inappropriate for answering real-world policy questions."

REFERENCES

Adelman, I., and S. Robinson (1978). *Income Distribution Policy in Developing Countries*. London: Oxford University Press.

Ahluwalia, M., and F. Lysy (1981). "Employment, Income Distribution, and Programs to Remedy Balance of Payments Difficulties." In *Economic Stabilization in Developing Countries*. See Cline and Weintraub (1981).

Armington, P. (1969). "A Theory of Demand for Products Distinguished by Place of Production." *IMF Staff Papers*, Vol. 16, pp. 159-78.

Arrow, K. J., and F. H. Hahn (1971). *General Competitive Analysis*. San Francisco: Holden-Day.

Bruno, M. (1976). "The Two-Sector Open Economy and the Real Exchange Rate." *American Economic Review*, Vol. 66, pp. 566-77.

Cline, W. R., and D. Weintraub, eds. (1981). *Economic Stabilization in Developing Countries*. Washington, D.C.: Brookings Institution.

Clower, R. (1965). "The Keynesian Counter-Revolution: A Theoretical Appraisal." In F. Hahn and F. Brechling, eds. *The Theory of Interest Rates*. London: Macmillan.

Cooper, R. J., and K. R. McLaren (1980). "The Orani-Macro Interface." Preliminary Working Paper No. IP-10, Impact Project, University of Melbourne.

Dervis, K. (1975). "Substitution, Employment, and Intertemporal Equilibrium in a Non-Linear Multi-Sector Planning Model for Turkey." *European Economic Review*, Vol. 6, pp. 77-96.

Dervis, K., J. de Melo, and S. Robinson (1981). "A General Equilibrium Analysis of Foreign Exchange Shortages in a Developing Economy." *Economic Journal*, Vol. 91, pp. 891-906.

——— (1982). *General Equilibrium Models for Development Policy*. Cambridge: Cambridge University Press.

Dervis, K., and S. Robinson (1978). "The Foreign Exchange Gap, Growth, and Industrial Strategy in Turkey, 1973-83." World Bank Staff Working Paper No. 306.

Dixit, A. (1981). "The Export of Capital Theory." *Journal of International Economics*, Vol. 11, No. 2, pp. 279-94.

Dornbusch, R. (1973). "Devaluation, Money, and Non-traded Goods." *American Economic Review*, Vol. 67, No. 5, pp. 871-83.

Fair, R. C. (1974). *A Model of Macroeconomic Activity*, Vol. 1. *The Theoretical Model*. Cambridge, Mass.: Ballinger.

Feltenstein, A. (1980). "A General Equilibrium Approach to the Analysis of Trade Restrictions with an Application to Argentina." *IMF Staff Papers*, Vol. 27, No. 4, pp. 749-84.

Fullerton, D., A. T. King, J. Shoven, and J. Whalley (1981). "Tax Integration in the U.S.: A General Equilibrium Approach." *American Economic Review*, Vol. 71, No. 4, pp. 677-91.

Green, D., and C. Higgins (1978). *A Macroeconomic Model of the Soviet Union*. New York: Academic Press.

Hudson, E., and D. Jorgenson (1978). "Energy Prices and the U.S. Economy, 1972-76." *Natural Resources Journal*, Vol. 18, No. 4, pp. 877-97.

Lysy, F., and L. Taylor (1980). "A Computable General Equilibrium Model for the Functional Distribution of Income: Experiments for Brazil, 1959-71."

In L. Taylor et al., eds., *Models of Growth and Distribution for Brazil.* Oxford: Oxford University Press.

Malinvaud, E. (1977). *The Theory of Unemployment Reconsidered.* Oxford: Basil Blackwell.

de Melo, J., and S. Robinson (1980). "The Impact of Trade Policies on Income Distribution in a Planning Model for Colombia." *Journal of Policy Modeling,* Vol. 2, No. 1, pp. 81–100.

——— (1982). "Trade Adjustment Policies and Income Distribution in Three Archetype Developing Economies." *Journal of Development Economics,* Vol. 10, No. 1, pp. 67–82.

Phelps, E. S. (1979). *Studies in Macroeconomic Theory,* Vol. 1: *Employment and Inflation.* New York: Academic Press.

Powell, A. (1981). "The Major Streams of Economy-Wide Modelling: Is Rapprochement Possible?" In J. Kmenta and J. B. Ramsey, eds., *Large Scale Econometric Models: Theory and Practice.* Amsterdam: North-Holland.

Robinson, S., and L. Tyson (1981). "A Computable General Equilibrium Model of the Yugoslav Economy." Mimeo., World Bank.

Sargent, T. S. (1979). *Macroeconomic Theory.* New York: Academic Press.

Taylor, L. (1979). *Macro Models for Developing Countries.* New York: McGraw-Hill.

——— (1980). "Macro Planning Models for Development: Current Issues and Perspectives." Paper prepared for the Symposium on Planning in Mexico, Mexico City, September 1980.

Weintraub, W. R. (1977). "The Micro Foundations of Macroeconomics: A Critical Survey." *Journal of Economic Literature,* Vol. 15, No. 1, pp. 1–23.

Comments on Chapters 5 and 6

Ronald I. McKinnon

Despite their difference in titles, both chapters have the same orientation. Starting with a nonmonetary general equilibrium model of an open economy with some input–output structure, how can one introduce money, bonds, and possibly other financial assets in such a way that the nominal price level and nominal interest rates are endogenously determined? How do fiscal deficits – government revenues less expenditures – add to these financial stocks so as to influence inflation, the balance of payments, and possibly real capital accumulation?

Starting with his large multisector "real" model, Feltenstein goes much further in adding the formal financial specifications necessary to link the fiscal deficit to changing stocks of money, bonds, and foreign indebtedness than do Robinson and Tyson. Because it is more specific, Feltenstein's chapter is an easier target for a discussant to criticize. The Robinson–Tyson chapter, on the other hand, is more a "wish list" of macroeconomic and financial relationships they would like to see grafted onto their "real" programming model of a developing economy. But very little grafting is actually done, and too many alternative approaches and considerations are thrown out for a discussant to encompass.

In common, however, both chapters fail to specify at the outset the level of financial development of the economy they are trying to model. Is it the United States with a highly developed primary securities market so that the government is unrestricted in the number of dollar-denominated bonds it may sell to cover any ongoing fiscal deficit? If so, the government need never issue either domestic money or bonds denominated in the foreign currency as instruments of deficit finance. Feltenstein believes his model is applicable to the United States, yet he assumes the government is constrained to always issuing money, foreign bonds, and domestic bonds in fixed proportions.

Feltenstein assumes that there is a fixed exchange rate and a single world money. So the domestic price level increases only insofar as the world money supply and world price level increase. This is in turn linked to the size of the domestic government's fiscal deficit. But then he faces the problem of having to model the rest of the world's demand for money, bonds, and goods – which he does arbitrarily by positing the existence of a single foreign consumer who demands goods and the three financial assets in exactly fixed proportions.

With only one world money, it is hard to see any empirical basis for Feltenstein's distinction between "foreign" bonds and "domestic" bonds. If they are both denominated in U.S. dollars, the basis for these different risk-return characteristics must somehow be associated with the identity of the issuer of the bonds. But in Feltenstein's model the U.S. government issues foreign bonds by borrowing abroad. Presumably foreign nationals also issue foreign bonds, although this mechanism for foreign bonds coming into existence is unclear. I conclude that, without introducing currency or exchange risk into Feltenstein's model, there is no logical basis for distinguishing between foreign and domestic bonds.

It is not clear how carryover stocks of bonds and money are treated because the model deals only with current flows of funds. Interest rates apparently don't influence the demand for money – there is no liquidity preference. Thus Feltenstein's macroeconomic simulations of the equilibrium price level and the rate of inflation lack credibility, as either a theoretical or an empirical exercise.

The Robinson–Tyson model would seem to apply to a less developed country. The "real" side is derived from ongoing research on development planning. Their ambitious agenda for future research (which is basically what their paper is) throws out all kinds of suggestions for introducing asset demand functions and money in order to make the price level and even possibly the exchange rate endogenously determined. Their discussion ranges widely over Keynesian, classical, and even Kaldorian macroeconomic approaches for accomplishing these ends.

What I missed was a specific list of believable financial specifications that adequately reflects the way capital markets work in a typical less developed country. From this starting point, one could seriously begin to model how government deficits get financed and what will be the consequences for ongoing price inflation, on the one hand, and the crowding out of private capital formation on the other. Open markets in primary securities either don't exist at all or are purely fringe operations in typical less developed countries. There may be some small credit markets associated with money lenders and village stores. Apart from foreign borrowing, however, the only large-scale organized capital market that the government and private borrowers may tap is the domestic banking system: the consolidated complex of central bank, commercial banks, savings banks, financiers, and so forth. Thus the banking system – and the way it is regulated through reserve requirements, interest restrictions, and other provisions for forced lending to the government or its assignees – must have center stage in any macro model of a developing economy. Yet representation of the banking system seems to be omitted entirely from the Robinson–Tyson agenda.

Let me illustrate briefly why it is important to incorporate bank regulations explicitly in any macroeconomic exercise. For a given fiscal deficit not covered by foreign borrowing, suppose the macro model builder wants to predict the resulting rate of price inflation in a typical less developed country. We know that the government must tap the banking system for finance, but it can do so either by imposing relatively high reserve requirements or by increasing the rate of issue of base money. Although less inflationary, the former route typically drives down real yields to depositors and drives up lending rates of interest to private borrowers, thus reducing private investment. On the other hand, if the government resorts mainly to the issue of base money without increasing reserve requirements, the rate of price inflation will be higher, although crowding out will be somewhat less. Therefore, the money supply mechanism must be carefully specified in any believable financial model of a less developed country, and so must be the demand functions for currency, sight deposits, interest-bearing term deposits, and so on. But those important considerations don't appear in the Robinson–Tyson "wish list."

Overall, how can we evaluate the efforts of Feltenstein and Robinson–Tyson to graft financial and monetary specifications onto micro general equilibrium models? Although perhaps useful to explore tentatively, at this stage it does not appear to me to be a promising future line of research. Micro general equilibrium models are better focused on relative commodity price changes and tax incidence over many sectors of the economy. Macroeconomic models are best kept much smaller in order to focus on questions of price level determination, money issue, the net trade balance, and the macroeconomic implications of government deficit finance. Too much excess baggage must be carried along when the two are joined for analyzing any specific problem. There is much to be said for the implicit traditional wisdom that has, hitherto, kept micro and macro analysis separate.

CHAPTER 7

General equilibrium analysis of regional fiscal incidence

Larry J. Kimbell and Glenn W. Harrison

1   Introduction

Two important and influential themes in applied general equilibrium analysis were initiated by Harberger (1962) and Scarf (1967, 1973), respectively: the use of analytic approximations to problems of differential tax incidence and the use of numerical simulation techniques to study arbitrary general equilibrium models. Our chapter discusses the application of general equilibrium numerical simulation techniques to the analysis of the regional incidence of fiscal policy.

Our general objective is to present a framework of analysis that incorporates the major elements of (i) the analytical approaches to tax incidence effects developed by Harberger (1962), Mieszkowski (1966, 1967, 1972), and McLure (1969, 1970, 1971); (ii) the implementation of constructive numerical approaches to general equilibrium comparative statics by Scarf (1967, 1973) and Shoven and Whalley (1972); and (iii) the use of interindustry transactions data in input–output models by Leontief (1966) and many others. Our specific objective is to provide an operational counterpart to the contributions of Mieszkowski and McLure, in the sense that Shoven and Whalley (1972) and Shoven (1976) have provided a counterpart to Harberger's work.

The structure of our paper is as follows. In Section 2 we examine the basic general equilibrium framework underlying the recent literature, noting the more important and sensitive theoretical issues raised by that framework. Section 3 presents our proposed general equilibrium numerical input–output (GENIO) framework for the analysis of these and other issues. A number of extensions to the earlier numerical simulation literature are noted. Finally in Section 4 we present several illustrative applica-

We are grateful to Glenn Graves, Charles McLure, Jr., Herbert Scarf, and participants of the NBER Conference on Applied General Equilibrium Analysis (San Diego, California, 1981) for comments. The National Science Foundation (Grant DAR-78-26309) has provided generous research support.

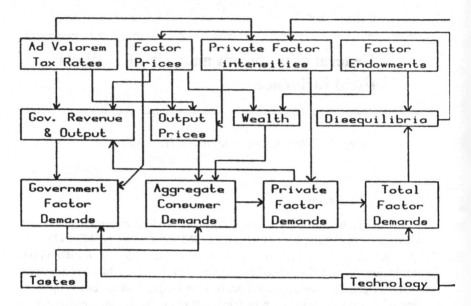

Figure 1. Basic general equilibrium interactions.

tions of our framework. The specific context for the work, and the regional partition used in the empirical application, concerns California versus the rest of the United States.

2   Theoretical issues

2.1   *Basic general equilibrium interactions*

In this section we introduce the overall equilibrium structure of our approach to the analysis of fiscal incidence. It is pedagogically useful to proceed in the rough algorithmic sequence adopted in searching for a new general equilibrium. Figure 1 illustrates this sequence in a simple flowchart. We see in Section 3 that this particular "recursive" sequence of calculations has a number of computational advantages.

Assume that some imaginary auctioneer or middleman proposes a vector of factor prices, expressed in terms of labor units (labor is the "numeraire"). Assuming constant returns to scale production functions,[1] cost-minimizing producers will choose to allocate factors in the same ratio for all levels of output: There is efficient "recipe" for producing a loaf of bread, and the input proportions of that recipe do not vary with the number of loaves produced. The assumption of profit maximization leads to the equality of (long-run) marginal cost with marginal revenue;

the assumption of "small" price-taking economic agents implies that marginal revenue is not a function of the output-level decision of any single entrepreneur. The further assumption of free entry into any industry leads to the key "zero-profit condition" allowing us to translate the factor prices and factor allocations prevailing into commodity prices. If we weight the amount of factor i used to produce a unit of output j [denoted $F(i,j)$] by the numeraire price of each factor i, and sum over all factors i, we have the marginal and average[2] cost of producing commodity j.

It follows from our earlier presumption of profit-maximizing producers, who are free to commit or remove resources from any given industry, that this average cost of producing the good is also equal to the price that it must be offered at. Producers offering the good at a higher price would earn "pure profits," attracting more producers into the industry; their added production, in aggregate, causes an excess supply at the old output price leading to a reduction in output price in order to clear the output market. Well-informed buyers will not purchase from the buyer offering the higher price, forcing producers offering the higher prices to lower their prices. All of the above is "action" that is presumed to occur behind the scenes of our model – we merely invoke the final equilibrium condition of zero profits. More succinctly, we have the condition that

$$p(j) = F(1,j) \cdot p(1) + F(2,j) \cdot p(2) + \cdots + F(n,j) \cdot p(n)$$

where we assume n factors in the economy. The condition holds for each output good j.

Note again the sequence of the algorithm: Given the n-dimensional vector of factor prices we derive the cost-minimizing allocation of factors in the production of each and every output good. These $F(i,j)$ terms are typically the result of lengthy calculations, depending on the structure and form of the production function for good j that is assumed. What is most important is that they are not related to the amount of j being produced; we may therefore proceed in one "closed" algorithmic step from the prevailing factor prices to the implied relative commodity prices.

Households are assumed to be endowed with certain physical quantities of the various factors. We assume that these factors are inelastically supplied. Each household is assumed to determine its "spending power" in terms of the numeraire by valuing these factors at prevailing factor prices. Households are assumed to allocate their spending power so determined and decide which commodities they wish to purchase. For this "calculation" they need three pieces of information: their preferences (embodied in the specification of their utility functions), the numeraire value of their factor endowment (given from their physical endowments and the prevailing factor prices), and finally relative commodity prices (which are derived in the way discussed earlier). By aggregating the planned purchases of each household for each commodity we arrive at a vector of final demands.[3]

Market equilibrium in the commodity markets is attained in an exceedingly simple way – producers just produce the quantity demanded in aggregate by households. This assumption determines the amount of output of each good *j* that is to be produced at the given factor prices, and therefore the derived demand for factors as inputs in that production.

Ignoring the influence of government activities for the time being, we proceed to consider the equilibrium of factor markets. This is where the lack of foresight of the auctioneer reveals itself and the "search" for a general equilibrium effectively begins. There was nothing in our preceding discussion to guarantee that the derived demand for factors as the result of the production of commodities would equal the existing endowment of factors. The initial set of factor prices was indeed arbitrary.[4] An obvious loop now occurs in the algorithm: If the derived demand for factors is not equal (within some close tolerance range) to the current-period endowment of the factor in each and every factor market, we must try another set of factor prices and try to get closer to an equilibrium. Computationally the search for a general equilibrium solution can be seen as a problem in minimizing the sum of the absolute values of the factor market disequilibria as a (highly nonlinear) function of the prevailing factor prices. It is possible to use standard algorithmic techniques to solve this problem (e.g., Newton–Raphson methods). Irrespective of how the solution is found, the important point at this stage is that it is identified by examining factor-market disequilibria only.[5]

There is much more to our framework than the simple interactions mentioned above, and these are introduced in due course below. One central feature of the models, however, should be noted – the role allowed government. In terms of the hypothetical sequence of decisions and events depicted above, government is assumed to enter at virtually all stages. The initial factor prices are "loaded" by some ad valorem tax on factors, affecting both the efficient factor allocation decisions of producers and the spending power of given physical factor endowments of households (thereby affecting the distribution of spending power directly). Similar taxes may be exacted on commodities, producing a direct "loading" on the prevailing relative commodity prices. The direct impact of this is on the allocation of spending power by households among the various commodities. This of course causes secondary influences in the factor markets, due to the derived demand for factors. The influence of the government, however, is felt in one further powerful manner – the way in which the revenue from this taxation[6] is spent. We assume that the government produces certain public goods. The essential distinction between private and public goods, for our purposes, is the nature of their consumption – private goods are rivalrously consumed,[7] public goods are not.[8] Naturally the production of public goods, requiring primary factor inputs, influences factor markets. The point to be made by the qualitative distinction between private and public goods is that the existing stock of the latter is a predetermined argument of the utility functions of private sector agents. Government provision of education is a prime, and properly controversial, example of some substitutability existing between a private good (private education) and a public good (government education). Our framework can deal explicitly with all of these influences of government.

2.2 *Regional incidence analysis*

The numerous analyses of tax incidence built on the original Harberger (1962) model have been surveyed by Mieszkowski (1967), Break (1974), and McLure (1975). This theoretical tradition has firmly established the advantages of general equilibrium analysis for a large number of policy issues. In this section we review several developments in terms of this tradition, identifying areas to which numerical simulation techniques may usefully contribute. We are particularly concerned with issues germane to *regional* incidence analysis.

Factor specificity and mobility: Within the Harberger tradition, McLure (1969, 1970, 1971) and Mieszkowski (1966, 1972) have examined the effects of assuming region-specific factors on the standard tax incidence results.[9] The notion of factor mobility in our framework can be usefully viewed as a particular configuration of sector-specific factoral usage. This is indeed how most of the literature has modeled factor mobility (see Section 3.2 below for further discussion).

The key result here is that regional taxes levied on regionally mobile factors (working capital, for example) will tend to fall on those factors that are specific to the region (land, for example). Clearly one would also expect the final incidence of regional taxes levied on region-specific factors to also fall on those factors. To the extent that the commodity prices of locally produced goods are impacted, there are said to be local "excise tax effects" on the industry arising from the factor tax changes.[10] If, additionally, other regions import goods from the taxing region, then there is "tax exporting" in the sense that consumers in other regions bear some of the burden of the regional tax. If local product prices change but few goods are exported, then there are excise tax effects with insignificant tax exporting.

These are seminal ideas,[11] and are central to any incidence analysis of regional taxes. We illustrate their importance in two applied simulations in Section 4 of the effects of regional tax changes. It should be noted that McLure (1975, p. 145) acknowledges that the original analyses producing these results "suffered from the necessity to lump the entire output of each region together into one aggregate commodity and the concomitant inability to consider partial taxes on only some products or some uses of a given factor in the region." We see in our simulations that numerical techniques are not similarly constrained.

Virtually identical ideas have appeared recently in an emerging theory of tariff incidence in international trade theory. Notable recent contributions include Dornbusch (1974), Clements (1979), Sjaasted (1980), and Sjaasted and Clements (1982). The key result of this literature is that the burden of a tariff on importables may fall mainly on exportables, rather than local nontraded goods.[12] This incidence depends on the import tariff elasticity of the price of local nontraded goods. If this elasticity is close to unity,[13] then the incidence of the tariff falls largely on exportables. If this elasticity is somewhat less than unity, the incidence is shared by exportables and nontraded goods.[14]

A number of alternative assumptions about the regional specificity of factors of production are widely used in incidence analysis. Heckscher-Ohlin models of international trade assume that factors may move freely between sectors in any region, but may not move between regions. A popular variant on these assumptions in the international trade literature is the Ricardo-Viner class of models that assume that one factor is able to move freely between sectors and another factor (or set of factors) is specific to each domestic sector. Again, no interregional factor mobility is assumed. A less popular variant on the Heckscher-Ohlin tradition, identified by Caves (1971), allows factors that are specific to certain sectors to move freely between regions providing they do not move between "different" sectors. Multinational mining companies, for example, tend to have an expertise in one sector and are highly mobile geographically.

Traditional Harberger-Mieszkowski-McLure (HMM) incidence analysis assumes one factor that is perfectly mobile between regions and one factor that is perfectly immobile. As noted earlier, however, the extent of intersectoral mobility was not really an issue here - the output of each region was aggregated into one output with no explicit discussion of its composition. We return to this issue below.

Three important modeling implications of our discussion may now be drawn. The first is that it is desirable to be able to contrast the results of incidence analyses of a particular policy that assume differing configurations of regional factor specificity. Apart from providing some common ground between international trade and HMM theoretical approaches, such contrasts often have considerable interpretative value with respect to model results. Factor specificity and immobility are widely regarded as constituting a reasonable characterization of the "short run," with intersectoral and interregional mobility a reasonable characterization of the "long run." We need not dwell on the limitations of such characterizations; the important point is that they do have substantial "story-telling" value in a general equilibrium analysis.

A second point, related to the first, is that we would like to be able to *readily* contrast alternative configurations on the spectrum of factor specificity and mobility. We shall see in Section 3 that numerical techniques are not limited to those configurations popularly adopted for analytical convenience.

The third general implication of dealing with factor specificity is the issue of computational feasibility. A general equilibrium model of a single region assuming a mere 10 sectors will have 2 factors if capital and labor are both sectorally mobile, and 11 factors if labor is sector-specific and capital is mobile. This modest enough extension raises the dimension of the search for an equilibrium from 1 relative factor price to 10 relative factor prices. A model of two regions assuming 10 sectors in each region will have 2 factors if capital and labor are regionally and sectorally mobile, 3 factors if labor is regionally immobile but still sectorally mobile within each region, and 21 factors if labor is regionally mobile and sector-specific. The reader can easily extend this counting exercise to the case of 3 or more original factors (e.g., energy, water) and 3 or more regions of interest. With current computer technology and *standard* solution algorithms, virtually any of these modestly realistic extensions would involve "considerable" computational expense. We propose a solution algorithm in Kimbell and Harrison (1983) and Section 3.3 below that allows rapid solutions to numerical models of the dimensions noted above.

Regional differentiation: The importance of intermediate inputs in international trade theory has grown in recent years; see Chang and Mayer (1973), Jones (1975), and Burgess (1980), inter alia. The theory of effective protection has a number of general equilibrium features[15] and is widely applied for policy purposes. It embodies the simple and important message that tariffs act as a subsidy to importables production and a tax on exportables production, since imported goods will typically be used directly or indirectly as intermediate inputs to exportables production. The relevance of this point for the extent of excise tax effects and tax exporting in regional incidence analysis is clear. Melvin (1979) indeed employs the effective protection methodology to estimate the incidence of the U.S. and Canadian corporate income tax structure on sectoral commodity prices. Interindustry trade flows have been allowed for in a number of recent general equilibrium models – see Dresch, Lin, and Stout (1977), Treddenick and Boadway (1977), Fullerton, Shoven, and Whalley (1978), DeFina (1980), and Fullerton, King, Shoven, and Whalley (1981).

Following Kuenne (1963, p. 398), we can divide spatial models into two basic types: "Those which take the spatial structure of the economy as given and which seek to determine the equilibrium patterns of prices and flows of goods over space, and those which add to these latter unknowns the spatial structure itself." As we shall see below in Section 3.2, the use of an interregional input–output (IO) accounting framework to calibrate our numerical model allows us to deal operationally with a regionally differentiated economy – the first type of spatial model referred to by Kuenne. The data on regional demand and value-added allow tastes and production functions to vary from region to region. Similarly, the interindustry trade data allow the "same" sector in different regions to have different (direct and indirect) own-region requirements of intermediate inputs.

One important idea in the analysis of regional fiscal incidence, provided by Tiebout (1956), focuses squarely on the possible endogeneity of the spatial fiscal structure. In Tiebout's analysis households "vote with their feet" by choosing a region in which to reside. Their choice of location depends on the public service mix[16] that a given region provides and the taxes it levies. In other words, households seek an optimal mix of regional taxes and local public goods. If there are a large number of small regions, each offering its own public service bundle and tax rate, the equilibrium location of residents may provide a solution that resembles the choices households would have made if they had fully revealed their preferences. Kimbell, Shih, and Shulman (1979) discuss the relevance of Tiebout mobility for the general equilibrium analysis of the Proposition 13 fiscal reform in California. It is possible to study such residential locational decisions in our framework if they are assumed to be made independently of the computation of a general equilibrium in our regionally differentiated model. In other words, we can solve for a given spatial configuration of households, *separately* "ask" households[17] whether they would like to move to another region,[18] move households to their preferred region,[19] and then re-solve the model *given* this conditionally preferred spatial distribution of households. After a sequence of such migrations, one would expect to obtain a stationary pattern of relative prices and no migratory inclinations. Modeling Tiebout mobility in terms of sequential comparative static general equilibrium solutions permits some explicit analysis of locational issues in terms of our general equilibrium framework.[20]

A number of recent studies have extended general equilibrium models in the Scarf tradition to deal with contemporaneous locational decisions. Important contributions in this area include MacKinnon (1974), King (1977), Arnott and MacKinnon (1977a, 1977b, 1978), and Richter (1978b, 1980).

3   A general equilibrium numerical input–output framework

3.1   *Overview*

In this section we introduce the numerical framework that we have developed to deal with several of the issues identified in Section 2. Although our approach is quite traditional, there are a number of novelties that we present in some detail.

The first major difference in our approach concerns the use of the general equilibrium structure described in Section 2.1 and illustrated in Figure 1. The advantage of this structure, in relation to the computational structure originally proposed by Scarf (1967), is that certain computational redundancies are removed for the class of models we happen to be interested in.[21] Specifically, the critical dimension of our search for a solution is the number of independent factor prices, which is just the number of primary factors in the model less one. The number of produced commodities has no fundamental influence on the search dimension, allowing us to build and solve models that utilize the detailed data available from input–output models on sectoral transactions. It should be noted that the structure of Scarf's algorithm can easily be modified to remove this computational redundancy.[22]

The second major difference concerns the algorithm used to solve for the general equilibrium. We have developed an exceedingly simple procedure, along the homely lines of the Walrasian auctioneer *tâtonnement* process, that displays several dramatic properties. The first such property is that, for a specified class of general equilibrium economies, the solution is a closed-form *analytic* solution. This means that one can simply compute the exact solution algebraically without *any* iterations. This result is independent of the number of primary factors and produced commodities. Since it is an analytic solution, there is, of course, no question of finding "good" starting values for factor prices. The dependence of this result on particular features of the model is noted below, and a proof that it is indeed the analytic solution offered in Kimbell and Harrison (1983). The second result is even more remarkable: This algorithm appears to be an excellent approximation to some undefined analytic solution for more general cases. In short, it is extremely fast for very general cases. What this second result means is that we may routinely solve for quite large problems. The implication here is that we are no longer limited by technique and/or computational resources to assume only two or three primary factors. This allows us to assume very detailed patterns of factor specificity and mobility in particular applications, as required by the analysis of regional fiscal incidence.

The third feature of our framework concerns the use of existing data from an input–output accounting framework to calibrate the model. Arguably, one of the most important developments in this field since the original contribution by Scarf (1967) has been the use of observed data to provide an empirical characterization of some kind in general equilibrium models. Input–output transactions tables are now routinely generated[23] for many countries and regions. Such tables provide the basic data necessary to minimally calibrate general equilibrium models: The value-added rows provide data on payments to primary factors and government (indirect taxes) by sector, the final demand columns provide expenditure data by domestic households and foreigners by sector, and the inter-industry transactions provide data on intermediate input requirements by sector. With extraneous estimates of certain key elasticities it is possible to identify all the necessary parameters of a simple general equilibrium model. For certain exercises these data are all that is needed; for other problems it is necessary to have recourse to essentially hypothetical parameter values. The important feature of our model is that it is flexible enough to incorporate an arbitrary input–output transactions table, providing it satisfies simple "adding-up" requirements.

In Section 3.2 we discuss the use of a general input–output accounting system in obtaining the "basic" data for our model, in Section 3.3 the crucial algorithmic features of our framework, and in Section 3.4 a number of immediate extensions to our framework.

3.2   The input–output accounting framework

Basic data: The typical input–output (IO) table provides all of the data necessary to calibrate a general equilibrium model allowing substitution in production and consumption. If extraneous estimates of certain elasticities of substitution can be obtained, from thin air or a literature survey, it is possible to calibrate more general (nested) functional forms with widely available IO data. In this section we discuss the use of such data, as a prelude to a discussion of the concept and computation of a benchmark equilibrium.

		Intermediate purchases 1 ... j ... n			Final demand C I G E				Σ = Gross output
	1	$X_{11} \dots X_{1j} \dots X_{1n}$			C_1	I_1	G_1	E_1	X_1
	$\vdots$	$\vdots$ $\vdots$ $\vdots$			$\vdots$	$\vdots$	$\vdots$	$\vdots$	$\vdots$
Producing sector	i	X_{i1} X_{ij} X_{in}			C_i	I_i	G_i	E_i	X_i
	$\vdots$	$\vdots$ $\vdots$ $\vdots$			$\vdots$	$\vdots$	$\vdots$	$\vdots$	$\vdots$
	n	$X_{n1} \dots X_{nj} \dots X_{nn}$			C_n	I_n	G_n	E_n	X_n

Value added	
Employee compensation	$EC_1 \dots EC_j \dots EC_n$
Profits	$PR_1 \dots PR_j \dots PR_n$
Interest	$IN_1 \dots IN_j \dots IN_n$
Depreciation	$DE_1 \dots DE_j \dots DE_n$
Indirect bus. taxes	$BT_1 \dots BT_j \dots BT_n$
Imports	$IM_1 \dots IM_j \dots IM_n$
Σ = Gross outlays	$X_1 \ \ \dots X_j \ \dots X_n$

Figure 2. Basic interindustry accounting system. Legend for final-demand components: C = consumption, I = investment, G = government expenditure, E = gross exports.

Figure 2 illustrates the basic IO accounting framework.[24] We shall be concerned with the use of three blocks of data from this table: the value-added rows, the final demand columns, and the matrix of interindustry transactions.

Each value-added row can be interpreted as the (value) payments to a particular factor – it is common to aggregate the rows for profit income, interest income, and depreciation to obtain the payments to the single factor of working capital. The employee compensation row provides data on payments to the factor of labor. The row that is typically labeled "Indirect Business Taxes" can be viewed for the moment as a general tax on value-added as a whole; we discuss its use in model-equivalent "ad valorem" form below. It is important to note that these rows provide *sectoral* data on factor payments, invariably for an exhaustive series of sectors. Imports often appear as a row in input–output tables, typically with some distinction being drawn between competitive imports[25] and noncompetitive imports.[26] The treatment of imports happens to be quite important for certain general equilibrium problems, particularly those involving open economies and trading regions. The ORANI model of

Dixon et al. (1982) is particularly sensitive to the assumed treatment of imports.[27] We return to the treatment of imports in the context of an interregional IO table below.

The final demand columns of the IO table provide data on expenditure in value units. The "household" types typically distinguished include consumers (consumption), investors (gross private capital formation), federal government (expenditure on current and capital account), state and local government, and foreigners (gross exports). Some tables provide further disaggregation of government expenditure, but this is not common. In any case, these categories at least provide the basis for more detailed attempts to disaggregate final expenditure on the basis of data from household expenditure surveys and/or taxation data. This block of data, as provided by the typical IO table, is probably the one that is least satisfactory for general equilibrium purposes.[28]

The final block of data provided by the IO table is of course the industry-by-industry matrix of intermediate input requirements. Each column of this matrix, divided elementwise by the value of that sector's total input usage, shows the direct per unit requirements of every other sector's output. It is common to assume that the intermediate input technology is of the standard fixed-coefficient Leontief type, and we follow convention here.

Data on individual household endowments are not obtainable from typical IO tables, and popular calibration procedures recognize this by adjusting the distribution of endowments across household types until the necessary budget constraints are satisfied.

Interregional data: It is possible to adapt essentially the same IO accounting framework to develop interregional transactions data. The typical procedure is to generate, by one method or another, matrices of direct own-region requirements and direct other-region requirements for each region considered. If we consider the simple case of just two regions, the former matrix represents the per unit requirements of each sector that are assumed to be met from own-region gross production; the latter matrix shows the per unit requirements of each sector that are assumed to be met by imports from the other region.[29] We shall concern ourselves here not with the methods used to construct such interregional tables,[30] but rather with the way in which it allows us to distinguish regions in terms of factor usage, expenditure patterns, and intermediate input technology.

Figure 3 illustrates the general interregional IO accounting framework used in this study for studying the regional incidence of government tax and expenditure policies. Regions are distinguished from sectors by the

	Intermediate purchases		Final demand	$\Sigma = $ Gross output
	Calif.	ROUS		
Producing region				
California	R^{11}	T^{12}	FD^1	X^1
ROUS	T^{21}	R^{22}	FD^2	X^2
Value added	VA^1	VA^2		
Imports	IM^1	IM^2		
$\Sigma = $ Gross outlays	X^1	X^2		

Figure 3. Interregional input–output accounting system. *Note:* Superscripts refer to regions (California = 1, ROUS = 2). See text for further explanation.

use of superscripts rather than subscripts. The R matrices represent own-region intersectoral transactions, and the T matrices represent inter-regional, intersectoral transactions. Similarly, the FD matrices represent final demand for the net output of each sector in each region, and the VA matrices represent value-added generated by each sector in each region. Figure 2 provides the accounting detail that Figure 3 glosses. Thus each regional FD matrix is $n \times 4$ (since we earlier distinguished four components of sectoral final demand), and each regional VA matrix is $5 \times n$ (since we distinguished five types of sectoral value-added). Each R and T matrix is $n \times n$, since we distinguish n sectors in each region.

Note that this interregional IO accounting framework is *qualitatively* identical to the accounting framework presented earlier (contrast Figure 2). The first block of sectors refers to one region (California here) and the second block of sectors to the other region (rest of U.S. – ROUS for short – here). Thus we identify the production of each good by the region in which that production is assumed to occur. This is the so-called Armington assumption, named after Armington (1969). It has been employed recently by Whalley (1980) and Brown and Whalley (1980) in an international context. One important area for future research is to allow goods that are distinguished solely by region to have an elasticity of substitution in consumption different from (and invariably higher than) goods that are produced in any single region. Our present models assume no such "nesting" of utility functions. One attractive feature of such nesting is the ability to replicate popular international trade assumptions about "small" economies (regions) effectively facing *given* relative commodity prices in some sectors.

As Isard (1951) emphasized many years ago, the use of such models of the spatial economy allows one to deal with a rich assortment of regional differentiation in tastes (each block of sectors has a particular expenditure pattern), factor usage (each block of sectors has distinct value-added shares), own-region intermediate production processes (each diagonal block of the interindustry matrix is distinct), and interregional trade flows (each off-diagonal block of the interindustry matrix is sector-specific). However, it is crucial that the limitations of this approach for the study of spatial issues be identified. Isard (1951, p. 328) notes:

> Constant production coefficients, interregionally viewed, mean unchanging supply channels. The model thus forces the assumption that the spatial extent of each line of production in each region is fixed with respect to its inputs. In this respect, no spatial lengthening or shortening of any line of production can be tolerated. Viewed otherwise, transport outlays or, in physical terms, distance inputs per unit of output of any line in any region are not permitted to change. Also, as a corollary, roughly fixed price ratios are assumed, so that substitution of distance inputs for other inputs, of transport outlays for other outlays, is precluded. In these respects, the underlying structure of the space-economy is held rigid.

As noted earlier in Section 2, we prefer to view our approach as dealing explicitly with many issues of *regional differentiation* and effectively ignoring the issues raised by allowing contemporaneous *regional location decisions*.

Factor specificity and mobility: A simple extension of the basic IO accounting framework, coupled with the powerful algorithm introduced in Kimbell and Harrison (1983) and discussed below, allows us to deal with relatively large problems and somewhat more "realistic" configurations of primary inputs. This extension is intended to allow us to deal with factor specificity in a general and intuitive manner. Suppose that we wished to distinguish the labor employed in California from the labor employed in the ROUS, to view labor as a region-specific or immobile factor. The procedure adopted is to view the payments by ROUS sectors to Californian labor as a null row vector, and the payments by California sectors to ROUS labor as a null row vector. Viewing California labor and ROUS labor as two distinct factors, each would be entitled to a separate row in the value-added block in the interregional IO accounting framework. Figure 4 illustrates this matrix configuration. Note that no adding-up constraints have been violated, by construction, and yet we have defined labor as being region-specific.

	Intermediate purchases		Final	Σ = Gross
	Calif.	ROUS	demand	output
Producing region				
California	R^{11}	T^{12}	FD^1	X^1
ROUS	T^{21}	R^{22}	FD^2	X^2
California labor	EC^1	$\bar{O}$		
ROUS labor	$\bar{O}$	EC^2		
Other value added	OVA^1	OVA^2		
Imports	IM^1	IM^2		
Σ = Gross outlays	X^1	X^2		

Figure 4. Specific factors in the accounting system. *Note:* "California labor" refers to employee compensation paid to labor directly working for California sectors.

This simple procedure obviously generalizes to allow any configuration of sector-specific factor usage.[31] Note also that many theorists have interpreted the two extreme cases of specific factors and sectorally mobile factors in terms of "short-run" and "long-run" resource allocation outcomes.[32] Our procedure for dealing with specific factors allows a simple contrast of these two types of outcomes, simply by altering the way the data are constructed. Moreover, it is an equally straightforward matter to deal with intermediate, "medium-run," configurations as desired. This opens the way to dealing with problems of great complexity and, depending on one's attitude to such modeling exercises, realism.

The computational effect of this important extension is to raise the dimensionality of the search for an equilibrium. As noted earlier, we believe that the algorithm discussed below allows us to proceed to use these extensions without undue concern over computational expense.

Parameter identification: There has been an increasing trend in the numerical simulation literature toward providing empirical versions of the economy under study. For many policy purposes this is clearly important, if for no other reason than their presumed relevance in the eyes of those who will act upon them. On a slightly more subtle level, however, budget constraints must "add up" for one even to define a general equilibrium solution. This is a transparent problem if one is willing to use purely hypothetical numbers, since the solution algorithm we propose in Figure 1 automatically ensures that budget constraints are met.

The truly important step in the generation of an empirical characterization occurs when the model is able to replicate the *essential* outcomes of the data it is fed. Specifically, we have in mind as "essential" the chosen factor intensities for each sector, the allocation of each household's spending power across commodities, and the aggregate allocation of final demand across commodities. The first item ensures that we *do* end up producing secondary energy with nontrivial amounts of primary energy. The second item is important for any study that is concerned with the distributional implications of any comparative static exercises with a general equilibrium model.[33] The last of these items ensures that we *do not* end up consuming a great deal of New York wine relative to California wine.[34]

Seminal contributions in the area of "general equilibrium accounting" for the United States, the United Kingdom, and Canada are provided by Fullerton, Shoven, and Whalley (1978), Piggott and Whalley (1983), and St-Hilaire and Whalley (1980). They have each successfully integrated wide varieties of national data to generate benchmark equilibria against which counterfactual simulations may be compared.[35] The problem of choosing parameter values for the underlying production and utility functions in a general equilibrium model may be usefully viewed from the perspective of the econometric identification of a system of structural equations. We use the available data on factor shares (by factor and sector) and expenditure shares (by sector and household type) along with the "identifying restrictions" of choice theory in order to work "backwards" to the parameters of the production and utility function that would generate those shares. Piggott and Whalley (1983, chapter 4) provide an excellent exposition of these standard calibration procedures.

The generation of an empirical general equilibrium model requires considerable attention to accounting detail and niceties and a liberal measure of common sense in deciding what is "essential" to the proposed application. Our efforts have been directed toward making the generation of such empirical characterizations revolve around the generation of reliable interregional input–output transactions data, on the simple rationale that one rarely has much else to work with.

3.3   *Algorithmic features*

The analytic factor price solution: The central thrust of our efforts to develop a faster and more accurate solution algorithm for general equilibrium models has been to sacrifice generality for closed-form analytic solutions to the various subproblems implied by a general equilibrium model. For the class of general equilibrium model considered here, the only iterative process involves the determination of equilibrium factor prices. Use of neoclassical production functions, as extended by fixed-coefficient intermediate input requirements, means that output prices are analytically determined by cost minimization and the zero-profit assumption.[36]

For a class of general equilibrium models, to be specified below, the closed-form solution is given by the following *analytic factor price solution:*

$$P(f) = [K(f)/K(1)]^{1/s}[X(f)/X(1)]^{-1/s}$$

for $f = 2$ to NFAC (number of factors in the model), with $P(1) = 1$ and

$$K(f) = \sum_{g=1}^{NCOM} a(g)^{s-1}B(g)^s d(g,f)^s T(g,f)^{-s}$$

and where $P(f)$ is the price of factor f; $D(f)$ is the demand for factor f; $X(f)$ is the (perfectly inelastic) aggregate supply of factor f; s is the elasticity of substitution in production (uniform across all industries) *and* consumption; $a(g)$ is the efficiency parameter for producing good g; NCOM is the number of produced goods (or commodities); $B(g)$ is the distribution parameter for good g in the constant elasticity of substitution (CES) utility function of the (single) consumer; $d(g,f)$ is the distribution parameter of factor f in the CES production function for good g; and $T(g,f)$ is unity plus the fractional rate of taxation on the use of factor f in industry g. The price of the first factor is taken without loss of generality to be the numeraire.

The analytic factor price solution is known for models that are general with respect to (i) any number of factors and goods; (ii) any pattern of distribution parameters in the single-level CES production functions or (single) utility function; (iii) any pattern of efficiency parameters in the production function; and (iv) any arbitrary pattern of factor taxes across factors and producing sectors. The exact solution does *not* apply to models with (i) more than one private household; (ii) any interindustry (input–output) flows; (iii) elasticities of substitution in production that vary from sector to sector; (iv) an elasticity of substitution in consumption different from the (uniform) elasticity of substitution in production; and (v) government factor demands that are not proportional to aggregate private industry factor demands.

The analytic factor price solution exhibits a property that we will call *systemwide separability,* since it implies that any changes in the tax rates on (nonnumeraire) factor f alter *only* the price of factor f. Equivalently, a change in the tax rates on the numeraire factor will change all other factor prices by exactly the same proportion. More formally,[37]

$$\frac{\partial[P(f)/P(k)]}{\partial[T(g,j)]}=0$$

for f, k, and j not equal, and for all such triples of f, k, and j. This property implies, not that the price of factor f adjusts enough to capitalize fully the tax changes – there can still be excise tax effects via changes in goods prices – but that the burden of increased taxes on one factor produces utterly no *relative* factor price changes among the other factors.

Assuming zero tax rates yield some insight into why systemwide separability holds, the analytic factor price solution leads to equations for factor intensities and output as follows:

$$F(g,f)=\frac{d(g,f)^{s}X(f)}{K(f)\cdot Z}$$

$$Q(g)=B(g)^{s}\cdot Z$$

where

$$Z=\left[\sum_{f=1}^{\text{NFAC}} d(g,f)^{s}K(f)^{-r}X(f)^{r}\right]^{1/r}$$

The allocation of factor f to the production of good g, $A(g,f)$, is simply the product of the relevant factor intensity and output:

$$A(g,f)=F(g,f)\cdot Q(g)$$
$$=\frac{d(g,f)^{s}B(g)^{s}X(f)}{K(f)}$$

Suppose the endowment of factor i increases, holding constant all other endowments and parameters. The ratio of the new factor allocation to the old factor allocation, for any arbitrary good g, becomes

$$A^{*}(i,g)/A(i,g)=X^{*}(i)/X(i)$$

$$A^{*}(g,f)/A(g,f)=1$$

for all f not equal to i, and where

$$X^{*}(i)=\text{new value of } X(i)$$

For all factors other than i the full allocation across all industries is completely invariant to changes in the endowment of factor i. Substituting for $A(g,f)$ yields the *factor use decomposition formula*:

$$\frac{F^{*}(g,f)}{F(g,f)}\frac{Q^{*}(g)}{Q(g)}=1 \tag{1}$$

The ratio of the output of good g *after* the expansion of the endowment of factor i to the output of good g *before* the endowment change,

$$Q^*(g)/Q(g)$$

is called the "expansion effect." It shows the proportion by which the use of factor f in producing good g would increase if output changed but factor prices were constant.[38] The ratio of the factor intensities,

$$F^*(g,f)/F(g,f)$$

is called the "substitution effect." It shows how the demand for factor f in producing good g would have changed, given the factor price changes, holding output constant. The factor use decomposition formula [Equation (1)] shows that the substitution effect is *identically equal to the reciprocal of the expansion effect* for all factors other than the one that changed, and for each and every industry. Essentially, the special restrictions involved in our analytic factor price solution are sufficient to make the expansion effect *identically offset* the substitution effect, leaving allocations other than $X(i)$ unchanged.[39]

This result also helps to explain a distinctive feature of the analytic factor price solution – the systemwide separability property. The CES family of production functions is strongly separable; that is, the marginal rate of substitution between factors f and j is invariant to changes in any other factor i, holding the inputs of f and j constant. An increase in the endowment of factor i, since it does not alter the amounts of f and j used in any production function (in a general equilibrium), leaves unchanged these marginal rates of substitution. The ratio of factor prices f and j is therefore invariant to changes in the endowment of factor i. Systemwide separability is therefore simply the result of strong separability of CES production functions, combined with the special result that allocations of factors other than i are invariant to changes in the endowment of factor i.

For any general equilibrium model the sum of factor demands across all industries equals the (inelastic) aggregate factor supply, before and after a change in endowments. In other words,

$$\frac{\sum_{g=1}^{\text{NCOM}} A^*(g,f)}{\sum_{g=1}^{\text{NCOM}} A(g,f)} = \frac{X^*(f)}{X(f)}$$

for all f. In our special case,

$$A^*(g,f)/A(g,f) = X^*(f)/X(f)$$

for all f,g pairs. Thus, what is special about our analytic factor price solution, in the case of zero taxes, is that the expansion effect is exactly offset by the substitution effect *in each and every industry.*

Even though the applications presented in Section 4 do not conform strictly to the conditions for a known analytic solution, systemwide separability tends to manifest itself repeatedly. Specifically, except for the effects of high tax rates on government revenues, and therefore government factor demands, many other factor prices change by exactly the same proportion relative to the numeraire. That is, a whole block of factor prices show the same percentage impacts.

One feature of our analytic factor price solution should be noted as particularly relevant for the study of regional fiscal incidence: the arbitrary pattern of distribution parameters in the CES production functions for each sector that is allowed. It is the adoption of alternative configurations of these parameters that allows us to examine alternative assumptions about factor specificity and mobility, as described earlier. Note that although our earlier discussion dealt with value share data and not distribution parameters, the latter may be obtained from the former for *given* values of the elasticity of substitution for each sector.

Some familiar analytic results: It is possible to analytically derive several standard HMM results with our analytic factor price solution, accepting the assumptions noted above for the existence of the closed-form solution. To simplify notation, let

$$h(g,f) = a(g)^{s-1} B(g)^s d(g,f)^s$$

and

$$M = K(1)^{-1/s} [X(f)/X(1)]^{-1/s}$$

Factor prices then become

$$P(f) = \left[\sum_{g=1}^{\text{NCOM}} h(g,f) T(g,f)^{-s} \right]^{1/s} \cdot M \tag{2}$$

for $f=2$ to NFAC and with $P(1)=1$. A standard HMM result emerges from Equation (2): If the tax expressions $T(g,f)$ are increased in proportion V for all uses of factor f (e.g., the property tax is increased in all regions), then factor price $P(f)$ changes by exactly the reciprocal of V. This result obtains by substituting $V \cdot T(g,f)$ into (2) and factoring out $1/V$. Capitalists bear fully a *uniform nationwide* increase in property taxes.

There are no excise tax effects in this case. The expression for product prices (obtained from the zero-profit equilibrium condition) becomes, with taxes:

$$P(g) = [1/a(g)] \left\{ \sum_{f=1}^{\text{NFAC}} d(g,f)^s [T(g,f) \cdot P(f)]^{1-s} \right\}^{1/(1-s)} \tag{3}$$

for $g=1$ to NCOM. Replace $P(f)$ in the expression for product prices by

$T(g,f) \cdot P(f)$ to obtain Equation (3). But increasing $T(g,f)$ by V, for all f, leads to $P(f)/V$, so the products $[T(g,f) \cdot V][P(f)/V] = T(g,f) \cdot P(f)$, and all product prices are invariant to a tax increase that is uniform across all factor uses.

Increasing the tax on *one use* of factor f is not the same, of course, as increasing taxes on all uses. In the original Harberger (1962) context the corporate profits tax was treated as levied on the use of capital in one sector, and in the Mieszkowski–McLure work on regional tax incidence an increase in property tax on one region is recognized as fundamentally different from a uniform nationwide tax change.

For expository convenience let $h(g,f) = 1$ in Equation (2), for all pairs g and f. In the base case let $T(g,f) = 1$, again for all g and f.[40] As the alternative, let the tax on the use of factor f in industry (or region) g increase by $V(g,f)$. The ratio of factor price f after the tax increase, $P(f)'$, to the price before the tax change, $P(f)$, becomes

$$\frac{P(f)'}{P(f)} = \left[\frac{G-1}{G} + \frac{1}{G \cdot V(g,f)^s} \right]^{1/s}$$

where G is the number of equally sized industries (or regions). It is obvious that as G grows larger the price of factor f is less and less affected (although it is always lower after the tax increase). The returns to a mobile factor are not significantly affected by a change in taxes on its usage in one small industry (or region).

These familiar results illustrate the potential analytical uses of the closed-form solution without any necessary numerical calculations.

The factor price revision rule: Useful as the analytic factor price solution may be, it does not appear to generalize to include certain important features of applied general equilibrium models (as noted earlier). It does, however, motivate a simple and powerful iterative algorithm for use in more general problems. Kimbell and Harrison (1983) examine these propositions in some detail.

The critical step in revising factor prices over iterations involves the following *factor price revision rule:*

Part 1. $\quad P(f, i+1) = P(f, i) \cdot [D(f)/X(f)]^{1/s}$

for $f = 1$ to NFAC, and where $P(f, i)$ is now the price of factor f at iteration i; and

Part 2 (Renormalize). $\quad P(f, i+1) \Leftarrow \dfrac{P(f, i+1)}{P(1, i+1)}$

for $f = 2$ to NFAC. The price of the first factor is taken without loss of generality to be the numeraire, and is simply reset to unity.

Notice that the factor price revision rule is a simple Walrasian rule that raises the price of a factor in excess demand, lowers the price of a factor in excess supply, and leaves unchanged the price of a factor with own demand equal to own supply.

The magnitude of the price revision, for a given ratio of demand to supply, is determined by the reciprocal of the elasticity of substitution. This is a *crucial discovery that critically influences the speed of convergence*. If the elasticity of substitution is very low, say .10, then the ratio of demand to supply in market f is raised to the 10th power in determining the price revision factor. If the elasticity of substitution is very high, say 10, then the 10th root of the ratio of demand to supply is the price revision factor. The low-elasticity revision rule causes far more "energetic" changes in factor prices than the high-elasticity case (for given values of the ratio of demand to supply).

We provide some computational experience with our factor price revision rule in the next section.

4   Applications

4.1   *A taxonomic illustration*

Structure of the economy: In this section we present several simulations of a hypothetical economy consisting of two regions each producing two private goods.[41] Using the "Armington assumption" noted in Section 3 we therefore distinguish four private commodities. Our hypothetical economy also includes two public goods, as described earlier in Section 2.1. One of these goods is produced with revenues generated by (factor) taxes that are specific to the good and region in which the factor is being used – this good may be regarded as a local public good. The other public good is produced with revenues generated by (factor) taxes that may vary with the good and factor being taxed, but are identical across regions – this good may be regarded as a national public good.

Each of the six commodities in our economy uses four *types* of primary factor. These are

  i.   A factor that is mobile between all regions and sectors
  ii. A factor that is mobile between sectors of the region in which the good is produced, but is not able to move to any other region
  iii. A factor that is specific to the production of a particular good and is able to move between regions
  iv. A factor that is specific to both a particular good and a particular region

Using our procedure for defining specific factors, the reader can confirm that our hypothetical economy has 1 factor of the first type, 2 factors of the second type (1 for each region), 3 factors of the third type (1 for each private good produced and 1 for the public good), and 7 factors of the fourth type (1 for each private and public good in each region, and 1 for the national public good). Our search for a general equilibrium solution therefore involves 12 relative factor prices (we define the completely mobile factor to be the numeraire). This configuration of factor specificity and immobility is designed to provide a complete taxonomy of such cases, extending earlier analyses in the HMM tradition. In addition, of course, we are able to study excise tax effects that may occur within regions and/or between regions.

For ease of interpretation of the simulation results, we have grossly simplified the production structure of this hypothetical economy: No intermediate trade between sectors or regions is assumed, the CES production functions for each good are calibrated with distribution parameters that take the value of 1 or 0 as the nature of the factor indicates, government taxes are assumed to be levied on each factor in each sector in each region (initially) at an "ad valorem" rate of 5%, a uniform elasticity of substitution (in production and consumption) of 2.0 is assumed, and each region is assumed to have only one household.[42]

Although conceptually simple and empirically spartan, this model is (i) large enough to illustrate the algorithmic power of our factor price revision rule; (ii) taxonomically complete enough to provide several extensions to the HMM literature; and (iii) small enough that we may present a policy simulation in some detail.

Some computational experience: Table 1 shows the speed of convergence to the general equilibrium set of 12 relative prices in terms of the absolute value of the maximum factor market disequilibria expressed as a percentage of the aggregate endowment of that factor.[43] The first run shown corresponds to the use of the unit vector as an initial guess at the equilibrium factor prices; in this case the factor price revision rule was able to solve the model described above in *nine* iterations.

The second run adopts starting values for factor prices that are deliberately disturbed "significantly" away from the (known) equilibrium solution. The sizable (maximum percentage) disequilibrium of 1423.977 (see iteration 1 for run 2 in Table 1) indicates what our algorithm had to overcome (relative to run 1). A new solution was found in *nine* iterations. Indeed, after the shock of the first iteration the rule tended to follow the convergence path of run 1.

The third run adopts the unit vector of factor prices as a starting point, but unlike run 1 assumes that intermediate trade is allowed between

Table 1. *Convergence experience*

Iteration	Percentage disequilibrium			
	Run 1	Run 2	Run 3	Run 4
1	90.000	1423.977	90.000	63.762
2	43.396	48.348	43.454	17.319
3	19.352	20.534	19.709	4.705
4	7.998	8.112	8.225	1.430
5	3.205	3.153	3.310	.468
6	1.269	1.225	1.312	.161
7	.500	.477	.517	.059
8	.196	.186	.203	—
9	.077	.073	.080	—

Note: Convergence is measured by the absolute value of
the maximum factor market disequilibrium expressed as
a percentage of the aggregate endowment.

commodities. The Leontief inverse used for this exercise was pseudo-randomly generated.[44] The convergence path again parallels that observed in run 1, with a solution (quite different from the solution found in run 1 or run 2) rapidly found.

The fourth run shown in Table 1 illustrates a common situation: Given the general equilibrium solution found in run 1 (or run 2), we search for a new solution after some policy perturbation. In this case we increase the local government tax on the fully mobile factor's use in good 1 in region 1 from 5% to 100%. The factor price revision rule is able to return us to a general equilibrium within a mere *seven* iterations.

Tax policy simulations: The simulations discussed below assume that the tax on the fully mobile factor is raised from an ad valorem rate of 5% to 100% on its use in the production of good 1 in region 1.

It is common in the analytical literature to distinguish tax and expenditure incidence by making some "equal-yield" assumptions about one side of the public accounts while altering the other side (e.g., assuming that an industry- and/or factor-specific tax cut is offset by a general "across-the-board" value-added tax increase of appropriate size). Shoven and Whalley (1977) provide an explicit computational approach to this issue, and Fullerton, Henderson, and Shoven (Chapter 9, this book) a critique of several numerical applications of the notion of "differential tax incidence." There are two objections to the use of such notions: (i) General equilibrium analysis is designed to deal with interdependencies of revenue sources and expenditures for all agent, and to single out the activities of one agent (government) for artificial treatment is illogical; and (ii) in a multigovernment economy (such as occurs invariably in a regional context) it is not clear what one should assume for the non-tax-change fiscal authority.[45]

The correct response to both of these objections is that the notion of "differential tax incidence" is essentially one motivated by pedagogic and expositional concerns[46] and that those concerns should indicate whether or not a particular procedure is useful. In the present context we shall examine the incidence of a particular tax increase by the region 1 government under two assumptions:

    a.   That the tax revenue is spent on the production of the local public good in region 1; and

    b.   That a uniform "across-the-board" value-added change in region 1 government taxes occurs such that its revenue does not change (in numeraire terms) from the base case.

In the first simulation our results represent a combination of tax *and* expenditure incidence. In the second simulation we make an equal-yield assumption with respect to the original taxing authority only (viz. the region 1 government); note that there will be some change in the expenditures of the region 2 government and the national government.

Our hypothetical economy is sufficiently similar to the model for which the analytic factor price solution is known to exist[47] that we may use that solution to motivate the nature of some of our simulation results. The nature of factor specificity in our model is that the distribution parameter $d(g,f)$ for factor f in the production function of good g is zero if the factor is unable to be used in that sector, and nonzero otherwise.[48] Recall from Equation (2) that if $d(g,f)=0$ for a given g and f associated with a change in taxes $T(g,f)$, then there is *no change* in the relative price of the nonused, nontaxed factor.[49] This result appears in one form or another in the simulations reported below. Specifically, there is typically a block of factors whose relative factor prices do not vary greatly from the numeraire or *at all* from each other.

Tables 2 and 3 present the incidence of an increase, from 5% to 100%, in the region 1 government tax on the use of the *fully mobile factor* in the production of good 1 in region 1. As noted earlier, we distinguish (a) overall fiscal (tax and expenditure) incidence results, and (b) "differential" equal-yield tax incidence results.

The tax increase leads to a shift in private good production away from good 1 in region 1 toward other commodities. In the equal-yield simulation this shift significantly favors good 2 in region 1 more than the goods in the nontaxed region. These relative shifts are reflected also in the

Table 2. *Incidence of tax on fully mobile factor (I)*

1. Percent change in demand for private goods

	(a) Region 1	Region 2	(b) Region 1	Region 2
Good 1	− 19.9	4.6	− 9.0	1.6
Good 2	4.2	4.6	4.7	1.6

2. Percent change in goods prices

	(a) Region 1	Region 2	(b) Region 1	Region 2
Good 1	22.1	6.8	9.8	3.9
Good 2	7.0	6.8	2.4	3.9

3. Percent changes in factor prices

	(a) Regionally mobile	Specific to R1	Specific to R2	(b) Regionally mobile	Specific to R1	Specific to R2
Goods-mobile	0	10.2	9.4	0	7.5	4.7
Good 1–specific	9.3	9.3	9.3	6.2	7.7	4.7
Good 2–specific	9.3	9.3	9.3	6.2	7.7	4.7
Gov't.-specific	24.2	55.3	13.4	3.6	1.2	4.7

Key: Factor 1 – fully mobile (between regions and sectors); 2 – sector specific/regionally mobile; 3 – sector-mobile/regionally immobile; 4 – fully specific (to a region and a sector).

excise tax effects on goods prices. Note the absence of any excise tax effects within the nontaxed region.

The changes in factor prices are shown relative to the taxed factor: There is a general increase in the relative price of all nontaxed factors. The systemwide separability of factor price effects on the taxed and non-taxed factors, discussed earlier in connection with our analytic factor price solution, is evident in the complete fiscal incidence results. Note the absence of any particular factor price capitalization effects on the factor specific to the tax base (good 1 in region 1).

When expenditure incidence is included there are sizable increases in the prices of factors that are specific to government and regionally mobile. The factors that are specific to some region but are able to move into the production of public goods also show a small additional factor price increase. Moreover, this additional increase is higher for the region 1 goods-mobile factor, since it is able to be employed by the taxing authority.

Table 3 presents an account of the detailed movements of the various factors in response to the tax policy. The sectoral movement of each factor as a percentage of the aggregate endowment[50] reveals the extent of the general equilibrium interactions present even in this simple hypothetical

Table 3. *Incidence of tax on fully mobile factor (II)*

4. *Factor movements (as percentage of aggregate endowment)*

Mobile factor

	(a) Region 1	Region 2	(b) Region 1	Region 2
Good 1	− 15.9	4.7	− 8.8	2.3
Good 2	4.7	4.7	3.9	2.3
S&L gov't.	1.2	.2	.02	.08
Fed. gov't.		.3		.1

Region-specific sectorally mobile factor

	(a) Region 1	Region 2	(b) Region 1	Region 2
Good 1	− .8	− .1	.2	0
Good 2	− .8	− .1	.2	0
S&L gov't.	1.7	.1	− .2	0
Fed. gov't.	− .04	.01	− .2	0

Sector-specific regionally mobile factor

	(a) Region 1	Region 2	Fed. gov't.	(b) Region 1	Region 2	Fed. gov't.
Good 1	0	0	—	1.4	− 1.4	—
Good 2	0	0	—	1.4	− 1.4	—
Government	28.3	− 8.3	− 19.8	− 2.3	1.1	1.3

5. *Factor changes for each private producing sector*

	Factor type					Factor type			
Sector (a)	1	2	3	4	(b) 1	2	3	4
Region 1								
Good 1	− 65.6	− .01	− 1.7	− .01	− 36.3	2.8	.4	0
Good 2	19.4	− .01	− 1.7	− .01	15.9	2.8	.4	0
Region 2								
Good 1	19.4	− .01	− .1	− .01	9.6	− 2.8	.02	0
Good 2	19.4	− .01	− .1	− .01	9.6	− 2.8	.02	0

6. *Factor use decomposition*

	Substitution effects				Expansion effects	Substitution effects				Expansion effects
Sector	(a) 1	2	3	4		(b) 1	2	3	4	
Region 1										
Good 1	− .85	.22	.20	.22	− .22	− .36	.12	.10	.09	− .09
Good 2	.14	− .05	− .06	− .04	.04	.10	− .02	− .04	− .05	0.5
Region 2										
Good 1	.13	− .05	− .05	− .05	.05	.08	− .05	− .02	− .02	.02
Good 2	.13	− .05	− .05	− .05	.05	.08	− .05	− .02	− .02	.02

Key: Factor 1 - fully mobile (between regions and sectors); 2 - sector-specific/regionally mobile; 3 - sector-mobile/regionally immobile; 4 - fully specific (to a region and a sector).

economy.[51] The mobile factor escapes the taxed sector, finding reemployment largely in the other private sectors. In the complete fiscal incidence simulation the region 1 government draws some of the government-specific regionally mobile factor away from the region 2 government and the national government.

Table 3 also presents an analysis of changes in factor use from the perspective of each private sector. The percentage change in the use of each factor type is shown, as well as a decomposition of that change into substitution and expansion effects using the factor use decomposition formula.

In the complete fiscal incidence simulation the taxed sector uses 65.6% less of the mobile factor after the tax change than it did before, and each of the other private sectors uses 19.4% more. In the equal-yield simulation good 2 in region 1 uses 15.9% more of the mobile factor, whereas the region 2 sectors only use 9.7% more. Note in the latter simulation that the region 1 sectors use more of their sector-specific regionally mobile factor.

The interpretation of these percentage changes is straightforward with the factor use decomposition formula, introduced earlier as Equation (1) and shown in Table 3 in log-ratio form. We are able to distinguish substitution and expansion effects on factor use. Consider the complete fiscal incidence simulation. The expansion effect shows a substantial decline in the production of good 1 in region 1,[52] and a small increase in the production of all other private sectors. In the case of the fully specific factors we see that their substitution effects, by definition, offset the corresponding expansion effects exactly. Note also the extent to which the substitution effects for the two partially mobile factors roughly offset the expansion effect for their sector.[53] The (negative) substitution effect for the fully mobile factor in the taxed sector reinforces the (negative) expansion effect. In the nontaxed private sectors the same reinforcement occurs, albeit qualitatively different. The overall sign pattern of the substitution effects is intuitive – the taxed sector uses more of the nontaxed factor and less of the taxed factor, and vice versa for the nontaxed sectors.

Now consider the decomposition of factor use changes in the equal-yield simulation. The sign patterns of the expansion and substitution effects are qualitatively the same as in the complete fiscal incidence simulation. However, we see that the substitution effects more than outweigh the expansion effects in several cases (most notably for the sector-specific regionally mobile factor).

4.2   A simple empirical model

An empirical model of the California and U.S. economies is under development by the UCLA Business Forecasting Project. This model has been

Table 4. *Impacts of capital tax reduction on relative prices*

	Percentage change relative to numeraire	
	California	Rest of U.S.
Factor	*Factor prices:*	
Capital	0	0
Labor	− 4.3	.005
Sector	*Output prices:*	
Agriculture	− 2.7	− .054
Mining	− 3.5	− .018
Construction	− 3.4	− .001
Food processing	− 4.6	− .003
Nondurables	− 4.5	− .050
Durables	− 3.4	− .030
Trans. & util.	− 4.1	− .041
Real estate	− 6.7	− .015
Services	− 4.3	− .024
Public enter.	− 3.8	− .006

Note: Capital is the numeraire, hence its price does not change; it is not region-specific.

brought to a prototype form that includes a 10-sector intermediate-good matrix for California and the rest of the United States, with explicit trade between the two regions. It represents consumer demand with only one household type per region. Since it lacks any distribution of income, it cannot have any meaningful progressive income tax system. Eventually the model will be used to evaluate the impacts of a major tax cut in property taxes in California, known as Proposition 13. At present we limit our focus to a reduction in factor taxes on capital. (See Christensen, Harrison, and Kimbell, 1982, for further applications.)

The empirical representation of California and the rest of the United States (ROUS) uses the 10 sectors shown in Table 4. Each industry typically buys from each other industry in its own region and from industries in the other region. There are five sources of final demands by industry: consumers in each region, state and local governments in each region, and the federal government.[54] For convenience and lack of data, consumers and state and local governments are assumed to buy goods directly only from their own region. Since these industries use intermediate goods from the other region, there is, of course, induced demand for the output of industries in the other region as well. The federal government demands goods from both regions.

Each industry uses two primary substitutable factors: capital, which is mobile across regions, and own-region labor. There are three factors: capital, California labor, and ROUS labor.

The case we examine is one in which the ad valorem factor tax rates levied by state and local governments in California on capital used by industries producing goods in California are reduced by 50%. The 50% reduction in the ad valorem tax rate on capital that is used in industries in California leads to an increase in the price of the mobile capital factor relative to wages in California. Alternatively, since the price of capital is the numeraire, California wages fall 4.3% with the tax rate reduction.

Induced wage effects in the rest of the United States are negligible – wages in the ROUS rise .005% relative to the price of capital. The capitalization effects are therefore strongly concentrated on the mobile factor and the California-specific factor.

If the tax reduction induced full capitalization in the price of capital, then there would be no excise tax effects. However, the mobility of capital leads to excise tax effects, especially for goods produced in California. The prices of goods produced in California fall (relative to the price of capital) for two reasons. First, the reduction in factor taxes lowers their costs of production even without changes in factor prices. Second, wage rates drop. Industries that are relatively capital-intensive (and that have relatively high capital factor taxes) receive proportionately higher reductions in capital costs, but benefit less from the wage reducton. Industries that are relatively labor-intensive also receive benefits in reduced wage costs. The largest price reduction in California industries is for real estate, which is highly capital-intensive.

Output prices in the ROUS drop slightly even though there are no directly relevant tax changes, no change in the price of capital, and a very slight increase in the price of labor in the ROUS. The reason is that industries in the ROUS use intermediate goods imported from California, and the prices of these goods drop (as discussed above).

5   Conclusion

Two major analytic traditions, those of Harberger-Mieszkowski-McLure and Scarf-Shoven-Whalley, form the basis of our efforts to develop empirical models of the incidence of fiscal policy on regional economies. Regional tax incidence theory leads naturally to the consideration of factors specific to regions and/or industries. This increase in numbers of factors, however, has previously been severely constrained by computational costs that increase rapidly with more dimensions. Our pursuit of solution techniques for dealing with large dimensionality led to the discovery of an admittedly special case that requires no computational search, since the exact algebraic solution is available. Explorations of a number of regional tax incidence issues can be pursued without the use of computer simulations if these restrictions are appropriate. Furthermore, in more general cases the iterative algorithm suggested by the closed-form solution provides a rapid and cost-effective solution technique.

Our analytic results, and the applications presented, show a strong tendency for the first-order effects of factor tax changes to concentrate in blocks of variables, with variables outside the directly affected sectors changing relative to the directly affected variables but not relative to one another. A large tax cut in one given region, such as the property tax reductions involved in Proposition 13, does not appear to propagate to other regions with significant force in the model specified. Other issues of regional fiscal incidence, specifically those that affect trade between regions or nations, need not necessarily show such strongly concentrated impacts.

Analysts of regional taxation and expenditure issues have been constrained by a lack of empirical models that stem from the Harberger–Mieszkowski–McLure tradition. Available models, however well they may serve specific policy purposes such as short-run revenue forecasting, generally lack solid analytic foundations and strong equilibrating market-like mechanisms. Our purpose is to enlarge the techniques regional fiscal analysts can use to examine the important longer-run issues that general equilibrium models seem well suited for. With the aid of such techniques, a great deal of applied work remains to be done within existing theoretical and empirical general equilibrium traditions.

NOTES

1. We presume that this production function is Leontief with respect to all inputs (intermediate and final), but that the primary factor input is a composite input that is produced with a Cobb–Douglas or constant elasticity of substitution (CES) specification. The efficient choice of primary inputs is therefore separable from the use of intermediate inputs. When we refer to Cobb–Douglas or CES production functions below it is assumed that we are referring just to the production of the composite primary input.
2. The marginal is equal to the average cost because of the constant returns assumptions. Note also that we ignore the use of intermediate inputs in this introductory discussion (with no essential loss in generality).
3. Note that household demands are *not* constrained to have unitary income elasticities.
4. Note that the starting values for the comparative static simulations of such models are not arbitrary in our framework. The "previous" solution or "benchmark equilibrium" provides a natural place to begin the search for a solution based on some *perturbation* of the conditions defining that initial

equilibrium. Moreover, we introduce several results in Kimbell and Harrison (1983) and Section 3.3 below that allow an *analytic* solution of a wide class of fully dimensioned general equilibrium models. These solutions serve as excellent starting values for more general models, as we explain and demonstrate in due course below.

5. This point is now widely recognized – see Fullerton, Shoven and Whalley (1978, p. 45) and the references cited therein.

6. Not to mention the value of the physical endowment of factors that the fiscal household may own.

7. That is, "If you want to eat that banana, you buy it!"

8. That is, one can contrast the views of different household types about the existing provision of particular public goods. Hawk: "I think we have too little defense expenditure!" Dove: "I think we have too much defense expenditure!" Quaker: "I think we shouldn't have any!" The point is that there is simply no way that these household types may *contemporaneously* choose to "enjoy" more or less of the public good than exists.

9. We shall often refer to a Harberger–Mieszkowski–McLure, or HMM, tradition in regional fiscal incidence analysis. We specifically refer here to the extensions of the Harberger (1962) model by Mieszkowski (1967, 1972) and McLure (1969, 1970, 1971). The choice of these three authors as representative of a long theoretical tradition is due to Break (1974, p. 131).

10. McLure (1977, p. 74) notes an important clarification of the popular expression "excise tax effects": "Whereas true excises are imposed upon *products* and distort only consumption decisions, differentials in property taxes (between regions or types of products) distort both production and consumption decisions.... Differential property taxes are identical to excise taxes only if factor proportions are fixed." We shall see in Section 4 the importance of the notion of excise tax effects in the interpretation of our simulations.

11. See Mayer (1974), Mussa (1974), and Jones (1975) for a discussion of related ideas in the international trade literature.

12. It is interesting to contrast McLure's (1975, p. 146) assessment of Mieszkowski's (1972) extension of the Harberger model: "Seen as a national tax levied at some uniform average rate, the local property tax reduces the net return to capital by roughly the amount of the tax, rather than being 'shifted' to consumers or reducing the rents paid on land. On the other hand, due to the mobility of capital, local differentials in property tax rates not matched by service differentials are likely to have what Mieszkowski calls 'excise tax effects' by raising (or lowering) the cost of capital to the local area imposing differentially higher (lower) taxes on property. Such excise effects are likely to be particularly important for so-called 'home' products, as opposed to 'export' goods." The empirical presumption obtained from the international trade application has been rather different (a heavier burden on exportables industries), but the analytical thrust has been similar.

13. Which would be the case if importables and nontradables are close substitutes in local production and consumption.

14. Sjaasted and Clements (1982) present some interesting evidence on the sensitivity of estimates of this elasticity to alternative parameter choices in an explicit general equilibrium model. This elasticity is a composite of four elasticities – those of the demand and supply of nontraded goods with respect to the prices of importables and nontraded goods. It is therefore sensitive to

the determinants of these elasticities. The simulations of the ORANI model reported in Dixon et al. (1979) imply that some 83% of an equiproportional tariff change on 112 sectors ends up as an excise tax on exporting industries. These simulations, however, were intended to be illustrative of the policy potential of ORANI, and did not incorporate any sensitivity analysis with respect to underlying parameters.

15. Along with a number of weaknesses from a general equilibrium perspective – see Cordon (1971, chapter 6), Kreinin, Ramsey, and Kmenta (1971), Evans (1971), and Johnson (1971, part IV).

16. Edel and Sclar (1974) found that although the Tiebout hypothesis appeared to be valid for school spending, no locational decisions appeared to have been made with respect to road maintenance expenditures for several communities in the Boston area. Thus, the *composition* of public services may be as important as the general *level* of public services in determining locational decisions.

17. Which may be distinguished on the basis of their tastes, their endowments, and their current location.

18. One basis for this decision could be the "true" cost of living for any particular household in any particular region. This evaluation could be made given the general equilibrium solution previously obtained. One may, therefore, observe households moving *to regions with lower wages* if they place a heavy enough weight (in their explicit utility function) on that region's local public good.

19. Some pragmatic distributed-lag mechanism could be used to avoid complete abandonment of any one region in a *single* period. One would tend to find economic forces slowing such heavy migration patterns down over *several* periods (e.g., with region-specific labor, outward migration would, ceteris paribus, tend to drive up local wages).

20. Richter (1978a) provides a direct extension of the Scarf framework to deal with regional locational decisions in the Tiebout sense.

21. Scarf's structure is more general than ours, but we have no foreseeable need to use that full generality for the problems that concern us. Certain aspects of that generality (such as the ability to handle joint production) raise problems in many applications. This does not justify ignoring such phenomena in general, but it does rationalize our desire to avoid them in certain applications.

22. By redefining the relevant unit simplex over factor-price and excess factor-demand space.

23. Albeit with long delays. Several official agencies are now exploring non-survey methods for updating these tables more frequently.

24. We deal throughout with industry-by-industry tables that are presumed to be expressed in producer's prices. The GEMTAP model of Fullerton, Shoven, and Whalley (1978) illustrates the use of industry-by-commodity absorption matrices, and the ORANI model of Dixon et al. (1982) the possible use of data on various pricing "margins."

25. Usually defined as imports in sectors that also show some nontrivial domestic production level.

26. Usually defined as imports in sectors that show no domestic production. Note that these definitions do not often relate to the pragmatic methods used to distinguish the two types of imports. In some cases tables based on alternative methods of allocation (direct and indirect) are provided.

27. This is entirely appropriate, given the open nature of the Australian economy.
28. One possible alternative is to substitute the results of systemwide estimates of particular demand systems for the available IO consumption data.
29. Whether or not they were produced in the other region.
30. General references on the empirical construction of interregional IO tables include Richardson (1972), Riefler (1973), and Round (1978).
31. For certain computational reasons (avoidance of "divide-by-zero" error messages) it is sometimes necessary to place numerical equivalents of an infinitesimal epsilon (ϵ) in the place of zero. This constraint refers only to the first factor, which plays an important algorithmic role in parameterizing production functions (see below); in general, it makes no noticeable difference to the numerical solution whether or not these zeros are indeed just epsilons. Less substantively, some economists like to think of every input to a CES production function as being economically essential, and may be offended by the use of zeros. To repeat: It makes no computational difference.
32. Amano (1977) correctly points out that "the emphasis on specific factors may lead to a danger of circular reasoning unless one can successfully explain the mechanism that determines the relative supply of those factors" (p. 131).
33. This is because the expenditure pattern of particular households is a critical input into any determination of the implied effect on their ("true" or functional) cost of living. It is common in standard computations of the incidence of particular taxes to distinguish their incidence by the level of household income (viz., how regressive or progressive is this tax?), and one can address these issues by distinguishing expenditure patterns by level of household income. Similarly, development theorists are increasingly concerned with the effects of alternative development strategies on income distribution within the nation. This concern, powerfully expressed in Chenery et al. (1974), is reinforced by the patterns of substitutability (particularly with respect to food prices) in household demand identified in Lluch, Powell, and Williams (1977) for less developed economies.
34. Which is an offensive proposition, aesthetically and literally.
35. Fullerton, Shoven, and Whalley (1978) also provide a facility to incorporate more recent data than their benchmark year. Whalley (1980) uses similar methods in an international context.
36. More general linear activity specifications, such as used by Scarf (1967, 1973), permit multiple outputs but also include output prices in the price vector space as additional dimensions. The linear activity approach does not have to define some goods as factors on an a priori basis, since a given good is a "factor" if it has a negative coefficient in any linear activity. We accept this restriction that factors be stipulated a priori as worth the gain in reduced dimensionality. Similarly, our way of specifying the role of government implies that the government budget constraint is imposed analytically and (unlike the approach of Fullerton, Shoven, and Whalley, 1978), does not add another dimension to the search.
37. *Proof:* Notice that $T(g,j)$ is not an argument of the formula for $P(f)/P(k)$.
38. Recall that the class of production functions currently being considered are homothetic and have constant returns to scale.
39. Note that this result is analogous to the familiar result that in the case of Cobb–Douglas production functions cross-price elasticities of factor demand

are identically zero, even though they are not zero for the more general CES case.

40. This means that no taxes are levied in the base case.
41. To avoid possible semantic snarls, we shall use the term *good* to refer to a production activity that may occur in either region (e.g., agriculture) and the term *commodity* to refer to a production activity in a specific region (e.g., Californian agriculture).
42. Each household is endowed with two units of the fully mobile factor; one unit of each of the regionally mobile, good-specific factors; two units of the own-region-specific factor that is mobile between goods; and one unit of each of the own-region-specific, good-specific factors.
43. Convergence was assumed when this criterion was less than .100.
44. With the restriction that off-diagonal elements take values between .3 and .5 and diagonal elements take values between 1 and 1.500. Run 1 essentially assumes that this is an identity matrix.
45. That is, changes in state and local government taxes will in general affect the tax revenues of the federal government (and vice versa). Ignoring the further complication of fiscal revenue equalization procedures, *should* one neutralize the impact on the federal government, and *how* should one do so (viz., by an "offsetting" change in state and local taxes, or an "offsetting" change in federal taxes, or some combination of both)? The importance of such fiscal interdependence in an applied context is discussed by Kimbell, Shih, and Shulman (1979).
46. This is not strictly true – some analytical approaches are algebraically intractable without some such assumption (e.g., our own analytic factor price solution concept, discussed earlier). Our present remarks refer more narrowly to numerical approaches.
47. In our hypothetical economy government factor demands are *not* proportional to aggregate private industry factor demands.
48. In our present model this parameter simply takes the value of zero or one.
49. If $d(g,f) = 0$ for a given g and f, then $h(g,f) = 0$ as defined earlier. The expression M is given parametrically for a change in the taxes of any non-numeraire factor. Finally note that the only element of the summation in Equation (2) that changes refers to the particular taxed good g, and that this element will be zero if the corresponding $h(g,f)$ term is zero.
50. Which is constant over the various simulations.
51. Note that the entire matrix of factor movements for the fully mobile factor sums to zero. Each of the *columns* of the region-specific sectorally mobile factor movements matrix sums to zero, and each of the *rows* of the sector-specific regionally mobile factor movements matrix sums to zero.
52. This is revealed in the 19.9% decline in the demand for this good, noted in Table 2.
53. This approximate offset lies at the heart of the systemwide separability property, and illustrates why our factor price revision rule incorporates the "first-order" properties that are *exact* in the analytic factor price solution.
54. Exports and imports from foreign countries are not explicitly modeled, but are included in consumption.

REFERENCES

Aaron, H. J. 1975. *Who Pays the Property Tax?* Washington, D.C.: Brookings Institution.

Amano, A. 1977. Specific Factors, Comparative Advantage, and International Investment. *Economica* 44:131–44.

Armington, P. S. 1969. A Theory of Demand for Products Distinguished by Place of Production. *IMF Staff Papers* 16:159–76.

Arnott, R. J., and MacKinnon, J. G. 1977a. The Effects of the Property Tax: A General Equilibrium Simulation. *Journal of Urban Economics* 4:389–407.

    1977b. The Effects of Urban Transportation Changes: A General Equilibrium Simulation. *Journal of Public Economics* 8:19–36.

    1978. Market and Shadow Land Rents with Congestion. *American Economic Review* 68:588–600.

Break, G. F. 1974. The Incidence and Economic Effects of Taxation. In Binder, A. S., and Solow, R. M., eds., *The Economics of Public Finance.* Washington, D.C.: Brookings Institution.

Brown, F., and Whalley, J. 1980. General Equilibrium Evaluations of Tariff-Cutting Proposals in the Tokyo Round and Comparisons with More Extensive Liberalisations of World Trade. *Economic Journal* 90:838–66.

Burgess, D. F. 1980. Protection, Real Wages, and the Neoclassical Ambiguity with Interindustry Flows. *Journal of Political Economy* 88:783–802.

Caves, R. E. 1971. The Industrial Economics of Foreign Investment. *Economica* 38:1–27.

Chang, W., and Mayer, W. 1973. Intermediate Goods in a General Equilibrium Trade Model. *International Economic Review* 14:447–59.

Chenery, H., Ahluwalia, M. S., Bell, C. L. G., Duloy, J. H., and Jolly, R. 1974. *Redistribution with Growth.* New York: Oxford University Press.

Christensen, M. N., Harrison, G. W., and Kimbell, L. J. 1982. Competition for California's Water: The Role of Energy. In Engelbert, E., ed., *Competition for California's Water: Alternative Resolutions.* Berkeley: University of California Press.

Corden, W. M. 1971. *The Theory of Protection.* Oxford: Clarendon Press.

DeFina, R. 1980. Equilibrium Differential Tax Analysis: A Computational Procedure and an Application. Research Paper No. 8009. Federal Reserve Bank of New York, Research and Statistics Function.

Dixon, P. B., Parmenter, B. R., Powell, A. A., and Vincent, D. P. 1979. The Agricultural Sector of ORANI 78: Theory, Data, and Application. Preliminary Working Paper #OP-25. Melbourne: IMPACT Project, Industries Assistance Commission.

Dixon, P. B., Parmenter, B. R., Sutton, J., and Vincent, D. P. 1982. *ORANI: A Multisectoral Model of the Australian Economy.* Amsterdam: North-Holland.

Dornbusch, R. 1974. Tariffs and Nontraded Goods. *Journal of International Economics* 4:177–85.

Dresch, S., Lin, A., and Stout, S. 1977. *Substituting a Value-Added Tax for the Corporate Income Tax.* NBER Fiscal Study No. 15. Cambridge: Ballinger.

Edel, M., and Sclar, E. 1974. Taxes, Spending, and Property Values: Supply Adjustment in a Tiebout–Oates Model. *Journal of Political Economy* 82:941–54.

Evans, H. D. 1971. Effects of Protection in a General Equilibrium Framework. *Review of Economics and Statistics* 53:147-56.

Fullerton, D., King, A., Shoven, J. B., and Whalley, J. 1981. Corporate Tax Integration in the United States: A General Equilibrium Approach. *American Economic Review* 71:677-91.

Fullerton, D., Shoven, J. B., and Whalley, J. 1978. General Equilibrium Analysis of U.S. Taxation Policy. In *1978 Compendium of Tax Research*. Washington, D.C.: Office of Tax Analysis, Department of Tax Research.

Harberger, A. C. 1962. The Incidence of the Corporate Income Tax. *Journal of Political Economy* 70:215-40.

Isard, W. 1951. Interregional and Regional Input-Output Analysis: A Model of a Space-Economy. *Review of Economics and Statistics* 33:318-28.

Johnson, H. G. 1971. *Aspects of the Theory of Tariffs*. Cambridge: Harvard University Press.

Jones, R. W. 1975. Income Distribution and Effective Protection in a Multicommodity Trade Model. *Journal of Economic Theory* 11:1-15.

Jones, R. W., and Schienkman, J. A. 1977. The Relevance of the Two-Sector Production Model of Trade Theory. *Journal of Political Economy* 85:900-35.

Kimbell, L. J. 1976. A General Equilibrium Analysis of Health-Consumption Externalities. *Applied Mathematics and Computation* 2:41-62.

Kimbell, L. J., and Harrison, G. W. 1983. On the Solution of General Equilibrium Models. Working Paper 8301C, January, Center for the Study of International Economic Relations, Department of Economics, University of Western Ontario.

Kimbell, L. J., Shih, A., and Shulman, D. 1979. A Framework for Investigating the Tax Incidence Effects of Proposition 13. *National Tax Journal* (Supplement) 32:313-24.

King, A. T. 1977. Computing General Equilibrium Prices for Spatial Economies. *Review of Economics and Statistics* 59:340-50.

Kreinin, M. E., Ramsey, J. B., and Kmenta, J. 1971. Factor Substitution and Effective Protection Reconsidered. *American Economic Review* 61:891-900.

Kuenne, R. E. 1963. *The Theory of General Economic Equilibrium*. Princeton: Princeton University Press.

Leontief, W. 1966. *Input-Output Economics*. New York: Oxford University Press.

Lluch, C., Powell, A. A., and Williams, R. A. 1977. *Patterns in Household Demand and Savings*. New York: Oxford University Press.

MacKinnon, J. G. 1974. Urban General Equilibrium Models and Simplicial Search Algorithms. *Journal of Urban Economics* 1:161-83.

Mayer, W. 1974. Short-Run and Long-Run Equilibrium for a Small Open Economy. *Journal of Political Economy* 82:955-68.

McLure, C. E., Jr. 1969. The Inter-regional Incidence of General Regional Taxes. *Public Finance* 24:457-83.

   1970. Taxation, Substitution, and Industrial Location. *Journal of Political Economy* 78:112-32.

   1971. Tax Incidence with Imperfect Factor Mobility. *Finanzarchiv* 30:27-48.

   1975. General Equilibrium Incidence Analysis: The Harberger Model after Ten Years. *Journal of Public Economics* 4:125-61.

   1977. The "New View" of the Property Tax: A Caveat. *National Tax Journal* 30:69-75.

Melvin, J. R. 1979. Short-Run Price Effects of the Corporate Income Tax and Implications for International Trade. *American Economic Review* 69:765-74.

Mieszkowski, P. 1966. The Comparative Efficiency of Tariffs and Other Tax-Subsidy Schemes as a Means of Obtaining Revenue or Protecting Domestic Production. *Journal of Political Economy* 74:587-99.

1967. On the Theory of Tax Incidence. *Journal of Political Economy* 75:250-62.

1972. The Property Tax: An Excise Tax or a Profits Tax? *Journal of Public Economics* 1:73-96.

Mussa, M. 1974. Tariffs and the Distribution of Income: The Importance of Factor Specificity, Substitutability, and Intensity in the Short and Long Run. *Journal of Political Economy* 82:1191-204.

Netzer, D. 1966. *Economics of the Property Tax.* Washington, D.C.: Brookings Institution.

Piggott, J. R., and Whalley, J. 1983. Economic Effects of U.K. Tax-Subsidy Policies: A General Equilibrium Appraisal. Manuscript, Department of Economics, University of Western Ontario.

Richardson, H. W. 1972. *Input-Output and Regional Economics.* New York: Wiley.

Richter, D. K. 1978a. Existence and Computation of a Tiebout General Equilibrium. *Econometrica* 46:779-805.

1978b. The Computation of Urban Land Use Equilibria. *Journal of Economic Theory* 19:1-27.

1980. A Computational Approach to Resource Allocation in Spatial Urban Models. *Regional Science and Urban Economics* 10:17-42.

Riefler, R. F. 1973. Interregional Input-Output: A State of the Arts Survey. In G. G. Judge and T. Takayama, eds., *Studies in Economic Planning over Space and Time,* Chap. 8. Amsterdam: North-Holland.

Round, J. I. 1978. On Estimating Trade Flows in Interregional Input-Output Models. *Regional Science and Urban Economics* 8:289-302.

Scarf, H. 1967. On the Computation of Equilibrium Prices. In *Ten Economic Essays in the Tradition of Irving Fisher.* New York: Wiley.

Scarf, H. (with T. Hansen). 1973. *The Computation of Economic Equilibria.* New Haven: Yale University Press.

Shoven, J. B. 1976. The Incidence and Efficiency Effects of Taxes on Income from Capital. *Journal of Political Economy* 84:1261-83.

Shoven, J. B., and Whalley, J. 1972. A General Equilibrium Calculation of the Effects of Differential Taxation of Income from Capital in the U.S. *Journal of Public Economics* 1:281-321.

1977. Equal Yield Tax Alternatives: General Equilibrium Computational Techniques. *Journal of Public Economics* 8:211-24.

Sjaasted, L. A. 1980. Commercial Policy, "True Tariffs," and Relative Prices. In J. Black and B. Hindley, eds., *Current Issues in Commercial Policy and Diplomacy.* London: Macmillan.

Sjaasted, L. A., and Clements, K. W. 1982. The Incidence of Protection: Theory and Measurement. In L. A. Sjaasted and H. Hesse, eds., *The Free Trade Movement in Latin America.* London: Macmillan.

St-Hilaire, F., and Whalley, J. 1980. A Microconsistent Equilibrium Data Set for Canada for Use in Tax Policy Analysis. Working Paper, December 1980. Department of Economics, University of Western Ontario.

Tiebout, C. M. 1956. A Pure Theory of Local Expenditures. *Journal of Political Economy* 64:416-24.

Treddenick, J., and Boadway, R. 1977. The General Equilibrium Effects of Commodity Taxes in an Economy with Inter-Industry Flows. *Public Finance Quarterly* 5:303–28.

Whalley, J. 1975. A General Equilibrium Assessment of the 1973 United Kingdom Tax Reform. *Economica* 42:139–61.

———. 1977. The United Kingdom Tax System, 1968–1970: Some Fixed Point Indications of Its Economic Impact. *Econometrica* 45:1837–58.

———. 1980. Discriminatory Features of Domestic Factor Tax Systems in a Goods Mobile-Factors Immobile Trade Model: An Empirical General Equilibrium Approach. *Journal of Political Economy* 88:1177–202.

Comments

Charles E. McLure, Jr.

As I contemplate developments in the general equilibrium analysis of tax incidence over the two decades since Harberger's model first appeared, I almost automatically ask what simple general equilibrium models tell us that partial equilibrium analysis does not and what we can learn from the large computational models of the 1970s that was not revealed by the simpler models of the 1960s. When I think in these terms, my answer to the first question begins with "interactions." When we draw a Marshallian demand curve, we may not think too much about interactions between markets, though they are clearly there in the form of various degrees of substitutability or complementarity between products. But when we draw a supply curve we are inevitably subsuming a great amount of detail about factor proportions, elasticities of substitution between factors in production, and the mobility or specificity of factors to particular industries or regions. Not only does general equilibrium analysis allow us to take account of these determinants of supply and "go behind the supply curve"; it forces us to do so, since otherwise we could not fully specify the model.

Because of the greater detail they include about interactions between industries and events in factor markets, general equilibrium models allow us to analyze many taxes more satisfactorily than we could using partial equilibrium analysis. Thus, partial equilibrium analysis might suffice if our concern were the incidence of an excise tax on cigarettes. But if the object of concern were a tax on one factor employed in that industry, we would have somewhat more difficulty in taking account of the inherently general equilibrium interactions in a partial equilibrium framework. Partial equilibrium analysis can also be inadequate for dealing with taxes that are more general than excises, rather than more partial. For example, if not cautiously applied, partial equilibrium analysis might suggest that a general payroll tax would be shifted to consumers of goods and services, especially those that are labor-intensive; but general equilibrium analysis would indicate that such a tax would be borne entirely by labor, if the supply of labor is not responsive to price. Mieszkowski combined these two important insights in his "new view" of the incidence of the property tax to note that on the average property taxes in the United States are probably borne largely by owners of property, but differentials from this average rate have excise effects that closely resemble the results under the "old view," which was based essentially on partial equilibrium reasoning.

While general equilibrium analysis is substantially more powerful than partial equilibrium analysis for some purposes, it explicitly raises problems that occur in a much attenuated form, if at all, in partial equilibrium analysis. These involve especially how to treat the use of tax revenues in incidence analysis. It is generally unsatisfactory just to ignore the use of revenues. Two standard practices are to assume that a given tax either replaces another of equal yield or finances a given package of public expenditures. Under the former approach, differential incidence analysis, it is impossible to untangle the results of the two taxes.

Under balanced budget incidence analysis, the situation is potentially even worse. Most obviously, if marginal public spending patterns differ from those in the private sector, transfer of purchasing power to the government will generally alter the prices of factors and products, and therefore affect the distribution of income, no matter what tax is used to raise the revenue. Thus tax incidence is likely to become contaminated with expenditure incidence. This led early practitioners of general equilibrium modeling to assume that marginal private and public spending patterns were identical, in order to be able to concentrate on tax incidence, without this contamination.

Beyond that, publicly provided services may either substitute for private goods and services or complement them. For example, urban transportation may displace private automobiles. But public marinas stimulate private demand for boats. Thus manufacturers of automobiles and boats can hardly be expected to be indifferent to the level of public expenditures on urban transportation and marinas. Only in recent years has the provision of public goods been included in general equilibrium models, and the state of that art is still rather rudimentary.

I tend to think of partial equilibrium models and general equilibrium models as being different in kind, for reasons stated above. By comparison, I think of the large-scale computational models as being similar in kind to the simpler general equilibrium models. But because they allow for the possibility of more goods, more factors, intermediate goods, and greater geographic differentiation, they can be much more powerful. This power is not necessarily reflected so much in qualitatively different answers as in the degree of disaggregation and precision that is possible in some applications. For some purposes the simpler models may suffice. But for others the large-scale computational models are absolutely essential.

It may be useful to harken back to earlier work on incidence theory in commenting on one limitation on the exact analytical solution that forces Kimbell and Harrison to use their new algorithm. The factor price revision rule cannot be used to produce an analytical solution when there is more than one consumer. This appears to be true because all disequilibria are concentrated in factor markets. When the rule adjusts factor prices in the light of existing excess supplies and demands, the distribution of income and consumption patterns changes, unless there is only one consumer or all consumers own factors in equal proportions. But if the factor price revision rule is used repeatedly in the Kimbell–Harrison algorithm to recalculate factor prices, based on demands resulting from the distribution of consumption power in the previous iteration, convergence occurs rapidly.

It is interesting to note that this limitation on the analytical solution is closely related to those found in the early Harberger literature and forces a similar simplifying assumption. In his original article, Harberger was concerned solely with what Musgrave has called incidence on the side of sources of income, that is, with effects on relative factor prices. To simplify the analysis he assumed that at the margin redistribution of income within the private sector made no difference for aggregate consumption patterns, by giving everyone the same marginal expenditure pattern. Since he was not examining effects on relative product prices and changes in the distribution of income resulting from such changes, he was not concerned that there would be no redistributional effect on the side of uses of income if average private spending patterns were also identical. Whereas Harberger sacrificed examination of the uses side of income in order to simplify his analysis, Kimbell and Harrison are forced to make the same sacrifice in order to obtain an exact analytical solution using their factor price revision rule. Whereas the uses side could be salvaged in the earlier analysis by assuming (usually implicitly) a nonunitary income elasticity of demand, Harrison and Kimbell can achieve the same result by using the powerful computational algorithm based on their factor price revision rule, rather than relying on an analytical solution.

If marginal private and public spending patterns diverge, the existence of government keeps the authors from having, in effect, a one-consumer model. But for the analysis of *tax* incidence it would be quite satisfactory to assume identical marginal public and private expenditure patterns, especially if incidence on the uses side is already being ignored by lumping all consumers together. But again, given the power of the Kimbell–Harrison algorithm for recalculating factor prices, this complication seems to make relatively little difference.

Given the emphasis I have placed on interactions as the key element of general equilibrium analysis, the systemwide separability that occurs under the special assumptions required for an analytical solution in the Kimbell–Harrison model is rather discouraging. Further research is clearly required in order to determine how much weight to put on this result, especially since there is a tendency for it to hold even when not all the very stringent requirements for an analytical solution are met.

Although it is well known that the choice of numeraire makes absolutely no difference for the ultimate incidence of a tax in general equilibrium analysis, results are sometimes easier to interpret under one numeraire than another. I have generally found it most useful in examining the incidence of taxes imposed in one state to use the output of the rest of the nation as the numeraire. In the present case the analog might be an index of the prices of the goods produced outside the taxing region. The authors' use of the taxed factor that is mobile between regions, as well as between sectors, as numeraire makes interpretation less straightforward than under the alternative I suggest. This would become more apparent if their analysis were extended to other taxes.

Kimbell and Harrison state that "the notion of 'differential tax incidence' is essentially one motivated by *pedagogic and expositional concerns*" (emphasis added). I am not totally ready to agree with this assessment, but even if one grants the authors' viewpoint, I think it unfortunate that they chose to proceed as they did in presenting the results of their analysis in Section 4.

I feel that in the present pedagogic exercise based entirely on hypothetical examples it would have been particularly useful to present the combined incidence of the balanced budget change as the result of two sets of changes: (a) imposition of the tax, on the assumption that public expenditure patterns do not differ from private patterns, at the margin; and (b) the actual assumed differences in marginal public and private expenditure patterns. Nothing would have been lost, and the separate effects of taxes and differences in public and private expenditure patterns would have been isolated. Had the authors been examining a real-world budgetary change, such as Proposition 13, the California initiative that reduced taxes and forced expenditure cuts, it would be useful to see the tax and expenditure effects isolated from each other in this way, as well as the overall balanced budget effect. I cannot agree with their argument that "to single out the activities of one agent (government) for artificial treatment is illogical." After all, the primary motive of their analysis is understanding of public policy. Besides, isolating these effects would facilitate comparison with results of simpler models.

Finally, I do not find Kimbell and Harrison's discussion of activity in the public sector satisfactory. The objection goes beyond my dislike for the way they have failed to isolate tax and expenditure incidence. There is no clear statement of how the government of the taxing state actually splits its expenditures between the various factors. Beyond that, there is no discussion of how benefits of public services affect private demands.

We are told that "the essential distinction between private and public goods, for our purpose, is the nature of their consumption – private goods are rivalrously consumed, public goods are not" and that "the existing stock of the latter is a predetermined argument in the utility functions of private sector agents." It is difficult to understand why the stock of public goods is said to be predetermined, when it appears to be determined simultaneously with private demands, because of feedback through changes in tax revenues. Moreover, we never learn what goods are provided publicly, exactly how (as complements or substitutes for private goods and factors) they enter utility or production functions, or even why the public sector does not purchase final products, rather than only factors. Given the generally high caliber of this chapter, this expositional deficiency is unfortunate.

These methodological comments carry over to the authors' research agenda. Proposition 13 included two important changes in the fiscal landscape of California: a reduction in the property tax and a reduction in public spending. For many purposes simulating the entire package is the proper approach. But I would like to see them decompose the overall effect of Proposition 13 into tax incidence and expenditure incidence. Decomposition would almost certainly indicate that the only important effect resulting from the reduction in property taxes per se was an increase in property values. The reduction in spending of the labor-intensive public sector in California presumably had an impact on wage rates that should not be confused with the tax effect. The latter effect would be particularly strong if it were felt only by workers specific to the public sector.

CHAPTER 8

Decomposing the impact of higher energy prices on long-term growth

Antonio M. Borges and Lawrence H. Goulder

1   Introduction: Energy analysis and general equilibrium modeling

Energy plays a vital role in production and consumption in the U.S. economy. As inputs into production and as consumption goods, energy products pervade all aspects of economic activity. Their prices and their availability influence markedly the decisions of every economic agent. And the nature of energy supply and the structure of energy markets have led to high levels of government intervention.

The desirability of careful modeling of energy problems has long been recognized.[1] After the disruptions in the world oil market in 1973–4, however, a reappraisal of the energy situation became essential. A great deal of economic research has been conducted since then, leading to important advances in methodology and empirical findings. The majority of these studies concentrate on the energy markets and discuss very specific issues of forecasting or regulation. Some address the broader questions of energy–economy interactions and the global impact of alternative energy policies. But only a few academic studies have attempted to model the implications of higher energy prices or of energy scarcity in a comprehensive manner.

The nature of the energy problems strongly invites methodologies based on a general equilibrium approach. The interactions between supply and demand, both within the energy markets as well as between the energy sector and the economy as a whole, are far too important to be neglected. The dramatic rise in energy prices has had a significant impact on the economy, generating a set of feedback effects on the energy markets that greatly influence the final reallocation of resources. The most

The authors wish to thank Alan Manne and John Shoven for most helpful comments and suggestions. The research leading to this project was supported by the Electric Power Research Institute and by the Office of Tax Analysis, U.S. Department of the Treasury.

consistent way to capture these interactions is to model the behavior of all agents in a general equilibrium framework.

The interest in general equilibrium modeling in the energy area is relatively recent. The first steps were taken in 1974 by Hudson and Jorgenson (1974), who combined an interindustry production model allowing for price-responsive input–output coefficients with a model of consumer behavior and a long-run growth model. Their main innovation consisted in integrating a neoclassical model of producer behavior with a standard input–output structure. Thus the substitutability between energy and other inputs as well as among the various energy products was captured, without sacrificing the consistency features of input–output models. Subsequent versions introduced additional innovations leading to what may be the most comprehensive general equilibrium energy model. Among its most significant features are a 36-sector production submodel where technological change can occur as a function not only of time but also of price changes,[2] and a model of consumer demand that accounts for specific characteristics of different household groups, based on an aggregation method originated by Lau.[3] Parameters of the model are estimated econometrically from time series data. Hudson and Jorgenson have used their model to assess the implications of the energy shocks of the 1970s and to predict the impact of certain types of energy conservation policies.

Another representative model of energy–economy interactions is Alan Manne's ETA-Macro, first presented in 1976.[4] It consists of a detailed energy technology assessment module describing various energy activities available at different points in time, combined with a simple specification of the interactions between the energy sector and the rest of the economy. Electric and nonelectric energy are treated as inputs into production, together with capital and labor. Flexibility in adjusting to higher energy costs is governed by the elasticity of substitution between energy and value-added. The production technology is of the putty-clay type. Unlike the Hudson–Jorgenson model, ETA-Macro deals explicitly with the energy resource base by assuming cumulative supply functions for primary energy. The solution of the model is based on intertemporal optimization, the maximization of utility from the stream of future consumption, given the resource base and the available energy technologies. The model has typically been used to simulate the impact of technological or regulatory constraints on energy supply such as a nuclear moratorium.

Recent research in energy continues to emphasize energy–economy interactions and attempts to reflect some "generalized" equilibrium assumptions. Several models have been developed along these lines, although none has the same comprehensive features and econometric foundation of the Hudson–Jorgenson model or the intertemporal optimization aspects of ETA-Macro. An overall evaluation of the research effort in the area of energy general equilibrium modeling shows that significant methodological advances have been achieved leading to important new results and energy policy implications. Perhaps the most visible outcome has been the analysis of the channels through which higher energy prices or energy scarcity may lead to slower economic growth. The impact of the new energy conditions on the demands for and the prices of primary factors has been identified. The dynamic effects on growth – through a decrease in the return to capital and the resulting drop in investment – have been forcefully argued by Hudson and Jorgenson. Often policy analysis has centered around estimating the cost, in terms of slower GNP growth, of reduced energy use.

This chapter attempts to contribute to the assessment of these energy–growth connections. The research stems from a general equilibrium model of the U.S. economy containing significant energy detail. The model follows directly in the tradition of the Shoven–Whalley tax analysis research[5] and incorporates some of the methodological advances of Hudson and Jorgenson. It introduces specific limitations on the domestic supply of certain forms of primary energy and explicitly treats the rents that accrue to owners of certain energy resources. It specifies the role of energy in production in various alternative ways to assess the significance of higher or lower flexibility and of complementarity between energy and capital. It recognizes the differences in the preferences of consumers as a function of their incomes and specifies a distinct demand system for each group of households. It models carefully the role of the government and extends the treatment of the foreign sector beyond the usual simple specification of other U.S. models.

The model is oriented toward energy policy simulation. The parameters of the model are obtained according to a benchmarking procedure that uses information from a consistent set of data for 1973, as well as information on key parameters obtained from econometric studies. Recent applications have emphasized the importance of taking into account certain feedbacks in analyzing energy policy. Indeed, a main feature of the energy crisis is the occurrence of large scarcity rents; the distribution of these rents often has consequences that overshadow some of the traditionally emphasized mechanisms of interaction between the energy sector and the economy.[6]

The specific application described in this chapter is an examination of the effects of higher-priced imported energy on the domestic economy. An attempt is made to identify the various channels through which higher energy prices lead to slower economic growth and to isolate them with the model. The impact of higher oil prices is simulated under alternative specifications of the model to obtain a quantified assessment of the relative importance of each of the mechanisms leading to slower economic growth. The policy significance of such an assessment should be apparent: Reducing the welfare losses associated with high-priced imported energy requires a clear understanding as to which energy–welfare connections are most important. The results from these simulations are compared with the results of others and with the views proposed in the theoretical literature.

2   Energy and growth: three hypotheses

The relationship between higher energy prices and slower growth of output and welfare is a central issue in energy general equilibrium modeling. The general equilibrium approach, however, usually deals with long-run effects, after all markets have cleared and all resources are optimally used. It is particularly well suited to analyze long-run welfare losses as a consequence of higher energy prices, beyond the short-run macroeconomic disturbances.

An accurate quantification of the impact on growth of more expensive energy has important implications from both the theoretical and the policy points of view. If growth is significantly reduced in the long run, the energy crisis acquires a new dimension that goes well beyond the current emphasis on short-run dislocations. From the modeling point of view, the change in the overall performance of the economy reveals the limitations in the use of partial equilibrium methods, even in studies that are concerned only with energy markets. In fact, the feedback effects on the energy markets of such a slowdown may offset the initial impacts of the change in relative energy prices. A number of implications for policy may also emerge. The indicated loss in welfare after a slowdown in growth may well justify substantial investments in the development of new technologies or in the expansion of the resource base. These modeling efforts may indicate that conservation policies are more costly than originally imagined. Or they may offer validity to measures that offset some of the adverse effects of energy on growth. The latter measures may include reduced taxes on capital that compensate for lower rates of return and help avoid reductions in investment.

Most researchers today agree that the impact of energy on growth is not negligible. Unfortunately, this is as far as the agreement goes. There is no consensus on the magnitude of energy's effect or on the relative importance of the channels through which it operates. A number of authors have examined a "direct" effect of energy on growth, an effect that is regulated by the elasticity of substitution between energy and other inputs. As shown, for example, by Hogan and Manne (1977), the direct impact of energy reduction varies drastically when the elasticity of substitution is .7 instead of, say .1. Yet most econometric estimates of this parameter range between .2 and .6, and span most of the relevant range of variation in terms of determining the impact of energy on growth.[7] To quote Manne: "These uncertainties associated with estimating the elasticity of substitution between energy and other inputs would appear to be at least as great as the geological uncertainties on petroleum and uranium resources" (Manne, 1977). Beyond the direct impact on GNP of higher energy prices, two other effects have been emphasized as contributing to slower economic growth: the savings–investment effect, consisting of the reduced capital accumulation as a consequence of lower rates of return to capital; and the terms-of-trade effect associated with the higher oil prices, given that a substantial component of oil supply is imported. The savings effect implies that the impact on long-term growth would be higher the larger the elasticity of saving with respect to the rate of return, and the larger the fall in the rate of return when energy prices increase; this effect is a consequence of the complementarity of energy and capital found by many econometric studies of the role of energy in production.[8]

The terms-of-trade effect is connected with the loss in real income that takes place when the relative price of imports increases. It implies that the higher energy prices have a quite different impact on the U.S. economy – which imports energy – relative to the economies of, for example, the United Kingdom or Norway – which are or soon will be self-sufficient – even if they face energy prices similar to those in the United States.

The three channels through which energy influences long-term growth in the United States are thus the direct effect on factor productivity, the savings effect, and the terms-of-trade effect. They naturally interact; for example, as GNP drops because of lower capital and labor productivity as a result of the direct effect, saving and capital accumulation will drop even if the rate of return to capital remained constant. But it is at least conceptually possible to try to isolate each one of them and thus evaluate them individually. A closer analysis of the arguments behind each of these three hypotheses may clarify the essential elements in each one and thus open the way for a quantification of their relative importance.

2.1   *The direct effect*

The direct effect has been explained by Hogan and Manne; it has also been discussed within a similar framework by Koopmans and Sweeney.[9] In its simplest form, it can be presented in the following way: Energy is

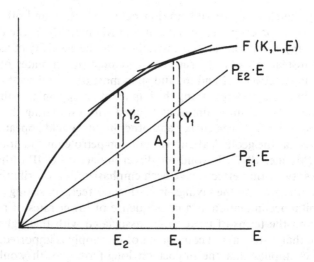

Figure 1. The direct effect on GNP of a higher energy price.

an input into production, as are capital and labor. But GNP or national income corresponds to the value of production minus the cost of energy inputs. Hence when the price of energy rises, GNP drops since the difference between the value of production and the cost of energy inputs is now smaller. This reasoning provides an upper bound on the GNP loss associated with higher energy prices: If the level of production does not change and the energy input remains fixed, the decrease in GNP will correspond to the increase in the energy price times the total quantity of energy used. As long as energy costs are a small percentage of the total value of production, the percentage reduction in GNP will be small – even for large increases in the price of energy.

This upper bound corresponds to rather pessimistic assumptions. In fact, as the price of energy increases it may be more efficient to use a smaller input of energy per unit of output. Clearly if the available set of technical alternatives permits easy substitution of other inputs for energy, the GNP loss associated with the higher energy prices will be small. Thus the small share of energy and the possibility of substituting other factors of production for energy might suggest that the long-term direct effect of higher energy costs on GNP is rather small.

These considerations are represented graphically in Figure 1. Assuming that total production F is a function of capital K, labor L, and energy E and denoting GNP by Y and the price of energy by P_e, the definition of GNP is

$$Y = F(K, L, E) - P_e E \tag{1}$$

Figure 1 represents total production and GNP as a function of energy input. If the price of energy is P_{e1}, the equilibrium level of energy input is E_1, since at the point the marginal productivity of energy (slope of F) equals P_{e1}; GNP is therefore Y_1. If the price of energy rises to P_{e2}, the upper bound for the GNP loss is A; however, at a price of P_{e2}, it is more efficient to use only E_2. In that case GNP will be equal to Y_2. The possibility of reducing the energy input, that is, making production more intensive in capital and labor, has reduced the GNP loss. Clearly Y_2 is larger than $Y_1 - A$, because the slope of F at E_1 is less than P_{e2}.

The magnitude of the direct effect on GNP of higher energy prices therefore depends on the degree of substitutability among factors of production. In a simple aggregate model, like the one used by Hogan and Manne, this is represented by a single parameter, the elasticity of substitution between energy and value-added. In a more disaggregated model, however, the role of energy in production and the flexibility of the technology vary a great deal from sector to sector. The share of energy in total value of production can also be quite different. Therefore, even if the overall impact on GNP is small, the effect on the level of output of certain individual sectors can be quite dramatic.

2.2   The savings effect

The savings effect has been emphasized above all by Hudson and Jorgenson.[10] It follows from the finding that in many sectors of production, capital and energy may be complements rather than substitutes.[11] Then, if energy prices increase, the demand for capital decreases and the rate of return to capital decreases. If saving is responsive to the rate of return, the higher energy prices may translate into less investment and therefore slower economic growth. The magnitude of this effect thus depends on the degree of capital-energy complementarity and on the elasticity of saving with respect to the rate of return.

The notion of capital-energy complementarity may seem counterintuitive. In fact, it is easy to cite examples of substitution of capital for energy as energy prices increase. However, this does not take into account the fact that there are other factors of production whose demands will also be affected by the higher energy prices. Any two factors taken separately must always be substitutes. Thus if other inputs, such as labor or materials, are kept fixed, a reduction of energy use per unit of output is only possible by increasing the capital input, that is, by substituting capital for energy. If, however, other inputs also vary, then higher energy prices may lead to less capital input. This will happen, for example, if the degree of substitutability between capital and energy is rather small and, in contrast, it is easy to substitute labor for both energy and capital.

Then, because of the limited substituability, the higher energy prices increase substantially the price of capital and energy taken as a composite input and induce the substitution of labor for both capital and energy. Thus, even if on a capital–energy isoquant the economy would be moving to a point with a higher K/E ratio, still the demand for capital will decrease as the intensity of labor rises relative to capital and energy taken together.[12]

The impact of higher energy prices or of a cut in energy supply on the rate of return to capital can be seen easily by using the definition of complementarity and substitutability based on the signs of the cross-partial second derivatives of the production function. Assume again that total production is a function of capital, labor, and energy:

$$F = F(K, L, E) \tag{2}$$

Capital and energy will be complements if

$$F_{ke} > 0 \tag{3}$$

that is, if a reduction of energy inputs reduces the marginal productivity of capital.[13] The substitutability between labor and energy and between labor and capital translates into

$$F_{le} < 0 \tag{4}$$

$$F_{kl} < 0 \tag{5}$$

These definitions clearly do not apply to the two-factor case under constant returns to scale, where the second-order cross-partial derivative must always be positive. But, as pointed out by Hogan, they are the most useful in the case of more than two factors.

If total capital and labor inputs are fixed, efficient production will correspond to

$$F_k = P_k \tag{6}$$

$$F_l = P_l \tag{7}$$

$$F_e = P_e \tag{8}$$

and

$$K = K^* \tag{9}$$

$$L = L^* \tag{10}$$

$$E = E^* \tag{11}$$

where K^*, L^*, and E^* are the total inputs of capital, labor, and energy, and the numeraire is the price of output. Then if the energy input is exogenously reduced, the changes in prices are given by

$$dP_k = F_{ke}\,dE \qquad (12)$$

$$dP_l = F_{le}\,dE \qquad (13)$$

$$dP_e = F_{ee}\,dE \qquad (14)$$

Since $dE < 0$, $dP_e > 0$ as expected, and the changes in the prices of labor and capital will depend on whether they are complements or substitutes with respect to energy. If $F_{ke} > 0$, $dP_k < 0$; if $F_{le} < 0$, $dP_l > 0$; the reduction of energy input (or higher energy prices) leads to a lower return to capital and a higher wage rate.

Moreover, if the labor input is allowed to vary in response to higher wage rates, the drop in the return to capital will be more pronounced. If q_l is the derivative of labor supply with respect to the wage rate, then

$$dL = q_l\,dP_l \qquad (15)$$

and the impact of rising prices and reduced use of energy will be given by

$$\frac{dP_k}{dE} = F_{ke} + \frac{F_{kl}F_{le}q_l}{1 - F_{ll}q_l} \qquad (16)$$

where the second term is positive and therefore translates into a larger drop in P_k.

Thus capital–energy complementarity leads to a reduction in the rate of return to capital; this will have an impact on investment if saving is responsive to rates of return.

To test the importance of this dynamic effect it is necessary to employ appropriate assumptions about the extent of capital–energy complementarity. The magnitude of the savings effect can be assessed by simulating an energy shock with various numerical values for the elasticity of saving with respect to the rate of return to capital. In their paper Hudson and Jorgenson (1978) attempt to isolate the dynamic effect by subtracting the direct effect from the total impact of a reduction in energy inputs. However, they take the direct effect to be

$$\frac{dK}{K}\,\theta_k + \frac{dL}{L}\,\theta_l + \frac{dE}{E}\,\theta_e + \frac{dM}{M}\,\theta_m \qquad (17)$$

where M denotes materials (intermediate inputs other than energy), and θ denotes the share of each factor in total cost. This provides only a first-order approximation, given that as the energy price changes the share of each factor will certainly change. It seems more accurate to compare the results from two different simulations of the same energy shock, with and without a positive elasticity of saving with respect to the rate of return to capital. In the one case the quantity of capital will respond over time to the lower rate of return, whereas in the other it will not.

2.3   *The terms-of-trade effect*

The terms-of-trade effect pertains to the loss in real income resulting from the higher price of energy imports. As imports become more expensive, additional resources must be diverted to pay for them, in particular through increased exports. This reduces what is left for consumption and investment and therefore lowers utility or welfare, current and future.

The terms-of-trade effect may seem identical to the direct effect: indeed in both cases the reduction of welfare arises because of the need to devote more resources to achieve the same supply of energy. And if the price of energy corresponds exactly to its cost, there is really no distinction between the two effects. In reality, however, the price of energy, in particular of crude oil, includes a substantial rent; that is, the resources paid by the U.S. economy to obtain a certain supply of oil exceed what is necessary to extract the oil from the ground.[14] This rent is quite substantial, both relative to the price of oil and in total absolute amount. Therefore, it can make a great deal of difference whether they are paid to U.S. producers or to foreigners.

With the type of diagram used previously, it is possible to show the significance of the terms-of-trade effect graphically. In Figure 2, P_{e1} is the initial price of energy, which is assumed to be its cost. As before, the equilibrium level of energy input is E_1 and GNP will be Y_1.

If the price of energy increases to P_{e2}, the new equilibrium will be E_2. Now two cases are possible: If the increase in P_e corresponds to an increase in the cost of producing energy, then the new level of GNP will be A. This is exactly as in the direct effect discussed above, and it does not matter whether energy is imported or supplied domestically. If, however, the increase in price is due to the monopoly power of suppliers, and therefore $P_{e2} - P_{e1}$ is simply a rent that producers extract from consumers, then the terms-of-trade effect may have a role to play. If all energy is imported, the rents will be paid to foreigners and the new level of GNP will still be A. If, on the other hand, all energy is produced domestically, these rents will be part of U.S. GNP, which will then amount to $A + B$. In this second case, a reduction in GNP also occurs ($A + B$ is less than Y_1); but the loss here is smaller and is simply the result of the inefficiency introduced by the monopoly behavior of energy suppliers.

The terms-of-trade effect may be, in many cases, the dominant consequence of the higher oil prices. It is the most obvious cost of the energy

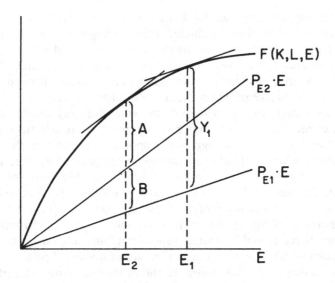

Figure 2. The terms-of-trade effect.

crisis for countries that have to import all of their energy. And in particular for less developed countries, the need to devote more resources to
exports, in order to pay for the higher oil bill, translates into much lower
levels of investment, since consumption is often already at an irreducible
minimum.[15] Recent work by Manne shows that the higher oil prices have
a much more serious impact on non–oil-producing less developed countries than on the industrialized countries exactly because of this effect.

Like the direct effect, the terms-of-trade effect also has consequences
over time: The lower level of GNP implies a reduced amount of saving
and therefore of investment. This drop in investment, however, is quite
different from the one resulting from the saving effect discussed above,
since it would happen even if the rate of return to capital should remain
constant.

2.4 Evaluating the three effects

The direct, dynamic, and the terms-of-trade effects are the three components of the impact of energy on long-term growth. They also correspond to as many hypotheses as to the main channels through which
higher oil prices reduce growth and welfare. Despite their conceptual
simplicity, these effects are difficult to isolate empirically. Yet to the
extent that these effects can be separated and their relative impact on
welfare ascertained, a good deal of useful information will become
available to those concerned with energy policy and analysis.

Several considerations suggest that a test of the relative importance of the different effects is best conducted with a disaggregated general equilibrium model. Indeed, some of the interactions discussed above cannot be analyzed except in a general equilibrium framework. All three effects imply changes in relative prices and supplies of all primary factors of production, the incidence of which depends on many feedbacks and cross-effects. Moreover, the consequences of reduced energy inputs, lower savings, or increased exports may be much more significant for certain sectors than for others; a disaggregated approach provides much richer information, which is hidden in one-sector models. Moreover, these effects have distributional consequences; since individual consumers are different, distributional changes can lead to different reallocations of resources, in ways that often offset initial changes.

The purpose of this chapter is to investigate these three hypotheses using a multisector, multiconsumer general equilibrium model. The tests will correspond to simulations of the impact of higher oil prices, under different assumptions with respect to the behavioral parameters of the economy.

To test the direct effect, the production structure will be modeled with different degrees of flexibility. By testing production submodels ranging from an almost pure fixed-coefficient case, where energy substitution within each sector is virtually impossible, to a Cobb–Douglas case, where the elasticity of substitution is 1, it will be possible to obtain upper and lower bounds on the direct impact of higher energy prices. As a more realistic case, an intermediate specification with limited substitution possibilities and capital–energy complementarity will also be presented.

The dynamic or savings effect will be tested by assuming complementarity between capital and energy and comparing cases where saving is a fixed proportion of income with cases where it depends positively on the rates of return to capital. Given the expected drop in the return to capital, the fixed-saving propensity case will naturally lead to higher investment and faster growth; the size of the difference, however, may be quite small.

Finally, the terms-of-trade effect can be analyzed by comparing the general case of substantial oil imports with a scenario where all energy is supplied domestically and, therefore, even though oil prices still increase, the rents associated with them remain within the United States.

By simulating the performance of the U.S. economy until the year 2001, a good measure of long-run effects can be obtained. The relative importance of each effect can be assessed from the level of GNP in real terms achieved in the year 2001 in each scenario, or by the growth rate until that year. It is also desirable to compare other welfare measures that take account of nonincome sources of welfare such as leisure. For this purpose the simulations will include comparisons of discounted utility flows for each group of consumers, based on the level of consumption of goods, services, and leisure in each year.

3 The model

The development of the model used in this chapter takes as a point of departure the Fullerton–Shoven–Whalley general equilibrium model of tax analysis in the U.S. economy. The main extensions necessary for energy analysis are a level of disaggregation compatible with the required detail in the energy markets both for producer and consumer goods, an explicit treatment of the rents associated with the scarcity of crude oil and natural gas in the United States, and a more comprehensive treatment of oil imports. Production submodels were also developed beyond the fixed-coefficient case used by Fullerton, Shoven, and Whalley, to account for the possibility of substituting other factors for energy as relative prices change. This section presents the main features of the model, discusses its strengths and weaknesses, and describes the main submodels in detail.

3.1 Basic structure

The general equilibrium nature of the model is reflected in the search for the vector of prices of producer goods, consumer goods, and services and factors of production that will clear all markets in each successive period. The equilibrium prices determine the optimal allocation of resources, given the endowments of capital, labor, and natural resources (oil and natural gas). Equilibria are linked recursively through time by the growth in the endowments. The solution of the model is therefore a sequence of general equilibria. Simulations cover the period from 1973 to 2001 at four-year intervals.

On the production side, technologies are represented with cost functions that exhibit constant returns to scale. There is no technological progress other than the increase in labor productivity reflected in a growth rate of the labor endowment in efficiency units that exceeds labor force growth. The technologies, however, will in general exhibit some flexibility, reflected in technical coefficients that respond to relative prices. Three alternative specifications are tested.

The domestic supply of crude oil and natural gas is determined as a function of the market (world) price of these fuels. The world price is specified exogenously. The responsiveness of domestic supply to prices

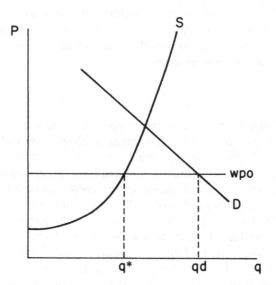

Figure 3. Demand, domestic supply, and imports of crude oil and natural gas in the model.

is governed by an exogenous elasticity parameter. An important aspect of these resources is the rents that they generate because of their exhaustible nature and the lack of pure competition in the world oil market. This model's treatment of the supply of oil and gas allows for such rents, since in general the world price of oil will exceed the domestic average cost determined by technology. The amount of oil and gas demanded at current prices that cannot be supplied domestically has to be imported. Figure 3 depicts the nature of domestic oil supply and demand. D is the demand curve for these fuels, S is the domestic supply curve; q^* is the amount supplied domestically, and *wpo* is the world market price for crude oil and natural gas (in Btu equivalents); $qd - q^*$ corresponds to imports.

On the demand side, the model represents the behavior of consumers, the government, investors, and foreigners. Consumers are grouped according to income and an individual demand system is specified for each consumer group. Each group has an endowment of capital and labor and, given prices, decides on how much to save and invest and how much to purchase of each consumer good. Investment is thus determined by saving, although it may include a foreign component if oil producers reinvest their revenues in the United States. The government levies taxes on production and consumption – taxes on factors of production, on output, on intermediate goods, and on the income, consumption, and, in

Table 1. *Classification of industries and consumer goods*

Industries	Consumer goods
1. Agriculture, forestry, fisheries	1. Food
2. Mining, excl. coal	2. Alcoholic beverages
3. Contract construction	3. Tobacco
4. Food and tobacco	4. Electricity
5. Textiles, apparel, leather	5. Gas utilities
6. Paper and printing	6. Other utilities
7. Chemicals and rubber	7. Housing
8. Lumber, furniture, stone	8. Furnishings
9. Metals, machinery, misc.	9. Appliances
manufacturing	10. Clothing and jewelry
10. Transportation equipment	11. Transportation
11. Motor vehicles	12. Motor vehicles, tires, and auto repair
12. Transportation	13. Services
13. Communication	14. Financial services
14. Water and sanitary services	15. Reading, recreation
15. Trade	16. Nondurable–nonfood household
16. Finance and insurance	items
17. Real estate	17. Gasoline and other fuels
18. Services	18. Savings
19. Government enterprises	
20. Coal mining	
21. Petroleum refining	
22. Electric utilities	
23. Gas utilities	
24. Crude petroleum and natural gas	

some cases, the rent included in the price of oil and natural gas (as in the case of the windfall profits tax). Revenues are used to redistribute income back to consumers and to buy goods and services, as well as capital and labor. The government budget deficit is assumed to be zero.

The foreign sector provides imports and purchases exports. Trade balance is assumed, but the exchange rate is not dealt with explicitly. Exports are scaled to match imports; thus foreigners can be regarded as consumers who purchase U.S. exports with the income from the sale of imports to the United States.

Table 1 presents the sectors of production and consumer goods defined by the model. The different household groups are shown in Table 2. This level of disaggregation was chosen to provide adequate detail in the energy markets and maximum information on intersectoral or intergroup differences within the constraints imposed by computational feasibility.

The model is parameterized based on econometric estimates of key parameters as well as information contained in a consistent data set for

Table 2. *Income classifications for consumer groups and number of households in each group (income in thousands of 1973 dollars; households in millions)*

Group	Income	Number	Group	Income	Number
1	0–3	14.149	7	8–10	8.563
2	3–4	6.683	8	10–12	7.565
3	4–5	6.236	9	12–15	9.774
4	5–6	6.107	10	15–20	10.220
5	6–7	5.042	11	20–25	4.589
6	7–8	4.755	12	25 +	5.033

the U.S. economy in 1973. The main sources of the data for the benchmark were the Bureau of the Census publications on input–output data on factor use by sector of production, Treasury Department data on consumer income and taxes, Bureau of Labor Statistics data on consumer expenditures, and the Organization for Economic Cooperation and Development (OECD) statistics on foreign trade. The construction of the benchmark and the procedures used to achieve internal consistency among data from different sources are described in Fullerton, Shoven, and Whalley (1977) and Borges (1980). The disaggregation level used in the production submodels presented here is different from the versions in those studies. However, the additional level of detail was obtained by further disaggregating the Shoven–Whalley benchmark with the use of the 1971 input–output data published by the Bureau of the Census. The model is solved in each period with Merrill's fixed-point algorithm.[16] As usual in this type of model, the algorithm deals only with factor prices and excess demands. The iterative solution starts with a guess as to the equilibrium factor prices. The production submodel is then solved to yield output prices corresponding to minimum cost. Factor prices determine the value of consumers' endowments. With this information and the output prices consumers make their decisions as to saving, labor supply, and current consumption. Total saving corresponds to investment, which together with consumption translates into final demand for each of the producer goods. Then the production submodel is used again to find the gross output and factor requirements necessary to meet final demand. Capital and labor demands are thus obtained and compared with the capital endowment and with the supply of labor, to determine net excess demands. If these are not zero, the algorithm searches efficiently for another vector of factor prices.

The general equilibrium problem has two additional dimensions necessary to achieve a balanced government budget and a trade balance. Government spending must equal tax revenues received. The government's tax receipts, however, depend on consumer incomes and expenditures and on production levels. These, however, cannot be determined if government spending is not known. The simultaneous determination of government spending and revenue calls for an additional dimension of the algorithm. A similar problem arises in the treatment of exports and imports. Thus the general equilibrium problem has a total of four dimensions. This is still within the limits of computational feasibility, even in the case when the 24-sector nonlinear production system has to be solved simultaneously in each iteration.

From period to period, endowments increase according to investment and labor force growth in efficiency units. Additionally, each scenario requires data on the world price of oil over time, the position and elasticity of the domestic supply function for oil and gas, and the rate of growth of import supplies (for imports other than oil and gas) by foreigners.

3.2 Strengths and weaknesses

The major strength of the model is its full general equilibrium nature. With all agents on their budget constraints and with individual behavior derived from maximization assumptions, the solution of the model requires that all markets clear. No transactions are conducted at prices other than equilibrium prices, and for every factor of production and every good or service, supply and demand match exactly. All interactions among markets are modeled and therefore all the feedback effects between the energy sector and the rest of the economy are accounted for. The general equilibrium structure is especially useful in analyzing energy issues. The dynamic or savings effect discussed above is a good illustration of the need to include important feedbacks; another one is the analysis of the impact of the windfall profits tax performed in other applications of the model.[17] Although this tax reduces substantially the income accruing to owners of capital – who are in general among the wealthiest household groups – the final impact on income distribution will depend crucially on how this revenue is spent; since government purchases are quite intensive in capital, if the revenue from this tax is spent in the same way as general revenues, the return to capital may actually increase, skewing income distribution more in favor of the wealthiest groups.

The level of disaggregation used in the model is another important advantage. In fact, as mentioned above, small aggregate effects often hide much more substantial consequences at the sectoral level. Rybczinski's theorem shows that on the supply side, the impact of a shock on one sector may even have a different sign from the impact on another sector. Moreover, the substitution away from energy when its price increases often consists simply of a change in the composition of output, with a reduction in the relative share of energy-intensive sectors, as a result of a decrease in the demand for their products. These effects cannot all be captured in an aggregate one-sector model, where all reactions to an energy shock must be represented by only two or three parameters.

The disaggregation of consumer groups also has significant advantages. Since it is not realistic to assume that all consumers behave alike, the explicit consideration of different preferences for different groups may lead to results that are often surprising. As an illustration, another result obtained under a previous application of the model is worth mentioning: Although the higher oil prices reduce the rate of return to capital because of capital–energy complementarity, they simultaneously generate rents that are distributed to owners of capital who have an above-average propensity to save. Thus it was found that under certain plausible scenarios higher energy prices actually increased saving and investment, in spite of the lower rate of return to capital.

The model also includes a careful treatment of all U.S. federal, state, and local taxes. These taxes introduce sizable wedges between prices paid by purchasers and prices received by suppliers, thereby generating inefficiency. The existence of inefficiencies, however, may significantly alter the evaluation of the impact of an energy shock, because it raises issues of second best.[18] These second-best effects can be captured by the model presented here, given that the decisions made by every agent take into account the taxes that currently exist in the United States.

The model is solved numerically, and after every change in the exogenous variables an entirely new equilibrium is computed. Therefore, the conclusions do not reflect any first-order approximations or the assumption of small changes.

Finally, the comparisons of various simulations can be based on welfare measures more meaningful than GNP or national income. Since consumer decisions are derived from utility maximization, it is always possible to compute how much utility each group receives in each scenario. For any two static equilibria, comparisons can then be based on compensating variations in income, that is, welfare changes can be evaluated by the amount of income each consumer would have to receive or lose to achieve the same level of utility. For dynamic solutions consisting of a sequence of equilibria, comparisons are based on the discounted present value of the utility derived from the consumption in each period.

Of course, the model also has some significant weaknesses. The model is not estimated econometrically. As described previously, only some key parameters are obtained from econometric studies. The remaining values are obtained by fitting the model to the 1973 benchmark, in a way designed to reproduce precisely the values of that data set in the solution for the first equilibrium.[19] All of the parameter values employed seem plausible and fall within an interval that corresponds to a consensus among modelers with respect to acceptable estimates. However, it is not possible to claim that the model has the accuracy required for forecasting. It is essentially a simulation model useful for revealing the relative magnitudes of certain impacts of higher energy prices.

All decisions in the model are made period by period, and all agents only use information available in the current period. Although consumers and producers make decisions with intertemporal implications, the model has no "look ahead" features. Economic agents assume future prices to be equal to the current ones. These agents therefore make decisions that, although reasonable according to current information, may lead to inferior solutions in the longer term. The myopia assumption may be more realistic than the assumption of full intertemporal optimization with perfect foresight, but it can potentially lead to implausible behavior, with agents making the same mistakes repeatedly in every period.

Consumer and producer behavior is modeled with full instantaneous adjustment, and adjustment costs are not modeled explicitly. As shown in many studies, the adjustments to an energy shock in the short run tend to be substantially smaller than in the long run. Energy consumption depends very much on the stock of capital – buildings, equipment, vehicles, appliances, etc. – that adjusts only gradually, as new vintages are introduced and obsolete ones replaced. Thus the absence of dynamic behavior leads to results that are clearly overoptimistic with respect to the short run. The simulations performed with the model must therefore be interpreted only as long-run implications of higher energy prices and not as representative of specific recent events.

The model, however, cannot be used for very-long-run simulations, since as mentioned above it includes no technological change other than Harrod-neutral labor productivity growth. Specific types of technological progress have been considered in other energy models.[20] Since these are not included in the model presented here, simulations should not be performed beyond a certain horizon. Thus the simulations are performed only through the end of the century, since it is unrealistic to assume that beyond that date the technology in place will still be correctly described by what was observed in 1973.

Finally, the model does not include financial assets and therefore forces all agents to be on their budget constraints. Even when investing, consumers are simply buying the right to a stream of capital services that this investment will produce. Since there are no bonds or money, no wealth effects exist and the interactions between portfolio choice and saving and consumption decisions cannot be studied. Similarly, the model cannot be used to simulate the impact of exogenous shocks on the general price level or to analyze the consequences of government deficits or of alternative ways of financing a trade deficit.

These weaknesses do not seem overwhelming – given the particular objectives of simulating the impact on resource allocation and long-term growth of higher energy prices. Still, they imply that the results should be interpreted cautiously, with no claims of forecasting accuracy, but as a contribution toward a better understanding of the most important interactions between energy and the economy.

3.3   *Functional forms and parameter values*

The production submodel consists of an input–output structure with some flexibility in technical coefficients. A technology is specified for each sector and is represented by a cost function. Using basic duality results, the technical coefficients can be obtained from the cost function given the prices of all inputs including taxes.[21] The degree of flexibility depends naturally on the choice of functional form for the cost function. Given the assumption of constant returns to scale, the technical coefficients are independent of the level of output, and output prices are independent of demand. The model's unit cost or price functions can be expressed by

$$p_i = p_i(p_1, p_2, \ldots, p_{23}, p_k, p_l, p_r), \qquad i = 1, 2, \ldots, 23 \qquad (18)$$

where p_i, $i = 1, 2, \ldots, 23$ is the output price a unit cost and p_k, p_l, and p_r are the prices of capital, labor, and imported inputs. For sector 24, the crude oil and natural gas sector, the output price, p_{24}, is determined exogenously by the world market price. A unit cost function still exists for this sector, but as indicated above this cost is generally less than the market price.

Given the values of p_{24}, p_k, p_l, and p_r, this system of 23 equations can be solved to yield the output prices for each sector that corresponds to minimum cost. Then the derivatives of the cost function with respect to each input price yield directly the corresponding input–output coefficient. The matrix of input–output coefficients that lead to minimum cost given the exogenous price is thus obtained. It can then be used to determine gross output and primary factor requirements for each level of final demands.

Three different functional forms of the unit cost functions were tested, to determine the sensitivity of the result to alternative assumptions as to the flexibility of the technology. The first one, applying to what will be called Model FC (for "fixed coefficients"), consists of a simple Leontief technology in all intermediate inputs and value-added, combined with a Cobb–Douglas nest for capital and labor. This is the least flexible technology used and will provide a lower bound to the set of plausible production technologies in an energy model. It can be represented as

$$P_i = \sum_{j=1}^{24} a_j p_j + a_r p_r + a_{va} y_i, \qquad i = 1, 23 \tag{19}$$

where

$$y_i = p_k^\alpha p_l^{1-\alpha}, \qquad i = 1, 23 \tag{20}$$

is the primary factor component of cost in each sector. (The subscript i has been removed from all coefficients for simplicity.) This model is parameterized entirely by benchmarking: the a_j, $j = 1, 23$ coefficients as well as a_r correspond to input–output coefficients as observed in the 1973 data set; α is the share of capital in value-added and can also be obtained from the benchmark.

A second set of functional forms, corresponding to a full Cobb–Douglas specification, define the production system of Model CD. The cost functions here are of the form

$$p_i = \prod_{j=1}^{24} p_j^{\alpha_j} p_k^{\alpha_k} p_l^{\alpha_l} \tag{21}$$

The flexibility exhibited by this functional form is much greater and in fact probably too optimistic. As is well known, the partial elasticities of substitution in this model are all 1. Here each factor has a fixed share in total cost. This implies, in particular, that an increase in the price of an energy input leads to an equal percentage reduction in the use of that input. Model CD will define an upper bound to the range of potential flexibility in production.

A third functional form gives rise to Model C, which represents a central or intermediate case, where flexibility is substantially reduced for certain key combinations of inputs and where, in particular, capital and energy are treated as fully complementary. Model C has a nested cost

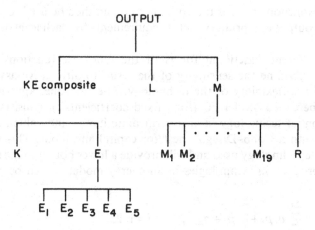

Figure 4. Structure of the production system for Model C.

structure, based on separability assumptions, that can be represented as in Figure 4. Here $M_1, M_2, \ldots, M_{19}$ are nonenergy intermediate inputs, corresponding to the outputs of sectors 1 through 19; R is imported units; and $E_1, E_2, \ldots, E_5$ are energy inputs, corresponding to the outputs of sectors 20 through 24. To achieve capital–energy complementarity it is sufficient that the elasticity of substitution between these two inputs within the KE nest be substantially smaller (even if positive) than the elasticity of substitution between the KE composite and L and M in the outer nest. To generate significant complementarity, and thus study adequately the dynamic effect, capital and energy are specified as fixed proportions of the KE composite, that is,

$$p_{ke} = a_k p_k + a_e p_e \qquad (22)$$

The outer nest remains Cobb–Douglas and thus imposes unitary elasticities of substitution between the KE composite, L and M; this corresponds to

$$p_i = p_{ke}^{\alpha_{ke}} p_l^{\alpha_l} p_m^{\alpha_m} \qquad (23)$$

Within the two materials and energy nests, a Cobb–Douglas structure is generally also used. It seems important, within the energy nest in particular, to allow for significant interfuel substitution possibilities. However, for certain energy sectors, this flexibility is not plausible; given the substantial increases in the price of crude oil and natural gas in all the simulations, it is more realistic to specify a fixed-coefficient technology in at least two sectors: the petroleum-refining sector and the gas utility sector. Although there is some possibility in these sectors to reduce the

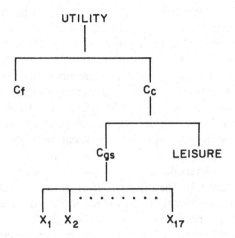

Figure 5. Structure of the consumer preference system.

crude oil or the natural gas input per unit of output, in particular by eliminating certain losses, these possibilities are very limited and very soon an increase in the output of refined products or of delivered natural gas requires a proportional increase in the input of the primary energy resource, despite higher and higher energy prices.

Given the multinested structure used in Model C and the combination of different functional forms, the production submodel can no longer be solved analytically, and a numerical analysis technique is used to solve the system of 23 equations,. yielding the output prices for each set of primary factors, imported inputs, and crude oil and natural gas prices.

All parameters of the submodel can still be obtained directly from the benchmark data set, given the assumption that all partial elasticities of substitution are either 0 or 1.

On the demand side of the model, complete demand systems are specified for each of the 12 consumer groups. These will determine saving and investment, labor supply, and current consumption of each of the 17 consumer goods and services. A multinested constant elasticity of substitution (CES) and Cobb–Douglas structure is used to represent consumer preferences.

In the model, consumer utility depends on future consumption, leisure, and current consumption of goods and services, as in Figure 5. Here C_f and C_c are future and current consumption, C_{gs} is consumption of goods and services, and $x_1, x_2, \ldots, x_{17}$ are the consumer goods available in the current period.

The intertemporal choice between current and future consumption and the labor–leisure choice are specified as CES subutility functions. The choice among the 17 consumer goods and services available in each period is based on a Cobb–Douglas specification.

Clearly, the choice between current and future consumption will determine the amount of saving in each period for each group of consumers. It will be a function of the relative price of future versus current consumption, which is in turn determined by the rate of return to capital. When a consumer saves, he in fact buys one unit of capital endowment that will produce a stream of capital services into the future. The return to saving will therefore be determined by the expected value of this stream of capital services, given by the expected price of capital, relative to the current cost of acquiring capital or investment goods. In the model consumers estimate the future price of capital to be equal to the current one, and consequently the expected return to saving matches the current rate of return to capital.

The intertemporal choice nest is again parameterized by benchmarking, with the additional information that the elasticity of saving with respect to the rate of return is .4.[22] Thus, each consumer will have utility functions with different parameters and in particular the percentage of income that is saved will differ across groups, reflecting the differences in behavior observed in 1973.

A similar functional form and parameterization method is used for the labor–leisure choice within the current consumption nest. The choice between leisure and income depends on the real wage rate, after taxes, and it is assumed that for all consumer groups the elasticity of the supply of labor with respect to the real wage rate is .15.[23] Again, this does not preclude differences in behavior; but all groups react in the same way to changes in the real wage rate.

Finally, the Cobb–Douglas nest to allocate current consumption among the 17 goods and services available is parameterized directly from the benchmark.

Formally each consumer preference system can be represented by

$$U = U\{C_f, G[\ell, h(x_1, x_2, \ldots, x_{17})]\} \tag{24}$$

where U and G are CES functions and h is Cobb–Douglas, and the symbols C_f and $x_1, x_2, \ldots, x_{17}$ have the meaning described above. The symbol ℓ stands for leisure.

In the comparisons of discounted streams of utility which will be used to evaluate the impact on welfare of higher oil prices, only the utility derived from the G function will be used. In fact, if the utility from future consumption were included in each period's total utility there would be double-counting. The particular nested structure used here is especially adequate for the evaluation of discounted utility from the *current* consumption of leisure, goods, and services.

Finally, given that the classification of consumer goods and services is not the same as the classification of producer goods, a transition matrix is employed to convert one into the other one. This is applied to all goods including savings, meaning that a unit of the savings good corresponds to a vector of producer goods in fixed proportion, as observed in 1973.

Government spending is modeled in a straightforward manner. Tax revenues are partly returned to consumers in the form of transfer payments, each group receiving a fixed share of the total. The remaining revenue is spent on purchases of goods, services, capital, and labor, following the maximization of the government's own Cobb–Douglas utility function; thus the share of government spending on each good or factor remains constant.

In the foreign sector, imports and exports are kept in balance.[24] Imports consist of certain types of intermediate inputs, as described in the production submodel, and of final demand imports. The latter are considered perfect substitutes for domestic outputs. They have the same price and are negative components of final demand. Their volume is fixed exogenously.

Exports are scaled up to match the total value of imports. Thus trade balance is imposed, on the assumption that imports are paid for with exports. There is no explicit treatment of exchange rates. Each production sector has a fixed share in total exports, implying that the quantity exported varies inversely with the domestic price.

4   Simulation results

4.1   *Reference case: no energy crisis*

The first important simulation is a reference case for assessing the welfare losses associated with energy scarcity and higher energy prices. In the reference case two highly unrealistic assumptions apply. First the domestic supply of all energy including oil and gas is taken to be perfectly elastic at the low cost determined by technology. This contrasts sharply with the nature of supply in the more realistic simulations described below, where a perfectly inelastic domestic supply function is imposed.[25] The second unrealistic assumption is that the world price of oil and gas will remain constant in real terms from 1973. The reference case thus implies no energy crisis. In such a case, the long-term growth rate of the economy is determined by the growth in the labor force; if capital grows more rapidly or less rapidly than the labor endowment, its relative price will change, inducing a change in saving behavior that eventually keeps the capital stock increasing at the same rate as the labor supply. However, to clear the reference case of any spurious effects resulting from relative price changes, the growth rate of the labor supply was chosen so as to keep the economy on a steady-state path starting in 1973. The growth rate that permits this is 2.76% per year. Here the labor endowment is measured in efficiency units. Its growth rate is meant to capture both population growth and increases in later productivity. To keep comparisons simple across all simulations, this rate was used in all scenarios, although it corresponds to a steady state only in the reference case.

Since capital, labor, and output all grow at the same rate, all relative prices remain constant. This is possible because there are no constraints on the supply of crude oil or any other energy resource, and because the price of oil as well as the price of imported inputs are fixed at their 1973 levels. Thus with constant returns to scale and homotheticity in consumer utility functions, all sectors grow at precisely the same rate, the technique of production does not change, and the pattern of final demand also remains fixed.

In this scenario, energy demands obviously grow at the same rate as the rest of the economy and therefore reach very high levels by 2001. The energy/GNP ratio is kept at 1. In particular, the total domestic supply of crude oil and natural gas in the United States climbs to almost 100 quads[26] (from its 1973 level of 44 quads). This is counterfactual, to say the least. But it is the very lack of realism of this scenario that makes it useful for evaluating the importance of the more likely conditions of domestic energy scarcity and higher energy prices.

National income and welfare – the latter is defined here as national income plus the value of leisure at current wage rates – more than double during this 28-year period. The total welfare of $3620.2 billion (at 1973 prices) will be used as the reference figure against which the losses imposed by higher oil prices or domestic supply constraints will be measured.

The main results from this case are presented in Table 3. Other results – presented in the Appendix – show that all prices remain equal to 1, all sectors grow at the same rate, and the composition of output remains fixed. As for energy demands in this unconstrained scenario, all energy requirements more than double, leading to a total consumption of primary energy of more than 160 quads by the end of the period (see the first column of Table 3).

Table 3. *No-energy-crisis case* (*oil price growth at 0%*)

Factor	Level in 2001	Annual growth rate, 1973–2001
GNP (billions of 1973 dollars)	2645.9	2.76
Welfare (national income plus value of leisure – billions of 1973 dollars)	3620.2	2.76
Primary energy		
Consumption (quads)	165.0	2.76
Import component (quads)	31.0	2.76

4.2 *Higher oil prices and energy scarcity*

To simulate the impact of higher oil prices and the scarcity of certain fossil fuels in the United States a scenario was developed with annual oil price increase of 8% from 1973 and a U.S. domestic oil and natural gas supply not to exceed the 1973 level of about 44 quads. The increase in the oil price leads to a cost per barrel of $58 in 2001 (1980 dollars). The constraint on the supply of domestic oil matches the consensus view that even with higher prices and the discovery of new reserves, the domestic supply of these two fuels will probably not increase. Additional elements of the scenario include the above mentioned 2.76% growth rate of labor supply and also a 2.76% assumed increase of final demand imports, except for imports of refined petroleum products that remain at their 1978 level. The impact of this scenario is determined by two sets of simulations. The first set contrasts the three different production submodels described above. They provide a type of sensitivity analysis, since they reveal the implications of different assumptions as to the flexibility of the technology. The impact of the higher oil prices will clearly be greater in the case of limited flexibility (Model FC) and smaller in the Cobb–Douglas case (Model CD).

The second set of simulations is designed to test the relative importance of the direct effect, the savings effect, and the terms-of-trade effect in the explanation of the reduction in welfare. In one case saving is fixed as a percentage of income; thus the dynamic effect on investment is eliminated. In another case, foreign oil producers receive as payment for the oil supplied to the U.S. only the equivalent of the cost of producing that oil domestically; since the market price is substantially higher than this cost, rents are generated on imported oil; these are distributed to U.S.

Table 4. *Results under alternative production specifications*

Factor	NEC	FC	CD	C
Oil price growth rate	0%	8%	8%	8%
Growth rates, 1973–2001				
GNP	2.76	2.35	2.70	2.56
Consumption	2.76	2.43	2.73	2.70
Investment	2.76	1.96	2.58	2.22
Government spending	2.76	2.26	2.66	2.34
Imports	2.76	4.83	2.51	2.52
Wage rate				
1973	1.0	1.0	1.0	1.0
2001	1.0	.868	.976	.962
Rate of return to capital				
1973	.04	.04	.04	.04
2001	.04	.0337	.0378	.0325
Welfare 2001 (billions of 1973 dollars)	3620.2	3252.1	3570.3	3474.7
% Change from NEC	—	− 10.2	− 1.4	− 4.0

households in proportion to their endowment of capital. The terms-of-trade effect then disappears since all rents are captured by U.S. domestic oil suppliers. In a third case, both the terms-of-trade and savings effects are eliminated; only the direct effect remains. These three cases are obtained with the most general of the production submodels (Model C).

The comparisons of results are based on welfare as defined above and on the present value of the utility from consumption.

4.3   Alternative specifications of the production submodel

The results obtained under the fixed coefficient (FC), Cobb–Douglas (CD), and multilevel or central (C) production models, as well as the case of no energy crisis (NEC), are presented in Tables 4 and 5. Detailed additional results from these simulations are presented in the Appendix.

The general impact of higher oil prices and limited domestic oil supply is clear: GNP growth rates decline, wage rates and returns to capital drop, and welfare losses are significant. Investment and capital accumulation suffer substantially. Relative prices vary markedly across sectors, and the composition of output is altered. All consumer groups have to face lower levels of consumption, and discounted utility decreases for all.

Table 5. *U.S. energy supply and demand in year 2001*

Factor	1973	2001 NEC	FC	CD	C
Oil price growth rate, 1973–2001	—	0%	8%	8%	8%
Electricity (sales - 10^9 kWh)	1703.2	3650.0	3146.5	3361.6	4761.8
Primary energy:					
Domestic supply					
Coal (quads)	14.37	30.80	31.66	29.26	47.04
Crude oil and natural gas (quads)	44.25	94.83[a]	44.25	17.89	42.05
Hydro, geothermal, and nuclear (quads)[b]	3.82	8.19	12.90	12.90	12.90
Imports					
Crude oil and natural gas (quads)	7.95	17.04	25.40	—	—
Refined products (quads)	6.58	14.10	6.58	6.58	6.58
Total primary energy consumed (quads)	76.97	164.96	120.79	66.36	108.57

[a] This highly unrealistic figure is for reference purposes only. It results from the counterfactual assumptions employed to define the reference or NEC case.
[b] Figures in the last three columns of this row derive from the assumptions that hydro and geothermal energy supplies remain at 1973 levels, and that nuclear provides 10 quads of energy in 2001.

These results obtained in all three cases but not always to the same degree. Naturally the impact of higher oil prices is most pronounced in the case of the least flexible technology (Model FC): GNP growth slows down to an annual rate of 2.35%. Wage rates drop substantially – by 13.2% – given that the labor force is still increasing at 2.76%. The decrease in the rate of return to capital and the slower growth rate of the economy as a whole lead to a much slower rate of growth of investment. Imports are increasing at 4.83% not in volume but in real terms, that is, after being deflated with the GNP price index. By the year 2001, welfare – national income plus the value of leisure – is 10% below welfare in the no-energy-crisis case.

Still, in spite of the fixed coefficients in production, there is some flexibility in the economy. This is achieved through changes in the composition of output, given that demand responds to changes in relative prices. Energy – and in particular oil-intensive goods – will have higher prices;

their demands will grow more slowly. In fact, as can be seen from Table 5, the consumption of total primary energy only increases at 1.62% per year (as compared with 2.35% for GNP).

The Cobb–Douglas case represents clearly an overoptimistic assumption as to the flexibility of production. The effect of the higher oil prices is very minor in terms of GNP growth. The composition of GNP changes much less, relative prices are much more stable, and the wage rate and the rate of return to capital drop very little. The total welfare loss by the year 2001 is only 1.4%. But the implausibility of the Cobb–Douglas case becomes more evident given the patently implausible results in the energy area. Since it is always possible to substitute other inputs for energy, and in particular for oil and natural gas, the total energy consumption actually decreases, thanks to a drop in the demand for those scarce fuels that is beyond the believable range. Although the Cobb–Douglas case is presented here as an upper bound on the flexibility admissible in the specification of the technology, it seems clear that it is not a realistic case, given its implications for energy demand. This conclusion highlights the importance of using disaggregated models and of evaluating the performance of the economy as a whole from the behavior of each sector. Although many might consider an elasticity of demand for primary energy of -1 as not altogether implausible, and even if the aggregate results obtained with such an assumption appear reasonable, when analyzing the implications of this specification for each type of energy form, its lack of realism surfaces.

The third simulation, referred to here as the central (Model C) case, uses the nested multilevel production model, with capital–energy complementarity and limited flexibility in certain energy supplying sectors. Given that some flexibility is assumed, the welfare consequences are considerably less severe than in the fixed coefficient case. GNP growth is now 2.56% per year, and the welfare loss in the year 2001 amounts to 4%. The strong capital energy complementarity leads to a sharp decrease in the rate of return to capital, which in 2001 is only 3.25%. Investment is hurt by this drop, as expected, and increases at only 2.22%. Relative prices change considerably, and output growth rates for different sectors reflect price changes and demand responses. Again all consumer groups lose with the worsening performance of the economy. Measuring by the ratio of discounted utility in this case relative to the reference case, it is clear that the biggest losers are the lower-income groups. This probably reflects their tendency to devote larger shares of income to the purchase of energy-intensive goods. The utility loss decreases monotonically with income, except for the highest-income group: Since the households in this group own a dominant share of the total capital stock, they are hurt substantially by the drop in the return to capital.

In this central case, energy consumption continues increasing but only at an annual rate of 1.23%. This is enough to lead to a cut in oil and natural gas demand sufficient to eliminate the imports of these two fuels by the year 2001. Only the imports of about 6.58 quads of refined petroleum products remain. This favorable result is due to high oil price assumed (almost $58 in 1980 dollars in 2001) and in the rather slow growth rate of GNP.

There are simultaneously significant compositional changes within the energy markets. Both electricity and coal play a much more relevant role, as expected.

These results indicate in detail the impact of the higher oil prices. The slowdown in growth is visible, structural changes follow price changes, important distributional effects are observed, and significant changes are predicted in the energy markets. The total welfare losses, or the decrease in the growth rate in GNP, may seem quite small. These are, however, long-term effects, and therefore persistent. Over two or three decades, their consequences become substantial. In fact, a drop in GNP growth from 2.76% per year to 2.56% leads to a loss in income over the period 1973–2001 of about $700 billion of 1973 dollars, when a discount rate of 4% is applied. This is an awesome figure that might justify a great effort of investment in research and development of energy-saving technologies or in the exploration of new sources of fuels.

Given this view of the impact of higher oil prices, it is now possible to use the model to attempt to decompose that impact into its three main effects.

4.4 Decomposing the impact of higher oil prices

To study the relative importance of each of the three effects of energy on growth, eight different simulations were performed, corresponding to two energy scenarios combined with four alternative versions of the model. The two scenarios consist of oil price growth rates of 4% and 8%, respectively, with the usual constraint that domestic supply of crude oil and natural gas not exceed its 1973 level. The four versions of the model attempt to isolate certain effects so that they can be studied individually. One version (C) is the central case described above; the model is used in its general form to simulate the full impact of the higher oil prices. The second version, central/fixed savings (C/FS), tries to determine what would happen if no savings effect existed; it corresponds to the central

Table 6. *Decomposition of the welfare cost of higher oil prices, I*

Factor	C	C/FS	C/NT	C/FS,NT
Oil price growth	4%	4%	4%	4%
Growth rates, 1973–2001				
GNP	2.67	2.69	2.70	2.71
Consumption	2.72	2.72	2.75	2.75
Investment	2.55	2.73	2.57	2.77
Government spending	2.59	2.59	2.60	2.60
Imports	3.23	3.26	2.74	2.76
Wage rate				
1973	1.0	1.0	1.0	1.0
2001	.987	.989	.988	.990
Rate of return to capital				
1973	.040	.040	.040	.040
2001	.037	.037	.037	.037
Welfare				
2001 (billions of 1973 dollars)	3552.3	3561.8	3576.0	3586.3
% Change from NEC	− 1.86	− 1.59	− 1.20	− .92
% of Total welfare loss	100%	85%	65%	50%

case specification except that saving no longer responds to changes in the rate of return to capital, but rather remains fixed relative to income in the private sector. The third version, central/no terms-of-trade effect (C/NT), attempts to eliminate the terms-of-trade effect; it is also based on the central case model, but it treats oil imports in a special way: Foreign oil is purchased at the cost at which it can be produced in the United States. Since the price of oil is still growing, important rents exist, but instead of accruing to foreigners these are distributed to capital owners in the United States. This is equivalent to a situation where oil prices increase because of a U.S.-owned cartel that has the ability to import oil at marginal cost and sell it in the domestic market at a fixed price. Finally, the last version (C/FS,NT) eliminates simultaneously the savings effect and the terms-of-trade effect: The remaining impact on growth must be attributed to the direct effect on factor productivity.

The results are summarized in Tables 6 and 7. With the central model (Model C), the general pattern of effects is similar under 4% and 8% oil price increases, although the individual effects are smaller when the oil price increases at the slower, 4% rate. The growth rate of GNP is 2.67% under 4% oil price increases and 2.56% under 8% oil price increases.

Table 7. *Decomposition of the welfare cost of higher oil prices, II*

Factor	C	C/FS	C/NT	C/FS,NT
Oil price growth	8%	8%	8%	8%
Growth rates, 1973–2001				
GNP	2.56	2.60	2.57	2.60
Consumption	2.70	2.69	2.70	2.69
Investment	2.22	2.74	2.23	2.74
Government spending	2.34	2.34	2.34	2.34
Imports	2.52	2.55	2.52	2.56
Wage rate				
1973	1.0	1.0	1.0	1.0
2001	.962	.967	.962	.967
Rate of return to capital				
1973	.040	.040	.040	.040
2001	.0325	.0319	.0325	.0319
Welfare				
2001 (billions of 1973 dollars)	3474.7	3497.2	3475.2	3498.0
% Change from NEC	−4.0	−3.38	−3.99	−3.36
% of Total welfare loss	100%	84.5%	99%	84%

This compares with a 2.76% growth rate in the reference case. Welfare falls 1.86% and 4.0% below the reference case under 4% and 8% oil price growth, respectively.

With 4% oil price increases, the following pattern emerges. When the savings effect is eliminated – the fixed savings or C/FS case – GNP growth is slightly faster. The faster GNP growth can be attributed to investment, which, as expected, grows faster than in the central case. In fact, investment now increases more rapidly than GNP; this is explained by the fact that private income is growing more rapidly than national income. The final welfare loss by the year 2001 is only 1.59% below the reference or no-energy-crises (NEC) case. The welfare loss in this C/FS case is 85% as large as the loss in the central (C) case. Therefore, the savings effect seems to be responsible for 15% of the welfare loss associated with higher oil prices.

In the case with no terms-of-trade effect – the C/NT case – it is clear that consumption grows slightly faster than in the C/FS case. The increase in imports is now much more moderate, given that the price of imported oil practically does not increase. The welfare loss by the year 2001 is approximately 1.2% below the NEC case. The loss is 65% as large as in

Table 8. *Contribution of individual effects to total welfare loss (oil price growth rate = 4%)*

Direct effect	50%
Savings effect	15%
Terms-of-trade effect	35%
Savings and terms-of-trade effects	50%
All three effects	100%

the central (C) case. The terms-of-trade effect thus accounts for 35% of the total effect.

Finally, when both the savings and terms-of-trade effect are eliminated simultaneously – the C/FS,NT case – the total welfare loss is significantly smaller. In this case higher investment growth coincides with slower import growth. By 2001 the welfare loss is only .92% below the NEC case, or 50% as large as in the central case. Thus the terms-of-trade effect and the savings effect combined account for 50% of the total welfare loss, the direct effect causing the remaining 50%. Since 50% is the sum of the two effects taken individually, there seems to be little interaction between them.

These results are summarized in Table 8.

When the oil price increases at 8% per year, the relative importance of the savings effects remains remarkably constant; but the terms-of-trade effect almost disappears because of the reduction and eventual elimination of oil imports by the end of the simulation period. As mentioned above, in the central case the total welfare loss by 2001 is of the order of 4%, with GNP growth during the 28-year period slowing down to 2.56%. If the savings effect is eliminated, GNP grows at 2.60% per year, as investment grows at a 2.74% annual rate. It is interesting to observe that the rate of return to capital declines even further to 3.19%; since investment increases rapidly, unaffected by the lower price of capital services, capital becomes relatively more abundant and its return falls. Ultimately the welfare loss relative to the NEC case is 3.38%, or 84.5% of the total loss in the central case. Thus the savings effect seems again to account for about 15% of the total welfare loss.

The terms-of-trade effect, on the other hand, is virtually negligible. Since oil imports decline to zero, as discussed above, the main differences between the central case and the C/NT case when the oil price grows at 8% occur during the initial periods while imports are still significant. In fact, even without any terms-of-trade effect during the whole period

Table 9. *Contribution of individual effects to total welfare loss (oil price growth rate = 8%)*

Direct effect	85%
Savings effect	15%
Terms-of-trade effect	1%
Savings and terms-of-trade effects	16%
All three effects	100%

the welfare loss by the year 2001 is still 3.99% or virtually the same as in the central case. This example illustrates the notion that the significance of the terms-of-trade effect depends on the percentage of energy that is imported.

Finally, when eliminating the savings and terms-of-trade effects simultaneously, the results are very similar to the C/FS effect, as would be expected since the terms-of-trade effect is negligible.

These results are presented in Table 9.

To summarize, the two oil price scenarios suggest that:

1. The direct effect on factor productivity is the dominant channel through which energy affects growth, at least in the United States; it accounts for 50% and 84% of the total welfare loss under 4% and 8% oil price growth, respectively.
2. The savings effect has a remarkably stable impact, corresponding in both cases to about 15% of the total loss, even though the rate of return to capital changes much more in one case than in the other.
3. The terms-of-trade effect depends naturally on the percentage of energy – in this case, oil – that is imported; if imports decline to zero, its impact will be negligible; in the case where imports remain positive, it accounts for 35% of the total loss.
4. The terms-of-trade and savings effects seem to have few interactions; together they account for a percentage of the total loss that corresponds closely to the sum of the losses accounted for by each individually.

5   Conclusions

This chapter presents the structure and results of a large-scale disaggregated general equilibrium model of the U.S. economy. The model is used to simulate the impact of higher energy prices on economic growth and to test the relative importance of three channels through which higher-priced energy affects growth. These channels are discussed and the nature of each of the effects leading to slower growth is clarified.

Higher energy prices induce changes in the pattern of demands that reduce energy input. These changes, however, are not costless: Other factors of production are not perfect substitutes for energy, and their supply is not perfectly elastic. The move away from energy is therefore reflected in lower output levels. How much lower depends on the degree of flexibility in the production technology and on the supply elasticity of other factors. The model is used to measure the impact of this reduction in overall productivity under three alternative specifications as to the flexibility of the production system.

Capital–energy complementarity has been identified as another source of lower levels of GNP in the long run. Higher energy prices reduce the demand for capital and therefore its rate of return; this induces lower saving and capital accumulation. This chapter briefly discusses the nature of capital–energy complementarity and assesses the significance of the associated savings–investment effect by comparing specifications where saving is and is not responsive to changes in the rate of return.

Finally, since a significant portion of the energy supply is imported, higher energy prices generate a terms-of-trade effect that also contributes to the decrease in real income. The terms-of-trade effect is explained, and it is shown that it exists only to the extent that rents included in the energy prices are paid to foreigners and not to domestic producers or consumers. The importance of this effect is analyzed by simulating cases where oil prices include substantial rents but the price paid to foreigners corresponds only to extraction cost.

The most important findings are useful both as insights into energy modeling and as tests of the relative significance of the three effects mentioned above.

The simulation of alternative production submodels shows that the degree of flexibility assumed for the technology will have some impact on the aggregate performance of the economy and will be crucial to the behavior of individual sectors, in particular in the energy area. It reveals the usefulness of using disaggregated approaches and provides evidence on the implications of capital–energy complementarity.

The decomposition of the impact of higher energy prices on growth is attempted under two different scenarios as to oil price increases. In both cases, the dominant channel through which energy affects growth seems to be the direct effect, that is, the reduction in the overall productivity of other factors of production as energy becomes more expensive. This indicates that, at least for the United States, the behavior of saving and the fact that some energy is imported seem to be less important elements of the energy problem. In fact, in both scenarios the savings effect seems to account for only 15% of the total welfare loss, in spite of the assumptions of strong capital–energy complementarity and of an elasticity of saving with respect to the rate of return of the order of .4. The terms-of-trade effect, on the other hand, is responsible for 35% of the total loss in welfare in one case and has a negligible impact in the other, where oil imports drop to zero.

All results are presented in detail. These reveal the effects of changing energy conditions on relative prices, on the composition of GNP and the structure of industrial output, and on consumers' utilities and general welfare.

Appendix A: Additional results from the four first simulations

Table A.1. *First case: no energy constraints (oil price growth rate = 0%)*

Sector	Price in 2001	Annual output growth rate (1973–2001)
1	1.0	2.76
2	1.0	2.76
3	1.0	2.76
4	1.0	2.76
5	1.0	2.76
6	1.0	2.76
7	1.0	2.76
8	1.0	2.76
9	1.0	2.76
10	1.0	2.76
11	1.0	2.76
12	1.0	2.76
13	1.0	2.76
14	1.0	2.76
15	1.0	2.76
16	1.0	2.76
17	1.0	2.76
18	1.0	2.76
19	1.0	2.76
20	1.0	2.76
21	1.0	2.76
22	1.0	2.76
23	1.0	2.76
24	1.0	2.76

Table A.2. *First case: no energy constraints* (*oil price growth rate*= 0%)

GNP and components	2001 (billions of 1973 dollars)	Annual growth rate (1973–2001)
GNP	2645.9	2.76
Consumption	1699.7	2.76
Investment	226.4	2.76
Government spending	719.9	2.76
Imports	181.2	2.76
National income	2681.6	2.76
Welfare (NI + value of leisure)	3619.6	2.76

Table A.3. *Second case: fixed-coefficient production system* (*oil price growth rate* = 8%)

Sector	Price in 2001	Annual output growth rate (1973–2001)
1	1.024	2.98
2	1.041	2.80
3	1.025	2.15
4	1.000	2.70
5	.986	2.80
6	.978	2.72
7	1.208	2.71
8	.963	2.59
9	.945	2.94
10	.922	3.17
11	.922	3.01
12	1.029	2.82
13	.928	2.63
14	1.001	2.58
15	.956	2.36
16	.915	2.70
17	.988	2.47
18	.951	2.68
19	.965	2.47
20	.988	2.86
21	4.357	1.78
22	1.153	2.22
23	3.313	.59
24	8.627	.00

Table A.4. *Second case: fixed-coefficient production system* (*oil price growth rate* = 8%)

GNP and components	2001 (billions of 1973 dollars)	Annual growth rate (1973–2001)
GNP	2364.9	2.35
Consumption	1554.4	2.43
Investment	181.7	1.96
Government spending	628.8	2.26
Imports	317.0	4.83
National income	2431.0	2.40
Welfare (NI + value of leisure)	3252.1	2.37

Present value of discounted utility: ratio of current to reference case

Household group	Ratio
1	.927
2	.931
3	.933
4	.935
5	.936
6	.937
7	.939
8	.939
9	.940
10	.941
11	.941
12	.928

Table A.5. *Third case: Cobb–Douglas production system* (*oil price growth rate* = 8%)

Sector	Price in 2001	Annual output growth rate (1973–2001)
1	1.024	2.59
2	1.026	2.48
3	1.021	2.51
4	1.016	2.67
5	1.010	2.68
6	1.008	1.65
7	1.076	2.43
8	1.004	2.60
9	.999	2.58
10	.992	2.66
11	.993	2.65

Table A.5. *(cont.)*

Sector	Price in 2001	Annual output growth rate (1973–2001)
12	1.022	2.53
13	.995	2.70
14	1.016	2.66
15	1.002	2.57
16	.991	2.74
17	1.015	2.62
18	1.000	2.69
19	1.005	2.66
20	1.011	2.57
21	2.608	− .31
22	1.061	2.46
23	1.945	.29
24	8.627	−3.18

Table A.6. *Third case: Cobb–Douglas production system (oil price growth rate = 8%)*

GNP and components	2001 (billions of 1973 dollars)	Annual growth rate (1973–2001)
GNP	2605.3	2.7
Consumption	1688.5	2.73
Investment	215.0	2.58
Government spending	701.7	2.66
Imports	169.2	2.51
National income	2653.1	2.71
Welfare (NI + value of leisure)	3570.3	2.71

Present value of discounted utility: ratio of current case to reference case

Household group	Ratio
1	.966
2	.969
3	.970
4	.971
5	.971
6	.972
7	.973
8	.973
9	.974
10	.975
11	.975
12	.973
Total	.973

Table A.7. *Fourth case: multilevel production system* (*oil price growth rate* = 8%)

Sector	Price in 2001	Annual output growth rate (1973–2001)
1	1.006	2.62
2	1.025	2.39
3	1.025	2.31
4	1.004	2.68
5	1.005	2.68
6	.997	2.64
7	1.118	2.31
8	.988	2.55
9	.982	2.54
10	.977	2.53
11	.959	2.67
12	1.030	2.55
13	.963	2.76
14	.993	2.73
15	.991	2.53
16	.950	2.88
17	.961	2.79
18	.987	2.71
19	.979	2.97
20	.992	4.33
21	3.542	.20
22	1.055	3.74
23	2.667	− .36
24	8.545	− .18

Table A.8. *Fourth case: multilevel production system* (*oil price growth rate* = 8%)

GNP and components	2001 (billions of 1973 dollars)	Annual growth rate (1973–2001)
GNP	2511.3	2.57
Consumption	1673.2	2.70
Investment	195.3	2.22
Government spending	642.9	2.34
Imports	169.9	2.52
National income	2579.1	2.61
Welfare (NI + value of leisure)	3463.5	2.61

Table A.8. *(cont.)*

Present value of discounted utility: ratio of current case to reference case	
Household group	Ratio
1	.945
2	.952
3	.956
4	.959
5	.960
6	.962
7	.965
8	.965
9	.967
10	.968
11	.967
12	.948
Total	.962

NOTES

1. Some representative preembargo energy research is contained in the essays in Macrakis (1974).
2. See Jorgenson and Fraumeni (1979).
3. See Jorgenson, Lau, and Stoker (1980).
4. See Manne (1976, 1977).
5. See Fullerton, Shoven, and Whalley (1978, 1981).
6. For a description of some main results obtained with previous applications of this model, see Borges (1980).
7. For a survey and analysis of various estimates of domestic oil and gas supply elasticities, see Energy Modeling Forum (1980).
8. See Berndt and Wood (1975, 1979).
9. See Sweeney (1979).
10. See, in particular, Hudson and Jorgenson (1978) and Jorgenson (1978).
11. Substitutability or complementarity, as discussed here, is completely determined by the nature of technology in the sector in question.
12. This argument is spelled out in Hogan (1977).
13. F_i is the partial derivative with respect to factor i, and F_{ij} is the cross-partial derivative with respect to factors i and j.
14. The notion of rent here is used broadly to include both user cost and monopoly rent.
15. An evaluation of the importance of energy's terms-of-trade effect to industrial nations and less developed countries is presented in a three-region model by Manne (1980).
16. See Merrill (1972).
17. See Borges (1980) and Goulder (1982).
18. For a presentation of this issue in an energy context, see Sweeney (1979).

19. For a more detailed discussion of the "calibration" approach, see the article by Mansur and Whalley in this volume.
20. The Hudson–Jorgenson model currently includes production technologies that change over time with the particular direction of change depending on relative prices of production factors. See Jorgenson and Fraumeni (1979). Manne's ETA-Macro accounts for technological progress in the energy sector by introducing new technologies at certain dates and rates.
21. The theoretical foundations for this technique are set forth in Shephard (1953).
22. This estimate is taken from Boskin (1978).
23. This is a rough average of the estimates obtained econometrically for various subsets of the labor force. See Brown and Deaton (1972).
24. If exports and imports did not balance, the model would have to provide for offsetting capital or reserves movements to insure overall balance of international flows. A different version of the model incorporates international capital movements and explores the implications of international reinvestment of surplus oil revenues on the part of the oil-exporting nations.
25. The model allows specification of any oil supply elasticity. In all simulations except for the reference case, this elasticity is taken to be zero: It is assumed that domestic supply will not exceed 1973 levels.
26. A quad is an energy unit equal to 10^{15} Btu (10 quadrillion British thermal units).

REFERENCES

Berndt, E. R., and Wood, D. O. (1975). "Technology, Prices, and the Derived Demand for Energy." *Review of Economics and Statistics,* Vol. 56, pp. 259–68.

Berndt, E., and Wood, D. (1979). "Engineering and Econometric Interpretations of Energy-Capital Complementarity." *American Economic Review,* Vol. 69, No. 3, pp. 342–54.

Borges, Antonio M. (1980). *Two General Equilibrium Models of the U.S. Economy.* Ph.D. diss., Department of Economics, Stanford University.

Boskin, Michael J. (1978). "Taxation, Saving, and the Rate of Interest." *Journal of Political Economy,* Vol. 86, Part 2, No. 2, pp. S3–S27.

Energy Modeling Forum (1980). "Aggregate Elasticities of Energy Demand." Energy Modeling Forum Final Report #4, Stanford University, August.

Fullerton, D., King, A., Shoven, J., and Whalley, J. (1981). "Corporate Tax Integration in the United States: A General Equilibrium Approach." *American Economic Review,* Vol. 71, No. 4, pp. 677–91.

Fullerton, D., Shoven, J., and Whalley, J. (1977). "Phase 5 Report on U.S. Treasury Contract TOS/76/41, Data Development for the GEMTAP Model." Prepared for the Office of Tax Analysis, Washington, D.C.

(1978). "General Equilibrium Analysis of U.S. Taxation Policy." In *1978 Compendium of Tax Research, Office of Tax Analysis.* Washington, D.C.: Department of the Treasury.

Goulder, Lawrence H. (1982). *A General Equilibrium Analysis of U.S. Energy Policy.* Ph.D. diss., Department of Economics, Stanford University.

Hitch, Charles (ed.) (1977). *Modeling Energy–Economy Interactions: Five Approaches.* Washington, D.C.: Resources for the Future.

Hogan, William (1977). "Capital Energy Complementarity in Aggregate Energy Economic Analysis." In *Energy and the Economy,* Vol. 2, Energy Modeling Forum Final Report #1. Stanford, Calif.: Stanford University.

Hogan, William W., and Manne, Alan S. (1977). "Energy–Economy Interactions: The Fable of the Elephant and the Rabbit?" In *Modeling Energy–Economy Interactions. See* Hitch (1977).

Hudson, Edward, and Jorgenson, Dale (1974). "U.S. Energy Policy and Economic Growth, 1975–2000." *Bell Journal of Economics and Management Science,* Vol. 5, No. 2, pp. 461–514.

——— (1978). "The Economic Impact of Policies to Reduce U.S. Energy Growth." *Resources and Energy,* Vol. 1, No. 3, pp. 205–29.

Jorgenson, Dale (1978). "The Role of Energy in the U.S. Economy." *National Tax Journal,* Vol. 31, No. 3, pp. 209–20.

Jorgenson, Dale, and Fraumeni, Barbara (1979). "Substitution and Technical Change in Production." Paper presented at the Conference on Economics of Substitution in Production with Special Reference to Natural Resources, Key Biscayne, Fla.

Jorgenson, D., Lau, L., and Stoker, T. (1980). "Welfare Comparison under Exact Aggregation." *American Economic Review,* Vol. 70, No. 2., pp. 268–72.

Macrakis, M. (ed.) (1974). *Energy: Demand, Conservation, and Institutional Problems.* Cambridge: MIT Press.

Manne, Alan S. (1976). "ETA: A Model for Energy Technology Assessment." *Bell Journal of Economics and Management Science,* Vol. 7, No. 2, pp. 379–406.

——— (1977). "ETA-MACRO: A Model of Energy Economy Interactions." In *Modeling Energy–Economy Interactions. See* Hitch (1977).

Manne, Alan S. (with the assistance of Sehun Kim) (1980). "Energy, International Trade, and Economic Growth." Department of Operations Research, Stanford University.

Merrill, O. H. (1972). "Applications and Extensions of an Algorithm that Computes Fixed Points of Certain Upper Semi-Continuous Point to Set Mappings." Ph.D. diss., University of Michigan, Ann Arbor.

Shephard, R. W. (1953). *Cost and Production Functions.* Princeton, N.J.: Princeton University Press.

Sweeney, James L. (1979). "Energy and Economic Growth: A Conceptual Framework," Occasional Paper EMF OP 3.0, Energy Modeling Forum, Stanford University.

Comments

Alan S. Manne

The Borges–Goulder chapter (hereafter abbreviated B-G) represents an instructive synthesis of much that has been learned about energy issues in recent years – and much that has been learned about applied general equilibrium analysis. Their work has the potential for a wide range of policy applications. The three-way quantitative decomposition appears quite plausible, and I am not inclined to challenge their conclusion that the "direct" effects dominate the savings and the terms-of-trade effects of a long-term gradual rise in energy prices. Experience with the ETA-MACRO model leads to similar results concerning the importance of direct effects versus those induced indirectly through the savings–investment link.

My principal concern about the general structure of the B-G model relates to its treatment of *time*. This is particularly important when we are analyzing the impacts of sudden shocks rather than a gradual long-term rise in energy prices. A "putty-clay" model of energy consumption may prove to be more useful in this case – and also for explaining the slowdown in overall economic productivity that occurred during the 1970s.

I will return to the putty-clay issue below, but let me begin with what the model suggests concerning the present state of the art of applied general equilibrium analysis. I will then focus upon the way in which time enters in this class of models, and will conclude with a series of miscellaneous observations.

From the B-G chapter, it is clear that we now have the ability to obtain numerical solutions to large-scale Walrasian models. This one contains:

Many agents (12 individual income groups plus the government sector);
Many physical commodities (24 industries); and
Many time periods (8 points of time, spaced at 4-year intervals from 1973 through 2001).

This level of aggregation is far more detailed than the artificial examples originally presented in Scarf's 1973 book, and it is impressive that the B-G model can nonetheless be solved by one of the earliest available fixed-point methods (Merrill's). How do B-G reduce their fixed-point problems to a search over a four-dimensional price simplex? The key idea appears to be a *recursive* rather than a fully intertemporal treatment of the system's dynamics. This permits B-G to operate with only four basic resources: capital, labor, a government budget, and a trade balance in each time period. From the prices on these resources, they then deduce product prices in each of the 24 industries, incomes for each of the 12 household groups, commodity demands, supplies, and in turn the vector label: excess demands for each of the four basic resources. Assuming stationary prices between successive time periods, it is straightforward to determine the allocation of resources between current consumption and savings – thereby determining the capital stock available during the following time period.

A recursive model dramatically reduces the burden of numerical computations, and it does not lead to any obvious biases in the B-G estimate of the importance of direct rather than indirect effects of rising energy prices. It can be argued that a recursive structure is a realistic approach, and that economic agents are myopic rather than clairvoyant with respect to the future. This type of model will generate a good approximation to an intertemporal equilibrium – provided that relative prices do not change too rapidly over time. Moreover, a recursive structure eliminates the need for arbitrary terminal conditions for a finite horizon.

There are, however, topics in energy policy analysis where a recursive approach may be misleading. The essence of the Hotelling–Nordhaus resource exhaustion paradigm is that each economic agent correctly anticipates a sequence of future prices and that today's energy markets are influenced by the length of time it will take to make a transition to high-cost "backstop" sources of supply. B-G avoid the resource exhaustion issue by postulating that domestic oil and gas supplies are limited in each individual time period, but not cumulatively. This shortcut seems satisfactory for many purposes but not, for example, energy R & D issues – where new sources of supply cannot make a significant contribution until after the year 2000.

Future prices also enter into "putty-clay" models of alternative techniques for energy conservation. By contrast, B-G deal only with the case of malleable capital, and they assume complete adjustment to price changes within each four-year time interval. They therefore limit their analysis to smooth long-term price trends, rather than sudden shocks such as the two that were experienced during the 1970s. Putty-clay assumptions can easily be built into recursive models. My vote would be to include this feature in future versions of the B-G project. Without some such assumption, it is difficult to be optimistic over long-term price elasticities of demand – given that the U.S. energy/GNP ratio declined by only 15% between 1973 and 1980.

Now for some miscellaneous observations:

1. Capital–energy complementarity may be related directly to the putty-clay issue. On this basis, one could observe short-run complementarity without necessarily concluding that this implies long-term complementarity of the type postulated in the "central" case.

2. B-G employ a flexible-price Walrasian framework. This is an additional reason why they deal with long-term trends rather than short-term monetary and unemployment phenomena. Also because of the flexible-price assumption, B-G do not deal with price controls within the domestic energy supply sector.

3. The description of foreign trade is sketchy. Can the United States really "scale up" its total volume of exports so as to overcome trade balance difficulties? Moreover, there is a unitary elasticity of substitution between individual sector-of-origin components of the export vector.

The combination of these two assumptions may well lead to an underestimate of the terms-of-trade effects of rising energy prices.

4. It is supposed that each household has homothetic indifference curves for all items of current consumption. This implies unitary *income* elasticities of demand – and hence is inconsistent with the saturation phenomena that have been suggested in some of the empirical energy literature. With less than unitary income elasticities, energy excise taxes would be regressive. It is entirely possible that such taxes would be less regressive than some groups have claimed, but this conclusion should not be a built-in result directly from the model's structure. If B-G enter into future controversies over the distribution of real incomes, it would be advisable for them to adopt a form of utility function that is more flexible than the homothetic one employed here.

Despite misgivings over this or that specific feature, let me conclude on a highly positive note. B-G have initiated an ambitious project – describing energy–economic interactions far more comprehensively than most studies. Their model is transparent and can be cross-checked by others. Their work has the potential to be applied to a wide range of policy issues, and I look forward to seeing future products of their collaboration.

CHAPTER 9

A comparison of methodologies in empirical general equilibrium models of taxation

*Don Fullerton, Yolanda K. Henderson,
and John B. Shoven*

1 Introduction

Since Arnold Harberger (1962, 1966) introduced a general equilibrium model of taxation two decades ago, his approach has been amended for the study of many economic issues. This chapter is concerned with the methodology of one line of the descendants of the Harberger model: empirical models of government expenditures and taxes. We have chosen for comparison eight models that meet our criteria of "empirical" and "public finance." Although many small models, including Harberger's, have been outfitted with plausible parameters and used for policy analysis, we have focused on models that have greater disaggregation, either in the number of producers or consumers, or both. These models are large enough so that they require computers for their solution. We have restricted our comparison to models whose primary purpose is evaluation of fiscal reform, rather than, for example, international trade, economic development, or regional issues. Though tax policies undoubtedly are an integral part of some of these other models, they are associated with additional methodological issues that are outside the scope of this chapter.[1]

This chapter is primarily about methodologies. We look at how these empirical public finance models have generalized the Harberger method.

We have received helpful comments on an earlier draft from Alan Auerbach, Charles Ballard, Wouter Keller, Larry Kimbell, Laurence Kotlikoff, Peter Mieszkowski, Jaime Serra-Puche, Joel Slemrod, and Wayne Thrisk, as well as other participants in the conference. We would like to thank Thomas Kronmiller for research assistance. This material is based on work supported by the National Bureau of Economic Research and by the National Science Foundation under Grants Nos. SES8025404 and DAR8019616. Any opinions, findings, and conclusions or recommendations expressed in this chapter are those of the authors and do not necessarily reflect the views of NBER or the National Science Foundation.

We also look at differences among them in their specifications. Sometimes these variations are due to differences in applications of these models. When the models are used for evaluating similar reforms, however, we examine results to determine the implications of alternative specifications. More briefly, we discuss some extensions that appear imminent, as well as theoretical innovations that have not yet been incorporated into empirical general equilibrium models.

We view this comparison of empirical general equilibrium models of taxation as an exercise that might eventually be conducted jointly by the proprietors of these various models. The authors of the current chapter are associated with the Fullerton-Shoven-Whalley model and its extensions. As such, we are more knowledgeable about sensitivity experiments using our models, and also have been able to perform some new experiments specifically for this chapter. We have inferred sensitivity results for other models analytically by examining published results. We recognize that this is only a second-best approach. The design and execution of common simulations have been tried successfully by builders of macroeconometric models (see Fromm and Klein, 1976), but only in a preliminary way for models of tax incidence (see Devarajan, Fullerton, and Musgrave, 1980). We hope that we have identified areas here where joint ventures might provide further understanding of general equilibrium models.

The discussion starts with brief overviews of the Harberger model and our selected models.

2   Harberger model

The Harberger model has been expounded in many articles in addition to his own. These include Mieszkowski (1967, 1969), McLure (1975), and Atkinson and Stiglitz (1980, lecture 6). Here, we set out the assumptions verbally; the other sources may be used for an algebraic description. Harberger's model was designed to examine the interindustry distortion from the corporate income tax. He assigned industries to the corporate and noncorporate sectors based on whether they were "heavily" or "lightly" taxed, according to data of Rosenberg (1969) for the United States, 1953-59.[2] Harberger's noncorporate sector included agriculture, housing, and crude oil and gas, while his corporate sector included all others. Each sector produced a single output in perfect competition using homogeneous, perfectly mobile labor and capital, the supplies of which were fixed in the aggregate. Harberger's results on the burden of the corporate income tax depended in part on the substitutability of labor and capital in production. This "factor substitution effect" (Mieszkowski

1967) was due to the fact that the corporate income tax was viewed as a differential tax on capital income only. Harberger simulated his model under a variety of assumptions on the elasticity of substitution in each sector.

On the demand side, the model was simpler. There was only one consumer, so that Harberger was limited to analyzing the functional, but not the personal, distribution of income. The government was assumed to display the same preferences as the consumer in spending its tax revenues. This specification is formally equivalent to a model in which consumer preferences are homothetic and in which tax revenue is returned as a lump-sum subsidy. Thus, using Mieszkowski's terminology, there was no "demand effect" because the model did not have different consumers purchasing different bundles of goods. There was an "output effect," however, because the extra tax was on output of only the corporate sector. Each sector's output could have a different price elasticity of demand, and each output could have different factor intensities.[3] Harberger had data on factor intensities and used a range of assumptions about demand elasticities.

The solution technique involved total differentiation, so that, technically speaking, the model was appropriate only for small changes in the tax code. As originally formulated, the model assumed no preexisting tax distortions but this was amended by Ballentine and Eris (1975). Shoven (1976) corrected Harberger's model for conceptual errors in the measurement of the surtax, as well as arithmetic errors. The often-quoted outcome of all these studies was that capitalists bear the full burden of the corporate income tax. Harberger's estimate of the efficiency cost, corrected by Shoven, was between 6% and 15% of the revenue generated, or .3% to .6% of GNP.

3   Empirical general equilibrium models of taxation

The general techniques of Harberger were quickly applied in models that relaxed some of the restrictive assumptions. The empirical models in our study are further elaborations of these earlier extensions. Shoven and Whalley (1972, 1973) and Shoven (1976) used the Scarf simplicial search algorithm to solve disaggregated versions of the Harberger model. With this new computational technique, they could properly examine large changes in the corporate tax rate. Feldstein (1974a, 1974b, 1978) studied capital income tax incidence by comparing steady states in a one-sector model with variable factor supply, and Ballentine (1978) developed the dynamic (steady-state) counterpart to Harberger's two-sector model. Boadway (1979) examined transitions between steady states. In the area

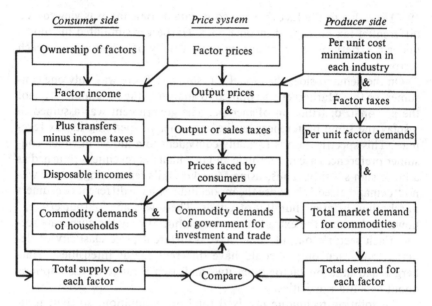

Figure 1. Diagram of a typical general equilibrium tax model. Competitive equilibrium is achieved when (1) demands equal supplies for all goods and factors; (2) zero profits (net of taxes) prevail in all industries; and (3) agents are on their budgets (e.g., total government expenditures equal receipts from taxes and from selling endowments of capital or "bonds").

of financial analysis, Feldstein and Slemrod (1980) examined the effects of the corporate income tax on portfolio allocation, and Feldstein, Green, and Sheshinski (1978) and Ballentine and McLure (1980) examined its effects on dividend payouts.

As might be expected, the results of these studies indicated a substantial range of answers on incidence of the corporate income tax. Particular findings will be mentioned below as we review specific features of applied general equilibrium models.

What is the profile of a "typical" applied general equilibrium model of taxation? Figure 1 provides an example. The prototypical model has several industrial sectors, in which fully mobile and homogeneous labor and capital are used in production in a profit-maximizing combination. There are several household groups, defined by income, that are endowed with labor and capital in varying amounts. These groups also derive income from government transfers. Households allocate their income across consumption goods according to principles of budget-constrained utility maximization. There are usually ad valorem taxes on incomes, factors, and outputs, and these enter into the appropriate production and consumption decisions. Equilibrium is reached when demand and supply are equal for all goods and factors. Generally, other features of the equilibrium are that producers receive no excess profits and that all agents are on their budget constraints. Solution for the equilibrium is accomplished by using a computer algorithm. Features such as endogenous factor supplies and financial assets are not part of the prototype model. As will be shown, none of the models in our survey adheres strictly to this blueprint.

The models included in our comparison are:

1. Piggott–Whalley (PW) (1976, 1982)
2. Fullerton–Shoven–Whalley (FSW) (1978, 1981,* 1983)
3. Ballentine–Thirsk (BT) (1979)
4. Keller (1980)
5. Serra-Puche (1979; Chapter 11, this book)
6. Slemrod (1980, 1983)
7. Fullerton–Gordon (FG) (1983)
8. Auerbach–Kotlikoff (AK) (1983)

The key features of these models are summarized in Table 1, which provides a structure for the discussion. The first five models in the list – those of Piggott and Whalley; Fullerton, Shoven, and Whalley; Ballentine and Thirsk; Keller; and Serra-Puche – are large, general-purpose models for different countries: the United Kingdom, the United States, Canada, the Netherlands, and Mexico, respectively. They each have considerable disaggregation of production and demand. They are designed to study a variety of taxes, transfers, and subsidies in addition to the corporate income tax. Despite these similarities, the authors have made different decisions on modeling factor mobility, aggregate factor supplies, budget balance, and the foreign sector.[4] They also employ different solution techniques.

The next two models, of Slemrod and of Fullerton and Gordon (an extension of the FSW model), are more fully specified than the previous models in the area of financial behavior. Yet they have interesting differences between them in how financial decisions are made by households and firms, in saving behavior, in disaggregation, and in parameter derivation. The FG model also differs from all the other models in that marginal tax rates on capital differ from average tax rates.[5]

The Auerbach–Kotlikoff model was designed for study of intergenerational incidence. It is also unique in its use of perfect foresight rather than myopic expectations.

*Fullerton, King, Shoven, and Whalley (1981).

Table 1. *Features of applied general equilibrium taxation models*

	Piggott–Whalley (1)	Fullerton–Shoven–Whalley (2)	Ballentine–Thirsk (3)	Keller (4)	Serra-Puche (5)	Slemrod (6)	Fullerton–Gordon (7)	Auerbach–Kotlikoff (8)
Country	U.K.	U.S.	Canada	Netherlands	Mexico	U.S.	U.S.	U.S.
Number of producers	33 CES	19 CES	7 CES	4 CES	14 Cobb–Douglas	4 Cobb–Douglas	19 CES	1 Cobb–Douglas
Number of consumers	100 Groups by occupation and income	12 Income groups	12 Income groups	2 Income groups	10 Income groups (urban & rural)	9 Income groups	12 Income groups	55 Age cohorts
Solution technique	Newton method	Merrill's algorithm	Linear approximation	Linear approximation	Merrill's algorithm	Gauss–Seidel iteration	Merrill's algorithm	Gauss–Seidel iteration
Year(s) of data	1973	1973	1969	1973	1977	1962/1977	1973	Plausible/hypothetical
Parameter deviation	Backward solution, exogenous parameters, and some separate estimation	Backward solution with selected exogenous parameters	Backward solution and sensitivity analysis	By assumption and backward solution	Backward solution	Plausible exogenous parameters with some backward solution	Backward solution, exogenous parameters, and some separate estimation	By assumption and sensitivity analysis

Factors of production	K, L, each mobile and homogeneous	K, L, each mobile and homogeneous	K, L, each mobile and homogeneous; land used in two sectors	K, skilled labor, unskilled labor, imports	K, rural labor, urban labor	K, L, each mobile and homogeneous, but risk varies by use	K, L, each mobile and homogeneous, but risk varies by use	K, L, each homogeneous (one sector)
Input–output matrix	Yes	Yes	Yes	Yes	Yes	No	Yes	No
Labor–leisure choice	Yes	Yes	No	Yes	No	No	Yes	No
Time path	Static equilibria only	Sequence of static equilibria	Static equilibria only	Static equilibria only	Static equilibria only	Static equilibria only	Sequence of static equilibria	Simultaneous solution for 200 years
Endogenous capital stock	Saving endogenous, K fixed in static calculation	Not in one period, but saving augments K through time	Fixed domestic capital, variable use of foreign capital	Saving endogenous, K fixed in static calculation	Saving endogenous, K fixed in static calculation	Fixed total capital	Not in one period, but saving augments K through time	Growing endogenously over time
Foresight/expectations	Myopic	Myopic	(No saving)	Fixed marginal propensity to save	Myopic	(No saving)	Myopic	Perfect

373

Table 1 *(cont.)*

	Piggott-Whalley (1)	Fullerton-Shoven-Whalley (2)	Ballentine-Thirsk (3)	Keller (4)	Serra-Puche (5)	Slemrod (6)	Fullerton-Gordon (7)	Auerbach-Kotlikoff (8)
Differing portfolios	In the data, yes; in the model, no	In the data, yes; in the model, no	No	In the data, yes; in the model, no	No	Different returns on 6 financial and real assets based on portfolio demands	Same as FSW, but tax rates on different assets reflect different portfolios	No
Risk	No separate risk premiums, all returns certain	No separate risk premiums, all returns certain	No separate risk premiums, all returns certain	No separate risk premiums, all returns certain	No separate risk premiums, all returns certain	Explicit variance in rates of return	Separate risk premiums dependent on asset and industry	No separate risk premiums, all returns certain
Government budget	Balanced, can calculate Lindahl solution	Balanced each period	Balanced	Balanced	Deficits allowed with government bonds	Balanced	Balanced each period	PV of expenditures = PV of revenue - initial debt (not balanced each period)
Equal tax yield	Allowed through broad-based sales tax	Allowed through lump-sum taxes or increased personal rates	Allowed through adjusting any rate	No; allows changed government spending	No	Allowed through increased personal rates	Allowed through lump-sum taxes or increased personal rates	Allowed through adjusting any rate

Taxes included	All major U.K. taxes and subsidies	All U.S. taxes	All major Canadian taxes and subsidies	Linear income tax, factor taxes, sales taxes	Income taxes, sales tax, VAT, tariffs	Corporate and personal income tax, property tax	All U.S. taxes	Capital tax, labor tax, consumption tax
Bankruptcy costs	No	No	No	No	No	No	Yes	No
Foreign sector	Balanced trade with Armington assumption	Balanced trade with constant elasticity	Imports and exports are distinct goods; balanced trade with flow of K	Foreign household sells distinct good (fixed world prices); balanced trade with flow of K	Unbalanced trade, but exogenous	None	Balanced trade, constant real value of trade in each good	None
Imperfect competition	No	No	No	No	No	No	No	No
Monetary policy	No	No	No	No	No	Liquid asset is a use of K	No	No
Involuntary unemployment	No	No	No	No	No	No	No	No
Policies evaluated	Housing subsidies, VAT, overall effects of each tax	Integration, consumption tax, VAT, capital or labor tax changes	Housing subsidies, intergovernmental grants	Changes in VAT, import levies, factor taxes, overall effects	VAT	Integration, effects of inflation	Integration	Consumption tax, capital vs. labor taxation

Table 1 *(cont.)*

	Piggott–Whalley (1)	Fullerton–Shoven–Whalley (2)	Ballentine–Thirsk (3)	Keller (4)	Serra-Puche (5)	Slemrod (6)	Fullerton–Gordon (7)	Auerbach–Kotlikoff (8)
Distributional effects	Calculates CV, EV, Gini coefficients, Atkinson measure social welfare	Changes to current income with Paasche or Laspeyres indices, CV or EV from static utility	Change to current income	Compensating and equivalent variations	Changes in utility measures	Changes to utility measures, based on current income and risk bearing	Same as FSW but not reported	Among age cohorts using utility measure
Efficiency effects:								
Intersectoral	Yes	Yes	Yes	Yes	Yes	Yes	Yes	No
Intertemporal	No	Yes	No	No	No	No	Yes	Yes
Debt/equity	No	No	No	No	No	Adjustments, but no efficiency loss of distortion	Yes	No
Dividend payout	No	No	No	No	No	Adjustments, but no efficiency loss of distortion	"Measured" at zero	No

376

4 Model comparisons

The remainder of the chapter is organized by methodological areas in which the applied models have contributed to the tax incidence literature. We review in turn: disaggregation, specification of the foreign sector, financial modeling, the measurement of effective tax rates, heterogeneity and imperfect mobility, factor supply, treatment of the government budget, and technical issues associated with implementation.

4.1 *Disaggregation*

a. *Production sectors:* The applied general equilibrium taxation models use disaggregated data on both production and consumption. We can delineate two levels of disaggregation of the production data: medium, including Slemrod (4 sectors), Keller (4), BT (7 domestic plus 1 foreign), and high, including FSW (19), Serra-Puche (14), PW (33 domestic plus 27 foreign). The AK model, designed to evaluate taxes on consumption and labor income, has no disaggregation of production.

Slemrod and BT preserved Harberger's specification of a homogeneous corporate sector, though each has refined the definition somewhat. For example, Slemrod correctly observed that the crude oil and gas industry is largely corporate despite its low rate of capital taxation. Each also disaggregated the noncorporate sector further. Slemrod's breakdown was composed of agriculture[6] and two types of housing, owner-occupied and rental. Because imputed rents and capital gains in the owner-occupied housing sector are virtually untaxed, there is a subsidy that causes misallocation of resources within housing and that is aggravated by inflation. BT separated out agriculture, as well as a homogeneous housing sector. Because of their interest in government expenditure programs, they distinguished urban transit services and local public services from other services. There are separate import and export sectors, as discussed in Section 4.2 below.

The FSW and PW models have disaggregation by industry, with each industry representing a fixed mix of corporate and noncorporate enterprises. With this specification, the effects of the corporate income tax are modeled directly. FSW, for example, have simulated elimination of taxation at the corporate level by deleting this component of capital income taxation in each industry and assigning corporate profits to taxation at the household level. This is in contrast to the Harberger approach, which equalized taxes in the corporate and noncorporate sectors. Tax rates differ from industry to industry not only because of the extent of incorporation, but also because of the differential tax reductions from investment tax credits and depreciation allowances.

The U.K. tax system, by contrast, has provided substantial relief from double taxation of dividends since 1973, when a partial integration measure was introduced. The advantage of disaggregation by industry in the PW model lies instead in the ability to evaluate specific capital subsidies, such as regional development grants and borrowing subsidies to nationalized industries.

These two models (FSW, PW) may be compared with the previous two (Slemrod, BT) with respect to housing and the foreign sector. The FSW model does not disaggregate the housing sector. The PW model, on the other hand, has private housing services and public (local authority) housing services. The latter category consists of subsidized rental housing and accounts for the majority of the rental housing stock in the United Kingdom. This ad valorem rent subsidy causes misallocation of resources.

Most industries in the PW model are composed of competing domestic and foreign producers, each subject to different tax rules. This treatment is described in Section 4.2 below.

b. *The benefits from disaggregation of production:* The foregoing description has shown that the applied general equilibrium models have disaggregated the Harberger sectors in many ways. In this section, we examine which degree of disaggregation is necessary on the grounds that Harberger argued were important, namely differences in tax rates, capital intensity, consumer price elasticities of demand for outputs, and degrees of factor substitution. We then take advantage of a feature of the FSW model that allows the level of aggregation to be changed. We use this feature to measure the importance of disaggregation in simulations of integration of corporate and personal income taxes.

The evidence on disaggregation appears to be that the "first-level" disaggregation – to a corporate sector, housing, and agriculture – is worthwhile because of differences in factor intensities. Further disaggregation of production is justified on other grounds, especially the existence of different tax rates by industry.

The disaggregated models show that production of housing services is by far the most capital-intensive industry. Other industries that rank fairly high in capital intensity are agriculture (in FSW and PW), utilities (in PW), and paper and printing and mining (in FSW).

In general, the evidence on demand elasticities for outputs and factors is not robust enough to point to significant interindustry differences. The FSW and Slemrod models assume Cobb-Douglas demands, so that, within an income class, relative expenditures on consumption goods are constant. Even though BT assume differential price elasticities, they conclude that the combined effects from capital/labor ratios and consumer demands generally produce a weak output effect. The one exception occurs when the relative price of land changes, since land is assumed to be used in only some sectors. The PW model has two layers of substitution elasticities among domestic goods. The elasticity of substitution between similar consumption items, such as coal and gas, is generally higher than the substitution between their aggregate and other "blocks" of goods. The elasticity of substitution between each pair of "blocks" is the same, one-half. Keller has similar blocking of commodities. In light of the BT findings, however, these differences in consumer demand elasticities may not be very important.

On the substitutability of capital for labor in production, Slemrod assumes Cobb–Douglas functions. The FSW, BT, and PW models use constant elasticity of substitution (CES) production functions, but the elasticities are close to 1 for most industries.[7] The most dramatic departure from this pattern is in housing, where Slemrod assumed that only capital is used in production, and where BT and PW posited a very low elasticity of substitution between capital and labor. There is another production-based argument for separating out housing and agriculture in the BT model, because land is a separate factor of production and is used only in these industries.

We turn next to our experiments with disaggregation of production. In the first part of Table 2, we review the results of Shoven (1976), who corrected two errors of Harberger (1966). He then applied the algorithmic approach to Harberger's 2-sector model and an alternative 12-sector model. When Harberger's simple arithmetic error was corrected, the efficiency gain from capital tax rate equalization was reduced. When his conceptual error on the definition of capital units was corrected, however, the efficiency gain estimate was increased approximately back to the original estimate. These corrected Harberger estimates are shown in row 1 of Table 2.

Row 2 shows that when the same data are used in the algorithmic approach, rather than the linear approximation, welfare gain estimates are changed only slightly. Row 3 shows that disaggregating the data to 12 producers has the effect of raising the estimate. This result can be explained intuitively as follows. The 2-sector model captures only the misallocation of capital between the two sectors, not within each sector. If the corporate sector is disaggregated into some high-tax industries and other relatively low-tax industries, as is possible with a 12-sector model, then further misallocations can be captured. Welfare gains from elimi-

Table 2. *Disaggregation experiments*

Elimination of surtax in the corporate sector

	Efficiency gain	
Model	$ Billions (1957)	% of NNP
1. Corrected Harberger model, 2 sectors	.625–1.79	.3–.6
2. Shoven–Whalley model using Scarf algorithm; 2 sectors and 2 consumers	.69–1.49	.3–.5
3. Shoven–Whalley model using Scarf algorithm; 12 sectors and 2 consumers	.92–2.11	.4–.7

Integration of the corporate and personal income tax

	"Dynamic" efficiency gain		"Static" efficiency gain	
Model	$ Billions (1973)	% of PV income	$ Billions (1973)	% of Expanded income
4. FSW model, 2 sectors (A)	87.8	.176	− 1.77	− .10
5. FSW model, 2 sectors (B)	219.8	.441	.79	.05
6. FSW model, 5 sectors	251.0	.503	.27	.02
7. FSW model, 19 sectors	344.4	.691	2.34	.14

Note: See text for further description. Rows 1–3 are taken from Shoven (1976). NNP = net national product; PV = present value.

nating these misallocations will be greater. A proof that welfare gains must increase with disaggregation for a policy that equalizes capital tax rates is given in Shoven (1973).

In the second part of Table 2, we display results from new simulations with the FSW model. These results are not really comparable to the earlier Shoven (1976) results, because the model is quite different. The "dynamic" efficiency gains refer to the present value of the sum of 12 consumers' compensating variations. This concept captures both intertemporal and intersectoral distortions, each of which is reduced through the integration of personal and corporate taxes. The "static" efficiency gains refer to the mean of Paasche and Laspeyres measures for the change in expanded national income (including leisure valued at the net-of-tax wage).

The two parts of Table 2 are also not comparable because full integration does not imply complete capital tax equalization. Some other tax distortions remain, including the low taxation of real estate caused by the nontaxable nature of imputed owner-occupant net rents. Integration is, however, comparable to the policy proposals simulated in some of the other models reviewed here. Integration, as we have defined it, includes the elimination of the corporate income tax, the full taxation of corporate income at the personal level, and the indexing of capital gains for inflation.[8] Table 3 shows the wide variation of the 19 capital tax rates of the FSW model before any policy change, as well as the lower and less varying capital tax rates implied by full integration.

Row 7 of Table 2 shows the results of integration for the full-sized (19-sector) FSW model. Static welfare gains as a percentage of income are much lower than for Shoven (1976) for at least two reasons. First, capital tax rates are not completely equalized as just discussed. Second, and more important, this model uses an equal-yield feature that increases personal tax rates multiplicatively until government can attain the same utility level as in the benchmark. Because all 12 personal tax rates are multiplied by the factor 1.16 in the new equilibrium, labor–leisure choices are further distorted. Welfare losses on that margin offset the gains from capital allocation improvements. The dynamic measure includes the same offsetting effect but also includes the gains on the intertemporal margin from capital tax reductions.

We are now prepared to address the following question: How much of the difference between the FSW results and other results are due to disaggregation in production? Our experiments make use of a variable aggregation procedure designed and built for the FSW model by Lawrence Goulder. We first aggregate to the two sectors defined by Harberger (and used by Shoven). In this two-sector model, called version A in the tables, the first sector includes agriculture, crude petroleum, and real estate, while the other sector includes all other private industry. Harberger divided the economy this way because the first sector was supposed to represent low-taxed industries.[9]

Our Table 3 shows that approximately the same ordering exists in the 1973 data set for the FSW model, except that the tax rate for petroleum refining is even lower than that for agriculture. This data set also includes "government enterprises" as an industry that was not considered in the 1957 data of Rosenberg (1969). This sector also has a very low tax rate on capital.

It thus makes sense to add petroleum refining and government enterprises to the low-tax sector, and we refer to this two-sector model as version B. The bottom of Table 3 shows that the selection of industries for

Table 3. *Capital tax rates (on net income) before and after integration,*
for each aggregation

	Capital tax rate	
Industry	Before	After
19 Industries		
1. Agriculture	.54	.46
2. Mining	.95	.71
3. Crude petroleum and gas	1.02	.70
4. Construction	2.10	.68
5. Food and tobacco	3.47	.88
6. Textile, apparel, and leather	2.53	.75
7. Paper and printing	1.63	.63
8. Petroleum refining	.46	.44
9. Chemicals and rubber	1.87	.60
10. Lumber, furniture, stone	.91	.52
11. Metals and machinery	1.72	.66
12. Transportation equipment	23.50	4.88
13. Motor vehicles	1.29	.47
14. Transportation, comm., util.	1.70	.89
15. Trade	1.85	.83
16. Finance and insurance	1.99	1.35
17. Real estate	.63	.56
18. Services	.86	.57
19. Government enterprises	.26	.26
(Weighted average)	.97	.61
5 Industries		
Agriculture	.54	.46
Real estate	.63	.56
Services	.86	.57
Government enterprises	.26	.26
All others	1.57	.76
(Weighted average)	.97	.61
2 Industries, version A		
Agric., crude pet., real estate (1,3,17)	.61	.54
All others	1.37	.69
(Weighted average)	.97	.61
2 Industries, version B		
Agric., crude, refined pet., real estate, gov't. ent. (1,3,8,17,19)	.58	.51
All others	1.62	.77
(Weighted average)	.97	.61

a two-sector model is very important. Benchmark capital tax rates for version A, corresponding to the Harberger aggregation, are considerably closer together than are the tax rates for version B. Equalization or integration cannot be expected to provide as great a gain in efficiency, especially since these distortions vary with the square of the surtax.

The efficiency gain results in rows 4 and 5 of Table 2 bear this out. Welfare gains from the "Harberger aggregation" are considerably smaller than from version B where the industries are more appropriately grouped.[10]

Next we aggregate the FSW model into groups of industries that are similar to the models of Slemrod (1983) and Keller (1980). Those models use four industries corresponding to agriculture, real estate, services, and other "corporate" industries.[11] We also break out government enterprises as a fifth industry, since this activity is not similar to other corporate activities. When this model is used to simulate integration, the welfare effects are shown in row 6 of Table 2.

Compare the dynamic measure for the "correct" 2-sector model of version B, the 5-sector model, and the 19-sector model. This measure increases from $220 billion (in 1973 dollars) to $251 billion, and to $344 billion, respectively. It would seem from this evidence that the 5-sector model does not do much to improve upon the 2-sector model. Indeed, when we look at the capital tax rates of Table 3, we see that the rates for the three private "noncorporate" industries are quite similar (.54, .63, .86) in the benchmark equilibrium. If the point of disaggregation is to capture differing effective tax rates, this is not the place to do it. The top of Table 3 reveals that there is more variance of tax rates among the industries of the corporate sector. This contrast explains the further change in welfare estimates from disaggregating to 19 industries. It is difficult to say whether further disaggregation would be warranted.

c. *Disaggregation of households:* Most of the applied general equilibrium models have disaggregated households by income class. A couple have also distinguished households by age, occupation, and family composition. In this section we survey what differences there are in the sources and uses of income by these classes and what additional insights may be gleaned by this disaggregation. The information on disaggregation is relevant not only for the basic tax structure that is under review, but also for the financing of the tax change, which may now have distributional effects as well.

The BT, FSW, Serra-Puche, and Slemrod models divide households into about a dozen groups by incomes. Serra-Puche distinguishes between urban and rural groups. Piggott and Whalley have 100 groupings by income, family composition, occupation, and work status. The latter two categories specify whether a household head is not employed, retired, or working in one of the following three occupations: manual employee, nonmanual employee, or self-employed. The Auerbach–Kotlikoff model has 55 age cohorts. During its working years, each cohort's wage grows at the fixed rate of increase of labor productivity; upon retirement, income consists of earnings from previous saving.

Where there is a progressive income tax, the range of marginal income tax rates may be taken as one indication of the degree and pattern of disaggregation of households by income. Comparing the FSW and Slemrod models of the United States, we see that the first disaggregates more finely at the low end of the scale, whereas the latter disaggregates more at the high end. The ranges of marginal tax rates in these models are 1–41% and 14–82%, respectively. This pattern corresponds to the emphasis of the Slemrod model on portfolio behavior; the distribution of wealth is more concentrated at the top than is income. Consumption data for very-high-income groups, by contrast, are not available, and were imputed in Slemrod's study. Slemrod's data on tax rates also reflects the tax law prior to the Revenue Act of 1964.

The use of marginal tax rates is less satisfactory for comparing the levels of disaggregation in models of different countries, since personal tax systems differ significantly. We can, however, compare incomes for the lowest and highest groups relative to the group with median income and look at the numbers of groups below and above the median income level. By these measures, the BT model's pattern of aggregation is roughly similar to that of the FSW model.[12]

We turn now to evidence on the difference among household groups in the sources and uses of income. On the factoral distribution of income, all the models with disaggregation only by income show a similar U-shaped pattern for the capital/labor ratio of income: The lowest- and highest-income groups receive the highest shares of their income from capital. Slemrod's data indicate that the very rich, those with income over $50,000 in 1962, derived almost all of their earnings from capital. For the low-income group, the data reflect the earnings pattern of retired persons. On this last point, the PW data are more specific. At least for the United Kingdom (and the range of incomes PW consider), the capital share of income is very high for retired persons[13] and self-employed persons. The differences among income groups within an occupation are in fact much less obvious. The AK model, with its stylized income pattern across households, has the capital income share rising monotonically with age.

There are two aspects to the uses side of household behavior: allocation to consumption categories and allocation to saving categories. For consumption, the models indicate that expenditure shares on food and housing each decline markedly with income. Expenditures on services, on the other hand, tend to rise somewhat with income. These patterns leave a progressive profile of consumption of manufactured products, which are produced by heavily corporate industries. The evidence on consumption, then, supports disaggregation of the production sectors into agriculture, housing, and other.

While consumption data support some disaggregation of income groups, a stronger argument for disaggregation may be made in models that have portfolio behavior. Slemrod's data show tremendous variation in asset holdings by income groups. In version B of his model, Slemrod distinguished six assets: corporate equity, taxable and tax-exempt debt, rental and owner-occupied housing, and liquid assets. The portfolio of the lowest group is about 70% in owner-occupied housing and liquid assets, whereas for the top group it is almost entirely in corporate equity and tax-exempt debt. Owner-occupied housing is the most important single asset for households with incomes under $25,000 (in 1962 dollars).

4.2   Foreign sector

The general equilibrium approach has long been used in models of international trade. Boadway and Treddenick (1978) extended this literature in modeling the effects of tariff policies on the allocation of resources across domestic industries. International trade is now part of the FSW model of the United States, as described in Goulder, Shoven, and Whalley (1983),[14] and of all the models that we review of other developed countries. All these models feature some form of balanced international trade, which sometimes refers just to net exports of goods and services, and sometimes encompasses capital flows as well. No models include flows of international reserves or a role for monetary policy.

Even within the area of commodity flows, there has been unexpected variation in modeling exports and imports. This may be due to data limitations in different countries. In the BT model, imports are aggregated to form one good and are considered to be imperfect substitutes for all other consumption goods. In Keller's model, imports are quasi-intermediate: Producing output involves substituting among domestically produced goods and foreign-produced goods as inputs. In PW, there is an explicit distinction between imports used for intermediate inputs and for final consumption. Consumers have CES demand functions between pairs of competing domestic and foreign goods, whereas intermediate imports are used in fixed proportions in production.

The treatment of exports is somewhat more uniform. In most cases, trade elasticities govern what fraction of a sector's output will be exported. In the Ballentine and Thirsk model, however, export production takes place in two export sectors, one of which is a price-taker in supply and the other of which has some market power in international trade.

These differing specifications make parameterization of elasticities of substitution difficult. Often the simplifications used in modeling do not correspond to the specifications in other empirical studies that are used to provide parameters (see Section 4.8a for a discussion of parameterization). In this situation, performing tests of alternative assumptions is important.

The model of the foreign sector is critical in evaluating changes from an origin-based tax to a destination-based tax, or vice versa. The corporate income tax is an example of the former: It is collected in the production of goods used for export but not for import. On the other hand, the value-added tax is generally rebated on exports and applied to imports. Shifts from one to the other could cause large changes in import and export prices and, depending upon trade elasticities, large changes in net exports. PW (for the U.K.) and Goulder, Shoven, and Whalley (for the U.S.) found that movements in terms of trade caused significant welfare changes.

Endogenizing capital flows may significantly change the evaluation of changing capital taxes, as Goulder, Shoven, and Whalley found for the United States. They estimated that the domestic welfare gain from corporate tax integration would be significantly increased if there were a fluid world capital market. The reduced tax would attract additional capital for which the U.S. economy would pay only the world net-of-tax rate of return to capital. However, the U.S. social benefits are equal to the gross of tax productivity of capital. On the other hand, Goulder, Shoven, and Whalley found that a world capital market may reduce the attractiveness of a consumption tax. In Section 4.5, we discuss some implications of the one-way capital flows assumed in the BT model.

4.3   Financial behavior

The aspects of general equilibrium tax models discussed so far have highlighted their use in studying intersectoral distortions. Models with financial behavior may be used for analysis of three additional distortions caused by personal and corporate income taxes. These are inefficiency in portfolio allocation, in the choice between debt and equity finance, and in dividend payout rates.

The general equilibrium tradition has been to define a unit of capital as that which earns one dollar net of all taxes in any use. Feldstein and Slemrod (1980) pointed out, however, that the income tax system in the United States leads to differences in net-of-tax earnings from capital in different uses and for different owners. As an example, take two individuals in different tax brackets, each of whom owns an unincorporated business in the same industry. Their gross returns would be identical, but the individual in the lower income bracket would earn a higher net rate of return. Feldstein and Slemrod have shown, on the other hand, that investment in the corporate sector is relatively more attractive – compared to investment in the noncorporate sector – for individuals in higher-income brackets. It is relatively less attractive for lower-income groups. Differences in these returns cause inefficiency in risk bearing. In addition, because these two types of capital are observed to be held by both income groups, a comparison of expected rates of return is not sufficient to describe portfolio behavior. Slemrod has incorporated these observations in his model. Capital is measured according to stocks, not capital income. Individuals make their portfolio choices by balancing off expected net rates of return against variances in returns.

Modeling portfolio choice is useful in examining the effects of income tax integration. This reform would make the after-tax rates of return in the corporate and noncorporate sectors more equal. Because of the initial discrepancies in these rates for different income classes, the tax reform would cause different shifts in asset holdings by income class. This finding is discussed in Section 4.5.

Another application of general equilibrium tax models that is affected by portfolios is the study of the effects of inflation on capital allocation. The deductibility of nominal interest payments from personal income tax liabilities provides a larger incentive for upper-income groups to leverage their investments. Reforms such as indexing for inflation would lower inefficiency caused by this discriminatory incentive to bear risk.

Corporate financial behavior has been modeled by Slemrod and by Fullerton and Gordon. The corporate income tax encourages debt rather than equity finance because of the deductibility of interest payments on debt but not of payments to shareholders. The personal income tax system taxes capital gains and dividends differently. For most holders of corporate equity, capital gains are taxed more lightly. This encourages firms to retain earnings rather than to pay out dividends.

Slemrod has modeled endogenous financial behavior by specifying that firms vary debt/equity ratios and dividend payout ratios in response to tax differentials. These response rates were taken from regression analysis. In his simulations of tax integration and indexing, the distortions in financing behavior turned out to be of secondary importance relative to the distortions in portfolio behavior.

Fullerton and Gordon have proceeded differently. By examining the marginal after-tax returns to investors from debt and equity finance, they concluded that investors as a group could save on taxes by any increases in the firm's debt/capital ratio. Offsetting this tax advantage of debt, however, a higher debt/capital ratio would imply a higher probability of default. Thus they modeled the firm's financing decision as a tradeoff between tax advantages and bankruptcy costs. Their simulation results indicated that this distortion in debt/equity choices accounts for a large efficiency loss. Motivated by the uncertainty of economic explanations for dividend behavior, on the other hand, FG posited that dividend payout rates were immaterial by assuming that in equilibrium the firm must value a dollar of dividends at the margin the same as a dollar of retentions.

Although the addition of endogenous financial behavior has enriched the study of distortions resulting from income taxes, it has also added to data collection problems. For the United States, the last comprehensive study of asset behavior was the 1962 Federal Reserve Survey of Consumer Finances. These data do not provide information on how portfolios are allocated when there is high inflation. This is particularly unfortunate because one of the purposes of adding endogenous financial behavior is to measure how the interaction of nonindexed taxation of capital and high inflation has affected financial decisions. The importance of distortions to financial behavior, indicated by Slemrod and FG, however, supports continued modeling efforts in this direction.

4.4   *Measurement of effective tax rates*

In modeling a country's tax code, there is the issue of whether average tax rates on income apply also at the margin. More generally, modelers face the problem of how to measure effective tax rates. These concerns arise both for the personal tax system and the corporate tax system.

Under a progressive personal income tax structure, marginal tax rates will be higher than average tax rates, and both will be higher at higher levels of income. To capture the progressivity of the personal income tax, some models (FSW, PW, Slemrod) treat the tax as a separate linear function of income for each household group. Under this treatment, however, each household faces a marginal tax rate that is unchanging even if simulations of a policy change show a redistribution of income. Slemrod

(1983) has gone on to endogenize the marginal tax rate, a significant modeling improvement. In his model, households make portfolio choices on the basis of the real after-tax rate of return to each asset, as well as its riskiness. The taxable income from each asset depends on provisions such as the taxation of nominal instead of real gains, the use of historical cost depreciation, and the tax-exempt status of some bonds. Taxable income is determined on the basis of the assets that are selected by the household. It may also be affected by other aspects of the simulation that tend to redistribute income. In the end, the marginal tax rate is calculated by applying an approximation of actual tax tables to the household's computed taxable income.

There are further reasons why average and marginal personal income tax rates may differ. For example, transfer payments, through their eligibility requirements, may impose an implicit high marginal tax rate on labor income. The extent of tax evasion may vary with the level of marginal tax rates. These are propositions that have arisen in the economics literature, but that have not been included in the general equilibrium models covered in our survey.

It is possible to model differences in average and marginal household tax rates even apart from the income tax. For example, property tax payments and contributions to public pensions may be nondistorting to the extent that they are payments for benefits received from the government, in the form of local public services and retirement income, respectively. The Fullerton–Gordon model includes such treatment.

The measurement of marginal income tax rates for industries is, if anything, more problematic. All models with the exception of that of Fullerton and Gordon assume that the average tax rate on capital income in each sector applies also at the margin. In most cases, the industry's total observed tax paid is divided by observed capital income to obtain a tax rate for use in the producer's decision of whether to employ the next unit of capital.

This procedure greatly simplifies the data requirements as well as the model itself. Average tax rates provide a relatively simple and complete summary of the actual tax law. They capture the low tax payments attributable to investment tax credits, accelerated depreciation allowances, and depletion, and they capture the high tax payments attributable to insufficient depreciation allowances based on historical cost when there is inflation. Average tax rates also capture the effects of many complex details of the tax law, such as export subsidies, treatment of financial intermediaries, and possibilities for alternative accounting practices. In contrast, use of marginal tax rates requires explicit treatment of indi-

vidual features of the tax code. In practice, therefore, marginal tax rates
have provided a measure of the tax that might be expected by looking at
a few major statutes. Because actual marginal tax rates are not observable, and because there are a variety of ways of incorporating a variety of
features of the tax law, correct measurement of marginal tax rates has
not been agreed upon.

The procedure of using observed tax rates as incentive tax rates, however, assumes away a number of reasons why average and marginal tax
rates might differ. First, the marginal investment may be financed by a
composition of debt and equity that is different from the composition of
previous investment. If these sources of finance are taxed differently,
then the average and marginal investments are taxed differently. Second,
unanticipated inflation reduces the real value of depreciation allowances
on past investments without necessarily affecting the expected real value
of depreciation allowances on the current marginal investment. Jorgenson and Sullivan (1981) argued that recent inflation rates have been
higher than expected in the United States, and have acted as a lump-sum
tax on investments already in place. Third, the average tax rate mixes investments with different tax treatments. The FSW average tax rates from
1973, for example, include taxes paid on some investments that were
made before the 1971 liberalization of depreciation allowances, whereas
the marginal rate in 1973 should reflect only the then-current law. Fourth,
transitory or windfall profits on past investments are subject to the statutory corporate tax rate, whereas the expected normal return to the marginal investment is affected also by investment tax credits and accelerated
depreciation allowances. Fifth, firms may have reasons unrelated to the
marginal investment for using charitable deductions, FIFO accounting,
longer-than-minimum asset lives, and other features affecting the average tax rate without necessarily affecting the marginal tax rate. Finally, if
some of the return to capital is treated as a risk premium, and if losses on
the marginal investment can be used to offset profits on other investments, then the corporate tax can be viewed as risk sharing by the government. As such, at least part of the tax receipts would not reflect any
marginal investment disincentives. Fullerton and Gordon have argued
that marginal tax rates are considerably less than average tax rates for
this reason.

Fullerton and Henderson (1981) estimated marginal tax rates for the
18 private industries of the FSW model, ignoring risk and using cost-of-
capital formulas similar to those of Hall and Jorgenson (1967). Just the
first five points above are sufficient to eliminate any similarity between
the average tax rates and these marginal rates. Using different formulations of the average tax rates from Commerce Department data and dif-

ferent formulations of the marginal tax rates from cost-of-capital formulas, Fullerton and Henderson obtained correlation coefficients that varied around zero and never exceeded .3.

Fullerton and Gordon used a more complicated version of the same cost-of-capital approach. Noting that the 7% government bill rate in 1973 included some inflation risk if not default risk, they started with 5% as the nominal risk-free rate of return. Since the actual (and possibly expected) inflation rate was 6%, the real risk-free return may have been zero or negative. Thus the total return to equity is a risk premium and essentially all of the corporate tax becomes nondistorting. The tax is related to benefits in that, with full loss offsets, the tax payments are just proper compensation to government for accepting a fraction of the risk. It is perhaps not surprising that when FG simulated the removal of this corporate tax, together with a yield-preserving increase in the personal income tax (which distorts labor–leisure decisions at the margin), they found resultant welfare losses.

A couple of objections have been raised to this modeling. First, corporate profits in the United States have always been positive since the end of the Great Depression. If there is no significant risk of negative corporate profits, then at least some positive part of the return must be risk-free. This point really raises some inconsistencies among the various sets of data and available theories. For if some positive part of corporate profits is a real risk-free return, and if investors can arbitrage, then why would the government bill rate provide a zero or negative real return? Fullerton and Gordon reparameterized their model with a small positive risk-free return and obtained substantially the same results as before.

Second, Bulow and Summers (1982) came to conclusions that are very different from those of Fullerton and Gordon when they considered risk, corporate profits, and the corporate income tax. They argued that most of the investment risk is not in the income flow from the investment. Rather, it is from recapitalizations of that income stream or from changes in stock and bond prices that result in capital gains or losses to the investor. The corporate income tax does not offset these price changes. Depreciation allowances, for example, are not adjusted for ex post changes in the value of the capital stock. Since these unexpected accrued capital gains are not subject to the same corporate tax rate, and unexpected accrued capital losses do not have the same loss offset, the FG story does not apply. The corporate tax does not reduce this important source of risk. Bulow and Summers concluded that the efficiency cost of the corporation income tax is close to what might be predicted from a model with marginal tax rates that are, on the whole, as high as average tax rates.

Our own conclusion, then, is that the FG model opens up the important possibility of different average and marginal tax rates. The data to implement that capability, however, are still subject to dispute.

4.5   Heterogeneity and imperfect mobility

Harberger introduced a framework in which capital and labor are each homogeneous, mobile across industries, and fixed in total supply. As general equilibrium models are increasingly applied to policy issues, this specification becomes less helpful in analyzing tax incidence, particularly over time. There has been relatively little improvement in this area, however, in the empirical general equilibrium models. The assumption that capital moves from industry to industry more quickly than it is added in the aggregate, for example, is a convenient though not compelling assumption in all the models. The PW model has households disaggregated by occupation, on the one hand, but, on the other hand, has labor being homogeneous and fully mobile in production. These examples of anomalous specifications should be viewed as temporary compromises along the path of development of these models. Some have modestly relaxed the homogeneity assumptions. Specifically, Keller has two different skill types for labor, Serra-Puche has both rural and urban labor, and BT include land as a separate factor of production.

In this section, we examine several attempts to relax assumptions of perfect mobility and homogeneity of factors. The examples here are quite diverse and include problems of time and geography. Although introduction of constraints affects efficiency gains, we show that this type of innovation is particularly instructive in analyzing incidence.

There are two very different studies that concern time constraints: AK's examination of rigidity of lifetime patterns of work and retirement and Fullerton's (1983) modeling of constraints in reallocation of capital across industries during finite time periods. The AK model has been applied to the study of replacement of an income tax by a wage tax and by a consumption tax. Their model traces the effects on 55 age cohorts and is particularly insightful in tracing the effects on different cohorts in the transition to the steady state, which they estimate takes about 40 years. Because the wage and consumption tax structures would have different effects on workers as opposed to retirees, and because cohorts are not mobile between these two occupational categories, these taxes would impose different burdens on different cohorts. Retirees, for example, would be worse off under a consumption tax than under an income tax of equal yield in present-value terms because the overall tax rate would have to be higher under the consumption tax. Conversely, retirees would be better off under the wage tax, since most of their income is derived from capital. On the other hand, some younger cohorts would lose in the transition to the steady state with a wage tax because their income loss from the tax rate increase is not fully offset in the short run by higher wages. In the long run, the higher capital/output ratios resulting from taxation of only labor income raise productivity and wage rates. Given that individuals are fixed in their pattern of work and retirement throughout their lives and given the infeasibility of levying age-specific taxes, AK found that the only way to obtain a Pareto-superior transition turns out to provide lower welfare gains for generations living in the posttransition years than the consumption tax would provide.

The other study that explored imperfect mobility of factors is Fullerton's alternative specification of the FSW model. His application concerned imperfect mobility of capital between industries. Because existing capital was modeled as industry-specific, capital could not be observed to move out of an industry at a rate faster than its rate of depreciation. In other words, capital could increase in an industry only as a result of saving being greater than depreciation and could not be physically moved from one industry to another. This is perhaps an upper bound to capital immobility, since it takes no account of the movability of items such as office equipment and trucks. Fullerton resimulated income tax integration under this specification and found that movement of capital out of several (largely noncorporate) industries was constrained. This implied a substantial reduction in efficiency gains in the first year, but not in subsequent years, when the constraint proved not to be binding.[15]

Another example of a heterogeneous capital stock is found in the BT model. Foreign-owned and domestically owned capital were assumed to be perfect substitutes in production. Domestic capital was fixed in aggregate supply and totally mobile across industries within the country. The specification of the supply of foreign-owned capital to Canada proved to be a key factor in incidence results, however. In the BT model, foreign capital moves into Canada based on gross rates of return rather than net rates of return. This was justified because Canadian corporate income tax payments are credited in computing tax liabilities in the home country; as long as the Canadian rate is below the home country rate, it does not affect capital flows into Canada. As a result of these assumptions on capital supply, a substantial portion of the burden of an increase in the corporate income tax in Canada is shifted onto foreigners.

In yet another context, Slemrod found that inflexible supply of some assets affected tax burdens. He found that a fixed supply of tax-exempt debt, in conjunction with a particular model of portfolio choice, caused those whose income was above $50,000 to lose with the passage of tax integration. The logic is as follows. The corporation effectively shelters income for upper-income groups, since the sum of the corporate income tax on a dollar of retained earnings plus the effective personal income tax on the resulting capital gains[16] is lower for them than the tax paid on a noncorporate investment, which is taxed at their (high) marginal personal income tax rate. For lower-income households, the opposite is true: The tax rate on income from corporate capital is higher than from noncorporate capital. With the passage of integration, the upper income group would prefer to shift out of corporate capital because for them it would be taxed at a higher rate. In Slemrod's model, they were limited in their possibility to invest in alternative assets that are taxed at a rate below their ordinary personal income tax rate. Housing is less heavily taxed, but this group's Cobb–Douglas preferences for owner-occupied housing restricted them to spending a fixed proportion of their income on housing, and the price of housing did not fall enough for them to transfer their entire desired reduction of corporate holdings into housing. Another possibility was tax-exempt debt. They were not able to transfer their holdings into this asset because its supply was held constant by the government.

4.6   Dynamic models

In this section, we discuss how factors of production have been allowed to grow over time. Of the models in our survey, only the AK, FSW, and FG models may be solved for a time sequence. In the AK model, each generation decides on its consumption and saving allocation for its entire lifetime, using perfect foresight expectations. Labor supply is exogenous.[17] The FSW and FG models have endogenous allocation over present and future consumption under myopic expectations and allow the current period's saving to augment capital in the next period.[18] Labor supply depends endogenously on the after-tax wage rate. Although the PW model is solved for only one period, two versions of it have, respectively, labor–leisure choice and saving behavior. The Serra-Puche model of Mexico also is a one-period model with saving but has no labor–leisure choice. We discuss saving aspects of the latter models here because these features make them readily adaptable to solving a sequence of equilibria.

a. *Labor–leisure choice:* The approach to modeling labor–leisure choice in the FSW and the PW models is based on applying an average figure from the literature for the elasticity of labor supply with respect to the after-tax wage. Although the implementation procedure appears to be straightforward, some of the assumptions that have to be made can affect the results.

In order to put this information into model-equivalent form, it is useful to look at the Slutsky equation in terms of labor supply elasticities:

$$\epsilon_{Lw} = \epsilon_{Lw}\big|_{\bar{u}} + \frac{L}{E}\epsilon_{LI}$$

where

L = labor supply
w = net wage
E = endowment of labor
I = expanded income (wE)
ϵ_{Lw} = uncompensated elasticity of L with respect to w
ϵ_{LI} = income elasticity of L
$\epsilon_{Lw}\big|_{\bar{u}}$ = compensated elasticity of L with respect to w

The compensated wage elasticity is positive, and the income elasticity is negative, so the uncompensated ϵ_{Lw} is of ambiguous sign.[19] Furthermore, if leisure is defined by $l = E - L$, then we have

$$\epsilon_{LI} = \frac{\partial L}{\partial I} \cdot \frac{I}{L} = \frac{\partial (E-l)}{\partial I} \cdot \frac{I}{E-l} = \frac{-\partial l}{\partial I} \cdot \frac{I}{l} \cdot \frac{l}{E-l} = -\epsilon_{lI} \cdot \frac{l}{L}$$

In a CES utility function defined over leisure and consumption, for example, ϵ_{lI} equals 1 and ϵ_{LI} would be $-l/L$. Thus

$$\epsilon_{Lw} = \epsilon_{Lw}\big|_{\bar{u}} - \frac{l}{E}$$

Now if the modeler uses a separately given estimate from the literature for the uncompensated elasticity ϵ_{Lw}, the compensated elasticity will vary directly with the postulated l/E ratio. In the U.K. model, for example, PW suppose that the normal laborer supplies 40 hours out of a possible 50-hour work week, so l/E is 1/5. In the U.S. model, FSW suppose a 40-hour week out of a possible 70-hour week, so l/E is set at 3/7. Thus the FSW income elasticity for labor is $-3/4$ and the PW income elasticity for labor is $-1/4$. If the two models used the same exogenous estimate for the uncompensated wage elasticity, then the FSW substitution effect (compensated wage elasticity) would be larger. For a zero uncompensated ϵ_{Lw}, for example, the compensated ϵ_{Lw} would be 3/7 and 1/5 for FSW and PW, respectively. Welfare costs depend on the compensated, not the uncompensated, elasticity of labor supply. The algebra above helps to explain the relatively large labor–leisure distortions caused in the FSW and FG models when they raise taxes on labor to achieve the same total tax revenue after full integration. These labor-related welfare losses offset capital-related welfare gains in these simulations.

To measure the importance of alternative assumptions about labor endowments, we repeated the tax integration experiment summarized in Table 2, using a 50-hour maximum work week in the FSW model. Under this assumption, integration of the corporate and personal income tax combined with restoration of a balanced government budget through upward scaling of income tax rates would produce a welfare gain of $512.5 billion. This is substantially higher than the $344.4 billion gain obtained earlier, with the assumption of a 70-hour potential work week.

The procedure of taking an average elasticity is, of course, a shortcut alternative to specifying different labor supply elasticities and labor endowments by household groups. The literature on labor supply elasticities indicates that there are sharp differences in (uncompensated) elasticities between males and females, primary and secondary workers, and prime-age and older workers (Hausman, 1981). This implies a need to reconcile labor supply behavior of income groups with evidence based on demographic characteristics. There is already some – but arbitrary – specification of demographic differences in the PW model, where it is assumed that households headed by a retired or nonemployed person have no sensitivity to tax rates in making their labor supply decisions. The demographic data on households in this model in fact could be exploited more in this area. The benefits to differentiating the labor supply elasticities by income group would be important, for example, in evaluating proposals that affect lower-income households, such as introduction of a negative income tax or changes in transfer programs.

The importance of modeling labor–leisure choice (using average elasticities) appears to vary with the experiment being performed and the existing tax structure, as well as depending on the specification of labor and leisure endowments. PW simulated the effects of elimination of all tax and subsidy distortions in the United Kingdom, with the revenue loss being made up by a broad-based sales tax. They reported only minimal differences in efficiency gains in simulations assuming, in turn, exogenous labor supply and a .125 elasticity of labor supply with respect to the after-tax wage rate. The labor–leisure distortion is apparently small compared to the very large interindustry distortions in the U.K. tax system caused by indirect taxes, especially housing subsidies and differential sales taxes.

An alternative view of the importance of the labor–leisure choice may be seen in simulations of full integration of personal and corporate income taxes by Fullerton, King, Shoven, and Whalley (FKSW) (1981). Given an assumed labor supply elasticity of .15, FKSW found that the efficiency gain from integration when the yield-preserving tax was multiplicative scaling of personal income tax rates was only about one-half of that when a lump-sum tax was used.

b. *Saving and capital formation:* In the Serra-Puche, FSW, and PW models, saving is equivalent to the purchase of a fixed-weight bundle of capital goods. To simplify the computations, these models assume that the capital stock is augmented with a one-year lag. Thus, the FSW model computes a sequence of static equilibria rather than dynamic equilibria. (The Serra-Puche and PW models compute only one equilibrium rather than a series.)

The specification of the mix of capital goods ignores composition effects, for example, between residential and nonresidential investments. Residential investment would be produced largely by the construction industry, whereas nonresidential investment goods would be produced by the manufacturing sector.

Saving behavior in the Serra-Puche model is based on a fixed proportion of income. In the FSW and PW models, it is based on the expected return, assuming myopic predictions. Both models take as their central estimate Boskin's (1978) .4 elasticity, but simulate elasticities between 0 and 2 for sensitivity analysis. The importance of this elasticity has been pointed out by Feldstein (1974a). The PW model then approximates the elasticity of substitution between current and future consumption as 1 plus the saving elasticity, whereas in the FSW model the relationship is solved explicitly.

PW found that the saving distortion is also a small factor compared to the largely intersectoral distortions of the British tax system.[20] They did find, however, fairly sizable efficiency gains if the income tax were replaced by a pure consumption tax, particularly when there was inflation. The large response in saving in both simulations, however, suggests continued efficiency gains in the long run. The Fullerton, Shoven, and Whalley (1983) study of the consumption tax in the United States also indicated potentially large efficiency gains. They showed huge sensitivity to the savings elasticity assumption, however.

The AK model has been used to examine the differential impacts of replacing the income tax by two taxes that eliminate the double taxation of saving, a consumption tax and a wage tax. Auerbach and Kotlikoff showed that, from the point of view of future generations, the consumption tax will be superior to the wage tax if, on average, wages are received earlier in life than consumption takes place. The utility differential was caused by the difference in the present value between these two streams of tax payments.

4.7   The government budget

In most models, the authors have assumed that the government budget is in balance. A tax reform that results in a revenue loss must therefore be matched by a tax increase or spending cut. In particular, a balanced budget is a necessary assumption in a model without paper assets, since deficits must be financed by an increase in government securities or by money creation.

The conventional wisdom in this field has been that the existence of a deficit does not change incidence or efficiency results. McLure (1970) has shown that in a Harberger-type model, allocation of resources depends only on relative prices, and not on absolute prices. General equilibrium models provide a solution only for relative prices; typically, the wage rate is taken as numeraire. Another equation is needed to close the model if absolute prices are to be derived. McLure illustrated his point by closing the model with the quantity equation for money. If a tax change is financed by money creation, this has no additional real effects on the economy, and therefore does not change economic decisions. The unimportance of financing effects does not carry over to a model with portfolio choice, however. Feldstein and Slemrod (1980) have shown, for example, that the corporate income tax may distort asset demand decisions even if it does not distort production decisions. Also, since the tax systems are generally nonneutral with respect to inflation, policies that affect absolute prices have allocational impacts. The potential for modeling unbalanced budgets is discussed below. First, however, we address the treatment of balancing the budget.

Budget balance in each period is a feature of all the models in the survey except the AK and Serra-Puche models, which have a government debt instrument. As shown in Table 1, the revenue yield may be equalized by different taxes in different models. With the specification of the behavior of different consumer groups, the choice of the equal-yield tax affects the efficiency and distributional results of the original policy change simulation. Financing by a consumption or broad-based sales tax usually introduces the least distortion of any available tax. An income tax should affect both labor–leisure choice and saving decisions and may be more progressive.

The choice of a particular budget-balancing technique may in fact obscure the incidence of a particular tax proposal and limit the usefulness of a model. Although a lump-sum equal-yield feature is not an option for policy makers, it may provide a useful benchmark for examining the incidence of a tax. Alternatively, several plausible equal-yield options may be compared. An example that shows how the choice of a budget-balancing measure may limit the information from a model is found in the set of simulations that Keller has performed. In this model, government always has a balanced budget, but does not acquire the same yield. When a tax change increases government revenue, the additional funds are spent in the proportions that previous revenues were spent. This amounts to an increased demand for skilled labor, because this factor makes up a high proportion of observed government expenditures. Thus Keller's simulated tax increases – whether on commodities or labor – tend to raise the wage of skilled labor. This result stems only from the higher demand for skilled labor caused by the budget-balancing expenditures. Keller compared his model results with those from partial equilibrium studies and attributed the differences to general equilibrium effects. This is a mistaken interpretation, since the partial equilibrium experiments did not include budget-balancing offsets to the tax changes.

Where a simulation measures not differential incidence but rather balanced budget incidence, it is important to model household preferences for public goods, in order to include the value of the change in government purchases in calculations of welfare change. This has been done by Keller, but not by Serra-Puche, despite his modeling of government expenditure policy to balance the budget.

The equal-yield feature is important to consider in comparing simulation results across models. But it is also necessary to be aware of other features of the models in interpreting the effect of the equal-yield tax. As one example, we compare the results of tax integration of Slemrod and FKSW. When both made up revenue losses by multiplicative scaling of personal income tax rates, Slemrod's efficiency gains were much larger. Comparing the features of the models, one might conclude that the importance of modeling financing decisions, considered by Slemrod and not FKSW, is greater than other differences in specification that would lessen the relative estimate of efficiency gains of the Slemrod model. (These latter differences include having fewer sectors and the specification of portfolio balance behavior.) This conclusion would not be correct, however, because Slemrod did not have endogenous saving or labor supply responses, while FKSW did. In this case, the correct comparison of efficiency gain would use the FKSW simulation with a lump-sum adjustment. When this is done, the results are in fact very similar.

In the AK model, the government budget constraint is that the present value of expenditures must equal the present value of revenue less the initial value of debt. Financing by money creation is not an option. Private and government capital are perfect substitutes in portfolios, but government debt is found to crowd out private capital formation. This phenomenon lowers potential efficiency gains when a tax reform is financed by issuing government bonds.

Introduction of money into the AK model would not be difficult on the supply side, since deficits are already a feature of the model. On the demand side, however, it would necessitate specifying portfolio decisions in a richer way. Since the model is not concerned with details of capital taxation, the distortionary effects of the inflationary impacts of money creation would not be extensive. A more promising model for this extension might be Slemrod's or Feltenstein's (this book). Serra-Puche's model has an initially unbalanced budget and is being expanded to include monetary phenomena. Slemrod already has portfolio behavior, with money and debt as available assets. Debt of the federal government would have to be separated from corporate debt in the data to model an unbalanced budget. Effective tax rates on capital are already a function of inflation, so that their specification would not be affected.

4.8   Technical operations

This section describes three technical aspects of operating applied general equilibrium models: parameterization procedures, solution methods, and measurement of efficiency and distributional gains.

a. *Parameterization:* Mansur and Whalley (Chapter 3, this book) go into detail in describing existing methods for parameterizing general equilibrium models and comparing these methods with stochastic estimation of parameters. Our discussion here is briefer, in light of their treatment of the subject and because models do not differ greatly in this respect.

The primary behavioral equations in general equilibrium tax models are production and demand equations. Elasticities of substitution between factors or goods are usually selected from previous econometric studies. This means either that a range of parameters is used, corresponding to the range of estimated values, or that specific estimates are chosen from particular studies.

There are problems with this procedure that are often acknowledged by modelers themselves. First, estimates of parameters may vary from study to study. Generally there are no clear rules for deciding among alternatives. This problem is exacerbated by the unclear time frame of general equilibrium models. For example, although there seems to be a systematic difference between cross-section and time-series estimates of the elasticity of substitution between capital and labor, FSW and PW took an average of estimates from these two types of studies rather than choosing one or the other. A second problem is the lack of estimates of some parameters. Sometimes the model builders have used estimates for the same concept for a different country. Piggott and Whalley, for example, used estimates of savings elasticities for the United States in their model of the United Kingdom. They compensated for this problem, however, by trying a wide range of estimates. At other times, the authors have estimated the missing parameters themselves. Fullerton and Gordon derived their own econometric estimates of parameters associated with bankruptcy costs. This was necessary because there is little empirical evidence on these costs.

When there is uncertainty about parameter values, the results are often subjected to sensitivity analysis, as described in several cases above. FSW (1978) reported experiments of the sensitivity of results to production elasticities in an early version of their model. They simulated elimination of the corporate income tax, varying the elasticity of substitution in production in all sectors from .5 to 2. In all cases consumers had Cobb–Douglas demands. For this experiment the welfare gain was almost exactly proportional to the production elasticity. PW (1982) have also reported sensitivities to both production and consumption elasticities. In both models the results indicate the importance of developing careful parameterization procedures.

Given exogenously determined substitution parameters, a technique of "backwards solution" has been used to determine the remaining parameters. For example, for CES production functions, FSW used outside studies to determine elasticities of substitution, then used benchmark data on labor and capital and assumed cost minimization under constant returns to scale to solve for the weighting parameter and the scale parameter. It must not be overlooked, however, that this is merely a calibration procedure used to match up the baseline solution with actual data. The backwards solution is a useful mechanical check on the programming of these models, but provides no assurance that the parameter estimates are reasonable. The residual parameters will take up the slack if there are errors in the substitution parameters. Also, even if the substitution elasticities are estimated correctly, but the production or consumption relationship is actually stochastic, the stochastic error for that period will show up in the residual parameters.

In fact, the choice of which parameters to make endogenous and exogenous is arbitrary, even though the results are not independent of the procedure selected. Authors have tried to follow the guideline of using outside estimates for scale-free parameters.

Another, less common, approach is to let some of the data be the residual. Slemrod used this procedure because his backwards solution for the coefficient of risk aversion did not come close to existing estimates. Instead of using backwards solution for parameters, he solved backwards for risk premiums that were implied by an exogenous risk-aversion parameter. The fact that Slemrod chose this procedure is probably an indication of the nonrobustness of the disaggregated data used in these models in general. Other authors (e.g., FSW) have noted the inconsistency of data, for example, on the sources and uses of income at a disaggregated level and have arbitrarily selected some data as superior and adjusted other data to match.

Reporting sensitivity of model results to the adjustment of data has not been as common as reporting the sensitivity with respect to parameter selection.[21] Model builders should consider both experiments, however. One example where implications of data selection were shown was in the FG simulation of income tax integration. Fullerton and Gordon examined the results under two estimates of the risk-free rate of return. The ambiguity of this concept stemmed from the fact that short-term government debt is riskless in nominal terms, but not in real terms.

b. *Solution techniques:* The Harberger model was solved by hand by taking linear approximations to production and consumption equations. Among the empirical models, this method is used for only the BT and Keller models. Because of the size of the matrices involved in these models, however, computation is done with the aid of a computer.

It is more common to use methods that properly handle large changes in tax rates. The remaining models are solved by three different techniques: a Newton-type method (PW), Gauss–Seidel iteration (AK, Slemrod), and a simplicial search method (FSW, Serra-Puche, and FG use Merrill's version of the Scarf algorithm).[22] In the case of the first two of these methods, successful convergence to an equilibrium depends in principle upon judicial selection of starting values and step size. Usually the benchmark values are used as starting values in alternate simulations. In fact, there have been no reports of cases, using these models, where there were convergence problems or where alternative starting points have affected the answer.[23]

Comparative data on computation costs of these methods are not readily available. Even when the same model is solved using the same technique on different computers, there may be substantial differences in computation costs (see Piggott and Whalley, 1982). It is possible that different solution techniques are preferred for different models, but there is no evidence on this.

The costs of the Gauss–Seidel method depend on efficient ordering of equations into simultaneous and recursive blocks. We have not found any discussion of this in the applied general equilibrium literature, however. The cost of using simplicial search algorithms varies exponentially with the number of dimensions on the simplex. The FSW and FG models have three dimensions, corresponding to the price of labor, the price of capital, and the revenue yield. Other prices and, in the case of FG, yields on assets are solved for as functions of the prices on the simplex.

The cost structure of these simplex algorithms is a deterrent to designing models with heterogeneous factors of production (see Fullerton, 1983). Future use of simplicial search methods will undoubtedly take advantage of innovations that reduce costs, such as the algorithm of van der Laan and Talman (1979). For the Newton method, Piggott and Whalley (1982) have reported that increasing the initial step size increases the efficiency of the search for a solution.

c. *Measurement of efficiency and distributional effects:* In the Harberger model, the efficiency cost of capital taxation was measured by movement of capital. Since a unit of capital was defined as the amount that earns a dollar net of all taxes, this change in capital could be interpreted in income terms and compared to GNP. Incidence was measured by the change in the price of capital relative to the size of the tax. The computational general equilibrium models, on the other hand, measure welfare changes and their distribution among households in terms of income changes. In the case of the BT model, this is based on comparison of real incomes between the policy simulation and the baseline. When there is an explicit utility function generating demands, the comparison is based on the change in income that would compensate each household for the tax changes. As is well known from index number theory, compensating and equivalent variation provide bounds on the welfare change. These should both be computed. When the utility function includes leisure, as in FSW, the measure used is "expanded" national income, which adds the value of leisure time to monetary income.

Welfare changes are more complicated in a dynamic model. In FSW (1983), a present-value calculation is used. This of course is sensitive to the assumption on the discount rate. In addition, FSW cautioned that present-value welfare gains should be measured only for the initial population, so that the steady-state growth rate does not distort the results.

Most models indicate distributional effects by measuring welfare changes for each household group. The PW model also calculates overall measures of the change in equality of incomes, such as the Gini coefficient.

5   Conclusion

Computational general equilibrium models have proven useful in the area of long-run analysis of alternative tax policies. A sizable number of studies have been completed examining policies such as a value-added tax, corporate and personal income tax integration, a consumption or expenditure tax, housing subsidies, and inflation indexation. We have surveyed several aspects of eight models and have found that they differ in structure in several areas. Clearly, researchers always face a tradeoff between simplicity and accuracy of detail, and in several areas (e.g., the level of disaggregation, the amount of substitution permitted) there is no "right" approach.

Although we feel that the general equilibrium approach is very appropriate for analyzing large tax policy changes, there are a number of areas in which all existing models of this type could be improved. The first thing that strikes us in surveying the work in this field is that the profession still has not reached a consensus on the value of the few "key" elasticity parameters. First among these is the elasticity of labor supply. Our examination of the sensitivity of results to this parameter strongly underlines its importance. In disaggregated models, what are needed are labor supply functions by age, income, and possibly marital status. The saving elasticity is probably the second most important parameter, at least for dynamic models. Again, disaggregated models call for these elasticities for each consumer class. Studies to date are far less conclusive on saving behavior than on labor supply.

The specification of the production side of the models could also be improved. Although there is some agreement about the elasticity of substitution of primary factors, issues such as technical change (induced either by changes in relative prices or by inventions) and substitution possibilities among intermediate inputs are neither resolved nor for the most part incorporated in the models we survey. The models uniformly assume perfect competition and constant returns to scale. Clearly, these assumptions are made as convenient abstractions. Incorporation of imperfect competition and government regulation would be useful.

Two areas that some of these models have begun to address are dynamic response and the modeling of financial markets and behavior. The economy may take a substantial period of time to adjust to the types of tax policies that are analyzed with these models. The impact may discriminate between generations, and life cycle modeling may be appropriate. With dynamic models, the issue of uncertainty and expectations regarding the future must be addressed.

General equilibrium models have traditionally emphasized the real economy at the expense of analyzing financial markets. This approach is less than satisfactory for tax analysis where financial flows are being taxed in nonneutral ways. As we have described in this chapter, several steps have been taken to include the modeling of financial behavior, but substantially more could be done in this area. Related to this is the treatment of government deficits. In order to handle adequately a government budget that is out of balance, a treatment of government bond markets is required. Our overall assessment is that both the areas of dynamics and financial behavior are ripe for further progress.

Finally, there are improvements that could be made in how the tax policies themselves are captured. For example, many of the models treat the personal income tax as a series of linear tax schedules. Higher-income households may face higher marginal tax rates, but each faces a constant marginal tax rate. This fails to capture the fact that a policy such as integrating corporate income into the personal tax base would cause people to be pushed into higher marginal tax rate brackets. So one area of possible improvement is a more accurate modeling of the progressive rate structure of the personal income tax.

Another aspect of policy modeling that could be improved is in the expenditure of the tax receipts. None of the models has correctly included the implicit marginal tax rates of many income transfer programs or adequately captured the demand for public goods. To some extent, this failure has been alleviated by those models that compare only tax policies of equal revenue yield. The assumption is then made that the expenditure distortions are unaffected by the tax alternatives being considered.

We do not mean to conclude this chapter on a negative note. Each of the models that we have surveyed is vastly richer than the 2×2 Harberger model from which they were derived. Empirical general equilibrium analysis has made great strides since the early 1970s and is now a useful tool for tax policy evaluation. We feel that these models can become even more valuable with further work and additional cross-fertilization between models under development.

NOTES

1. This chapter is not intended to survey all general equilibrium models related to taxation. Instead, we hope to learn about problems in designing a tax model by looking in depth at only a few of them. The choice of these eight models is ultimately arbitrary, however. By concentrating on nationwide allocation effections of tax policy, in particular, we omit regional considerations and expenditure-side considerations. See, for example, Richter (1975) and Kimbell and Harrison (Chapter 7, this book). Other general equilibrium models include Dungan (1980), which simulates tax and expenditure changes in Canada but which is primarily concerned with monetary policy, foreign exchange, and macroeconomic effects. Whalley (1980) describes a world model with four major trading blocs, while Boadway and Treddenick (1978) have a trade model of Canada. Aspects of trade, taxes, and development are addressed in models by Adelman and Robinson (1978) for Korea, Feltenstein (1980) for Argentina, de Melo (1978) for Colombia, and Dervis, de Melo, and Robinson (1981). Development models are described in Dervis, de Melo, and Robinson (1982).

2. The Rosenberg (1969) data and the aggregation by Harberger are discussed below.
3. The term *output effect* refers to the effect on the demand for the output of the industry where a factor of production is being taxed.
4. A version of the Ballentine–Thirsk model may be used to examine inter-regional incidence of taxation. This version is not reviewed here.
5. Except where otherwise specified, the description of the Fullerton–Shoven–Whalley model is applicable to the Fullerton–Gordon model as well. The FG model is discussed only where it differs from the FSW model.
6. In the earlier version, Slemrod (1980), agriculture was not distinguished from the corporate sector.
7. These choices do not necessarily indicate that industries have similar rates of substitution between factors. PW, for example, estimate production functions for the United Kingdom and derive quite varying elasticities that they use in sensitivity experiments. The "standard case" choices are based on average findings in the literature, a procedure that tends to minimize inter-industry differences.
8. In such a plan, the corporate share price as a basis for capital gains purposes would be increased by the already taxed retained earnings.
9. If we look only at corporate income taxes and property taxes in Harberger's 1957 data from Rosenberg (1969), we see that these three industries did not have the lowest tax rates. Agriculture had the lowest rate, followed by crude petroleum, refined petroleum, and then the real estate sector. However, Harberger added imputations for the personal income tax on capital income from each sector. He assumed that 70% of net capital income in real estate was from untaxed imputed rents of owner-occupants, and that the other 30% from rental housing was taxed at a 20% personal rate. He assumed that farm income (net of other taxes) faced a 15% personal rate, but that crude petroleum income had depletion and similar privileges to offset any personal taxes. Finally, for all parts of the corporate sector, Harberger assumed a 20% effective rate that reflects a 40% personal tax on the half of earnings assumed to be distributed. Because refined petroleum was grouped with the corporate sector, Harberger's total tax on that industry was increased by personal taxes. The FSW model makes similar imputations for personal taxes of each sector, but these are based on the actual proportions of noncorporate earnings, retained corporate earnings, and distributed corporate earnings of each industry. In the 1973 data, petroleum refining starts with a low corporate rate due to depletion and retains a low rate after personal tax imputations.
10. Harberger grouped his industries appropriately given his personal tax imputations. The other grouping is more appropriate given the 1973 data and FSW personal tax imputations.
11. We were not able to disaggregate real estate into owner-occupied and rental housing, as in the Slemrod model.
12. The median income for the United Kingdom was not provided in PW (1982).
13. This statement is less true for their "type III" households, which are composed of either two adults and more than one child or of more than two adults. This group has significant labor income.
14. The first of four formulations in the Goulder, Shoven, and Whalley (1983) paper has been added as a standard feature of the FSW model. The specification features constant elasticity demand functions for foreigners' behavior, no Armington product heterogeneity, and no international capital flows.

This version of the FSW model was used in the simulations presented in Table 2. An earlier specification of the trade sector, also described in the Goulder, Shoven, and Whalley article, was used in the previously published papers on the FSW model.

15. The constraints on movement of capital out of housing might be binding for a longer period of time if the low economic depreciation rates of Fullerton and Gordon (1983) were used.

16. This rate is reduced both by statutory preferential treatment and by deferral of realization.

17. In a very recent version of their model Auerbach and Kotlikoff have modeled labor–leisure decisions.

18. Recent work by Bovenberg and Keller (1981) has added a similar capability to Keller's model.

19. Estimates of ϵ_{Lw} are generally zero or negative for prime-age males and between zero and one for females and other groups. Fullerton (1982) reviews these estimates and finds .15 to be a plausible aggregate elasticity, but household differences here can warrant disaggregation on a basis other than income.

20. The modeling of the personal income tax also diminishes estimates of the distortion of saving decisions. The top income tax rate in the PW model is 30%, reflecting the proportional structure for most income levels. At high income levels, however, investment income is taxed at a higher marginal rate. This feature of the tax system was ignored even for groups where it appears to be operative.

21. In some cases, tests of sensitivity to elasticity parameters may be interpreted as tests of data as well. In the case of labor supply, selection of labor supply elasticity and labor endowment affect the results in a similar manner. See Section 4.6a for further discussion.

22. For a short description of gradient methods, including the Newton method and the Gauss–Seidel procedure, see Goldfeld and Quandt (1972). The Scarf algorithm is described briefly in Shoven and Whalley (1972, 1973), and in more detail in Scarf (1973). Piggott and Whalley (1982, chapter 7) provide an excellent discussion of the Newton, Scarf, and Merrill techniques in applied general equilibrium models.

23. Existence of a unique equilibrium depends upon the specification of the model, and testing for multiple equilibria is prudent, regardless of the solution technique. For discussion of models with multiple equilibria, see Kehoe (1980).

REFERENCES

Adelman, I., and Robinson, S. 1978. *Income distribution policy in developing countries*. Stanford, Calif.: Stanford University Press.

Atkinson, A. B., and Stiglitz, J. E. 1980. *Lectures in public economics*. New York: McGraw Hill.

Auerbach, A. J., and Kotlikoff, L. J. 1983. National savings, economic welfare, and the structure of taxation. In Feldstein, M. S., ed., *Behavioral simulation methods in tax policy analysis*. Chicago: University of Chicago Press.

Ballentine, J. G. 1978. The incidence of a corporation income tax in a growing economy. *Journal of Political Economy* 86:863–75.

Ballentine, J. G., and Eris, I. 1975. On the general equilibrium analysis of tax incidence. *Journal of Political Economy* 83:633–44.

Ballentine, J. G., and McLure, C. E., Jr. 1980. Taxation and corporate financial policy. *Quarterly Journal of Economics* 94:351–72.

Ballentine, J. G., and Thirsk, W. 1979. *The fiscal incidence of some experiments in fiscal federalism.* Ottawa: Canadian Mortgage and Housing Corporation.

Boadway, R. 1979. Long-run tax incidence: A comparative dynamic approach. *Review of Economic Studies* 46:505–11.

Boadway, R., and Treddenick, J. M. 1978. A general equilibrium computation of the effects of the Canadian tariff structure. *Canadian Journal of Economics* 11:424–46.

Boskin, M. J. 1978. Taxation, saving, and the rate of interest. *Journal of Political Economy* 86:S3–S27.

Bovenberg, A. L., and Keller, W. J. 1981. Dynamics and nonlinearities in applied general equilibrium models. Central Bureau of Statistics, the Netherlands. Mimeo.

Bulow, J. I., and Summers, L. H. 1982. The taxation of risky assets. National Bureau of Economic Research. Mimeo.

Dervis, K., de Melo, J., and Robinson, S. 1981. A general equilibrium analysis of foreign exchange shortages in a developing economy. *Economic Journal* 91:891–906.

——— 1982. *General equilibrium models for development policy.* Cambridge: Cambridge University Press.

Devarajan, S., Fullerton, D., and Musgrave, R. 1980. Estimating the distribution of tax burdens: A comparison of different approaches. *Journal of Public Economics* 13:155–82.

Dungan, D. P. 1980. An empirical multi-sectoral Walrasian–Keynesian model of the Canadian economy. Ph.D. diss., Princeton University.

Feldstein, M. S. 1974a. The incidence of a capital income tax in a growing economy with variable savings rates. *Review of Economic Studies* 41:505–13.

——— 1974b. Tax incidence in a growing economy with variable factor supply. *Quarterly Journal of Economics* 88:S51–S73.

——— 1978. The welfare cost of capital income taxation. *Journal of Political Economy* 86:S29–S51.

Feldstein, M. S., Green, J., and Sheshinski, E. 1978. Inflation and taxes in a growing economy with debt and equity finance. *Journal of Political Economy* 86:S53–S70.

Feldstein, M. S., and Slemrod, J. 1980. Personal taxation, portfolio choice, and the effect of the corporation income tax. *Journal of Political Economy* 88:854–66.

Feltenstein, A. 1980. A general equilibrium approach to the analysis of trade restrictions, with an application to Argentina. In International Monetary Fund, *Staff Papers,* Vol. 27, No. 4. Washington, D.C.

Fromm, G., and Klein, L. R. 1976. The NBER/NSF model comparison seminar: An analysis of results. In Klein, L. R., and Burmeister, E., eds., *Econometric model performance: Comparative simulation studies of the U.S. economy.* Philadelphia: University of Pennsylvania Press.

Fullerton, D. 1982. On the possibility of an inverse relationship between tax rates and government revenues. *Journal of Public Economics,* 19:3–22.

1983. The transition losses of partially mobile industry specific capital. *Quarterly Journal of Economics,* 83(1):107–25.

Fullerton, D., and Gordon, R. H. 1983. A reexamination of tax distortions in general equilibrium models. In Feldstein, M. S., ed., *Behavioral simulation methods in tax policy analysis.* Chicago: University of Chicago Press.

Fullerton, D., and Henderson, Y. K. 1981. Long run effects of the Accelerated Cost Recovery System. National Bureau of Economic Research Working Paper No. 828.

Fullerton, D., King, A. T., Shoven, J. B., and Whalley, J. 1981. Tax integration in the U.S.: A general equilibrium approach. *American Economic Review* 71:677–91.

Fullerton, D., Shoven, J. B., and Whalley, J. 1978. General equilibrium analysis of U.S. taxation policy. In U.S. Treasury Department, *1978 compendium of tax research.* Washington, D.C.: U.S. Government Printing Office.

1983. Replacing the U.S. income tax with a progressive consumption tax: A sequenced general equilibrium approach. *Journal of Public Economics,* 20: 1–21.

Goldfield, S. M., and Quandt, R. E. 1972. *Nonlinear methods in econometrics.* Amsterdam: North-Holland.

Goulder, L. H., Shoven, J. B., and Whalley, J. 1983. Domestic tax policy and the foreign sector: The importance of alternative foreign policy formulations to results from a general equilibrium tax analysis model. In Feldstein, M. S., ed., *Behavioral simulation methods in tax policy analysis.* Chicago: University of Chicago Press.

Hall, R. E., and Jorgenson, D. W. 1967. Tax policy and investment behavior. *American Economic Review* 57:391–414.

Harberger, A. C. 1962. The incidence of the corporation tax. *Journal of Political Economy* 70:215–40.

1966. Efficiency effects of taxes on income from capital. In Krzyzaniak, M., ed., *Effects of corporation income tax.* Detroit: Wayne State University Press.

1976. The incidence and efficiency of taxes on income from capital: A reply. *Journal of Political Economy* 84:1285–92.

Hausman, J. 1981. Labor supply. In Aaron, H., and Pechman, J., eds., *How taxes affect economic behavior.* Washington, D.C.: Brookings Institution.

Jorgenson, D. W., and Sullivan, M. A. 1981. Inflation and corporate capital recovery. In Hulten, C. R., ed., *Depreciation, inflation, and the taxation of income from capital.* Washington, D.C.: Urban Institute.

Kehoe, T. 1980. Uniqueness of equilibrium in production economies. Department of Economics Working Paper #271, Massachusetts Institute of Technology.

Keller, W. J. 1980. *Tax incidence: A general equilibrium approach.* Amsterdam: North-Holland.

van der Laan, G., and Talman, A. J. J. 1979. A restart algorithm for computing fixed point without an extra dimension. *Mathematical Programming,* 17: 74–84.

McLure, C. E., Jr. 1970. Tax incidence, absolute prices, and macroeconomic policy. *Quarterly Journal of Economics* 84:254–67.

1975. General equilibrium analysis: The Harberger model after ten years. *Journal of Public Economics* 4:125–61.

de Melo, J. 1978. Estimating the costs of protection: A general equilibrium approach. *Quarterly Journal of Economics* 42:209-26.

Mieszkowski, P. 1967. On the theory of tax incidence. *Journal of Political Economy* 75:250-62.

———. 1969. Tax incidence theory: The effects of taxes on the distribution of income. *Journal of Economic Literature* 7:1103-24.

Piggott, J. R., and Whalley, J. 1976. General equilibrium investigations of U.K. tax subsidy policy: A progress report. In Artis, M. J., and Nobay, A. R., eds., *Studies in modern economic analysis*. Oxford: Blackwell.

———. 1982. Economic effects of U.K. tax-subsidy policies: A general equilibrium appraisal. New York: Macmillan.

Richter, D. 1975. Existence of general equilibrium in multi-regional economies with public goods. *International Economic Review* 16:201-21.

Rosenberg, L. G. 1969. Taxation of income from capital, by industry group. In Harberger, A. C., and Bailey, M. J., eds., *The taxation of income from capital*. Washington, D.C.: Brookings Institution.

Scarf, H. E. (with the collaboration of Terje Hansen). 1973. *The computation of economic equilibria*. New Haven: Yale University Press.

Serra-Puche, J. J. 1979. A computational general equilibrium model for the Mexican economy: An analysis of fiscal policies. Ph.D. diss., Yale University.

Shoven, J. B. 1973. General equilibrium with taxes: Existence, computation, and a capital income taxation application. Ph.D. diss., Yale University.

———. 1976. The incidence and efficiency effects of taxes on income from capital. *Journal of Political Economy* 84:1261-83.

Shoven, J. B., and Whalley, J. 1972. A general equilibrium calculation of the effects of differential taxation from capital in the U.S. *Journal of Public Economics* 1:281-321.

———. 1973. General equilibrium with taxes: A computational procedure and an existence proof. *Review of Economic Studies* 40:475-89.

Slemrod, J. B. 1980. A general equilibrium model of capital income taxation. Ph.D. diss., Harvard University.

———. 1983. A general equilibrium model of taxation with endogenous financial behavior. In Feldstein, M. S., ed., *Behavioral simulation methods in tax policy analysis*. Chicago: University of Chicago Press.

Whalley, J. 1980. Discriminating features of domestic factor tax systems in a goods mobile-factors immobile trade model: An empirical general equilibrium approach. *Journal of Political Economy* 88:1177-202.

Comments

Peter Mieszkowski

The authors of this chapter and John Whalley have been the leaders in analyzing the general equilibrium effects of alternative tax policy. They began by extending the work of Arnold Harberger (1962, 1966) and have consistently developed the scope and complexity of the neoclassical approach to tax analysis. In previous papers they have incorporated work-leisure choice, the savings decision, foreign trade, and international capital movements, and have analyzed the static and dynamic impacts of various tax policy changes on the economic welfare of 12 income groups.

In two recent contributions, Fullerton, King, Shoven, and Whalley (1981) and Fullerton, Shoven, and Whalley (FSW) (1983) have analyzed corporate tax integration and the effects of replacing the income tax with a progressive consumption tax. The work is most impressive; a wide range of policy alternatives are analyzed under a number of different sets of parameter values. This research has yielded a basic approach by which we evaluate alternative tax policies. The work by Fullerton, Shoven, and Whalley takes its place beside the econometric work on the effects of taxes and social security on economic behavior as the most important contribution to quantitative public economics since the early 1970s.

Fullerton, Henderson, and Shoven's contribution to this volume is a chapter on methodology that compares the alternative specifications of different models. Their discussion concerns disaggregation, the foreign sector, financial behavior, the measurement of effective taxes, imperfect mobility, dynamic considerations, government budget, and technical operations.

The chapter is only partially successful in conveying the accomplishments of past research and the relative importance of various theoretical issues and alternative specifications. The authors, perhaps because of their modesty, cite relatively few results from this previous work, and their very important accomplishments are understated. The significance of alternative specification and key parameters would have been clearer if additional results had been presented.

One of the most illuminating sections of the chapter, developed by means of a number of results, demonstrates the importance of disaggregating production sectors and capturing the misallocation resulting from tax rate differences within the corporate sector. Also demonstrated is the importance of the selection of industries for a two-sector model.

In contrast to the complete and effective discussion of disaggregation, the discussion of the foreign sector is very terse. Goulder, Shoven, and Whalley (1983) have demonstrated the importance of international capital and foreign tax credits for domestic tax policy. A superior policy when the economy is closed, or when foreign capital movements are insensitive to rates of return, may decrease a country's welfare when capital is highly mobile internationally.

Goulder, Shoven, and Whalley find that the gains of corporate tax integration increase with the degree of response of international capital movements, whereas the reverse is true of the introduction of a consumption tax (a savings deduction). Concretely, a present value gain of $326 billion for this policy change without capital mobility turns into a $486 billion loss with responsive international capital movements.

A more complete discussion of results would also have strengthened the authors' presentation of the importance of the assumption, made in the FSW model, that the after-tax rate of return for a particular income group is the same in all sectors and on all assets. Slemrod's contributions (1980, 1983) are significant as he allows for these differences. High-income groups have a tax incentive to hold disproportionate amounts of tax-exempt municipal debt and corporate equity.

By disaggregating high-income groups – income in excess of $22,500 – into six groups, Slemrod is able to show the variations among these groups and demonstrate that corporate tax integration benefits all income groups, except the very wealthy. Another experiment, indexation for inflation, shows how varied the impacts of inflation are on different groups. For example, inflation decreases the cost of housing for the wealthy and increases it for moderate-income groups. In part, the new insights gained by Slemrod are the result of greater disaggregation at higher income levels. However, his basic contribution is the specification of financial assets and the effect of taxes on portfolio choice.

Fullerton and Gordon (1983), building on the theoretical work of Gordon (1981), have raised two fundamental conceptual issues. The first is how effective tax rates are to be calculated and whether average and marginal tax rates are equal. The second is whether the corporate tax is largely a tax on returns to risk and is therefore nondistortionary.

As pointed out by Fullerton, Henderson, and Shoven (FHS), there are a number of reasons why average and marginal tax rates may vary. It is well known that a cash flow corporate income tax that allows instantaneous depreciation for new capital expenditures and no deduction for interest on debt is nondistortionary. With a 50% tax rate the government puts up 50% of the funds for marginal investments in return for 50% of gross profits. Such a tax system may collect substantial tax revenues on intramarginal profits. For example, petroleum companies may pay large taxes on windfall profits but, because of the expensing of dry wells and intangible drilling expenses, pay no tax on marginal investments.

The distinction between average and marginal tax rates seems particularly relevant following the dramatic shortening of asset lives in the Tax Act of 1981. The combination of accelerated depreciation and deduction of interest on debt has probably eliminated the corporate tax on investment in many industries. Also, the calculation of effective tax rates from statutory tax information will integrate general equilibrium models of taxation with the investment literature that emphasizes cost of capital.

Whether the corporate tax is a tax on risk taking and is nondistortionary is a fundamental issue that bears on the welfare effects of corporate tax integration and the elimination of the corporate tax under a progressive expenditure tax. However, Harberger and FSW have assumed an exogenous financial structure for corporations, independent of taxes. The reasons for the coexistence of equity and debt are not explored, and it is assumed that the corporate tax will increase the cost of equity by the amount of the tax.

The Fullerton–Gordon proposition that the return to equity is primarily a return for risks implies that by sharing in income *and* risk the corporate tax does not distort equity investment as the government shares in risk in proportion to its share in income.

There are two responses to this point. One is to argue that the very low real return to riskless assets observed in the 1970s is atypical and not representative of long-run equilibrium. The real rate of return on debt in 1982 is much higher than in 1973. But Ibbotson and Sinquefeld (1979) report a substantial premium on equity, about 9 percentage points over the last 50 years.

The second point is made by Bulow and Summers (1982) who argue that the earlier analyses of taxes assume no risk in asset prices. Bulow-Summers maintain that when the uncertainty in the market value of a firm's assets and hence its stock market value are accounted for, the corporate tax that shares in income risk, but not price risk, will distort corporate investment by increasing the required tax on corporate investment.

I follow FHS in supporting the Bulow-Summers argument. Their basic point – that an investment is risky largely because of the uncertainty in its market (terminal) value – sits very well with common sense. The Bulow-Summers conclusion is also consistent with the claims of corporate officials that they shift the corporate tax by increasing the required rate of return on investment. However, the Fullerton–Gordon modeling of the effects of the corporate tax, while extreme, raises a fundamental point that should be incorporated in a more general approach; otherwise the range of estimates on the effects of corporate tax integration and related policies is too wide to be very helpful for policy.

REFERENCES

Bulow, J. I., and Summers, L. H. 1982. The taxation of risky assets. National Bureau of Economic Research, Discussion Paper No. 897, Cambridge, Mass.

Fullerton, D., and Gordon, R. H. 1983. A reexamination of tax distortions in general equilibrium models. In Feldstein, M. S., ed., *Behavioral simulation methods in tax policy analysis*. Chicago: University of Chicago Press.

Fullerton, D., King, A. T., Shoven, J. B., and Whalley, J. 1981. Tax integration in the U.S.: A general equilibrium approach. *American Economic Review* 71:677–91.

Fullerton, D., Shoven, J. B., and Whalley, J. 1983. Replacing the U.S. income tax with a progressive consumption tax: A sequenced general equilibrium approach. *Journal of Public Economics*, 20:1–21.

Gordon, R. H. 1981. Taxation of corporate capital income: Tax revenues vs. tax distortions. Bell Laboratories Economics Discussion Paper #212. September.

Goulder, L. H., Shoven, J. B., and Whalley, J. 1983. Domestic tax policy and the foreign sector: The importance of alternative foreign policy formulations to results from a general equilibrium tax analysis model. In Feldstein, M. S., ed., *Behavioral simulation methods in tax policy analysis*. Chicago: University of Chicago Press.

Harberger, A. C. 1962. The incidence of the corporation tax. *Journal of Political Economy* 70:215–40.

———. 1966. Efficiency effects of taxes on income from capital. In Krzyzaniak, M., ed., *Effects of corporation income tax*. Detroit: Wayne State University Press.

Ibbotson, Roger G., and Sinquefeld, Rex A. 1979. *Stocks, Bonds, Bills, and Inflation: Historical Returns (1926–78) and Supplements*. Charlottesville, Va.: Financial Analysts' Research Foundation.

Shoven, J. B., and Whalley, J. 1972. A general equilibrium calculation of the effects of differential taxation of income from capital in the U.S. *Journal of Public Economics* 1:281–321.

———. 1973. General equilibrium with taxes: A computational procedure and an existence proof. *Review of Economic Studies* 40:475–89.

Slemrod, J. B. 1980. A general equilibrium model of capital income taxation. Ph.D. diss., Harvard University.

———. 1983. A general equilibrium model of taxation with endogenous financial behavior. In Feldstein, M. S., ed., *Behavioral simulation methods in tax policy analysis*. Chicago: University of Chicago Press.

CHAPTER 10

Planning models and general equilibrium activity analysis

Victor Ginsburgh and Jean Waelbroeck

1   Introduction

One of the important trends in model building for developing countries has been the CGE (computable general equilibrium) approach introduced by Adelman and Robinson (1978). This can describe systems in which there are several groups of utility-maximizing consumers, extending the approach of Johansen (1960) and others, which had described general equilibrium models with one group of consumers. These models tend to play the role of the so-called planning models (using linear programming), which were quite fashionable 10 to 15 years ago. The passing of the planning models has to a significant extent been due to the growing realization of their theoretical weaknesses; Taylor's paper (1975) gave the coup de grace.

In recent years, Ginsburgh and Waelbroeck (1975) and Manne (1977) have been developing what the first two have called the AGE (activity analysis general equilibrium) approach, which starts from Koopmans's activity analysis; the first implementation of this type of ideas is by Dixon (1975).

The goal of this chapter is to illustrate that the approach is capable of giving a second lease on life to "planning models" – subject to modification of their specification and solution procedure. This is important, for the planning models did provide a way of using the technological data available to planners,[1] a function that the CGE models cannot easily take over. The CGE models, on the other hand, are cheaper to solve than the traditional planning models, and a fortiori cheaper than the more complex AGE models.

The chapter is organized as follows. Section 2 shows how programming models should theoretically be constructed so that their solutions generate general (competitive) equilibria. Section 3 shows how to represent concave (convex) functions by linear programming. The treatment of inelastic foreign demand and supply is discussed in Section 4, the treatment of capital accumulation and saving in Section 5. To illustrate these concepts, they are applied to Sandee's well-known planning model for India (Section 6).

2   The relation between competitive equilibrium and plan

Users of empirical "planning" models have invoked implicitly one of the fundamental theorems of welfare economics, which relates the concept of "competitive equilibrium" to that of "plan," formulated as a mathematical program. This theorem states that a competitive equilibrium is the solution of a mathematical program; in the very special case of one single agent the converse is also true.

To state the version of the theorem that we need, we define the following variables: x, y, and ω are n-vectors (there are n commodities) of consumption, production, and initial resources (land etc.); X and Y are convex consumption and production sets; p is a vector of prices; $U(x)$ is the utility function of the unique consumer.

Definition 2.1. Competitive equilibrium for a one-agent closed economy. The allocation $\bar{x}, \bar{y}$ supported by the price vector $\bar{p} \geqslant 0$ is a competitive equilibrium if

 (a) $\bar{x}$ maximizes $U(x)$ subject to $\bar{p} \cdot x \leqslant \bar{p} \cdot \omega + \bar{p} \cdot \bar{y}$, $x \in X$
 (b) $\bar{y}$ maximizes $\bar{p} \cdot y$ subject to $y \in Y$
 (c) $\bar{x} - \bar{y} - \omega \leqslant 0$; $p \cdot (\bar{x} - \bar{y} - \omega) = 0$

In this definition, (a) describes the utility maximization problem of the consumer, subject to his budget constraint at given prices $\bar{p}$; the right-hand side of the budget constraint is the consumer's income; (b) describes the profit maximization problem of the producer, at given prices and subject to technological constraints; (c) states that consumption of each commodity is bounded by supply, whereas if, for a certain commodity there is excess supply, the price is zero.

Definition 2.2. "Planning model." The planning model simply looks for a solution that maximizes utility, subject to feasibility constraints:

$$\max U(x) \quad \text{subject to} \quad x - y - \omega \leqslant 0, \quad x \in X, \quad y \in Y$$

The theorem that links the two definitions can now be stated as:

Theorem 2.1 (Karlin, 1959): If $U(x)$ is concave, the optimal primal solution $\bar{x}, \bar{y}$ and the optimal dual prices $\bar{p}$ (associated with $x - y - \omega \leqslant 0$) of the planning model are a competitive equilibrium, that is, satisfy conditions (a), (b), and (c) of Definition 2.1.

We do not give the proof, which can be found in Karlin (1959, pp. 294–7); but we observe that, as a consequence of the Kuhn–Tucker theorem, the optimal solution of the planning model satisfies $\bar{p} \cdot (\bar{x} - \bar{y} - \omega) = 0$; this also shows that for $x = \bar{x}$, the budget constraint of the consumer is satisfied. This observation is crucial to the understanding of the rest of the argument.

Planners have modified the basic format of the model, mainly in two ways:

1. Because linear programming is so much easier to use than nonlinear programming, they have tended to consider only linear utility functions that are separable and imply constant marginal utilities of commodities[2] and linear consumption and production sets.
2. They have tried to take into account international trade and investment.

3   Linearization of nonlinear functions

Let us first consider the consequences of a linear utility function, say $c \cdot x$, and assume the constraints to be linear. The planning model then boils down to a linear program; the difficulty faced by linear planning models originates in a theorem that states that, if a linear program is feasible and the solution set-bounded, there exists an optimal solution in which the number of nonzero variables, including slacks, does not exceed the number of constraints, other than nonnegativity constraints. Thus, out of the $2n$ variables (n consumptions and n productions), at most n will be positive. The situation is even worse if n export and import activities are allowed for. To prevent such extreme solutions, one has to increase the number of constraints; and since it is very hard to find enough economically meaningful constraints, builders of planning models have improvised a complex assortment of bounds on production, consumption, and import and export levels, without careful justification. For instance, production is bounded above or below in recognition of "resource constraints that limit expansion" or of "the social costs of a rapid reduction of output"; consumption is constrained to fluctuate between upper and lower bounds because "the planner's ability to influence consumption patterns is not unlimited"; and so forth.

The result is, in effect, to define a small cage out of which the optimal solution cannot escape. This is good diplomacy, as policy makers can then please governments by presenting solutions that both look reasonable and are claimed to optimal. But this is neither good economics nor a reasonable way of formulating economic policy.

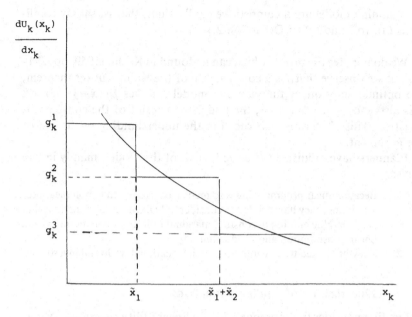

Figure 1. Stepwise approximation of a separable concave utility function.

Planners do also compute shadow prices that can be used for project analysis and other forms of decentralized decision making. But the arbitrary bounds introduced pick up shadow prices that have no clear meaning and distort the dual solution. How, for instance, should one interpret, in a decentralized decision-making context, the shadow price of a constraint expressing "the inability of planners to distort consumption patterns beyond given limits"?

This can be avoided by linearizing nonlinear utility functions. This is discussed at length in Ginsburgh and Waelbroeck (1981). We will thus present the approach briefly.

If the utility function is separable, it can be written as $U(x) = \sum_{k=1}^{n} U_k(x_k)$, where x_k is consumption of good k. If marginal utility of each good is positive and decreasing, each component $U_k(x_k)$ can be approximated with arbitrary accuracy by steps as illustrated in Figure 1, and the utility function can be represented by the linear program

$$U(x) = \max \sum_k \sum_s g_k^s x_k^s$$

subject to

$$\sum_s x_k^s \le x_k, \qquad k = 1, 2, \ldots, n$$

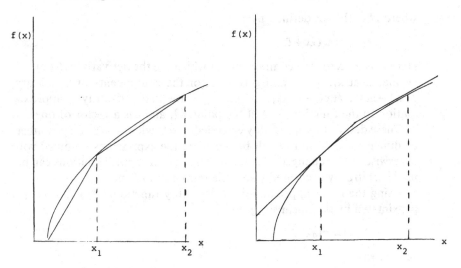

Figure 2. Inner and outer approximations of a convex set.

$$0 \leqslant x_k^s \leqslant \bar{x}_k^s, \quad s = 1, 2, \ldots, S, \quad k = 1, 2, \ldots, n$$

Here g_k^s is the average value of the marginal utility of good k on step s, and $\bar{x}_k^s$ is a given bound.

This formulation introduces a large number of additional constraints into the model, freeing the solution from the straightjacket apparently imposed by linear programming theory.

For a nonseparable utility function the representation is based on the fact that if $U(x)$ is concave, $C = \{x, U \mid U \leqslant U(x)\}$ is a convex set in R^{n+1}, bounded above by the graph of the utility function; $U(x)$ can now be defined by the mathematical program

$$U(x) = \max U$$

subject to

$$(U, x) \in C \qquad \text{for given} \quad x \in X$$

As a convex set, C can be approximated in two ways, which are illustrated in Figure 2.

In Figure 2, a grid $X = [x_1 x_2 x_3 \ldots]$ is defined to approximate the convex set bounded above by a concave function $f(x)$.

In the sequel, we discuss the use in models of the outer approximation only. There is no difficulty in implementing the ideas using the inner approximation.

The outer approximation is defined by

$$C = \{x, f(x) \mid x, f(x) \in H\}$$

where H is the set defined by

$$\epsilon \cdot f(x) \leqslant Gx + \tilde{g}$$

Here G is a vector the components of which are the derivatives $df(x)/dx$ evaluated at $x_1, x_2, \ldots$ and g is a vector the components of which are $f(x_1) - g_1 x_1$, $f(x_2) - g_2 x_2, \ldots$ [$g_i x_i + \tilde{g}_i$ is the first-order Taylor approximation to the function $f(x)$ at the point x_i], and ϵ is a vector of ones.

These definitions are readily extended to sets with an arbitrary number of dimensions. X and G will be matrices; the expressions obtained will otherwise not be changed. Also, it is clear that the approximations can be made arbitrarily accurate by suitable refinement of the grid.

Using the outer approximation, the utility function $U(x)$ can be approximated by the linear program

$$U(x) = \max U$$

subject to

$$\epsilon U - Gx \leqslant \tilde{g} \qquad \text{for given } x \geqslant 0$$

which is easy to introduce into a linear programming model of an economy.

As to production sets, it is well known that they can be represented by linear inequalities. It is seen, therefore, that there is no difficulty in using linear programming to represent equilibrium problems of general type, provided only that this involves concave utility functions and convex production sets.

4   The introduction of international trade

Let us next consider the introduction of international trade; to do this, define a vector of net imports

$$m - e = x - y - \omega$$

and note that the budget constraint of the consumer can now be written $p \cdot (m - e) \leqslant 0$ instead of $p \cdot (x - y - \omega) \leqslant 0$. In condition (c) of Definition 2.1, $x - y - \omega$ will be replaced by $x - y - \omega - (m - e)$. Suppose we now try to generate a competitive allocation for this economy by solving the following "planning model" $\max U(x)$ subject to $x - y - \omega - (m - e) \leqslant 0$, $x \in X$, $y \in Y$. At the optimal point, by the Kuhn-Tucker theorem, we have

$$\bar{p} \cdot (\bar{x} - \bar{y} - \omega - (\bar{m} - \bar{e})) = 0$$

but nothing guarantees that this satisfies also the budget constraint $\bar{p} \cdot (\bar{m} - \bar{e}) \leqslant 0$. If we want this to be satisfied, we need to impose it;

but since we do not know $\bar{p}$ beforehand, we impose a constraint $p^w \cdot (m - e) \leqslant 0$, where p^w is a vector of "given world prices." This can be justified on grounds of the "small country assumption," but nevertheless implies infinitely elastic export demand and import supply. It is not surprising to trade economists that planning models based on such assumptions have solutions implying extreme specialization: Very few goods are produced and exported; domestic demand of the other goods is entirely met by imports.

A correct solution to this problem is provided by an existence theorem for a competitive equilibrium due to Negishi (1960). To simplify the presentation, we state the results for an economy without production, but the results hold in the general case. Let x_i and ω_i be the consumer i's ($i = 1, 2, \ldots, m$) consumption and initial endowment; $U_i(x_i)$ is his (monotonic and concave) utility function, and x_i his (convex) consumption set.

Definition 4.1. Competitive equilibrium for an m-agent closed economy. The allocation $\bar{x}_1, \ldots, \bar{x}_m$ supported by a price vector $\bar{p} \geqslant 0$ is a competitive equilibrium if

(a) $\bar{x}_i$ maximizes $U_i(x_i)$ subject to the budget constraint $\bar{p} \cdot x_i \leqslant \bar{p} \cdot \omega_i$ and feasibility $x_i \in X_i$, for all $i = 1, 2, \ldots, m$

(b) $\sum_i \bar{x}_i \leqslant \sum_i \omega_i$; $\bar{p} \cdot (\sum_i \bar{x}_i - \sum_i \omega_i) = 0$

Theorem 4.1 (Negishi): There exist positive scalars $\bar{\alpha}_1, \ldots, \bar{\alpha}_m$, $\sum \bar{\alpha}_i = 1$ such that the primal and dual solutions of the mathematical program $\sum_i \alpha_i U_i(x_i)$ subject to $\sum_i x_i \leqslant \sum_i \omega_i$, $x_i \in X_i$ for all i, satisfy conditions (a) and (b) above; $\bar{p}$ is the vector of shadow prices associated with $\sum_i x_i \leqslant \sum_i \omega_i$.

The main point to observe here is that for this specific choice of α values, the budget constraints will all be satisfied as equalities [combine $\bar{p} \cdot x_i \leqslant \bar{p} \cdot \omega_i$ and $\bar{p} \cdot (\sum_i \bar{x}_i - \sum_i \omega_i) = 0$].

In the general m-consumer case, the search for the equilibrium welfare weights $\bar{\alpha}_i$ is difficult. In a two-agent case (the country and the rest of the world), however, the solution is straightforward. Consider the problem $\max \alpha_1 U_1(x_1) + \alpha_2 U_2(x_2)$ ($\alpha_1 + \alpha_2 = 1$) subject to $x_1 + x_2 \leqslant \omega_1 + \omega_2$, $X_1 = X_2 = \Omega^+$. Solving the problem with $\alpha_1 = 1$ (and $\alpha_2 = 0$) will give a solution $p \cdot x_1 = \omega_1 + \omega_2$, $x_2 = 0$ such that $p \cdot x_1 > p \cdot \omega_1$, $p \cdot x_2 < p \cdot \omega_2$; whereas if $\alpha_2 = 1$ ($\alpha_1 = 0$), we end up with $x_1 = 0$, $x_2 = \omega_1 + \omega_2$, and $p \cdot x_1 < p \cdot \omega_1$, $p \cdot x_2 > p \cdot \omega_2$. So, when we decrease α_1 from 1 to 0, there is a value $\bar{\alpha}_1$ such that the optimal $\bar{p}$, $\bar{x}_i$ satisfy the budget constraint of consumer 1.[3] Because of the Walras law $\bar{p} \cdot (\bar{x}_1 + \bar{x}_2) = \bar{p} \cdot (\omega_1 + \omega_2)$, for this value $\bar{\alpha}_1$ (and $\bar{\alpha}_2$), the budget constraint of the second consumer will also hold as an equality.

These considerations lead to a very easy computational procedure to find a two-agent equilibrium. It involves parameterizing the objective function, giving to α_1 values between 1 and 0. It is readily proved that a continuous *tâtonnement* process in which α_1 is adjusted according to the rule

$$\frac{d\alpha_1}{dt} = p(\alpha) \cdot \omega_1 - p(\alpha) \cdot x_1(\alpha)$$

converges to an equilibrium.[4] Computers can handle only discrete processes; these will identify an arbitrarily small interval in which the equilibrium $\bar{\alpha}_1$ lies.

Negishi's theorem seems to imply that complete models should built for the country and for the "rest of the world," which would be difficult. Construction of the latter model is of course not practical. It is, however, possible to use a device of international trade theory, the trade welfare function, relating the welfare of a country to its imports and exports. Let $U(x)$ be the utility function of the country. The trade welfare function defines the maximum utility the country can reach for given values of exports $\bar{e} \in E$, imports $\bar{m} \in M$, and initial resources. Here E, M are sets of feasible exports and imports. This is

$$V(\bar{e}, \bar{m}) \max U(x)$$

subject to

$$x - y \leqslant m - \bar{e} + \omega, \quad y \in Y, \quad x \in X, \quad \bar{m} \in M, \quad \bar{e} \in E$$

This trade welfare function, which is concave if $U(x)$ is concave and Y and X convex, can be represented by linear programming along the lines of Section 3 and used to determine exports and imports of the rest of the world.

The model of an open economy facing inelastic foreign demand would then have the following form:

Program 4.2

$$\max \alpha U(x) + (1 - \alpha) V(e, m), \qquad 0 \leqslant \alpha \leqslant 1$$

subject to

$$x - y - m + e \leqslant \omega, \quad x \in X, \quad y \in Y, \quad e \in E, \quad m \in M$$

with α such that $p \cdot (m - e) = 0$, where p is the vector of dual prices associated with $x - y - m + e \leqslant \omega$. Note that the balance-of-payments constraint $p \cdot (m - e) = 0$ does not appear in the programming model; this constraint is bilinear in prices and volumes and the model cannot be solved as a linear program; nonlinear programming would be of no help either, since there is no nonlinear programming computing technique that can solve models involving constraints that are bilinear in primal and dual variables.

The model can be solved as suggested earlier by gradually increasing values of α (starting at $\alpha = 0$) or by *tâtonnement;* both are guaranteed to produce a solution.

Computational procedure 1

Initialization: Choose a value $\alpha = \alpha^0$. Set $t = 0$.
    Iteration t:

Phase 1. Function evaluation: Solve Program 4.2. Compute $B(\alpha^t) = -p^t \cdot e^t + p^t \cdot m^t$, where p, e, and m are optimal dual prices, exports, and imports. If $B(\alpha^t) \approx 0$, stop. The solution of the program is an equilibrium. If not, go to phase 2.

Phase 2. Parameter revision: Use the following difference equation to update α:

$$\alpha^{t+1} = \alpha^t + \lambda B(\alpha^t)$$

where λ is a positive scalar. Set $t = t + 1$ and go to the next iteration.

We are in fact using Program 4.2 to evaluate the function $B(\alpha)$; in phase 2 we look for the value $\bar{\alpha}$ that solves $B(\alpha) = 0$. The solution of Program 4.2 with $\alpha = \bar{\alpha}$ is an equilibrium.

5   Investment and saving

From a formal point of view, if the number of periods is finite, multiperiod equilibrium is no more complicated than equilibrium for one period. Each agent maximizes an intertemporal utility function subject to an intertemporal balance constraint. The modeling approach sketched above is applicable.

Attempts to implement this idea have led to disappointing results. The problem is similar to that encountered using trade models with infinitely elastic foreign demand and supply: The model generates a highly unstable path of consumption and saving, with big consumption splurges in some years and very high saving in others. It is possible to smooth out these paths by defining for each period a utility function that implies a sharply decreasing marginal utility of income, but this is rather artificial as very little is known about the way in which utility changes as income rises. Our view is that it is the theory of intertemporal consumption decisions that is unrealistic: consumers know so little about future incomes and prices that they make saving decisions on the basis of "rules of thumb" related to present incomes and prices rather than optimally on the basis of forecasts of future prices and incomes; we assume that they use saving functions similar to those that appear in Keynesian models. These ideas lead to the following consumer utility maximization problem:

$$\max U(x)$$

subject to

$$\bar{p} \cdot x + \bar{\sigma} \leqslant p \cdot (\omega + \bar{y}), \qquad x \in X$$

where $\bar{\sigma}$ is, say, a constant fraction γ of income:

$$\bar{\sigma} = \gamma \bar{p} \cdot (\omega + \bar{y})$$

For investment, there arises the well-known problem of terminal conditions. Because in practice models must have a finite horizon, it is necessary to fix terminal prices of capital goods or the terminal pattern of investment in some sensible way. Here again many devices have been proposed, the best (but expensive to solve) being to follow Goreux and Manne (1973) in choosing a horizon much beyond the practical plan period to minimize the impact on decisions of the arbitrary terminal conditions.

We shall not offer judgment on all the devices that have been proposed to deal with these two problems. What we shall emphasize rather is that if the constraints imposed to reflect the observed stability of saving patterns are included in the optimizing model, the latter will imply an inefficient use of resources, and hence its results cannot be interpreted as an equilibrium.

To make the point clear, it is enough to consider a simple case, which corresponds to a widely used model structure.

To simplify the presentation, we assume no lag between production and investment. Let v_0 and y_0 represent initial-year investment and production; assume investment increases with Δ every year, reaching $v_0 + T\Delta$ during the terminal year T; accumulated investment is then $Tv_0 + \frac{1}{2}T(T-1)\Delta$. Since there is no lag, if, to simplify further, output in calendar year T is related to investment up to the middle of year T, accumulated investment is $Tv_0 + \frac{1}{2}T^2\Delta$. Initial capacity is κy_0, where κ is a matrix of capital coefficients. Hence, terminal capital stocks will be equal to

$$\kappa y_0 + Tv_0 + \frac{1}{2} T^2\Delta = K_0 + \frac{T}{2} v$$

where $K_0 = \kappa y_0 + T v_0$ and $v = T\Delta$. This leads to the following producer profit maximization problem:

$$\max \bar{p} \cdot y$$

subject to

$$\kappa y \leqslant K_0 + \frac{T}{2} \bar{v}, \qquad y \in Y$$

with $\bar{v}$ given.

The general equilibrium model is now:

Definition 5.1. Competitive equilibrium for a one-agent closed economy with investment. The allocation $\bar{x}, \bar{y}, \bar{v}$ supported by the price vector $\bar{p} \geqslant 0$ is a competitive equilibrium if

    (a) $\bar{x}$ maximizes $U(x)$ subject to $\bar{p} \cdot x + \bar{\sigma} \leqslant \bar{p} \cdot (\omega + \bar{y})$, $x \in X$

    (b) $\bar{y}$ maximizes $\bar{p} \cdot y$ subject to $\kappa y \leqslant K_0 + (T/2) \bar{v}$, $y \in Y$

    (c) $\bar{x} - \bar{y} + \bar{v} - \omega \leqslant 0$; $\bar{p} \cdot (\bar{x} - \bar{y} + \bar{v} - \omega) = 0$; $\bar{\sigma} = \bar{p} \cdot \bar{v}$

The $\bar{\sigma} = \bar{p} \cdot \bar{v}$ is simply the equilibrium condition stating that ex post, saving equals investment.

Let us now set up the following one-period "planning model":

Definition 5.2. Planning model with investment

$$\max U(x)$$

subject to

$$x - y + v - \omega \leqslant 0 \qquad \text{(dual prices} = p)$$

$$\kappa y - \frac{T}{2} v \leqslant K_0 \qquad \text{(dual prices} = r)$$

$$x \in X, \qquad y \in Y$$

At the optimal point of this program, the budget constraint will be satisfied, since

$$\bar{p} \cdot \bar{x} + \bar{p} \cdot \bar{v} = \bar{p} \cdot \omega + \bar{p} \cdot \bar{y}$$

but nothing guarantees

$$p^I \cdot v \leqslant \gamma p^I \cdot (\omega + \bar{y}) \qquad \text{(dual prices} = u_\gamma)$$

at given prices p^I.

As pointed out in particular by Taylor (1975), the dual of the system does not make sense from an economic point of view. At the optimum, the dual constraint reads

$$p + u_\gamma p' = \frac{T}{2} r$$

imposing that for every investment good i, r_i should be equal to $2/T$ times a weighted average of the market price p_i of the good and the "given" price p_i' of that good. Moreover, if $x_i > 0$, we also have

$$\frac{\partial U(x)}{\partial x_i} = p_i = \frac{T}{2} r_i - u_\gamma p_i'$$

which is a very strange way of evaluating marginal utilities.

More fundamentally, the model of Definition 5.2 with a saving constraint does not even guarantee efficient use of resources. To see this, solve Model 5.2 (with a saving constraint) and obtain the optimal value $\bar{v}$. Construct then the following model without saving constraint (since it has no general equilibrium interpretation):

Model 5.3

$$\max U(x)$$

subject to

$$x - y \leqslant \omega - \bar{v}, \quad \kappa y \leqslant K_0 + \frac{T}{2} \bar{v}, \quad x \in X, \quad y \in Y$$

It is clear that the optimal $\bar{v}$ is feasible for Model 5.3; if the dual prices $\bar{p}_i$ of the first program are not all equal, it is easy to construct an example (with a linear utility function) in which the optimum of Model 5.3 exceeds that of the first program.

We now formulate a computational procedure, which is closely related to the procedure described in Section 4. The similarity between Program 5.2 and Program 4.2 is that in both cases, there is an equation, bilinear in prices and volumes, that has to be satisfied. In Program 4.2 it is the balance of payments; here it is the saving investment identity.

Computational procedure 2

Initialization: Choose initial values $v = v^0$. Set $t = 0$.
    Iteration t:

Phase 1. Function evaluation: Solve Program 5.2. Then compute

$$\sigma(v') = \gamma p' \cdot (\omega + y') : p' \cdot v'$$

where v' is a given vector of investments, while p' and y' are solutions of Program 5.2. If $\sigma(v') \approx 1$, stop. The saving equation is satisfied. If not, go to phase 2.

Phase 2. Parameter revision: Use the following difference equations to update v':

$$v'^{+1} = \sigma(v')^\mu v'$$

where μ is a positive scalar. Set $t = t + 1$ and go to the next iteration.

As in the preceding section, the program is used to evaluate a function $\sigma(v)$ [earlier we evaluated $B(\alpha)$], and we look in phase 2 for the value $v = \bar{v}$ that solves $\sigma(\bar{v}) = 1$. The solution of Program 5.2 for $v = \bar{v}$ is an equilibrium.

However, if there are several capital goods, a more flexible procedure is needed that reflects the fact that new capital v' is putty, so that it can be allocated optimally between the various types of equipment. This allocation should reflect the prices of the different capital goods.

We need an "aggregate capital constraint" in which the different capital goods are evaluated at prices that reflect marginal cost. Define:

Program 5.4

$$\max U(x)$$

subject to

$$x - y + v - \omega \leqslant 0 \qquad \text{(dual prices} = p)$$

$$p \cdot \kappa y - \frac{T}{2} p \cdot v \leqslant p \cdot K_0 \qquad \text{(dual prices} = r)$$

$$x \in X, \quad y \in Y$$

and consider the following algorithm:

Computational procedure 3

Initialization: Choose initial values $v = v^0$ and $p = p^{-1}$. Set $t = 0$.
  Iteration t:

Phase 1. Function evaluation: Solve Program 5.4. Then compute

$$\sigma(v', p') = \gamma p' \cdot (\omega + y') : p' \cdot v' \qquad \text{and} \qquad v(v', p') = \frac{2}{T}(\kappa y' - K_0)$$

where p^t and y^t are solutions of Program 5.4. If $\sigma(\cdot) \simeq 1$ and $v(\cdot) \simeq v^t$, stop. The saving equation is satisfied and each $\kappa y - (T/2)v \leqslant K_0$ constraint is binding. If not, go to phase 2.

Phase 2. Parameter revision: Use the following difference equation to update v^t:

$$v^{t+1} = \sigma(v^t, p^t)^\mu v^t$$

where μ is a positive scalar. Set $t = t + 1$ and go to the next iteration.

6   An application to Sandee's model for India

We illustrate the procedure by applying it to Sandee's model for India, one of the first planning models ever built, which served as a prototype for much of the later work.[5] The model's simplicity, clean design, and small size make it very suitable as the basis of an illustration. This of course does not mean that we are somehow correcting errors that it embodies. Sandee meant it as a tool for planning calculations, not as a description of how a competitive market might function in India. We also are not pretending that our adaptation of the model produces a satisfactory description of such a market: A substantially larger and more complex system would be necessary. Our goal is to show, for readers familiar with the planning model literature, how a simple but rather typical model would have to be transformed to generate a solution that satisfies the canons of general equilibrium theory. In that spirit, we do not hesitate to invent coefficients where needed, without bothering to estimate them.

6.1   The constraints of Sandee's model

The model includes 13 sectors[6] and the following equations:

Supply-demand balances for commodities

$$\underset{\text{Production}}{-y_k} \; + \; \underset{\substack{\text{Demand for} \\ \text{commodity } k \text{ by} \\ \text{industries}}}{\textstyle\sum_h a_{kh} y_h} \; + \; \underset{\text{Consumption}}{x_k} \; + \; \underset{\text{Investment}}{v_k}$$

$$+ \; \underset{\substack{\text{Consumption} \\ \text{of fertilizer} \\ \text{by agriculture}}}{y_k^*} \; + \; \underset{\text{Exports}}{e_k} \; - \; \underset{\text{Imports}}{m_k} \; \leqslant \; \underset{\substack{\text{Exogenous} \\ \text{right-hand} \\ \text{side}}}{\omega_k} \qquad (6.1)$$

This equation, defined for $k = 1, 2, \ldots, 13$ is the classical input–output identity; x_k (consumption) is defined for $k=1, 2, 7, 10, 12,$ and 13; v_k (investment) for $k=8, 9,$ and 11; y_k^* (consumption of fertilizer by agriculture) for $k=6$; and e_k (exports) and m_k (imports) for $k=1, 2, 3, 6, 8$ to $10,$ and 12. Finally, we denote by p_k the dual price picked up by this balance and refer to it as the domestic price of commodity k.

Capital goods balances

$$-(T/2)v_k \;+\; \Sigma_h \, \kappa_{kh} y_h \;+\; v^* \;\leqslant\; K_{0k} \qquad (6.2)$$

| Capital created during the planning period | Capital required by sectors except by irrigation | Capital investment in irrigation | Initial capital |

Such equations are defined for $k=8, 9,$ and 11; v^* is defined only for $k=11$; T is the time horizon (10 years), while v_k is investment embodied in good k.

Agricultural production function

$$y_1 \;-\; b_1 y^* \;-\; b_2 v^* \;-\; b_3 a^* \;=\; b_4 \qquad (6.3)$$

| Agricultural supply | Fertilizer inputs | Irrigation projects | Extension services | Constant |

with the following bounds for the inputs:

$$y^* \leqslant \bar{y}^*, \quad -\bar{v}^* \leqslant v^* \leqslant \bar{v}^* \quad a^* \leqslant \bar{a}^*$$

Constraints on imports and exports: Sandee introduces upper and lower bounds for exports and imports to exclude solutions that do not appear credible. These are generally of the form

$$e_k \leqslant \bar{e}_k, \quad m_k \leqslant \bar{m}_k$$

for $k=1, 2, 6, 9, 10,$ and 12.

For steel and for heavy engineering, the upper bounds on imports depend on production. Sandee makes it clear that this reflects a policy objective of import substitution. The formulation is

$$m_k - \mu_k y_k \leqslant 0 \qquad \text{for} \quad k=3 \text{ and } 8 \qquad (6.4)$$

Constant-prices balance-of-payments constraint: The import and export constraints are complemented by a balance-of-payments constraint, expressed at fixed (unit) prices:

$$\Sigma_h \, m_h - \Sigma_h \, e_h \leqslant 0 \qquad (6.5)$$

| Imports | Exports |

Consumption bounds: The constraints involving consumption are defined as follows:

$$-\bar{x}_k^- \quad \leqslant \quad x_k \quad -\gamma_k \, \Sigma_h \, x_h \leqslant \quad \bar{x}_k^+, \qquad k=1,2,7,13 \qquad (6.6)$$

| Lower bound | Consumption | Share of consumption evaluated at unit price | Upper bound |

Each consumption is allowed a limited freedom around the rigid Engel pattern $\gamma_k \, \Sigma_h \, x_h$. Only one such constraint is defined for the sum of large-scale and small-scale manufactured goods:

$$-\bar{x}_*^- \leqslant x_{10}+x_{12}-\gamma_* \, \Sigma_h \, x_h \leqslant \bar{x}_*^+$$

As small-scale manufactured goods are cheaper than goods produced by large-scale enterprises,[7] it is necessary to set a lower limit to production of the latter. This is achieved by an Engel constraint, always tight in practice:

$$x_{10} \leqslant \gamma_{10} \, \Sigma_h \, x_h - x_{10}$$

Saving behavior: The consumption constraints are complemented by a fixed (unit)–prices saving constraint

$$\Sigma_h \, v_h = \gamma \, \Sigma_h \, x_h \qquad (6.7)$$

Objective function: The objective finally is the maximization of total consumption:

$$\max \Sigma_h \, x_h \qquad (6.8)$$

6.2   A general equilibrium interpretation of the system

Can we recognize in Sandee's model the classical components of a general equilibrium model – consumers' maximizing behavior, consumption sets, and initial resources; producers' maximizing behavior and production sets?

There are two groups of consumers: Indians and the rest of the world. Indians own their country's producers and initial stock of capital. Their maximizing behavior differs from that usually assumed: They maximize utility subject to setting aside for investment a fixed fraction of their income. It is easy to see that (6.6) and (6.8) are equivalent to a utility function of the type defined in Section 3:

$$\max U_I = M \, \Sigma_h \, x_h^1 + \Sigma_h \, x_h^2 + 0 \, \Sigma_h \, x_h^3$$

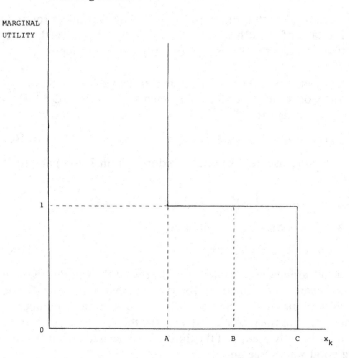

Figure 3. Approximation of India's utility function. At point A, $x_k = \gamma_k \sum x_h - \bar{x}_k$; at B, $x_k = \gamma_k \sum x_h$; at C, $x_k = \bar{x}_k^+ + \bar{x}_k^-$.

$$x_k^1 \leqslant \gamma_k \sum_h x_h - \bar{x}_k^-, \quad x_k^2 \leqslant \bar{x}_k^+ + \bar{x}_k^-, \quad x_k^3 \text{ unbounded},$$

$$x_k = x_k^1 + x_k^2 + x_k^3 \tag{6.9}$$

where M is arbitrarily large. This is a utility function of the type described by Figure 1. For given total consumption $\sum_h x_h$, marginal utility of good k as a function of x_k is represented in Figure 3. It should be noted that the whole schedule shifts to the right when total consumption increases.

The consumption sets are implicitly the positive orthant; in fact, the model rules out solutions that would imply starvation.

By the Walras law the budget constraint of India (and of the rest of the world) will be satisfied if the balance of the payments is in equilibrium.

A clearer view of the Indian production set is obtained if the agricultural production function is translated into a formulation closer to standard activity analysis. Examination of (6.3) shows that there are four agricultural technologies, each of which can be used up to a given upper bound. They all have the same input coefficients; only capital coefficients differ.

The production set is thus described by 16 activity vectors (4 for agriculture, 1 for each of the other sectors) and upper bounds on the agricultural activities, reflecting somewhat brutally the decreasing returns in agriculture.

Sandee's model is not meant to include a trade welfare function for the rest of the world, but it can be interpreted as if it did. Indeed, (6.4) and (6.5) are equivalent to

$$\max V_{rw} = \Sigma_h (e_h - m_h), \qquad e_k \leqslant \bar{e}_k, \quad m_k \leqslant \bar{m}_k, \quad V_{rw} = 0 \qquad (6.10a)$$

Or, if it is desired to use the form described in Section 3, (6.4) and (6.5) are equivalent to

$$\max V_{rw} = M \Sigma_h t_h^1 + \Sigma_h t_h^2 + 0 \Sigma_h t_h^3$$

$$-\infty \leqslant t_k^1 \leqslant -\bar{m}_k, \quad 0 \leqslant t_k^2 \leqslant \bar{m}_k + \bar{e}_k,$$

$$0 \leqslant t_k^3 \leqslant \infty, \quad \Sigma_s t_k^s = e_k - m_k \qquad (6.10b)$$

where M is arbitrarily large. The utility of the rest of the world is the sum of piecewise-linear utility functions for the different goods, where the marginal utility of imports of the rest of the world is the large number M for the first step, 1 for the second, and 0 for the third; in practice the first step will always be fully used, and the third would be used only if the corresponding good was a free good.

A trade welfare function is thus implicitly set up and set equal to zero. A solution of Sandee's model is therefore a kind of Pareto optimum in which India's welfare is maximized, subject to a fixed value of the rest of the world's welfare.

The budget constraint of the rest of the world, obviously, is its balance-of-payments constraint.

The production set, consumption set, and initial resources of the rest of the world do not have to be defined, since they are subsumed by the trade welfare function.

6.3   Modifications of Sandee's model

We list the modifications introduced in decreasing order of importance.

Current-prices balance-of-payments constraint: It is essential to replace the constant-prices balance-of-payments constraint (6.5) by a current-prices balance-of-payments constraint:[8]

$$\underset{\substack{\text{Value of} \\ \text{imports}}}{\Sigma_h p_{mh} m_h} - \underset{\substack{\text{Value of} \\ \text{exports}}}{\Sigma_h p_{eh} e_h} = 0 \qquad (6.11)$$

Current-prices saving function: It is not sensible to assume that consumers determine their saving by a constant-prices constraint. We have accordingly replaced (6.7) by

$$\Sigma_h \, p_h v_h - \gamma \, \Sigma_h \, p_h x_h = 0 \qquad (6.12)$$

Value of   Value of
investment   consumption

There would be no difficulty in using a more complex function, provided that it depends only on current and past prices and quantities.[9]

Indian utility function: While theoretically acceptable, the utility function implied by Sandee's model does not produce reasonable price behavior. Accordingly this was replaced by a function which generates piecewise-linear indifference surfaces:

$$U_I(\cdot) = \Sigma_h \, x_h - \Sigma_h \, \Sigma_{s=1}^2 \, \phi_h^s (x_h^{s+} + x_h^{s-})$$

Utility   Utility of commodities consumed

$$x_k \quad - \quad \gamma_k \, \Sigma_h \, x_h \quad - \Sigma_{s=1}^2 (x_k^{s+} - x_k^{s-}) = 0$$

Consumption   Consumption on   Deviation from
           equal prices   equal prices
           Engel ray   Engel ray

$$x_k^{s+} \leqslant \bar{x}_k^s, \quad x_k^{s-} \leqslant \bar{x}_k^s; \qquad s=1,2 \qquad (6.13)$$

Linearization bounds

Trade welfare function of the rest of the world: For the same reason, the trade welfare function of the rest of the world was replaced by a system that also implies more complex piecewise-linear indifference surfaces:

$$V_{rw}(\cdot) = \Sigma_h \, \Sigma_s \, \psi_{eh}^s \, e_h^s - \Sigma_h \, \Sigma_s \, \psi_{mh}^s \, m_h^s$$

Utility   Utility derived   Disutility derived
        from Indian   from exports
        exports   to India

$$e_k = \Sigma_s \, e_k^s, \quad m_k = \Sigma_s \, m_k^s,$$

$$e_k^s \leqslant \bar{e}_k^s, \quad m_k^s \leqslant \bar{m}_k^s; \qquad s=1,\dots,8 \qquad (6.14)$$

Linearization bounds

Each "step" defines the region over which the marginal utility of a good is constant.

Solution procedure

As explained, the programming model is solved as part of a "function evaluation" phase of the calculations, in which functions $B(\cdot)$ and $\sigma(\cdot)$

are evaluated. If $B(\cdot) \approx 0$ and $\sigma(\cdot) \approx 1$, the procedure stops and the solution is an equilibrium. If not, the arguments of the two functions are revised using an appropriate rule. In the solution procedure both computational procedures 1 and 3 are used.

Define first an aggregate capital constraint

$$\sum_k p_k \sum_h \kappa_{kh} y_h + p_{11} v^* - \frac{T}{2} \sum_k p_k v_k \leqslant \sum_k p_k K_{0k} \qquad (6.15)$$

where k takes the values 8, 9, and 11.

Initialization: Choose initial values for $\alpha = \alpha^0$, $v = v^0$, and $p = p^{-1}$; set $t = 0$.

Iteration t:

Phase 1. Function evaluation: Maximize $\alpha^t U_t + (1 - \alpha^t) V_{rw}$ subject to (6.1) with v^t given, (6.3), constraints appearing (6.13) and (6.14), and (6.15).

Compute

$$B(\cdot) = -p_e^t \cdot e^t + p_m^t \cdot m^t$$

$$\sigma(\cdot) = \gamma p^t \cdot x^t : p^t \cdot v^t$$

$$v(\cdot) = \frac{2}{T}(\kappa y^t - K_0)$$

If $B(\cdot) \approx 0$, $\sigma(\cdot) \approx 1$, and $v(\cdot) \approx v^t$, stop. If not, go to phase 2.

Phase 2. Parameter revision: Use the following difference equations to update α and v:

$$\alpha^{t+1} = \alpha^t + \lambda B(\cdot)$$

$$v^{t+1} = \sigma(\cdot)^\mu v^t$$

Set $p^{t+1} = p^t$. Set $t = t + 1$ and go to the next iteration.

7   Results

Several sets of prices coexist in linear programming planning models of the traditional type. These are the dual prices of the balance constraints, the exogenous import and export prices in the balance of payments, and the national prices that would match the marginal utilities of consumers. These three sets are made compatible by wedges representing the dual prices of the bounds introduced to exclude "unreasonable" optimal solutions.

Table 1 reproduces the prices generated by Sandee's original model.

Table 1. *Price system in the programming model*

Sector	World trade prices	Dual prices of export bounds	Production prices	Dual prices of consump- tion bounds	Marginal utilities
Agriculture	1.497	.801	.696	—	—
Food	1.497	.717	.780	− .084	.696
Steel	1.497	1.080	2.577	—	—
Electricity	—	—	3.364	—	—
Coal	—	—	1.697	—	—
Fertilizers	1.497	.700	2.197	—	—
Transport	—	—	1.631	− .935	.696
Heavy equip.	1.497	1.814	3.311	—	—
Other equip.	1.497	0	1.497	—	—
Large-scale manufact.	1.597	0	1.497	− .800	.697
Construction	—	—	1.003	—	—
Small-scale manufact.	—	—	.670	.026	.696
Housing	—	—	3.808	− 3.112	.696

Note: The sign (+) is attributed to the dual variable if the upper bound is effective, the sign (−) if the lower bound is.

High values of the wedge variables mean that the corresponding bounds have a high cost. It can be expected, therefore, that replacing Sandee's utility functions (6.9) and (6.10) by functions (6.13) and (6.14), which imply more flexibility of consumption and trade patterns, will change the primal solution substantially. This is confirmed by Table 2.[10] (We have not included steel and heavy equipment.)

The table illustrates that with the more flexible specification the economy does exploit its comparative advantages more fully. And this is basically what a good planning model should do. Is it really correct to call an "optimal plan" the solution of a model that includes consumption and trade bounds the changing of which has a very high payoff to the policy maker?

As the coefficients of the utility function of the equilibrium model were set quite arbitrarily, we make no claim for realism of the equilibrium version of the model. It is perhaps possible that the export bounds imposed by Sandee reflected the pessimism about foreign markets characterizing Indian thinking at the time; this brought about self-fulfilling policies oriented to import substitution, preventing the country from taking advantage of the opportunities that were available. The more flexible equilibrium approach might have revealed the scope for specialization that India failed to exploit.

Table 2. *Patterns of consumption and trade in the programming and equilibrium versions of the model*

| Sector | Programming version | | | | Equilibrium version | |
| | Volume | | Dual prices of bounds | | Volume | |
	Net exports	Consumption	Net exports	Consumption	Net exports	Consumption
Agriculture	94	3426	.801	—	127	3409
Food	177	457	.717	− .084	500	910
Fertilizers	− 350	—	.700	—	− 595	—
Transport	—	629	—	− .935	—	522
Other equip.	− 614	—	0	—	142	—
Large-scale manufact.	814	342	0	− .800	1100	0
Small-scale manufact.	—	1261	—	.026	—	2047
Housing	—	569	—	− 3.112	—	370

Table 3. *Exports and imports in the two versions of the model, at current and constant prices*

Evaluation prices	Programming version	Equilibrium version
Exports evaluated at unit prices (as % of imports at those prices)	100	202
Exports evaluated at prices implied by model (as % of imports at those prices)	76	100

Note: Imports and exports are evaluated at the dual prices of the supply–demand balances, net of the quasi-tariffs implied by the import quotas affecting steel and heavy equipment.

The other major finding is the large difference between the constant- and current-prices balance of payments. Table 3 gives the relevant figures.

Using a constant-prices balance of payments therefore implies a striking distortion of the costs of imports and exports. The reason for the unfavorable terms of trade is of course that the country exports (imports) what it is able to produce at low (high) costs.

Table 4. *Rates of return to capital in the programming model*

Sector	Rate	Sector	Rate
Irrigation	.323	Transport	.212
Extension services	.323	Heavy equip.	.267
Food manufact.	.283	Other equip.	.285
Steel	.261	Large-scale manufact.	.282
Electricity	.276	Construction	.258
Coal	.321	Small-scale manufact.	.308
Fertilizer	.264	Housing	.323

Table 5. *Saving, investment, consumption, and capital output ratios in the two models*

	Magnitudes evaluated at	
Factor	Prices implied by the model	Unit prices
Programming model		
Investment	2,980	2,153
Consumption	4,683	6,729
Saving ratio	.64	.32
Increase in GNP	8,882	7,663
Increase of capital	10,765	14,900
Incremental COR	1.21	1.94
Equilibrium model		
Investment	1,967	1,473
Consumption	6,368	7,259
Saving ratio	.31	.20
Increase in GNP	8,341	9,607
Increase of capital	9,835	7,365
Incremental COR	1.18	.77

Note: COR = capital output ratio.

For the same reason, the exchange rates implied by the two models are remarkably different. The shadow exchange rate of the programming model is 1.50 versus .82 in the equilibrium model: Foreign trade is extremely valuable in the first model as it provides opportunities to buy at unit prices highly valuable goods and to sell at unit prices goods that can be produced very cheaply. These opportunities vanish in the equilibrium model, since world prices equal Indian marginal costs.[11]

What are the rates of return to capital in the two models? In the equilibrium version this rate is unique and equal to .241. We have seen (Section 5) that in a programming model that treats capital accumulation as Sandee does there is a rate of return to capital for each activity. These are, however, reasonably close to each other, as Table 4 shows.

Finally, Table 5 compares some important macroeconomic values for the two models; goods are evaluated both at the prices implied by the model (shadow prices) and at the unit prices, as is done in Sandee's formulation.

Specifying the saving function at constant prices does make considerable difference because capital goods are relatively more expensive at the prices implied by the model than at unit prices. As the proper way to cost goods is to evaluate them at marginal cost, it is seen that it is not 32% but 64% of consumption that is allocated to capital accumulation in Sandee's model.

NOTES

1. On the importance of this type of data, see, for instance, Koopmans's (1979) recent arguments.
2. There are a few exceptions, such as Goreux and Manne (1973) and Goreux (1977), who use piecewise-linear functions.
3. As $\bar{p} \cdot (x_i - \omega_i)$ defines an upper semicontinuous correspondence, the equilibrium value $\bar{\alpha}_1$ may imply consumptions and prices that do not satisfy the budget constraint, in addition to the equilibrium $\bar{p}, \bar{x}_i$ vectors.
4. See, e.g., Mantel (1971).
5. The model was published by a rather obscure Indian publishing house and is not easy to obtain; thus many later workers drew their inspiration from papers that used Sandee's work, rather than directly from Sandee's model.
6. Agriculture, food, steel, electricity, coal, fertilizers, transport, heavy equipment, other equipment, large-scale manufacturing, construction, small-scale manufacturing, and housing. These sectors are indexed from 1 to 13, respectively.
7. Input–output and capital coefficients in the small-scale manufacturing sector are smaller than (or equal to) those of the large-scale manufacturing sector.
8. Trade prices p_{mk}, p_{ek} may differ from domestic prices p_k if there are import or export quotas such as in (6.4), the shadow price of which is equivalent to a tariff.
9. For example, consumption could depend on expected prices, whereas price expectations depend on current and past prices via adaptive mechanisms.
10. We have not included steel and heavy equipment in the comparison, since the trade wedge variables for these goods are interpreted as the tariff equivalent of import quotas and are therefore present in the equilibrium as well as in the programming solution.
11. The results illustrate how dangerous it is to use the shadow exchange rate in a programming model to calculate the true value of foreign exchange to a country.

REFERENCES

Adelman, I., and Robinson, S. (1978). *Income Distribution Policy in Developing Countries*. Oxford: Oxford University Press.

Dixon, P. (1975). *The Theory of Joint Maximization*. Amsterdam: North-Holland.

Ginsburgh, V., and Waelbroeck, J. (1975). "A General Equilibrium Model of World Trade, Part I: Full Format Computation of Economic Equilibria." Cowles Foundation Discussion Paper 412.

(1981). *Activity Analysis and General Equilibrium Modelling*. Amsterdam: North-Holland.

Goreux, L. (1977). *Interdependence in Planning: Multilevel Programming Studies of the Ivory Coast*. Baltimore: Johns Hopkins Press.

Goreux, L., and Manne, A., eds. (1973). *Multi-Level Planning: Case Studies in Mexico*. Amsterdam: North-Holland.

Johansen, L. (1960). *A Multi-Sectoral Study of Economic Growth*. Amsterdam: North-Holland.

Karlin, S. (1959). *Mathematical Methods and Theory in Games, Programming, and Economics*. London: Pergamon Press.

Koopmans, T. C. (1979). "Economics among the Sciences." *American Economic Review, 69,* 1–13.

Lluch, C., Powell, A., and Williams, R. (1977). *Patterns in Household Demand and Saving*. Baltimore: Johns Hopkins Press.

Manne, A. (1977). "General Equilibrium with Activity Analysis." In C. Hitch, ed., *Modeling Energy-Economy Interactions: Five Approaches*. Washington, D.C.: Resources for the Future.

Manne, A., Chao, H., and Wilson, R. (1980). "Computation of Competitive Equilibria by a Sequence of Linear Progams." *Econometrica, 48,* No. 7, 1595–1615.

Mantel, R. R. (1971). "The Welfare Adjustment Process: Its Stability Properties." *International Economic Review, 12,* 415–30.

Negishi, T. (1960). "Welfare Economics and the Existence of an Equilibrium for a Competitive Economy." *Metroeconomica, 12,* 92–7.

Sandee, J. (1960). *A Demonstration Planning Model for India*. Bombay: Asia Publishing House.

Taylor, L. (1975). "Theoretical Foundations and Technical Implications." In C. Blitzer, P. Clark, and L. Taylor, eds., *Economy-Wide Models and Development Planning*. Oxford: Oxford University Press.

Comments

Robert M. Stern

I shall first make some general comments on the Ginsburgh–Waelbroeck chapter and then address a number of important international economic policy issues in the context of what computable general equilibrium (CGE) models may or may not have to offer.

Ginsburgh–Waelbroeck

1. An important issue that is not addressed fully in the chapter is the rationale for an economywide "planning" model as compared to a CGE model. The authors mention the availability and use of technological data as the main motivation for their choice of a linear programming (LP) model. However, although technological data availability is undoubtedly important, it does not follow that one should opt necessarily for an economywide LP model. Indeed, it may well be that an LP model is better suited in terms of data requirements for particular sectors (e.g., agriculture, energy) than for an entire economy. It may be possible accordingly to embed the LP sectoral model(s) in an economywide CGE model. This has apparently been done on occasion, although it is by no means an easy empirical task to combine data from the two models. Moreover, there may be some difficulties in obtaining consistency in the prices generated from the two approaches. If it is true therefore that the LP model is more appropriate for sectoral applications, the issues just mentioned become of greater importance than the economywide application addressed in the chapter.

2. The authors' use of an LP model is made possible by their representation of the consumer utility function in a stepwise fashion in order to deal with the nonlinearities involved. Computationally, this is designed to get around the introduction of arbitrary constraints often resorted to in earlier work and to obviate the need to use nonlinear programming (NLP). The representation of utility and production functions in both LP and CGE models is of course a matter of great concern. One can debate the merits of the formulations adopted that often seem to be guided more by tractability than by economic reality. If the authors were to choose some alternative representation for smoothing the utility function, this would most probably necessitate more complex modeling methods and in particular the use of NLP. The question that then arises concerns the feasibility and cost of using NLP, which may perhaps be less forbidding than the authors suggest.

3. The authors are no doubt aware of the simplicity of the "balance-of-payments" constraint in their LP model since it refers only to exports and imports of merchandise. What is missing, of course, is international capital movements and the implied changes in stocks of assets that more realistically would alter the balance-of-payments constraint by permitting a country to augment its domestic savings by means of international borrowing. Further, the LP model assumes a fixed exchange rate and thus abstracts from the interim effects of exchange rate flexibility as well as possible foreign exchange market intervention by the central bank. The

omission of these financial influences can no doubt be defended on grounds that they have no effect in general equilibrium. But this omission may nonetheless limit the use and relevance of the LP model in particular circumstances.

4. Again, for simplicity, the authors have chosen to represent investment and saving in a one-period model. This abstracts from the intertemporal optimization that is obviously important but may require an explicit dynamic model. Moreover, the possibility of international borrowing mentioned above would have to be considered in defining both the balance-of-payments constraint and the investment-saving relationship through time.

5. The authors have chosen Sandee's LP model of India to demonstrate the application of their procedure. This raises the issue noted above of the suitability of economywide LP models. Presumably, these models may be most appropriate for an economy with a relatively simple technological structure. This may have been the case for India in the late 1950s, but it would appear to be much less relevant for India in the 1980s in view of the further development that has occurred over the years in the industrial sector and the relatively greater importance of manufactured goods in India's foreign trade. There may be other less developed countries for which an economywide LP model may be appropriate. But this remains to be seen. The point then is that such models may be best suited for individual sectors because of the availability of technological data.

6. My final concern is whether there is a formal equivalence between LP and CGE models in terms of the design of policy experiments and the evaluation of results. My impression is that CGE models may be more flexible and adaptable than LP models, especially for policy experimentation in advanced industrialized countries. LP models may have their place, but it seems more limited than the thrust of this chapter would lead one to believe.

Modeling and analysis of international economic policy issues

In recent years, there has been considerable progress in the application of large-scale disaggregated models of world trade to important international economic policy issues. The most noteworthy efforts include the general equilibrium model developed by Whalley (1980) and the Michigan model of world production and trade developed by Deardorff and Stern (1981). The Deardorff–Stern model is comparative-static and focuses on short- and medium-run impacts of changes in policy rather than seeking a full equilibrium solution as in Whalley's model. Both models have been used to analyze the economic effects of the Tokyo Round reductions in tariff and nontariff barriers (NTBs) to trade, the effects of domestic factor and commodity taxes in the major industrialized countries, and other selected issues of commercial policy. Given what these models have accomplished, it might be useful to juxtapose them in relation to the important international economic issues of the day in order to determine what contribution, if any, the models may make. In proceeding, I shall confine my remarks to the CGE type of model, typified by Whalley, since this is what is germane to this book. The areas of policy to be considered involve international trade, international investment, and certain aspects of macro–international–financial and micro interactions.

International trade

With respect to international trade, the major policy concerns involve (1) continuing assessment of existing trade and domestic policies and the evaluation of policy alternatives; (2) problems of adjustment, especially in the advanced industrialized countries; and (3) ramifications of industrial policies.

Since the conclusion of the Tokyo Round in 1979, tariffs in most of the industrialized countries have been reduced to relatively very low levels. The Tokyo Round also resulted in agreement on a series of codes governing the use of various NTBs, with the objective of liberalizing the impact of restrictive measures especially in government procurement, agriculture, customs valuation procedures, and import licensing. Although the existence of NTBs is extensively documented, it is unfortunately very difficult to express them in terms of price and quantity equivalents and thus to assess their impact on trade and domestic variables. Both Deardorff–Stern and Whalley have some crude approximations of existing NTBs in their models, and calculations of their partial or complete removal suggest sizable impacts on world trade and welfare. However, until more accurate representation of NTBs is completed, calculations of their effects derived from a CGE or any other type of model are at best educated guesses.[1] In this regard, attention has been shifting recently to the identification and possible lowering or removal of barriers to international trade in services (e.g., shipping, banking, insurance, communications, information flows, etc.). A ministerial meeting was held in November 1982 in Geneva under the auspices of the General Agreement on Tariffs and Trade (GATT), and liberalization of trade in services was prominent on the agenda for study and possible future negotiations. It thus appears that NTBs to trade in goods and services are currently the dominant policy concerns. Given the difficulties of representing the various NTBs empirically, it seems fair to say that data requirements are a major stumbling block in the further application of CGE multilateral trade models.

If one takes a national rather than a multilateral view of trade policy, CGE models may have an important role to play especially in developing countries. Several of these countries have liberalized their trade and payments regimes in the past 10–15 years and as a consequence have greatly increased their exports and imports of manufactures in trade with the advanced countries. Having achieved success, these developing countries can be expected to liberalize their policies even further and their examples may motivate other countries to do the same. One of the great advantages of CGE models is that they can be disaggregated in a variety of ways across producing sectors and households to reflect the economic structure and policies of a given country. Experiments can then be conducted by using a CGE model to help identify the changes that may occur and the benefits realized from alternative changes in policies.

The shifting currents of trade over a period of time will necessitate movements of labor and capital domestically. An important issue for policy is how industries respond especially to competition from imports in terms of the magnitude of adjustment and the speed with which it occurs. This is especially the case for labor displacement. The impact of trade liberalization on employment was of major concern in the Tokyo Round, and it was a central focus in the initial development and application of the Deardorff–Stern model. In order to analyze adjustments in factor markets, there is a need to model markets in disequilibrium. A factor such as physical capital can be assumed to be sector-specific whereas labor may be assumed to be mobile. Further, consideration should be given to the appropriate time horizon over which adjustment will take place. These are matters that are difficult to model in most circumstances. They are not of direct concern, however, for a CGE model that is premised on the clearing of all markets in a full, competitive solution. Thus, CGE modeling must of necessity abstract from this whole range of disequilibrium and dynamic questions that are often at the center of policy concern. This is not to say that we presently have other models that can cope adequately with these questions. But it does suggest that CGE models have definite limitations with regard to the kinds of trade policy issues that can be addressed.

There has been much discussion recently, especially in the United States, of the need for industrial policies to help bolster declining industries and to foster the development of new industries. Japan is often cited as a case in point where industrial policies have supposedly been of great significance in shaping that nation's structure of production and trade. In principle, the tax-subsidy aspects of industrial policies should lend themselves to analysis by means of a CGE model. There may be some difficulty, however, in using a CGE model for this purpose because of the need to deal with capital accumulation and intersectoral shifts in capital.

International investment

The foreign direct investment activities of multinational corporations and the resulting effects on trade and domestic variables in the investing and host countries are of unquestionable importance. There are many issues and problems involving the behavior and control of multinationals that pose difficult problems for modeling and analysis. One of the most obvious is that many of the firms involved may exercise some degree of monopoly power that can persist over a long period of time. Since CGE models are based on competitive, profit-maximizing behavior of firms, there may be a significant element of unreality in applying these models in circumstances where there are significant departures from competition that may be reflected especially in pricing and investment decisions.

International macro–micro interactions

In the construction and implementation of CGE models, the focus is on efficiency in resource use and utility maximization. It is standard, therefore, to abstract from macroeconomic considerations, in particular how governments may respond to particular changes in exogenous policy or other variables, and the asset portfolio behavior of households and firms. It is convenient, of course, to assume that macroeconomic considerations do not matter, but this may do great violence to reality and therefore cloud the interpretation and acceptability of the analytical results based on CGE models. Three somewhat interrelated examples may be cited to illustrate the issues involved.

The first example concerns the adaptation to changes in energy prices. There are clearly important microeconomic changes that will occur in response to the changes in relative prices, but there may be significant macro effects as well stemming from the balance-of-payments and stabilization policy changes that will take place. It is difficult to imagine that there will be no real, allocative effects associated with the macro changes.

A second example involves the possible sectoral impacts of changes in exchange rates. The variability of exchange rates since the advent of floating in 1973 has at times been of great magnitude. The changes involved have dwarfed the changes in commercial policies that have occurred, the tariff reductions in the Tokyo Round being a case in point.

These changes in exchange rates are bound to have important sectoral impacts in terms of resource allocation and welfare. Yet there has been very little attention devoted to the analysis of these impacts. The reason no doubt is that exchange rate effects are ruled out in the equilibrium properties of a CGE model. If one wished to analyze these effects, it would therefore be necessary to adapt the model so that it can handle markets that are in disequilibrium. Such an undertaking may be considered beyond the scope of CGE models as presently conceived. If so, this could constitute a notable limitation of these models.

The final example involves changes in monetary and fiscal policies that are designed for short- and medium-run stabilization purposes, but may have differential effects across sectors that would be reflected both domestically and internationally. As mentioned above, these macro-stabilization measures will affect financial asset decisions as well and in turn may have real effects.

The implication of the foregoing examples is that more attention needs to be given to the macroeconomic assumptions that are being made in CGE models and to the possible extension and elaboration of these models so as to permit macro–financial–micro interactions to be taken more explicitly into account. Macro-type issues are simply too important to assume away.

NOTES

1. Alan V. Deardorff and I are preparing a work, *The Theory and Measurement of Nontariff Barriers to International Trade,* that reviews the literature on NTBs and attempts to synthesize the existing estimates of NTBs and their impact on trade and domestic variables for a variety of countries and goods.

REFERENCES

Deardorff, Alan V., and Stern, Robert M. 1981. A disaggregated model of world production and trade, applied to the Tokyo Round. *Journal of Policy Modeling* 3:127-52. .

Whalley, John. 1980. Discriminatory features of domestic factor tax systems in a goods mobile–factors immobile trade model: An empirical general equilibrium approach. *Journal of Political Economy* 88:1177-202.

CHAPTER 11

A general equilibrium model for the Mexican economy

Jaime Serra-Puche

1   Introduction

A general equilibrium model (GEM) provides an analytical framework in which widely different policies can be examined. Once the basic model has been specified and implemented with actual data, various policies can be studied with only minor modifications. The GEM for Mexico that we present here has been used to analyze unemployment, energy, domestic commerce, protection policies, and tax incidence. Currently, we are making an effort to introduce a financial sector that integrates real and monetary phenomena. The advantage of this unified approach is the attention paid to details of the economy beyond the immediate interest of particular study, which are often omitted from partial equilibrium analyses.

The present chapter is devoted to the analysis of tax incidence. In particular, we examine the impact on income distribution and resource allocation of the 1980 Mexican value-added tax (VAT). In 1980, in a major reform, Mexico shifted from a system of indirect turnover taxes to a consumption value-added tax system. Presumably, this change will have different effects on the various productive sectors and on the different income groups of the economy; only a general equilibrium framework would make it possible to capture these effects without ignoring the simultaneous adjustment of the main economic variables.

The next section describes the model following its natural divisions. We then present the computation of the original equilibrium, which is the benchmark for the comparative statics exercises performed later on.

This work is part of MEGAMEX, a project sponsored by the Banco de Mexico, on which Timothy Kehoe and I worked during 1981 and 1982. I am grateful to Timothy Kehoe and also to the other members of the project, especially David Backus and Leopoldo Solis. Gabriel Vera of the Banco provided invaluable assistance in assembling the data for the model. Rodolfo de la Torre and Sanjay Srivastava provided technical help. I am solely responsible for any errors.

Section 4 analyzes the introduction of the value-added tax in its two stages. Finally, we use Section 5 to evaluate this tax reform and to present the main conclusions of the study.

2   The model

The structure of the GEM that we have built for Mexico is basically the same as that of Serra-Puche (1979, 1981). It is a static Walrasian general equilibrium model solved using a variant of Scarf's algorithm for computing fixed points. The model brings together demand and production decisions to determine equilibrium prices (p^*), equilibrium activity levels (y^*), and equilibrium tax revenue (R^*). In equilibrium no activity makes positive profits and demand equals supply in every sector. Various consumers choose bundles of commodities to maximize utility. Similarly, producers select those combinations of factors of production that maximize their profits. It is also assumed that there is full employment and perfect mobility of three factors, which are inelastically supplied. Thus, the model allows for equilibrium analysis of income distribution and resource allocation.

Let us describe the model in detail. We shall discuss, following the natural division of the model, the production side of the economy, the government, the demand side of the economy, and the investment and foreign sectors. The economy has 14 production sectors, 3 nonconsumption demand sectors, and 3 factors of production (rural labor, urban labor, and capital). We have included a conversion matrix that transforms the final demand for 15 specific goods into implicit demands for the 14 production sectors. The total number of goods and sectors, including factors of production, is then 35.

2.1   Production

Production combines a fixed-coefficient, Leontief system for intermediate inputs and value-added with constant elasticity of substitution (CES) production functions that generate value-added from the three factors. This permits us to utilize data from the Mexican input–output matrix without unduly restricting the range of substitution possibilities.

To be more precise, the production function for sector j is

$$Q_j = \min(A_j, \mathrm{VA}_j), \qquad j = 1, \ldots, 17 \tag{1}$$

where A_j represents the intermediate inputs for sector j:

$$A_j = \min_{i=j}\left(\frac{x_{ij}}{|a_{ij}|}\right), \qquad j = 1, \ldots, 17 \tag{2}$$

where x_{ij} represents the physical quantities of input i used in the production of j, and a_{ij} is a nonpositive number that represents the minimal input of input i required to produce a_{jj} units of output of j.

VA_j represents the value added in sector j, which is produced from the three factors according to a CES production function:

$$VA_j = c_j \left[\sum_{k=1}^{3} \delta_{kj} x_{kj}^{-\rho_j} \right]^{-1/\rho_j}, \qquad j=1,\ldots,17 \qquad (3)$$

where c_j is the efficiency parameter; δ_{kj} is the distribution, or input intensity, parameter of input k; ρ_j is the substitution parameter; and X_{kj} is use of factor k, all for sector j.

These production functions can be arranged in an activity analysis matrix A of the following form:

$$A = \begin{bmatrix} a_{11} & \cdots & a_{1n} \\ a_{21} & \cdots & a_{2n} \\ \vdots & & \vdots \\ a_{n1} & \cdots & a_{nn} \\ l_{r1}(q) & \cdots & l_{rn}(q) \\ l_{u1}(q) & \cdots & l_{un}(q) \\ K_1(q) & \cdots & K_n(q) \end{bmatrix} \qquad (4)$$

where the labor and capital requirements (l_{rj}, l_{uj}, K_j) are functions of factor prices (q). Requirements of intermediate inputs a_{ij} are technical coefficients that do not depend on prices. The combination of primary factors does depend on factor prices, however, since producers choose the combination that minimizes their after-tax cost of production. Forming the respective Lagrangian, we get

$$\min\left[L_j = \sum_{k=1}^{3} q_k X_{kj} + \lambda \left[VA_j - c_j \left(\sum_{k=1}^{3} \delta_{kj} X_{kj}^{-\rho_j} \right)^{-1/\rho_j} \right] \right],$$
$$j=1,\ldots,17 \qquad (5)$$

where q_k is the price of factor k. This leads to the following demand for factor k in sector j:[1]

$$X_{kj} = \frac{VA_j}{c_j} \cdot \left[\sum_{i=1}^{3} \delta_{ij} \left[\frac{q_k/\delta_{kj}}{q_i/\delta_{ij}} \right]^{-\rho_j/(1+\rho_j)} \right]^{1/\rho_j},$$
$$k=1,2,3, \quad j=1,\ldots,17 \qquad (6)$$

The l_{rj}, l_{uj}, and K_j elements in the activity analysis matrix A are determined by (6), normalized by total production in sector j. Thus, production in the model is represented by an activity analysis matrix (4), which allows for substitution only among the primary factors of production, which has as many activities as the economy has sectors, and does not permit joint production.

2.2   Government

The government in this model collects taxes and purchases commodities. Tax revenues and expenditures are closely related although, as we shall see, the government's budget need not be balanced.

There are three kinds of taxes: income taxes, sales taxes, and tariffs. The income tax can be described as follows. Each consumer group h, with income Y_h, faces an income tax rate i_h. The group h is taxed on the value of its factor endowment (ω_h) prior to production and before payment of any taxes. Thus, group h will pay, for any factor price q_k,

$$I_h = i_h \sum_{k=1}^{3} q_k \omega_{kh} \tag{7}$$

The income tax revenue received by the government is then

$$I = \sum_{h=1}^{10} I_h \tag{8}$$

where 10 is the number of consumer groups.

The pattern of indirect taxation in Mexico was extremely complex prior to the value-added tax reform. In addition to having a general turnover tax rate (*impuesto sobre ingresos mercantiles*), the Mexican tax system had a large number of special taxes applied to specific sectors. Our computation of the original equilibrium takes full account of this tax system, and so does the specification. Let c_{if} and c_{il} be the ad valorem tax rates imposed on the purchase of final and intermediate goods, respectively, which are weighted sums of all the tax rates that apply to good i.[2] The total payments collected from this tax are

$$C_i = \sum_{j=1}^{17} |a_{ij}| p_i c_{il} y_j + \sum_{h=1}^{10} X_{ih} p_i c_{if} \tag{9}$$

where y_j is the activity level of activity j, p_i is the price of good i, and X_{ih} is the demand of group h for good i, which will be derived below. Therefore, the total revenue to the government from sales taxes is given by

$$C = \sum_{i=1}^{32} C_i \tag{10}$$

This specification takes account of the "cascade" effect of this turnover tax system: The total tax is reflected in the final price of the good after going through all the stages of production and commercialization. The more stages the good goes through, the larger is the cascade effect of the tax.

Finally, the government is assumed to tax imports. As we shall describe below, imports in the original specification are noncompetitive and are assumed to be a homogeneous good. This good is obtained from the export activity in the activity analysis matrix A (a_M). Thus, the model has an aggregate tariff that applies to this good when used as an input. (The implicit final demand for imports is reflected in the conversion matrix.) All those activities that use imports as inputs to the production process face this aggregate tariff. The revenue from taxing imports is[3]

$$T = \sum_{j=1}^{17} |a_{Mj}| p_M t_j y_j \tag{11}$$

Therefore, the government's total revenue R is

$$R = I + C + T \tag{12}$$

In addition to tax collections, the model also incorporates transfers and tax rebates by having each consumer group receive, in lump-sum form, a fraction of government revenue:

$$R_h = \alpha_h R \tag{13}$$

where $\sum_{h=1}^{10} \alpha_h = 1 - \alpha_G$, and α_G is the share of the total revenue that the government retains (α_h and $\alpha_G \geqslant 0$).[4]

The government's total revenue is generated by taxing income and domestic and foreign transactions. The tax rates used in the model are the effective average tax rates. Tax evasion is considered to be neutral. The rate of tax evasion is independent, within this model, of the source and level of income as well as of the type of good. The lack of information about evasion and its distribution makes it impossible to look for nonneutral criteria to distribute the effect of evasion when computing the effective tax rates.

Let us now turn to the expenditure side of the government's budget. The government may be viewed as purchasing the various commodities of the model in fixed proportions. That is, it maximizes a Leontief-type utility function and is constrained by its income:

$$Y_G = q_3 \omega_{3G} + p_V \omega_{VG} + \alpha_G R \tag{14}$$

where p_V and ω_{VG} are respectively the price and the endowment of capital tomorrow in the hands of the government (see below for an explanation of capital tomorrow) and ω_{3G} is the government's initial endowment of physical capital. A useful device in this regard is for the government to purchase an artificial good, government services, which is produced from goods and factors with the same type of technology as described previously.

An interesting feature of the model is that the government may spend more than it receives. Such a deficit on current expenditures appears exogenously above as a positive endowment of capital tomorrow in the government's budget constraint. This endowment is equal to the actual government deficit when evaluated at 1977 prices. Implicitly the government issues bonds that are purchased by consumers in place of physical capital.

To summarize, the government taxes income and domestic and foreign transactions. The tax revenue, plus the government's capital endowment and the endowment of bonds (capital tomorrow), constrain the maximization of its utility function. This function has only two nonzero fixed coefficients: demand for government services and demand for capital tomorrow (investment). Government services are produced by combining commodities in fixed proportion and factors with a CES technology. The government endowment of bonds is equal to the current government's deficit.

2.3   Demand

The demand side of the economy is represented by 10 groups of domestic consumers differentiated according to their average income, by the government, already described, and by a foreign consumer that represents the rest of the world. These consumers are different because their initial endowments and their utility functions are different. Let us describe how the domestic consumers behave. The "rest of the world" shall be described later on.

Prior to production each consumer group owns capital and labor that, when evaluated at market prices, produce the group's income. The consumer groups are assumed to maximize their utility functions subject to their respective income constraints.

Let ω_{kh} be a nonnegative endowment of factor k of group h. If the nonnegative q_k represents the prevailing market price, then the income of group h is

$$Y_h = \sum_{k=1}^{3} q_k \omega_{kh} \tag{15}$$

which is obtained by renting the group's endowments ω_{kh} $(k=1,\ldots,3)$ at market prices. Given Y_h, consumer group h maximizes its utility function. We assume, due to data constraints, that the utility function is of the Cobb–Douglas form:

$$U_h(X) = \sum_{i=18}^{32} b_{ih} \log X_{ih} \tag{16}$$

Given the existence of taxes, as well as the possibility of transfers from the government, the budget constraint for consumer group h may be written as

$$\sum_{k=1}^{3} q_k \omega_{kh} + R_h = \sum_{i=18}^{32} p_i X_{ih} + i_h \sum_{k=1}^{3} q_k \omega_{kh} + \sum_{i=18}^{32} p_i X_{ih} c_{if} \tag{17}$$

The Lagrangian for group h is

$$\max\left[L_h = \sum_{i=18}^{32} b_{ih} \log X_{ih} + \lambda \left[\sum_{k=1}^{3} q_k \omega_{kh}(1 - i_h) + R_h - \sum_{i=18}^{32} p_i (1 + c_{if}) X_{ih} \right]\right] \tag{18}$$

First-order conditions lead to the following demand for good i by group h:

$$X_{ih} = \frac{b_{ih}[\sum_{k=1}^{3} q_k \omega_{kh}(1 - i_h) + R_h]}{p_i(1 + c_{if})},$$

$$h = 1, \ldots, 10, \quad i = 18, \ldots, 32 \tag{19}$$

which is a constant proportion (b_{ih}) of the real disposable income and transfers received by group h. This proportion is easily observed in the household survey information. Thus, demand responds to changes in commodity prices and to factor prices (income). These individual demand functions lead to the market demand functions,

$$X_i = \sum_h^{10} X_{ih}, \quad i = 18, \ldots, 32 \tag{20}$$

which are the sum of the individual demands over all consumers. For goods 18 to 32, these market demands are equal to the excess demand functions since there are no initial endowments of i for $i = 18, \ldots, 32$. These market demand functions are continuous for all strictly positive price vectors and satisfy the following version of Walras's law:

$$\sum_{h=1}^{10} \sum_{i=18}^{32} p_i X_{ih}(1 + c_{if}) + \sum_{h=1}^{10} \sum_{k=1}^{3} q_k \omega_{kh} i_h = R \tag{21}$$

for all vectors (p, q) and R.

2.4   Foreign sector

As we said before, the original specification of the model assumes that all imports are noncompetitive and compose a homogeneous good, which is partially obtained with the foreign exchange generated by the exports. This relationship is expressed in the activity analysis matrix A by a final column a_M:

$$a_M = (a_{1M}, a_{2M}, \ldots, a_{17M}) \tag{22}$$

where a_{iM}, $i \neq M$, is a nonpositive number that represents the exports of commodity i per a_{MM} units of imports. This expression for the import–export activity assumes a fixed export composition.

The imports that cannot be paid for by the foreign exchange generated from exports – that is, the deficit in the trade balance – are generated by incurring debt with the rest of the world (ROW). The model has a 12th "consumer" called ROW, which is endowed with "imports" in the amount of the actual trade deficit and only demands our capital tomorrow. In other words, the ROW lends to the country, by demanding capital tomorrow, the trade deficit that the country incurs. Behind this argument, the ROW has a Leontief utility function, with $a_{iROW} = 1$ ($i = $ capital tomorrow), which is maximized subject to the ROW's budget constraint $p_M \omega_{MROW}$ (p_M is the price of imports and ω_{MROW} is the original endowment of imports in the hands of the ROW and equals the trade deficit). This demand pattern is implicitly a fixed-coefficient demand for the exports of the model.

This specification determines the balance of trade exogenously and thus does not allow for the analysis of any external disequilibrium of the economy. It also limits the analysis of commercial policies and protection by reducing the tariff structure to only one aggregate tariff that applies to this homogeneous good formed by the noncompetitive imports. This specification facilitates the inclusion of the trade deficit within the general equilibrium framework, however, adding a greater content of realism and consistency to the computation of the original equilibrium.

2.5   Investment

The model we presented above is static. However, we must account for the investment taking place during the period of analysis. We introduce an investment activity that produces a "good" called capital tomorrow (V), as opposed to capital today (K used in production). This activity is represented by a final column in matrix A:

$$a_V = (a_{1V}, a_{2V}, \ldots, a_{17V}) \tag{23}$$

where a_{iV}, $i \neq V$, is a nonpositive number that represents the investment purchases from sector i per a_{VV} units of total investment. Activity a_V "produces" V using the proportions of investment per sector:[5]

$$|a_{il}| = \text{investment purchases from sector } i \qquad (24)$$

and a_{VV} = total investment. Only the government has an original endowment of this good, and it is demanded by the consumer groups, the government itself, and the ROW. Consumer group h's demand for V is

$$X_{Vh} = \frac{(1 - \text{APC}_h)[Y_h(1 - i_h) + R_h]}{p_V(1 + c_{Vf})} \qquad (25)$$

where APC_h is the average propensity to consume of consumer group h.[6] The sum over all individuals must equal total private savings in the economy:

$$S = \sum_{h=1}^{10} X_{Vh} \qquad (26)$$

The ROW also demands this commodity and only this commodity. The ROW's demand is $X_{V\text{ROW}}$, which is identical to the trade deficit and, through the budget constraint, to the market value of the ROW's endowment of imports.

Finally, the government also demands this good in the fixed proportions given by the ratio of government investment in the period to total government expenditure in the period. However, the government's deficit is covered by an original endowment of V, as expressed in Equation (14). Thus, the total physical investment in the economy is given by

$$V = S + \text{GI} + \text{TD} - \text{GD} \qquad (27)$$

where GI is government investment (X_{VG}), TD is the trade deficit ($X_{V\text{ROW}}$), and GD is the government deficit (ω_{VG}). In other words, total investment in the economy is the excess demand for V in the model:

$$\text{ED}_V = \sum_{h=1}^{10} X_{Vh} + X_{V\text{ROW}} + X_{VG} - \omega_{VG} \qquad (28)$$

The role of V is to include investment in the model. By definition, V cannot be used in production in the current period and, even though it is demanded in this period, it cannot be consumed.

2.6 Equilibrium conditions and the algorithm

It is assumed that the activity analysis matrix A satisfies, using vector notation,

$$Ay \geq 0 \qquad (29)$$

where y is a nonnegative vector of activity levels. On the other hand, the market demands in Equation (20) are continuous for positive price vectors, homogeneous of degree zero in prices and total revenue, and satisfy the version of Walras's law (21) given previously.

Let π denote the price vector (p, q). A vector π^*, a total revenue R^*, and a nonnegative vector of activity levels y^* are a solution to the general equilibrium problem if

$$X_T = Ay^* + \omega \tag{30}$$

where ω is the vector of total endowments.[7] Define the matrix $\bar{A}$ by the rule

$$\bar{a}_{ij} = a_{ij} - t_{ij}|a_{ij}|, \qquad i = 1, \ldots, 35, \quad j = 1, \ldots, 32 \tag{31}$$

Here t_{ij} is the ad valorem tax rate on production or use of good i by sector j. We require that the price vector π^* satisfy the additional condition that

$$\pi^* \bar{A} \leqslant 0 \tag{32}$$

with strict equality if $y^* > 0$. In other words, π^*, R^*, and y^* represent an equilibrium solution if demand equals supply in all sectors (30) and all activities make zero profits after payment of taxes (32).

The model is solved numerically by using a modified version of Scarf's algorithm. For the simplicial subdivision of the simplex, we use Merrill's method, which makes the computation more efficient for a given goal of accuracy.[8] Furthermore, since our matrix A has as many activities as the model has sectors, and all the intermediate demands enter with a fixed-coefficient specification, it is very efficient to divide the model into two markets: the commodity and the factor markets. The fixed-point search is done only within the factor market.

This division of markets is done by dividing matrix A into $\begin{bmatrix} A_1 \\ A_2 \end{bmatrix}$, where A_1 has the elements of A_j in Equation (2) and A_2 the elements of VA_j in Equation (3). The zero-profit condition in Equation (32) may be expressed as

$$p\bar{A}_1 = -q\bar{A}_2(q) \tag{33}$$

where p is the vector of commodity prices and q the vector of factor prices. Now $\bar{A}_1$ and $\bar{A}_2$ are the matrices A_1 and A_2 net of taxes. The simplex search is done for vector q with Scarf's standard rules of grid labeling. Commodity prices are formed by simply inverting $\bar{A}_1$:

$$p = -q\bar{A}_2(q)\bar{A}_1^{-1} \tag{34}$$

which implies that once the factor prices have been computed, the commodity prices are automatically computed. There is a necessary iterative process until vectors p^* and q^* are found.[9] This version of the algorithm has proven to be quite efficient, as we shall show below, since it reduces dramatically the dimensions of the simplex.

3   The original equilibrium

The purpose of the original equilibrium is twofold: It is used as the bench-mark for the comparative static exercises and it also constitutes a consisten-cy check of the data. The original equilibrium is intended to be a "replica" of the Mexican economy in the period of analysis (1977). The information has been collected from different sources and thus some incompatibilities arise. Fortunately, the calibration of the model leads to very satisfactory results, as we shall see below. The model values of the variables are equal, with a high degree of accuracy, to the actual values. The solution of inconsistencies in information, as well as the calibration of the model, make the original equilibrium a good benchmark for the simulation.

The original equilibrium is given historically. Although uniqueness cannot be ensured, we assume that such an equilibrium is locally stable for shifts in the parameters of the model.[10]

The production side of the economy has been integrated by using the input–output matrix of Mexico for 1970 and, using the row and column sum (RAS) method, we have updated it to 1977. From this matrix we have built the activity analysis matrix, which has 14 production sectors, 3 nonconsumption demand sectors, and 3 factors of production (see the Appendix for a description of the sectors). The intermediate demands are derived from the interindustry transactions of the input–output table. The value-added parameters, required for the computation of the demand for primary factors, have been computed under the assumption of profit maximization. The substitution parameters (ρ_j) have been assumed to be zero in all sectors, due to the lack of reliable estimates. This leads to a Cobb–Douglas specification for all the production functions. Results of sensitivity tests on the ρ_j are given in Serra-Puche (1979). The distribu-tion parameters (δ_j) are derived from the first-order conditions by as-suming all prices to be equal to one, their equilibrium values in the bench-mark simulation. The efficiency parameter (c_j) is subject to calibration, to ensure that the model's total production per sector is identical to the actual values. In the Appendix we present the values of the parameters for the different sectors of the model.

The consumer-demand side of the economy has been obtained from the household survey of Mexico for 1977. The information has been aggregated so as to have 10 different consumer groups, divided into 5 different income brackets in rural and urban areas.[11] The demand para-meters (b_{ih}) were obtained from the shares of expenditure on good i by consumer group h, and adjusted so as to have the market demands equal to the final private consumption column in the input–output matrix. The initial endowments of the consumer groups were also adjusted to match value-added in the activity analysis matrix.

Nevertheless, the demand parameters are given for specific goods and not for sectors. Consumers do not demand agriculture as such, but goods that use its output – for example, bread. Furthermore, consumers purchase in commercial establishments, implicitly demanding commercial services. To solve this incompatibility between the aggregation in the activity analysis matrix and the demand parameters, we have built a conversion matrix Z:

$$Z = \begin{bmatrix} Z_{1,18} & \cdots & Z_{1,32} \\ Z_{2,18} & \cdots & Z_{2,32} \\ \vdots & & \vdots \\ Z_{32,18} & \cdots & Z_{32,32} \end{bmatrix} \tag{35}$$

There are 15 final consumption goods (i) and 14 sectors of production (j). Coefficient Z_{ji}, $i \neq j$, is a nonpositive number that represents the demand of output j when consumers purchase Z_{ii}, $i = 18, \ldots, 32$, units of final good i. For example, when consumers acquire bread, they implicitly demand the outputs from agriculture (1), food products (4), and commerce (11). Thus, matrix Z converts final consumption demand into demand for the production sectors, including the markups generated in the commercialization process. (For a description of the consumers and sectors of the Z matrix, see the Appendix.) Hence the aggregation followed in the model, which explains the rather messy combination of indices in Section 2 above, is 14 sectors of production, 3 sectors of nonconsumption demand (investment, government, and foreign sector), 15 final consumption goods, and 3 factors of production – in total, 35.

The information on the government activity was taken from the input-output matrix, including the value-added parameters. As for the tax information, which is very important in this work, we carefully aggregated the actual tax rates so as to match our aggregation. For indirect taxes, our original specification includes the turnover tax and the special taxes specific to particular goods. The tax that each good in our model faces is a weighted average of effective rates. Once the correct aggregation has been done, we compute effective tax rates by finding the turnover tax and the special tax rates that yield the actual government revenue in 1977. In this case, we are assuming neutrality of tax evasion within the sector or aggregate good.

As far as the income tax is concerned, we derive the effective rates while keeping the whole income tax structure unchanged. Here, evasion is assumed to be neutral across consumers and independent of the income source, since we are dealing with aggregate income tax rates that yield the correct revenue value.

The tariff and the export taxes are computed simply by finding the rates that yield the actual revenues, without too many complications, since imports are one homogeneous good and all exports face the same tax rate.

The foreign-sector information only requires the trade deficit of Mexico for 1977, which is consistent with the rest of the variables. Finally, we take into account the government's deficit in 1977, which, as we said, is included in the ω_g vector in the entry that corresponds to capital tomorrow.

Thus, we compute the original equilibrium in order to replicate the Mexican economy in 1977. All the data required for the computation are presented in the Appendix. These data were adjusted for consistency and, as we shall show next, this set of information led to a rather faithful and accurate representation of the economy in 1977. Let us describe it.

Units were chosen so that all equilibrium prices and final activity levels are equal to one. For this latter normalization, it was necessary to include total net production per sector in the diagonal of the activity analysis matrix. All the elements of the price vector are exactly equal to one.[12] Similarly, all activity levels are also one, and yield the correct tax revenue from indirect taxes, as shown in Table 1.

These first results show the accuracy of the replica we have built. All the model values are equal to the actual values, since the activity levels and the prices are identical to one. At the same time the zero-profit condition is satisfied, and supply equals demand.

The government's revenue from taxation is also identical to the actual 1977 government revenue in Mexico, as the reader can verify by comparing the results in Table 2 with the information on major macroeconomic variables in the Appendix.

The use of factors of production also coincides with the actual values of the economy. As it is presented in Table 3, the activity analysis matrix includes the fixed coefficients for intermediate demands, which are exogenously given to the model, and the primary factor coefficients, which are determined by the computation of the equilibrium. Rows 33, 34, and 35 represent the total demand for rural labor, urban labor, and capital of the different sectors of the economy. Agriculture (1), commerce (11), and services (13) are the sectors that demand the most capital in absolute terms. Government (15), on the other hand, is the biggest user of urban labor, also in absolute terms. Of course, the biggest absolute demand for rural labor takes place in the agriculture activity (1). The reader should bear in mind that the category capital is defined in a residual manner and it actually includes all those inputs within value-added that are not labor or indirect taxes. Some of the sectors have labor/capital

Table 1. *Activity levels and indirect tax revenue - original equilibrium*

Sector	Level	Revenue - indirect taxes (billions of 1977 pesos)
1	1.000000	.33632
2	1.000000	1.25072
3	1.000000	9.09806
4	1.000000	9.25871
5	1.000000	3.81015
6	1.000000	2.20945
7	1.000000	5.74886
8	1.000000	1.53543
9	1.000000	12.06850
10	1.000000	1.34623
11	1.000000	0
12	1.000000	1.10808
13	1.000000	5.38648
14	1.000000	3.46925
15	1.000000	.07775
16	1.000000	15.50500
17	1.000000	3.98452
18	1.000000	.63780
19	1.000000	.12850
20	1.000000	6.40540
21	1.000000	0
22	1.000000	.61460
23	.999998	.03060
24	1.000000	10.46590
25	1.000000	3.54060
26	1.000000	2.66450
27	1.000000	3.61810
28	1.000000	.89100
29	1.000000	.82500
30	1.000001	.12520
31	.999999	.49590
32	1.000000	6.79340

Table 2. *Government tax revenue - original equilibrium (billions of 1977 pesos)*

Source	Revenue
Income taxes	93.386
Indirect taxes	123.430
Total	216.816

460

Table 3. *Activity analysis matrix for Mexico – original equilibrium (tens of billions of 1977 pesos)*

	Sector								
	1	2	3	4	5	6	7	8	9
Sectors									
1	20.690319	– .003080	0	– 7.842960	– .692241	– .204184	– .045776	– .001399	– .043396
2	– .012504	2.692462	– .033167	– .009138	– .001632	– .004813	– .146399	– .273644	– .584002
3	– .386824	– .080761	6.030017	– .256777	– .048114	– .058785	– .582603	– .184713	– .168538
4	– .835908	0	0	22.842354	– .082110	– .015994	– .115602	0	– .000173
5	– .091950	– .014911	– .003238	– .223287	12.354725	– .113036	– .120920	– .005097	– .074996
6	– .094095	– .016720	– .006723	– .338549	– .116186	4.953083	– .383239	– .163134	– .307536
7	– .698656	– .051647	– .056708	– .200954	– .696366	– .157530	– .239138	– .081281	– .402463
8	– .023365	– .002053	– .005727	– .176300	– .001640	– .006140	8.085218	– .913666	– .083894
9	– .177817	– .049662	– .179180	– .399398	– .082737	– .104349	– .228585	3.074278	16.928360
10	– .102661	– .066432	– .051120	– .210913	– .115305	– .078031	– .137485	– .157921	– .278626
11	– .654885	– .264421	– .077430	– 2.136966	– 1.133147	– .594312	– .290341	– .336722	– 2.349486
12	– .058954	– .012177	– .122171	– .149593	– .071119	– .054022	– 1.146988	– .066216	– .183953
13	– .102921	– .082393	– .117286	– .430294	– .178737	– .106665	– .306163	– .141645	– .335402
14	0	0	0	0	0	0	0	0	0
15	0	0	0	0	0	0	0	0	0
16	– .094016	– .108373	– .142483	– .603664	– .332938	– .366528	– 1.645148	– .231806	– 2.995016
17	0	0	0	0	0	0	0	0	0
Factors									
33	– 4.004791	– .333939	– .130315	– .714260	– .556389	– .272365	– .042637	– .272419	– .464877
34	– .886751	– .299389	– 2.336642	– 2.012621	– 3.048371	– 1.003875	– .955645	– .542743	– 3.162847
35	–12.430589	– 1.181432	– 1.858019	– 6.211110	– 4.816679	– 1.591509	– 1.431505	– 1.227104	– 4.286304

461

Table 3 (cont.)

	Sector							
	10	11	12	13	14	15	16	17
Sectors								
1	– .000724	0	0	.033951	0	.008062	– 2.120121	.941948
2	– .006366	– .003842	– .002438	– .016811	.166597	– .004259	– 1.342222	.078837
3	– .473404	– .514931	– .596906	– .212742	– .434599	– .136703	– .450265	.044658
4	– .000218	0	0	.049877	0	.009575	– 1.910163	.472312
5	– .002655	– .195650	– .004701	.155283	– .008919	.021378	– 1.562226	.530308
6	– .024620	– .422892	– .036713	.256192	– .751538	.106000	.198117	.240082
7	– .005010	– .215466	– .205166	.653795	– .500083	.086212	.509270	.540629
8	– .002681	– .003448	– .007405	.090606	– 2.564288	.034731	.121865	.136324
9	– .081812	– .331164	– .192865	.796404	– 2.346225	.159021	1.447901	5.183658
10	3.103760	– .558953	– .017249	.210773	– .081921	.139867	0	0
11	– .073012	49.430362	– .329271	.869101	– 1.806880	– .121831	– 1.046713	– 4.644212
12	– .003432	– .102353	5.882912	.127259	– .404390	– .062817	.298841	.202440
13	– .065475	– 2.459816	– .245593	28.009989	– .264283	3.155773	.0287505	.077599
14	0	0	0	0	19.734900	0	0	– 19.734900
15	0	0	0	0	0	19.555200	0	0
16	– .125591	0	– .310789	– .468266	– .494578	– .092270	12.586909	– 4.728642
17	0	0	0	0	0	0	0	37.955000
Factors								
33	– .226144	– 2.220716	– .356153	– 1.617244	– 1.914736	– 2.567393	0	0
34	– .788458	– 7.727462	– 1.391844	– 7.396960	– 4.115907	– 12.467906	0	0
35	– 1.089535	– 34.673670	– 2.075010	– 14.516075	– 3.533032	.373626	0	0

Table 4. *Utility indices for
consumer groups – original
equilibrium*

Consumer group (h)	Utility index ($\sum_{i=17}^{32} b_{ih} \log X_{ih}$)
1	-1.75542
2	$-.14055$
3	$-.63716$
4	$-.31005$
5	$.30958$
6	$-.27533$
7	1.23851
8	$.30696$
9	1.46091
10	$-.44134$

ratios that seemed to be too small; that is explained by the definition of capital. The lack of data does not allow us to break down this category or to distinguish it from other "primary" (produced in former periods) inputs. The income distribution analysis concentrates on the final allocation per consumer and good after production takes place. Given the consumer group's form of the utility functions and their final demand for the different goods, we can compute utility indices for each consumer group. The utility indices per consumer group in the original equilibrium are shown in Table 4.

Table 4 gives utility indices for the original income distribution in the model. Policy-induced changes in these indices will show the distributional effects of the policy being simulated. Whereas intergroup comparisons are not possible, interequilibrium comparison is allowed within each consumer group. This latter comparison will indicate the effects of the different policies to be simulated on income distribution.

Hence, we have built a faithful representation of the Mexican economy for 1977. The values endogenously determined by the model are identical to the actual values in the Mexican national accounts for 1977. All prices and activity levels are one; all activities make zero profits; demand equals supply in all sectors. Tax revenues are also consistent with the actual values.

In summary, the computation of the original equilibrium yields vectors of equilibrium prices and of activity levels, as well as values of government tax revenue, that lead to the computation of total production, value-added, factor shares, demand, and supply. The algorithm also computes the capital and labor coefficients that indicate whether production is more or less capital-intensive or labor-intensive. Lastly, this computation leads to the final allocation of produced commodities, which is used to compute the utility indices.

The original equilibrium represents a benchmark for the comparative static analysis of the tax reform under study, which shall be introduced in two different stages as shown in the next section.

4   The introduction of the value-added tax

The introduction of the value-added tax (VAT) in Mexico responded to the belief that this tax system, as opposed to the turnover tax system, is a more efficient and transparent tool of fiscal policy. In the first place, under a consumption value-added tax regime, the fiscal authorities can formulate discriminatory policies with more accuracy than with the cascade system. Under VAT, the exemption of particular goods or sectors from the payment of the tax follows more directly than under the turnover regime. From the authorities' point of view, even ignoring the general equilibrium effects, policy making is more transparent under a regime where the tax does not accumulate through the stages of production and commercialization. It is often claimed that income distribution targets can be reached more easily under the VAT system than under the turnover system, since in the latter case it is more difficult to obtain complete exemption of specific goods (zero tax rate). This argument, of course, ignores factor price adjustments.

It is also argued that the VAT system may facilitate, for the same reason mentioned above, export promotion policies. Exports are easily exempted, so as to improve their competitiveness with respect to the rest of the world, under the VAT regime. This was not the case under the previous system where the tax had a cascade effect. On the other hand, a small open economy must choose a tariff structure equivalent to the domestic indirect tax structure. The VAT system allows for these optimal adjustments better than the turnover regime. Finally, the fractional payment system introduced with the VAT (any VAT refund requires the receipts of payment of the tax) makes tax evasion less likely to occur, since agents are under mutual surveillance.

The substitution of VAT for the turnover tax was accompanied by the elimination of several special taxes. The VAT was not introduced with a uniform rate, since some sectors and regions were treated differently.[13] In particular, the agriculture sector was exempted from tax payments, as well as some final nonprocessed foodstuffs. Several professional services were also exempted. Furthermore, all border transactions were taxed with a 6% rate instead of the 10% rate for the rest of the regions and nonexempted sectors. The VAT also substituted export taxes and import tariffs for all the in-bond industries' demand for imports (temporary imports).

The computation of the effective VAT rate in our model takes into account all these exemptions. Since the aggregation in the official documents differs from ours, we introduced the tax rate that substitutes for the original turnover tax rate by using the following expression for the tax on sector/good j:

$$t_j = \sum_{l=1}^{L} \alpha_l t_l^{VAT} + \sum_{l=1}^{L} \alpha_l t_l^{SP} \tag{36}$$

where L is the number of subsectors within sector j; t_l^{VAT} and t_l^{SP} the VAT rate and the special tax rate, respectively, faced by subsector l; and α_l ($\geqslant 0$) is the share of subsector l in the total production of sector j.

Hence, the turnover and export taxes disappear, and the new tax rates (t_j) enter the model by only taxing final transactions and thus eliminating the cascade effects. These exemptions respond to allocation, fiscal, and distributive incentives by ignoring the tax yield. The introduction of the tax, in this form, does not respond to constant-yield criteria, as the reader shall see below.[14]

We first simulate the introduction of the VAT (which took place in January 1980) as explained above, and later we will simulate the second stage of the tax reform (January 1981). The first stage introduced, as we said before, a 10% tax rate, except for all border transactions (6%), agriculture and nonprocessed foodstuffs (0%), and some professional services (0%). A good deal of special taxes disappear except for those faced by sectors 20 and 24.

The introduction of VAT alters all the prices in the model, as can be seen in Table 5. The new prices in Table 5 show the percentage change with respect to the original equilibrium, since all prices in the original equilibrium were equal to one. The change in the price of petroleum and petrochemicals (sector 3), which dropped by more than 14%, is due to the removal of the turnover tax and, above all, of the additional effective special tax rate of more than 4%. The overall tax rate faced by the sector prior to VAT was 15%. The price of transportation in its final form (29) also dropped substantially because petroleum refinery products (e.g., gasoline, diesel fuel) make up a significant portion of the inputs demanded by that sector. The rest of the prices changed in smaller percentages.

The prices of factors also moved. The capital/urban labor price ratio increased by 4.5% and the capital/rural labor price ratio increased by

Table 5. *Equilibrium market prices in VAT 1 (numéraire = urban labor)*

Sector	Price	Sector	Price	Sector	Price	Sector	Price
1	1.021694	9	.924816	17	.956334	25	1.069076
2	.996633	10	.947112	18	.992560	26	1.025729
3	.857635	11	1.029022	19	1.010137	27	.997970
4	.975073	12	.975318	20	.039499	28	1.006818
5	.982159	13	.998411	21	1.079636	29	.913596
6	.961970	14	.970723	22	1.023223	30	.976613
7	.911147	15	.999633	23	1.038722	31	1.028584
8	.957745	16	.854362	24	.047867.	32	1.002222
						Factors	
						33	1.018183
						34	1.000000
						35	1.045399

Table 6. *Factor coefficients in VAT 1 (percentage change)*

		Sector								
Factor		1	2	3	4	5	6	7	8	9
33	(L_R)	1.82	1.43	.16	1.44	.86	.84	.85	1.11	.71
34	(L_N)	3.67	3.27	1.98	3.28	2.69	2.67	2.68	2.95	2.54
35	(K)	− .83	−1.21	−2.45	−1.20	−1.77	−1.79	−1.78	−1.52	−1.91

		Sector				
Factor		10	11	12	13	14
33	(L_R)	.69	1.75	.78	1.07	.20
34	(L_N)	2.52	3.60	2.61	2.90	2.02
35	(K)	−1.93	− .90	−1.84	−1.56	−2.41

2.7%. This is a result of the higher increases in activity levels of capital-intensive sectors, as we shall see below. If the relative price of factors had not been allowed to adjust, this policy would have had very negative effects on employment. By letting these prices adjust, we allow some sectors of the economy to use more labor-intensive techniques, as shown in the changes of the primary factor coefficients in Table 6.

The urban labor/rural labor price ratio went down almost 2%, which is explained by the increase of the activity levels of those sectors that

Table 7. *Activity levels and tariff revenue in VAT 1*

Sector	Level	Tariff revenue (billions of 1977 pesos)
1	1.009962	.07106
2	1.027687	.08335
3	1.038161	.11070
4	1.020742	.46092
5	.980446	.24430
6	1.017803	.27919
7	1.014825	1.24947
8	1.025141	.17784
9	1.033485	2.31650
10	1.012440	.09516
11	1.009944	0
12	1.082201	.25171
13	1.007765	.35317
14	1.032382	.38212
15	.862804	.05958
16	1.026983	0
17	1.032382	3.65347
18	1.037434	0
19	1.017162	0
20	1.047921	0
21	.952599	0
22	1.004313	0
23	.989432	0
24	.981578	0
25	.962073	0
26	1.002606	0
27	1.030368	0
28	1.022102	0
29	1.125792	0
30	1.052490	0
31	.999340	0
32	1.025517	0

demand rural labor more intensively than urban labor – for example, agriculture. The income distribution effects of this change in relative prices are positive since they reduce overall inequality, as we shall see below.

The activity levels also changed substantially. As shown in Table 7, the level of production in agriculture went up, which was expected, since agriculture was exempted from the VAT. This table also includes final goods: the changes in total production of the consumption goods. The level shows the percentage change in production due to the introduction of VAT, since these levels were exactly one in the original equilibrium (Table 1). The only production sector that has a decreasing activity level is textiles (5). This is explained largely by the fact that this sector did not have a very high turnover effect under the previous fiscal regime: A 2.8% turnover tax rate, with a rather small cascade effect, was changed to a 9.02% consumption value-added tax rate, which affected negatively the final demand for clothing (25), which is, among final goods, the main user of textiles output.

The rest of the production sectors increased their level of activity. Since agriculture (1) was already facing a relatively small turnover tax rate, the final effect on its level of production is not very substantial. Food products still face several special taxes that apply mostly to the sector "other groceries" (20) in final transactions. Thus, the increase in activity is a modest 4.7%.

The reduction in the price of petroleum and petrochemicals, together with a 3.8% increase in its level of production, is reflected in the larger increases in transportation in both intermediate (12) and final (29) activity levels. The special tax removal from sector 3, and the removal of the turnover tax faced originally by sector 12 itself, eliminated the rather high cascade effect faced by transportation. This sector improved notably after the tax reform.

Those final goods that do not go through many stages of production and commercialization seem to be affected by the policy. Fresh fruits and vegetables (21) and fish (23) suffered declines in their activity levels. They were facing a turnover tax that, through the cascade effect, turned out to be less than the VAT they are facing with the new regime. Hence, the tax change did encourage the production sectors that the government wanted to encourage, but only some of the final products were actually given incentives by this policy. Two-thirds of the final sectors of foodstuffs (18–23) have increased their total supply. The beverages sector (24) was negatively affected by the special tax regime to which it is subject. Its relative position, after the tax reform, is worse than before.

The changes in the import activity suggest that if the trade deficit had not been fixed, this policy would have had negative effects on the trade balance of the economy. The specification of the model does not allow us to analyze the order of magnitude of such effects.

The tax burden decreased considerably. As shown in Table 7, the supply of government services went down 13.7%. Tax revenue decreased 19.6% (174.2 billion pesos, using urban labor as a numeraire) as a result of the change in the tax regime. As we mentioned previously, the constant-

Table 8. *Utility indices for consumer groups in VAT 1*

Consumer group	Change in utility index
1	2.2
2	23.7
3	4.1
4	8.3
5	4.3
6	9.1
7	1.7
8	14.6
9	2.7
10	7.2

yield criterion was not actually taken into account when the policy was formulated. Although the 10% rate might have been the rate to keep the tax revenue constant, as the authorities claimed, the exemptions and the removal of several special taxes brought the tax revenue down. This fiscal sacrifice will have positive effects on resource allocation, according to the model's predictions.

Income distribution improved as a result of the policy change. Given the positive incentives received by agriculture, the urban–rural income differential decreases, according to the model results. Since rural average income is lower than urban average income, the decrease in the urban labor/rural labor price ratio improves the overall income distribution. As the reader will notice in Table 8, all the consumer groups are better off as a result of the lowering of the tax burden. Of course, the provision of the public good, government services, has gone down, as mentioned previously. Our analysis of the incidence of the tax reform assumes implicitly that the reduction in this public good has no effect on the utility index of any consumer group. However, the improvement among rural groups exceeds that of the urban groups.

Whereas income distribution improves across sectors (urban–rural), it is not clear that it improves across income brackets. Although the highest increase observed is in the utility index of the rural poor group, the richer rural groups also improve notably. The lack of progressivity in this tax reform is basically explained by the dominant increase in the price of capital (8.7%). Both labor/capital price ratios went down.

In January 1981, a year after the introduction of the VAT, the Mexican

Table 9. *Equilibrium market prices in VAT 2 (numéraire = urban labor)*

Sector	Price	Sector	Price	Sector	Price	Sector	Price
1	1.035636	9	.934656	17	.966523	25	1.081180
2	.978101	10	.956186	18	1.005362	26	1.037813
3	.864400	11	1.042404	19	1.023438	27	1.009288
4	.987364	12	.985120	20	.942530	28	1.018442
5	.992621	13	1.009257	21	1.037978	29	.922726
6	.972321	14	.980018	22	1.000240	30	.988106
7	.921114	15	1.003462	23	1.015687	31	1.040114
8	.968456	16	.864544	24	1.061321	32	1.013045
						Factors	
						33	1.027955
						34	1.000000
						35	1.062630

authorities decided, taking advantage of the transparency of this tool, to exempt all the foodstuff products, mainly to improve the purchasing power of the poor and low-income groups, which had been deteriorating with inflation. In terms of our aggregation, this tax change implies the removal of the consumption VAT faced by other groceries (20), fresh fruits and vegetables (21), meat (22), and fish (23).

The introduction of this exemption (VAT 2) had the expected effects in many respects. In terms of prices, we observe a pattern similar to the one observed in VAT 1, as shown in Table 9.

The similarity of the changes in the relative prices indicates that these exemptions did not alter the system of prices. The prices of factors also changed in the same directions. The increase in the price of capital is higher than in VAT 1. Again, there is a tendency to use more labor-intensive techniques in production once the price adjustment takes place. The demands for both labors (urban and rural) increase per unit of production in all sectors, and the capital coefficients also go down in every sector.

The urban labor/rural labor price ratio goes down by almost 3%, which is also explained by relatively higher increases in the activities of production of those sectors, such as agriculture, that use rural labor more intensively than urban labor.

The tax exemption does have the expected effects on the activity levels. As shown in Table 10, all the target sectors increase their activity levels. The most noteworthy changes in activity levels are in sectors 20–23.

Table 10. *Activity levels and tariff revenue in VAT 2*

Sector	Level	Tariff revenue (billions of 1977 pesos)
1	1.028740	.07244
2	1.023389	.08307
3	1.038212	.11079
4	1.039779	.46988
5	.979198	.24418
6	1.016229	.27898
7	1.014178	1.24965
8	1.019316	.17697
9	1.029198	2.30870
10	1.012371	.09523
11	.015642	0
12	1.081270	.25169
13	1.004270	.35222
14	1.023655	.37919
15	.828266	.05724
16	1.022680	0
17	1.023655	3.62543
18	1.035921	0
19	1.014425	0
20	1.103582	0
21	1.001592	0
22	1.038174	0
23	1.022508	0
24	.979712	0
25	.961091	0
26	1.001641	0
27	1.029146	0
28	1.021069	0
29	1.126031	0
30	1.051241	0
31	.998180	0
32	1.025190	0

While in VAT 1 only two-thirds of the foodstuff sectors increased their activity levels, in VAT 2 all the sectors have increased their level of production. In particular, sectors 21 and 23 improved because of the consumption VAT exemptions. Sectors 18 and 19 were better off in VAT 1, since the tradeoff within food production favored the other sectors. With respect to the production sectors, it is clear that agriculture (1) and other

Table 11. *Utility indices for consumer groups in VAT 2*

Consumer group	Change in utility index
1	.72
2	13.5
3	1.3
4	4.5
5	1.8
6	4.7
7	.34
8	2.6
9	.28
10	2.0

foods (4) are better off in VAT 2. Except for commerce (11), the rest of the production sectors were better off in VAT 1. The tax exemption induced a tradeoff in favor of the target sectors.

The supply of government services decreased 17.2% with respect to the original equilibrium and 4% with respect to VAT 1. The tax burden also decreased, as the tax revenue (165.3 billion pesos, using urban labor as a numeraire) went down by 23.7% with respect to original equilibrium 1 and by 5.1% with respect to VAT 1. This sacrifice of tax revenue was expected when the policy was first implemented. Again, our income distribution appraisals assume that everybody benefits equally from the government activities.

The change in the import activity shows a smaller increase in VAT 2 than in VAT 1. If the trade deficit had not been exogenously fixed, the balance of trade would have deteriorated less in VAT 2 than in VAT 1.

In terms of income distribution, there is an apparent Pareto improvement, as in VAT 1. The improvement of all the utility indices is explained by the large decline of the tax burden. The distribution of this improvement favors the rural groups, however, as shown in Table 11. The changes in the indices have been computed with respect to VAT 1, so as to capture the net effect on income distribution of the consumption VAT exemption for foodstuffs.

This policy has effects very similar to those of VAT 1. Income distribution improves due to the differential effects across sectors, in favor of rural groups. The pattern of the changes across income brackets is not progressive, due to the increase in the price, and the distribution among groups, of capital.

5   Conclusions and final remarks

The model is designed to capture the general equilibrium effects of changes in parameters such as taxes. The use of the model determines the directions of the changes and allows an appreciation of how the economy functions and reacts to different shocks. Although the simulation results include precise measures of the effects of the shocks introduced, the user should have more confidence in the direction than the size of the change indicated. This analytical tool should be used to evaluate policies by comparing their orientation with the direction of the effects as predicted by the model.

In the analysis of tax incidence we discovered a few potential shortcomings of the model. In the first place, this model allows all the prices to adjust, whereas the real economy does have some fixed prices. In particular, we do not take into account the stickiness of the wage and its effects on unemployment. Also, the specification of the foreign sector does not allow an endogenous determination of the trade deficit.[15] Both phenomena (unemployment and the trade deficit) seem to play important roles in the Mexican economy.

Within this framework, the present work simulated and evaluated the effects of the substitution of a consumption value-added tax regime (in two stages) for a turnover indirect tax regime. The two major conclusions of this work have been that resource allocation moved in favor of the target sectors (agriculture and foodstuffs) and that income distribution improved, reducing the differentials between urban and rural groups. These results show that the introduction of VAT is compatible with the overall thrust of the Mexican government's current policies, in which the stimulation of agricultural production and the relative improvement of the income of the rural groups have high priority.

Appendix

This appendix contains a list of the sectors, the consumers, and the major macroeconomic variables of the Mexican economy in 1977. It also presents the conversion matrix (Z), the utility function parameters (b_i), the efficiency and distribution parameters in the production functions (δ_j, c_j), the endowments of the consumers (ω_h), and the tax rates.

List of sectors

Production

1. Agriculture
2. Mining
3. Petroleum and petrochemicals
4. Food products
5. Textiles
6. Wood products
7. Chemical products
8. Nonmetal production
9. Machinery and automobiles
10. Electric energy
11. Commerce
12. Transportation
13. Services
14. Construction

Nonconsumption demand

15. Government services
16. Imports–exports
17. Fixed investment and inventory accumulation (capital tomorrow)

Consumption demand

18. Bread and cereals
19. Milk and eggs
20. Other groceries
21. Fresh fruits and vegetables
22. Meat
23. Fish
24. Beverages
25. Clothing
26. Furniture
27. Electronic products
28. Medical products
29. Transportation
30. Educational articles
31. Articles for personal care
32. Services

Factors of production

33. Rural labor
34. Urban labor
35. Capital and other factors

List of consumers

1. Urban poor (0–1800 pesos per month net income)
2. Rural poor (0–1800)
3. Urban low-income (1801–3150)
4. Rural low-income (1801–3150)
5. Urban low to middle-income (3151–5725)
6. Rural low to middle-income (3151–5725)
7. Urban middle-income (5726–13,400)
8. Rural middle-income (5726–13,400)
9. Urban upper-income (13,401 and up)
10. Rural upper-income (13,401 and up)
11. Government
12. Foreign sector

Major macroeconomic variables in Mexico (billions of 1977 pesos)

Wages and salaries	638.318
Returns to capital and other factors	755.534
Capital consumption allowance	157.418
Indirect taxes	123.430
Gross national product	1674.700

474

Private consumption	1101.127
Government consumption	195.552
Gross investment	379.550
Exports	176.062
Imports	− 177.591
Gross national product	1674.700
Import taxes	10.735
Export taxes	15.505
Indirect taxes paid by producers	49.953
Indirect taxes paid by consumers	47.236
Total indirect taxes	123.430
Indirect taxes	123.430
Income taxes	93.386
Income from capital and other factors	14.00
Total government revenues	230.816
Government consumption	195.552
Government investment	98.750
Total government expenditures	294.302
Government expenditures	294.302
Government revenues	− 230.816
Government deficit	63.486
Wages and salaries	638.318
Returns to capital and other factors	755.534
Government capital income	− 14.000
Capital consumption allowance	157.418
Private income	1537.270
Private income	1537.270
Private consumption	− 1101.127
Income taxes	− 93.386
Gross savings	342.757
Imports	177.591
Exports	− 176.062
Trade deficit	1.529
Gross savings	342.757
Trade deficit	1.529
Government deficit	− 63.486
Private investment	280.800
Private investment	280.800
Government investment	98.750
Total investment	379.550
Fixed investment	399.100
Inventory accumulation	40.450
Total investment	379.550

Conversion matrix (Z) (tens of billions of 1977 pesos):

	18	19	20	21	22	23	24	25
1.	-1.425370	-1.647905	-1.136032	-3.738113	-.332541	-.226320	0	0
2.	0	0	-.005791	0	0	0	0	0
3.	0	0	0	0	0	0	0	0
4.	-4.958296	-.999017	-5.013866	0	-4.777702	-.237736	-3.363805	-8.537893
5.	0	0	0	0	0	0	0	0
6.	0	0	0	0	0	0	0	-.067294
7.	0	0	0	0	0	0	0	0
8.	0	0	0	0	0	0	0	0
9.	0	0	0	0	0	0	0	0
10.	0	0	0	0	0	0	0	0
11.	-2.975354	-1.533688	-2.733032	-1.978457	-2.637943	-.199379	-4.555052	-6.901595
12.	0	0	0	0	0	0	0	-.136816
13.	0	0	0	0	0	0	0	0
14.	0	0	0	0	0	0	0	0
15.	0	0	0	0	0	0	0	0
16.	0	0	0	0	0	0	0	0
17.	0	0	0	0	0	0	0	0
18.	9.422800	0	0	0	0	0	0	0
19.	0	4.193460	0	0	0	0	0	0
20.	0	0	9.529261	0	0	0	0	0
21.	0	0	0	5.71657	0	0	0	0
22.	0	0	0	0	7.809646	0	0	0
23.	0	0	0	0	0	.666495	0	0
24.	0	0	0	0	0	0	8.965448	0
25.	0	0	0	0	0	0	0	15.997657
26.	0	0	0	0	0	0	0	0
27.	0	0	0	0	0	0	0	0
28.	0	0	0	0	0	0	0	0
29.	0	0	0	0	0	0	0	0
30.	0	0	0	0	0	0	0	0
31.	0	0	0	0	0	0	0	0
32.	0	0	0	0	0	0	0	0

	26	27	28	29	30	31	32
1.	0	0	0	0	0	0	-.246196
2.	0	0	0	-.930764	0	0	0
3.	0	0	0	0	0	0	-.467931
4.	0	0	0	0	0	0	0
5.	-.412440	-.275835	0	0	0	0	-.004036
6.	-.961121	-.047245	-1.043909	-.075432	-.482382	-.551498	0
7.	-1.094757	-.340974	0	-1.364185	0	0	0
8.	-.523171	-.044811	-.029579	0	0	0	-.896505
9.	-1.042889	-2.656651	0	0	0	0	-.168706
10.	0	0	-.895674	-.920213	0	-.460106	-.134364
11.	-2.882106	-2.492243	0	-3.545008	-.368085	0	-18.837514
12.	0	0	0	-.622853	0	-.450872	0
13.	0	0	0	0	0	0	0
14.	0	0	0	0	0	0	0
15.	0	0	0	0	0	0	0
16.	0	0	0	0	0	0	0
17.	0	0	0	0	0	0	0
18.	0	0	0	0	0	0	0
19.	0	0	0	0	0	0	0
20.	0	0	0	0	0	0	0
21.	0	0	0	0	0	0	0
22.	0	0	0	0	0	0	0
23.	0	0	0	0	0	0	0
24.	0	0	0	0	0	0	0
25.	0	0	0	0	0	0	0
26.	7.182934	6.219569	0	0	0	0	0
27.	0	0	2.058262	0	0	0	0
28.	0	0	0	0	0	0	0
29.	0	0	0	8.540955	0	0	0
30.	0	0	0	0	.862987	0	0
31.	0	0	0	0	0	1.512067	0
32.	0	0	0	0	0	0	21.434590

Utility parameters and endowments:

	Income groups				
Good	1	2	3	4	5
17	.2998692	.2184588	.2650147	.1589905	.1516540
18	.1094570	.1882454	.0961469	.1453307	.0844406
19	.4671240	.0251506	.0440289	.0358856	.0447625
20	.0967575	.1195329	.0773011	.1018984	.0771810
21	.0565412	.0694367	.0533166	.0601286	.0538618
22	.0875501	.0514502	.0838017	.0635650	.0863294
23	.0045101	.0030577	.0046419	.0042449	.0056099
24	.0610519	.0837458	.0781064	.0990019	.0750952
25	.0448967	.0876805	.0688132	.1125858	.1089388
26	.0379558	.0518021	.0434016	.0584625	.0573554
27	.0109825	.0114259	.0186416	.2384858	.0395105
28	.0136593	.0172653	.0117978	.0197818	.0138018
29	.0287714	.0126714	.0380144	.0212988	.0425540
30	.0022082	.0039120	.0049522	.0577110	.0057065
31	.0092953	.0065511	.0105686	.0099833	.0123851
32	.0897815	.0496135	.1014526	.0792252	.1408136

Endowments (billions of 1977 pesos)

Rural labor	—	24.364079	—	33.080724	—
Urban labor	3.947726	—	24.719532	—	92.458871
Capital	13.124833	62.596001	32.324842	52.619278	75.293355

	Income groups				
Good	6	7	8	9	10
17	.1457390	.2008161	.3706541	.3332217	.0204065
18	.1026330	.0497371	.0484789	.0205797	.0251377
19	.0362926	.0316915	.0220340	.0174120	.0183137
20	.0957508	.0636303	.0538610	.0389004	.0458806
21	.0524465	.0383174	.0300508	.0220113	.0239579
22	.0537511	.0536746	.0536501	.0361498	.0266506
23	.0048926	.0050195	.0041226	.0043521	.0041661
24	.0917352	.0620104	.0594110	.0360575	.0462758
25	.1347254	.1249518	.1021151	.1077326	.1149935
26	.0645297	.0488722	.0476178	.0437523	.0462824
27	.0443762	.0476180	.0415679	.0555470	.0549848
28	.0179162	.0140778	.0135134	.0130019	.0094704
29	.0396333	.0631193	.0708473	.0842506	.0846597
30	.0064470	.0070161	.0061004	.0059519	.0040433
31	.0116459	.0126266	.0089897	.0089280	.0082268
32	.0974856	.1768210	.0669858	.1721512	.4665501

Endowments (billions of 1977 pesos)

Rural labor	38.786712	—	46.596938	—	14.115326
Urban labor	—	211.062933	—	149.185159	—
Capital	54.882450	207.005560	88.062716	275.735026	37.307943

Value-added parameters:

Sector	δ_{j,L_R}	δ_{j,L_U}	$\delta_{j,k}$	VA_j/c_j	ρ_j
1	.23119505	.05119182	.71761313	8.3572420	0
2	.18401255	.16497437	.65101308	.7465865	0
3	.03013072	.54026710	.42960218	1.9411404	0
4	.07991280	.22517598	.69491123	4.0541828	0
5	.06606817	.36197743	.57195440	3.5391569	0
6	.09497521	.35005679	.55496800	1.1453516	0
7	.01754766	.39330397	.58914837	1.1481316	0
8	.13339067	.26575532	.60085401	.8082353	0
9	.05874093	.39965065	.54160843	3.3316332	0
10	.10747566	.37471813	.51780621	.8151113	0
11	.04976746	.17317665	.77705589	23.3183197	0
12	.09316054	.36407037	.54276909	1.5225660	0
13	.06873035	.31435921	.61691044	10.0995269	0
14	.20020920	.43036882	.36942198	3.3375315	0

Aggregate tax rates

Consumer group	Income tax rates
1	0
2	0
3	0
4	0
5	0
6	0
7	.071448
8	.071448
9	.113141
10	.113141

Sector/good	Turnover	VAT 1	VAT 2	Tariff	Export tax
1	.001242			.08426343	
2	.043060			.08426343	
3	.148888			.08426343	
4	.038307			.08426343	
5	.028568			.08426343	
6	.038372			.08426343	
7	.052949			.08426343	
8	.034241			.08426343	
9	.056383			.08426343	
10	.039964			.08426343	

Sector/good	Turnover	VAT 1	VAT 2	Tariff	Export tax
11	0			.08426343	
12	.014384			.08426343	
13	.017821			.08426343	
14	.015467			.08426343	
15	0			.08426343	
16	0			.08426343	.12318354
17	0			.08426343	
18	.006769	0	0	.08426343	
19	.003064	0	0	.08426343	
20	.067218	.055048	0	.08426343	
21	0	.054095	0	.08426343	
22	.007870	.036063	0	.08426343	
23	.004591	.036063	0	.08426343	
24	.116736	.179158	.179158	.08426343	
25	.022132	.090158	.090158	.08426343	
26	.037095	.090158	.090158	.08426343	
27	.058173	.090158	.090158	.08426343	
28	.043289	.090158	.090158	.08426343	
29	.126742	.090158	.090158	.08426343	
30	.014508	0	0	.08426343	
31	.032796	.090158	.090158	.08426343	
32	.031694	.041923	.041923	.08426343	

NOTES

1. The form of the demand for factor k in sector j when $\rho_j = 0$ would be

$$X_{kj} = \frac{VA_j}{c_j} \prod_i \left[\frac{q_i \delta_{kj}}{q_k \delta_{ij}} \right]^{\delta_{ij}}, \qquad j = 1, \ldots, 17$$

which will be the case in the computation of the original equilibrium due to the lack of data and of reliable estimates of ρ_j for the Mexican economy.

2. Although $c_{if} = c_{il}$, we distinguish between the two rates because whereas c_{il} enters in the activity analysis matrix (with $c_{il} = 0$ for the diagonal elements, $i = j$), c_{if} enters in the demand functions for the consumer groups. Note that c_{if} could also enter in the conversion matrix.

3. We also consider an aggregate export tax that applies to the export activity in matrix A. In Equation (11) this tax would be represented by t_j when $j = m$.

4. For the computation of the original equilibrium it is assumed that $\alpha_G = 1$.

5. In the actual computation, we choose units so as to have activity levels equal to one representing the actual levels of gross production per sector.

6. Note that $\sum_{i=18}^{32} b_{hi} + [1 - APC_h] = 1$.

7. The only "produced" goods of which there are positive original endowments are capital tomorrow and imports, which take care of the government and trade deficits, respectively.

8. For a very complete description of this method see Scarf (1977).

9. See Helpmann (1976).

10. See Kehoe (1980).

11. Urban consumer groups are defined as those having their residence in towns with more than 10,000 inhabitants. Rural groups live in settlements of fewer than 10,000 residents.
12. The solution was obtained after 25 Merrill loops. The computation of the final equilibrium took under 20 seconds of computing time in the IBM 370/168.
13. Since VAT was not introduced uniformly, it is important to distinguish between the consumption value-added tax that we are introducing in the model and the income value-added tax, because due to the nonuniform tax rates they are not equivalent.
14. For simulations with constant-yield restrictions and uniform tax rates, see Shoven and Whalley (1977) and Serra-Puche (1979).
15. See Kehoe and Serra-Puche (1981).

REFERENCES

Banco de Mexico, S.A. 1980. *Información Económica: Producto Interno Bruto y Gasto, 1970-1979.* Mexico City.
Fullerton, D. A., King, A., Shoven, J., and Whalley, J. 1981. "Corporate Tax Integration in the United States: A General Equilibrium Approach." *American Economic Review* 71(4):677-91.
Fullerton, D., Shoven, J., and Whalley, J. 1983. "Replacing the U.S. Income Tax with a Progressive Consumption Tax: A Sequenced General Equilibrium Approach." *Journal of Public Economics* 20:1-21.
Harris, R., and MacKinnon, J. 1977. "A Simple Technique for Computing Optimal Tax Equilibria." Discussion Paper No. 270, Department of Economics, Queen's University. Kingston, Ontario.
Heady, C., and Mitra, P. 1977. "The Computation of Linear Taxation." Mimeo.
Helpman, E. 1976. "Solutions of General Equilibrium Problems for a Trading World." *Econometrica* 44:547-59.
Kehoe, T. 1980. "Uniqueness of Equilibrium in Production Economies." Working Paper No. 271, Department of Economics, Massachusetts Institute of Technology.
Kehoe, T., and Serra-Puche, J. 1981. "The Impact of the 1980 Fiscal Reform on Unemployment in Mexico." Mimeo.
MacKinnon, J. 1976. "General Equilibrium with Taxes." Discussion Paper No. 200, Institute for Economic Research, Queen's University. Kingston, Ontario.
Scarf, H. 1977. "The Computation of Equilibrium Prices: An Exposition." Cowles Foundation Discussion Paper No. 473, Yale University.
Scarf, H. (with the collaboration of T. Hansen). 1973. *The Computation of Economic Equilibria.* New Haven: Yale University Press.
Secretaría de Programación y Presupuesto. *Matriz de Insumo-Producto de México, Año 1970,* Vol. 1. Mexico City: Secretaría de Programación y Presupuesto.
   1980. *Encuesta Nacional de Ingresos y Gastos Familiares en 1977.* Mexico City: Secretaría de Programación y Presupuesto.
Secretaría de Programación y Presupuesto and Banco de México, S.A. 1980. *Submatriz de Consumo Privado por Objeto del Gasto y Rama de Actividad Económica de Origen, Año 1970.* Mexico City: Secretaría de Programación y Presupuesto.

Serra-Puche, J. 1979. "A Computational General Equilibrium Model for the Mexican Economy: An Analysis of Fiscal Policies." Ph.D diss., Yale University.
   1981. *Politicas Fiscales en Mexico: Un Enfoque de Equilibrio General.* Mexico City: El Colegio de Mexico.
Shoven, J. 1974. "A Proof of the Existence of a General Equilibrium with *ad Valorem* Commodity Taxes." *Journal of Economic Theory* 8:1-25.
   1973. "General Equilibrium with Taxes: A Computational Procedure and an Existence Proof." *Review of Economic Studies* 40:475-90.
   1974. "On the Computation of Competitive Equilibria on International Markets with Tariffs." *Journal of International Economics* 4:341-54.
   1977. "Equal Yield Tax Alternatives: General Equilibrium Computational Techniques." *Journal of Public Economics* 8:211-24.

Comments

Sherman Robinson

This chapter involves analysis that could fruitfully draw on two separate strands of work with applied general equilibrium models. The first strand includes models that have been built since the early 1970s to study tax incidence and other public finance issues in developed countries. The second strand includes models of developing countries and really started with input–output and linear programming models in the 1950s and 1960s, and extends through the computable general equilibrium (CGE) models developed in the 1970s. The model used by Serra-Puche, although applied to a developing country, is very much in the first tradition. Although the application of the public finance model to Mexico is quite interesting and represents a useful first step in the adaptation of such models to developing countries, it would have benefited from a closer reading of the large and rapidly expanding literature using multisector models of developing countries.

Some specifications that may be acceptable in tax models applied to developed countries are either suspect or clearly inappropriate in a model of a developing country. For example, the assumption that capital is freely mobile across sectors and will be allocated so as to equate rental rates in all sectors assumes a degree of perfection in capital markets that is not consistent with empirical observation in developing countries. And the assumption that capital in the service and agricultural sectors is the same "stuff" as in the industrial sectors (i.e., capital goods are the same, regardless of sector of destination) is clearly wrong and will cause trouble in a model of a developing country in which manufacturing represents only about a quarter of GDP.

In the Serra-Puche model of Mexico, the largest sectors in terms of value-added are (in decreasing order): commerce, trade, and agriculture (see Serra-Puche's Table 3). In the development literature, there has been a tendency to take account of their importance by segmenting models and treating these special sectors separately. For example, it is often assumed that agricultural labor is not freely mobile across sectors, and that therefore migration must be considered explicitly. But in this model, "rural" and "urban" labor appear in all sectors and there is no restriction on labor or capital mobility across sectors. Similarly, the service and trade sectors are often viewed as having a rather special role in the economy, with a quite different technology from the productive sectors. For example, one view is that the "urban traditional" sector (including the service sectors), provides a kind of labor sink for the rest of the economy – a residual employer that sops up the underemployed. Such structural features are characteristic of many developing countries, have been much studied, and will have a significant impact on how changes in tax policy affect the economy. In this model, however, there is no special consideration of any of these important sectors.

Although probably acceptable for a study of taxes, the treatment of foreign trade in the model – with its fixed coefficients and simple treatment of the balance of payments – is clearly unsatisfactory for any serious analysis of trade and/or industrial policy. Again, there has been much work in the development literature on the role of foreign trade and of the impact that different policies have on the structure of production, exports, and imports. Such issues are clearly very important in Mexico, particularly given the importance of oil, and a computable general equilibrium model would seem to be an ideal tool for studying them. To address such issues, however, more work is required on the specification of international trade and of the role of the exchange rate and the balance of payments than is evident in the current version of the model.

The Serra-Puche chapter is a good example of work in the public finance tradition of applied general equilibrium models and, on reflection, I think that the basic thrust of my comments also applies to other work in this tradition. This work has remained strongly rooted in the Walrasian model and has tended to retain assumptions of perfect markets that modelers working on developing countries abandoned years ago and those working in developed countries should be questioning. Indeed, some of the discussion in the presentation of these models seems to strain much too hard to retain its links with the Walrasian model. For example, Serra-Puche speaks of the government as maximizing a utility function (Leontief-type, in his case). As a behavioral assumption, this is not at all persuasive as a justification for what is really an ad hoc specification of government expenditure behavior. The real point is that for the purposes of a tax study, the assumption of fixed expenditures shares for government is realistic enough – especially when one also often restricts the analysis to "equal-yield" tax scenarios. Appeals to utility functions seem superfluous. In more ambitious models that seek to capture "realistic" macroeconomic mechanisms, imperfect markets, and behavior of agents other than simply consumers and producers, the Walrasian paradigm will be stretched even thinner. For example, in a model in which one seeks to "endogenize" the government as an active agent pursuing, say, stabilization policy, it would be pointless to pursue the analogy of the government acting like any other consumer maximizing utility subject to a budget constraint. As we move to more realistic models and seek to make statements about how real-world economies will react to changes in policies, it seems to me that we must also be careful in how we justify our behavioral specifications. The pure Walrasian model is a very abstract construct. Although it provides a useful and necessary starting point for applied models, it should not end up being a straightjacket.

CHAPTER 12

Extending the ORANI model of the Australian economy: adding foreign investment to a miniature version

Peter B. Dixon, B. R. Parmenter, and Russell J. Rimmer

1   Introduction

ORANI is a large multisectoral model of the Australian economy.[1] In standard applications it identifies 113 industries, 230 commodities (115 domestically produced and 115 imported), 9 types of labor, 7 types of agricultural land, and 113 types of capital (one for each industry). It contains explicit modeling, at this disaggregated level, of many types of commodity and factor flows – for example, inputs to current production, inputs to capital creation, household consumption, exports and margin services (retail, wholesale, and transport). The multiproduct characteristics of production in Australian agricultural industries are also explicitly modeled, and a facility is included for disaggregating economywide results to the regional (state) level.

The reason for including so much detail in ORANI is to facilitate its use by a variety of government agencies with interests in different spheres of economic policy. Among the agencies that have used the model are the Industries Assistance Commission, the Bureau of Agricultural Economics, and the Premier's Department of South Australia. Applications of ORANI made by these agencies and other groups include simulations of the effects on industries, occupations, and regions of changes in tariffs, the exploitation of mineral resources, changes in world commodity prices, changes in the exchange rate, the adoption of import parity pricing for oil products, subsidies to ailing industries, the move toward equal pay for women, changes in real wages, and the adoption of Keynesian demand stimulation policies. Each of these applications draws upon different aspects of the model's detail.

In handling such a large model, three features of our procedures have been helpful. The first is that the theoretical structure has been kept simple. Lags are not explicitly included and similar behavioral assumptions and function forms are employed for each industry. Consequently, results from ORANI can be explained intuitively in terms of the model's theory. Second, we solve the model by linear approximations. This enables us to obtain solutions at modest cost, and has the additional advantages of allowing flexibility in the selection of exogenous variables and of facilitating changes to the structure of the model. Finally, we have devised miniature versions of the model for experimenting with new developments prior to their implementation in the main model.

In Section 2 of the chapter we outline the theory of our computing procedure, including a method for overcoming the problem of linearization errors. In Section 3 we introduce the current miniature version of ORANI (MO81). With MO81 we are experimenting with ways of accounting explicitly for capital inflow in long-run simulations. Foreign investment is important to the long-run development of the Australian economy but is not a crucial consideration in the short-run problems that have been the subjects of most ORANI applications to date. Results of our experiments are reported in Section 4. This section also includes an illustration of our method for eliminating linearization errors. Section 5 contains conclusions.

2   Computing ORANI solutions: theoretical overview

The ORANI model can be represented as a system of m equations in n variables, with $n > m$:

$$F(X) = 0 \tag{2.1}$$

where X is an $n \times 1$ vector of variables (demands, prices, employment levels, etc.) and F is an m-component vector of differentiable functions. In each application of ORANI, the equations are interpreted as referring to one point of time (the solution year), although the point of time chosen varies with applications. For example, in a study of the long-run effects of a change in protection, the solution year might be 1990. Then (2.1) would be interpreted as saying that in 1990, demand will equal supply, prices will equal costs, and so forth. For a study of short-run effects, the solution year might be 1984. As we will see, the choice of the solution year has implications for (a) the choice of values for various parameters, (b) the setting of the initial solution, and (c) the allocation of variables between the endogenous and exogenous categories.

Whereas the selection of the $(n - m)$ variables to be treated as exogenous varies across applications of the model, in any particular application we can denote the endogenous variables by the $m \times 1$ vector X_1 and the exogenous variables by the $(n-m) \times 1$ vector X_2. Then (2.1) can be rewritten as

$$F(X_1, X_2) = 0 \tag{2.2}$$

and a solution for the model can be written as a system of m equations of the form

$$X_1 = G(X_2) \tag{2.3}$$

where

$$F(G(X_2), X_2) = 0 \tag{2.4}$$

for all X_2 in some subset of R^{n-m}. In computations with ORANI, we are concerned with the effects on the endogenous variables of given changes to the exogenous variables. Thus the computational problem is to evaluate ΔX_1, where

$$\Delta X_1 = G(X_2^F) - G(X_2^I) \tag{2.5}$$

and where X_2^I and X_2^F are the initial and final values for the exogenous variables.

The numbers of equations and variables in ORANI is extremely large and the F vector includes a variety of functional forms. However, in all ORANI computations we have two important pieces of information. First, we know an initial solution, (X_1^I, X_2^I). That is, we have a set of values for demands, prices, employment levels, and so on such that

$$F(X_1^I, X_2^I) = 0 \tag{2.6}$$

This initial solution is provided by the demands, prices, employment levels, and so on revealed in the initial-situation input–output data. These data are the source of parameters relating to cost shares, sales shares, and so on in the system (2.1). If the solution year chosen for an application of ORANI is 1990, then the initial-situation input–output data are a balanced set of input–output tables for 1990. These tables can be constructed by simply applying a uniform expansion factor to all flows in the most recently published input–output accounts. Alternatively, their construction could be based on detailed forecasts. In most of our work with ORANI, we have implicitly adopted the simple mechanical approach.[2] We have, therefore, reported results from the model in the following way: If we increase tariffs by 25%, then in 1990 the output of cars will be $x\%$ higher than it would have been without the change in tariffs. The value assumed, $X^I(\text{cars})$, for what output would have been is part of our mechanically projected input–output data. If our aim were to produce a projection of the form

$$X^F(\text{cars}) = X^I(\text{cars})\left(1 + \frac{x}{100}\right)$$

for the output of cars in 1990 under an increase in tariffs, then our assumed value for $X^I(\text{cars})$ would be vital. However, in applications of ORANI, we have concentrated on the percentage change results x. These are comparatively insensitive to plausible variations in X^I.

The second piece of information we have is how to evaluate any selected components of an $m \times n$ matrix $A(X)$, which has the property that

$$A(X) = F_X(X)\hat{X} \tag{2.7}$$

for all X satisfying (2.1), where $F_X(X)$ is the $m \times n$ matrix of first-order partial derivatives of F with respect to X and $\hat{}$ denotes a diagonal matrix.

The derivation of an $A(X)$ matrix is straightforward for ORANI, and we believe this is true for most members of the current generation of computable general equilibrium models. The task is to translate the system (2.1) into a percentage-change or elasticities form. The system becomes

$$A(X)x = 0 \tag{2.8}$$

where, for X satisfying (2.1), the ijth element of $A(X)$ is given by

$$A_{ij}(X) = \frac{\partial F^i}{\partial X(j)} X(j)$$

and where the jth component of x [denoted by $x(j)$] is the percentage change in the jth variable [denoted by $X(j)$],[3] that is,

$$x(j) = 100\left(\frac{d(X(j))}{X(j)}\right) \tag{2.9}$$

The A_{ij} often turn out to be cost shares or sales shares. Assume, for example, that the ith equation in (2.1) is

$$F^i(X) = \frac{Q_1 + Q_2}{Q} - 1 = 0 \tag{2.10}$$

where Q_1 and Q_2 are demands by agents 1 and 2 and Q is total sales. Then

$$\left(\frac{\partial F^i}{\partial Q_r}\right)Q_r = \frac{Q_r}{Q}, \qquad r = 1, 2 \tag{2.11}$$

and

$$\left(\frac{\partial F^i}{\partial Q}\right)Q = -\frac{Q_1 + Q_2}{Q^2}Q \tag{2.12}$$

Letting Q_1, Q_2, and Q be the first three variables, we can write the ith row of $A(X)$ as

$$A_{i\cdot}(X) = (S_1, S_2, -1, 0, \ldots, 0) \tag{2.13}$$

where

$$S_r = Q_r/Q, \qquad r = 1, 2 \tag{2.14}$$

Thus, $A_{i1}(X)$ and $A_{i2}(X)$ are the shares of agents 1 and 2 in total sales. It is worth noting that in deriving (2.13), we have simplified (2.12). This explains the comment following (2.7). The $A(X)$ that we compute for ORANI necessarily satisfies (2.7) only for X satisfying (2.1). In our example, the third element in the ith row of $A(X)$ is

$$A_{i3}(X) = -1$$

This coincides with the value for $(\partial F/\partial Q)Q$ given in (2.12) only if Q_1, Q_2, and Q satisfy (2.10).

To make use of the $A(X)$ matrix in solving the computational problem (2.5), we reformulate the problem as one in numerical integration. We start by differentiating (2.4) to obtain

$$F_1(X_1, X_2)G_2(X_2) + F_2(X_1, X_2) = 0 \tag{2.15}$$

where X_2 is in the relevant subset of R^{n-m} and X_1 and X_2 jointly satisfy (2.2). Here F_1 and F_2 are $m \times m$ and $m \times (n-m)$ submatrices of F_X. Now F_1 contains the derivatives with respect to the endogenous variables X_1, and F_2 contains the derivatives with respect to the exogenous variables X_2. And G_2 is the $m \times (n-m)$ matrix of first-order partial derivatives of G.

Next, we assume that

$$\text{determinant}\left\{F_1\left(X_1^I, X_2^I\right)\right\} \neq 0 \tag{2.16}$$

This is a sufficient condition to ensure the existence in a neighborhood of (X_1^I, X_2^I) of a unique vector of G functions [functions satisfying (2.4)] passing through (X_1^I, X_2^I) (see the implicit functions theorem – Apostol, 1957, pp. 146–8). It also allows us to rearrange (2.15) as

$$G_2(X_2) = -F_1^{-1}(X_1, X_2)F_2(X_1, X_2) \tag{2.17}$$

where it is understood that (X_1, X_2) is in a neighborhood of (X_1^I, X_2^I) and that X_1 and X_2 jointly satisfy (2.2).

Finally, we substitute from (2.7) into (2.17). This gives

$$G_2(X_2) = -\hat{X}_1 A_1^{-1}(X) A_2(X) \hat{X}_2^{-1} \tag{2.18}$$

for all (X_1, X_2) satisfying (2.2) and lying in a neighborhood of (X_1^I, X_2^I). Thus, for any value of (X_1, X_2), we can evaluate a matrix $B(X_1, X_2)$ that has the property that

$$G_2(X_2) = B(X_1, X_2) \tag{2.19}$$

for all X_1 and X_2 satisfying (2.2) and lying in a neighborhood of (X_1^I, X_2^I). The formula for B is the right-hand side of (2.18).

The computation of ΔX_1 in (2.5) can now be handled as a standard problem in numerical integration. We have an initial point (X_1^I, X_2^I) satisfying

$$X_1^I = G(X_2^I) \tag{2.20}$$

and we have a formula, (2.18), for evaluating the derivatives of G. We can proceed by, for example, Euler's method. We divide the change in the exogenous variables, ΔX_2 $(= X_2^F - X_2^I)$, into n equal parts. Then we approximate $G(X_2^F) - G(X_2^I)$ by

$$(\Delta X_1)^n = \sum_{q=0}^{n-1} (\Delta X_1)_q^n \tag{2.21}$$

where the $(\Delta X_1)_q^n$ are given by

$$(\Delta X_1)_0^n = \frac{1}{n} B(X_1^I, X_2^I) \Delta X_2 \tag{2.22}$$

and

$$(\Delta X_1)_q^n = \frac{1}{n} B\left(X_1^I + \sum_{r=0}^{q-1} (\Delta X_1)_r^n, \ X_2^I + \frac{q}{n} \Delta X_2\right) \Delta X_2$$
$$\text{for} \quad q = 1, \ldots, n-1 \tag{2.23}$$

If we set $n = 1$, our approximation is

$$G(X_2^F) - G(X_2^I) \approx B(X_1^I, X_2^I) \Delta X_2 \tag{2.24}$$

This is Johansen's (1960) approach. If we set $n = 2$, then we obtain

$$G(X_2^F) - G(X_2^I) \approx \tfrac{1}{2} B(X_1^I, X_2^I) \Delta X_2$$
$$+ \tfrac{1}{2} B(X_1^I + (\Delta X_1)_0^2, \ X_2^I + \tfrac{1}{2}\Delta X_2) \Delta X_2 \tag{2.25}$$

where

$$(\Delta X_1)_0^2 = \tfrac{1}{2} B(X_1^I, X_2^I) \Delta X_2 \tag{2.26}$$

With the first term on the right-hand side of (2.25) we approximate the effect on X_1 of moving X_2 from X_2^I to $X_2^I + \frac{1}{2}\Delta X_2$. In the second term, B is reevaluated to give an estimate of $G_2(X_2^I + \frac{1}{2}\Delta X_2)$. Then this estimate is used in approximating the effect on X_1 of moving X_2 from $X_2^I + \frac{1}{2}\Delta X_2$ to X_2^F.

Provided that the derivatives of B satisfy various boundedness conditions [these are detailed in Dixon, Parmenter, Sutton, and Vincent (1982) (DPSV), sec. 35], it can be shown that

$$\lim_{n \to \infty} (\Delta X_1)^n = G(X_2^F) - G(X_2^I) \tag{2.27}$$

Our experience (see Section 5) with applications of ORANI suggests that $G(X_2^F) - G(X_2^I)$ can usually be approximated to a high level of accuracy using a low value of n. Here $n = 2$ is normally adequate.

3 A miniature version of ORANI, MO81

3.1 Introduction

Tables 1–4 set out the miniature version of ORANI, MO81. Table 1 lists the equations in the percentage-change form (2.8). Tables 2 and 4 define the variables and coefficients appearing in Table 1. Three possible selections for the exogenous variables are given in Table 3. In Table 4 we have also given examples of how the coefficients are evaluated for our miniature model using hypothetical input–output data. These data are discussed in Section 4 of the chapter. We have chosen to locate Table 4 together with the data tables (Tables 5 and 6) in subsection 4.1.

The equations in ORANI can be classified under five headings: (I) final demands, (II) industry inputs and outputs, (III) zero-pure-profit conditions, (IV) market clearing, and (V) miscellaneous. This last group includes definitions of various aggregates such as the balance of trade and the consumer price index. In MO81 we have added a category VI, macroeconomic closure. This category includes an aggregate consumption function and equations describing the foreign share in capitalist income. In the current ORANI model the macro aggregates are usually treated as being exogenous and no explicit consideration is given to the foreign share in domestic capital. At present we are using MO81 to experiment with various equations that will allow a more complete treatment of these variables. Results from these experiments are discussed in Section 4.

In describing MO81, we will first work through the equations in categories I–V. In Section 3.3 we will consider the closure options that are available in a model restricted to these categories. This will indicate the

Table 1. The MO8I equations: a linear system in percentage changes

Identifier	Equation	Subscript range[a]	Number	Description
I. Final demands				
(T1)	$x_{(is)}^{(3)} = c^R - \left(p_{(is)}^{(3)} - \sum_{r=1}^{2} S_{(ir)}^{(3)} p_{(ir)}^{(3)} \right)$	$i=1,\dots,g$ $s=1,2$	$2g$	Household demands for commodities
(T2)	$x_{(is)j}^{(2)} = y_j - \left(p_{(is)j}^{(2)} - \sum_{r=1}^{2} S_{(ir)j}^{(2)} p_{(ir)j}^{(2)} \right)$	$i=1,\dots,g$ $s=1,2$ $j=1,\dots,h$	$2gh$	Demands for inputs to capital creation
(T3)	$p_{(i1)}^* = -\gamma_i x_{(i1)}^{(4)} + f_{(i1)}^{(4)}$	$i=1,\dots,g$	g	Export demand functions
II. Industry inputs and outputs				
(T4)	$x_{(is)j}^{(1)} = z_j - \left(p_{(is)j}^{(1)} - \sum_{r=1}^{2} S_{(ir)j}^{(1)} p_{(ir)j}^{(1)} \right)$	$i=1,\dots,g+1$ $j=1,\dots,h$ $s=1,2$	$2(g+1)h$	Demands for intermediate and primary factor inputs
(T5)	$x_{(i1)j}^{(0)} = z_j + \left(p_{(i1)}^{(0)} - \sum_{q=1}^{g} H_{(q1)j}^{(0)} p_{(q1)}^{(0)} \right)$	$i=1,\dots,g$ $j=1,\dots,h$	gh	Commodity supplies by industry
III. Zero-pure-profit conditions				
(T6)	$\sum_{q=1}^{g} H_{(q1)j}^{(0)} p_{(q1)}^{(0)} = \sum_{i=1}^{g+1} \sum_{s=1}^{2} H_{(is)j}^{(1)} p_{(is)j}^{(1)}$	$j=1,\dots,h$	h	Zero pure profits in production
(T7)	$p_{(i2)}^* + t_i + \phi = p_{(i2)}^{(0)}$	$i=1,\dots,g$	g	Zero pure profits in importing

(T8) $p^*_{(i1)} + v_i + \phi = p^{(4)}_{(i1)}$ $i=1,\ldots,g$ g Zero pure profits in exporting

(T9) $\pi_j = \sum_{i=1}^{g} \sum_{s=1}^{2} H^{(2)}_{(is)j} p^{(2)}_{(is)j}$ $j=1,\ldots,h$ h Zero pure profits in capital creation

(T10) $p^{(k)}_{(is)} = p^{(0)}_{(is)}$ $i=1,\ldots,g,$ $s=1$ for $k=4,$ $s=1,2$ for $k=3$ $3g$ Zero pure profits in the distribution of goods

(T11) $p^{(k)}_{(is)j} = p^{(0)}_{(is)}$ $i=1,\ldots,g,$ $s=1,2,$ $j=1,\ldots,h,$ $k=1,2$ $4gh$

IV. Market clearing

(T12) $\displaystyle\sum_{j=1}^{h} x^{(0)}_{(q1)j} W^{(0)}_{(q1)j} = \sum_{k=1}^{2} \sum_{j=1}^{h} x^{(k)}_{(q1)j} W^{(k)}_{(q1)j} + \sum_{k=3}^{4} x^{(k)}_{(q1)} W^{(k)}_{(q1)}$ $q=1,\ldots,g$ g Demand equals supply for domestically produced commodities

(T13) $\displaystyle\sum_{j=1}^{h} x^{(1)}_{(g+1,1)j} W^{(1)}_{(g+1,1)j} = l$ 1 Demand for labor equals employment of labor

(T14) $x^{(1)}_{(g+1,2)j} = k_j$ $j=1,\ldots,h$ h Demand equals employment of capital in each industry

V. Miscellaneous equations

(T15) $\displaystyle x^{(0)}_{(q2)} = \sum_{k=1}^{2} \sum_{j=1}^{h} x^{(k)}_{(q2)j} W^{(k)}_{(q2)j} + x^{(3)}_{(q2)} W^{(3)}_{(q2)}$ $q=1,\ldots,g$ g Import volumes

(T16) $\displaystyle m = \sum_{q=1}^{g} M_{(q2)}(p^*_{(q2)} + x^{(0)}_{(q2)})$ 1 Foreign currency value of imports

(T17) $\displaystyle e = \sum_{q=1}^{g} E_{(q1)}(p^*_{(q1)} + x^{(4)}_{(q1)})$ 1 Foreign currency value of exports

(T18) $\Delta B = (Ee - Mm)/100$ 1 Balance of trade

Table 1 (cont.)

Identifier	Equation	Subscript range[a]	Number	Description
(T19)	$\xi^{(3)} = \sum_{i=1}^{g} \sum_{s=1}^{2} H_{(is)}^{(3)} p_{(is)}^{(3)}$		1	Consumer price index
(T20)	$c^R = c - \xi^{(3)}$		1	Real aggregate consumption
(T21)	$y^R = \sum_{j=1}^{h} W_j^y y_j$		1	Aggregate real investment
(T22)	$\pi = \sum_{j=1}^{h} W_j^y \pi_j$		1	Investment goods price index
(T23)	$f_R = c^R - y^R$		1	Ratio of real aggregates
(T24)	$r_j = (p_{(g+1,2)j}^{(1)} - \pi_j) Q_j$	$j=1,\ldots,h$	h	Rates of return on capital in each industry
(T25)	$y_j = f_j^{(1)} k_j + I_j^{(2)} B_j (r_j - \omega) + f_j^{(2)}$	$j=1,\ldots,h$	h	Investment in each industry
(T26)	$k = \sum_{j=1}^{h} W_j^k k_j$		1	Aggregate capital stock
(T27)	$t = \sum_{i=1}^{g} (t_i^t t_i + p_{(i2)}^* + x_{(i2)}^{(0)} + \phi) \Upsilon_i^t$		1	Aggregate tariff revenue
(T28)	$v = \sum_{i=1}^{g} (\xi_i^v v_i + p_{(i1)}^* + x_{(i1)}^{(4)} + \phi) \Upsilon_i^v$		1	Aggregate export subsidies
(T29)	$p_{(g+1,1)j}^{(1)} = I_{(g+1,1)j} \xi^{(3)} + f_{(g+1,1)j} + f_{(g+1,1)}$	$j=1,\ldots,h$	h	Wage indexation
(T30)	$r_j = r + f_j^r$	$j=1,\ldots,h$	h	Relative rates of return

Total number of equations in categories I–V $= 9gh + 10g + 9h + 12$

495

VI. Macroeconomic closure

(T31) $$c = f_c + \psi_1\left(\sum_{j=1}^{h}(p_{(g+1,1)j}^{(1)} + x_{(g+1,1)j}^{(1)})N_{(g+1,1)j}\right) + \psi_2 t$$
$$-\psi_3 v + \psi_4\left(q + \sum_{j=1}^{h}(p_{(g+1,2)j}^{(1)} + x_{(g+1,2)j}^{(1)})N_{(g+1,2)j}\right)$$
　　　　1　　Consumption function

(T32) $$u = (s-\pi)\left(\frac{U+1}{\tau U}\right)$$
　　　　1

(T33) $$q + k = u\Gamma$$
　　　　1　　Determination of the domestic ownership share in the capital stock

(T34) $$s = c - f_c/(1-F_c)$$
　　　　1

Total number of equations in category VI = 4

Total number of equations in the complete model = $9gh + 10g + 9h + 16$

Note: The variables and coefficients are defined in Tables 2 and 4.

[a] The number of domestically produced goods is g, the number of imported goods is g, and the number of industries is h. In standard applications of ORANI, $g = 115$ and $h = 113$. Some ORANI industries produce several goods and some goods are produced by several industries. In MO81, $g = 2$ and $h = 2$.

Table 2. *The MO81 variables*

Variable	Subscript range[a]	Number	Description
Variables appearing in categories I–V			
$x_{(is)}^{(3)}$	$i=1,\ldots,g$ $s=1,2$	$2g$	Household demands for commodities
$x_{(is)j}^{(k)}$	$i=1,\ldots,g$ $s=1,2$ $j=1,\ldots,h$ $k=1,2$	$4gh$	Demands for inputs of commodities for current production ($k=1$) and capital creation ($k=2$)
$x_{(g+1,s)j}^{(1)}$	$j=1,\ldots,h$ $s=1,2$	$2h$	Demands for labor ($s=1$) and capital ($s=2$) by industry
$x_{(i1)}^{(4)}$	$i=1,\ldots,g$	g	Export volumes
$x_{(q2)}^{(0)}$	$q=1,\ldots,g$	g	Import volumes
$x_{(i1)j}^{(0)}$	$i=1,\ldots,g$ $j=1,\ldots,h$	gh	Commodity supplies by industry
z_j	$j=1,\ldots,h$	h	Industry activity levels
c		1	Aggregate consumption
c^R		1	Real aggregate consumption
y^R		1	Real aggregate investment
y_j	$j=1,\ldots,h$	h	Capital creation for each industry
l		1	Aggregate employment
k_j	$j=1,\ldots,h$	h	Employment of capital in each industry
k		1	Aggregate capital employed
m		1	Foreign currency value of imports
e		1	Foreign currency value of exports
ΔB		1	Balance of trade
$p_{(is)}^{(k)}$	$i=1,\ldots,g,$ $s=1$ for $k=4,$ $s=1,2$ for $k=3$	$3g$	Prices paid by households and exporters for commodities
$p_{(is)j}^{(k)}$	$i=1,\ldots,g$ $j=1,\ldots,h$ $s=1,2$ $k=1,2$	$4gh$	Prices paid by industries for commodity inputs to production and capital creation
$p_{(is)}^{(0)}$	$i=1,\ldots,g$ $s=1,2$	$2g$	Basic prices of domestic and imported commodities
$p_{(g+1,s)j}^{(1)}$	$j=1,\ldots,h$ $s=1,2$	$2h$	Prices paid by industries for use of primary factors ($s=1$ for labor and $s=2$ for capital)
$p_{(i1)}^{*}$	$i=1,\ldots,g$	g	Foreign currency prices of exports
$p_{(i2)}^{*}$	$i=1,\ldots,g$	g	Foreign currency prices of imports
π_j	$j=1,\ldots,h$	h	Prices of units of capital

Table 2 *(cont.)*

Variable	Subscript range[a]	Number	Description
π		1	Investment goods price index
$\xi^{(3)}$		1	Consumer price index
r_j	$j=1,\ldots,h$	h	Rates of return on capital in each industry
r		1	⎧ Useful variables for exogenizing relative rates of
f_j^r		h	⎩ return while endogenizing absolute rates of return
$f_{(i1)}^{(4)}$	$i=1,\ldots,g$	g	Shifts in foreign export demands
f_R		1	Ratio of real aggregate consumption to real aggregate investment
$f_j^{(2)}$	$j=1,\ldots,h$	h	Shift variable in industry investment equations
$f_{(g+1,1)j}$	$j=1,\ldots,h$	h	Variable used to allow variations across industries in wage rate movements
$f_{(g+1,1)}$		1	Normally interpreted as the real wage rate
ϕ		1	Exchange rate ($Aus./$U.S.)
v_i	$i=1,\ldots,g$	g	One plus ad valorem export subsidies
t_i	$i=1,\ldots,g$	g	One plus ad valorem tariff rates
v		1	Aggregate export subsidy
t		1	Aggregate tariff revenue
ω		1	Expected rate of return in all industries, adjusted for risk

Total number of
variables in categories I–V $= 9gh + 14g + 12h + 17$

Additional variables introduced in category VI

f_c		1	Shift in the average propensity to consume
q		1	Domestic share in the ownership of capital
u		1	Rate of growth in real domestic saving over the period 0 to τ
s		1	Domestic saving

Number of
additional
variables $=4$

Total number of
variables in categories I–VI $= 9gh + 15g + 12h + 21$

[a] The number of domestically produced goods is g, the number of imported goods is g, and the number of industries is h. In standard applications of ORANI, $g=115$ and $h=113$. Some ORANI industries produce several goods, and some goods are produced by several industries. In MO81, $g=2$ and $h=2$.

Table 3. *Typical lists of exogenous variables*

(1) Short-run restricted model	(2) Long-run restricted model	(3) Long-run complete model	Number of variables
$p^*_{(i2)}$	$p^*_{(i2)}$	$p^*_{(i2)}$	g
$f^{(4)}_{(i1)}$	$f^{(4)}_{(i1)}$	$f^{(4)}_{(i1)}$	g
t_i	t_i	t_i	g
$v_q \forall q \in G$	$v_q \forall q \in G$	$v_q \forall q \in G$	g
$x^{(4)}_{(q1)} \forall q \notin G$	$x^{(4)}_{(q1)} \forall q \notin G$	$x^{(4)}_{(q1)} \forall q \notin G$	
k_j	r_j	r_j	h
$f_{(g+1,1)j}$	$f_{(g+1,1)j}$	$f_{(g+1,1)j}$	h
$f_{(g+1,1)}$	l	l	1
$f^{(2)}_j$	$f^{(2)}_j$	$f^{(2)}_j$	h
c^R	f_R	f_c	1
y^R	ΔB	ω	1
r	r	r	1
ϕ	ϕ	ϕ	1

Total number of exogenous variables $= 4g + 3h + 5$

possibilities available in the current version of ORANI. Then in Section 3.4 we will consider the equations in category VI. The additional closure options that are available in the complete model are discussed in Section 3.5.

3.2   The equations of MO81, categories I–V

Category I – final demands: ORANI includes equations describing final demands by households, capital creators, foreigners (export demands), and the government. Only the first three types appear in our miniature version.

Underlying the estimation of the ORANI household-demand functions is the assumption of constrained utility maximization. It is assumed that $X^{(3)}_{(is)}$, $i = 1, \ldots, g$, $s = 1, 2$, maximizes

$$U(X^{(3)}_{(11)}, \ldots, X^{(3)}_{(g1)}; X^{(3)}_{(12)}, \ldots, X^{(3)}_{(g2)}) \tag{3.1}$$

subject to

$$\sum_{i=1}^{g} \sum_{s=1}^{2} P^{(3)}_{(is)} X^{(3)}_{(is)} = C \tag{3.2}$$

where U is a utility function describing household preferences, C is aggregate household expenditure, and $X_{(is)}^{(3)}$ and $P_{(is)}^{(3)}$ are household consumption and the price to households of good i from source s. The superscript (3) is used to denote households. [Later we will be using superscript (1) to denote intermediate usage, superscript (2) to denote demands for inputs to capital creation, and superscript (4) to denote export demands.] Source 1 (i.e., $s=1$) is domestic supplies, while $s=2$ indicates foreign supplies, that is, imports. Thus domestic and imported commodities are treated as distinct. For example, domestically produced cars are treated as different products from imported cars although the two are modeled as being good substitutes. Much of the econometric effort associated with ORANI has been concerned with estimating elasticities of substitution between imported and domestic products belonging to the same input-output categories. [Details are in DPSV, sec. 29(a).] By handling imported and domestic products as imperfect substitutes, we avoid the unsatisfactory consequences of either of the two extremes frequently found in modeling exercises. On the one hand, the assumption of perfect substitutability, which is implied when imported cars and domestic cars are treated as the same product, is inconsistent with the empirical observation that prices of imported and domestic commodities can move independently of each other without causing the exclusion of either product from the market. At the other extreme, the quantity share of imports in each market is assumed to be fixed, that is, imports are treated as noncompetitive. The implied assumption, that the elasticity of substitution between imported and domestic cars is zero, is inconsistent with the observation that the quantity share of imported cars in the domestic market responds to changes in the relative prices of imported and domestic products.

On solving problem (3.1)–(3.2), we obtain demand functions of the form

$$X_{(is)}^{(3)} = f_{(is)}^{(3)}(P_{(11)}^{(3)}, \ldots, P_{(g1)}^{(3)}; P_{(12)}^{(3)}, \ldots, P_{(g2)}^{(3)}; C),$$

$$i=1,\ldots,g, \quad s=1,2 \quad (3.3)$$

In our miniature model, we assume that the utility function (3.1) has the form

$$U = \min_{i=1,\ldots,g} \left\{ \frac{X_{(i\cdot)}^{(3)}}{A_{(i\cdot)}^{(3)}} \right\} \quad (3.4)$$

where the $A_{(i\cdot)}^{(3)}$ are positive parameters and the $X_{(i\cdot)}^{(3)}$ are defined by

$$X_{(i\cdot)}^{(3)} = \text{Cobb-Douglas}\{X_{(i1)}^{(3)}, X_{(i2)}^{(3)}\} \quad \text{for} \quad i=1,\ldots,g \quad (3.5)$$

This specification implies that consumers derive utility from "effective"

units of goods $1, 2, \ldots, g$, where an effective unit of good i is an aggregation of units of domestically produced and imported good i. The aggregation is defined by a Cobb–Douglas function. Of course, both (3.4) and
(3.5) could be replaced by more general forms. In ORANI, the equations
corresponding to these have, respectively, additive and CES forms (see
DPSV, sec. 14). Under (3.4) and (3.5), however, the percentage-change
form of (3.3) is very simple. One representation is that given in Equation
(T1) of Table 1. There we have used c^R (the percentage change in *real*
household expenditure) rather than c, where c^R is defined in the table by
(T20) and (T19).

Without going through the derivation, it is easy to justify (T1). First,
we notice that it implies that the expenditure elasticity of demand for
each good is 1. This follows from the homotheticity of the utility function
(3.4)–(3.5). Second, at any fixed level of real expenditure (c^R), (T1) implies that the demand for good i from either source is independent of the
price of good j from either source for all $j \neq i$. This follows from the
adoption of the Leontief form in (3.4). Finally, (T1) implies that the elasticity of substitution ($\sigma_i^{(3)}$) between alternative sources of good i is unity,
that is,

$$\sigma_i^{(3)} \equiv \frac{\eta_{(is)(it)}}{S_{(it)}^{(3)}} = 1 \qquad \text{for} \quad s \neq t \qquad (3.6)$$

where $S_{(it)}^{(3)}$ is the share of good i from source t in household expenditure
on good i, and $\eta_{(is)(it)}$ is the compensated (fixed real expenditure) elasticity of demand for good i from source s with respect to changes in the
price of good i from source t. A unitary substitution elasticity would be
expected in view of the Cobb–Douglas assumption, (3.5).

The second set of final-demand equations in MO81 describe inputs to
capital creation (buildings, plant, and equipment). We assume that for
each industry j, $j = 1, \ldots, h$, these inputs

$$X_{(is)j}^{(2)}, \qquad i = 1, \ldots, g, \quad s = 1, 2$$

are chosen to minimize

$$\sum_{i=1}^{g} \sum_{s=1}^{2} P_{(is)j}^{(2)} X_{(is)j}^{(2)} \qquad (3.7)$$

subject to

$$Y_j = \min_{i=1, \ldots, g} \left\{ \frac{X_{(i \cdot)j}^{(2)}}{A_{(i \cdot)j}^{(2)}} \right\} \qquad (3.8)$$

and

$$X_{(i \cdot)j}^{(2)} = \text{Cobb–Douglas}\{ X_{(i1)j}^{(2)}, X_{(i2)j}^{(2)} \} \qquad \text{for} \quad i = 1, \ldots, g \quad (3.9)$$

where $A^{(2)}_{(i\cdot)j}$ is a positive parameter, $X^{(2)}_{(is)j}$ is the quantity of good i from source s used in creating capital for industry j, $P^{(2)}_{(is)j}$ is the price to industry j of its inputs of (is) used for capital creation, $X^{(2)}_{(i\cdot)j}$ is the "effective" input of good i to industry j for capital creation, and Y_j is the number of units of capital created for industry j. Thus, whatever the value of Y_j, industry j is assumed to choose its inputs to minimize the costs of creating Y_j units of capital. The technology for creating capital is described by (3.8) and (3.9). Primary factors do not appear in either of these equations. The use of primary factors in creating buildings and so forth is accounted for via the inputs from the construction industry. Equations (3.8) and (3.9) are close to those adopted in ORANI. However, in ORANI, (3.9) is generalized to the CES form.

On solving problem (3.7)–(3.9), we obtain demand functions of the form

$$X^{(2)}_{(is)j} = f^{(2)}_{(is)j}(P^{(2)}_{(11)j}, \ldots, P^{(2)}_{(g1)j}; P^{(2)}_{(12)j}, \ldots, P^{(2)}_{(g2)j}; Y_j),$$

$$\text{for} \quad i = 1, \ldots, g, \quad s = 1, 2, \quad \text{and} \quad j = 1, \ldots, h \qquad (3.10)$$

Under the specification (3.8)–(3.9), the percentage-change form of (3.10) reduces to (T2).

The third set of final-demand equations in Table 1 describe demands for exports. Export-demand functions in MO81 (and ORANI) take the form

$$P^*_{(i1)} = (X^{(4)}_{(i1)})^{-\gamma_i} F^{(4)}_{(i1)}, \qquad i = 1, \ldots, g \qquad (3.11)$$

where $P^*_{(i1)}$ is the foreign currency receipt per unit of export of good i, $X^{(4)}_{(i1)}$ is the volume of exports of good i, and $F^{(4)}_{(i1)}$ is an export-demand shift variable. Now $F^{(4)}_{(i1)}$ will increase if there is an increase in foreign demand. The nonnegative parameter γ_i is the reciprocal of the foreign elasticity of demand for good $(i1)$. The percentage-change form of (3.11) is (T3).

No satisfactory econometric estimates are available for export-demand elasticities $(1/\gamma_i)$ for Australian products. In most ORANI computations, numbers ranging from 1.3 to 20 have been used with the particular number chosen for each commodity depending on Australia's share in the relevant world market and on views about demand elasticities in importing countries. [Details are in DPSV, sec. 29(f).]

Export demand functions for all g domestic commodities are specified in MO81 (and ORANI). For commodities that are not exported, $X^{(4)}_{(i1)}$ can be fixed exogenously at an appropriately small level. This procedure is computationally more convenient than including export demand equations for some commodities and not for others.

Category II – industry inputs and outputs: Each industry in MO81 is assumed to choose its inputs to minimize the cost of achieving its activity or overall output level. The cost minimization problems produce functions explaining demands for intermediate and primary factor inputs in terms of industry activity levels and input prices. Equation (T4) arises from assuming that industry j chooses its inputs of domestically produced and imported materials, $X^{(1)}_{(is)j}$, $i=1,\ldots,g$, $s=1,2$, its input of labor, $X^{(1)}_{(g+1,1)j}$, and its input of capital, $X^{(1)}_{(g+1,2)j}$, to minimize

$$\sum_{i=1}^{g+1} \sum_{s=1}^{2} P^{(1)}_{(is)j} X^{(1)}_{(is)j} \tag{3.12}$$

subject to

$$Z_j = \min_{i=1,\ldots,g+1} \left\{ \frac{X^{(1)}_{(i\cdot)j}}{A^{(1)}_{(i\cdot)j}} \right\} \tag{3.13}$$

and

$$X^{(1)}_{(i\cdot)j} = \text{Cobb-Douglas}\{X^{(1)}_{(i1)j}, X^{(1)}_{(i2)j}\}, \quad i=1,\ldots,g+1 \tag{3.14}$$

where the $A^{(1)}_{(i\cdot)j}$ are positive parameters; $P^{(1)}_{(is)j}$, for $i=1,\ldots,g$, $s=1,2$, is the price to industry j of good i from source s to be used as in intermediate input; $P^{(1)}_{(g+1,s)j}$ is the price to industry j of primary factor (denoted by subscript $g+1$) of type s ($s=1$ for labor and $s=2$ for capital), and Z_j is the activity level in industry j.

To explain the commodity composition of each industry's output, we solve a revenue maximization problem. Equation (T5) is derived via the problem of choosing

$$X^{(0)}_{(i1)j}, \quad i=1,\ldots,g \quad (j\text{'s commodity outputs})$$

to maximize revenue,

$$\sum_{i=1}^{g} P^{(0)}_{(i1)} X^{(0)}_{(i1)j} \tag{3.15}$$

subject to the transformation constraint

$$Z_j = \left(\sum_{i=1}^{g} (X^{(0)}_{(i1)j})^2 A^{(0)}_{(i1)j} \right)^{1/2} \tag{3.16}$$

where the $A^{(0)}_{(i1)j}$ are positive parameters and $P^{(0)}_{(i1)}$ is the basic price for domestically produced good i. [This price carries no j subscript because it is assumed in MO81 (and ORANI) that all producers of good $(i1)$ receive the same price.]

Thus, each industry is modeled as if it makes two separate sets of decisions. First, it chooses a vector of inputs to minimize the cost of giving

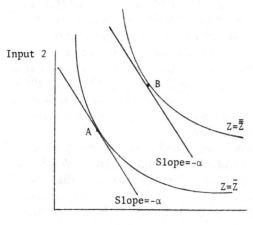

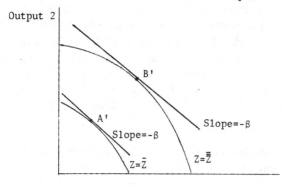

Figure 1. Isoquants and transformation frontiers. If the ratios of input and output prices are α and β, respectively, and $Z = \bar{Z}$, then the input combination will be at A and the output combination will be at A'. If Z is set at the higher value, $\bar{\bar{Z}}$, then the input and output combinations move to B and B'.

itself a particular production possibilities set. Then, from that set, it chooses the revenue-maximizing commodity output combination. (The situation is illustrated in Figure 1 for the two-input, two-output case.) The separation of the input and output problems implies that inputs are not specific to products. This simplification is suitable where the principal inputs are of a general nature – for example, labor, tractors, and fertilizer in an agricultural industry.

In ORANI, the cost-minimizing problems are more elaborate than (3.12)–(3.14). Agricultural land is included as a primary factor and labor is subdivided into 9 skill categories. The CES function and Hanoch's (1971) CRESH function appear instead of the Cobb–Douglas functions in (3.14). However, the Leontief form is retained in the ORANI equations corresponding to (3.13). Efforts were made to estimate substitution elasticities between capital and labor in general and between labor skill categories. These efforts are reported in DPSV, sec. 29(b) and 29(c). Although some success was achieved in estimating averages over all industries for the various substitution elasticities, no satisfactory results were obtained for individual industries.

Revenue maximization problems are specified in ORANI only for the agricultural industries. Nonagricultural commodities are modeled as if they are produced by single-product industries. The generalization to multiproduct production functions was considered worthwhile in modeling the agricultural sector because most Australian farms are multiproduct enterprises and Australian farmers frequently shift their output mixes between wheat, wool, cattle, and other products in response to changes in product prices. Estimates of various pairwise product transformation elasticities are available for three Australian agricultural industries defined on a regional basis: high-rainfall zone farming, pastoral zone farming, and wheat–sheep zone farming. Details of these estimates and of the CRETH functional form used to specify the transformation frontiers are in DPSV, secs. 12 and 29(d), and Vincent, Dixon, and Powell (1980).

Category III – zero-pure-profit conditions: The zero-pure-profit conditions, (T6), in our miniature version of ORANI equate the percentage changes in revenue per unit of activity in each industry to the percentage change in costs per unit of activity. Because the production functions (3.13)–(3.14) and (3.16) exhibit constant returns to scale, no quantity variables appear in (T6). Revenue and costs per unit of activity are functions of output and input prices alone. Thus, percentage changes in revenue and costs per unit of activity are appropriately weighted averages of percentage changes in output and input prices.

Equations (T7) and (T8) are derived from

$$P^*_{(i2)} T_i \Phi = P^{(0)}_{(i2)}, \qquad i = 1, \ldots, g \tag{3.17}$$

and

$$P^*_{(i1)} V_i \Phi = P^{(4)}_{(i1)}, \qquad i = 1, \ldots, g \tag{3.18}$$

Equation (3.17) relates the basic price of imported product i ($P^{(0)}_{(i2)}$) to the costs of importing, that is, the foreign currency cost ($P^*_{(i2)}$) converted by the exchange rate (Φ) and inflated by the power of the tariff (T_i).[4]

Similarly, Equation (3.18) relates the costs of exporting domestic commodity i [its at port price $(P_{(i1)}^{(4)})$] to the receipt from exporting, that is, the foreign currency price $(P_{(i1)}^*)$ converted by the exchange rate and inflated by the power of the export subsidy (V_i). In the case of nonexportables, the export subsidy can be treated as an endogenous variable. Then the relevant component of (3.18) simply defines the value of the export subsidy, a variable that may be meaningless but that is also harmless. Thus (3.18) has no unfortunate implications for the way in which the model determines domestic prices of nonexportables.

The fourth zero-pure-profit condition in Table 1, (T9), equates the percentage change in the price of a unit of capital for industry j with the percentage change in the cost of constructing such a unit. The technology for producing capital for industry j exhibits constant returns to scale [see (3.8)–(3.9)]. Consequently, the percentage change in the cost of a unit of capital for industry j is simply a weighted average of the percentage changes in the relevant input prices where the weights are cost shares.

The final two zero-pure-profit conditions, (T10) and (T11), provide the link between purchasers' prices and basic prices. In MO81 there is no allowance for transport, wholesale, retail, or other margins costs. Thus, in MO81 the absence of pure profits in the distribution of goods implies that purchasers' prices are equal to basic prices. In ORANI there is a detailed treatment of margins. Changes in purchasers' prices are modeled as reflecting not only changes in basic prices but also changes in the prices of margin services and changes in sales taxes.

Category VI – market clearing: Condition (T12) equates percentage changes in demands and supplies for domestically produced goods. The percentage change in the supply of domestically produced good q is a weighted average of the percentage changes in the supplies of this good by each industry. Imports are not added to domestic production in determining total supplies. This is because commodities from foreign and domestic sources are treated as distinct. The percentage change in the demand for domestically produced good q is a weighted average of the percentage changes in demands by intermediate users, capital creators, households, and foreigners.

Equations (T13) and (T14) are the percentage-change forms of the equations

$$\sum_{j=1}^{h} X_{(g+1,1)j}^{(1)} = L \tag{3.19}$$

and

$$X_{(g+1,2)j} = K_j, \qquad j = 1, \ldots, h \tag{3.20}$$

The left-hand sides of (3.19) and (3.20) are respectively the economywide demand for labor and the demand for capital by industry j. Capital is assumed to be industry-specific. Thus demands for capital are not aggregated across industries. On the right-hand sides of (3.19) and (3.20) are respectively the employment level for labor and the employment of capital of type j. Thus we are assuming that demands for factors are satisfied. This does not mean that we are necessarily assuming full employment. Although we could set L and K_j exogenously at full-employment levels, an obvious alternative is to set some factor prices exogenously and to let the model determine the corresponding factor employment levels. Under this latter specification our assumption would be that some factor markets are slack, that is, supply constraints play no role in determining employment levels for some factors.

Category V - miscellaneous equations: Equations (T15)-(T18), (T27), and (T28) are concerned with trade aggregates. Equation (T15) gives the percentage change in the imports of each commodity as a weighted average of the percentage changes in demands by intermediate users, capital creators, and households. Equations (T16) and (T17) define the percentage changes in the foreign currency values of aggregate imports and exports. Equation (T18) defines the change in the balance of trade. The change is used rather than the percentage of change because the balance of trade is a variable whose value can have either sign. There are obvious difficulties in using percentage changes for variables whose values can pass through zero. Equations (T27) and (T28) are derived from the equations

$$T = \sum_{i=1}^{g} (T_i - 1) P^*_{(i2)} \Phi X^{(0)}_{(i2)} \tag{3.21}$$

and

$$V = \sum_{i=1}^{g} (V_i - 1) P^*_{(i1)} \Phi X^{(4)}_{(i1)} \tag{3.22}$$

where T is the aggregate collection of tariff revenue and V is the aggregate payment of export subsidies.

Equations (T19)-(T23) and (T26) define various macro indices. In (T19) and (T22), the percentage changes in the consumer price index and the investment-goods price index are defined as weighted averages of percentage changes in commodity prices and the prices of units of capital. Equations (T20) and (T21) define the percentage changes in real consumption expenditure and real investment expenditure and (T23) defines the percentage change in the ratio of these two variables. Equation (T26) provides an index of the size of the aggregate capital stock. It defines the percentage change in the economy's capital stock as a weighted average of the percentage changes in the capital stocks of the industries.

Equations (T24) and (T25) tie down the percentage changes in investment by industry, y_j, $j=1,\ldots,h$. Equation (T24), which gives the percentage changes in the rates of return on capital in each industry, is derived from the equation

$$R_j = \frac{P^{(1)}_{(g+1,2)j}}{\Pi_j} - D_j, \qquad j=1,\ldots,h \tag{3.23}$$

where R_j is the rate of return on capital in industry j, $P^{(1)}_{(g+1,2)j}/\Pi_j$ is the ratio of the rental price to the purchase price of a unit of capital in industry j, and D_j is the rate of depreciation. The D_j values are assumed to be technologically fixed.

There are a variety of theories about investment that are consistent with (T25). One such theory starts with the assumption that investors are cautious. They behave as if they expect that expansions in the capital stock of any industry will lower the rate of return on the industry's capital. More particularly, investors in industry j behave as if their expectations in the solution year concerning the response of their rate of return in the following year (R_j^+) to changes in the size of the industry's capital stock are described by the equation

$$R_j^+ = R_j \left(\frac{K_j^+}{K_j} \right)^{-\beta_j} \tag{3.24}$$

where R_j is the rate of return in the solution year, K_j is the capital stock in the solution year, and K_j^+ is the "planned" capital stock, that is, the level planned in the solution year for the following year; β_j is a positive parameter. If the planned capital stock is the same as the current capital stock, then (3.24) implies that the rate of return expected for the future is the current rate of return. If, however, investment plans are set so that K_j^+/K_j will reach A (see Figure 2), then investors will behave as if they expect the rate of return to fall to B.

Next, we assume that investment plans are set as if they are intended to equate expected rates of return across industries, that is, there exists a number Ω such that

$$R_j \left(\frac{K_j^+}{K_j} \right)^{-\beta_j} = \Omega, \qquad j=1,\ldots,h \tag{3.25}$$

Finally, we assume that

$$K_j^+ = K_j(1-D_j) + Y_j, \qquad j=1,\ldots,h \tag{3.26}$$

That is, planned capital stock is the sum of current capital stock (appropriately depreciated) and current investment.

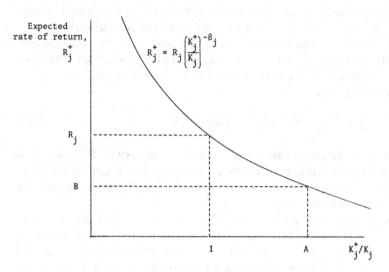

Figure 2. Expected rate-of-return schedule for industry j.

In percentage-change form, (3.25) and (3.26) become

$$r_j - \beta_j(k_j^+ - k_j) = \omega, \qquad j = 1, \ldots, h \tag{3.27}$$

and

$$k_j^+ = k_j(1 - \Delta_j) + y_j \Delta_j, \qquad j = 1, \ldots, h \tag{3.28}$$

where

$$\Delta_j = Y_j / K_j^+, \qquad j = 1, \ldots, h$$

On using (3.28) to eliminate k_j^+ from (3.27) we obtain

$$y_j = k_j + B_j(r_j - \omega), \qquad j = 1, \ldots, h \tag{3.29}$$

where[5]

$$B_j = \frac{1}{\beta_j \Delta_j}, \qquad j = 1, \ldots, h \tag{3.30}$$

In (T25) we have shown (3.29) with two extra coefficients, $I_j^{(1)}$ and $I_j^{(2)}$, and an extra variable $f_j^{(2)}$. If we set all the $I_j^{(1)}$ values and $I_j^{(2)}$ values at one and the $f_j^{(2)}$ values at zero, then (T25) reduces to (3.29). However, (T25) allows other possibilities. For some industries, the investment theory set out in Equations (3.24)–(3.26) might not be considered appropriate, for example, in government-dominated industries investment might be considered to be independent of changes in rates of return. In such cases, $I_j^{(1)}$ and $I_j^{(2)}$ can be set at zero and the percentage change in investment in industry j can be determined by the exogenously chosen value for $f_j^{(2)}$. Another possibility is to set just $I_j^{(2)}$ at zero. For example, we might wish to specify investment by industry j as

$$Y_j = (H_j + D_j)K_j, \qquad j = 1, \ldots, h \qquad (3.31)$$

where H_j, the rate of growth of capital in industry j in the solution year, is treated as a constant. This specification is popular in long-run planning models. With H_j and D_j held constant, (3.31) reduces to

$$y_j = k_j, \qquad j = 1, \ldots, h \qquad (3.32)$$

Equation (3.32) can be accommodated in (T25) by setting $I_j^{(1)}$ at one and $I_j^{(2)}$ and the variable $f_j^{(2)}$ at zero.

Rather than treating the H_j terms as constants, we could assume that

$$K_j = K_j(0)(1 + H_j)^\tau \qquad (3.33)$$

that is,

$$H_j = \left(\frac{K_j}{K_j(0)} \right)^{1/\tau} - 1 \qquad (3.34)$$

where $K_j(0)$ is the capital stock in industry j in the base year, the base year being τ years before the solution year. Under (3.31) and (3.34) we are assuming that growth rates in the solution year are the same as the average growth rates established between the base year and the solution year. With the H_j terms treated as variables, the percentage-change form of (3.31) is

$$y_j = h_j \frac{H_j}{H_j + D_j} + k_j, \qquad j = 1, \ldots, h \qquad (3.35)$$

Equation (3.34) implies that

$$h_j = \frac{1}{\tau} \frac{H_j + 1}{H_j} k_j, \qquad j = 1, \ldots, h \qquad (3.36)$$

Substitution of (3.36) into (3.35) gives

$$y_j = \left(\frac{H_j + 1}{\tau(H_j + D_j)} + 1 \right) k_j, \qquad j = 1, \ldots, h \qquad (3.37)$$

To accommodate (3.37) by (T25), we set

$$I_j^{(1)} = \left(\frac{H_j + 1}{\tau(H_j + D_j)} + 1 \right), \qquad j = 1, \ldots, h \qquad (3.38)$$

Again, $I_j^{(2)}$ and $f_j^{(2)}$ are set at zero for all j.

The final pair of equations for discussion in this section is (T29) and (T30). Equation (T29) allows flexibility in the treatment of wages. If we fix the coefficient $I_{(g+1,1)j}$ at one for all j and the variable $f_{(g+1,1)j}$ at zero, then $f_{(g+1,1)}$ is the percentage change in real wages in each industry.

Variations in relative wages across industries can be introduced by using nonuniform values for the $f_{(g+1,1)j}$, $j=1,\ldots,h$. The effects of policy changes and other economic shocks in an environment of partial wage indexation can be studied by setting the $I_{(g+1,1)j}$ at values different from one. Equation (T30) is useful if we wish to assume that all rates of return move by the same endogenously determined percentage. We simply set f_j^r exogenously at zero for all j and treat r as an exogenous variable. Exogenously determined changes in the relative rates of return can be handled by assigning different values to the f_j^r for different j. If the f_j^r are treated as endogenous variables, then (T30) has no influence on results from the model apart from the values for the f_j^r terms themselves.

3.3   Closure options in MO81 restricted to categories I–V

In this section we consider the closure options available in the restricted MO81 model formed by Equations (T1)–(T30), that is, categories I–V in Table 1. This restricted model has $9gh+10g+9h+12$ equations and $9gh+14g+12h+17$ variables (see Tables 1 and 2). It can be closed by treating $4g+3h+5$ variables as exogenous. Columns 1 and 2 of Table 3 give two lists of exogenous variables that could be used in the restricted model. The first list is suitable for studies of the short-run effects of tariff changes and the like, and the second is suitable for long-run studies. Other choices of exogenous variables are available for both short- and long-run simulations.

The first two variables, $p_{(i2)}^*$ and $f_{(i1)}^{(4)}$, in columns 1 and 2 of Table 3 are the percentage changes in the foreign currency prices of imports and the percentage shifts in the export-demand curves. MO81, in common with ORANI, contains no equations describing either the conditions of supply of foreign products or the positions of foreign-demand curves for domestic products. It is difficult, therefore, to imagine a plausible MO81 experiment in which either $p_{(i2)}^*$ or $f_{(i1)}^{(4)}$ is treated as endogenous. By placing $p_{(i2)}^*$ in the exogenous category we are adopting the small-country assumption on the import side; that is, the prices of imports are independent of local demands. Because Australia is a major supplier of wool, wheat, sugar, and various mineral products, the small-country assumption is not appropriate on the export side. Consequently, it is only the positions of the foreign-demand curves that are exogenized. With $p_{(i2)}^*$ and $f_{(i1)}^{(4)}$ exogenous, we are allowing for the computation of answers to questions of the form: What were (or will be) the effects of past (or projected) changes in foreign import supply prices and foreign export demands?

The third group of exogenous variables in columns 1 and 2 of Table 3 are the tariffs. In most ORANI computations, the tariffs have been exogenous. It is possible, however, to conduct experiments in which some or all the tariffs are endogenous. For example, we might wish to compute the level of protection that would be required to maintain current employment levels in footwear, say, in the face of exogenously given movements in foreign prices, domestic wages and the exchange rate. For such a computation, footwear employment would replace the footwear tariff on the exogenous list.

The fourth set of exogenous variables is a selection of export subsidies and export levels. In most ORANI computations, the set G contains the labels of Australia's major export commodities. For these commodities, the model is allowed to explain export levels and foreign currency export prices are allowed to play a dominant role in determining domestic prices. Notice that if v_i is exogenous, then $p_{(i1)}^{(4)}$ will fully reflect movements in $p_{(i1)}^*$ via (T8). For commodities not included in G, the export volume is exogenous and the foreign currency export price does not influence the domestic price. As we noted earlier, if v_i is endogenous, then the only role of the ith component of (T8) is in the determination of the value of v_i. Nonexportables and minor export commodities are usually excluded from G.

The fifth set of variables in columns 1 and 2 of Table 3 are capital stocks (column 1) and rates of return (column 2). For short-run analysis, where the solution year is only 1 or 2 years ahead, the effects of tariff changes and so forth on capital stocks are ignored. It is assumed that the shock (e.g., tariff change) under investigation can affect the allocation of investment across industries but that insufficient time passes for capital stocks to reach levels noticeably different from those they would have reached in the absence of the shock. For long-run analysis, where the solution year is, say, 10 years ahead, it is assumed that rates of return are unaffected by the shock under investigation. The assumption is that in the long run, industries that are favored by the shock will grow relative to other industries until rates of return are restored to their historic norms. Thus, we are assuming that tariff changes and so on affect rates of return in the short run and capital stocks in the long run.

The sixth and seventh sets of exogenous variables concern wages and aggregate employment. We will assume that the coefficient $I_{(g+1,1)j}$ appearing in (T29) is unity for all j. Thus, the percentage change in real wages payable in industry j is $(f_{(g+1,1)j}+f_{(g+1,1)})$. In the short run, movements in real wages in Australia tend to be dominated by political pressures operating through and around a central wage-setting tribunal (the Conciliation and Arbitration Commission). Thus, in analyzing the short-run effects of economic changes, it is realistic to treat $f_{(g+1,1)j}$ and $f_{(g+1,1)}$ as exogenous variables. In the long run, however, real wages have adjusted in a way that is consistent with the maintenance of approximately full employment. Where a long-run focus is adopted, it is appropriate to assume that changes in the aggregate level of employment are determined by demographic factors and are independent of tariff changes and the like. That is, it is appropriate to treat l as an exogenous variable and to allow the overall level of real wages to adjust to shocks via the endogenous treatment of $f_{(g+1,1)}$. Even in long-run simulations, the $f_{(g+1,1)j}$ would usually be treated as exogenous in models such as MO81 and ORANI. These models have no equations explaining industry-specific wage rates. MO81 has just one type of labor that is free to move between industries. In standard applications, ORANI recognizes nine types of labor. These labor types are distinguished on an occupational (not an industrial) basis.

The eighth set of variables in columns 1 and 2 of Table 3 are the shift terms $(f_j^{(2)})$ that appear in the investment equations, (T25). Their role was explained following (3.30) in Section 3.2.

The next two variables listed in column 1 of Table 3 are the percentage changes in real aggregate household expenditure and real aggregate investment, c^R and y^R.[6] By including these in column 1 we are setting an economic environment in which real aggregate demand is controllable independently of other variables appearing in the column. The underlying assumption is that policy makers have available macro instruments, not included in our model, by which they can influence c^R and y^R, at least in the short run. Another option is to set exogenously the change in the balance of trade, ΔB, and the percentage change in the ratio of consumption to investment, f_R. Then our model would indicate the change in real domestic absorption that would need to accompany a tariff cut, say, in order to maintain a target level for the balance of trade.

Neither of these options (exogenizing c^R and y^R or ΔB and f_R) is satisfactory for long-run analysis. In the absence of a better alternative, the second option is shown in column 2 of Table 3 as the standard long-run macro closure for the restricted MO81 model. (This is also the standard closure used in long-run ORANI simulations.) The problem is that for long-run simulations it is desirable to treat all the variables c^R, y^R, ΔB, and f_R as endogenous. For example, our model might indicate that a tariff reform in 1981 would cause a 10% increase in the amount of capital in 1990 consistent with earning the exogenously given rates of return, R_j, $j = 1, \ldots, h$. That is, we might obtain the result

$$k = 10 \tag{3.39}$$

where k is the percentage change in the aggregate capital stock defined in Equation (T26). The effect of the tariff reform on consumption, investment, and the balance of trade would then depend on (among other things) the way in which the 10% extra expansion in the capital stock over the period 1981–1990 was financed. If the extra capital is owned mainly by foreign investors, then we could expect the income accruing from it in 1990 to be reflected in an increased balance-of-trade surplus to finance additional profit repatriation. On the other hand, if the extra capital were domestically owned, then the income accruing from it in 1990 would increase domestic absorption (c^R and y^R). In ORANI and the restricted version of MO81, there is no explicit consideration of domestic and foreign ownership. In Section 3.4 we consider a way of rectifying this deficiency.

The second last variable in columns 1 and 2 of Table 3 is r. In Table 1, r appears only in Equation (T30). As explained in our discussion of this equation in Section 3.2, r will normally be set exogenously. The exception is when we wish to exogenize relative rates of return across industries without exogenizing absolute rates of return. Then we can exclude r and r_j, $j = 1, \ldots, h$, from the list of exogenous variables and include k (the percentage change in the aggregate capital stock) and f_j^r, $j = 1, \ldots, h$ [the shift terms in (T30)]. When k and the f_j^r terms replace r and the r_j terms as exogenous variables, we are assuming that tariff changes and other shocks have no effect on long-run capital accumulation or on relative rates of return, but that they can affect the average rate of return across all industries. The exogenous treatment of k is attractive in ORANI and the restricted version of MO81 when we wish to draw conclusions about efficiency and gains and losses to the domestic economy. For example, if we were interested in the welfare effects of a tariff reform, then we might set

$$k = l = 0$$

and compute the effects of the tariff change on the level of production arising from a fixed level of resources. The difficulty with letting k move is that ORANI and the restricted version of MO81 give no indication of capital ownership. Hence, they give no indication of how a changed level of capitalist income would be allocated between domestic residents and foreigners.

The last variable in columns 1 and 2 of Table 3 is the percentage change in the exchange rate, ϕ. It acts as a numeraire; that is, it determines the percentage change in the absolute price level. Natural alternatives to ϕ as the numeraire include the average wage rate and the consumer price index.

3.4   *Macro equations in MO81, category VI*

For a small open economy such as Australia's, a reasonable assumption in long-run analysis is that rates of return on capital are exogenous. A tariff reform, for example, might be expected to affect rates of return in the short run. But for the long run, we can assume that adjustments in the level of foreign investment will force domestic rates of return into line with foreign rates of return.

There is no difficulty in exogenizing rates of return in ORANI and allowing capital stocks to adjust. However, as we have seen in the previous section, there is a problem in determining the implied levels of foreign ownership of domestic capital. Because ORANI, as presently constituted, includes no domestic savings function, the model provides no basis for projecting the share of capital accumulation that is financed from domestic sources. In this section we show how MO81 can be expanded to accommodate domestic savings and domestic and foreign ownership. A similar expansion of ORANI is planned as part of our future research.

The first step is to add a consumption function. We assume that in the solution year (1990, say) consumption is related to domestic income by

$$C = F_c \left[\sum_{j=1}^{h} P^{(1)}_{(g+1,1)j} X^{(1)}_{(g+1,1)j} + Q \left(\sum_{j=1}^{h} P^{(1)}_{(g+1,2)j} X^{(1)}_{(g+1,2)j} \right) + T - V \right]$$

(3.40)

Here F_c is the average propensity to consume. The first term inside the square brackets is total labor income; Q is the domestic share in the ownership of capital. Thus, the second term in the square brackets is the capital income accruing to domestic residents; T and V are tariff revenue and export subsidies. In the context of MO81, the sum of the terms in the square brackets is the total income of domestic residents.

In percentage-change form, (3.40) becomes (T31) in Table 1 where the ψ_i terms are the ratios of labor income, tariff revenue, export subsidies, and domestic capitalist income to total domestic income. Here $N_{(g+1,1)j}$ and $N_{(g+1,2)j}$ are industry j's shares in total labor and capital income.

Equation (T31) introduces two variables not appearing in the earlier equations in Table 1: f_c, the percentage change in the average propensity to consume, and q, the percentage change in the domestic share of capitalist income. In long-run simulations, it is reasonable to set f_c exogenously at zero. To tie down q, we require some additional equations.

We assume that

$$Q(\tau) \left(\sum_{j=1}^{h} \Pi_j(\tau) K_j(\tau) \right) = Q(0) \left(\sum_{j=1}^{h} \Pi_j(\tau) K_j(0)(1-D_j)^\tau \right) + S^* \quad (3.41)$$

where

$$S^* = \sum_{t=0}^{\tau-1} \left(\frac{S(t)}{\sum_{j=1}^{h} \Pi_j(t) Y_j(t)} \right) \left(\sum_{j=1}^{h} \Pi_j(\tau) Y_j(t)(1-D_j)^{\tau-t-1} \right) \quad (3.42)$$

The first point to note about these two equations is that we have added explicit time arguments to the variables. Time τ is the solution year, 1990 say, and time 0 is the base year, 1981 say. The base year can usually be interpreted as the year in which the tariff reform or other shock under investigation is introduced. The τ arguments are not strictly necessary in (3.41) and (3.42). Our convention until now has been to represent variables for the solution year without time arguments. However, expressions containing variables from several different points of time are probably clearer if we include all the time arguments.

Equation (3.41) says that the value of the domestically owned capital stock in the solution year (year τ) equals the depreciated value of the domestically owned base year capital stock plus S^*, the depreciated value of domestically owned capital acquired between the base year and the solution year. In more detail, the left-hand side of (3.41) is the value[7] of the capital stock in the solution year, $\sum_j \Pi_j(\tau) K_j(\tau)$, multiplied by the domestic share $Q(\tau)$. The first term on the right-hand side is the value in the solution year of what remains of the base period capital stock $[(\sum_j \Pi_j(\tau) K_j(0)(1-D_j)^\tau)]$ multiplied by the share $[(Q(0))]$ that is domestically owned. (Here D_j is the annual rate of depreciation of the capital used by industry j.) The second term on the right-hand side of (3.41), S^*, is defined by (3.42). In (3.42) we assume that the amount of capital installed for industry j at time $t+1$ is $Y_j(t)$, that is, the investment at time t. Of this, the amount remaining by the solution year is $Y_j(t)(1-D_j)^{\tau-t-1}$. Thus, the total value in the solution year of capital installed as a result of investment at time t is $\sum_j \Pi_j(\tau) Y_j(t)(1-D_j)^{\tau-t-1}$. The share of this capital that is domestically owned is assumed to be the ratio for time t of domestic savings $S(t)$ to investment $\sum_j \Pi_j(t) Y_j(t)$. For Australia, it is realistic to suppose that the savings/investment ratio will remain below unity over at least the next 10 years. However, (3.42) is interpretable even when savings exceeds investment in some periods. For those periods, (3.42) implies that domestic investors buy some existing units of capital from foreign owners.

For the purposes of our miniature model, it is legitimate to simplify (3.41) and (3.42) by assuming that

$$\Pi_j(t) = \Pi(t), \quad \text{for} \quad j=1,\ldots,h \quad \text{and} \quad t=0,\ldots,\tau \quad (3.43)$$

and

$$D_j = D \quad \text{for} \quad j=1,\ldots,h \quad (3.44)$$

Equations (3.43) and (3.44) imply that the costs of constructing units of capital and depreciation rates are identical across industries. These assumptions would be justified if the technologies for constructing capital,

(3.8)–(3.9), were identical for all j. This is, in fact, assumed in our implementation of MO81 (see Section 4.2). Under (3.43) and (3.44), Equations (3.41) and (3.42) may be combined and written as

$$Q(\tau)\left(\sum_j K_j(\tau)\right)=Q(0)\left(\sum_j K_j(0)\right)(1-D)^\tau$$

$$+\sum_{t=0}^{\tau-1}(S(t)/\Pi(t))(1-D)^{\tau-t-1} \qquad (3.45)$$

To make use of (3.45), we must provide an explanation for the stream of real savings $[(S(t)/\Pi(t), t=1,\ldots,\tau-1)]$ over the period between the base year and the solution year. We assume that real savings grow exponentially, that is,

$$\frac{S(t)}{\Pi(t)}=\frac{S(0)}{\Pi(0)}(1+U)^t, \qquad t=1,\ldots,\tau-1 \qquad (3.46)$$

where

$$U=\left(\frac{S(\tau)/\Pi(\tau)}{S(0)/\Pi(0)}\right)^{1/\tau}-1 \qquad (3.47)$$

Then on substituting from (3.46) into (3.45) we obtain

$$Q(\tau)K(\tau)=Q(0)K(0)(1-D)^\tau+\frac{S(0)}{\Pi(0)}\left(\frac{(1+U)^\tau-(1-D)^\tau}{D+U}\right) \qquad (3.48)$$

where we have denoted the economy's aggregate capital stocks at times τ and 0 by $K(\tau)$ and $K(0)$. We treat $K(0)$, $S(0)$, $\Pi(0)$, $Q(0)$, and D as constants. Thus, in linear percentage-change form, (3.47) and (3.48) reduce to (T32) and (T33) where the coefficient in (T33) is

$$\Gamma=\left[\left(\frac{U\tau}{1+U}\right)\left(\frac{(1+U)^\tau}{(1+U)^\tau-(1-D)^\tau}\right)-\frac{U}{D+U}\right]$$

$$\times\left(\frac{Q(\tau)K(\tau)-Q(0)K(0)(1-D)^\tau}{Q(\tau)K(\tau)}\right) \qquad (3.49)$$

Equation (T34) in Table 1 relates percentage changes in consumption to percentage changes in savings. It is the percentage-change form of

$$S=\left(\frac{1-F_c}{F_c}\right)C \qquad (3.50)$$

where (3.50) follows from (3.40).

3.5   Closure of MO81 when category VI is included

Category VI in Table 1 adds four equations and four variables to the model set out in categories I–V. The four new variables are f_c, the percentage change in the average propensity to consume; u, the percentage change in the growth rate of real domestic savings over the period from the base year to the solution year, that is, year 0 to year τ; s, the percentage change in savings in year τ; and q, the percentage change in the domestic share in the ownership of the capital stock. Because we have added equal numbers of equations and variables, the closure options discussed in Section 3.3 are still available. Results from the restricted model can be regarded as coming from the complete model with f_c, u, s, and q treated endogenously. If these variables are endogenous, then values for the remaining endogenous variables can be computed without reference to the category VI equations.

The main reason for adding the category VI equations is to allow consumption (c^R), investment (y^R), the balance of trade (ΔB), and the consumption/investment ratio (f_R) all to be endogenous in a long-run simulation. This can be done by selecting the exogenous variables shown in column 3 of Table 3. In constrast with column 2 (the preferred long-run closure in the restricted model), in column 3 we have replaced f_R and ΔB with f_c and ω.

By exogenizing f_c, we are linking consumption to domestic income. This is possible in the expanded MO81 model because we have added the consumption function (T31) and sufficient equations to explain domestic income. In particular, we have added sufficient equations to explain the domestic share in capital income. By exogenizing ω, we are allowing (T25) to explain not only the allocation of investment across industries but also total investment.

4   Implementation of MO81

4.1   The data for MO81 and the initial evaluation of the coefficients in Table 1

Data for MO81 are set out in Tables 5 and 6. These data are purely hypothetical. They are illustrative of the input–output data base that will be required for implementing a version of ORANI extended to include the types of equations appearing in category VI of Table 1.

In Table 4, we have indicated how the information in Tables 5 and 6 is used to give initial values for the coefficients of the equations in Table 1.

Table 4. *The MO81 coefficients and parameters appearing in Table 1*

Equation	Coefficient or parameter	Description and evaluation[a]
(T1)	$S_{(ir)}^{(3)}$	Share of good i from source r in household purchases of good i; e.g., initially $S_{(11)}^{(3)} = 19.55/(19.55 + 1.63)$.
(T2)	$S_{(ir)j}^{(2)}$	Share of good i from source r in industry j's purchases of good i to be used as an input to capital creation; e.g., initially $S_{(11)1}^{(2)} = 1$, initial value for $S_{(22)1}^{(2)} = 3.26/(9.78 + 3.26)$.
(T3)	γ_i	Reciprocal of the foreign (export) demand elasticity for good i. Values adopted were $\gamma_1 = .5$, $\gamma_2 = .05$.
(T4)	$S_{(ir)j}^{(1)}$	For $i = 1, 2$, this is the share of good i from source r in industry j's purchases of good i to be used as an intermediate input; e.g., initially $S_{(11)1}^{(1)} = 16.28/(16.28 + 1.63)$. For $i = 3$, this is the share of labor ($r = 1$) or the share of capital ($r = 2$) in industry j's payments to primary factors; e.g., initially $S_{(31)1}^{(1)} = 32.57/(32.57 + 8.14 + 8.14)$.
(T5)	$H_{(q1)j}^{(0)}$	Share of total revenue in industry j accounted for by sales of good q; e.g., initially $H_{(11)1}^{(0)} = 73.30/(73.30 + 26.06)$.
(T6)	$H_{(q1)j}^{(0)}$	Covered under (T5).
	$H_{(is)j}^{(1)}$	Share of input (is) in the total costs of production in industry j; e.g., initially $H_{(11)1}^{(1)} = 16.28/99.36$, $H_{(32)1}^{(1)} = 16.28/99.36$, $H_{(31)2}^{(1)} = 32.57/71.67$.
(T7)	None	—
(T8)	None	—
(T9)	$H_{(is)j}^{(2)}$	Share of input (is) in the total cost of capital creation for industry j; e.g., initially $H_{(11)1}^{(2)} = 3.26/16.29$, $H_{(12)1}^{(2)} = 0$, $H_{(21)2}^{(2)} = 4.89/8.14$.
(T10)	None	—
(T11)	None	—
(T12)	$W_{(q1)j}^{(0)}$	Share of the total output of ($q1$) accounted for by industry j; e.g., initially $W_{(11)1}^{(0)} = 73.30/87.96$, $W_{(11)2}^{(0)} = 14.66/87.96$.
	$W_{(q1)j}^{(k)}$	Share of the total purchases of ($q1$) accounted for by industry j for purpose k ($k = 1$, intermediate demand; $k = 2$, input to capital creation); e.g., initially $W_{(11)1}^{(1)} = 16.28/87.96$, $W_{(11)2}^{(2)} = 1.63/87.96$, $W_{(21)2}^{(2)} = 4.89/83.07$.
	$W_{(q1)}^{(k)}$	Share of the total purchases of ($q1$) accounted for by final user k ($k = 3$, households; $k = 4$, exports); e.g., initially $W_{(11)}^{(3)} = 19.55/87.96$, $W_{(11)}^{(4)} = 34.21/87.96$.
(T13)	$W_{(g+1,1)j}^{(1)}$	Share of the total demand for primary factor of type 1 (i.e., labor) accounted for by industry j; e.g., initially $W_{(g+1,1)2}^{(1)} = 32.57/65.16$.
(T14)	None	—

Table 4 *(cont.)*

Equation	Coefficient or parameter	Description and evaluation[a]
(T15)	$W^{(k)}_{(q2)j}$	Share of total purchases of imported good q accounted for by industry j for purpose k; e.g., initially $W^{(1)}_{(12)1} = 1.63/16.29$, $W^{(2)}_{(22)2} = 1.63/27.69$. *Note:* The denominator in these shares is the basic value (including duty) of the sales of good ($q2$).
	$W^{(3)}_{(q2)}$	Share of total purchases of good ($q2$) accounted for by households; initially $W^{(3)}_{(12)} = 1.63/16.29$, $W^{(3)}_{(22)} = 11.40/27.69$.
(T16)	$M_{(q2)}$	Share of the total foreign currency value of imports accounted for by imports of good ($q2$); initially $M_{(12)} = 14.66/34.21$, $M_{(22)} = 19.55/34.21$.
(T17)	$E_{(q1)}$	Share of the total foreign currency value of exports accounted for by exports of good ($q1$); initially $E_{(11)} = 1$, $E_{(21)} = 0$. *Note:* There are no export taxes or subsidies in the data.
(T18)	E	Foreign currency value of exports; initially $E = 34.21$.
	M	Foreign currency value of imports; initially $M = 34.21$.
(T19)	$H^{(3)}_{(is)}$	Share of household expenditure devoted to good (is); e.g., initially, $H^{(3)}_{(11)} = 19.55/74.93$.
(T20)	None	—
(T21)	W^y_j	Share of total investment accounted for by industry j; initially $W^y_1 = 16.29/24.43$, $W^y_2 = 8.14/24.43$.
(T22)	W^y_j	Covered under (T21).
(T23)	None	—
(T24)	Q_j	$Q_j = (R_j + D_j)/R_j$; i.e., Q_j is the ratio of the gross to the net rate of return in industry j. From Table 6, $D_1 = 8.14/162.89$, $D_2 = 4.07/81.45$ (these are treated as constants). Initially $R_1 = 8.14/162.89$, $R_2 = 4.07/81.45$. Hence, initially $Q_j = 2$ for $j = 1, 2$.
(T25)	$I^{(1)}_j, I^{(2)}_j$	Users of the model set values according to how investment by industry is to be modeled (see discussion of category V in Section 3.2). Where formulas such as (3.38) are used, the H_j are valued according to (3.34) using values for $K_j(0)$ and K_j from Tables 5 and 6. For example, where $\tau = 10$, the initial value for H_1 is $(162.89/100)^{.1} - 1$.
	B_j	$B_j = 1/\beta_j \Delta_j$, where β_j is the elasticity of the expected rate of return schedule for industry j and Δ_j is the ratio of investment in the solution year to capital stock in the following year. For $j = 1, 2$, we set $\beta_j = 30$. Initially $\Delta_1 = 16.29/[162.89(.95) + 16.29]$ and $\Delta_2 = 8.14/[81.45(.95) + 8.14]$. *Note:* None of the results reported in Section 4 is affected by the value used for B_j.

Table 4 *(cont.)*

Equation	Coefficient or parameter	Description and evaluation[a]
(T26)	W_j^k	Share of the total capital stock accounted for by industry j. Initially, $W_1^k = 162.89/244.34$, $W_2^k = 81.45/244.34$.
(T27)	ζ_i^t	$\zeta_i^t = T_i/(T_i - 1)$, i.e., ζ_i^t is the ratio of the power of the tariff on good i to the ad valorem rate. Initially $\zeta_1^t = 16.30/1.63$, $\zeta_2^t = 27.69/8.14$.
	Υ_i^t	Share of total tariff revenue accounted for by tariffs on good i. Initially, $\Upsilon_1^t = 1.63/9.77$, $\Upsilon_2^t = 8.14/9.77$.
(T28)	ζ_i^v	$\zeta_i^v = V_i/(V_i - 1)$, i.e., ζ_i^v is the ratio of the power of the export subsidy on good i to the ad valorem rate.
	Υ_i^v	Share of total export subsidies accounted for by export subsidies on good i. *Note:* Our data base shows no export subsidies. Hence, in our computations, (T28) and the variable v are deleted.
(T29)	$I_{(g+1,1)j}$	User-determined wage-indexing parameter (see the end of Section 3.2).
(T30)	None	—
(T31)	ψ_i	ψ_i, $i = 1, \ldots, 4$ are the shares in domestic income accounted for by wage income, tariff revenue, export subsidies, and capital income accruing to domestic capitalists. In Table 6, wage income is 65.16, tariff revenue is 9.77, export subsidies are 0, and domestic capitalist income is $(24.44)(183.26/244.34) = 18.33$. Thus, domestic income is 93.24 and initially we have $\psi_1 = .70$, $\psi_2 = .10$, $\psi_3 = 0$, and $\psi_4 = .20$.
	$N_{(g+1,1)j}$	Share of industry j in total wage payments. Initially $N_{(g+1,1)1} = 32.57/65.16$, $N_{(g+1,1)2} = 32.57/65.16$.
	$N_{(g+1,2)j}$	Share of industry j in total returns to capital. Initially $N_{(g+1,2)1} = 16.28/24.44$, $N_{(g+1,2)2} = 8.14/24.44$.
(T32)	$(U+1)/\tau U$	In the base year (see Table 5) domestic income is 40 (wages) plus 6 (tariff revenue) plus $15(112.5/150)$ (domestically accruing capital income), i.e., domestic income is 57.25. Consumption is 46, leaving savings $S(0) = 11.25$. In the solution year (see Table 6) domestic income is 93.24 (see the discussion of ψ_i earlier in this table). Consumption is 74.93, leaving $S(\tau) = 18.31$. Commodity prices are constant as we move from Table 5 to Table 6 (see discussion at beginning of Section 4.1). In particular, initially, $\Pi(\tau)/\Pi(0) = 1$. Hence, the initial value for U is $(18.31/11.25)^{-1} - 1 = .05$. With $\tau = 10$, we find that the initial value for the coefficient in (T32) is $1.05/.50 = 2.10$.

Table 4 *(cont.)*

Equation	Coefficient or parameter	Description and evaluation[a]
(T33)	Γ	See Equation (3.49). With $\tau = 10$, $D = .05$, $Q(0) = .75$, $K(0) = 150$, and U, $Q(\tau)$, and $K(\tau)$ having initial values .05, .75 and 244.34, respectively, Γ has an initial value of .160.
(T34)	$1 / (1 - F_c)$	Initially F_c equals $(74.93/93.24) = .80$; i.e., F_c is the ratio of consumption to domestic income. This gives an initial value for the coefficient in (T34) of 5.0.

[a]Except when otherwise indicated, the initial share values were computed from the solution-year input–output data, i.e., Table 6.

Data are required for two points of time, the base year (year 0) and the solution year (year τ). In implementing MO81 we have set τ equal to 10. The data for the solution year are used to evaluate the share coefficients (cost shares, sales shares, and revenue shares). Both base year and solution year data are necessary for evaluating the growth-related coefficients: U in (T32), Γ in (T33), and the H_j terms used in some variants of (T25). As explained earlier (see Section 2), data for the solution year must be obtained by projection. In the present exercise, Table 6 was obtained from Table 5 by assuming a growth rate of 5% per annum for 10 years in all commodity and primary factor flows and zero growth in all prices.

Two further points concerning the input–output data are worth mentioning. First, as we noted in Section 2, these data provide an initial solution, X^I, to (2.1). To obtain X^I, a convention is required with respect to quantity units. The most convenient approach is to define the quantity units so that all initial prices for commodities and primary factors in the solution year are unity. Then we can simply read the value flows in Table 6 as quantity flows. The balancing properties of Table 6 ensure that the quantity flows satisfy the market-clearing conditions and that the value of production in each industry equals the value of inputs. We may assume that the free parameters are set so that the other equations in MO81 are also satisfied. For example, the exponents in the Cobb–Douglas function (3.5) can be assumed to be set at 19.55/21.18 and 1.63/21.18 for $i = 1$ and 42.35/53.75 and 11.40/53.75 for $i = 2$.

Second, we note that the data in Table 6 are in accord with the simplifying assumptions (3.43) and (3.44). The inputs used to create a unit of

Table 5. Input–output data base for MO81 for year 0, the base year

Factor	Intermediate inputs to industries		Gross fixed capital formation by industries		Household consumption	Exports	Negative of import duty	Row totals
	Ind. 1	Ind. 2	Ind. 1	Ind. 2				
Domestic commodities								
Commodity 1	10	8	2	1	12	21	—	54
Commodity 2	15	1	6	3	26	0	—	51
Imported commodities								
Commodity 1	1	8	0	0	1	—	−1	9
Commodity 2	5	2	2	1	7	—	−5	12
Labor	20	20	—	—	—	—	—	40
Gross operating surplus								
Depreciation	5	2.5	—	—	—	—	—	7.5
Net profit	5	2.5	—	—	—	—	—	7.5
Total costs	61	44	10	5	46	21	−6	181
Domestic commodity outputs								
Commodity 1	45	9	—	—	—	—	—	54
Commodity 2	16	35	—	—	—	—	—	51
Domestically owned capital stocks	75	37.5	—	—	—	—	—	112.5
Foreign-owned capital stocks	25	12.5	—	—	—	—	—	37.5
Total capital	100	50	—	—	—	—	—	150

Table 6. *Input–output data base for MO81 for year τ, the solution year*

Factor	Intermediate inputs to industries		Gross fixed capital formation by industries		Household consumption	Exports	Negative of import duty	Row totals
	Ind. 1	Ind. 2	Ind. 1	Ind. 2				
Domestic commodities								
Commodity 1	16.28	13.03	3.26	1.63	19.55	34.21	—	87.96
Commodity 2	24.43	1.63	9.78	4.89	42.35	0	—	83.07
Imported commodities								
Commodity 1	1.63	13.03	0	0	1.63	—	−1.63	14.66
Commodity 2	8.14	3.26	3.26	1.63	11.40	—	−8.14	19.55
Labor	32.57	32.57	—	—	—	—		65.16
Gross operating surplus								
Depreciation	8.14	4.07	—	—	—	—	—	12.22
Net profit	8.14	4.07	—	—	—	—	—	12.22
Total costs	99.36	71.67	16.29	8.14	74.93	34.21	−9.77	294.84
Domestic commodity outputs								
Commodity 1	73.30	14.66			—	—	—	87.96
Commodity 2	26.06	57.01			—	—	—	83.07
Domestically owned capital stocks	122.17	61.09	—	—	—	—	—	183.26
Foreign-owned capital stocks	40.72	20.36	—	—	—	—	—	61.08
Total capital	162.89	81.45	—	—	—	—	—	244.34

Note: τ = 10. All flows shown here are obtained from the corresponding flows in Table 5 by multiplying by (1.05)[10].

Table 7. *Effects of a 3.4% increase in the ad valorem tariff rate on good 2: long-run simulations*

Variable	(1) Standard long-run simulation available with restricted model	(2) Standard long-run simulation available with complete model
Gross domestic product[a]	$- .06$	$- .06$
Aggregate capital (k)	$- .40$	$- .40$
Aggregate employment (l)	0^b	0^b
Real aggregate consumption (c^R)	$- .06$	.05
Real aggregate investment (y^R)	$- .06$	$- .40$
$100\Delta B/\text{GDP}$	0^b	.00
Imports, foreign currency value (m)	$- .27$	$- .28$
Exports, foreign currency value (e)	$- .27$	$- .27$
Domestic ownership share (q)	.63	.40
Average propensity to consume (f_c)	$- .16$	0^b
Activity level, industry 1 (z_1)	$- .48$	$- .47$
Activity level, industry 2 (z_2)	.33	.33

Note: All projections are percentage changes except those for ΔB. Changes in the balance of trade are expressed as a percentage of GDP. Results should be interpreted as deviations from the values that the variables would have reached in the solution year in the absence of the tariff change.
[a]Calculated as the appropriately weighted sum of c^R, y^R, and $100\Delta B/\text{GDP}$.
[b]Set exogenously.

capital for industry 1 are identical to those used for industry 2. The rate of depreciation of capital in both industries is 5%.

4.2   Illustrative results: the effects of a 3.4% increase in the ad valorem tariff rate on commodity 2

In Table 7 we report two simulations of the effects of a 1% increase in the power of the tariff on good 2 (the main import-competing commodity). This is equivalent to a 3.4% increase in the ad valorem rate. [Notice from Table 6 that the initial value of T_2 is $1.42 = (8.14 + 19.55)/19.55$].

In making the computations we relied on the Johansen approach, (2.24). That is, we computed x_1 according to

$$x_1 = -A_1^{-1}(X^I) A_2(X^I) x_2 \tag{4.1}$$

where x_1 and x_2 are the vectors of percentage changes in the endogenous and exogenous variables. The only nonzero component of x_2 in the simulations was t_2 which was set at 1. In simulation 1 (column 1 of Table 7), the list of exogenous variables was that given in column 2 of Table 3. In simulation 2, the exogenous variables were those listed in column 3 of Table 3. In both simulations, the wage-indexation parameters, $I_{(g+1,1)j}$, $j = 1, 2$, in (T29) were set at unity. In simulation 1, $I_j^{(1)}$ and $I_j^{(2)}$ appearing in (T25) were also set at unity, that is, (3.29) applies. Because ω is endogenous in this simulation, the role of (T25) is confined to allocating investment across industries. Now ω adjusts so that the y_j values emerging from (T25) are consistent with aggregate investment that is assumed to move in line with aggregate consumption. The allocation of investment across industries is of little importance in our miniature model because the technology for building capital is identical for the two industries. Thus, shifts of investment expenditure between the two industries in the solution year have no effect on input demands. In simulation 2, we set $I_j^{(1)} = 1$ and $I_j^{(2)} = 0$ for all j; that is, (3.32) applies. Experiments with (3.37) have also been conducted. However, for long-run simulations, (3.32) seems more reasonable. The argument is that after 10 years, growth rates in capital stocks will have settled back to reflect the underlying growth in productivity and the size of the labor force. Capital growth rates in year 10 are assumed to be independent of the adjustments caused by the tariff change to the growth rates for the period 0 to 10. Notice, finally, that with $I_j^{(2)} = 0$, the value chosen in simulation 2 for the exogenous variable ω has no bearing on the results.

Simulation 1 is illustrative of the current ORANI model in standard long-run mode. In particular, it is assumed that the change in the tariff on good 2 has no effect on the balance of trade or on the ratio of consumption to investment. Consumption and investment are assumed to move by the same percentage as GDP. In simulation 2 it is assumed that the change in the tariff does not affect the average propensity to consume; that is, consumption changes by the same percentage as income accruing to domestic residents.

The most obvious feature of the results in Table 7 is their similarity in the two experiments for all variables except those relating to the composition of domestic absorption (c^R, y^R, f_c, and q). In both simulations the tariff change increases activity by the main producer (industry 2) of good 2 and depresses the main exporter (industry 1). The resulting effects on GDP depend on the sizes of (a) the efficiency losses, (b) the favorable terms-of-trade effects, and (c) the contractions in the capital stocks necessary to maintain rates of return. The sizes of these three effects of the tariff increase are not very sensitive to changes in the composition of domestic absorption.

In analyzing the results we found it helpful to make a third simulation of the effects of the tariff increase. The same conditions were assumed as in simulation 2 except that we held the aggregate capital stock fixed and allowed the economywide average rate of return to be endogenous. (Compared with simulation 2, in this third simulation, k and the f_j^r terms set at zero, replaced r and the r_j terms in the exogenous category; see Section 3.3.) We found that with $k = 0$, the tariff increase caused GDP to increase by .04%. The terms-of-trade effect dominated the conventional efficiency losses. The tariff increase also reduced the real rentals on units of capital because the production of exports (good 1) is relatively capital-intensive. Real capital income fell by .31% and real noncapital income (wages and tariff revenue) rose by .15%. We have assumed that domestic residents own all of the noncapital income (which accounts for 80% of their total income in the solution year) and 75% of the capital income. Thus, in the fixed-capital experiment, the percentage change in the real income of domestic residents is

$$x_d^R = .8(.15) + .2(-.31) = .06$$

This is also the percentage change in real consumption (c^R).

To arrive at the results in simulation 2, we must now allow for the reduction in the size of the capital stock necessary to restore rates of return (and thus real rentals) to their original levels. The necessary change is $k = -.40$. The same is true for simulation 1 (see Table 7). This yields a reduction in GDP given, to a good approximation, by

$$GDP = S_K k = .25(-.40) = -.10$$

where $S_K = .25$ is the capital share in value-added shown in our data base. The net effect on GDP of the tariff increase in simulation 2 (and in simulation 1) is the sum of the effect with capital fixed and the effect of the reduction in the capital stock, that is,

$$GDP = .04 - .10 = -.06$$

Despite this reduction in GDP, the result for consumption $(c^R = .05)$ in column 2 of Table 7 remains close to that in the fixed-capital case where c^R is .06, that is, the reduction in the size of the capital stock has a negligible impact on the amount of domestically owned income. This is because there is a negligible effect on the amount of domestically owned capital.[8] The explanation depends on two relationships. First, other things being equal, as domestic income (and thus savings) increases so does domestic ownership of capital. By substituting from (T32) and (T33) and by assuming that $(s - \pi) = x_d^R$, we obtain

$$q+k=\frac{\Gamma(1+U)}{\tau U}x_d^R \qquad (4.2)$$

where $q+k$ is the percentage change in the domestic ownership of capital. Second, other things being equal, as domestic ownership of capital increases, so does domestic income. Starting from

$$X_d^R = X^R - (1-Q)KW_K^R \qquad (4.3)$$

where X_d^R is real domestic income, X^R is total real income (GDP), W_K^R is the real rental on units of capital, and K is the capital stock, we obtain, in percentage-change form,

$$x_d^R = x^R\left(\frac{X^R}{X_d^R}\right) - (k+w_K^R)\left(\frac{(1-Q)KW_K^R}{X_d^R}\right) + q\left(\frac{QKW_K^R}{X_d^R}\right) \qquad (4.4)$$

From our data base, $\Gamma = .16$, $(1+U)/\tau U = 2.1$, $(X^R/X_d^R) = 1.066$, $[(1-Q)KW_K^R/X_d^R] = .066$, and $(QKW_K^R/X_d^R) = .197$. With a .40% reduction in capital stock, we have found that $x^R = -.10$, and $w_K^R = .31$. Thus, with $k = -.40$, (4.2) and (4.4) reduce to

$$q = .40 + .34x_d^R \qquad (4.5)$$

and

$$x_d^R = -.10 + .197q \qquad (4.6)$$

implying that $q = .396$, $x_d^R = -.01$, and $(q+k) = .004$.

The final result in column 2 of Table 7 that warrants explanation is for the change in the balance of trade. This is close to zero because the percentage change in real domestic absorption turns out to be close to the percentage change in real GDP. In our miniature model real domestic absorption is made up of consumption and investment. The result in column 2 for real consumption has already been explained. The percentage change in real investment (y^R) is equal to the percentage change in aggregate capital by assumption. In our data base, the shares of consumption and investment in absorption are .75 and .25, respectively. Thus, we have

$$a = .75(.05) - .25(.40)$$
$$= -.06 \qquad (4.7)$$

where a is the percentage change in real absorption.

In simulation 1 the change in the balance of trade is set exogenously at zero and the GDP result is very close to that in simulation 2. Thus, aggregate absorption is approximately the same in simulations 1 and 2.

Table 8. Selection of results for an elimination of the tariff on good 2 computed by Euler's method: standard long-run simulation available with the complete version of MO81

| Variable | Computed projections[a] | | | | | | Extrapolations[b] | | Percentage errors | |
	(1) 1-step	(2) 2-step	(3) 4-step	(4) 8-step	(5) 16-step	(6) 32-step	(7) 1- to 2-step	(8) 16- to 32-step	(9) Johansen $\left[\frac{(1)}{(8)}-1\right]100$	(10) 1–2 step extrapolation $\left[\frac{(7)}{(8)}-1\right]100$
GDP	1.79	1.33	1.05	.89	.82	.77	.86	.73	143.3	16.7
u	− .70	− 2.47	− 3.54	− 4.12	− 4.43	− 4.59	− 4.24	− 4.75	− 85.2	− 10.7
c^R	− 1.39	− 2.29	− 2.83	− 3.12	− 3.28	− 3.36	− 3.18	− 3.44	− 59.5	− 7.4
y^R	11.75	12.98	13.80	14.28	14.55	14.69	14.20	14.83	− 20.7	− 4.2
m	8.14	9.40	10.22	10.70	10.95	11.09	10.67	11.22	− 27.4	− 4.9
e	8.02	9.07	9.71	10.06	10.25	10.34	10.13	10.44	− 23.2	− 3.0
ΔB	− .04	− .11	− .18	.21	.24	.25	− .19	.26	− 84.7	− 26.3
$\xi^{(3)}$	− 8.88	− 9.50	− 9.85	− 10.03	− 10.13	− 10.17	− 10.13	− 10.22	− 13.2	− .9
z_1	13.90	15.61	16.71	17.34	17.68	17.85	17.33	18.03	− 22.9	− 3.9
z_2	− 9.63	− 11.03	− 11.90	− 12.39	− 12.66	− 12.79	− 12.43	− 12.93	− 25.5	− 3.8
q	− 11.87	− 12.56	− 13.01	− 13.27	− 13.41	− 13.49	− 13.25	− 13.56	− 12.5	− 2.3
t	− 66.35	− 77.80	− 82.55	− 84.35	− 85.08	− 85.39	− 89.24	− 85.71	− 22.6	4.1

[a]Column 1 contains results from a Johansen-style solution computed according to Equation (2.24). Columns 2–6 were computed via the n-step Euler method (2.21)–(2.23) for $n = 2, 4, 8, 16,$ and 32, respectively.

[b]Column 7 was calculated from columns 1 and 2 via (4.9) with $n = 1$. Column 8 was calculated in an analogous way from columns 5 and 6. The results in column 8 are assumed to be free from linearization errors and are used as the exact solution to the model in calculating the percentage errors given in columns 9 and 10.

However, the allocation of absorption between consumption and investment is different. In simulation 1, both consumption and investment are forced to move with GDP. Consequently, compared with simulation 2, simulation 1 shows a reduction in the consumption/investment ratio. In fact, the increase in the domestic ownership share of capital (and thus in domestically accruing income) is greater in simulation 1 than in simulation 2, but there is a marked fall in the average propensity to consume in simulation 1.

4.3   An illustration of Euler's method in computing MO81 results

The results reported in the previous section were computed from MO81 using the Johansen method, (4.1). We can have confidence in this method if the exogenous shock is small. In this subsection, we examine the effects of a large shock: complete elimination of the tariff on good 2. Our interest is in how sensitive the results are to the method by which they are computed. We will compare results computed using Euler's method, (2.21)–(2.23), for various values of n (the number of steps) including $n = 1$ (Johansen's method).

Table 8 contains results for the 100% reduction in the tariff on good 2 computed under the same assumptions as in simulation 2 in Table 7. Results in column 1 of Table 8 (i.e., the Johansen-style results) could be calculated from the results in column 2 of Table 7 by multiplying the latter by $-100/3.4 = -29.4$. In columns 2–6 of Table 8 we give Euler-style results for n equal to 2, 4, 8, 16, and 32.

The n-step results were computed by breaking the change in the exogenous variable (T_2) into n equal parts. The initial value of T_2 in our data (Table 6) is 1.42. A 100% cut in the ad valorem tariff rate on good 2 reduces this to 1.00. Thus, in the first step of the n-step procedure, we applied (4.1) to compute the effects on the endogenous variables of the exogenous shock

$$(t_2)_0^n = -\left(\frac{0.42/n}{1.42}\right)100$$

The results of this computation were used in updating the entire data base. This involved the updating of input–output flows (defined as the product of a price and a quantity) according to the formula

$$(\text{flow})_1^n = (\text{flow})_0\left(1 + \frac{p_0^n}{100}\right)\left(1 + \frac{q_0^n}{100}\right)$$

where $(\text{flow})_0$ and $(\text{flow})_1^n$ are the initial and updated values of the flow, and p_0^n and q_0^n are respectively the relevant components of the x_1 and x_2

vectors in the first application of (4.1). Using the updated flows, we re-evaluated the matrix $-A_1^{-1}A_2$. Then, at the second step of the n-step procedure this reevaluated matrix was used to derive the effects on the endogenous variables of the exogenous shock

$$(t_2)_1^n = -\left(\frac{0.42/n}{1.42 - 0.42/n}\right)100$$

The cycle of data updates, reevaluations of the matrix $-A_1^{-1}A_2$, recalculations of the exogenous shock $(t_2)_q^n$, and recomputations of solution values for the endogenous variables was then repeated a further $n-2$ times. The final results in the n-step column in Table 8 are of the form

$$(x)^n = \left(\prod_{q=0}^{n-1}\left(1 + \frac{x_q^n}{100}\right) - 1\right)100$$

where x_q^n is the solution value or exogenous input for variable x at the $(q+1)$th step of the procedure.

Columns 1–6 of Table 8 reveal that for any endogenous variable the results of the different Euler computations exhibit (approximately) the following relationship:

$$(x)^{2n} - (x)^n = 2[(x)^{4n} - (x)^{2n}] \tag{4.8}$$

This suggests that we can calculate $(x)^\infty$ by extrapolating from results generated by Euler-style computations using small numbers of steps. Relationship (4.8) implies the extrapolation rule

$$(x)^\infty = (x)^{2n} + [(x)^{2n} - (x)^n] \tag{4.9}$$

If (4.8) were to apply exactly in our results, we could obtain $(x)^\infty$ by extrapolation from a two-step Euler computation and a one-step computation. In fact, (4.8) applies only approximately, with the results conforming more closely to the relationship as n increases. In columns 7 and 8 of Table 8 we report two sets of extrapolations [generated via (4.9)]. Those in column 7 were computed with $n=1$ and for those in column 8 we used $n=16$. Column 8 is assumed to be free from linearization errors, that is, to be an accurate solution to the nonlinear form of MO81. Columns 9 and 10 contain the percentage deviations of the Johansen results (column 1) and the results generated via (4.9) with $n=1$ (column 7) from the linearization-error-free results (column 8).

The errors associated with the Johansen-style results (column 9) average about 40%. It must be noted that the exogenous shock in this experiment is very large in comparison to the types of shocks that are normally under consideration by policy makers. Our experience with MO81 subjected to more modest shocks is that the Johansen errors are typically much smaller than those evident in Table 8.[9] Column 10 of the table shows that extrapolation based on only the one-step and two-step Euler computations dramatically reduces the errors. With few exceptions, errors in column 10 do not exceed 5%. Errors of this size could not normally be regarded as serious in comparison to those introduced by data inaccuracies and the simplifications of reality imposed by theoretical assumptions.

5   Conclusion

MO81 is a model of ORANI. In building ORANI, we have used MO81 and its predecessors to try out new ideas. Because ORANI is very large, we have found that it is sensible to devise small, simplified versions for experimenting with potential improvements and extensions before attempting to implement them in the main system. In this chapter we have described two sets of experiments with MO81: one concerned with the solution procedure, and the other concerned with long-run macroeconomic closure and foreign ownership of capital.

Originally, Johansen's linearization method was the solution procedure adopted for ORANI. This method has advantages in terms of flexibility and cheapness, but it introduces uncontrolled linearization errors. In Section 4.3 we showed how Euler's method combined with extrapolation can be used to produce MO81 results in which the linearization errors are negligible. Encouraged by similar results from an earlier version of MO81, we committed resources to programming the Euler method for ORANI. Results from ORANI follow the same pattern as those in the minature versions. Consequently, we have been able to effectively eliminate linearization errors from ORANI computations without either a significant loss of computing flexibility or a serious increase in costs. Examples for ORANI of Euler-style solutions with extrapolation are in DPSV (sec. 47). The theoretical justification for the method is given in DPSV (chap. 5). Our view is that the method could be applied successfully to many of the current generation of general equilibrium models. In fact, it has been used with satisfactory results in recent work by Bovenberg and Keller (1981) on a model quite different from ORANI.

To date, our work on long-run closure and foreign ownership has gone no further than this chapter. Results from MO81, extended to deal with these issues, have proved interpretable and have not indicated any obvious flaws in our approach. However, before proceeding to add a category VI to ORANI, we will carry out further experiments with MO81. It would be useful to know, for example, whether our conclusion that reductions in capital have little impact on the amount of domestically owned capital depends on particular features of the MO81 data base used in this chapter or whether this is a more general result. It would also be useful to know more about the role of τ (the time between the base year and the solution year). So far we have fixed τ at 10 in all experiments. Would our results be very different if τ were 5 or 15?

NOTES

1. Full documentation is given in Dixon, Parmenter, Sutton, and Vincent (DPSV), 1982.
2. In fact, we have calculated cost shares, sales shares, etc. from base period input–output accounts without any explicit forward projection. These shares are unaffected by a uniform expansion of all flows.
3. We use lower-case letters for percentage changes in the variables denoted by the corresponding upper-case letters. In writing (2.8) and (2.9) we have assumed that none of the components of X is zero. It is convenient, for the present (and not limiting in any practical sense), to think of all the ORANI variables as being positive. Later we will see that for one variable, the balance of trade, it is the change (not the percentage) that appears in ORANI computations.
4. That is, one plus the ad valorem rate.
5. The estimation of the B_j for ORANI is described in DPSV, sec. 29(g).
6. Notice that the variable ω appearing in (T25) is treated endogenously. It adjusts so that the y_j, $j = 1, \ldots, h$, are consistent with the exogenously given value for y^R. (We assume that the coefficients $I_j^{(2)}$ are not all zero.) Where ω is endogenous, (T25) can be thought of as determining the allocation of investment across industries while leaving the overall level of investment to be determined elsewhere.
7. We value units of industry j's capital stock existing in the solution year at their cost of construction, $\Pi_j(\tau)$. In view of our assumption of a one-period gestation lag in the creation of capital [see (3.26)], it might be considered appropriate to value existing capital at more than $\Pi_j(\tau)$ per unit. We have found it convenient to use $\Pi_j(\tau)$; i.e., we value capital at time τ assuming that rentals for the year have already been paid and that depreciation has already taken place. In fact, as we will see, the valuation chosen is not critical. Under the assumptions we will be adopting, the $\Pi_j(\tau)$ terms cancel out of (3.41)–(3.42).
8. Recall that employment of labor is held fixed. The argument in the text will establish that the reduction in capital has little effect on the amount of domestically owned capital. It follows that it has little effect on the amount of employed, domestically owned resources. Thus, there is little effect on the overall level of domestic income although there is a redistribution of income in favor of domestic capitalists and away from labor.
9. See DPSV, sec. 8.4.

REFERENCES

Apostol, Tom M. (1957). *Mathematical Analysis: A Modern Approach to Advanced Calculus.* Reading, Mass.: Addison-Wesley.

Bovenberg, A. L., and Keller, W. J. (1981). "Dynamics and Nonlinearities in Applied General Equilibrium Models." Working paper M1-8-208, Central Bureau voor de Statistiek, Voorburg, Netherlands.

Dixon, P. B., Parmenter, B. R., Sutton, J., and Vincent, D. P. (1982). *ORANI: A Multisectoral Model of the Australian Economy.* Amsterdam: North-Holland.

Hanoch, Giora (1971). "CRESH Production Functions." *Econometrica* 39: 695–712.

Johansen, L. (1960). *A Multi-Sectoral Study of Economic Growth.* Amsterdam: North-Holland.

Vincent, D. P., Dixon, P. B., and Powell, A. A. (1980). "The Estimation of Supply Response in Australian Agriculture: The CRESH/CRETH Production System." *International Economic Review* 21:221–42.

Comments

John Whalley

The present chapter is principally devoted to (1) a summary of existing work with the ORANI model on Australia; (2) a description of a miniaturized version of the model, referred to as MO81; and (3) discussion of solution methods for the model. The treatment of foreign investment, in spite of the title, only accounts for a small portion of the chapter. A set of illustrative results are provided for MO81 for a 3.4% increase in the tariff on the second good for a hypothetical data set.

My remarks are concerned with some of the broader issues of general equilibrium modeling which are raised by the chapter. I have relatively little to say about solution methods. The ORANI model is solved using linearization methods that for relatively small changes seem to work extremely well. Computational experience with other models discussed in this book appears to indicate that solution method, per se, is not a major issue with applied models in current use. Instead, the main focus seems now to be on theoretical underpinnings and interpretation of model findings; this is the direction I take here.

Issue orientation, model structure, and theoretical underpinnings

The ORANI model is perhaps the most impressive of the various recent applied general equilibrium models in its complexity, use of data, and amount of effort involved in its construction. To my mind, it also clearly illustrates the dilemmas that face modelers in the choice of basic model on which the elaboration should build. I wish to illustrate these dilemmas

by taking a "non-ORANI," simplified view of evaluating policy proposals for Australia, focusing on the issue of impacts of a tariff increase
in Australia.

A trade theorist, innocent of large models, might assume that Australia is a small, open, price-taking economy with the implication that no
complex general equilibrium model is necessary to evaluate impacts of
tariff changes. All prices are given by the rest of the world. The impact of
any change in policy, whether it be domestic taxes or tariffs or whatever,
simply involves adding on the appropriate distortions. Discounting difficulties with time and investment in the gains from trade literature, Australia would gain from the removal of a tariff (assuming no other distortions are present) because there is only a domestic distortion effect and
no terms-of-trade impact. In building a numerical general equilibrium
model to evaluate tariff changes in a relatively small, open economy like
Australia the key issue thus appears to be the departure one makes from
the simplest model of a small, open, price-taking economy. Where does
the price endogeneity come from that leads to the complex general equilibrium structure?

The basic difference between this orientation and that in ORANI is
(1) the issue orientation, and (2) the need for careful theoretical underpinnings if the welfare analysis that the theorist thinks of can be done.
The issue orientation results in the main focus of modeling being on
the external sector and its links back into the economy. The theoretical
requirements suggest a traditional full-employment, relative-price-based
Walrasian structure.

The way the ORANI model has been designed does not seem to reflect
this concern with the trade sector. The orientation I have outlined suggests worrying primarily about the external sector and moving from that
to domestic linkages. Instead, the external sector is specified in ORANI
so as to "close" the model whereas to a theorist the external sector specification would, in all probability, "drive" the model. This set of issues
deriving from basic orientation in model building is equally crucial for
the treatment of foreign investment, to which I return below.

Given the importance of specifying carefully the departures from a
simple small, open economy model, it is perhaps worth discussing how
they might arise. The first and perhaps obvious departure involves the
differentiation between traded and nontraded goods. A typical ratio of
values of traded to nontraded goods in a small, open economy, such as
Australia, would be in the neighborhood of one. Roughly one-half of
activity is in the traded goods sector and half in the nontraded goods sector, where government services are particularly significant. But with this
departure the key parameters in the model become the elasticities of sub-

stitution in demand and production between fixprice traded and flexprice nontraded goods.

A further and equally significant departure arises when one tries to accommodate estimated trade elasticities for small economies, since they are typically low. If one examines, for instance, the compendium of trade elasticities produced by Stern, Francis, and Schumacher (1976), one finds that the "best guess" export price elasticity for Australia is $-.74$, lower than that for the United States. For many people, including myself, these low values of estimated trade elasticities for small economies are somewhat puzzling. However, if these values are accepted, accommodating them produces further and sharper departures from the small, open economy assumption. The crucial thing then becomes how these elasticities are incorporated (see Whalley and Yeung, 1980).

Because of its orientation, ORANI is, in my mind at least, quite sharply differentiated from some of the other models discussed in this book. Its basic objective seems to me to be to provide a forecasting tool, and not to produce applied welfare analysis as is the case with most of the tax and trade models. Because of its forecasting orientation, this model departs from the "purist" classical general equilibrium structure that one emphasizes in applied welfare analysis. Its general approach is one of equilibrium interdependence, but with a number of departures from a pure model, which to a welfare economist makes its interpretation difficult. The model contains such parameters as an average propensity to consume, which does not seem to come from utility maximization. In the treatment of investment expenditures there is an exogenous adjustment parameter that determines the change in the desired capital stock of each industry in light of changes in the rate of return on capital.

Although this type of model feature makes interpretation of any model findings difficult in terms of welfare analysis, a defense is that there really is no welfare calculation presented of who gains and who loses from a particular policy change. Instead, ORANI is to be used as an expanded form of forecasting device that goes beyond the macro models that have been prominent in the literature in the 1970s and 1980s.

I have troubles with ORANI as a forecasting device because major disturbances in individual sectors of the economy primarily reflect macro fluctuations rather than micro-induced effects of relatively small changes in policy parameters. To my eye an implicit macro model of somewhat simple proportions is built into ORANI. A Keynesian structure is used with no well-defined monetary sector. The price level is not determined by the rate of growth of the money supply. There is no equation that determines the natural rate of unemployment. There is no clear determination of real growth performance in the economy.

The defense for the welfare-oriented models is that the macro disturbances in the economy are put on one side in doing the welfare analysis. What happens to real growth rates? What happens to the rate of unemployment? What happens to the inflation rate? These are all things that are left to the macro forecasters, and a partition between macro and micro issues is assumed. The micro welfare analysis is done on the assumption of full employment, even though full employment does not come to pass. It seems to me, however, that the forecasting approach of ORANI cannot avoid these issues in quite the same way.

The treatment of foreign investment

In the extensions to incorporate foreign investment similar issues of modeling orientation and theoretical underpinnings arise. It appears that a simple equation is first used to determine the desired capital stock of an industry. This involves taking the change induced in the economywide rate of return and calculating the desired capital stock of an industry. The sum of the changes determines investment. The model determination of domestic and foreign investment follows using the ratio of domestic savings to economywide investment. A key elasticity parameter β_j for each industry enters this calculation. This parameter is not discussed in detail in the text, but it appears that this part of the model is not rooted in any form of utility maximization.

More significant, perhaps, is the contrast with a more traditional approach to determination of investment that focuses not on individual industries but on the economy in aggregate. The demand and supply sides of the investment goods market depend only indirectly on how much capital is currently employed in individual industries. Savers make decisions on the basis of the anticipated rate of return on capital, which they can realize by investing in any industry. Changes in the individual industries will, of course, determine the demand for capital goods, but the kind of modeling that is used in ORANI would seem to be "nontraditional." In ORANI, savings behavior reflects the propensity to consume that is assumed in macro module. Household savings do not depend on the rate of return on capital. The division of investment between domestic and foreign savings in any industry reflects the domestic savings/investment ratio in aggregate.

Theorists would probably find this treatment less than satisfactory since the treatment of inward foreign investment reflects neither investment decisions based on rates of return on capital nor the outcome of a portfolio choice problem accounting for the composition of domestic and foreign capital formation. In fact, basic divisions and disagreements dominate the current literature on inward foreign investment, and it would seem that these cannot be avoided in designing a model like ORANI. The recent literature, including Harberger (1980) and Feldstein and Horioka (1980), raises the issue of whether or not there is an international capital market. This seems to be a central issue in this whole area, and nowhere is this discussion or debate reflected in the ORANI model.

Results

In spite of the length of this chapter there is only one table of results. It reports the effects of a 3.4% increase in the ad valorem tariff rate on good 2 using hypothetical data for MO81. Good 2 is the major import in the data set. The table reports results from a "standard" long-run simulation available with "complete" and "restricted" models. The "restricted" model has an exogenous trade balance and ratio of consumption to investment, whereas the complete model does not. The two sets of results reported unfortunately do not seem to allow the reader to ascertain the impact of the change in treatment of foreign investment on model performance.

In both cases, the impact of an increase in the tariff rate is to reduce the value of gross domestic product. It reduces the aggregate capital stock whereas aggregate employment is left unchanged because there is a market-clearing condition for labor and a fixed labor supply. The reduction in employment of aggregate capital, in turn, reflects a reduction in aggregate investment. In the "restricted" case, aggregate consumption falls, whereas in the "complete" case consumption rises. Imports and exports fall by approximately the same amount.

The reduction in aggregate investment in both cases seems to follow from the fact that in the data the protected industry is labor-intensive and the increase in the output level of the labor-intensive industry results in a fall in investment. The opposite sign of impacts on consumption is more difficult to trace through. A further point is that if a long-run simulation represents a steady state, should it be true that the percentage change in investment is also the same as the percentage change in aggregate capital? One is a flow and one is a stock, and these two are not the same. Also, the domestic ownership share of capital is reported, but there is little discussion of what model features determine this or of what interpretation can be placed on the calculations.

To summarize my remarks, the ORANI model is perhaps the most impressive in scope of the first generation of applied equilibrium models. It seems to me to be different from some of the other models that are described in this book because of its forecasting rather than applied welfare orientation. It has had large amounts of resources devoted to it and has generated a level of elaboration that is at times perhaps a little hard for the outsider to grasp. The impressive research output from this modeling effort has raised many issues of design that will give second and subsequent generations of modelers food for thought.

REFERENCES

Feldstein, M., and C. Horioka (1980). "Domestic Savings and International Capital Flows." *Economic Journal,* Vol. 90, No. 358:314–29.
Harberger, A. C. (1980). "Vignettes on the World Capital Market." *American Economic Review,* Vol. 70, No. 2:331-7.
Stern, R. M., J. Francis, and B. Schumacher (1976). *Price Elasticities in International Trade.* New York: Macmillan.
Whalley, J., and B. Yeung (1980). "External Sector Closing Rules in Applied General Equilibrium Models." Working Paper, Centre for the Study of International Economic Relations, University of Western Ontario.